Praise for *Learning Cocos2L*

"If you're looking to create an iPhone or iPad game, *Learning Cocos2D* should be the first book on your shopping list. Rod and Ray do a phenomenal job of taking you through the entire process from concept to app, clearly explaining both how to do each step as well as why you're dong it."

—Jeff LaMarche, Principal, MartianCraft, LLC, and coauthor of *Beginning iPhone Development* (Apress, 2009)

"This book provides an excellent introduction to iOS 2D game development. Beyond that, the book also provides one of the best introductions to Box2D available. I am truly impressed with the detail and depth of Box2D coverage."

—Erin Catto, creator of Box2D

"Warning: reading this book will make you *need* to write a game! *Learning Cocos2D* is a great fast-forward into writing the next hit game for iOS— definitely a must for the aspiring indie iOS game developer (regardless of experience level)! Thanks, Rod and Ray, for letting me skip the learning curve; you've really saved my bacon!"

—Eric Hayes, Principle Engineer, Brewmium LLC (and Indie iOS Developer)

"*Learning Cocos2D* is an outstanding read, and I highly recommend it to any iOS developer wanting to get into game development with Cocos2D. This book gave me the knowledge and confidence I needed to write an iOS game without having to be a math and OpenGL whiz."

—Kirby Turner, White Peak Software, Inc.

"*Learning Cocos2D* is both an entertaining and informative book; it covers everything you need to know about creating games using Cocos2D."

—Fahim Farook, RookSoft (rooksoft.co.nz)

"This is the premiere book on Cocos2D! After reading this book you will have a firm grasp of the framework, and you will be able to create a few different types of games. Rod and Ray get you quickly up to speed with the basics in the first group of chapters. The later chapters cover the more advanced features, such as parallax scrolling, CocosDenshion, Box2D, Chipmunk, particle systems, and Apple Game Center. The authors' writing style is descriptive, concise, and fun to read. This book is a must have!"

—Nick Waynik, iOS Developer

Learning Cocos2D

Learning Cocos2D

A Hands-On Guide to Building iOS Games with Cocos2D, Box2D, and Chipmunk

Rod Strougo

Ray Wenderlich

↟Addison-Wesley

Upper Saddle River, NJ · Boston · Indianapolis · San Francisco
New York · Toronto · Montreal · London · Munich · Paris · Madrid
Capetown · Sydney · Tokyo · Singapore · Mexico City

Many of the designations used by manufacturers and sellers to distinguish their products are claimed as trademarks. Where those designations appear in this book, and the publisher was aware of a trademark claim, the designations have been printed with initial capital letters or in all capitals.

The authors and publisher have taken care in the preparation of this book, but make no expressed or implied warranty of any kind and assume no responsibility for errors or omissions. No liability is assumed for incidental or consequential damages in connection with or arising out of the use of the information or programs contained herein.

The publisher offers excellent discounts on this book when ordered in quantity for bulk purchases or special sales, which may include electronic versions and/or custom covers and content particular to your business, training goals, marketing focus, and branding interests. For more information, please contact:

U.S. Corporate and Government Sales
(800) 382-3419
corpsales@pearsontechgroup.com

For sales outside the United States please contact:

International Sales
international@pearson.com

Visit us on the Web: informit.com/aw

Library of Congress Cataloging-in-Publication Data
Strougo, Rod, 1976-
  Learning Cocos2D : a hands-on guide to building iOS games with
Cocos2D, Box2D, and Chipmunk / Rod Strougo, Ray Wenderlich.
       p.   cm.
  Includes index.
  ISBN-13: 978-0-321-73562-1 (pbk. : alk. paper)
  ISBN-10: 0-321-73562-5 (pbk. : alk. paper)
  1. iPhone (Smartphone)—Programming. 2. iPad (Computer)—Programming.
  3. Computer games—Programming. I. Wenderlich, Ray, 1980- II. Title.
  QA76.8.I64S87 2011
  794.8'1526—dc23

                                      2011014419

ISBN-13: 978-0-321-73562-1
ISBN-10:   0-321-73562-5
Text printed in the United States on recycled paper at RR Donnelley in Crawfordsville, Indiana.
Second printing, August 2011

Editor-in-Chief
Mark Taub

Acquisitions Editor
Chuck Toporek

Managing Editor
John Fuller

Project Editor
Anna Popick

Copy Editor
Carol Lallier

Indexer
Jack Lewis

Proofreader
Lori Newhouse

Editorial Assistant
Olivia Basegio

Cover Designer
Chuti Prasertsith

Compositor
The CIP Group

Dedicated to my wife, Agata.
—Rod

Dedicated to my wife, Vicki.
—Ray

Contents at a Glance

Contents

Preface

So you want to be a game developer?

Developing games for the iPhone or iPad can be a lot of fun. It is one of the few things we can do to feel like a kid again. Everyone, it seems, has an idea for a game, and what better platform to develop for than the iPhone and iPad?

What stops most people from actually developing a game, though, is that game development covers a wide swath of computer science skills—graphics, audio, networking—and at times it can seem like you are drinking from a fire hose. When you are first getting started, becoming comfortable with Objective-C can seem like a huge task, especially if you start to look at things like OpenGL ES, OpenAL, and other lower-level APIs for your game.

Writing a game for the iPhone and iPad does not have to be that difficult—and it isn't. To help simplify the task of building 2D games, look no further than Cocos2D.

You no longer have to deal with low-level OpenGL programming APIs to make games for the iPhone, and you don't need to be a math or physics expert. There's a much faster and easier way—use a free and popular open source game programming framework called Cocos2D. Cocos2D is extremely fun and easy to use, and with it you can skip the low-level details and focus on what makes your game different and special!

This book teaches you how to use Cocos2D to make your own games, taking you step by step through the process of making an actual game that's on the App Store right now! The game you build in this book is called *Space Viking* and is the story of a kick-ass Viking transported to an alien planet. In the process of making the game, you get hands-on experience with all of the most important elements in Cocos2D and see how everything fits together to make a complete game.

Download the Game!

You can download *Space Viking* from the App Store: *http://itunes.apple.com/us/app/ space-vikings/id400657526mt=8*. The game is free, so go ahead and download it, start playing around with it, and see if you're good enough to get all of the achievements!

Think of this book as an epic-length tutorial, showing you how you can make a real game with Cocos2D from the bottom up. You'll be coding along with the book, and we explain things step by step. By the time you've finished reading and working through this book, you'll have made a complete game. Best of all, you'll have the confidence and knowledge it takes to make your own.

Each chapter describes in detail a specific component within the game along with the technology required to support it, be it a tile map editor or some effect we're creating with Cocos2D, Box2D, or Chipmunk. Once an introduction to the functionality and technology is complete, the chapter provides details on how the component has been implemented within *Space Viking*. This combination of theory and real-world implementation helps to fill the void left by other game-development books.

What Is Cocos2D?

Cocos2D *(www.cocos2d-iphone.org)* is an open source Objective-C framework for making 2D games for the iOS and Mac OS X, which includes developing for the iPhone, iPod touch, the iPad, and the Mac. Cocos2D can either be included as a library to your project in Xcode or automatically added when you create a new game using the included Cocos2D templates.

Cocos2D uses OpenGL ES for graphics rendering, giving you all of the speed and performance of the graphics processor (GPU) on your device. Cocos2D includes a host of other features and capabilities, which you'll learn more about as you work through the tutorial in this book.

Cocos2D started life as a Python framework for doing 2D games. In late 2008, it was ported to the iPhone and rewritten in Objective-C. There are now additional ports of Cocos2D to Ruby, Java (Android), and even Mono (C#/.NET).

> **Note**
>
> Cocos2D has an active and vibrant community of contributors and supporters. The Cocos2D forums *(www.cocos2d-iphone.org/forum)* are very active and an excellent resource for learning and troubleshooting as well as keeping up to date on the latest developments of Cocos2D.

Why You Should Use Cocos2D

Cocos2D lets you focus on your core game instead of on low-level APIs. The App Store marketplace is very fluid and evolves rapidly. Prototyping and developing your game quickly is crucial for success in the App Store, and Cocos2D is the best tool for helping you quickly develop your game without getting bogged down trying to learn OpenGL ES or OpenAL.

Cocos2D also includes a host of utility classes such as the `TextureCache`, which automatically caches your graphics, providing for faster and smoother gameplay. `TextureCache` operates in the background and is one of the many functions of Cocos2D that you don't even have to know how to use; it functions transparently to you. Other useful utilities include font rendering, sprite sheets, a robust sound system, and many more.

Cocos2D is a great prototyping tool. You can quickly make a game in as little as an hour (or however long it takes you to read Chapter 2). You are reading this book because you want to make games for the iPhone and iPad, and using Cocos2D is the quickest way to get there—bar none.

Cocos2D Key Features

Still unsure if Cocos2D is right for you? Well, check out some of these amazing features of Cocos2D that can make developing your next game a lot easier.

Actions

Actions are one of the most powerful features in Cocos2D. Actions allow you to move, scale, and manipulate sprites and other objects with ease. As an example, to smoothly move a space cargo ship across the screen 400 pixels to the right in 5 seconds, all the code you need is:

```
CCAction *moveAction = [CCMoveBy actionWithDuration:5.0f
                                  position:CGPointMake(400.0f,0.0f)];
[spaceCargoShipSprite runAction:moveAction];
```

That's it; just two lines of code! Figure P.1 illustrates the moveAction on the space cargo ship.

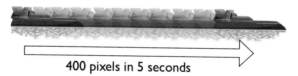

400 pixels in 5 seconds

Figure P.1   Illustrating the effect of the moveAction on the Space
Cargo Ship sprite

There are many kinds of built-in actions in Cocos2D: rotate, scale, jump, blink, fade, tint, animation, and more. You can also chain actions together and call custom callbacks for neat effects with very little code.

Built-In Font Support

Cocos2D makes it very easy to deal with text, which is important for games in menu systems, score displays, debugging, and more. Cocos2D includes support for embedded TrueType fonts and also a fast bitmap font-rendering system, so you can display text to the screen with just a few lines of code.

An Extensive Effects Library

Cocos2D includes a powerful particle system that makes it easy to add cool effects such as smoke, fire, rain, and snow to your games. Also, Cocos2D includes built-in effects, such as flip and fading, to transition between screens in your game.

Great for TileMap Games

Cocos2D includes built-in support for tile-mapped games, which is great when you have a large game world made up of small reusable images. Cocos2D also makes it easy to move the camera around to implement scrolling backgrounds or levels. Finally, there is support for parallax scrolling, which gives your game the illusion of 3D depth and perspective.

Audio/Sound Support

The sound engine included with Cocos2D allows for easy use of the power of OpenAL without having to dive into the lower level APIs. With Cocos2D's sound engine, you can play background music or sound effects with just a single line of code!

Two Powerful Physics Engines

Also bundled with Cocos2D are two powerful physics engines, Box2D and Chipmunk, both of which are fantastic for games. You can add a whole new level of realism to your games and create entire new gameplay types by using game physics—without having to be a math guru.

Important Concepts

Before we get started, it's important to make sure you're familiar with some important concepts about Cocos2D and game programming in general.

Sprite

You will see the term *sprite* used often in game development. A sprite is an image that can be moved independently of other images on the screen. A sprite could be the player character, an enemy, or a larger image used in the background. In practice, sprites are made from your PNG or PVRTC image files. Once loaded in memory, a sprite is converted into a texture used by the iPhone GPU to render onscreen.

Singleton

A *singleton* is a special kind of Objective-C class, which can have only one instance. An example of this is an iPhone app's Application Delegate class, or the Director class in Cocos2D. When you call a singleton instance in your code, you always get back the one instance of this class, regardless of which class called it.

OpenGL ES

OpenGL ES is a mobile version (ES stands for *Embedded Systems*) of the Open Graphics Language (OpenGL). It is the closest you can get on the iPhone or iPad to sending zeros and ones to the GPU. OpenGL ES is the fastest way to render graphics on the iPhone or iPad, and due to its origin, it is a low-level API. If you are new to game development, OpenGL ES can have a steep learning curve, but luckily you don't need to know OpenGL ES to use Cocos2D.

The two versions of OpenGL ES supported on the iPhone and iPad are 1.1 and 2.0. There are plans in the Cocos2D roadmap to support OpenGL ES 2.0, although currently only version 1.1 is supported.

Languages and Screen Resolutions

Cocos2D is written in Objective-C, the same language as Cocoa Touch and the majority of the Apple iOS APIs. In Objective-C it is important to understand some basic memory-management techniques, as it is a good foundation for you to become an efficient game developer on the iOS platform. Cocos2D supports all of the native resolutions on the iOS devices, from the original iPhone to the iPad to the retina display on the iPhone 4.

2D versus 3D

You first learn to walk before you can run. The same is true for game development; you have to learn how to make 2D games before diving into the deeper concepts of 3D games. There are some 3D effects and transitions in Cocos2D, such as a 3D wave effect and an orbit camera move; however, most of the functionality is geared toward 2D games and graphics.

Cocos2D is designed for 2D games (hence the 2D in the name), as are the tutorials and examples in this book. If you want to make 3D games, you should look into different frameworks, such as Unity, the Unreal Engine, or direct OpenGL.

The Game behind the Book: Space Viking

This book takes you through the process of creating a full-featured Cocos2D-based game for the iPhone and iPad. The game you build in this book is called *Space Viking*. If you want to try *Space Viking* now, you can download a free version of the game from the App Store *(http://itunes.apple.com/us/app/id400657526)* and install it on your iPhone, iPod touch, or iPad.

Of course, if you are more patient, you can build the game yourself and load it onto your device after working through the chapters in this book. There is no greater learning experience than having the ability to test a game as you're building it. Not only can you learn how to build a game, but you can also go back and tweak the code a bit to change things around to see what sort of effect something has on the gameplay. Good things come to those who wait.

This book teaches you how to use all of the features and capabilities of Cocos2D, but more important, how to apply them to a real game. By the time you are done, you will have the knowledge and experience needed to get your own game in the App Store. The concepts you learn from building *Space Viking* apply to a variety of games from action to puzzle.

Space Viking's Story

Every game starts in the depths of your imagination, with a character and storyline that gets transformed into a game. This is the story of *Space Viking*.

In the future, the descendants of Earth are forced into colonizing planets outside our own solar system. In order to create hospitable environments, huge interplanetary machines extract giant chunks of ice from Northern Europe and Greenland and send it across the galaxy to these planets. Unbeknown to the scientists, one of these chunks contains Ole the Viking, who eons ago fell into an icy river on his way home from defeating barbarian tribes. Encased in an icy tomb for centuries, Ole awakens thousands of years later—and light years from home—after being warmed by an alien sun, as shown in Figure P.2.

Figure P.2   Ole awakens on the alien planet

You get to play as Ole the Viking and battle the aliens on this strange world in hopes of finding a way to return Ole to his native land and time.

You control Ole's movement to the right and left by using the thumb joystick on the left side of the screen. On the right side are buttons for jumping and attacking. Ole starts out with only his fists. In later levels Ole finds his trusty mallet, and you use the accelerometer to control him in the physics levels.

Space Viking is an action and adventure game, with the emphasis on *action*. The goal was to create a real game from the ground up so you could learn not only Cocos2D but also how to use it in a real full-featured game. The idea for the game came from concept art that Eric Stevens, a graphic artist and fellow game devotee, developed earlier when we were discussing game ideas to make next.

Space Viking consists of a number of levels, each of which demonstrates a specific area of Cocos2D or gameplay type. For example, the first level is a side-scrolling beat 'em up, and the fourth level is a mine cart racing level that shows off the game physics found in Box2D and Chipmunk. Our hope is that you can reuse parts of Space Viking to make your own game once you've finished this book! That's right: you can freely reuse the code in this book to build your own game.

Organization of This Book

The goal of this book is to teach you about game development using Cocos2D as you build Space Viking (and learn more about the quest and story of Ole the Viking). You start with a simple level and some basic game mechanics and work your way up to creating levels with physics and particle systems and finally to a complete game by the end of the book.

First you learn the basics of Cocos2D and build a small level with basic running and jumping movements for Ole. Part II shows you how to add animations, actions, effects, and even text to Space Viking. Part III takes the game further, adding more levels and scenes, sounds, and scrolling to the gameplay. In Part IV realism is brought into the game with the Box2D and Chipmunk physics engines. Finally in Part V, you learn how to add a particle system, add high scores, connect to social networks, and debug and optimize Space Viking to round out some best practices for the games you will build in the future.

There are 17 chapters and one appendix in the book, each dealing with a specific area of creating Space Viking.

- **Part I: Getting Started with Cocos2D**

  Learn how to get Cocos2D installed and start using it to create Space Viking. Learn how to add animations and movements to Ole and his enemies.

  - **Chapter 1: Hello, Cocos2D**

    This chapter covers how to install Cocos2D framework and templates in Xcode and some companion tools that make developing games easier. These tools are freely available and facilitate the creation of the elements used by Cocos2D.

  - **Chapter 2: Hello, Space Viking**

    Here you create the basic Space Viking game, which you build upon throughout the book. You start out with just a basic Cocos2D template and add the hero (Ole the Viking) to the scene. In the second part of this chapter, you add the methods to handle the touch inputs, including moving Ole around and making him jump.

- **Chapter 3: Introduction to Cocos2D Animations and Actions**

  In this chapter, you learn how to make the game look much more realistic by adding animations to Ole as he moves around the scene.

- **Chapter 4: Simple Collision Detection and the First Enemy**

  In this chapter, you learn how to implement simple collision detection and add the first enemy to your *Space Viking* game, so Ole can start to fight his way off the planet!

- **Part II: More Enemies and More Fun**

  Learn how to create more complex enemies for Ole to battle and in the process learn about Cocos2D actions and effects. Finish up with a live, onscreen debugging system using Cocos2D text capabilities.

  - **Chapter 5: More Actions, Effects, and Cocos2D Scheduler**

    Actions are a key concept in Cocos2D—they are an easy way to move objects around, make them grow or disappear, and much more. In this chapter, you put them in practice by adding power-ups and weapons to the level, and you learn some other important Cocos2D capabilities, such as effects and the scheduler.

  - **Chapter 6: Text, Fonts, and the Written Word**

    Most games have text in them at some point, and *Space Viking* is no exception. In this chapter, you learn how to add text to your games using the different methods available in Cocos2D.

- **Part III: From Level to Game**

  Learn how to expand the *Space Viking* level into a full game by adding menus, sound, and scrolling.

  - **Chapter 7: Main Menu, Level Completed, and Credits Scenes**

    Almost all games have more than one screen (or "scene," as it's called in Cocos2D); there's usually a main menu, main game scene, level completed, and credits scene at the very least. In this chapter, you learn how to create multiple scenes by implementing them in *Space Viking*!

  - **Chapter 8: Pump Up the Volume!**

    Adding sound effects and music to a game can make a huge difference. Cocos2D makes it really easy with the CocosDenshion sound engine, so in this chapter you give it a try!

  - **Chapter 9: When the World Gets Bigger: Adding Scrolling**

    A lot of games have a bigger world than can fit on one screen, so the world needs to scroll as the player moves through it. This can be tricky to get right, so this chapter shows you how by converting the beat-'em-up into a side-scroller, using Cocos2D tile maps for improved performance.

- **Part IV: Physics Engines**

  With the Box2D and Chipmunk physics engines that come with Cocos2D, you can add some amazing effects to your games, such as gravity, realistic collisions, and even ragdoll effects! In these chapters you get a chance to add some physics-based levels to *Space Viking*, from simple to advanced!

  - **Chapter 10: Basic Game Physics: Adding Realism with Box2D**

    Just as Cocos2D makes it easy to make games for the iPhone without knowing low-level OpenGL details, Box2D makes it easy to add physics to your game objects without having to be a math expert. In this chapter, you learn how to get started with Box2D by making a fun puzzle game where objects move according to gravity.

  - **Chapter 11: Intermediate Game Physics: Modeling, Racing, and Leaping**

    This chapter shows you some of the really neat stuff you can do with Box2D by making the start of a side-scrolling cart-racing game. In the process, you learn how to model arbitrary shapes, add joints to restrict movement of physics bodies, and much more!

  - **Chapter 12: Advanced Game Physics: Even Better than the Real Thing**

    In this chapter, you make the cart-racing level even more amazing by adding spikes to dodge and an epic boss fight at the end. You learn more about joints, how to detect collisions, and how to add enemy logic as well.

  - **Chapter 13: The Chipmunk Physics Engine (No Alvin Required)**

    The second physics engine that comes with Cocos2D, called Chipmunk, is similar to Box2D. This chapter shows you how to use Chipmunk, compares it to Box2D, and gives you hands-on practice by making a Metroid-style escape level.

- **Part V: Particle Systems, Game Center, and Performance**

  Learn how to quickly create and add particle systems to your games, how to integrate with Apple's Game Center for online leaderboards and achievements, and some performance tips and tricks to keep your game running fast.

  - **Chapter 14: Particle Systems: Creating Fire, Snow, Ice, and More**

    Using Cocos2D's particle system, you can add some amazing special effects to your game—extremely easily! In this chapter, you learn how to use particle systems to add some special effects to *Space Viking*, such as ship exhaust.

  - **Chapter 15: Achievements and Leaderboards with Game Center**

    With Apple's Game Center, you can easily add achievements and leaderboards to your games, which makes things more fun for players and also might help you sell more copies! This chapter covers how to set things up in *Space Viking*, step by step.

- ### Chapter 16: Performance Optimizations

  In this chapter, you learn how to tackle some of the most common challenges and issues you will face in optimizing and getting the most out of your Cocos2D game. You get hands-on experience debugging the most common performance issues and applying solutions.

- ### Chapter 17: Conclusion

  This final chapter recaps what you learned and describes where you can go next: into 3D, using Cocos2D on other platforms such as Android, and more advanced game-development topics.

- ### Appendix: Principal Classes of Cocos2D

  The Appendix provides an overview of the main classes you will be using and interacting with in Cocos2D.

By the time you've finished reading this book, you'll have practical experience making an awesome game from scratch! You can then take the concepts you've learned (and even some of the code!) and use it to turn your own game into a reality.

Audience for This Book

The audience for this book includes developers who are put off by game-making because they anticipate a long and complex learning curve. Many developers want to write games but don't know where to start with game development or the Cocos2D framework. This book is a hands-on guide, which takes you from the very beginning of using Cocos2D to applying the advanced physics concepts in Box2D and Chipmunk.

This book is targeted to developers interested in creating games for iOS devices, including the iPhone, iPad, and iPod touch. The book assumes a basic understanding of Objective-C, Cocoa Touch, and the Xcode tools. You are not expected to know any lower-level APIs (Core Audio, OpenGL ES, etc.), as these are used internally by Cocos2D.

Who This Book Is For

If you are already developing applications for the iPhone of other platform but want to make a move from utility applications to games, then this book is for you. It builds on the development knowledge you already have and leads you into game development by describing the terminology, technology, and tools required as well as providing real-world implementation examples.

Who This Book Isn't For

If you already have a grasp of the workflow required to create a game or you have a firm game idea that you know will require OpenGL ES for 3D graphics, then this is not the book for you.

It is expected that before you read this book you are already familiar with Objective-C, C, Xcode, and Interface Builder. While the implementations described in this book have been kept as simple as possible, and the use of C is limited, a firm foundation in these languages is required.

The following books can help provide you with the grounding you need to work through this book:

- *Cocoa Programming for Mac OS X, Third Edition,* by Aaron Hillegass (Addison-Wesley, 2008)

- *Learning Objective-C 2.0* by Robert Clair (Addison-Wesley, 2011)

- *Programming in Objective-C 2.0* by Stephen G. Kochan (Addison-Wesley, 2009)

- *Cocoa Design Patterns* by Erik M. Buck and Donald A. Yacktman (Addison-Wesley, 2009)

- *The iPhone Developer's Cookbook, Second Edition,* by Erica Sadun (Addison-Wesley, 2010)

- *Core Animation: Simplified Animation Techniques for Mac and iPhone Development* by Marcus Zarra and Matt Long (Addison-Wesley, 2010)

- *iPhone Programming: The Big Nerd Ranch Guide* by Aaron Hillegass and Joe Conway (Big Nerd Ranch, Inc., 2010)

- *Learning iOS Game Programming: A Hands-On Guide to Building Your First iPhone Game* by Michael Daley (Addison-Wesley, 2011)

These books, along with other resources you'll find on the web, will help you learn more about how to program for the Mac and iPhone, giving you a deeper knowledge about the Objective-C language and the Cocoa frameworks.

Source Code, Tutorial Videos, and Forums

Access to information is not limited only to the book. The complete, fully commented source code for *Space Viking* is also included, along with video tutorials (available at *http://cocos2Dbook.com*) that take you visually through the concepts of each chapter.

There is plenty of code to review throughout the book, along with exercises for you to try out, so it is assumed you have access to the Apple developer tools such as Xcode and the iPhone SDK. Both of these can be downloaded from the Apple iPhone Dev Center: *http://developer.apple.com/iphone.*

If you want to work with your fellow students as you work through the book, feel free to check out the book's forums at *http://cocos2dbook.com/forums/.*

Acknowledgments

This book would not have been possible without the hard work, support, and kindness of the following people:

- First of all, thanks to our editor, Chuck Toporek, and his assistant, Olivia Basegio. Chuck patiently helped and encouraged us during the entire process (even though we are both first-time authors!) and has managed all of the work it takes to convert a simple Word document into the actual book you're holding today. Olivia was extremely helpful through the entire process of keeping everyone coordinated and the tech reviews coming in. Thanks again to both of you in making this book a reality!

- Another person at Addison-Wesley whom we want to thank is Chuti Prasertsith, who designed the cover for the book.

- A huge thanks to the lead developer and coordinator of Cocos2D, Ricardo Quesada (also known as Riq), along with the other Cocos2D contributors, such as Steve Oldmeadow and many others. Without Riq and his team's hard work and dedication to making Cocos2D into the amazing framework and community that it is today, this book just wouldn't exist. Also, we believe that Cocos2D has made a huge positive difference in many people's lives by enabling them to accomplish a lifelong dream—to make their own games. Riq maintains Cocos2D as his full-time job, so if you'd like to make a donation to thank him for his hard work, you can do so at *www.cocos2d-iphone.org/store*. Riq also sells source code for his game *Sapus Tongue* and a great physics editor called Level-SVG. You can find out more about both at *www.sapusmedia.com*.

- Also, thank you to Erin Catto (the lead developer of Box2D) and Scott Lembcke (the lead developer of Chipmunk) for their work on their amazing physics libraries. Similarly to Riq's work on Cocos2D, Erin's and Scott's work has enabled countless programmers to create cool physics-based games quickly and easily. Erin and Scott are extremely dedicated to supporting their libraries and community, and even kindly donated their time in reviewing the physics chapters of this book. If you'd like to donate to Erin or Scott for their hard work on their libraries, you can do so by following the links at *www.box2d.org* and *http://code.google.com/p/chipmunk-physics*.

- A big thanks to Steve Oldmeadow, the lead developer of CocosDenshion, the sound engine behind Cocos2D. Steve provided assistance and time in reviewing the chapter on audio. Steve's work has allowed many game developers to quickly and easily add music and sound effects to their games.

- Eric Stevens is an American fine artist who moonlights as a game illustrator. Years of good times and bad music contributed to the initial concept of *Space Viking*. Eric worked closely with us to bring Ole and everything you see in *Space Viking* to life. Eric maintains an illustration site at *http://imagedesk.org*, and you can see his paintings at several galleries in the Southwest and at *http://ericstevensart.com*.

- Mike Weiser is the musician who made the rocking soundtrack and sound effects for *Space Viking*. We think the music made a huge difference in *Space Viking* and really set the tone we were hoping for. A special thanks to Andrew Peplinski for the Viking grunts and Rulon Brown for conducting the choir that you hear in the beginning of the game. Mike has made music for lots of popular iOS games, and you can check him out at *www.mikeweisermusic.com*.

- A huge thanks to our technical reviewers: Farim Farook, Marc Hebert, Mark Hurley, Mike Leonardi, and Nick Waynik. These guys did a great job catching all of our boneheaded mistakes and giving us some great advice on how to make each chapter the best it could be. Thank you so much, guys!

Each of us also has some personal "thank yous" to make.

From Rod Strougo

I thank my wife and family for being ever patient while I was working on this book. There were countless evenings when I was hidden away in my office writing, editing, coding. Without Agata's support and understanding, there is no way this book could exist. Our older son, Alexander, was two and a half during the writing of this book, and he helped beta test *Space Viking*, while Anton was born as I was finishing the last chapters. Thank you for all the encouragement, love, and support, Agata.

I would also like to thank Ray for stepping in and writing the Box2D, Chipmunk, and Game Center chapters. Ray did a fantastic job on in-depth coverage of Box2D and Chipmunk, while adding some fun levels to *Space Viking*.

From Ray Wenderlich

First of all, a huge thank you to my wife and best friend, Vicki Wenderlich, for her constant support, encouragement, and advice throughout this entire process. Without her, I wouldn't be making iOS apps today, and they definitely wouldn't look as good! Also, thank you to my amazing family. You believed in me through the ups and downs of being an indie iOS developer and supported me the entire way. Thank you so much!

Finally, I thank all of the readers and supporters of my iOS tutorial blog at *www. raywenderlich.com*. Without your interest, encouragement, and support, I wouldn't have been as motivated to keep writing all the tutorials and might have never had the opportunity to write this book. Thank you so much for making this possible, and I hope you enjoy this book!

About the Authors

Rod Strougo is the founder and lead developer of the studio Prop Group at *www.prop.gr*. Rod's journey in physics and games started way back with an Apple][, writing games in Basic. From the early passion in games, Rod's career moved to enterprise software development, spending 10 years writing software for IBM and recently for a large telecom company. These days Rod enjoys helping others get started on their paths to making games. Originally from Rio de Janeiro, Brazil, Rod lives in Atlanta, Georgia, with his wife and sons.

Ray Wenderlich is an iPhone developer and gamer and the founder of Razeware, LLC. Ray is passionate about both making apps and teaching others the techniques to make them. He has written a bunch of tutorials about iOS development, available at *www.raywenderlich.com*.

Part I

Getting Started with Cocos2D

Learn how to install Cocos2D and start using it to create *Space Viking*. Learn how to add animations and movements to Ole the Viking and his enemies.

- Chapter 1: "Hello, Cocos2D"
- Chapter 2: "Hello, Space Viking"
- Chapter 3: "Introduction to Cocos2D Animations and Actions"
- Chapter 4: "Simple Collision Detection and the First Enemy"

1

Hello, Cocos2D

Cocos2D is incredibly fun and easy to use. In this chapter you will learn how to install Cocos2D, integrate it with Xcode, and make a simple HelloWorld app. You'll then add a space cargo ship to the app and have it move around the screen, with just a few lines of code, as shown in Figure 1.1.

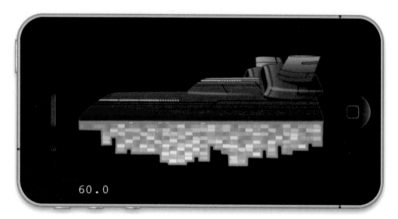

Figure 1.1   The space cargo ship that you will add to your HelloWorld app

After you create this simple app, you will get a chance to go behind the scenes and see how the Cocos2D template code generated for you works and try running the app on your own iPhone or iPad.

> **Note**
>
> It is assumed you have already signed up for Apple's iPhone Developer program and downloaded and installed Xcode on your Mac. You should also have some knowledge of Objective-C syntax. For more information and references on how to get started with these, please see the preface.

This chapter walks you through the process of downloading and installing Cocos2D and inte-grating it with Xcode. Once Cocos2D is installed, you'll build a simple HelloWorld app and test it in the iPhone Simulator. You will learn exactly what each line in the HelloWorld program does as well as how to get HelloWorld on your iOS device.

Ready? Okay then, let's get started!

Downloading and Installing Cocos2D

This section walks you through the process of downloading and installing Cocos2D. Before you can start creating your first Cocos2D game, you need to download Cocos2D and get the templates installed in Xcode.

Downloading Cocos2D

The official Cocos2D project is hosted on GitHub, but the latest stable and tested releases are available from the Cocos2D homepage under the download tab at *www.cocos2d-iphone.org/download*. Figure 1.2 shows the Cocos2D download page.

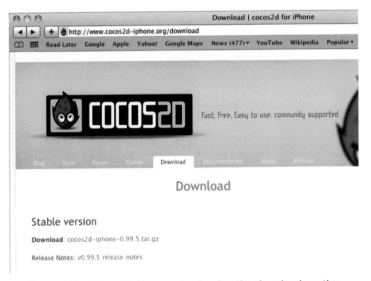

Figure 1.2   Cocos2D homepage showing the download section

To get Cocos2D on your Mac:

1. Create a folder called *Cocos2D* on your Mac and download the latest stable version that you see on the *www.cocos2d-iphone.org/download* site.

2. Double-click on the *gzipped tar* file, and Finder will automatically extract the file into a *cocos2d-iphone-VERSION* subfolder.

In this subfolder is where you will find the *install_templates.sh* script that you
need to run next.

Installing the Cocos2D Templates

Installing the Cocos2D templates is the same whether you downloaded a gzipped
archive shown in the previous section or cloned the latest version from the develop
branch using Git. To start:

1. Open **Terminal** and navigate to the *Cocos2D* folder that you created in the previous section. You can use the **cd** command to change folders.

2. Once inside the *Cocos2D* folder, use the **cd** command once more to change folders so that you are inside the *cocos2d-iphone* subfolder. You can see a listing of the
   cocos2d-iphone subfolder in Figure 1.3.

   ```
   $ cd cocos2d-iphone
   ```

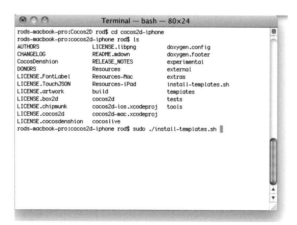

Figure 1.3   Looking inside the cocos2d-iphone subdirectory

3. Run the *install-templates.sh* script by entering the following command:

   ```
   $ sudo ./install-templates.sh
   ```

4. When prompted, enter your password.

The *install-templates.sh* script copies the three Cocos2D templates into the Xcode folder. That is all it takes to install the Cocos2D templates. Restart Xcode if you had it running while installing the templates, and you will be ready to create a Cocos2D *HelloWorld* in the next section.

Creating Your First Cocos2D HelloWorld

No more delays: time to dive in to the code. In this section you will learn to use the Cocos2D templates that you installed earlier and to build the Cocos2D *HelloWorld* sample. No programming introduction is complete without a proper "Hello World."

Inspecting the Cocos2D Templates

Fire up Xcode, and from Xcode's menu, select **File > New Project** and select the **iOS/User Templates** section. You should see three Cocos2D templates, as shown in Figure 1.4, under the User Templates section. The first template is for an application with just Cocos2D, the second for a Cocos2D with Box2D application, and the third for a Cocos2D with Chipmunk application.

Figure 1.4   Cocos2D templates in Xcode

> **Tip**
> Make sure you select **Application** under the iOS and User Templates section.

The three Cocos2D templates provide three different versions of a simple *HelloWorld* application. The Cocos2D Application template has just Cocos2D and is what you will use to create the *HelloWorld* app. The Box2D template creates a mini Box2D *HelloWorld* where you can drop boxes into the screen with physics simulation. The Chipmunk template creates a mini Chipmunk project where you can create multiple bodies and try out collisions.

When you are building your own games, these three templates are key to getting your game started quickly. The Box2D and Chipmunk projects contain all of the wiring between Cocos2D and the physics engines. Even the Cocos2D-only template comes already connected with an application delegate and runs without you having to type any code.

Building the Cocos2D HelloWorld Project

Let's build the basic Cocos2D *HelloWorld* project. Once you've built this one, you should take a stab at building the Cocos2D+Box2D and Cocos2D+Chipmunk examples, too.

1. Launch Xcode and select **File > New Project** from the menu.

2. Select the **Cocos2D template** (without Box2D or Chipmunk).

3. Name this project *CCHelloWorld*, as shown in Figure 1.5.

Figure 1.5   Creating the Cocos2D HelloWorld sample

4. In Xcode on the Scheme dropdown, select **CCHelloWorld** and the **iPhone Simulator** (4.2 or the latest iOS you have installed on your system), as shown in Figure 1.6.

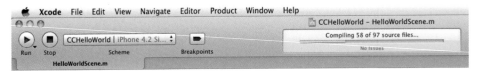

Figure 1.6   Showing the CCHelloWorld and iPhone Simulator on the Scheme dropdown

5. In Xcode, click **Run**.

You now have a fully functional Cocos2D *HelloWorld* app running in the iPhone Simulator, as shown in Figure 1.7.

Figure 1.7   The Cocos2D HelloWorld app running in the iPhone Simulator

The Cocos2D *CCHelloWorld* project is already set up for iPhone and iPad from the start; there is no need to transition it or do anything else. If you select iPad Simulator under the Scheme dropdown and click **Run**, you will see *CCHelloWorld* running on the iPad, as shown in Figure 1.8.

Figure 1.8   The Cocos2D HelloWorld app running in the iPad Simulator

Taking HelloWorld Further

While displaying "Hello World" on the screen is a good first step, you are learning about Cocos2D to create games, so why not add a quick space cargo ship here and make it move?

To start, locate the *SpaceCargoShip* folder included with the resources for this chapter. The *SpaceCargoShip* folder contains the *SpaceCargoShip.png*, which is the image of—what else?—the alien's space cargo ship.

In Xcode with the *HelloWorld* project opened:

1. Drag the *SpaceCargoShip* folder into the *CCHelloWorld* project and select **Copy items into destination group's folder**. You are merely adding the *SpaceCargoShip* folder and PNG to your *CCHelloWorld* project so that it is included with your app.

2. Open the `HelloWorldScene.m` class and, in the `init` method, add the lines shown in Listing 1.1.

Listing 1.1   **Adding the space cargo ship onscreen**

```
CCSprite *spaceCargoShip = [CCSprite
                           spriteWithFile:@"SpaceCargoShip.png"];
[spaceCargoShip setPosition:ccp(size.width/2, size.height/2)];
[self addChild:spaceCargoShip];
```

Click **Run**, and you should see the space cargo ship in the middle of the screen, as shown in Figure 1.9.

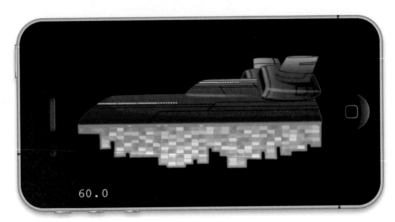

Figure 1.9   Space cargo ship in HelloWorld

Only three lines of code, and you already have a space cargo ship on your iOS device. You will learn in-depth about the details behind the lines in Listing 1.1 in the next chapters.

Adding Movement

A ship is supposed to move around, and moving sprites in Cocos2D is really easy. Add the lines shown in Listing 1.2 right below the lines you added for the space cargo ship.

Listing 1.2   **Code to move the spaceCargoShip in HelloWorldScene.m**

```
id moveAction = [CCMoveTo actionWithDuration:5.0f
                                  position:ccp(0, size.height/2)];
[spaceCargoShip runAction:moveAction];
```

Click **Run** and watch your space cargo ship move slowly to the left side of the screen. How about that—just five short lines of code and you have a moving ship on your iOS device. It only gets better from here.

> **Note**
>
> If you are having issues with your *HelloWorld* crashing with an error message saying **cocos2d: Couldn't add image:SpaceCargoShip.png in CCTextureCache**, make sure you have properly copied the *SpaceCargoShip* folder to your *CCHelloWorld* project. You can always check your work against the completed *CCHelloWorld* project located with the resources for this book.

Hopefully, this has been one of the simplest *HelloWorld* programs you have tried out: you only had to type five lines of code. Getting started with Cocos2D is easy, and you can render some amazing effects and graphics with very little code. In the next chapter you will start building *Space Viking* by putting Ole the Viking and the controls on the screen. You will go from this *HelloWorld* to a Viking you can move on the screen in one short chapter.

The rest of this chapter explains in detail what each line in *HelloWorld* does, as well as how to generate builds for your iOS device. If you don't want to learn what is happening "behind the scenes," feel free to skip ahead to the next chapter and start creating your *Space Viking* game.

For the More Curious: Understanding the Cocos2D HelloWorld

If you are curious about how the Cocos2D application template works, this section covers the most important pieces.

Scenes and Nodes

The first step to understanding the Cocos2D template code is to understand the concepts of scenes, layers, and nodes.

Cocos2D games are made up of scenes (CCScenes), and the director (CCDirector) is responsible for running scenes. The Cocos2D Director runs only one scene at a time. For example, Figure 1.10 shows how you might have the CCDirector running a scene with a main menu on it at one point, and switch to another scene with the gameplay later.

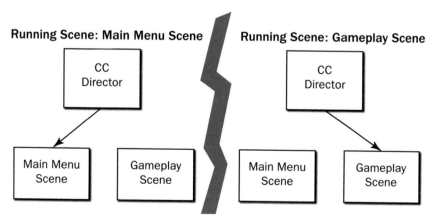

Figure 1.10   Cocos2D Director running Main Menu Scene and then Gameplay Scene

Each scene in Cocos2D consists of one or more layers, which are composited on top of each other. For example, in building *Space Viking* you will create two layers in the first scene: one on the bottom to contain the background, and one on the top to contain the moving characters and action.

Each layer (CCLayer) can in turn have sprites (CCSprite), labels (CCLabel), and other objects you want to display onscreen. If you remember, when you added SpaceCargoShip, you created a new sprite and then added it as a child of the layer.

You can see an example of how the hierarchy of Cocos2D nodes fits together in Figure 1.11.

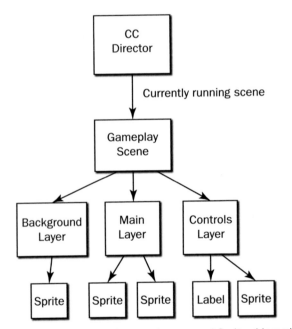

Figure 1.11   Cocos2D Scenes, Layers, and Sprites hierarchy

In Xcode, go to the *Classes* folder and open the *CCHelloWorldAppDelegate.m* file.

Look inside the applicationDidFinishLaunching method, which is where the Cocos2D Director (CCDirector) is set up and instantiated. On line 113, you will see the following, which is where HelloWorld scene is allocated and run:

```
[[CCDirector sharedDirector] runWithScene: [HelloWorld scene]];
```

In the *HelloWorld* sample, the CCDirector allocates the HelloWorld scene and then proceeds to run it, calling all of the schedulers and draw calls of the scene and its children.

Open up *HelloWorldScene.m* and find the scene method that creates a new scene, as shown in Listing 1.3.

Listing 1.3   **Inside the HelloWorldScene.m +(id)scene method**

```
+(id) scene
{
    // 'scene' is an autorelease object.
    CCScene *scene = [CCScene node];

    // 'layer' is an autorelease object.
    HelloWorld *layer = [HelloWorld node];

    // add layer as a child to scene
    [scene addChild: layer];

    // return the scene
    return scene;
}
```

The first line of code creates a new instance of CCScene by calling [CCScene node], which is shorthand for [[[CCScene alloc] init] autorelease]. It then creates a new instance of the HelloWorld layer, adds it as a child of the CCScene, and returns the new scene.

When the HelloWorld layer is called, the init method is called, which contains the code shown in Listing 1.4.

Listing 1.4   **Inside the HelloWorldScene.m –(id)init method for HelloWorld Layer**

```
// Create and initialize a Label
CCLabelTTL* label = [CCLabelTTL labelWithString:@"Hello World"
fontName:@"Marker Felt" fontSize:64];

// Ask CCDirector for the window size
CGSize size = [[CCDirector sharedDirector] winSize];

// Position the label at the center of the screen
label.position =  ccp( size.width /2 , size.height/2 );

// Add the label as a child to this Layer
[self addChild: label];
```

This creates a label saying "Hello World" and sets its position to the center of the screen. It then adds the label as a child of the HelloWorld layer.

So in summary, the CCDirector needs to know which scene to run. Inside of applicationDidFinishLaunching, the template calls the [HelloWorld scene] method to create a new CCScene with a single layer as a child—the HelloWorld layer. The init function of the HelloWorld layer creates a label and adds it as a child of the layer. At that point, you have "Hello World" showing onscreen.

From the Beginning

At this point we've covered the most critical parts of the template—how the scene gets run and how the label gets added to the scene. But if you're still curious, here's some additional information about the remaining template code automatically created for you.

When the *HelloWorld* app first starts, the int main(int argc, char *argv[]) function inside of the *main.m* file is executed by the iOS. The main function allocates the memory pool the *HelloWorld* application will use and has the UIApplication-Main run the CCHelloWorldAppDelegate class. It is in the application delegate class that *HelloWorld* comes to life, with the instantiation of the Cocos2D Director. Listing 1.5 covers the applicationDidFinishLaunching method that is called by the UIApplicationMain when CCHelloWorld is loaded and ready to start running.

Listing 1.5 applicationDidFinishLaunching in CCHelloWorldAppDelegate.m class

```
- (void) applicationDidFinishLaunching:(UIApplication*)application
{
    // Init the window
    window = [[UIWindow alloc] initWithFrame:[
                                    [UIScreen mainScreen] bounds]];
    // Try to use CADisplayLink director
    // if it fails (SDK < 3.1) use the default director
    if( ! [CCDirector setDirectorType:kCCDirectorTypeDisplayLink] )
        [CCDirector setDirectorType:kCCDirectorTypeDefault]; // 1

    CCDirector *director = [CCDirector sharedDirector]; // 2

    // Init the View Controller
    viewController = [[RootViewController alloc]
                        initWithNibName:nil bundle:nil];
    viewController.wantsFullScreenLayout = YES; // 3

    // Create the EAGLView manually
    // 1. Create a RGB565 format. Alternative: RGBA8
    // 2. depth format of 0 bit. Use 16 or 24 bit for 3d effects,
    //     like CCPageTurnTransition
    EAGLView *glView = [EAGLView viewWithFrame:[window bounds]
                            pixelFormat:kEAGLColorFormatRGB565
                            depthFormat:0]; // 4
```

```
// attach the openglView to the director
[director setOpenGLView:glView];

// By default, this template only supports Landscape orientations.
// Edit the RootViewController.m file to edit the supported
// orientations.
#if GAME_AUTOROTATION == kGameAutorotationUIViewController
  [director setDeviceOrientation:kCCDeviceOrientationPortrait];
#else
  [director setDeviceOrientation:kCCDeviceOrientationLandscapeLeft];
#endif // 5

[director setAnimationInterval:1.0/60]; // 6
[director setDisplayFPS:YES]; // 7


// make the OpenGLView a child of the view controller
[viewController setView:glView]; // 8

// make the View Controller a child of the main window
[window addSubview: viewController.view];
[window makeKeyAndVisible]; // 9

// Default texture format for PNG/BMP/TIFF/JPEG/GIF images
// It can be RGBA8888, RGBA4444, RGB5_A1, RGB565
[CCTexture2D setDefaultAlphaPixelFormat:
                kCCTexture2DPixelFormat_RGBA8888]; // 10
// Removes the startup flicker
[self removeStartupFlicker]; // 11
// Run the intro Scene
[[CCDirector sharedDirector] runWithScene:
                        [HelloWorld scene]]; // 12
}
```

The first step is to initialize the UIWindow where the View Controller and EAGLView will be attached. The UIWindow is set to full screen, and the EAGLView is where all of the OpenGL ES calls are going to be sent. Next, the Application Delegate:

1. Tries to set up Cocos2D to use the DisplayLink Director available on iOS 3.1 and higher. The DisplayLink Director allows Cocos2D to be called right before the device needs to display the current image onscreen, so that the updates and render cycles are in sync with the screen refresh interval.

2. Instantiates the Cocos2D Director singleton.

3. Instantiates the view controller that will contain the EAGLView and will inform Cocos2D of any orientation changes when the device switches between portrait and landscape orientations.

4. Creates the `EAGLView`, which is used to render your game. Cocos2D will use the `EAGLView` to send the OpenGL ES commands to the OpenGL ES driver.

5. Sets the orientation to either portrait or landscape. If you are using the View Controller created by the Cocos2D template, you will need to modify the `shouldAutorotateToInterfaceOrientation` in the *RootViewController.m* class to support the orientations you need in your game.

6. Sets the animation interval to 60 times per second, which is the default mode for Cocos2D. Normally, Cocos2D tries to update the screen at the fastest rate (60 times per second).

7. Sets the Frames Per Second (FPS) display to be on and active. Cocos2D has the option of calculating the average frames per second that your game is running at and display it on the bottom left corner of the screen. The FPS display can be really useful in troubleshooting game performance. The FPS display is off by default; this line turns it on.

8. Adds the `EAGLView` as a child to the `RootViewController` so that it will be rendered.

9. Adds the `RootViewController` to the `UIWindow` and makes it active, allowing for the `RootViewController` and more importantly the `EAGLView` to start rendering elements on the screen.

10. Sets the Cocos2D texture format. Note that by default Cocos2D uses the highest bit depth for your images. In later chapters you will learn how to use images with a lower bit depth to save on memory usage.

11. Removes the startup flicker if your game runs only in landscape orientation. If your game runs only in a landscape orientation, Cocos2D needs to briefly load and display the *Default.png* image to avoid a flicker from the splash screen *(Default.png)* to black.

12. Instantiates the `HelloWorld` scene, which in turn instantiates the `HelloWorld` layer, and starts running the `HelloWorld` scene. At this point, the "Hello World" label is visible on the screen.

The Cocos2D Director is responsible for running the game loop and rendering all of the graphics in your game. Since the director is running the game loop, it can control when the game runs, pauses, or stops. Looking at Listing 1.6, you can see the methods in the application delegate that call the director in response to events from the iPhone operating system, including pause and resume.

Listing 1.6   Methods inside of CCHelloWorldAppDelegate.m

```
- (void)applicationWillResignActive:(UIApplication *)application {
    [[CCDirector sharedDirector] pause];                          // 1
}
```

```
- (void)applicationDidBecomeActive:(UIApplication *)application {
    [[CCDirector sharedDirector] resume];                          // 2
}


- (void)applicationDidReceiveMemoryWarning:(UIApplication *)application {
    [[CCDirector sharedDirector] purgeCachedData];                 // 3
}


- (void)applicationWillTerminate:(UIApplication *)application {
    CCDirector *director = [CCDirector sharedDirector];
    [[director openGLView] removeFromSuperview];
    [viewController release];
    [window release];
    [director end];                                                // 4
}


- (void)applicationSignificantTimeChange:(UIApplication *)application {
    [[CCDirector sharedDirector] setNextDeltaTimeZero:YES];        // 5
}
```

1. Pauses the game and all timers if the application is paused by the operating system. This event occurs when the user locks the iPad or iPhone screen while playing a game or when an incoming call or other similar event forces the game to the background.

2. Resumes the game and all timers when the application is brought back into the foreground by the operating system. This event occurs when the user unlocks the iPad or iPhone screen after locking it with the game running or resumes a game after the call is complete.

3. Removes from memory any sprite textures that are not being used at the moment in response to a low-memory warning. This call dumps all of the cached texture and bitmap fonts data that is not currently in use to render graphics onscreen.

Note

Your image files (PNGs, PVR) are loaded into OpenGL ES textures in a format that the GPU can understand. The Cocos2D sprites are your link to these textures, which are used by the Cocos2D Director and OpenGL ES to render your game. Cocos2D includes a texture cache manager to maintain any textures you use cached in memory. Keeping textures cached in memory greatly speeds up the creation of new sprites that utilize previously used textures. The disadvantage of keeping textures cached is the additional memory overhead. If the application receives a low-memory warning, Cocos2D moves quickly to remove from memory any textures not actively in use. It is important to always remember to deallocate your layers and scenes once you have moved from one scene to another, and remove any unused textures and other assets, to keep your memory footprint as small as possible.

4. Ends the director and detaches the EAGLView from the application's UIWindow. This ends the game loop, removes all textures from memory, and clears all of the scheduler timers. This command also forces the director to deallocate the currently running scene, including all of its layers and sprites. The applicationWillTerminate event is called when the user quits the game.

5. Sets the delta time between the last event call and the current event call to zero. This method is called if a significant amount of time has passed between event calls, usually due to the iPhone readjusting the system time for daylight savings or varying clocks on mobile phone towers. Physics inside of games and other calculations are sensitive to large time changes, and it is useful to reset the amount of time elapsed *(delta)* to zero if it is too large. If you were to try to run the update methods with a large delta value (several seconds at once, or several minutes), it would throw off the calculations and result in strange behavior and rendering effects. You will learn more about delta times in Part IV of this book.

If you follow the order of execution, the AppDelegate starts when the application is launched. The AppDelegate starts up the director and in turn calls on the director to run the HelloWorld scene. The HelloWorld scene has one layer, and that layer contains a label with the words "Hello World." The label is added as a child to the HelloWorld layer, which is a child of the scene. The director starts rendering the scene and its children, displaying the label (i.e., *Hello World*) onscreen.

> **Note**
>
> The 60.0 number on the bottom-left corner in Figure 1.9 is the frames per second at which Cocos2D is rendering the scene. This information is useful for debugging purposes because it allows you to see the frame rate your game is running. If you wish to disable it (which you will need to do when you ship your final app), you can go into the AppDelegate and remove the following line:
>
> ```
> [director setDisplayFPS:YES];
> ```

Looking Further into the Cocos2D Source Code

One of the great features of Cocos2D is that all of the source code is available and included in your projects, making it easy to look behind the scenes and see how the rendering and other tasks are being done. Not only Cocos2D but also the source code for CocosDenshion, Box2D, and Chipmunk are included in the projects that you create from the Cocos2D templates. You can look at any part of the source code if you ever have a question about what a particular method does or how it is implemented. To see a method, select the method or variable in Xcode, right-click (or Control-click), and choose **Jump to Definition** or press **Control-z-D** while the method or variable is selected. Figure 1.12 shows the **Jump to Definition** selection in the Xcode pop-up menu.

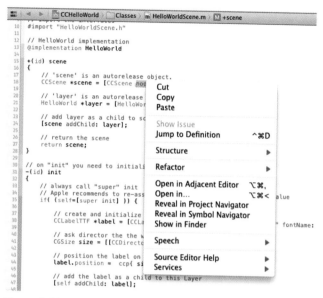

Figure 1.12   Jump to Definition option in the Xcode right-click
pop-up menu

To see the **Jump to Definition** in action:

1. Open the *HelloWorldScene.m* file.

2. On line 18, select the `node` method and right-click.

3. In the Xcode pop-up menu, select **Jump to Definition**. Xcode should open *CCNode.m* for you and show you the code in Listing 1.7.

Listing 1.7   **The node method inside of CCNode.m**

```
#pragma mark CCNode - Init & cleanup

+(id) node
{
    return [[[self alloc] init] autorelease];
}
```

Cocos2D has a large collection of utility and helper methods that can save you time and typing. As an example, in the Cocos2D Director there exist the methods `convertToGL` and `convertToUI` for converting a point between UIKit and OpenGL ES coordinate systems. In addition to utility and helper methods, Cocos2D has a set of macros to shorten some of the repetitive calls your code would contain.

The ccp macro is one you will use numerous times, and it is just a shortcut to the CGPointMake method. The following is the code behind the ccp macro.

```
/** Helper macro that creates a CGPoint
 @return CGPoint
 @since v0.7.2
 */
#define ccp(__X__,__Y__) CGPointMake(__X__,__Y__)
```

If you see an unknown method or macro, do not hesitate to jump to the definition of that bit of code. The Cocos2D source is well documented and is easy to understand with some practice. Knowing the helper methods, or at least how to find them, is key to becoming an efficient Cocos2D game developer.

The next section covers how to get *HelloWorld* and any other games you create onto your iPhone, iPad, or iPod touch.

Getting CCHelloWorld on Your iPhone or iPad

The first step to getting *CCHelloWorld* on your device is to sign up for an iPhone Developer account with Apple *(http://developer.apple.com/iphone)*. Figure 1.13 shows the iPhone Developer Portal.

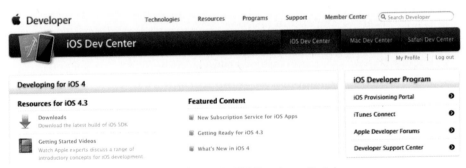

Figure 1.13   Apple iOS Developer Portal

Starting with Xcode 3.2.3, there are two ways to manage your builds for the iOS devices. You can let Xcode automatically configure the provisioning profile for your apps, or you can manually create and use an Ad Hoc profile from the iOS Developer Portal.

Letting Xcode Do Everything for You

Provisioning profiles is one of the biggest hurdles to new developers on the iOS platform. You spend all your time getting your game code working just right on the simulator, only to have to deal with code signing in order to get the game on an actual device. Apple has made this process a lot simpler starting with Xcode 3.2.3. To let Xcode configure the provisioning profiles on your behalf:

1. Make sure your iPhone or iPad is connected via USB.
2. In the Xcode menu, select **Window > Organizer**.
3. Select the **Devices** section.
4. Press the button marked **Use for Development**.
5. When prompted, enter your credentials for the iPhone Developer Program.

That's it! Xcode automatically sends your device UDID to Apple, creates a special provisioning profile called "Team Provisioning Profile," and sets everything up for you. After a minute or so, your Organizer window should look similar to Figure 1.14.

Figure 1.14   Xcode Organizer window with iPad configured for development

Building for Your iPhone or iPad

Under the Scheme dropdown menu, select *CCHelloWorld* and your iPhone or iPad device. You should see your iPad or iPhone listed if it is connected via USB.

If you select **Run**, Xcode will build a version of *CCHelloWorld* for the ARM processors on the iPad or iPhone and then copy *CCHelloWorld* to your device.

Summary

In this chapter you downloaded the source code for Cocos2D and installed the
Cocos2D templates into Xcode. You quickly created a HelloWorld app and added a
moving Space Cargo Ship in just a few lines of code. Additionally, you covered the
basics of Cocos2D Director, scenes, and layers, and what the Cocos2D templates
provide.

In the next chapter you get a chance to dive deeper into Cocos2D and start building the *Space Viking* game. If you are ready, turn the page and start on your journey to
get Ole the Viking moving around and fighting off the alien robots.

Challenges

1. Open the Cocos2D Xcode project included with the Cocos2D source you
    downloaded and run some of the included tests, such as the **SpriteTest**. The
    Cocos2D project file is located inside the *cocos2d-iphone* subfolder where you
    cloned or downloaded Cocos2D earlier in this chapter. To run the **SpriteTest**,
    select it under the Scheme dropdown, as shown in Figure 1.15.

Figure 1.15   SpriteTest selected under the Scheme dropdown in Xcode

2. Create a Cocos2D Box2D application and a Cocos2D Chipmunk application
    and run them on the simulator or your iOS device. Play around with the physics
    engines you will learn about in Part IV of this book.

2

Hello, Space Viking

In the previous chapter you installed Cocos2D on your system, including the templates that are used by Xcode. You also learned about some of the companion tools you will be using in later chapters. Now it is time to start your journey creating Space Viking *by putting Ole the Viking onscreen and moving him around. In this chapter you will deal only with the iPad version of* Space Viking; *later in the book you will cover in detail techniques and practices to adapt and scale a game from iPad down to the iPhone.*

You will start by creating the basic Space Viking *game project, which you will build upon throughout the rest of the book. You will begin with a basic Cocos2D template and add two sprites, one for the background and the other for Ole the Viking. In the second part of this chapter you will learn how to add the methods needed to handle the touch inputs, including moving your Viking and making him jump. If you are ready, open up Xcode to get started with* Space Viking!

Creating the SpaceViking Project

Space Viking is your key to learning Cocos2D as you progress through this book. All games have to start somewhere, and *Space Viking* starts life as a Cocos2D template project. The first thing you need to do is create a new Cocos2D project in Xcode, so go ahead and launch Xcode and create the project:

1. Open Xcode and select **Create a New Xcode Project**.
2. Choose the **Cocos2D** template (without Box2D or Chipmunk) under the iOS section.
3. Enter *SpaceViking* as the name of the product, and select **Next**.
4. Select a location to save your *SpaceViking* project, and click **Create**.

The location of the Cocos2D templates in Xcode are shown in Figure 2.1. Depending on what version of Cocos2D you have installed, your templates might have different revision numbers.

Figure 2.1   Cocos2D templates in Xcode

These are the same two steps you performed in Chapter 1, "Hello, Cocos2D," and if you press **Run** in Xcode, you will see the Cocos2D *HelloWorld* sample. You will be creating *Space Viking* specifically for the iPad, and you will learn how to scale it down for the iPhone in later chapters. The Cocos2D templates are set up to create an iPhone game by default, requiring you to quickly transition the project in Xcode before getting started with the coding.

Creating the Space Viking Classes

At this point you have a project template game app, running on both the iPhone and iPad at full-screen resolution. Leaving the *HelloWorld* files as reference, it is time to start creating the classes needed for *Space Viking*. The first step is to add the *Images* folder that you downloaded from the book site to the *SpaceViking* project.

> **Note**
> For this chapter you need the *Images* folder included with the resources for this book. You must download the resources from the InformIT website (*www.informit.com/title/9780321735621*). Once you download the disk image, go to the folder for Chapter 2.

Next you need to make it so Xcode pulls the *Images* folder into your project and copies the files into the *SpaceViking* project's directory.

5. With the *SpaceViking* project opened in Xcode, drag the *Images* folder from a Finder window into your *SpaceViking* project.

6. On the sheet that drops down, make sure that the **Copy items into destination group's folder** is checked and click **Finish**, as shown in Figure 2.2.

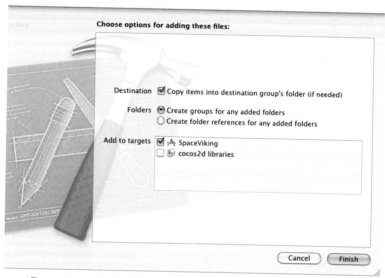

Figure 2.2   Xcode Add Files dialog with the copy items checkbox turned ON

Warning

The **Copy items into destination group's folder** option is needed when you want to copy files to your project from another location on your system. If you leave this checkbox unchecked, the files will only be linked into your project, meaning the files will exist only in their original folder outside of your project. In *Space Viking*, you want the *Images* folder inside your project folder just in case you decide to move the downloaded *Images* folder later on.

If you look in the *Images* folder, you will see the PNG files that you will use on this version of the game. These include the background image and the first frame you will use for Ole the Viking. Now that the images are part of the project, you can move on and create the background layer and gameplay layers followed by the gameplay scene, which will contain both layers.

> **Note**
>
> The *Images* folder you copied into the *Space Viking* Xcode project contains the various icon file images used for *Space Viking*'s app icon. The Cocos2D templates already contain *icon.png, Icon@2x.png, Icon-Small.png, Icon-Small@2x.png, Icon-Small-50.png, Icon-72.png,* and *Default.png* files in the *Resources* folder, so you need to delete them from the project before proceeding.

Creating the Background Layer

As noted earlier, the Cocos2D Director is responsible for running the scene, and each scene in Cocos2D is made up of layers. As each layer is initialized, an `init` method is called. The `init` method is the perfect location to create and initialize the sprites used in each layer. The background of *Space Viking* will have one sprite containing the background image centered onscreen. In later versions of *Space Viking*, you will add scrolling backgrounds and animations.

1. In Xcode, select the *Classes* folder and right-click, choosing **New File** from the contextual menu.

2. On the dialog that drops down, select the **iOS\Cocoa Touch class** on the left panel and **Objective-C class**, and then click **Next**, as shown in Figure 2.3.

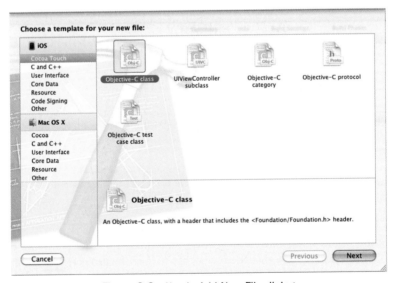

Figure 2.3   Xcode Add New File dialog

3. For the Subclass field, enter *CCLayer* and click **Next**.

4. In the Save As field, type in *BackgroundLayer.m* and click **Save**. Figure 2.4 shows the Add new file window.

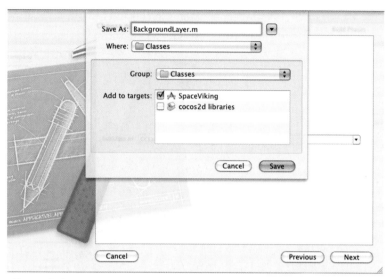

Figure 2.4   Adding the BackgroundLayer.m class to SpaceViking in Xcode

Open the *BackgroundLayer.h* header file.

Add a #import line for Cocos2D, and change the BackgroundLayer class to inherit from CCLayer instead of NSObject. Listing 2.1 shows the complete *BackgroundLayer.h* file.

Listing 2.1   **BackgroundLayer.h**

```
#import <Foundation/Foundation.h>
#import "cocos2d.h"

@interface BackgroundLayer : CCLayer {

}

@end
```

Switch to the *BackgroundLayer.m* implementation file so you can add the init method and the background sprite.

Tip

Whether you're using a MacBook, MacBook Pro, or Apple's Magic TrackPad, you can use a three-finger swipe up or down to switch between the header *.h* and the implementation *.m* files quickly in Xcode. Just swipe up or down to move between the header and implementation files. You can also use the keyboard combination of Option+Command+Up Arrow to switch between header and implementation files.

Open the *BackgroundLayer.m* implementation file and add the -(id)init method, as shown in Listing 2.2.

Listing 2.2   **BackgroundLayer.m**

```
//   BackgroundLayer.m
//   SpaceViking
#import "BackgroundLayer.h"

@implementation BackgroundLayer
-(id)init {
    self = [super init];                                       // 1
    if (self != nil) {                                         // 2
// 3
        CCSprite *backgroundImage;
    if (UI_USER_INTERFACE_IDIOM() == UIUserInterfaceIdiomPad) {
            // Indicates game is running on iPad
            backgroundImage = [CCSprite
             spriteWithFile:@"background.png"];
    } else {
            backgroundImage = [CCSprite
             spriteWithFile:@"backgroundiPhone.png"];
        }

        CGSize screenSize = [[CCDirector sharedDirector] winSize]; // 4
        [backgroundImage setPosition:
         CGPointMake(screenSize.width/2, screenSize.height/2)];    // 5

        [self addChild:backgroundImage z:0 tag:0];                 // 6

    }
    return self;                                              // 7

}
@end
```

The first two lines of this method are standard boilerplate code from Apple's template; it checks that the parent/super class is initialized and not nil. Now let's take a closer look at what's going on in that init method; the following list refers to the numbered/commented lines in Listing 2.2.

1. Creates an initialized instance of the superclass of the BackgroundLayer class, which in this case is CCLayer.

2. Checks to make sure this instance is not nil.

3. Checks to see if *Space Viking* is running on the iPad or the iPhone. If the iPad is selected, then the *background.png* image is used for the background; otherwise, when running on the iPhone, the *backgroundiPhone.png* is selected. If you look

inside of the *Images/Backgrounds* folder you copied into your project, you will see there are two iPhone backgrounds, *backgroundIiPhone.png* and *backgroundiPhone-hd.png*. Cocos2D automatically detects the iPhone 4 Retina display and will use the higher resolution image. The `spriteWithFile` method call creates a texture from the image file and associates it with the `CCSprite` object. The sprite's dimensions and corresponding geometry are set to the image dimensions.

4. Gets the screen size from the Cocos2D Director. On the iPad, this returns 1024 × 768 pixels.

5. Sets the position of the `backgroundImage` sprite to the center of the screen.

   The Cocos2D coordinate system has (0,0) at the bottom left of the screen. Cocos2D positions sprites according to their center points. Make sure to always take into account the dimensions of your sprite when using the `setPosition` method.

6. Adds the `backgroundImage` to the `backgroundLayer` with the z and `tag` values set to zero. The z values are used by Cocos2D to composite the sprites and layers onscreen. The higher the z value, the closer to the front of the screen an object is. For sprites, you need to keep track of which layer the sprite is in, as well. If a sprite has a z value of 100 but is still in the backmost layer (with the lowest z value), it will be rendered behind other sprites in layers with a higher z value.

7. Returns the newly initialized `BackgroundLayer` class.

> **Tip**
>
> The UIKit coordinate system has the origin (0,0) at the upper left of the screen. However, Cocos2D uses the OpenGL ES coordinate system, which places the origin (0,0) at the lower left of the screen.
>
> To combat this, the Cocos2D utility functions `convertToGL` and `convertToUI` allow for easy conversions between points in the UIKit coordinate system and the OpenGL ES coordinate system. You will use these functions when trying to get the location of a touch event, converting it from UIKit to OpenGL ES coordinates.

The background layer in this chapter contains just one image; later in the book you will learn how to add tile maps and scrolling to the *Space Viking* game. Let's continue to the `GameplayLayer` and `GameScene` classes, which you will use to wire up the background layer into the game.

The Gameplay Layer: Adding Ole the Viking to the Game

You are well on your way to a functional game. Now it is time to add Ole the Viking to the scene. You use a separate layer to house all of your actors and actions, including Ole the Viking. In Xcode, you need to create a new `GameplayLayer` class and the sprite that will hold the image of Ole. In the next chapter, you add enemies and animations to the `GameplayLayer`.

1. In Xcode, select and right-click on the *SpaceViking Classes* folder.
2. Choose **New File** and select **iOS\Cocoa Touch\Objective-C class** as the type.
3. For the Subclass field, enter *CCLayer* and click **Next**.
4. Enter *GameplayLayer.m* for the filename, and click **Save**. Xcode automatically creates the header file for you, setting up the basics so that all you need to do is add any instance variables or properties to the header file.
5. Open the *GameplayLayer.h* header file and add the #import line for Cocos2D and an instance variable called vikingSprite, which holds the sprite, as shown in Listing 2.3.

The changed *GameplayLayer.h* header is shown in Listing 2.3.

Listing 2.3   **GameplayLayer.h**

```
#import <Foundation/Foundation.h>
#import "cocos2d.h"
@interface GameplayLayer : CCLayer {
    CCSprite *vikingSprite;
}
@end
```

Move to the implementation *(GameplayLayer.m)* file and add the init method, as shown in Listing 2.4.

Listing 2.4   **GameplayLayer.m**

```
//   GameplayLayer.m
//   SpaceViking

#import "GameplayLayer.h"

@implementation GameplayLayer
-(id)init {
    self = [super init];
    if (self != nil) {
        CGSize screenSize = [CCDirector sharedDirector].winSize;  // 1
        // enable touches
        self.isTouchEnabled = YES;                                // 2
        vikingSprite = [CCSprite spriteWithFile:@"sv_anim_1.png"];// 3
        [vikingSprite setPosition:
            CGPointMake(screenSize.width/2,
                        screenSize.height*0.17f)];                // 4
        [self addChild:vikingSprite];                             // 5
                                                                  // 6
        if (UI_USER_INTERFACE_IDIOM() != UIUserInterfaceIdiomPad) {
            // If NOT on the iPad, scale down Ole
```

```
            // In your games, use this to load art sized for the device
            [vikingSprite setScaleX:screenSize.width/1024.0f];
            [vikingSprite setScaleY:screenSize.height/768.0f];
        }
    }
    return self;
}
@end
```

Now let's take a look at what's happening in Listing 2.4:

1. Gets the screen size from the Cocos2D Director. On the iPad, this returns 1024 × 768 pixels.

2. Informs Cocos2D that the gameplayLayer will receive touch events.

3. Allocates and initializes the vikingSprite instance variable with the image *viking1.png*.

4. Sets the position of the vikingSprite onscreen. The screenSize.width/2 parameter takes the current screen width (1024 pixels on the iPad) and divides it by two. This places the Viking 512 pixels to the right of the screen, dead center on the X-axis. The Y-axis is being set to 130 pixels up from the bottom. Recall that the OpenGL ES and Cocos2D coordinate system has (0,0) at the bottom left of the screen. The use of 130.0f instead of 130 is because this method expects a float value instead of an integer value. You are skipping a conversion from integer to float here by providing the value in float format.

5. Adds the vikingSprite to the GameplayLayer. Having the vikingSprite as a child of the layer enables it to be rendered on the screen by Cocos2D.

6. Scales down the vikingSprite if *Space Viking* is **not** running on the iPad, resizing it to fit the screen resolution. In your games and in later chapters, you will want to use this check to load the appropriate iPhone/iPod touch artwork. In order to keep things simple, this example just scales down the Viking image.

> **Warning**
>
> Please ensure that you copied the *Images* folder into your project with the *background.png* and *sv_anim_1.png* image files. While *Space Viking* will compile without those images, you will get a runtime crash with the error message **cocos2d: Couldn't add image:sv_anim_1.png in CCTextureCache.**

The GameScene Class: Connecting the Layers in a Scene

You now have the two layers in the *Space Viking* game: one with the background and one with Ole the Viking. The next step is to have both of these layers as children of a Scene object. The Cocos2D Director executes the game run loop and "runs" a particular scene. At the moment, your game will have just one scene, the GameScene. You'll see how to add more scenes to Cocos2D and transition between them in Chapter 7, "Main Menu, Level Completed, and Credit Scenes."

Creating the GameScene

Select and right-click on the *Classes* folder, and then choose **New File**.

Select the **iOS\Cocoa Touch\Objective-C class** and click **Next**. For the Subclass field, enter *CCScene* and click **Next**. Type in *GameScene.m* under the **File Name** and click **Save**.

Open up *GameScene.h* and add the #import lines for Cocos2D, BackgroundLayer, and GameplayLayer classes. Listing 2.5 shows the full *GameScene.h* header file.

Listing 2.5   **GameScene.h**

```
#import <Foundation/Foundation.h>
#import "cocos2d.h"
#import "BackgroundLayer.h"
#import "GameplayLayer.h"
@interface GameScene : CCScene {
}
@end
```

Switch to the *GameScene.m* implementation file. Here you will add the init method to create and add the BackgroundLayer and GameplayLayer instances to the GameScene class. Listing 2.6 shows the init method inside the *GameScene.m* implementation file.

Listing 2.6   **GameScene.m (add between @implementation and @end)**

```
-(id)init {
    self = [super init];
    if (self != nil) {
        // Background Layer
        BackgroundLayer *backgroundLayer = [BackgroundLayer node]; // 1
        [self addChild:backgroundLayer z:0];                       // 2
        // Gameplay Layer
        GameplayLayer *gameplayLayer = [GameplayLayer node];       // 3
        [self addChild:gameplayLayer z:5];                         // 4
    }
    return self;
}
```

Here is what is happening in the init method of GameScene:

1. Instantiates the backgroundLayer object. The node method call is just a shortcut for the alloc and init methods combined.

2. Adds the `backgroundLayer` to the scene with a z value of zero.

3. Instantiates the `gameplayLayer` object.

4. Adds the `gameplayLayer` object to the scene with a z value of 5. Since the z value of the `gameplayLayer` is higher than the z value of `backgroundLayer`, it will be composited in front of the `backgroundLayer`.

As you can see in Listing 2.6, Cocos2D scenes can be pretty simple, acting as a container for the `CCLayers` in your game. Most of the functionality you will create in *Space Viking* will be restricted to the `CCLayers` in the game.

In Xcode press **z–B** or select **Build** from the Product menu to ensure that you have not made any typos or errors in entering the code thus far. *Space Viking* should have a clean build at this point. In the next section you will add the code to make the director run the `GameScene` instead of `HelloWorld`.

A Note on z Values

Cocos2D is a 2D game engine, but because it uses OpenGL ES for all rendering, it knows about the third dimension (depth), otherwise known as the z *value*. In 3D engines the z value is used in the compositing stage to specify what objects or sprites are in front and behind. In Cocos2D the z value determines the order in which your `CCNodes` (sprites, layers, etc.) will be drawn. All of the sprites in your layers have z values, and the layers themselves have z values in the scenes. The z value of 0 (zero) denotes the furthest point from the screen, while a positive z value is closer to the screen. If you have two sprites in the same layer, one with a z value of 10 and another with a z value of 20, the one with a z value of 20 is in front. Figure 2.5 shows the background and gameplay layers in *Space Viking*, with the background layer having the lower z value.

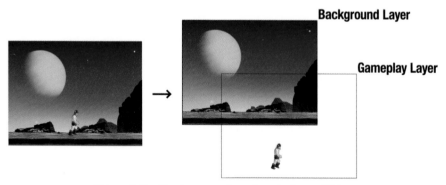

Figure 2.5   The layers and z values in Space Viking

Commanding the Cocos2D Director

In the *SpaceViking* project, the Cocos2D Director is set to instantiate and run the `HelloWorld` scene. You need to change the director call so that it runs the `GameScene` instead.

1. Open the *SpaceVikingAppDelegate.m* implementation file.

2. At the top of the file, add an import for the `GameScene` class in the *SpaceVikingAppDelegate.m* implementation file, as shown in Listing 2.7.

Listing 2.7   **SpaceVikingAppDelegate.m**

```
#import "cocos2d.h"
#import "SpaceVikingsAppDelegate.h"
#import "GameConfig.h"
#import "HelloWorldScene.h"
#import "RootViewController.h"
#import "GameScene.h"

@implementation SpaceVikingAppDelegate
```

3. Scroll down and uncomment the following lines in order to enable the higher resolution images in the iPhone 4's retina display:

```
// Enables High Res mode (Retina Display) on iPhone 4 and maintains
// low res on all other devices
if( ! [director enableRetinaDisplay:YES] )
    CCLOG(@"Retina Display Not supported");
```

When you remove the comments from this line in the Application Delegate, Cocos2D will always look for files with a -hd suffix. In this chapter this means that the `BackgroundLayer` will use *backgroundiPhone-hd.png* on the iPhone 4 and *backgroundiPhone.png* on the older iPhone and iPod touch devices.

4. Scroll down and find the `-applicationDidFinishLaunching` method. Then find and comment out the following line:

```
// [[CCDirector sharedDirector] runWithScene: [HelloWorld scene]];
```

5. In its place add a line to indicate you want the director to run the `GameScene`.

```
[[CCDirector sharedDirector] runWithScene:[GameScene node]];
```

This line instructs the director to allocate and instantiate the `GameScene` class and then run it. Your `GameScene` class contains the background and gameplay layers, and running the scene causes any layers contained in it to render to the screen.

If you select the iPad Simulator from the Scheme dropdown and click **Run**, you will see the *Space Viking* game with Ole the Viking in the middle of the alien world background. Figure 2.6 shows *Space Viking* running on the iPad Simulator.

Figure 2.6   Space Viking running on the iPad Simulator

Adding Movement

It took only a few pages to get your Viking and background on the iPad screen. Now you have to work on getting Ole to move around. Luckily, Cocos2D makes the job of moving and animating sprites easy. In *Space Viking*, you will use a thumb joystick on the left side to move Ole and buttons on the right to attack and jump. In Cocos2D, touch events are sent to the layers that subscribe to those events. You have already set your `GameplayLayer` class to receive touch events, and all you have to do now is implement the methods that will be called when the touch events occur.

Importing the Joystick Classes

In *Space Viking* you will use an Open Source joystick project called SneakyInput. It is included with the resource files for this chapter. SneakyInput is one of many joystick projects and options available to use with Cocos2D. To add the SneakyInput joystick to your *SpaceViking* project:

1. In Xcode select your *SpaceViking* project.
2. Right-click and select **Add > Files**.

3. Browse to the location of the *Resources* folder you downloaded for this chapter and select the *JoystickClasses* folder.

4. Ensure that **Copy items into destination group's folder** is selected, and click **Add**.

Now that you have the `SneakyInput` joystick classes in your *SpaceViking* project, the next step is to utilize those classes in the `GameplayLayer` class.

> **Note**
>
> The `SneakyInput` joystick classes are not part of the main Cocos2D distribution at this time. The `applyJoystick` method used in *Space Viking* borrows some of the code from the SneakyInput samples. You can view and check out the latest code for SneakyInput at the GitHub repository located at *https://github.com/sneakyness/SneakyInput*.

Adding the Joystick and Buttons

Open up the *GameplayLayer.h* header file and add the `#import` statements for the `SneakyInput` classes. Along with the import statements, add three instance variables for the joystick and two buttons, as shown in Listing 2.8.

Listing 2.8 **GameplayLayer.h**

```
//   GameplayLayer.h
//   SpaceViking

#import <Foundation/Foundation.h>
#import "cocos2d.h"
#import "SneakyJoystick.h"
#import "SneakyButton.h"
#import "SneakyButtonSkinnedBase.h"
#import "SneakyJoystickSkinnedBase.h"

@interface GameplayLayer : CCLayer {
    CCSprite *vikingSprite;
    SneakyJoystick *leftJoystick;
    SneakyButton *jumpButton;
    SneakyButton *attackButton;
}
@end
```

The `leftJoystick` will be the thumb stick used to move Ole left and right. The jump and attack buttons will trigger jump and attack actions, respectively.

In the *GameplayLayer.m* implementation file, add a method called `-(void)init-JoystickAndButtons()` above the `-(id)init` method in order to initialize the joystick and buttons. This method is called from the `init` method. Listing 2.9 shows the contents of the `initJoystickAndButtons` method.

Listing 2.9   **GameplayLayer.m –(void)initJoystickAndButtons()**

```
-(void)initJoystickAndButtons {
    CGSize screenSize = [CCDirector sharedDirector].winSize;      // 1
    CGRect joystickBaseDimensions =
            CGRectMake(0, 0, 128.0f, 128.0f);                     // 2
    CGRect jumpButtonDimensions =
            CGRectMake(0, 0, 64.0f, 64.0f);
    CGRect attackButtonDimensions =
            CGRectMake(0, 0, 64.0f, 64.0f);
    CGPoint joystickBasePosition;                                 // 3
    CGPoint jumpButtonPosition;
    CGPoint attackButtonPosition;

    if (UI_USER_INTERFACE_IDIOM() == UIUserInterfaceIdiomPad) {   // 4
        // The device is an iPad running iPhone 3.2 or later.
        CCLOG(@"Positioning Joystick and Buttons for iPad");
        joystickBasePosition = ccp(screenSize.width*0.0625f,
                                   screenSize.height*0.052f);

        jumpButtonPosition = ccp(screenSize.width*0.946f,
                                 screenSize.height*0.052f);

        attackButtonPosition = ccp(screenSize.width*0.947f,
                                   screenSize.height*0.169f);
    } else {
        // The device is an iPhone or iPod touch.
        CCLOG(@"Positioning Joystick and Buttons for iPhone");
        joystickBasePosition = ccp(screenSize.width*0.07f,
                                   screenSize.height*0.11f);

        jumpButtonPosition = ccp(screenSize.width*0.93f,
                                 screenSize.height*0.11f);

        attackButtonPosition = ccp(screenSize.width*0.93f,
                                   screenSize.height*0.35f);
    }

    SneakyJoystickSkinnedBase *joystickBase =
    [[[SneakyJoystickSkinnedBase alloc] init] autorelease];       // 5
    joystickBase.position = joystickBasePosition;                 // 6
    joystickBase.backgroundSprite =
    [CCSprite spriteWithFile:@"dpadDown.png"];                    // 7
    joystickBase.thumbSprite =
    [CCSprite spriteWithFile:@"joystickDown.png"];                // 8
    joystickBase.joystick = [[SneakyJoystick alloc]
                        initWithRect:joystickBaseDimensions];     // 9
```

```
    leftJoystick = [joystickBase.joystick retain];              // 10
    [self addChild:joystickBase];                               // 11

    SneakyButtonSkinnedBase *jumpButtonBase =
    [[[SneakyButtonSkinnedBase alloc] init] autorelease];       // 12
    jumpButtonBase.position = jumpButtonPosition;               // 13
    jumpButtonBase.defaultSprite =
    [CCSprite spriteWithFile:@"jumpUp.png"];                    // 14
    jumpButtonBase.activatedSprite =
    [CCSprite spriteWithFile:@"jumpDown.png"];                  // 15
    jumpButtonBase.pressSprite =
    [CCSprite spriteWithFile:@"jumpDown.png"];                  // 16
    jumpButtonBase.button = [[SneakyButton alloc]
                            initWithRect:jumpButtonDimensions];  // 17
    jumpButton = [jumpButtonBase.button retain];                // 18
    jumpButton.isToggleable = NO;                               // 19
    [self addChild:jumpButtonBase];                             // 20

    SneakyButtonSkinnedBase *attackButtonBase =
[[[SneakyButtonSkinnedBase alloc] init] autorelease];           // 21
    attackButtonBase.position = attackButtonPosition;           // 22
    attackButtonBase.defaultSprite = [CCSprite
spriteWithFile:@"handUp.png"];                                  // 23
    attackButtonBase.activatedSprite = [CCSprite
spriteWithFile:@"handDown.png"];                                // 24
    attackButtonBase.pressSprite = [CCSprite
spriteWithFile:@"handDown.png"];                                // 25
    attackButtonBase.button = [[SneakyButton alloc]
initWithRect:attackButtonDimensions];                           // 26
    attackButton = [attackButtonBase.button retain];            // 27
    attackButton.isToggleable = NO;                             // 28
    [self addChild:attackButtonBase];                           // 29
}
```

The initJoystickAndButtons method gets the SneakyJoystick classes all set up and connected to your *Space Viking* game. Here is what happens in the method, line by line:

1. Gets the screenSize from the Cocos2D Director. The screenSize is used to calculate the positioning of the joystick and buttons.

2. Sets up the touch dimensions for the joystick and buttons. The joystick touch dimensions are a rectangle of size 128 × 128 pixels. The jump and attack buttons dimensions are a rectangle of size 64 × 64 pixels.

3. Creates the three CGPoint variables that are used to position the joystick and buttons.

4. Determines if *Space Viking* is running on an iPad or iPhone/iPod touch. In iOS 3.2 and later, this is the best way to determine what device your game is running on. Depending on whether the iPad or iPhone/iPod touch is detected, the positions for the joystick and buttons are set up. This if/else block uses a calculation for the values so that if the iPad dimensions change, the joystick and buttons will still be in their proper place.

5. Allocates and initializes a joystick base. The joystick base will contain the actual joystick and the sprites used to show the static joystick directional pad (DPAD) and the moveable thumb portion of the joystick.

6. Sets the position of the joystick base to the value corresponding to either iPad or iPhone dimensions.

7. Sets the background image of the joystick to the *dpadDown.png* image. In *Space Viking* this is a Viking rune–styled directional pad.

8. Sets the thumb portion of the joystick to the *joystickDown.png* image. This is the image players will move around with their thumbs or fingers.

9. Sets the joystick touch area to be a rectangle of 128 × 128 pixels, based on the value of `joystickBaseDimensions` variable.

10. Assigns the joystick component of the joystick base to the `GameplayLayer` `leftJoystick` instance variable. Later in this chapter you will query the `leftJoystick` thumb component position to move Ole the Viking around the screen.

11. Adds the joystick base to the `GameplayLayer` instance, making it visible on the lower-left portion of the screen.

Lines 5 through 11 set up the thumb joystick to move Ole the Viking around the screen. Lines 12 through 29 set up the attack and jump buttons.

12. Allocates and initializes the jump button base.

13. Sets the base position onscreen.

14. Sets the up position of the jump button base to the *jumpUp.png* image. This is the state of the button if it is not being pressed.

15. Sets the activated position of the jump button base to the *jumpDown.png* image. This is the state of the button if it is toggled to on or down.

16. Sets the down position of the jump button base. This is the state of the button when the player presses it. Cocos2D textures are cached, so having the same image for the down and activated states of this button loads the *jumpDown.png* image only once in memory.

17. Sets the touch area of the button to a rectangle of 64 × 64 pixels.

18. Assigns the button component of the jump button base to the `GameplayLayer` `jumpButton` instance variable. In the `applyJoystick` method further in this

chapter, you will query the jumpButton object to determine if the player is pressing the button.

19. Sets this button to not act as a toggle. If a button has isToggleable set to YES, pressing it alternates the button state from ON to OFF. If the button has isToggleable set to NO, it turns OFF as soon as the player lifts his or her finger from it.

20. Adds the jump button base to the GameplayLayer instance, making it visible on the lower-right portion of the screen.

Lines 21 through 29 are the same as lines 12 through 20, except they set up the attack button instead of the jump button. Now that you have the joystick and buttons initialized, it is time to add code to check them and connect the joystick movements to Ole the Viking.

Applying Joystick Movements to Ole the Viking

In the *GameplayLayer.m* implementation file, add a method called applyJoystick below the initJoystickAndButtons method, as shown in Listing 2.10. This method is called every time the position of Ole the Viking needs to be adjusted based on the position of the joystick.

Listing 2.10   The applyJoystick method in gameplayLayer.m

```
-(void)applyJoystick:(SneakyJoystick *)aJoystick toNode:(CCNode
*)tempNode forTimeDelta:(float)deltaTime
{
    CGPoint scaledVelocity = ccpMult(aJoystick.velocity, 1024.0f); // 1

    CGPoint newPosition =
        ccp(tempNode.position.x + scaledVelocity.x * deltaTime,
        tempNode.position.y + scaledVelocity.y * deltaTime);        // 2

    [tempNode setPosition:newPosition];                             // 3

    if (jumpButton.active == YES) {
        CCLOG(@"Jump button is pressed.");                          // 4
    }
    if (attackButton.active == YES) {
        CCLOG(@"Attack button is pressed.");                        // 5
    }
}
```

1. Gets the velocity from the joystick object and multiplies it by 1024, which is used here because it is the size of the iPad screen. The velocity can be multiplied

by different factors to make Ole the Viking move faster or slower in relation to the movement of the joystick.

2. Creates a new position based on the current `tempNode` position, the joystick velocity, and how much time has elapsed between the last time this method was called and now. In Listing 2.11 you will see that `tempNode` contains a reference to the `vikingSprite` instance variable.

3. Sets the `tempNode` position to the newly calculated position. Here `tempNode` is really a reference to `vikingSprite`, so this call is placing Ole the Viking at a new position.

4. Checks if the jump button is pressed, and if so, prints a message to the Console.

5. Checks if the attack button is pressed, and if so, prints a message to the Console.

In the `applyJoystick` method, the jump and attack buttons only cause messages to be displayed to the Console. In the next chapter you will learn about Cocos2D animations and add the code to enable Ole the Viking to jump and attack.

> **Note**
>
> CCLOG is a Cocos2D macro for the `NSLog` method. If *Space Viking* is being compiled with an active configuration of Debug, then this line compiles to an `NSLog` statement; otherwise, it compiles down, in essence, to an empty line. If you want to have CCLOG active even on a Distribution configuration, you can set the `COCOS2D_DEBUG` `#define` to a number higher than zero. CCLOG is useful to keep your Console log messages active in the Debug configuration and inactive for builds you plan to release via Ad Hoc distribution or to the AppStore.

After the `applyJoystick` method in *GameplayLayer.m*, add a method called `update`, as shown in Listing 2.11.

Listing 2.11   **The update method in GameplayLayer.m (after applyJoystick)**

```
#pragma mark -
#pragma mark Update Method
-(void) update:(ccTime)deltaTime
{
    [self applyJoystick:leftJoystick toNode:vikingSprite
forTimeDelta:deltaTime];
}
```

The `update` method is called before every frame of *Space Viking* is to be rendered. The Cocos2D Director runs the *Space Viking* game loop at 60 frames per second, so the `update` method is called approximately 60 times a second. Here the `update` method calls the `applyJoystick` method shown in Listing 2.10, passing it the `vikingSprite` object and how much time (`deltaTime`) has elapsed between the last update call and now.

Finally, it is time to add the last bit of code that initializes the buttons and calls the update method before each frame is rendered. In the `init` method of `GameplayLayer`, add the following two lines right after `[self addChild:vikingSprite];` as shown in Listing 2.12.

Listing 2.12 **Joystick initialization and update scheduler setup in init inside of gameplayLayer.m**

```
[self initJoystickAndButtons];          // 7
[self scheduleUpdate];                   // 8
```

Line 7 calls the `initJoystickAndButtons` method covered in Listing 2.9, setting up the joystick and the two buttons. Line 8 is a call to the Cocos2D scheduler to call the update method every time this layer is set to be rendered on the screen. The `scheduleUpdate` call is new as of Cocos2D version 0.99.3.

Click **Run** in Xcode and you should see the *Space Viking* game with the joystick on the bottom-left side and the buttons on the right side. Figure 2.7 shows Space Viking with the controls in place on the iPad Simulator.

Figure 2.7   Space Viking with joystick, jump, and attack buttons

> **Note**
>
> The artwork you are using is designed for the iPad, but the code you entered for the Viking, background, joystick, and buttons will allow it to work on the iPad or iPhone/iPod touch.

A Word on Instance Variables

You may have noticed that you used a `vikingSprite` instance variable to keep track of Ole's sprite object. You then kept the instance variable pointing to the `viking-Sprite` so that you could update his position. Cocos2D automatically retains the sprites that are added as children to the layers and optionally can mark each sprite with a unique integer tag. You can use this tag mechanism to avoid having to keep instance variables of your character sprites. If you set an integer constant of `kVikingSprite` to be 10 and change the `addChild` line as follows:

```
#define kVikingSprite 10
[self addChild:tempSprite z:0 tag:kVikingSprite];
```

Then, when you want to access Ole's sprite object to change the position, you can get it from the `GameplayLayer` with the `getChildByTag` method call.

```
CCSprite *tempSprite = [self getChildByTag:kVikingSprite];
```

Using the tag feature of Cocos2D can simplify memory management in your Cocos2D games. You will explore tags and their use in later chapters.

At this point you hopefully have the first glimpse of the *Space Viking* game that you can hold in your hands, with thoughts of what it will become. With your confidence slowly building, it is time to cover some of the graphics work needed before you can move on with the coding intricacies. In particular, it is important to understand what texture atlases are and why you should use them.

Terminology Review

These three terms, covered briefly in Chapter 1, are worth spending a few minutes reviewing. Understanding these terms is key to building a solid foundation and becoming an efficient Cocos2D game developer.

- **Image Files**
  Your characters start out as images on the flash storage of the iPhone/iPad. The format of files is typically PNG or JPEG. Once the images are loaded into memory, they are stored in an uncompressed texture format. PNG is the preferred format for images on the iOS devices.

- **Texture**
  The image file of your character has to be decompressed and possibly converted into a format that the iPhone and iPad GPU can understand and loaded into RAM before it can be used. The loaded image in RAM is referred to as a texture. The GPU can natively handle a few compressed formats such as PVRTC; others have to be stored as uncompressed image data. This is what OpenGL ES draws on the screen. The decompression of your images is why a PNG image may be small in flash storage but in memory takes up much more as it is stored uncompressed.

- **Texture Atlas or Sprite Sheet**
  In order to save on memory and reduce the amount of wasted empty space in
  your textures, you want to combine them into one larger texture, called a texture
  atlas. The texture atlas is simply a large texture, containing your images, from
  which smaller textures for each of your images can be cut or extracted from.
  Imagine a large sheet of paper with photographs glued to it. You can cut out
  each of the photographs from the single larger sheet. If you want to hand some-
  one all the photos at once, you just hand over the sheet. One of the keys to getting more graphical performance is handing OpenGL ES as few textures as you
  can in one pass by having a lot of textures combined into the texture atlas. The
  key is in batching the draw calls and reducing the number of textures OpenGL
  ES binds to, both accomplished by using a texture atlas in Cocos2D via the
  `CCSpriteBatchNode`.

Texture atlases can seem a hard concept to grasp at first. To better understand why
they are used, continue to the next section, which further explains atlases and walks
you through creating the atlas used in *Space Viking*.

Texture Atlases

Life is filled with constraints, and game development is no different. In fact, game
development is always pushing to get the most performance out of the limited hardware at hand. A common issue that developers face is slow performance after they get
a large number of sprites on the screen. You create your game in much the same way
you did in this chapter, where all of the graphic elements are individual CCSprites.
Everything is going fine, until you start to have 15 or 20 elements onscreen and you
notice your frame rate plummeting. The more elements you add, the quicker it drops.
Even if you take out game logic, and just move the CCSprites on the screen, your
game keeps slowing down as you add CCSprites. There can be many reasons for the
performance problems; one of the most common is too many texture context switches
caused by using individual CCSprites instead of a CCSpriteBatchNode. In a nutshell,
you are doing too many OpenGL ES calls, and having all the images as separate textures is more work and memory than the GPU can handle in the time allotted for a
single frame. One of the easiest solutions to implement is the use of texture atlases.

If you look inside the code for a CCSprite, you will notice that a -(void)draw
method gets called on every frame. Inside that draw method are the actual OpenGL ES
calls to draw the sprite on the screen. For each sprite, OpenGL ES has to bind to the
texture for that CCSprite and then draw (also called rendering) the sprite onscreen.

There is one more layer that occurs before the pixels show up on the screen: an
OpenGL ES driver provided by the iOS that converts the OpenGL ES calls into the
actual hardware assembly code to perform the actions on the GPU. You don't have
to know the driver details, only that each OpenGL ES call has the cost of a few CPU
cycles for the OpenGL ES driver. Your game will run faster if you do all of your rendering work with the least number of OpenGL ES calls.

Here is a way to visualize all of this. Think of yourself in the role of OpenGL ES, and the game needs you to draw a scene of a typical beach. This scene has the sand, the water, and some beach umbrellas. If the game is just using CCSprites, then it has to first give you the image for the sand and ask you to draw it, then give you the image of the ocean and ask you to draw it. It would continue like this until all of the images are drawn/rendered onscreen. This quickly becomes very tedious, and you might begin to wonder why the game cannot give you all of the image files at once. It turns out you can send all of the textures to OpenGL ES at once, and the way to do that is with CCSpriteBatchNode and texture atlases.

The CCSpriteBatchNode is a special class in Cocos2D that can act as the parent to a host of CCSprites. It sits between the CCLayer and the CCSprites. Just as the name states, if you use CCSpriteBatchNode, all of the draw calls for the CCSprites are batched and done at once. The large performance savings is not from just batching the calls together but from combining all of the little textures into one large texture that OpenGL ES has to bind just once.

The last point bears repeating. All of the OpenGL ES bind calls get reduced to one call. If you have 100 CCSprites under a CCSpriteBatchNode, you have only one OpenGL ES bind call instead of 100.

The large texture is called a texture atlas or sprite sheet, and it is simply a texture big enough to fit all the smaller textures you need inside of it. If you think about the beach scene example, this would be a large piece of paper from which you could cut out the sand texture, the ocean texture, and all of the beach umbrella textures.

Technical Details of Textures and Texture Atlases

Memory is a precious resource on the iPhone and iPad. The less memory used, the better your game performs. The iPhone and iPad utilize a shared memory system, which means that the GPU does not have its own memory; rather, it uses up some of the main system memory for storing textures and geometry. The memory limitations are especially apparent on the older iPhone, iPod touch, and iPhone 3G devices that were limited to 128MB of memory. Aggravating the memory constraints is the padding of images to texture with power-of-two sizes in their length and width.

The GPU inside older versions of the iPhone and iPod can store textures internally only in power-of-two sizes. While the iPhone 3GS, iPhone 4, and iPad can use non–power-of-two textures, doing so comes with a large performance penalty. Cocos2D is set up by default to pad all textures to power-of-two sizes for maximum compatibility, although you can change this in the *ccConfig.h* file.

To understand what the power-of-two size and texture padding means, here is a quick hands-on example. Take a piece of paper, or any drawing tool, and draw a square. Label the height and width as 256, to represent a 256 × 256 pixel texture. Now draw another square, this time 129 × 129 pixels in size, just slightly over half the height and half the width. The smaller square will represent your 129 × 129 pixel image stored as a 256 × 256 texture. Look at your drawing: about three-quarters of the texture space is wasted! Figure 2.8 illustrates this point, showing a 129 × 129 pixel sprite inside of a 256 × 256 texture. Regardless of the bit depth of your images, only about one-quarter of the memory this image is using is actually utilized to display anything—the rest is wasted. By utilizing tightly packed texture atlases you can avoid this wasted space.

Every byte of texture memory has to be copied from one location in memory that the CPU addresses to the area used by the GPU. Using extra texture memory has a lot of negative effects, and as you can imagine, the effects get worse and worse as you

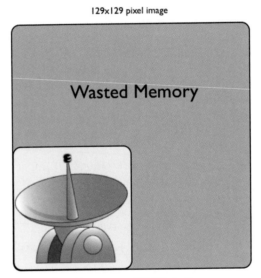

Figure 2.8   Example of wasted memory: a 129 × 129 pixel image
padded out to 256 × 256

increase the number nonbatched CCSprites on the screen. Table 2.1 shows the texture sizes supported by the current Apple mobile hardware.

Table 2.1   **The Power-of-Two Sizes Support on the Older Generation**

Device	Maximum Texture Width	Maximum Texture Height
iPhone, iPhone 3G, iPod touch (first and second generation)	1024 pixels	1024 pixels
iPhone 3GS, iPhone 4, iPad, iPod touch (third generation and later)	2048 pixels	2048 pixels

The combined wasted memory from using individual textures as well as the individual OpenGL ES bind texture calls can really work against you and slow down your game. Figure 2.9 illustrates how individual Viking and Radar Dish textures are stored in comparison with a texture atlas combining all of the textures needed for this scene in *Space Viking*.

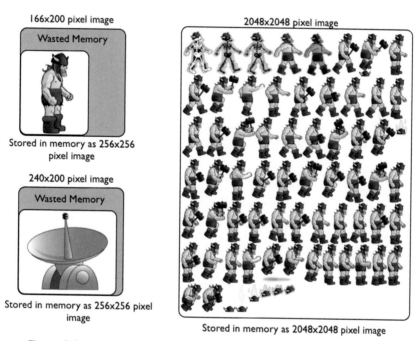

Figure 2.9   Example of wasted memory with individual images versus a texture atlas

There is one more key advantage of using a texture atlas. Often, a significant part of your images contains transparent space, and this space contains no pixel color data but takes up memory just the same. Most texture atlas software, such as Zwoptex and TexturePacker, can overlap the transparent space between two or more images. Zwoptex and TexturePacker keep track of your original image size, including the transparent space, and Cocos2D can automatically adjust your sprites to make up for the trimmed transparent space.

If all of this does not make complete sense yet, do not worry—it will soon. Keep in mind these reasons why you want to use a texture atlas:

Top Reasons to Use a Texture Atlas/Sprite Sheet

1. Reduced OpenGL ES bind calls—the more images contained in the texture atlas, the greater the reduction.

2. Reduced memory footprint for the images stored as textures in memory.

3. Easy method to trim and save on transparent space in your images, allowing for more images/texture in the same space.

4. Zwoptex and TexturePacker are fully supported by Cocos2D, so creating and using texture atlases is painless.

> **Note**
>
> For the texture atlas to be efficient, you will want it to contain as many images as possible. The scene1 texture atlas in this chapter has quite a bit of empty space that we will fill in with weapons in Chapter 5, "More Actions, Effects, and Cocos2D Scheduler." Always try to have the smallest texture atlas possible, with the least empty space, in your games.

In your games, you may have one or more texture atlases depending on what objects you need for each scene or level. In *Space Viking* you will have one texture atlas for this scene and another for the underground mining scene that you will discover in Chapter 10, "Basic Game Physics: Adding Realism with Box2D." The next step is to actually create the texture atlas for the first scene in *Space Viking*, and then you will be ready to dive back into the code in Chapter 4, "Simple Collision Detection and the First Enemy."

Creating the Scene 1 Texture Atlas

Texture atlases provide significant improvement in game performance with minimal effort on your part. In the first scene of *Space Viking*, you will have one texture atlas containing the Viking, all the enemy characters, and power-ups. There are two great tools available for quickly creating texture atlases: TexturePacker and Zwoptex. This book covers how to use TexturePacker or Zwoptex to create the texture atlas for *Space Viking*.

Zwoptex can be found at *http://zwoptexapp.com*.

TexturePacker can be found at *http://texturepacker.com*.

The next step is to create the scene 1 texture atlas that will be used in Chapter 3, "Introduction to Cocos2D Animations and Actions," and beyond.

Texture Packer Instructions

1. Start the Texture Packer Application.

2. For each of the following subfolders in *Resources\Images for Texture Atlases* for this chapter, select **Add Folder** in the top toolbar and choose the folder:

   Detrius

   EnemyRobot

   ImpactEffects

PowerUps

Radar

SpaceCargoShip

Teleport Effects

Viking

Be sure to use the Add Images button and not the Add Folders button, so that TexturePacker does not include the path as the key to the image coordinates.

3. In the toolbar to the left, make sure that the Data Format is set to **cocos2d**.

4. Click **Publish**, and when prompted for a name, enter *scene1atlas*. It will save two files (*scene1atlas.png* and *scene1atlas.plist*) to the folder you choose, so note where you save it for use later (see Figure 2.10).

Figure 2.10   Creating the scene1atlas texture atlas in TexturePacker

Zwoptex Instructions

1. Start the Zwoptex Application.

2. Select **File > New**.

3. Click the **Import+** button and select the images from the following folders inside the *Resources\Images for Texture Atlases* folder for this chapter:

Detrius

EnemyRobot

ImpactEffects

PowerUps

Radar

SpaceCargoShip

Teleport Effects

Viking

4. Change the Canvas dimensions to have a width of **2048** pixels and height of **2048** pixels.

5. Select **Max Rect** as the algorithm on the left panel.

6. Set the padding to 1 pixel, by entering **1px** on the padding text box.

7. Click the **Apply** button so that Zwoptex lays out your images.

8. Select **File > Save** and name this Texture Atlas *scene1atlas*.

9. Click **Publish** on the menu, and then click **Publish Settings**.

10. Make sure the **Coordinates Format** is set to **cocos2d**, and click **Save**.

11. Click **Publish** on the menu again, and then press the **Publish** button on the pop-down notification. This will create two files, *scene1atlas.png* and *scene1atlas.plist*, in the same folder where you saved the texture atlas in step 8 (see Figure 2.11).

Figure 2.11   Creating the scene1atlas texture atlas in Zwoptex

That was simple right? With a few clicks, you combined all of the images needed for this level of *Space Viking* in one texture atlas and exported the atlas and coordinates file that will be used by Cocos2D.

You will need two more texture atlases for when *Space Viking* is running on the iPhone and on the iPhone 4's retina display. You can create them following the same steps, except they should be named *scene1atlasiPhone* and *scene1atlasiPhone-hd* (png and plist files). You can find all of the completed texture atlases in the resources folder for this chapter.

If you are wondering how Cocos2D knows to extract your individual images from the texture atlas, the coordinates *plist* file is what provides the key. If you open the *scene1atlas.plist* file in Xcode, you will see that it contains the coordinates for each image you imported as well as each image's original size before it was trimmed.

Your texture atlas should look similar to the one in Figure 2.10 or 2.11. The order of the sprites is not important; you just need to ensure that they are all present in the texture atlas.

Adding the Scene 1 Texture Atlas to Space Viking

1. In Xcode, open the *SpaceViking* project.
2. Select the *Images* folder.
3. Right-click and select **Add Files**.
4. Browse to the directory where you saved the *scene1atlas*, select the *scene1atlas.png* and *scene1atlas.plist* files, and click **Add**.
5. Ensure that the **Copy items to destination group's folder** is selected and click **Add**.

   You should see the *scene1atlas.png* and *scene1atlas.plist* files under your *Images* folder.

6. Follow the same steps to add the *scene1atlasiPhone* (png and plist) and *scene1atlas-iPhone-hd* (png and plist) texture atlases. These two texture atlases provide the graphics for *Space Viking* on the iPhone and iPhone 4.

In Chapter 4, you will use this texture atlas to provide the graphics for all of the characters in *Space Viking*. Since you only have Ole onscreen at the moment, the texture atlas does not buy you much performance. Don't worry: you will soon add enemies and even a space cargo ship to your *Space Viking* game.

> **Warning**
>
> Make sure you have the scene1atlas.png, scene1atlas.plist, scene1atlasiPhone.png, scene1atlasiPhone.plist, scene1atlasiPhone-hd.png, and scene1atlasiPhone-hd.plist files in Xcode; otherwise, you will not be able to get the *SpaceViking* project running when you reach the end of the next chapter.

For the More Curious: Testing Out CCSpriteBatchNode

While Chapter 4 goes into detail on how to set up and use CCSpriteBatchNode, you might be interested in getting it working now. It is very simple, and you can do it with just five lines of code.

In the init method of *GameplayLayer.m*:

1. Comment out the lines marked //3 and //5, which previously created the Viking CCSprite and added it to the GameplayLayer.

2. Add the lines shown in Listing 2.13.

Listing 2.13 Using CCSpriteBatchNode in init method of GameplayLayer.m

```
//vikingSprite = [CCSprite spriteWithFile:@"sv_anim_1.png"]; // 3

CCSpriteBatchNode *chapter2SpriteBatchNode;
    if (UI_USER_INTERFACE_IDIOM() == UIUserInterfaceIdiomPad) {
        [[CCSpriteFrameCache sharedSpriteFrameCache]
         addSpriteFramesWithFile:@"scene1atlas.plist"];       // 3.1
         chapter2SpriteBatchNode =
         [CCSpriteBatchNode
          batchNodeWithFile:@"scene1atlas.png"];               // 3.2
    } else {
        [[CCSpriteFrameCache sharedSpriteFrameCache]
         addSpriteFramesWithFile:@"scene1atlasiPhone.plist"];// 3.1
         chapter2SpriteBatchNode =
         [CCSpriteBatchNode
          batchNodeWithFile:@"scene1atlasiPhone.png"];         // 3.2
    }
      vikingSprite =
    [CCSprite spriteWithSpriteFrameName:@"sv_anim_1.png"];    // 3.3


    [chapter2SpriteBatchNode addChild:vikingSprite];          // 3.4


    [self addChild:chapter2SpriteBatchNode];                  // 3.5

 [vikingSprite setPosition:
  CGPointMake(screenSize.width/2,
              screenSize.height*0.17f)];                      // 4
    //[self addChild:vikingSprite];                           // 5
```

The new lines you added (3.1 through 3.5) work as follows:

3.1 Loads the `CCSpriteFrames` into the Cocos2D cache. The frames are the dimensions and location of all of the images inside of the texture atlas. This *plist* is what allows Cocos2D to extract the images from the texture atlas PNG and render them onscreen. The frames also allow Cocos2D to recreate the trimmed transparent space that Zwoptex or TexturePacker removed in creating the texture atlas. Once more, you see the check for `UI_USER_INTERFACE_IDIOM()`, which determines if *Space Viking* is running on the iPad or the iPhone. If Cocos2D detects a Retina display on the iPhone, it will automatically load the `-hd` versions of the *png* and *plist* files *(scene1atlasiPhone-hd.png)*.

3.2 Creates the `CCSpriteBatchNode` and loads it with the large texture atlas image.

These two steps are all that are needed to create and set up a `CCSpriteBatchNode`. Next you need only add `CCSprites` to the `CCSpriteBatchNode` and add the `CCSpriteBatchNode` to the layer, and Cocos2D takes care of the rest.

3.3 Creates the `vikingSprite` with only the name of the frame that Cocos2D should use to extract the image from the texture atlas.

3.4 Adds the `vikingSprite` to the `CCSpriteBatchNode` so that the `vikingSprite` will be rendered by the `CCSpriteBatchNode` and not by itself.

3.5 Adds the `CCSpriteBatchNode` to the layer so that all of the children (`CCSprites`) of the `CCSpriteBatchNode` can be rendered onscreen in one pass.

The steps required to use a texture atlas in Cocos2D are loading the sprite frames into the cache and creating a `CCSpriteBatchNode` with the texture atlas image. From then on, the `CCSpriteBatchNode` will render any sprite you create from the texture atlas and add to the `CCSpriteBatchNode` in one pass. In this chapter, you only have the lonely Ole the Viking, so there is no performance advantage to using a texture atlas. In later chapters with enemies, weapons, and more, the texture atlas and `CCSpriteBatchNode` both are key to maintaining good game performance.

> **Warning**
>
> Remember to comment out the original line adding the `vikingSprite` directly to the layer, as shown in Listing 2.13. A `CCSprite` can only be a child to either the `CCLayer` or the `CCSpriteBatchNode`, and not both. If you leave the line in there, you will get a runtime crash with an assert warning you of the problem.

Fixing Slow Performance on iPhone 3G and Older Devices

As a default Cocos2D uses the `RootViewController` (`UIViewController`) to determine the orientation of the device and properly rotate both the Cocos2D (OpenGL ES) and any UIKit elements you may have onscreen. If you leave it at the default setting, then Cocos2D will render as if it is in the portrait orientation and leave it up the `UIViewController` to rotate the rendered content. While not a problem on newer devices, on the iPhone 3G and older devices, it causes quite a bit of overhead, capping your maximum frames per second at 40 instead of the full 60fps. You can easily change this setting so that Cocos2D Director handles the rotation, and have your game running at 60fps even on the original iPhone. The only caveat is that if you do overlay UIKit elements, such as a `UIButton` on top of Cocos2D, you will have to manually rotate them.

Space Viking does not use any UIKit elements: everything including the menus uses Cocos2D.

To change the screen rotation control from the `UIViewController` to the Cocos2D Director, make the change shown in Listing 2.14 in your *GameConfig.h* file, located in the *Classes* folder.

Listing 2.14   **Changes to GameConfig.h file**

```
// For iPhone 3GS and newer, comment out for Space Viking
//#define GAME_AUTOROTATION kGameAutorotationUIViewController

// For iPhone 3G and older (runs better)
#define GAME_AUTOROTATION kGameAutorotationCCDirector
```

Summary

If you have followed all of the steps in this chapter, you now have a very basic version of *Space Viking* running on your iPad. You have implemented a joystick and buttons and connected the game logic to move Ole the Viking around the screen. You have also learned about texture atlases and created the texture atlas that will be used in the first level of *Space Viking*.

In the next chapter, you will add animations to Ole the Viking so that his walking and jumping are more fluid. You will also learn how to add other characters to *Space Viking* and wire up Ole's attack button so he can fight off the alien hordes.

Challenges

1. Modify the `scaledVelocity` calculation in `applyJoystick` to have a factor of `10.0f` instead of `1024.0f`. What happens when you try to move Ole around with the joystick? What about with a factor of `10000.0f`?

2. Change the `newPosition` calculation in `applyJoystick` to not include the `deltaTime`. What happens when you try to move Ole around using the joystick?

Hint

You need to remove `deltaTime` from this line:

```
CGPoint newPosition =
        ccp(tempNode.position.x + scaledVelocity.x * deltaTime,
        tempNode.position.y + scaledVelocity.y * deltaTime); // 2
```

3. Add left and right limits for Ole the Viking so he does not move offscreen even if the player moves the joystick left or right continuously. (Hint: `vikingSprite`'s x coordinate is the variable you have to limit.)

Bonus

Modify the `applyJoystick` method in `GameplayLayer` so the joystick only changes Ole's x coordinates, leaving the y coordinate intact.

3

Introduction to Cocos2D Animations and Actions

In Chapter 2, "Hello, Space Viking," you learned the basics of Cocos2D and created a scene with two layers: background and gameplay. You got a Viking sprite moving around on the screen, and hopefully, you whet your appetite for continuing on to the full-featured game. In this chapter you will learn about actions and animations and in the process start to build a flexible framework for Space Viking. *As you read this chapter, keep in mind that you can reuse this framework to create your own games in the future.*

A quick word of warning: this chapter and the next one are very code heavy, but do not be alarmed—we go through it step by step and explain everything along the way. Game development covers the gamut of the computer science (CompSci) discipline, and you are going to learn various facets of CompSci in the writing of Space Viking. *Do not hesitate to refer back to this chapter to make sure all the concepts are firmly entrenched in your mind.*

Ready? Let's begin!

Animations in Cocos2D

Adding animations into your game is easy with Cocos2D. You already learned how to create and add sprites to your layers and to get those sprites rendered onscreen. Animations in Cocos2D are just like old flipbook-style paper animations: all animations are just individual image frames being switched multiple times per second. Technically, this means your sprites have their display frames changed to different textures with a set delay between the time each texture is displayed.

There are two steps to animate your sprites:

- Create a `CCAnimation` to specify the set of images/textures in your animation, called frames.

- Create a `CCAnimate` action, and "run" it on a sprite. A `CCAnimate` action specifies the `CCAnimation` to use and the delay to use between its frames.

To recap, you first create a CCAnimation to store the frames or images in your animation. You then create a CCAnimate action to run the animation.

The easiest way to understand how this works is to try out two quick examples. Don't worry, the first example is short, just a few lines of code.

1. Open the *SpaceViking* project in Xcode.

2. Drag the *an1_anim_1, 2, 3*, and *4 png* files from the *Resources/Enemy Robot Animation* folder for this chapter into your *SpaceViking* project.

   The *an1_anim_1.png* through *an1_anim_4.png* are used in this animation example. After this chapter, you can remove them, as you will learn to drive the animations from the texture atlas you created in Chapter 2.

3. Open the GameplayLayer.m class and navigate to the init method.

4. Add the lines shown in Listing 3.1 to the init method above the line [self initJoystickAndButtons];.

Listing 3.1 **Adding an animation to Space Viking**

```
// Animation example with a Sprite (not a CCSpriteBatchNode)
CCSprite *animatingRobot = [CCSprite
                        spriteWithFile:@"an1_anim1.png"];   // 1
[animatingRobot setPosition:ccp([vikingSprite position].x + 50.0f,
                        [vikingSprite position].y)];        // 2
[self addChild:animatingRobot];                             // 3

CCAnimation *robotAnim = [CCAnimation animation];           // 4
[robotAnim addFrameWithFilename:@"an1_anim2.png"];          // 5
[robotAnim addFrameWithFilename:@"an1_anim3.png"];
[robotAnim addFrameWithFilename:@"an1_anim4.png"];

id robotAnimationAction =
    [CCAnimate actionWithDuration:0.5f
                    animation:robotAnim
            restoreOriginalFrame:YES];                      // 6
id repeatRobotAnimation =
    [CCRepeatForever actionWithAction:robotAnimationAction]; // 7
[animatingRobot runAction:repeatRobotAnimation];            // 8
```

In Listing 3.1 you are adding an animating enemy robot to the right of Ole. Here is what is going on in the code step by step:

1. Creates and initializes a CCSprite of the animating robot, with the image *an1_anim1.png.*

2. Sets the position of the robot to 50 points to the right of Ole. If you wanted the exact pixel position of the Viking, you would use the call to positionInPixels instead of position.

3. Adds the `animatingRobot` to the `GameplayLayer`. Up to this point the steps in creating and adding a `CCSprite` to a `CCLayer` should be familiar, as you learned it in the previous chapter.

4. Creates and initializes a new `CCAnimation` named `robotAnim`. In this line the `robotAnim` is created but empty.

5. Adds the animation frames to the `robotAnim` animation. Three frames are added by passing in the filenames for each.

6. Creates the `robotAnimationAction` that is responsible for running the animation. The delay between frames is set to half a second (`0.5f`), the animation to use is set to `robotAnim`, and the flag is set to restore the original frame. The restore original frame flag informs the `CCAnimate` action to do a bit of work at the end of the animation and reset the `CCSprite` to the display frame it was showing before the animation started. In other words, when the animation ends, the `CCSprite` reverts back to its original image.

7. Creates an action to repeat the animation forever. In Chapter 4, "Simple Collision Detection and the First Enemy," you will learn how to use actions to drive behavior in *Space Viking*. For now, just know that the `CCRepeatForever` action keeps repeating the robot animation.

8. Informs the `animatingRobot` `CCSprite` to run the animation in an endless loop.

Click **Run** in Xcode and watch the robot walk in place next to the Viking. Figure 3.1 shows the robot on the iPad Simulator.

Figure 3.1   Animating robot next to Ole

As you can see, creating animations in Cocos2D is easy. The code in Listing 3.1 works with regular CCSprites, but if your CCSprites are being rendered by a CCSpriteBatchNode, the code requires a couple of modifications. The CCSprite-Frames you use for your animation must get their textures from the texture atlas used by the CCSpriteBatchNode. The best way to understand this is to see it in action. Copy the contents of Listing 3.2 directly below the code you created earlier in Listing 3.1.

Listing 3.2   Animations using a CCSprite rendered by CCSpriteBatchNode

```
// Animation example with a CCSpriteBatchNode
CCAnimation *exampleAnim = [CCAnimation animation];
[exampleAnim addFrame:
  [[CCSpriteFrameCache sharedSpriteFrameCache]
    spriteFrameByName:@"sv_anim_2.png"]];

[exampleAnim addFrame:
  [[CCSpriteFrameCache sharedSpriteFrameCache]
    spriteFrameByName:@"sv_anim_3.png"]];

[exampleAnim addFrame:
  [[CCSpriteFrameCache sharedSpriteFrameCache]
    spriteFrameByName:@"sv_anim_4.png"]];

id animateAction =
 [CCAnimate actionWithDuration:0.5f
                    animation:exampleAnim
         restoreOriginalFrame:NO];
id repeatAction =
  [CCRepeatForever actionWithAction:animateAction];

[vikingSprite runAction:repeatAction];
```

Recall from Chapter 2 that you used TexturePacker or Zwoptex to create a big sprite sheet image with all of the images for *Space Viking*, and a property list containing the coordinates for each image in the sprite sheet. You then added code to use the addSpriteFramesWithFile method to load the property list, which makes Cocos2D cache the coordinates for each individual image so you can look them up later. Looking them up is simple—you just use the spriteFrameByName method, which returns a CCSpriteFrame object containing the location information.

To set up a CCAnimation, you need to specify each CCSpriteFrame in the animation. So in Listing 3.2, the only difference is that addFrame is used instead of addFrameWithFilename. This way, you can specify the CCSpriteFrames that are already in the cache from the sprite sheet's property list.

Once the CCAnimation object is populated, the rest of the code is the same, setting up an action to play the animation and assigning it to the vikingSprite.

The important takeaway here is that when you are creating animations for sprites using a texture atlas, the animation frames must come from the same texture atlas. If you want to animate a sprite, make sure you put all of the frames of the animation in the same sprite sheet—otherwise it will not work.

Note on EnemyRobot Size

If you ran Listing 3.1 on a device other than the iPad, you may have noticed the EnemyRobot's size was larger then the Viking. The first code you typed in for this chapter uses just plain CCSprites, which are sized for the iPad, without checking for UI_USER_INTERFACE_IDIOM() to determine if you are running on an iPhone or iPad. All subsequent code you will write for *Space Viking* uses the texture atlases you created in Chapter 2 and will select the correct texture atlas depending on what iOS device you are running the game on (iPhone, iPhone 4, or iPad).

In *Space Viking* the frame rate is set to 60 frames per second (fps). By changing the delay between frames, you can control how long each frame is onscreen. If you need to keep a set of frames onscreen longer than others, you can add them multiple times to the CCAnimation object. Remember, Cocos2D caches the textures used by each frame; repeating a frame does not consume much additional memory.

Warning

The code in Listing 3.2 assumes you completed all of the steps in the previous chapter in setting up the CCSpriteBatchNode. If you encounter any issues, remember to refer back to the sample code included with this chapter.

Don't worry if you don't completely understand all of this yet: you will have a chance to see how it all ties together in the code listings in this chapter. Just remember that in order to play an animation, you must use a CCAnimate action, and you can always refer back to this code for a working example.

There are many characters in *Space Viking*, each with several animations. Typing out each frame for every animation would quickly become tedious and bloat your code with line after line of just addFrame calls. Each CCAnimation and CCAnimate action has two components: a delay between frames and a list of sprite frames to progress through. This kind of animation data is best stored in property list *(plist)* files separate from your code. This chapter covers the *plist* files and code you need to set up for the character animations in *Space Viking*.

At this point you have made quite a bit of progress. You have the beginnings of a Cocos2D game and already have animating characters onscreen with joystick control. The animations in *Space Viking* will be used to bring characters to life with walking, jumping, crouching, and attacking moves. The rest of this chapter builds on what you learned to set the foundations for *Space Viking*, including a large portion of code you can reuse in your own games.

Note

Before moving on, be sure to comment out the lines of code you added from Listings 3.1 and 3.2: they are examples only and are not used in the rest of the book.

For the More Curious: CCAnimationCache

Cocos2D comes bundled with a `CCAnimationCache` singleton that can cache all of your animations. Instead of storing the animations as instance variables, you can store them in the `CCAnimationCache` and retrieve them as needed. This is really useful if you have a lot of `CCSprites` in your game all using the same animations. A good example is a shooting game with similar enemies, such as the classic Space Invaders or R-Type.

There are two items you should be aware of when using the `CCAnimationCache`:

1. When retrieving the animation, you should check that it is not `nil`. The `CCAnimationCache` can purge animations if asked via the `purgeShared-AnimationCache` call.
   If the animation you ask is no longer cached, it will return `nil`.
2. Any animations you wish to keep around should be retained so that if they are purged from the cache, they will still be available to your objects.

Using `CCAnimationCache` is really easy. You create the animation as you did in the listings in this chapter and then add them to the `CCAnimationCache` as follows:

```
[[CCAnimationCache sharedAnimationCache]
            addAnimation:animationToCache
                name:@"AnimationName"];
```

The `CCAnimation` called `animationToCache` is now stored in the `CCAnimation-Cache` singleton. When you want to use the cached animation, you can retrieve it by using:

```
CCAnimation *myAnimation = [[CCAnimationCache sharedAnimationCache]
                animationByName:@"AnimationName"];
```

In *SpaceViking* the choice was made to store the animations as instance variables because it was deemed easier to understand and use. In your games do not hesitate to use the `CCAnimationCache`, especially in cases where you have several objects using the same animations.

Space Viking Design Basics

In Chapter 2 you had a very simple game with a Viking character and joystick controls to move him around. You could continue building a game this way, but the `Gameplay` layer would grow very large and quickly become unmanageable. The goal of this book is to provide you with the knowledge and skills needed for game development with

Cocos2D and also to provide a sample game with code you can reuse in your own games.

Each game object in *Space Viking* has some logic behind it, not just the graphical sprite/image component. Enemies have to have a primitive artificial intelligence (AI) and be able to patrol the scene, attack Ole the Viking, and react to attacks. In addition to enemies, there are power-ups for better weapons and health and other objects. Instead of having all of the logic in one massive file, each object in the game has its own class to contain the portions of code needed. Game logic used by more than one object is included once in the classes those objects inherit from, such as `GameObject` or `GameCharacter`.

Thinking in Terms of Objects

From this chapter on, you will implement the logic for *Space Viking* by separating the functionality of each character or game element into distinct objects. Each object is implemented in Objective-C by a class, including a header and an implementation file.

One way of thinking about how classes or object-oriented programming works is to model everyday objects and see how their object/class structure works. Take the example of modeling a dog such as the golden retriever.

In designing objects, you always want to go from abstract to specific. In the case of the golden retriever, you might start with a `Mammal` object.

The `Mammal` object would contain all of the basics for all animals, like the nervous system component, a skeletal system component, and a muscular system component. From the `Mammal` object, you could have a `Canine` object, which would be a more specific type of `mammal`. The `Canine` object would have four legs, ability to bark, and all of the traits that exist across all dogs. Finally, you would have a `Golden-Retriever` object, which would be a more specific type of `Canine` object containing `GoldenRetriever`-specific features.

When converting the objects into classes, the `Mammal` object would be a class, the `Canine` object a subclass of `Mammal`, and `GoldenRetriever` a subclass of `Canine`. Each component of the objects can be either an instance variable (`ivar`) or an object itself if it has complex functionality. Hair color could be stored as an `ivar`, but the skeletal system component would be made up of several objects in order to model the complex functionality of the bones and joints.

When designing the objects and classes for your games, remember to think from abstract to specific, with the more abstract classes at the top of your hierarchy. The methods that are common to your objects and classes should be moved up into their parent objects or further up the hierarchy. If you have a method that is needed in two classes, ask yourself if you would not be better off having that method in the parent object. If you need a refresher on object-oriented programming, take a look at the classic *Object-Oriented Programming*, by Peter Coad and Jill Nicola (Prentice-Hall, 1993).

In *Space Viking* each game object has its own class, which encapsulates the AI needed by that object. The objects share common methods that they can use to query each other as to their state, present location, and other attributes. To understand how all of these objects fit together, it is best to start with the topmost object in the hierarchy, the GameObject:

- GameObject

  The GameObject class inherits from CCSprite and contains methods common to all GameObjects, including a method to update the object on every frame and another to change its state. Since GameObject itself inherits from CCSprite, it already knows how to render textures onscreen. Remember that CCSprites can render themselves or be rendered by a CCSpriteBatchNode. All of the objects in *Space Viking* inherit directly or indirectly from the GameObject class.

- GameCharacter

  The GameCharacter class inherits from GameObject and is the foundation of the "characters" in the game. It contains some additional methods and functionality needed by the characters in *Space Viking*. The Viking, EnemyRobot, RadarDish, and PhaserBullet all inherit from GameCharacter.

- Viking

  The Viking class inherits from GameCharacter and contains the logic and code needed to move Ole the Viking around according to your joystick input and to launch attacks and react to attacks from the other enemies in the game.

- RadarDish

  The RadarDish is a nonmoving enemy that serves as Ole's introduction to the alien world. It sits on the corner, scanning for our Viking until it detects him. Think of the radar dish as an easy enemy that does not fight back. It is important to understand how the RadarDish works because all of the other enemies in *Space Viking* are more complex versions of it. The RadarDish class inherits from the GameCharacter class.

- SpaceCargoShip

  The alien world is actually a large mining planet. The aliens are always moving cargo on and off the planet. When the alien ship passes near the ground, some objects always tend to fall off. Maybe some of these objects will be useful to Ole the Viking? The SpaceCargoShip inherits from the GameObject class.

- Mallet

  Long ago, Ole was separated from his beloved mallet when he fell into the icy river. If he ever finds it again, he will be armed with a mighty weapon to fend off the aliens. The Mallet class inherits from GameObject class and is one of the power-ups in the first scene in *Space Viking*.

- Health

  The Health class represents the health power-ups in *Space Viking*. Even though Ole is a mighty Viking, he does get hungry after fighting, and the health power-ups restore Ole's health. The Health class inherits from the GameObject class.

> **Note**
>
> You will create these classes for *Space Viking* in this chapter. In Chapter 4, you will add the enemy robot and phaser beams that the robot fires at Ole. The actions and animation system in Cocos2D is used extensively by the GameObjects in *Space Viking*, and it is covered in detail in the next section.

Figure 3.2 shows the inheritance and makeup of the Viking and RadarDish classes and how they are added to the scene 1 CCSpriteBatchNode, which in turn is added to the GameplayLayer. Recall that in Cocos2D, the CCScenes contain CCLayers, the CCLayers contain objects, in our case the CCSpriteBatchNode, which then contains the Viking and RadarDish classes.

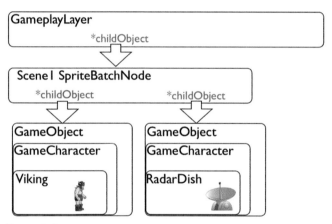

Figure 3.2   Class hierarchy of the Viking and RadarDish classes

A Word on Artificial Intelligence

Depending on the type of game you are creating, the demands of the in-game AI will vastly differ. If you were making a racing game, the enemy cars only have to make their way around the track and avoid each other, while a real-time strategy game would require a more complex AI. In many games the AI is represented as state machines, with distinct operations at each state. In *Space Viking* the enemy AI is a very simplistic state machine, going between walking, attacking, and taking damage states. The complexity of the AI in your games is limited only by your imagination and how much computing time you want to devote to it in your game.

Actions and Animation Basics in Cocos2D

Actions are a powerful mechanism in Cocos2D to control the movement, transition, and effects of your objects. All CCNode objects are able to run actions, and since CCSprites inherit from CCNodes, all Cocos2D actions can be run on CCSprites. The Viking and RadarDish objects inherit from GameCharacter, which in turns inherits from GameObject and CCSprite, allowing your characters to have all of the built-in logic to run actions. In Chapter 2 you moved Ole the Viking's sprite by changing the position variable of the sprite. Suppose you wanted to move Ole from the left to the right of the screen 200 pixels in 2 seconds. The following move action would accomplish this for you.

```
CCAction *moveAction = [CCMoveBy actionWithDuration:2.0f
                                   position:ccp(200.0f,0.0f)];
[vikingSprite runAction:moveAction];
```

That's all it takes to do the animation—*just two lines of code!* Figure 3.3 illustrates the moveAction effect on the Viking sprite.

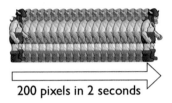

200 pixels in 2 seconds

Figure 3.3   Effect of the CCMoveBy action on the Viking CCSprite

You don't have to worry about how many pixels you should move on each update call because Cocos2D automatically calculates and moves your sprite in the correct increments. There are many actions in Cocos2D: move, jump, scale, and rotate are just a few of the most frequently used ones. In Chapter 5, "More Actions, Effects, and Cocos2D's Scheduler," you will learn more details about actions, including complex callbacks into your code. For now you will use the following actions:

- CCAnimate

  Runs a particular animation with a set delay between each frame. This action is what you use to play an animation.

- CCJumpBy

  Simulates a parabolic jump automatically, given the height of the jump and the horizontal distance to cover. This action is used to give Ole the Viking a realistic jump arc.

- CCRepeatForever

  Repeats the action indefinitely. It has the effect of running an action on an infinite loop until stopAction: or stopAllActions is called.

- CCSequence

  Sequences two or more actions together so that after the first action completes, the second action is run.

- CCSpawn

  Fires off two or more actions simultaneously. CCSpawn is very useful for combining actions, such as a jump animation with the CCJumpBy action.

In this chapter you will use actions to drive the animations, including Ole the Viking's jump and attack movements. The next section covers adding animations via property lists.

Using Property List Files to Store Animation Data

Property list files (more commonly referred to as "plist files") contain XML data used to define a set of properties used by your app or game. In *Space Viking* you will also use the plist files to store an NSDictionary of the settings you need to create and load the CCAnimations. Xcode has built-in support for creating and editing plist files, making it very easy to use plists in your projects.

Of course, you could include all of the information from these plist files directly in your code, but then every time you want to make an animation change, you would have to change your code and recompile. Having the animation data in plist files keeps your code smaller and allows you to have your artist help with the setup and tweaking of the animation frames and delays. I have found that it is not good practice to hard-code the animation data. Having it separate helps compartmentalize the code and makes it easier on you when you visit the same code months later.

In *Space Viking* each object is in its own class, such as Viking and RadarDish. Each object then points to its own plist file for information on how to set up its animations. For example, in the case of the RadarDish, the *RadarDish.plist* file contains data for the takingAHit, blowingUp, tilting, and transmitting animations.

NSDictionary objects are just what the class name suggests: a set of key-value pairs. In *Space Viking* the plist files contain mini-dictionaries for each animation with a filename prefix, a delay amount, and the listing of animation frames for a particular animation. The quickest way to wrap your head around this is to create one, so let's get moving (excuse the pun).

Starting with the simplest enemy in *Space Viking*, the RadarDish, open Xcode:

1. Right- or Control-click on the *SpaceViking* project and select **New Group**.

2. Click on the new group and change the name to *Plists*. You will use this group to organize all of the animation plist files used in *Space Viking*.

3. Selecting the *Plists* group, right- or Control-click and select **New File**.

4. Select the **Resource** section under iOS on the left, and then select **Property List** for the type of file and click **Next**.

5. Enter *RadarDish.plist* for the filename, and then click **Finish**.

Xcode creates and opens the *RadarDish.plist* file for you. The next step is to add the items needed for a particular RadarDish animation. Figure 3.4 shows the *RadarDish. plist* file you will create in this section.

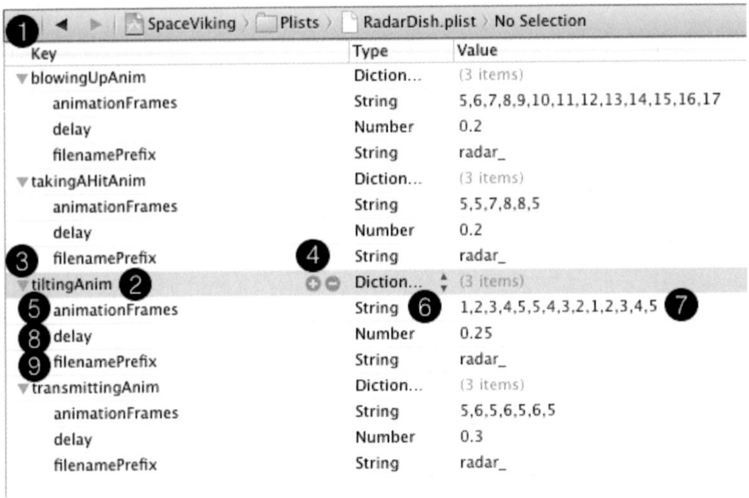

Figure 3.4   RadarDish.plist file

The first animation is for the tilting movement that the RadarDish performs when it is first created. This animation consists of a series of frames showing the dish tilting down and then back up. With the *RadarDish.plist* file open in Xcode, do the following (the numbers in the list correspond to the numbered callouts in Figure 3.4):

1. Select the *RadarDish.plist* file and in the empty editor area, right-click, selecting **Add Row**.

2. For the Key column, enter tiltingAnim, then change the type to Dictionary. This step means you have created a subdictionary inside the main root dictionary to store the data for the tilting animation. After you set the type to Dictionary, you'll notice a disclosure triangle next to tiltingAnim in the Key column.

3. Click the **disclosure triangle** next to tiltingAnim so it faces down; this opens the dictionary so you can add items to tiltingAnim's dictionary.

4. Click the **+** button next to the `tiltingAnim` key to add a row to the `tiltingAnim` dictionary.

5. Click on the **Key** field and enter `animationFrames`.

6. Leave the type as `String`.

7. In the **Value** field, enter `1,2,3,4,5,5,4,3,2,1,2,3,4,5`.

8. Add another item under `tiltingAnim` by clicking the **+** sign next to the `animationFrames` field, set the key in the new row to `delay`, the type to **Number**, and the value to `0.25`.

9. Create a final item under `tiltingAnim`, setting the key to `filenamePrefix`, the type to `String`, and the value to `radar_`.

To verify that you created these items correctly under the `tiltingAnim`, click on the disclosure triangle to the right of `tiltingAnim` to collapse it. All three items should disappear from view. If they do not, right-click on the item that did not disappear and select **shift item right**.

Repeat these steps for `takingAHitAnim`, `blowingUpAnim`, and `transmittingAnim` mini-animation dictionaries, entering the values shown in Figure 3.4.

One of the key benefits of having the animation data in plists is that it frees you up from having to go into your code to change the animation data. In fact, if you are working with an artist or animator in your games, they can often build these files as they create the animations for you. Later in this chapter you will see how to read the animation plists using a method included in the `GameObject` class and called by each object in *Space Viking*.

> **Note**
>
> While it is important to understand how the plist files are used in *Space Viking*, it's not worth your time to type them in by hand for the purposes of learning how to make this game. So before you continue, download the plist files along with the source code for this chapter at the InformIT website (*www.informit.com/title/9780321735621*).
>
> Once you've downloaded the files, add the plist files to your project inside the *Plists* group (*EnemyRobot.plist, Health.plist, Mallet.plist, RadarDish.plist,* and *Viking.plist*).
>
> Be sure to remember to add these files to your project, because without them, the rest of this code won't work!

Organization, Constants, and Common Protocols

In the next sections you will create a host of classes for use in *Space Viking*. In each subsequent chapter you will add more functionality and more classes. In order to keep your sanity, it is best to start organizing the source code inside of Xcode.

To start, create some groups in Xcode to help keep the new classes you are going to create organized.

1. Open Xcode, and under the Groups and Files section, select the *Classes* folder.

2. With the *Classes* folder selected, you can either press **Option-z-N** or right-click on the *Classes* folder and select **New Group** from the contextual menu. Create the following groups:

   - Constants
   - Scenes
   - Layers
   - GameObjects
   - EnemyObjects
   - PowerUps
   - Singletons

3. Drag the *GameScene.h* and *GameScene.m* files into the *Scenes* group.

4. Drag the *BackgroundLayer* and *GameplayLayer* .h and .m files into the *Layers* group.

5. Finally, drag the *SpaceVikingAppDelegate* .h and .m files into the *Singletons* group.

At this point your *SpaceViking* project layout should be similar to the one shown in Figure 3.5. The order of the groups is not important, only that they exist under *Classes* to keep your code organized. If you still have your *HelloWorldScene* .m and .h files inside your *SpaceViking* project, you can safely delete them.

Figure 3.5   Xcode Groups and File panel showing the groups created
under the Classes folder in Space Viking

Creating the Constants File

Space Viking has some static values that you will want to use in more than one class. For this purpose, you create a *Constants.h* header file, which contains all of the `#define` statements and other constants used by more than one class in *Space Viking*.

Now that you have the groups in place to keep *Space Viking* organized, it is time to add the `Constants` and `CommonProtocol` classes.

1. In Xcode, select the *Constants* group (**Classes > Constants**).

2. Select **File > New File (z-N**, or right-click on the *Constants* folder and select **New File** from the contextual menu), and then select **C and C++** category under iOS, and choose the **Header File** option.

3. Enter *Constants.h* for the filename and click **Finish**.

4. Select the *Constants.h* file and enter the text shown in Listing 3.3.

Listing 3.3 **Constants.h header file**

```
//  Constants.h
// Constants used in SpaceViking

#define kVikingSpriteZValue 100
#define kVikingSpriteTagValue 0
#define kVikingIdleTimer 3.0f
#define kVikingFistDamage 10
#define kVikingMalletDamage 40
#define kRadarDishTagValue 10
```

When you add a sprite to your layer, you can give it a z-order. In *Space Viking*, we give a unique z-order to each of the sprites to make it very clear which sprites are on the top and which are behind. The `kVikingSpriteZValue` is used to keep Ole the Viking in front of the other game characters. The number 100 is arbitrary, and it only has to be larger than the number of objects added to the same `CCSpriteBatchNode`. In other words, a z value of 0 is the backmost object, while positive numbers are in front, with the highest number being the object rendered in front of all of the others. If there were 500 enemy objects in *Space Viking*, you would want to make this number higher, such as 501 or 600.

Each `CCNode` object can hold an optional tag value: a unique integer value that other nodes can use to retrieve it. The enemy objects in *Space Viking* will use the `kVikingSpriteTagValue` to get the Viking object from the `CCSpriteBatchNode` and query the Viking's position and state. The default value of the tag is `kCCNodeTagInvalid` (-1), so 0 is a valid tag to use. Similarly, `kRadarDishTagValue` will be used in Chapter 5 to get a reference to the `RadarDish` class from the `CCBatchNode`.

Finally, there is a setting for the idle timer for the `Viking`, currently set to 3 seconds (as noted by 3.0f). If Ole is idle for 3 seconds, the `Viking` will perform a breathing action to entice the player to keep going. The tags are just unique integer values you can assign to any CCNode and use the values to retrieve a reference to the CCNode from their parent class.

Common Protocols File

Protocols in Objective-C are similar to interfaces in other languages such as Java. To put it simply, protocols allow you to specify the methods that a class will respond to, without knowing how those methods are implemented. Think of protocols as a contract stating that the class adhering to the protocol will respond to the methods defined in that protocol.

In *Space Viking* the EnemyRobot class has to ask the GameplayLayer to create a phaserBullet when the robot is attacking Ole the Viking. It does not make sense for EnemyRobot to just import GameplayLayer because of all of the other classes that GameplayLayer itself imports. By creating a GameplayLayer delegate protocol, the EnemyRobot class can access just the method it needs in GameplayLayer. To EnemyRobot, GameplayLayer only has the three methods shown in the Gameplay-LayerDelegate protocol in Listing 3.4.

To create the *CommonProtocols.h* file:

1. In Xcode, select the *Constants* group.

2. Select **File > New File** (z-N, or right-click on the *Constants* folder and select **New File** from the contextual menu), and then select **C and C++** category and the **Header File** option.

3. Enter *CommonProtocols.h* for the filename, and click **Finish**.

4. Select the *CommonProtocols.h* file and enter the text shown in Listing 3.4.

Listing 3.4 **CommonProtocols.h header file**

```
//   CommonProtocols.h
//   SpaceViking

typedef enum {
    kDirectionLeft,
    kDirectionRight
} PhaserDirection;

typedef enum {
    kStateSpawning,
    kStateIdle,
    kStateCrouching,
    kStateStandingUp,
    kStateWalking,
    kStateAttacking,
    kStateJumping,
    kStateBreathing,
```

```
    kStateTakingDamage,
    kStateDead,
    kStateTraveling,
    kStateRotating,
    kStateDrilling,
    kStateAfterJumping
} CharacterStates; // 1

typedef enum {
    kObjectTypeNone,
    kPowerUpTypeHealth,
    kPowerUpTypeMallet,
    kEnemyTypeRadarDish,
    kEnemyTypeSpaceCargoShip,
    kEnemyTypeAlienRobot,
    kEnemyTypePhaser,
    kVikingType,
    kSkullType,
    kRockType,
    kMeteorType,
    kFrozenVikingType,
    kIceType,
    kLongBlockType,
    kCartType,
    kSpikesType,
    kDiggerType,
    kGroundType
} GameObjectType;

@protocol GameplayLayerDelegate
-(void)createObjectOfType:(GameObjectType)objectType
            withHealth:(int)initialHealth
            atLocation:(CGPoint)spawnLocation
            withZValue:(int)ZValue;

-(void)createPhaserWithDirection:(PhaserDirection)phaserDirection
                  andPosition:(CGPoint)spawnPosition;
@end
```

The typedef enum lines simply ask the compiler to create a special variable type that can have only the values defined for that particular type, as shown in Listing 3.4. Instead of keeping a numeric value for each possible state for the characters in *Space Viking* and trying to remember that a value of 1 represents idle and 4 represents walking, you can just reference meaningful identifiers such as kStateIdle or kStateWalking. It makes the code in *Space Viking* much more readable and easier to understand.

The `GameplayLayerDelegate` protocol defines two methods that the characters in *Space Viking* will use. In particular, the `SpaceCargoShip` and the `EnemyRobot` use these methods to have the `GameplayLayer` create the power-ups and the phaser bullets. The `SpaceCargoShip` does not have to know anything further about the `GameplayLayer`, only that it responds to these two methods. Using protocols can hide the complexity of the implementation and allow your game code to be more modular and reusable. If you want to later replace the `GameplayLayer` with another class, all you need to do is ensure that the new class adheres to the `GameplayLayer-Delegate` protocol.

With these two header files out of the way, it is time to create the `GameObject` and `GameCharacter` classes.

The GameObject and GameCharacter Classes

The `GameObject` and `GameCharacter` classes are the foundations of the in-game elements in *Space Viking*. The `Viking`, `RadarDish`, and `EnemyRobot` classes all inherit functionality from `GameObject` and `GameCharacter`. These base classes can serve as a model that you can use when building your own games. The `GameObject` class contains the functionality need to read the property list files you created earlier in this chapter, allowing all of the *Space Viking* objects to set up their animations based on these files.

Creating the GameObject

The `GameObject` class is the starting point for all of the objects in *Space Viking*. The `GameObject` class inherits from the `CCSprite` class, allowing it the ability to run actions and know how to render its texture. The `GameObject` class adds some specific methods and instance variables used by your *Space Viking* game.

Follow these steps to create the `GameObject` header and implementation files:

1. In Xcode, select the *GameObjects* group and right-click.
2. From the contextual menu, select **New File**, and choose the **Cocoa Touch** category under iOS and **Objective-C** class as the file type, and click **Next**.
3. For the Subclass field, enter *CCSprite* and click **Next**.
4. Enter *GameObject* for the filename and click **Save**.

Open the *GameObject.h* header file and change the contents to match the code in Listing 3.5.

Listing 3.5 **GameObject.h header file**

```
//   GameObject.h
//   SpaceViking
//
```

```
#import <Foundation/Foundation.h>
#import "cocos2d.h"
#import "Constants.h"
#import "CommonProtocols.h"

@interface GameObject : CCSprite {
    BOOL isActive;
    BOOL reactsToScreenBoundaries;
    CGSize screenSize;
    GameObjectType gameObjectType;
}
@property (readwrite) BOOL isActive;
@property (readwrite) BOOL reactsToScreenBoundaries;
@property (readwrite) CGSize screenSize;
@property (readwrite) GameObjectType gameObjectType;
-(void)changeState:(CharacterStates)newState;
-(void)updateStateWithDeltaTime:(ccTime)deltaTime
andListOfGameObjects:(CCArray*)listOfGameObjects;
-(CGRect)adjustedBoundingBox;
-(CCAnimation*)loadPlistForAnimationWithName:(NSString*)animationName
andClassName:(NSString*)className;
@end
```

Take a close look at the @interface declaration line. The GameObject :
CCSprite code is what sets up the GameObject class as a subclass of CCSprite. All
of the methods available to the CCSprite are now part of GameObject. You can see
defined in Listing 3.5 some of the instance variables you will use in *Space Viking* that
are not part of the base CCSprite class. In addition to the instance variables, there are
the changeState, updateStateWithDeltaTime, adjustedBoundingBox, and
loadPlistForAnimationWithName methods. To see what these methods do, open
the GameObject.m implementation file and replace the content with the code shown
in Listings 3.6 and 3.7.

Listing 3.6   GameObject.m implementation file (part 1 of 2)

```
//   GameObject.m
//   SpaceViking
//
#import "GameObject.h"

@implementation GameObject
@synthesize reactsToScreenBoundaries;
@synthesize screenSize;
@synthesize isActive;
@synthesize gameObjectType;
```

```
-(id) init {
    if((self=[super init])){
        CCLOG(@"GameObject init");
        screenSize = [CCDirector sharedDirector].winSize;
        isActive = TRUE;
        gameObjectType = kObjectTypeNone;
    }
    return self;
}


-(void)changeState:(CharacterStates)newState {
    CCLOG(@"GameObject->changeState method should be overridden");
}


-(void)updateStateWithDeltaTime:(ccTime)deltaTime
andListOfGameObjects:(CCArray*)listOfGameObjects {
    CCLOG(@"updateStateWithDeltaTime method should be overridden");
}


-(CGRect)adjustedBoundingBox {
    CCLOG(@"GameObect adjustedBoundingBox should be overridden");
    return [self boundingBox];
}
```

The first part of *GameObject.m* in Listing 3.6 has the `init` method that sets up the default values for the instance variables and calls the superclass initializer; in this case, `CCSprite`. Looking at these three methods, you can see that `updateStateWith-DeltaTime` and `adjustedBoundingBox` are stubs and do nothing more than call `CCLOG` to warn that they should be overridden. This is because you will not be using the `GameObject` class directly; instead, you will use it as the base for the other object classes in *Space Viking*. This means that the `Viking`, `SpaceCargoShip`, and other classes should have methods with the same name, essentially overriding these three default methods.

The `updateStateWithDeltaTime` method is what the `GameplayLayer` class calls to update game objects on every frame. This method also contains the AI for the objects and is where the objects perform the actions that define their individual behavior.

The `changeState` method is used by the objects to transition from one state to another. The state change often triggers custom animations that represent each state.

Finally, the `adjustedBoundingBox` method does exactly what the name implies. In your game objects, this method adjusts the default sprite's bounding box to compensate for the transparent space. Figure 3.6 shows the transparent space around the `Viking` sprite with a padding of 26 pixels behind and 66 pixels in front of the `Viking`. If you were to just take the default `CCSprite boundingBox`, it would include these transparent pixels, and your collision detection would be inaccurate. Objects in your game would come into contact before the meaningful/nontranparent part of the graphics ever touched.

Figure 3.6   Transparent space around the Viking sprite/image

A Word on Bounding Boxes

The bounding boxes in Cocos2D are actually what are referred to as axis-aligned bounding boxes, or AABB for short. This is simply a box around your sprite texture (your image), with the axis of the box lined up with the axis of the coordinate system being used. The bounding box is really useful in determining when two or more objects are overlapping or colliding, without having to resort to a physics engine.

In Listing 3.7 you can see the `loadPlistForAnimationWithName` method, which is responsible for setting up the animations based on the data stored in the plist files. This method is declared and implemented in `GameObject`, but it is actually called and used by the individual classes such as the `RadarDish` and `Viking`. This method is passed the animation name as well as the class name. The class name is used to find the plist file, since the files are named after the classes they belong to, such as *RadarDish. plist* for the `RadarDish` class. Each plist file dictionary may contain several mini-dictionaries for each animation, and the animation name is used to extract the specific dictionary for the animation name passed in. Add the contents of Listing 3.7 below the code you just entered in *GameObject.m.*

Listing 3.7   **GameObject.m implementation file (part 2 of 2)**

```
-(CCAnimation*)loadPlistForAnimationWithName:(NSString*)animationName
andClassName:(NSString*)className {

    CCAnimation *animationToReturn = nil;
    NSString *fullFileName =
    [NSString stringWithFormat:@"%@.plist",className];
    NSString *plistPath;

    // 1: Get the Path to the plist file
    NSString *rootPath =
    [NSSearchPathForDirectoriesInDomains(NSDocumentDirectory,
```

```objc
                NSUserDomainMask, YES) objectAtIndex:0];
        plistPath = [rootPath stringByAppendingPathComponent:fullFileName];
        if (![[NSFileManager defaultManager] fileExistsAtPath:plistPath]) {
            plistPath = [[NSBundle mainBundle]
                            pathForResource:className ofType:@"plist"];
        }

        // 2: Read in the plist file
        NSDictionary *plistDictionary =
        [NSDictionary dictionaryWithContentsOfFile:plistPath];

        // 3: If the plistDictionary was null, the file was not found.
        if (plistDictionary == nil) {
            CCLOG(@"Error reading plist: %@.plist", className);
            return nil; // No Plist Dictionary or file found
        }

        // 4: Get just the mini-dictionary for this animation
        NSDictionary *animationSettings =
        [plistDictionary objectForKey:animationName];
        if (animationSettings == nil) {
            CCLOG(@"Could not locate AnimationWithName:%@",animationName);
            return nil;
        }

        // 5: Get the delay value for the animation
        float animationDelay =
        [[animationSettings objectForKey:@"delay"] floatValue];
        animationToReturn = [CCAnimation animation];
        [animationToReturn setDelay:animationDelay];

        // 6: Add the frames to the animation
        NSString *animationFramePrefix =
        [animationSettings objectForKey:@"filenamePrefix"];
        NSString *animationFrames =
        [animationSettings objectForKey:@"animationFrames"];
        NSArray *animationFrameNumbers =
        [animationFrames componentsSeparatedByString:@","];

        for (NSString *frameNumber in animationFrameNumbers) {
            NSString *frameName =
            [NSString stringWithFormat:@"%@%@.png",
             animationFramePrefix,frameNumber];
            [animationToReturn addFrame:
             [[CCSpriteFrameCache sharedSpriteFrameCache]
              spriteFrameByName:frameName]];
        }
```

```
        return animationToReturn;
}
@end
```

Now let's examine the sections in Listing 3.7, as noted by the numbered comment lines in the code:

- Sections 1 and 2 are from the standard Apple templates on reading property list files:
  - Section 1 tries to get the actual file system path to the property list file. This is where the `className` that was passed into the method is used to try to determine the path from the application bundle.
  - Section 2 uses built-in methods to read and parse the property list file, returning a dictionary with the entire contents of the plist file. This is an `NSDictionary` containing all of the animation mini-dictionaries in this single file.
- Section 3 is just a quick check to make sure the `NSDictionary` was not empty.
- Section 4 is where the mini-dictionary for the particular animation passed in as `animationName` is extracted. The mini-dictionary (named `animation-Settings` in the code) contains the filename prefix, delay, and list of animation frames. After extracting the `animationSettings` dictionary, a quick check is made to ensure it is not empty.
- In Section 5, the `delay` value is retrieved from `animationSettings`, and the `CCAnimation` object is created with the delay. Since the delay is often fractions of a second, this is stored as a float value. You can have the delay in the `CCAnimate` action as you learned, or as part of the `CCAnimation` object itself.
- Section 6 is where all of the animation frames are loaded into the animation. The first step is to get the prefix for the filename for each of the frames. (For example, the `RadarDish` animations use the `radar_` prefix.) The next step is to break apart the string of frame numbers into an `NSArray` of just the number themselves. A convenient `NSString` method called `componentsSeparated-ByString` allows you to split up the string into comma-separated values in one line of code. The `for` loop iterates through the `NSArray` of frame numbers and adds the `CCSpriteFrame` to the animation. Each frame number becomes a call to add a `CCSpriteFrame` where the name consists of the prefix, the frame number, and *.png*. Finally, the newly created and loaded animation is returned.

The key point to understand about the code in Listing 3.7 is that by using the `loadPlistForAnimationWithName` method, you can load the animation settings for all of the game objects in *Space Viking*. If you look closely at section 7, you will see the key names `filenamePrefix` and `animationFrames`, which you set up in the plist files at the beginning of this chapter. Make sure your *GameObject.m* implementation file contains the code from both Listings 3.6 and 3.7.

At the end of each section in this chapter, it is good practice for you to build the project and ensure you have not introduced any typos or errors. Use ⌘-B or select **Build** from the Product menu to build the project.

Creating the GameCharacter Class

In *Space Viking*, power-ups and the SpaceCargoShip inherit directly from GameObject, as their behavior is very simple. The other objects in *Space Viking* inherit from the GameCharacter class, providing these objects with a state machine brain. The GameCharacter class provides instance variables for holding the current state as well as the character's health. The class also provides a handy method to ensure that all of the game elements remain within the boundaries of the screen. To create the GameCharacter header and implementation files:

1. In Xcode, right-click on the *GameObjects* group.
2. Select **New File**, and choose the **Cocoa Touch category** under iOS and **Objective-C** class as the file type, and click **Next.**
3. For the Subclass field, enter *GameObject* and click **Next**.
4. Enter *GameCharacter* for the filename and click **Finish**.

Open the *GameCharacter.h* header file and change the contents to match the code in Listing 3.8.

Listing 3.8   **GameCharacter.h header file**

```
//   GameCharacter.h
//   SpaceViking

#import <Foundation/Foundation.h>
#import "GameObject.h"

@interface GameCharacter : GameObject {
    int characterHealth;
    CharacterStates characterState;
}

-(void)checkAndClampSpritePosition;
-(int)getWeaponDamage;

@property (readwrite) int characterHealth;
@property (readwrite) CharacterStates characterState;
@end
```

In Listing 3.8, you can see that two new instance variables and methods are added to all objects inheriting from GameCharacter. Open the GameCharacter.m implementation file and replace the template code with the contents of Listing 3.9.

Listing 3.9 **GameCharacter.m implementation file**

```objc
//  GameCharacter.m
//  SpaceViking

#import "GameCharacter.h"

@implementation GameCharacter
@synthesize characterHealth;
@synthesize characterState;

-(void) dealloc {
    [super dealloc];
}

-(int)getWeaponDamage {
    // Default to zero damage
    CCLOG(@"getWeaponDamage should be overridden");
    return 0;
}

-(void)checkAndClampSpritePosition {
    CGPoint currentSpritePosition = [self position];

    if (UI_USER_INTERFACE_IDIOM() == UIUserInterfaceIdiomPad) {
        // Clamp for the iPad
        if (currentSpritePosition.x < 30.0f) {
            [self setPosition:ccp(30.0f, currentSpritePosition.y)];
        } else if (currentSpritePosition.x > 1000.0f) {
            [self setPosition:ccp(1000.0f, currentSpritePosition.y)];
        }
    } else {
        // Clamp for iPhone, iPhone 4, or iPod touch
        if (currentSpritePosition.x < 24.0f) {
            [self setPosition:ccp(24.0f, currentSpritePosition.y)];
        } else if (currentSpritePosition.x > 456.0f) {
            [self setPosition:ccp(456.0f, currentSpritePosition.y)];
        }
    }
}
@end
```

The getWeaponDamage method provides a quick method to determine how much damage to inflict when an enemy or the Viking attacks. In the Viking this value will change if Ole is using his fists or the Mallet.

The checkAndClampSpritePosition is used to ensure that an object stays in the confines of the screen. It checks the current object's position and repositions the object if it is too far to the left or right of the screen. This is useful for keeping Ole the Viking and his enemies onscreen at all times. By having this method in the `GameCharacter` class, you can avoid typing redundant code in each of your game character classes.

Tip on Points Versus Pixels

Remember that Cocos2D uses a point system to help position objects on the normal iPhone display (480 × 320 pixels) and the retina display (960 × 640 pixels). In the nonretina display a point equals a pixel, but in the retina display a point equals two pixels. When you set Ole's position to 24 points, on an iPhone 3G or 3GS it equates to exactly 24 pixels from the left side. On an iPhone 4 with the retina display it is 48 pixels from the left side. In both cases, to the player Ole will look like he is in the exact same position onscreen. You can read more about the points system in Cocos2D at *www.cocos2d-iphone.org/wiki/doku.php/ prog_guide:how_to_develop_retinadisplay_games_in_cocos2d.*

Once more, hit ⌘-**B** or select **Build** from the Product menu to make sure your code is free of typos and errors. Having created the `GameObject` and the `GameCharacter` classes, in the next chapter you will dive in a little deeper and get into the first enemy Ole the Viking will encounter.

Summary

In this chapter you learned about Cocos2D animations, the `CCAnimationCache`, and the game design that you will use for *Space Viking*. Although you cannot see tangible results yet, it was necessary to set up the groundwork in order to add enemies and more to the game. When you are ready, flip over to Chapter 4 and learn how to add the menacing `RadarDish` enemy to SpaceViking.

Challenges

1. Think about your own game: How would you design the classes and hierarchy of your objects?

2. How would you modify the method `loadPlistForAnimationWithName` inside of `GameObject` so that the `CCAnimations` are added to the `CCAnimationCache`?

> **Hint**
> If you are stumped, look at the commented-out solution inside the source code for this chapter.

4

Simple Collision Detection and the First Enemy

In the previous chapter you learned the basics of Cocos2D animations and actions. You also started building a flexible framework for Space Viking. *In this chapter you go further and create the first enemy for Ole to do battle with. In the process you learn how to implement a simple system for collision detection and the artificial intelligence brain of the enemies in* Space Viking.

There is a significant amount of code necessary in this chapter to drive the behavior of Ole and the RadarDish. Take your time understanding how these classes work, as they are the foundation and models for the rest of the classes in Space Viking.

Ready to defeat the aliens?

Creating the Radar Dish and Viking Classes

From just a `CCSprite` to a fully animated character, Ole the Viking takes the plunge from simple to advanced from here on out. In this section you create the `RadarDish` and `Viking` classes to encapsulate the logic needed by each, including all of the animations. The `RadarDish` class is worth a close look, as all of the enemy characters in *Space Viking* are modeled after it.

Creating the RadarDish Class

In this first scene, there is a suspicious radar dish on the right side of the screen. It scans for foreign creatures such as Ole. Ole needs to find a way to destroy the radar dish before it alerts the enemy robots of his presence. Fortunately, Ole knows two ways to deal with such problems: his left and right fists. Create the new `RadarDish` class in Xcode by following these steps:

1. In Xcode, right-click on the *EnemyObjects* group.
2. Select **New File**, choose the **Cocoa Touch category** under iOS and **Objective-C class** as the file type, and click **Next**.

3. For the Subclass field, enter *GameCharacter* and click **Next**.

4. Enter *RadarDish* for the filename and click **Finish**.

Open the *RadarDish.h* header file and change the contents to match the code in Listing 4.1.

Listing 4.1   **RadarDish.h header file**

```
//   RadarDish.h
//   SpaceViking
//
#import <Foundation/Foundation.h>
#import "GameCharacter.h"

@interface RadarDish : GameCharacter {
    CCAnimation *tiltingAnim;
    CCAnimation *transmittingAnim;
    CCAnimation *takingAHitAnim;
    CCAnimation *blowingUpAnim;
    GameCharacter *vikingCharacter;

}
@property (nonatomic, retain) CCAnimation *tiltingAnim;
@property (nonatomic, retain) CCAnimation *transmittingAnim;
@property (nonatomic, retain) CCAnimation *takingAHitAnim;
@property (nonatomic, retain) CCAnimation *blowingUpAnim;

@end
```

Looking at Listing 4.1 you can see that the `RadarDish` class inherits from the `GameCharacter` class and that it defines four `CCAnimation` instance variables. There is also an instance variable to hold a pointer back to the `Viking` character.

Why the vikingCharacter Variable Is of Type GameCharacter and Not of Type Viking Class

If you look carefully at Listing 4.1, you will notice that the `vikingCharacter` instance variable is of type `GameCharacter` and not of type `Viking`. This is because the `RadarDish` class needs access only to the methods defined in `GameCharacter` and not to the full `Viking` class.

Having an instance variable of type `GameCharacter` here allows for the `RadarDish` class to not have to know anything further about the `Viking` object except that it is a `GameCharacter`. You are free to add features to the `Viking` class without fear that it will break any functionality in `RadarDish`. If you were to change the main character in a future version of *Space Viking*, the code would still function fine, since that new main character class too would, presumably, be derived from the GameCharacter class.

Listings 4.2, 4.3, and 4.4 show the contents of the *RadarDish.m* implementation file. The changeState and updateStateWithDelta time methods are crucial to understand, as they are the most basic versions of what you will find in all of the characters in *Space Viking*. While reading this code, keep in mind that the RadarDish is a simple enemy that never moves or attacks the Viking. The RadarDish does take damage from the Viking, eventually blowing up by moving to a dead state. Listing 4.2 covers the top portion of the *RadarDish.m* implementation file, including the changeState method. Open the *RadarDish.m* implementation file and replace the code so that it matches the contents in Listings 4.2, 4.3, and 4.4.

Listing 4.2   **RadarDish.m implementation file (top portion)**

```
// RadarDish.m
// SpaceViking
#import "RadarDish.h"

@implementation RadarDish
@synthesize tiltingAnim;
@synthesize transmittingAnim;
@synthesize takingAHitAnim;
@synthesize blowingUpAnim;

- (void) dealloc{
    [tiltingAnim release];
    [transmittingAnim release];
    [takingAHitAnim release];
    [blowingUpAnim release];
    [super dealloc];
}

-(void)changeState:(CharacterStates)newState {
    [self stopAllActions];
    id action = nil;
    [self setCharacterState:newState];

    switch (newState) {
        case kStateSpawning:
            CCLOG(@"RadarDish->Starting the Spawning Animation");
            action = [CCAnimate actionWithAnimation:tiltingAnim
                            restoreOriginalFrame:NO];
            break;
```

```
        case kStateIdle:
            CCLOG(@"RadarDish->Changing State to Idle");
            action = [CCAnimate actionWithAnimation:transmittingAnim
                                 restoreOriginalFrame:NO];
            break;

        case kStateTakingDamage:
            CCLOG(@"RadarDish->Changing State to TakingDamage");
            characterHealth =
             characterHealth - [vikingCharacter getWeaponDamage];
            if (characterHealth <= 0.0f) {
                [self changeState:kStateDead];
            } else {
                action = [CCAnimate actionWithAnimation:takingAHitAnim
                                    restoreOriginalFrame:NO];
            }
            break;

        case kStateDead:
            CCLOG(@"RadarDish->Changing State to Dead");
            action = [CCAnimate actionWithAnimation:blowingUpAnim
                                 restoreOriginalFrame:NO];
            break;

        default:
            CCLOG(@"Unhandled state %d in RadarDish", newState);
            break;
    }
    if (action != nil) {
        [self runAction:action];
    }
}
```

The changeState method is called when the RadarDish needs to transition between states. In the beginning of this chapter you were introduced to state machines, and the changeState method is what allows for transitions to different states in the miniscule "brain" of the RadarDish. The RadarDish brain can exist in one of four states: spawning, idle, taking damage, or dead. In the listings that follow, you will see that the RadarDish is initialized in the spawning state when it is created, and then through the updateStateWithDeltaTime method it will move through the four states.

When the updateStateWithDeltaTime determines that the RadarDish needs to change its state, the changeState method is called. Looking at Listing 4.2, you can recap what the switch state is doing as follows:

- **Spawning** (kStateSpawning)

  Starts up the RadarDish with the tilting animation, which is the dish moving up and down.

- **Idle** (kStateIdle)

  Runs the transmitting animation, which is the RadarDish blinking.

- **Taking Damage** (kStateTakingDamage)

  Runs the taking damage animation, showing a hit to the RadarDish. The RadarDish health is reduced according to the type of weapon being used against it.

- **Dead** (kStateDead)

  The RadarDish plays a death animation of it blowing up. This state occurs once the RadarDish health is at or below zero.

The next section of the RadarDish implementation file is covered in Listing 4.3, showing the updateStateWithDeltaTime method.

Listing 4.3   **RadarDish.m implementation file (middle portion)**

```
-(void)updateStateWithDeltaTime:(ccTime)deltaTime
andListOfGameObjects:(CCArray*)listOfGameObjects {
    if (characterState == kStateDead)
        return;                                            // 1

    vikingCharacter =
    (GameCharacter*)[[self parent]
      getChildByTag:kVikingSpriteTagValue];                // 2


    CGRect vikingBoudingBox =
            [vikingCharacter adjustedBoundingBox];          // 3
    CharacterStates vikingState = [vikingCharacter
                                characterState];            // 4

    // Calculate if the Viking is attacking and nearby
    if ((vikingState == kStateAttacking) &&
        (CGRectIntersectsRect([self adjustedBoundingBox],
vikingBoudingBox))) {                                      // 5
        if (characterState != kStateTakingDamage) {
            // If RadarDish is NOT already taking Damage
            [self changeState:kStateTakingDamage];
            return;
        }
    }
```

```
if ((([self numberOfRunningActions] == 0) &&
    (characterState != kStateDead)) {
    CCLOG(@"Going to Idle");
    [self changeState:kStateIdle];                          // 6
    return;
  }
}
}
```

Now let's examine the numbered lines of the code:

1. Checks if the `RadarDish` is already dead. If it is, this method is short-circuited and returned. If the `RadarDish` is dead, there is nothing to update.

2. Gets the `Viking` character object from the `RadarDish` parent. All of *Space Viking*'s objects are children of the scene `SpriteBatchNode`, referred to here as the parent. The `Viking` in particular was added to the `SpriteBatchNode` with a particular `tag`, referred to by the constant `kVikingSpriteTagValue`. By obtaining a reference to the `Viking` object, the `RadarDish` can determine if the `Viking` is nearby and attacking the `RadarDish`. (Listing 4.3 contains the code that sets up the `kVikingSpriteTagValue` constant.)

3. Gets the `Viking` character's adjusted bounding box.

4. Gets the `Viking` character's state.

5. Determines if the `Viking` is nearby and attacking. If the adjusted bounding boxes for the `Viking` and the `RadarDish` overlap, and the `Viking` is in his attack phase, the `RadarDish` can be certain that the `Viking` is attacking it. The call to `changeState:kStateTakingDamage` will alter the `RadarDish` animation to reflect the attack and reduce the `RadarDish` character's health.

6. Resets the transmission animation on the `RadarDish`. If the `RadarDish` is not currently playing an animation, and it is not dead, it is reset to idle so that the transmission animation can restart.

The last part of the *RadarDish.m* implementation file is the longest but least complicated. There is an `initAnimations` method, which sets up all of the `RadarDish` animations, and an `init` method that initializes the `RadarDish` and sets up the starting values for the instance variables. Add the contents of Listing 4.4 to your *RadarDish.m* implementation file.

Listing 4.4 RadarDish.m implementation file (bottom portion)

```
-(void)initAnimations {
    [self setTiltingAnim:
    [self loadPlistForAnimationWithName:@"tiltingAnim"
    andClassName:NSStringFromClass([self class])]];
```

```
    [self setTransmittingAnim:
     [self loadPlistForAnimationWithName:@"transmittingAnim"
      andClassName:NSStringFromClass([self class])]];

    [self setTakingAHitAnim:
     [self loadPlistForAnimationWithName:@"takingAHitAnim"
      andClassName:NSStringFromClass([self class])]];

    [self setBlowingUpAnim:
     [self loadPlistForAnimationWithName:@"blowingUpAnim"
      andClassName:NSStringFromClass([self class])]];
}
-(id) init {
    if( (self=[super init]) ) {
        CCLOG(@"### RadarDish initialized");
        [self initAnimations];                          // 1
        characterHealth = 100.0f;                        // 2
        gameObjectType = kEnemyTypeRadarDish;            // 3
        [self changeState:kStateSpawning];               // 4
    }
    return self;
}
@end
```

The initAnimations method calls the loadPlistForAnimationWithName method you declared in the GameObject class. The name of the animation to load is passed along with the class name. Note the convenience method NSStringFrom-Class is used to get an NSString from the class name, in this case RadarDish. The class name is used to find the correct plist file for the object, since the plist files have a name corresponding to the class. The following occurs in the init method:

1. Calls the initAnimations method, which sets up all of the animations for the RadarDish. The frame's coordinates and textures were already loaded and cached by Cocos2D when the texture atlas files (*scene1atlas.png* and *scene1atlas.plist*) were loaded by the GameplayLayer class.

2. Sets the initial health of the RadarDish to a value of 100.

3. Sets the RadarDish to be a Game Object of type kEnemyTypeRadarDish.

4. Initializes the state of the RadarDish to spawning. Looking back at Listing 4.2, you can see that this starts the tilting animation, which is followed by the transmitting animation when the RadarDish moves from spawning to an idle state.

There is a little more work left before you can have this chapter's game running on your device. You need to add the Viking class and make some changes to the GameplayLayer class. It is important to understand how the updateStateWith-DeltaTime and the changeState methods in RadarDish control the state of the

AI brain. These same two methods are used to drive the brain of all of the other game characters, including Ole the Viking.

Creating the Viking Class

In the previous chapter, Ole the Viking was nothing more than a CCSprite. In this chapter you pull him out into his own class complete with animations and a state machine to transition him through his various states. If the Viking class code starts to look daunting, refer back to the RadarDish class: the Viking is simply a game character like the RadarDish, albeit with more functionality. Create the new Viking class in Xcode by:

1. In Xcode, right-click on the *GameObjects* group.

2. Select **Add > New File**, choose the **Cocoa Touch category** under iOS and **Objective-C class** as the file type, and click **Next**.

3. For the Subclass field, enter *GameCharacter* and click **Next**.

4. Enter *Viking* for the filename and click **Save**.

Open the *Viking.h* header file and change the contents to match the code in Listing 4.5.

Listing 4.5   **Viking.h header file**

```
//  Viking.h
//  SpaceViking
#import <Foundation/Foundation.h>
#import "GameCharacter.h"
#import "SneakyButton.h"
#import "SneakyJoystick.h"
typedef enum {
    kLeftHook,
    kRightHook
} LastPunchType;

@interface Viking : GameCharacter  {
    LastPunchType myLastPunch;
    BOOL isCarryingMallet;
    CCSpriteFrame *standingFrame;

    // Standing, breathing, and walking
    CCAnimation *breathingAnim;
    CCAnimation *breathingMalletAnim;
    CCAnimation *walkingAnim;
    CCAnimation *walkingMalletAnim;
```

```
    // Crouching, standing up, and Jumping
    CCAnimation *crouchingAnim;
    CCAnimation *crouchingMalletAnim;
    CCAnimation *standingUpAnim;
    CCAnimation *standingUpMalletAnim;
    CCAnimation *jumpingAnim;
    CCAnimation *jumpingMalletAnim;
    CCAnimation *afterJumpingAnim;
    CCAnimation *afterJumpingMalletAnim;

    // Punching
    CCAnimation *rightPunchAnim;
    CCAnimation *leftPunchAnim;
    CCAnimation *malletPunchAnim;

    // Taking Damage and Death
    CCAnimation *phaserShockAnim;
    CCAnimation *deathAnim;

    SneakyJoystick *joystick;
    SneakyButton *jumpButton ;
    SneakyButton *attackButton;

    float millisecondsStayingIdle;
}
// Standing, Breathing, Walking
@property (nonatomic, retain) CCAnimation *breathingAnim;
@property (nonatomic, retain) CCAnimation *breathingMalletAnim;
@property (nonatomic, retain) CCAnimation *walkingAnim;
@property (nonatomic, retain) CCAnimation *walkingMalletAnim;

// Crouching, Standing Up, Jumping
@property (nonatomic, retain) CCAnimation *crouchingAnim;
@property (nonatomic, retain) CCAnimation *crouchingMalletAnim;
@property (nonatomic, retain) CCAnimation *standingUpAnim;
@property (nonatomic, retain) CCAnimation *standingUpMalletAnim;
@property (nonatomic, retain) CCAnimation *jumpingAnim;
@property (nonatomic, retain) CCAnimation *jumpingMalletAnim;
@property (nonatomic, retain) CCAnimation *afterJumpingAnim;
@property (nonatomic, retain) CCAnimation *afterJumpingMalletAnim;

// Punching
@property (nonatomic, retain) CCAnimation *rightPunchAnim;
@property (nonatomic, retain) CCAnimation *leftPunchAnim;
@property (nonatomic, retain) CCAnimation *malletPunchAnim;
```

```
// Taking Damage and Death
@property (nonatomic, retain) CCAnimation *phaserShockAnim;
@property (nonatomic, retain) CCAnimation *deathAnim;

@property (nonatomic,assign) SneakyJoystick *joystick;
@property (nonatomic,assign) SneakyButton *jumpButton;
@property (nonatomic,assign) SneakyButton *attackButton;
@end
```

Listing 4.5 shows the large number of animations that are possible with the Viking character as well as instance variables to point to the onscreen joystick and button controls.

The key items to note are the typedef enumerator for the left and right punches, an instance variable to store what the last punch thrown was, and a float to keep track of how long the player has been idle. The code for the Viking implementation file is a bit on the lengthy side, hence it is broken up into four Listings, 4.6 through 4.9. Open the *Viking.m* implementation file and replace the code so that it matches the contents in Listings 4.6, 4.7, 4.8, and 4.9.

Listing 4.6   **Viking.m implementation file (part 1 of 4)**

```
//  Viking.m
//  SpaceViking
#import "Viking.h"

@implementation Viking
@synthesize joystick;
@synthesize jumpButton ;
@synthesize attackButton;

// Standing, Breathing, Walking
@synthesize breathingAnim;
@synthesize breathingMalletAnim;
@synthesize walkingAnim;
@synthesize walkingMalletAnim;
// Crouching, Standing Up, Jumping
@synthesize crouchingAnim;
@synthesize crouchingMalletAnim;
@synthesize standingUpAnim;
@synthesize standingUpMalletAnim;
@synthesize jumpingAnim;
@synthesize jumpingMalletAnim;
@synthesize afterJumpingAnim;
@synthesize afterJumpingMalletAnim;
// Punching
@synthesize rightPunchAnim;
```

```objc
@synthesize leftPunchAnim;
@synthesize malletPunchAnim;
// Taking Damage and Death
@synthesize phaserShockAnim;
@synthesize deathAnim;

- (void) dealloc {
    joystick = nil;
    jumpButton = nil;
    attackButton = nil;
    [breathingAnim release];
    [breathingMalletAnim release];
    [walkingAnim release];
    [walkingMalletAnim release];
    [crouchingAnim release];
    [crouchingMalletAnim release];
    [standingUpAnim release];
    [standingUpMalletAnim release];
    [jumpingAnim release];
    [jumpingMalletAnim release];
    [afterJumpingAnim release];
    [afterJumpingMalletAnim release];
    [rightPunchAnim release];
    [leftPunchAnim release];
    [malletPunchAnim release];
    [phaserShockAnim release];
    [deathAnim release];

    [super dealloc];
}

-(BOOL)isCarryingWeapon {
    return isCarryingMallet;
}

-(int)getWeaponDamage {
    if (isCarryingMallet) {
        return kVikingMalletDamage;
    }
    return kVikingFistDamage;
}
-(void)applyJoystick:(SneakyJoystick *)aJoystick forTimeDelta:(float)
deltaTime
{
    CGPoint scaledVelocity = ccpMult(aJoystick.velocity, 128.0f);
    CGPoint oldPosition = [self position];
    CGPoint newPosition =
```

```
    ccp(oldPosition.x +
        scaledVelocity.x * deltaTime,
        oldPosition.y);                                        // 1
    [self setPosition:newPosition];                            // 2

    if (oldPosition.x > newPosition.x) {
        self.flipX = YES;                                      // 3
    } else {
        self.flipX = NO;
    }
}

-(void)checkAndClampSpritePosition {
    if (self.characterState != kStateJumping) {
        if ([self position].y > 110.0f)
            [self setPosition:ccp([self position].x,110.0f)];
    }
    [super checkAndClampSpritePosition];
}
```

At the beginning of the *Viking.m* implementation file is the dealloc method. Far wiser Objective-C developers than this author have commented on the benefits of having your dealloc method up top and near your synthesize statements. The idea behind this move is to make sure you are deallocating any and all instance variables, therefore avoiding one of the main causes of memory leaks in Objective-C code.

Following the dealloc method, you have the isCarryingWeapon method, but since it is self-explanatory, move on to the applyJoystick method. This method is similar to the one back in Chapter 2, "Hello, Space Viking," Listing 2.10, but it has been modified to deal only with Ole's movement and removes the handling for the jump or attack buttons. The first change to applyJoystick is the creation of the oldPosition variable to track the Viking's position before it is moved. Looking at the applyJoystick method in Listing 4.6, take a note of the following key lines:

1. Sets the new position based on the velocity of the joystick, but only in the x-axis. The y position stays constant, making it so Ole only walks to the left or right, and not up or down.

2. Moves the Viking to the new position.

3. Compares the old position with the new position, flipping the Viking horizontally if needed. If you look closely at the Viking images, he is facing to the right by default. If this method determines that the old position is to the right of the new position, Ole is moving to the left, and his pixels have to be flipped horizontally. If you don't flip Ole horizontally, he will look like he is trying to do the moonwalk when you move him to the left. It is a cool effect but not useful for your Viking.

Cocos2D has two built-in functions you will make use of frequently: flipX and flipY. These functions flip the pixels of a texture along the x- or y-axis, allowing you to display a mirror image of your graphics without having to have left- and right-facing copies of each image for each character. Figure 4.1 shows the effect of flipX on the Viking texture. This is a really handy feature to have, since it helps reduce the size of your application, and it keeps you from having to create images for every possible state.

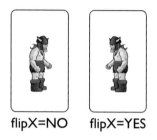

flipX=NO   flipX=YES

Figure 4.1   Effects of the flipX function on the Viking texture or graphic

The next section of the *Viking.m* implementation file covers the changeState method. As you learned with the RadarDish class, the changeState method is used to transition the character from one state to another and to start the appropriate animations for each state. Copy the contents of Listing 4.7 into your *Viking.m* class.

Listing 4.7   **Viking.m implementation file (part 2 of 4)**

```
#pragma mark -
-(void)changeState:(CharacterStates)newState {
    [self stopAllActions];
    id action = nil;
    id movementAction = nil;
    CGPoint newPosition;
    [self setCharacterState:newState];

    switch (newState) {
        case kStateIdle:
            if (isCarryingMallet) {
                [self setDisplayFrame:[[CCSpriteFrameCache
                    sharedSpriteFrameCache]
                    spriteFrameByName:@"sv_mallet_1.png"]];
            } else {
                [self setDisplayFrame:[[CCSpriteFrameCache
                    sharedSpriteFrameCache]
                    spriteFrameByName:@"sv_anim_1.png"]];
            }
            break;
```

```
case kStateWalking:
    if (isCarryingMallet) {
        action =
            [CCAnimate actionWithAnimation:walkingMalletAnim
                        restoreOriginalFrame:NO];
    } else {
        action =
            [CCAnimate actionWithAnimation:walkingAnim
                        restoreOriginalFrame:NO];
    }
    break;


case kStateCrouching:
    if (isCarryingMallet) {
        action =
            [CCAnimate actionWithAnimation:crouchingMalletAnim
                        restoreOriginalFrame:NO];
    } else {
        action =
            [CCAnimate actionWithAnimation:crouchingAnim
                        restoreOriginalFrame:NO];
    }
    break;

case kStateStandingUp:
    if (isCarryingMallet) {
        action =
            [CCAnimate actionWithAnimation:standingUpMalletAnim
                        restoreOriginalFrame:NO];

    } else {
        action =
            [CCAnimate actionWithAnimation:standingUpAnim
                        restoreOriginalFrame:NO];
    }
    break;

case kStateBreathing:
    if (isCarryingMallet) {
        action =
            [CCAnimate actionWithAnimation:breathingMalletAnim
                        restoreOriginalFrame:YES];
    } else {
        action =
            [CCAnimate actionWithAnimation:breathingAnim
                        restoreOriginalFrame:YES];
    }
    break;
```

```
case kStateJumping:
    newPosition = ccp(screenSize.width * 0.2f, 0.0f);
    if ([self flipX] == YES) {
        newPosition = ccp(newPosition.x * -1.0f, 0.0f);
    }
    movementAction = [CCJumpBy actionWithDuration:0.5f
                                        position:newPosition
                                          height:160.0f
                                           jumps:1];

    if (isCarryingMallet) {
        // Viking Jumping animation with the Mallet
        action = [CCSequence actions:
                    [CCAnimate
                        actionWithAnimation:crouchingMalletAnim
                        restoreOriginalFrame:NO],
                    [CCSpawn actions:
                     [CCAnimate
                        actionWithAnimation:jumpingMalletAnim
                        restoreOriginalFrame:YES],
                     movementAction,
                     nil],
                    [CCAnimate
                        actionWithAnimation:afterJumpingMalletAnim
                        restoreOriginalFrame:NO],
                    nil];
    } else {
        // Viking Jumping animation without the Mallet
        action = [CCSequence actions:
                    [CCAnimate
                        actionWithAnimation:crouchingAnim
                        restoreOriginalFrame:NO],
                    [CCSpawn actions:
                     [CCAnimate
                        actionWithAnimation:jumpingAnim
                        restoreOriginalFrame:YES],
                     movementAction,
                     nil],
                    [CCAnimate
                        actionWithAnimation:afterJumpingAnim
                        restoreOriginalFrame:NO],
                    nil];
    }
    break;

case kStateAttacking:
    if (isCarryingMallet == YES) {
```

```
                    action = [CCAnimate
                                actionWithAnimation:malletPunchAnim
                                restoreOriginalFrame:YES];
                } else {
                    if (kLeftHook == myLastPunch) {
                        // Execute a right hook
                        myLastPunch = kRightHook;
                        action = [CCAnimate
                                    actionWithAnimation:rightPunchAnim
                                    restoreOriginalFrame:NO];
                    } else {
                        // Execute a left hook
                        myLastPunch = kLeftHook;
                        action = [CCAnimate
                                    actionWithAnimation:leftPunchAnim
                                    restoreOriginalFrame:NO];
                    }
                }
                break;

        case kStateTakingDamage:
            self.characterHealth = self.characterHealth - 10.0f;
            action = [CCAnimate
                        actionWithAnimation:phaserShockAnim
                        restoreOriginalFrame:YES];
            break;

        case kStateDead:
            action = [CCAnimate
                        actionWithAnimation:deathAnim
                        restoreOriginalFrame:NO];
            break;

        default:
            break;
    }
    if (action != nil) {
        [self runAction:action];
    }
}
```

The first part of the changeState method stops any running actions, including animations. Any running actions would be a part of a previous state of the Viking and would no longer be valid. Following the first line, the Viking state is set to the new state value, and a switch statement is used to carry out the animations for the new state. A few items are important to note:

1. Method variables cannot be declared inside a `switch` statement, as they would be out of scope as soon as the code exited the `switch` statement. Your `id action` variable is declared above the `switch` statement but initialized inside the `switch` branches.

2. Most of the states have two animations: one for the `Viking` with the `Mallet` and one without. The `isCarryingMallet` Boolean instance variable is key in determining which animation to play.

3. An action in Cocos2D can be made up of other actions in that it can be a compound action. The `switch` branch taken when the `Viking` state is `kState-Jumping` has a compound action made up of `CCSequence`, `CCAnimate`, `CCSpawn`, and `CCJumpBy` actions. The `CCJumpBy` action provides the parabolic movement for Ole the Viking, while the `CCAnimate` actions play the crouching, jumping, and landing animations. The `CCSpawn` action allows for more than one action to be started at the same time, in this case the `CCJumpBy` and `CCAnimate` animation action of Ole jumping. The `CCSequence` action ties it all together by making Ole crouch down, then jump, and finally land on his feet in sequence.

4. Taking a closer look at the `kStateTakingDamage switch` branch, you can see that after the animation completes, Ole reverts back to the frame that was displaying before the animation started. In this state transition, the `CCAnimate` action has the `restoreOriginalFrame` set to `YES`. The end effect of `restore-OriginalFrame` is that Ole will animate receiving a hit, and then return to looking as he did before the hit took place.

The first line of Listing 4.7 might be rather odd-looking: `#pragma mark`. The `pragma mark` serves as a formatting guide to Xcode and is not seen by the compiler. After the words `#pragma mark` you can place any text you would like displayed in the Xcode pulldown for this file. If you have just a hyphen (-), Xcode will create a separate section for that portion of the file. Using `pragma mark` can make your code easier to navigate. Figure 4.2 shows the effects of the `pragma mark` statements in the completed *Viking.m* file.

Figure 4.2   The effect of the pragma mark statements in the Xcode
pulldown menus

The next section of the *Viking.m* file covers the `updateStateWithDeltaTime` and the `adjustedBoundingBox` methods. Copy the contents of Listing 4.8 into your *Viking.m* file immediately following the `changeState` method.

Listing 4.8   **Viking.m implementation file (part 3 of 4)**

```
#pragma mark -
-(void)updateStateWithDeltaTime:(ccTime)deltaTime
andListOfGameObjects:(CCArray*)listOfGameObjects {
    if (self.characterState == kStateDead)
        return; // Nothing to do if the Viking is dead

    if ((self.characterState == kStateTakingDamage) &&
        ([self numberOfRunningActions] > 0))
        return; // Currently playing the taking damage animation

    // Check for collisions
    // Change this to keep the object count from querying it each time
    CGRect myBoundingBox = [self adjustedBoundingBox];
    for (GameCharacter *character in listOfGameObjects) {
        // This is Ole the Viking himself
        // No need to check collision with one's self
        if ([character tag] == kVikingSpriteTagValue)
            continue;

        CGRect characterBox = [character adjustedBoundingBox];
        if (CGRectIntersectsRect(myBoundingBox, characterBox)) {
            // Remove the PhaserBullet from the scene
            if ([character gameObjectType] == kEnemyTypePhaser) {
                [self changeState:kStateTakingDamage];
                [character changeState:kStateDead];
            } else if ([character gameObjectType] ==
                        kPowerUpTypeMallet) {
                // Update the frame to indicate Viking is
                // carrying the mallet
                isCarryingMallet = YES;
                [self changeState:kStateIdle];
                // Remove the Mallet from the scene
                [character changeState:kStateDead];
            } else if ([character gameObjectType] ==
                        kPowerUpTypeHealth) {
                [self setCharacterHealth:100.0f];
                // Remove the health power-up from the scene
                [character changeState:kStateDead];
            }
        }
    }
}
```

```
        [self checkAndClampSpritePosition];
        if ((self.characterState == kStateIdle) ||
            (self.characterState == kStateWalking) ||
            (self.characterState == kStateCrouching) ||
            (self.characterState == kStateStandingUp) ||
            (self.characterState == kStateBreathing)) {

            if (jumpButton.active) {
                [self changeState:kStateJumping];
            } else if (attackButton.active) {
                [self changeState:kStateAttacking];
            } else if ((joystick.velocity.x == 0.0f) &&
                        (joystick.velocity.y == 0.0f)) {
                if (self.characterState == kStateCrouching)
                    [self changeState:kStateStandingUp];
            } else if (joystick.velocity.y < -0.45f) {
                if (self.characterState != kStateCrouching)
                    [self changeState:kStateCrouching];
            } else if (joystick.velocity.x != 0.0f) { // dpad moving
                if (self.characterState != kStateWalking)
                    [self changeState:kStateWalking];
                [self applyJoystick:joystick
                        forTimeDelta:deltaTime];
            }
        }

        if ([self numberOfRunningActions] == 0) {
            // Not playing an animation
            if (self.characterHealth <= 0.0f) {
                [self changeState:kStateDead];
            } else if (self.characterState == kStateIdle) {
                millisecondsStayingIdle = millisecondsStayingIdle +
                                          deltaTime;
                if (millisecondsStayingIdle > kVikingIdleTimer) {
                    [self changeState:kStateBreathing];
                }
            } else if ((self.characterState != kStateCrouching) &&
                        (self.characterState != kStateIdle)){
                millisecondsStayingIdle = 0.0f;
                [self changeState:kStateIdle];
            }
        }
    }
}


#pragma mark -
-(CGRect)adjustedBoundingBox {
    // Adjust the bouding box to the size of the sprite
    // without the transparent space
```

```
CGRect vikingBoundingBox = [self boundingBox];
float xOffset;
float xCropAmount = vikingBoundingBox.size.width * 0.5482f;
float yCropAmount = vikingBoundingBox.size.height * 0.095f;

if ([self flipX] == NO) {
    // Viking is facing to the rigth, back is on the left
    xOffset = vikingBoundingBox.size.width * 0.1566f;
} else {
    // Viking is facing to the left; back is facing right
    xOffset = vikingBoundingBox.size.width * 0.4217f;
}
vikingBoundingBox =
CGRectMake(vikingBoundingBox.origin.x + xOffset,
        vikingBoundingBox.origin.y,
        vikingBoundingBox.size.width - xCropAmount,
        vikingBoundingBox.size.height - yCropAmount);

if (characterState == kStateCrouching) {
    // Shrink the bounding box to 56% of height
    // 88 pixels on top on iPad
    vikingBoundingBox = CGRectMake(vikingBoundingBox.origin.x,
    vikingBoundingBox.origin.y,
    vikingBoundingBox.size.width,
    vikingBoundingBox.size.height * 0.56f);
}

return vikingBoundingBox;
}
```

In the same manner as the RadarDish updateStateWithDeltaMethod worked, this method also returns immediately if the Viking is dead. There is no need to update a dead Viking because he won't be going anywhere.

If the Viking is in the middle of playing, the taking damage animation is played. This method again short-circuits and returns. The taking damage animation is blocking in that the player cannot do anything else while Ole the Viking is being shocked.

If the Viking is not taking damage or is dead, then the next step is to check what objects are coming in contact with the Viking. If there are objects in contact with the Viking, he checks to see if they are:

- Phaser: Changes the Viking state to taking damage.
- Mallet power-up: Gives Ole the Viking the mallet, a fearsome weapon.
- Health power-up: Ole's health is restored back to 100.

After checking for contacts, often called *collisions*, a quick call is made to the checkAndClampSpritePosition method to ensure that the Viking sprite stays within the boundaries of the screen.

The next `if` statement block checks the state of the joystick, jump, and attack buttons and changes the state of the `Viking` to reflect which controls are being pressed. The `if` statement executes only if the `Viking` is not currently carrying out a blocking animation, such as jumping.

Lastly the `Viking` class reaches a section of the `updateStateWithDeltaTime` method that handles what happens when there are no animations currently running. Cocos2D has a convenience method on `CCNodes` that reports back the number of actions running against a particular `CCNode` object. If you recall from the beginning of this chapter, all animations have to be run by a `CCAnimate` action. Once the animation for a state completes, the `numberOfRunningActions` will return zero for the `Viking`, and this block of code will reset the `Viking`'s state.

If the health is zero or less, the `Viking` will move into the dead state. Otherwise, if `Viking` is idle, a counter is incremented indicating how many seconds the player has been idle. Once that counter reaches a set limit, the `Viking` will play a heavy breathing animation. Finally, if the `Viking` is not already idle or crouching, he will move back into the idle state.

> **Note**
>
> The breathing animation is just a little bonus move to try to get the player to focus back on the game. If the joystick has been idle for more than 3 seconds, the `Viking` will let out a few deep breaths as if to say "Come on! I have aliens to fight here, let's get going!"

After the `updateStateWithDeltaTime` method, there is the `adjustedBoundingBox` method you declared inside the `GameObject` class. In Chapter 3, "Introduction to Cocos2D Animations and Actions," Figure 3.6 illustrated the transparent space in the `Viking` texture between the actual `Viking` and the edges of the image/texture. This method compensates for the transparent pixels by returning an adjusted bounding box that does not include the transparent pixels. The `flipX` parameter is used to determine which side the `Viking` is facing, as fewer pixels are trimmed off the back of the `Viking` image than the front.

The last part of the *Viking.m* implementation file sets up the animations inside the `initAnimations` method and the instance variables inside the `init` method. Once more, copy the contents of Listing 4.9 into your *Viking.m* implementation file immediately following the end of the `adjustedBoundingBox` method.

Listing 4.9   Viking.m implementation file (part 4 of 4)

```
#pragma mark -
-(void)initAnimations {

    [self setBreathingAnim:[self loadPlistForAnimationWithName:
@"breathingAnim" andClassName:NSStringFromClass([self class])]];

    [self setBreathingMalletAnim:[self loadPlistForAnimationWithName:
@"breathingMalletAnim" andClassName:NSStringFromClass([self class])]];
```

```
    [self setWalkingAnim:[self loadPlistForAnimationWithName:
@"walkingAnim" andClassName:NSStringFromClass([self class])]];

    [self setWalkingMalletAnim:[self loadPlistForAnimationWithName:
@"walkingMalletAnim" andClassName:NSStringFromClass([self class])]];

    [self setCrouchingAnim:[self loadPlistForAnimationWithName:
@"crouchingAnim" andClassName:NSStringFromClass([self class])]];

    [self setCrouchingMalletAnim:[self loadPlistForAnimationWithName:
@"crouchingMalletAnim" andClassName:NSStringFromClass([self class])]];

    [self setStandingUpAnim:[self loadPlistForAnimationWithName:
@"standingUpAnim" andClassName:NSStringFromClass([self class])]];

    [self setStandingUpMalletAnim:[self loadPlistForAnimationWithName:
@"standingUpMalletAnim" andClassName:NSStringFromClass([self class])]];

    [self setJumpingAnim:[self loadPlistForAnimationWithName:
@"jumpingAnim" andClassName:NSStringFromClass([self class])]];

    [self setJumpingMalletAnim:[self loadPlistForAnimationWithName:
@"jumpingMalletAnim" andClassName:NSStringFromClass([self class])]];

    [self setAfterJumpingAnim:[self loadPlistForAnimationWithName:
@"afterJumpingAnim" andClassName:NSStringFromClass([self class])]];

    [self setAfterJumpingMalletAnim:[self loadPlistForAnimationWithName:
@"afterJumpingMalletAnim" andClassName:NSStringFromClass([self class])]];

    // Punches
    [self setRightPunchAnim:[self loadPlistForAnimationWithName:
@"rightPunchAnim" andClassName:NSStringFromClass([self class])]];

    [self setLeftPunchAnim:[self loadPlistForAnimationWithName:
@"leftPunchAnim" andClassName:NSStringFromClass([self class])]];

    [self setMalletPunchAnim:[self loadPlistForAnimationWithName:
@"malletPunchAnim" andClassName:NSStringFromClass([self class])]];

    // Taking Damage and Death
    [self setPhaserShockAnim:[self loadPlistForAnimationWithName:
@"phaserShockAnim" andClassName:NSStringFromClass([self class])]];

    [self setDeathAnim:[self loadPlistForAnimationWithName:
@"vikingDeathAnim" andClassName:NSStringFromClass([self class])]];

}
```

```
#pragma mark -
-(id) init {
    if( (self=[super init]) ) {
        joystick = nil;
        jumpButton = nil;
        attackButton = nil;
        self.gameObjectType = kVikingType;
        myLastPunch = kRightHook;
        millisecondsStayingIdle = 0.0f;
        isCarryingMallet = NO;
        [self initAnimations];


    }
    return self;
}
@end
```

The initAnimation method, while quite long, is very basic in that it only initializes all of the Viking animations based on the display frames already loaded from the *scene1atlas.plist* file in the GameplayLayer class. The init method sets up the instance variables to their starting values.

Final Steps

The final step for this chapter is to make some changes to the GameplayLayer class so it loads the RadarDish and Viking onto the layer. Once these changes are made to the GameplayLayer files, you will have a working and playable version of *Space Viking* in your hands.

The GameplayLayer Class

The GameplayLayer class has a few changes to the header file. There is an additional import for the *CommonProtocols.h* file and the vikingSprite has been removed; instead there is a CCSpriteBatchNode called sceneSpriteBatchNode. Move your *GameplayLayer.h* and *GameplayLayer.m* files into the *Layers Group* folder in Xcode and ensure that your *GameplayLayer.h* header file has the same contents as Listing 4.10.

Listing 4.10   **GameplayLayer.h header file**

```
//  GameplayLayer.h
//  SpaceViking

#import <Foundation/Foundation.h>
#import "cocos2d.h"
#import "SneakyJoystick.h"
```

```
#import "SneakyButton.h"
#import "SneakyButtonSkinnedBase.h"
#import "SneakyJoystickSkinnedBase.h"
#import "Constants.h"
#import "CommonProtocols.h"
#import "RadarDish.h"
#import "Viking.h"

@interface GameplayLayer : CCLayer <GameplayLayerDelegate> {
    CCSprite *vikingSprite;
    SneakyJoystick *leftJoystick;
    SneakyButton *jumpButton;
    SneakyButton *attackButton;
    CCSpriteBatchNode *sceneSpriteBatchNode;
}

@end
```

The initJoystickAndButtons method of GameplayLayer stays the same as in Chapter 3. The rest of the GameplayLayer class requires changes to use the new CCSpriteBatchNode instance. Listings 4.11, 4.12, 4.13, and 4.14 cover the code for *GameplayLayer.m*. Replace the code in your *GameplayLayer.m* implementation file with the code in the next four listings.

Listing 4.11   **GameplayLayer.m implementation file (part 1 of 4)**

```
//  GameplayLayer.m
//  SpaceViking

#import "GameplayLayer.h"
@implementation GameplayLayer
- (void) dealloc {
    [leftJoystick release];
    [jumpButton release];
    [attackButton release];
    [super dealloc];
}

-(void)initJoystickAndButtons {
    CGSize screenSize = [CCDirector sharedDirector].winSize;        // 1
    // 2
    CGRect joystickBaseDimensions = CGRectMake(0, 0, 128.0f, 128.0f);
    CGRect jumpButtonDimensions = CGRectMake(0, 0, 64.0f, 64.0f);
    CGRect attackButtonDimensions = CGRectMake(0, 0, 64.0f, 64.0f);
    // 3
    CGPoint joystickBasePosition;
```

```
CGPoint jumpButtonPosition;
CGPoint attackButtonPosition;
// 4
if (UI_USER_INTERFACE_IDIOM() == UIUserInterfaceIdiomPad) {
    // The device is an iPad running iPhone 3.2 or later.
    CCLOG(@"Positioning Joystick and Buttons for iPad");
    joystickBasePosition = ccp(screenSize.width*0.0625f,
                               screenSize.height*0.052f);

    jumpButtonPosition = ccp(screenSize.width*0.946f,
                             screenSize.height*0.052f);

    attackButtonPosition = ccp(screenSize.width*0.947f,
                               screenSize.height*0.169f);
} else {
    // The device is an iPhone or iPod touch.
    CCLOG(@"Positioning Joystick and Buttons for iPhone");

    joystickBasePosition = ccp(screenSize.width*0.07f,
                               screenSize.height*0.11f);

    jumpButtonPosition = ccp(screenSize.width*0.93f,
                             screenSize.height*0.11f);

    attackButtonPosition = ccp(screenSize.width*0.93f,
                               screenSize.height*0.35f);
}

SneakyJoystickSkinnedBase *joystickBase =
[[[SneakyJoystickSkinnedBase alloc] init] autorelease];
joystickBase.position = joystickBasePosition;
joystickBase.backgroundSprite =
[CCSprite spriteWithFile:@"dpadDown.png"];
joystickBase.thumbSprite =
[CCSprite spriteWithFile:@"joystickDown.png"];
joystickBase.joystick = [[SneakyJoystick alloc]
                          initWithRect:joystickBaseDimensions];
leftJoystick = [joystickBase.joystick retain];
[self addChild:joystickBase];

SneakyButtonSkinnedBase *jumpButtonBase =
[[[SneakyButtonSkinnedBase alloc] init] autorelease];
jumpButtonBase.position = jumpButtonPosition;
jumpButtonBase.defaultSprite =
[CCSprite spriteWithFile:@"jumpUp.png"];
jumpButtonBase.activatedSprite =
[CCSprite spriteWithFile:@"jumpDown.png"];
```

```
    jumpButtonBase.pressSprite =
    [CCSprite spriteWithFile:@"jumpDown.png"];
    jumpButtonBase.button = [[SneakyButton alloc]
                            initWithRect:jumpButtonDimensions];
    jumpButton = [jumpButtonBase.button retain];
    jumpButton.isToggleable = NO;
    [self addChild:jumpButtonBase];

    SneakyButtonSkinnedBase *attackButtonBase = [[[SneakyButtonSkinnedBase
alloc] init] autorelease];
    attackButtonBase.position = attackButtonPosition;
    attackButtonBase.defaultSprite = [CCSprite spriteWithFile:
@"handUp.png"];
    attackButtonBase.activatedSprite = [CCSprite
spriteWithFile:@"handDown.png"];
    attackButtonBase.pressSprite = [CCSprite spriteWithFile:
@"handDown.png"];
    attackButtonBase.button = [[SneakyButton alloc] initWithRect:
attackButtonDimensions];
    attackButton = [attackButtonBase.button retain];
    attackButton.isToggleable = NO;
    [self addChild:attackButtonBase];
}
```

The initJoystick method remains unchanged from previous chapters. The directional pad (DPad) as well as the jump and attack buttons are set up and added to the GameplayLayer. The high z values ensure that the joystick controls appear on top of all the other graphical elements in the GameplayLayer.

Listing 4.12   **GameplayLayer.m implementation file (part 2 of 4)**

```
#pragma mark -
#pragma mark Update Method
-(void) update:(ccTime)deltaTime {
    CCArray *listOfGameObjects =
            [sceneSpriteBatchNode children];                    // 1
    for (GameCharacter *tempChar in listOfGameObjects) {        // 2
        [tempChar updateStateWithDeltaTime:deltaTime andListOfGameObjects:
                    listOfGameObjects];                         // 3
    }
}
```

The update method is the run loop for the entire GameplayLayer. The CCSpriteBatchNode object contains a list of all of the CCSprites for which it will handle the rendering, batching their OpenGL ES draw calls. The update method does the following:

1. Gets the list of all of the children CCSprites rendered by the CCSpriteBatch-Node. In *Space Viking* this is a list of all of the GameCharacters, including the Viking and his enemies.

2. Iterates through each of the Game Characters, calls their updateStateWith-DeltaTime method, and passes a pointer to the list of all Game Characters. If you look back at the updateStateWithDeltaTime code in *Viking.m*, you can see the list of Game Characters used to check for power-ups and phaser blasts. Power-ups and aliens with phaser beams are covered in the next chapter.

3. Calls the updateStateWithDeltaTime method on each of the Game Characters. This call allows for all of the characters to update their individual states to determine if they are colliding with any other objects in the game.

The next section of code in *GameplayLayer.m* (Listing 4.13) contains the methods for creating the enemies and a placeholder for creating the phaser blast.

Listing 4.13   **GameplayLayer.m implementation file (part 3 of 4)**

```
#pragma mark -
-(void)createObjectOfType:(GameObjectType)objectType
              withHealth:(int)initialHealth
              atLocation:(CGPoint)spawnLocation
              withZValue:(int)ZValue {

    if (objectType == kEnemyTypeRadarDish) {
        CCLOG(@"Creating the Radar Enemy");
        RadarDish *radarDish = [[RadarDish alloc] initWithSpriteFrameName:
@"radar_1.png"];
        [radarDish setCharacterHealth:initialHealth];
        [radarDish setPosition:spawnLocation];
        [sceneSpriteBatchNode addChild:radarDish
                            z:ZValue
                            tag:kRadarDishTagValue];
        [radarDish release];
    }


}

-(void)createPhaserWithDirection:(PhaserDirection)phaserDirection
andPosition:(CGPoint)spawnPosition {
    CCLOG(@"Placeholder for Chapter 5, see below");
    return;
}
```

The createObjectOfType method sets up the RadarDish object using the CCSpriteBatchNode and adds it to the layer. This method is expanded upon in

Chapter 5, "More Actions, Effects, and Cocos2D Scheduler," to include the other enemies in the *Space Viking* world.

The last code listing for *GameplayLayer.m* covers the init method. Copy the contents of Listing 4.14 into your *GameplayLayer.m* file.

Listing 4.14   **GameplayLayer.m implementation file (part 4 of 4)**

```
-(id)init {
    self = [super init];
    if (self != nil) {
        CGSize screenSize = [CCDirector sharedDirector].winSize;
        // enable touches
        self.isTouchEnabled = YES;

        srandom(time(NULL)); // Seeds the random number generator

    if (UI_USER_INTERFACE_IDIOM() == UIUserInterfaceIdiomPad) {
        [[CCSpriteFrameCache sharedSpriteFrameCache]
          addSpriteFramesWithFile:@"scene1atlas.plist"];            // 1
        sceneSpriteBatchNode =
          [CCSpriteBatchNode batchNodeWithFile:@"scene1atlas.png"]; // 2
    } else {
        [[CCSpriteFrameCache sharedSpriteFrameCache]
          addSpriteFramesWithFile:@"scene1atlasiPhone.plist"];      // 1
        sceneSpriteBatchNode =
          [CCSpriteBatchNode
           batchNodeWithFile:@"scene1atlasiPhone.png"];             // 2
    }
        [self addChild:sceneSpriteBatchNode z:0];                   // 3
        [self initJoystickAndButtons];                              // 4
        Viking *viking = [[Viking alloc]
            initWithSpriteFrame:[[CCSpriteFrameCache
                sharedSpriteFrameCache]
                spriteFrameByName:@"sv_anim_1.png"]];               // 5
        [viking setJoystick:leftJoystick];
        [viking setJumpButton:jumpButton];
        [viking setAttackButton:attackButton];
        [viking setPosition:ccp(screenSize.width * 0.35f,
                                screenSize.height * 0.14f)];
        [viking setCharacterHealth:100];

        [sceneSpriteBatchNode
            addChild:viking
                z:kVikingSpriteZValue
                tag:kVikingSpriteTagValue];                         // 6
```

```
        [self createObjectOfType:kEnemyTypeRadarDish
                    withHealth:100
                    atLocation:ccp(screenSize.width * 0.878f,
                                    screenSize.height * 0.13f)
                    withZValue:10];                              // 7


        [self scheduleUpdate];                                   // 8
    }
    return self;
}
@end
```

Some key lines have been added since Chapter 2; they support the use of the
CCSpriteBatchNode class and texture atlas:

1. Adds all of the frame dimensions specified in *scene1atlas.plist* to the Cocos2D
   Sprite Frame Cache. This will allow any CCSprite to be created by referencing
   one of the frames/images in the texture atlas. This line is also key in loading up
   the animations, since they reference spriteFrames loaded by the CCSprite-
   FrameCache here.

2. Initializes the CCSpriteBatchNode with the texture atlas image. The image
   scene1atlas.png becomes the master texture used by all of the CCSprites under
   the CCSpriteBatchNode. In *Space Viking* these are all of the GameObjects in
   the game, from the Viking to the Mallet power-up and the enemies.

3. Adds the CCSpriteBatchNode to the layer so it and all of its children (the
   GameObjects) are rendered onscreen.

4. Initializes the Joystick DPad and buttons.

5. Creates the Viking character using the already cached sprite frame of the
   Viking standing.

6. Adds the Viking to the CCSpriteBatchNode. The CCSpriteBatchNode
   does all of the rendering for the GameObjects. Therefore, the objects have
   to be added to the CCSpriteBatchNode and *not* to the layer. It is important
   to remember that the objects drawn from the texture atlas are added to the
   CCSpriteBatchNode and only the CCSpriteBatchNode is added to the
   CCLayer.

7. Adds the RadarDish to the CCSpriteBatchNode. The RadarDish health is
   set to 100 and the location as 87% of the screen width to the right (900 pixels
   from the left of the screen on the iPad) and 13% of the screen height (100 pixels
   from the bottom).

The percentages are used instead of hard point values so that the same game will
work on the iPhone, iPhone 4, and iPad. Although the screen width and height

ratios between the iPhones and iPad are a little different, they are close enough to work for the placement of objects in *Space Viking*.

8. Sets up a scheduler call that will fire the update method in *GameplayLayer.m* on every frame.

Now that you have added code to handle the RadarDish, the Viking, and the texture atlas, it is time to test out *Space Viking*. If you select **Run** from Xcode, you should see the *Space Viking* game in the iPad Simulator, as shown in Figure 4.3.

Figure 4.3   Space Viking with the RadarDish in place

Summary

If you made it through, great work—you've gotten a simple Cocos2D game working, and you've learned a lot in the process! You learned about texture atlases, actions, and animations. You utilized the texture atlas you created in the previous chapter to render all of the GameObjects in *Space Viking*. You created the enemy RadarDish and gave Ole the power to go over there and destroy it to bits. In the process you learned how to implement a simple state machine brain (AI) for the RadarDish and for the Viking. You have also set up the groundwork for *Space Viking* to have multiple enemies onscreen at once, each with its own AI state machines. The CCArray of objects you pass in GameplayLayer to each character on the updateStateWithDeltaTime call will allow for the enemy objects to send messages to each other and even coordinate attacks against the Viking.

Since you just wrote so much code, you might want to take a few moments to examine the code in more detail and make sure you understand how it all fits together. It's important to make sure you understand how things work so far, since you'll be building more on top of what you've built here in the rest of the chapters.

In the next chapter, you will dive deeper into Cocos2D actions, learn to use some of the built-in effects, and add more enemies to *Space Viking*. When you are ready, turn the page and learn how to add a mean alien robot that shoots phaser beams.

Challenges

1. Try changing the RadarDish animation delay on the takingAHitAnim to 1.0f seconds instead of 0.2f in the *RadarDish.plist* file. What happens when you click **Run** and Ole attacks the RadarDish?

2. How would you add another instance of the RadarDish on the left side of the screen facing in the opposite direction?

Hint

You can use the CCFlipX action to flip the RadarDish pixels horizontally.

3. How would you detect when the RadarDish object is destroyed and alert the player that the level is complete?

Hint

You can extract the RadarDish object from the sceneSpriteBatchNode by using the unique tag assigned to the RadarDish.

Part II

More Enemies and More Fun

Learn how to create more complex enemies for Ole to battle and in the process learn about Cocos2D actions and effects. Finish up with a live, onscreen debugging system using Cocos2D text capabilities.

- Chapter 5: "More Actions, Effects, and Cocos2D Scheduler"
- Chapter 6: "Text, Fonts, and the Written Word"

More Actions, Effects, and Cocos2D Scheduler

In Chapters 3 and 4 you created the foundation for the Space Viking game, added Ole the Viking and a radar dish to the scene, and wired up all of the controls. In this chapter you will add an enemy robot, the massive space cargo ship, and several power-ups to help Ole. You will learn how to create a complex enemy that can chase after and attack the player. You will also learn about the Cocos2D scheduler and how to use the Cocos2D built-in effects.

Terminology Review

Before you begin with Chapter 5, there are a few terms worth reviewing.

- **Protocols in Objective-C**

  Protocols in Objective-C are a way to declare methods, which are implemented by any class conforming to the protocol. Using protocols can help you have a loose coupling between your classes, where they know as little about each other as possible, allowing them to be interchanged more easily. If you are coming from another language such as Java, protocols are similar to interfaces. In SpaceViking the GameplayLayer adheres to the GameplayLayerDelegate protocol, which defines two methods. The EnemyRobot uses one of these methods to create a PhaserBullet, and the SpaceCargoShip uses the other method to create the power-ups. By using a protocol, the only thing that the SpaceCargoShip and the EnemyRobot need to know about the GameplayLayer is that it conforms to the protocol, and not all of the other classes that GameplayLayer imports.

- **Loose Coupling**

  Loose coupling is when two classes only know what public methods each other respond to and not the internal details or actual instance of the classes. Two classes that are loosely coupled can be replaced as long as the methods they expect to call on each other exist in the new classes. In SpaceViking you will use loose coupling between the EnemyRobot and the GameplayLayer. If at a later point you were to replace the GameplayLayer class with another

CCLayer, you would just need to ensure that it too responds to the one method required by the EnemyRobot, defined in the GameplayLayerDelegate protocol.

- **Delegates**
  Delegates are classes that carry out specific functionality on behalf of other classes. In SpaceViking the GameplayLayer will act as a delegate for the SpaceCargoShip and EnemyRobot. The GameplayLayer will create power-ups and PhaserBullets on behalf of the SpaceCargoShip and EnemyRobot classes.

Power-Ups

When Ole first appears in *Space Viking*, he is armed only with his fists. While he does pack a powerful punch, Ole will still need the help of his trusty mallet to inflict damage more quickly on the enemy RadarDish and robot. As you might have guessed, the mallet is a power-up. The power-ups are dropped from the SpaceCargoShip, but before you can code the ship, you have to add the power-ups and their logic to your *Space Viking* game. With the *SpaceViking* project opened in Xcode, you can start by creating the Mallet and Health power-up classes.

Mallet Power-Up

It is good practice to continue the organization in your *SpaceViking* Xcode project that you started in Chapter 4, "Simple Collision Detection and First Enemy." You will create the Mallet and Health classes inside of the *PowerUps* group you previously created.

To create the Mallet class, first select the *PowerUps* group.

1. Right-click and select **New File**.
2. Select the **Cocoa Touch category** under iOS and the **Objective-C class** type and click **Next**.
3. For the Subclass field, enter *GameObject* and click **Next**.
4. Enter *Mallet.m* for the filename and click **Save**.

After Xcode creates the header and implementation files for you, replace the contents of the *Mallet.h* file with the code in Listing 5.1.

Listing 5.1   Mallet.h header file

```
//  Mallet.h
//  SpaceViking
//
#import <Foundation/Foundation.h>
#import "GameObject.h"
```

```
@interface Mallet : GameObject {
    CCAnimation *malletAnim;
}
@property (nonatomic, retain) CCAnimation *malletAnim;
@end
```

The power-up objects in *Space Viking* are very simple, consisting of nothing more than a simple animation. As you can see in Listing 5.1, the `Mallet` object inherits from `GameObject` and contains a single animation stored in the `malletAnim` instance variable. The `Mallet` implementation is equally short: switch to the *Mallet.m* implementation file and replace the contents with the code in Listing 5.2.

Listing 5.2   **Mallet.m implementation file**

```
//  Mallet.m
//  SpaceViking
//
#import "Mallet.h"
@implementation Mallet
@synthesize malletAnim;

- (void) dealloc {
    [malletAnim release];
    [super dealloc];
}

-(void)changeState:(CharacterStates)newState {
    if (newState == kStateSpawning) {
        id action = [CCRepeatForever actionWithAction:
                        [CCAnimate actionWithAnimation:malletAnim
restoreOriginalFrame:NO]];
        [self runAction:action];
    } else {
        [self setVisible:NO]; // Picked up
        [self removeFromParentAndCleanup:YES];
    }
}

-(void)updateStateWithDeltaTime:(ccTime)deltaTime
andListOfGameObjects:(CCArray*)listOfGameObjects {
    float groundHeight = screenSize.height * 0.065f;

    if ([self position].y > groundHeight)
        [self setPosition:ccp([self position].x,
        [self position].y - 5.0f)];
}
```

```
-(void)initAnimations {
    [self setMalletAnim:
      [self loadPlistForAnimationWithName:@"malletAnim"
        andClassName:NSStringFromClass([self class])]];
}
-(id) init
{
    if( (self=[super init]) )
    {
        screenSize = [CCDirector sharedDirector].winSize;
        gameObjectType = kPowerUpTypeMallet;
        [self initAnimations];
        [self changeState:kStateSpawning];

    }
    return self;
}
@end
```

The `Mallet` is initialized by first calling `initAnimations` and then setting its state to `kStateSpawning`. The `initAnimations` method loads the `malletAnim` animation based on the animation frames listed in *Mallet.plist*. The `changeState` method then sets up a `CCRepeatForever` animation of the mallet spinning around.

If look closely in the else block in the `changeState` method, you can see that transitioning to any other state will cause the `Mallet` object to remove itself from the game. The Viking character will use this to signal to the `Mallet` that it has been picked up and that it should disappear.

> **Tip**
> If you have any animations you need to repeat, the `CCRepeat` and `CCRepeatForever` actions are what you should use. It frees you from having to restart those animations each time they finish.

The other power-up in this scene is the `Health` power-up. The next section covers the steps needed to add it to *Space Viking*.

Health Power-Up

The `Health` power-up comes in the form of a sandwich, which Ole can consume, restoring his health to 100%. It may seem odd to have a sandwich fall from a space cargo ship on an alien planet, but hey, aliens have to eat, too. So go ahead and create a new class to represent the `Health` power-up using the following steps:
In Xcode, right-click on the *PowerUps* folder and select **New File**.

1. Select the **Cocoa Touch category** under iOS and the **Objective-C class** type and click **Next**.
2. For the Subclass field, enter *GameObject* and click **Next**.

3. Enter *Health.m* for the filename and ensure that the "Also create Health.h" checkbox is selected. Click **Finish**.

Replace the contents of the *Health.h* header file with the code in Listing 5.3.

Listing 5.3   **Health.h header file**

```
// Health.h
// SpaceViking
//
#import <Foundation/Foundation.h>
#import "GameObject.h"

@interface Health : GameObject {
    CCAnimation *healthAnim;
}
@property (nonatomic, retain) CCAnimation *healthAnim;
@end
```

Open the *Health.m* implementation file and replace the code with the contents of Listing 5.4.

Listing 5.4   **Health.m implementation file**

```
// Health.m
// SpaceViking
//
#import "Health.h"
@implementation Health
@synthesize healthAnim;

-(void) dealloc {
    [healthAnim release];
    [super dealloc];
}

-(void)changeState:(CharacterStates)newState {
    if (newState == kStateSpawning) {
        id action = [CCRepeatForever actionWithAction:
                    [CCAnimate actionWithAnimation:healthAnim
                              restoreOriginalFrame:NO]];
        [self runAction:action];
    } else {
        [self setVisible:NO];// Picked up
        [self removeFromParentAndCleanup:YES];
    }
}
```

```
-(void)updateStateWithDeltaTime:(ccTime)deltaTime
andListOfGameObjects:(CCArray*)listOfGameObjects {
    float groundHeight = screenSize.height * 0.065f;

    if ([self position].y > groundHeight)
        [self setPosition:ccp([self position].x,
                             [self position].y - 5.0f)];
}

-(void)initAnimations {
    [self setHealthAnim:
     [self loadPlistForAnimationWithName:@"healthAnim"
      andClassName:NSStringFromClass([self class])]];
}
-(id) init
{
    if( (self=[super init]) )
    {
        screenSize = [CCDirector sharedDirector].winSize;
        [self initAnimations];
        [self changeState:kStateSpawning];
        gameObjectType = kPowerUpTypeHealth;

    }
    return self;
}
@end
```

The Health power-up is identical to the Mallet power-up except for the animation that is repeated while the power-up is onscreen. The gameObjectType is set in the init method of both power-ups and is the variable the Viking will use to detect and pick up the power-ups. Now that you have both power-ups created, you need to add a way to get them in the game, which brings you to the SpaceCargoShip.

Space Cargo Ship

The SpaceCargoShip is a massive freight vehicle that travels to and from the alien planet. The SpaceCargoShip travels back and forth on the screen, getting closer on each pass. When it is closest to the Viking, it drops a power-up. The SpaceCargoShip is an example of how you can add a background animation that interacts with the game. To create the SpaceCargoShip:

1. In Xcode, right-click on the *GameObjects* folder and select **New File**.

2. Select the **Cocoa Touch category** under iOS and the **Objective-C class** type and click **Next**.

3. For the Subclass field, enter *GameObject* and click **Next**.

4. Enter *SpaceCargoShip.m* for the filename and click **Save**.

Replace the contents of the *SpaceCargoShip.h* header file with the code in Listing 5.5.

Listing 5.5 **SpaceCargoShip.h header file**

```
//   SpaceCargoShip.h
//   SpaceViking
//
#import <Foundation/Foundation.h>
#import "GameObject.h"

@interface SpaceCargoShip : GameObject {
    BOOL hasDroppedMallet;
    id <GameplayLayerDelegate> delegate;
}
@property (nonatomic,assign) id <GameplayLayerDelegate> delegate;
@end
```

The SpaceCargoShip does not contain any animations; instead it uses a set of CCMoves and CCScale actions to achieve the motion effects. The SpaceCargoShip has an instance variable to keep track if it has already dropped the Mallet and an object reference back to the GameplayLayerDelegate. The delegate instance variable is the link from the SpaceCargoShip back to the gameplayLayer, allowing the ship to ask the GameplayLayer to create a power-up.

Having the SpaceCargoShip only know about the delegate frees it from having a tight coupling with the GameplayLayer class. In fact, you could replace the GameplayLayer class with any other class that implements the GameplayLayerDelegate protocol.

The next step is to set up the SpaceCargoShip implementation file. Open the *SpaceCargoShip.m* implementation file and replace the code with the contents of Listing 5.6.

Listing 5.6 **SpaceCargoShip.m implementation file**

```
//   SpaceCargoShip.m
//   SpaceViking
//
#import "SpaceCargoShip.h"

@implementation SpaceCargoShip
@synthesize delegate;

-(void)dropCargo {
    CGPoint cargoDropPosition = ccp(screenSize.width/2,
                                    screenSize.height);
    if (hasDroppedMallet == NO) {
        CCLOG(@"SpaceCargoShip --> Mallet Powerup was created!");
```

```
            hasDroppedMallet = YES;
            [delegate createObjectOfType:kPowerUpTypeMallet withHealth:0.0f
               atLocation:cargoDropPosition withZValue:50];
        } else {
            CCLOG(@"SpaceCargoShip --> Health Powerup was created!");
            [delegate createObjectOfType:kPowerUpTypeHealth withHealth:0.0f
             atLocation:cargoDropPosition withZValue:50];
        }
    }

-(id) init
{
    if( (self=[super init]) )
    {
        CCLOG(@"SpaceCargoShip init");
        hasDroppedMallet = NO;
        float shipHeight = screenSize.height * 0.71f;
        CGPoint position1 = ccp(screenSize.width * -0.48f, shipHeight);
        CGPoint position2 = ccp(screenSize.width * 2.0f, shipHeight);
        CGPoint position3 = ccp(position2.x * -1.0f, shipHeight);
        CGPoint offScreen = ccp(screenSize.width * -1.0f,
                                screenSize.height * -1.0f);

        id action = [CCRepeatForever actionWithAction:
                     [CCSequence actions:
                      [CCDelayTime actionWithDuration:2.0f],
                      [CCMoveTo actionWithDuration:0.01f
                                           position:position1],
                      [CCScaleTo actionWithDuration:0.01f scale:0.5f],
                      [CCFlipX actionWithFlipX:YES],
                      [CCMoveTo actionWithDuration:8.5f
                                           position:position2],
                      [CCScaleTo actionWithDuration:0.1f scale:1.0f],
                      [CCFlipX actionWithFlipX:NO],
                      [CCMoveTo actionWithDuration:7.5
                                           position:position3],
                      [CCScaleTo actionWithDuration:0.1f scale:2.0f],
                      [CCFlipX actionWithFlipX:YES],
                      [CCMoveTo actionWithDuration:6.5f
                                           position:position2],
                      [CCFlipX actionWithFlipX:NO],
                      [CCScaleTo actionWithDuration:0.1f scale:2.0f],
                      [CCMoveTo actionWithDuration:5.5
                                           position:position3],
                      [CCFlipX actionWithFlipX:YES],
                      [CCScaleTo actionWithDuration:0.1f scale:4.0f],
                      [CCMoveTo actionWithDuration:4.5f
                                           position:position2],
```

```
                    [CCCallFunc actionWithTarget:
                     self selector:@selector(dropCargo)],
                    [CCMoveTo actionWithDuration:0.0f
                                        position:offScreen],
                nil]
               ];
       [self runAction:action];

    }
    return self;
}

@end
```

The `dropCargo` method of the space cargo ship gets called when the ship is closest to the viewer. This method checks to see if the `Mallet` has been dropped; if not, it calls on the `GameplayDelegate` to drop the `Mallet`. If the `Mallet` has been dropped, it asks for the `Health` power-up to be dropped. This one method call is what sets in motion the code in `GameplayLayer` to create and add the power-ups to the game.

The `init` method consists of a long chain of actions wrapped around a `CCRepeatForever`. If you take a close look at the actions, you can see that there are `CCMoveTo`, `CCFlipX`, and `CCScaleTo` actions wrapped inside a `CCSequence` action. The `CCSequence` action is in turn wrapped inside a `CCRepeatForever`.

You can use this same setup for background animations in your games, where you script the animations as a series of nested `CCActions`. To keep the ship from appearing too often, a `CCDelayAction` is called on the beginning of the sequence, pausing the action sequence before it starts, and on every repeat.

At this point you have added the power-ups and the `SpaceCargoShip` to drop those power-ups on the screen. The next step is to create the `EnemyRobot`, and then add the final bits of code to `GameplayLayer` and `Viking` so that Ole can fight off the `EnemyRobot`.

Enemy Robot

The enemy robot is Ole's main opponent in the first scene of *Space Viking*. While the `RadarDish` will sit quietly in the corner, the enemy robot doesn't mess around—he pulls out a phaser and shoots to kill!

However, the enemy robot has a weak point. Modeled after the 1960s Ultraman TV shows, the enemy robot is a humanoid with poor vision. Maybe Ole can figure a way to sneak behind the robot and take him out?

Creating the Enemy Robot

The `EnemyRobot` is set up just like the `RadarDish` enemy you created in the previous chapter. It has all of the AI included in a single `EnemyRobot` class that inherits from `GameCharacter`.

1. Right-click on the *EnemyObjects* folder and select **New File**.
2. Select the **Cocoa Touch category** under iOS and the **Objective-C class** type and click **Next**.
3. For the Subclass field, enter *GameCharacter* and click **Next**.
4. Enter *EnemyRobot.m* for the filename and click **Save**.

Open the *EnemyRobot.h* header file and replace the template code with the contents for Listing 5.7.

Listing 5.7   EnemyRobot.h header file

```
//   EnemyRobot.h
//   SpaceViking
//
#import <Foundation/Foundation.h>
#import "GameCharacter.h"
@interface EnemyRobot : GameCharacter {
    CCAnimation *robotWalkingAnim;

    CCAnimation *raisePhaserAnim;
    CCAnimation *shootPhaserAnim;
    CCAnimation *lowerPhaserAnim;

    CCAnimation *torsoHitAnim;
    CCAnimation *headHitAnim;
    CCAnimation *robotDeathAnim;

    BOOL isVikingWithinBoundingBox;
    BOOL isVikingWithinSight;

    GameCharacter *vikingCharacter;
    id <GameplayLayerDelegate> delegate;


}
@property (nonatomic,assign) id <GameplayLayerDelegate> delegate;
@property (nonatomic, retain) CCAnimation *robotWalkingAnim;
@property (nonatomic, retain) CCAnimation *raisePhaserAnim;
@property (nonatomic, retain) CCAnimation *shootPhaserAnim;
@property (nonatomic, retain) CCAnimation *lowerPhaserAnim;
@property (nonatomic, retain) CCAnimation *torsoHitAnim;
```

```
@property (nonatomic, retain) CCAnimation *headHitAnim;
@property (nonatomic, retain) CCAnimation *robotDeathAnim;
-(void)initAnimations;
@end
```

The first part of Listing 5.7 is very similar to what you saw on `RadarDish`, as the `EnemyRobot` class inherits from `GameCharacter` class and has a set of instance variables for the animations. Toward the end of Listing 5.7 is the `<GameplayLayer-Delegate>` instance variable of type `id`. In the previous chapter in Listing 4.2, you created a `CommonProtocols` file that defined the `GameplayLayerDelegate` protocol. This protocol defines what methods a class conforming to the protocol can be expected to implement. In the case of the `EnemyRobot`, the `GameplayLayer-Delegate` is what will allow the `EnemyRobot` to ask the `GameplayLayer` to create a `PhaserBullet` object. By using a protocol here, the `EnemyRobot` class does not have to know any further details about the `GameplayLayer`, only that it responds to the `createPhaserWithDirection` method.

The *Space Viking* game in this book is designed not only to provide a sample of a full working game but also to give you the components you can reuse in your own games. The idea is to not reinvent the wheel but rather spend your time on making your games better. An issue that comes up frequently during game development is how to alert the `CCLayer` or `CCScene` in a game that some event has occurred. For instance, maybe the player has died and the game over animation needs to play. *Space Viking* has two actions the `CCLayer` (`GameplayLayer`) must perform for the characters: creating a phaser beam and dropping a power-up. Using protocols allows the game objects to be loosely coupled with the `CCLayer` and therefore gives you the most flexibility when it comes to changing the `CCLayer` or game objects at a later date. When you encounter the same condition in your games, refer back to this design and chapter.

The `EnemyRobot` implementation file is lengthy, as the robot has a significant amount of logic. The implementation details are split into the next four sections. So be sure to include all of the code in Listings 5.8 through 5.11 in your *EnemyRobot.m* implementation file.

Listing 5.8   EnemyRobot.m implementation file (part **1 of 4**)

```
//   EnemyRobot.m
//   SpaceViking
//
#import "EnemyRobot.h"
@implementation EnemyRobot
@synthesize delegate;
@synthesize robotWalkingAnim;
@synthesize raisePhaserAnim;
@synthesize shootPhaserAnim;
```

```
@synthesize lowerPhaserAnim;
@synthesize torsoHitAnim;
@synthesize headHitAnim;
@synthesize robotDeathAnim;
-(void) dealloc {
    delegate = nil;
    [robotWalkingAnim release];
    [raisePhaserAnim release];
    [shootPhaserAnim release];
    [lowerPhaserAnim release];
    [torsoHitAnim release];
    [headHitAnim release];
    [robotDeathAnim release];

    [super dealloc];
}

-(void)shootPhaser {
    CGPoint phaserFiringPosition;
    PhaserDirection phaserDir;
    CGRect boundingBox = [self boundingBox];
    CGPoint position = [self position];

    float xPosition = position.x + boundingBox.size.width * 0.542f;
    float yPosition = position.y + boundingBox.size.height * 0.25f;

    if ([self flipX]) {
        CCLOG(@"Facing right, Firing to the right");
        phaserDir = kDirectionRight;
    } else {
        CCLOG(@"Facing left, Firing to the left");
        xPosition = xPosition * -1.0f; // Reverse direction
        phaserDir = kDirectionLeft;
    }
    phaserFiringPosition = ccp(xPosition, yPosition);
    [delegate createPhaserWithDirection:phaserDir
     andPosition:phaserFiringPosition];
}

-(CGRect)eyesightBoundingBox {
    // Eyesight is 3 robot widths in the direction the robot is facing.
    CGRect robotSightBoundingBox;
    CGRect robotBoundingBox = [self adjustedBoundingBox];
    if ([self flipX]) {
        robotSightBoundingBox = CGRectMake(robotBoundingBox.origin.x,
                                           robotBoundingBox.origin.y,
```

```
        robotBoundingBox.size.width*3.0f,
        robotBoundingBox.size.height);
    } else {
        robotSightBoundingBox =
          CGRectMake(robotBoundingBox.origin.x -
                       (robotBoundingBox.size.width*2.0f),
                       robotBoundingBox.origin.y,
                       robotBoundingBox.size.width*3.0f,
                       robotBoundingBox.size.height);
    }
    return robotSightBoundingBox;
}
```

The `EnemyRobot` implementation file starts with the `@synthesize` statement for the delegate variable, which is the link to the `gameplayLayer`. The first method immediately following it is the `dealloc` method, which takes care to set the delegate to `nil`, releasing any references to it.

The `shootPhaser` method takes the current direction the `EnemyRobot` is facing and asks the delegate (the `GameplayLayer`) to create a phaser bullet moving in that direction. The `createPhaserWithDirection` method was declared in the `GameplayLayerDelegate` protocol, and you will add the implementation details later in this chapter.

Following the `shootPhaser` is the `eyesightBoundingBox` method, which calculates how far the `EnemyRobot` can see. This method creates an eyesight box three times the width of the enemy. This method is used by the `EnemyRobot` to figure out if it can "see" the Viking and change state so that it can attack Ole. The `EnemyRobot` uses bounding boxes to approximate the vision; later on you can see how to use ray casting to simulate an enemy's line of sight.

The next listing has the contents of the `changeState` method that is used by the `EnemyRobot` to alternate states and animations. Copy the contents of Listing 5.9 into the *EnemyRobot.m* implementation file below the `eyesightBoundingBox` method.

Listing 5.9   **EnemyRobot.m implementation file (part 2 of 4)**

```
-(void)changeState:(CharacterStates)newState {
    if (characterState == kStateDead)
        return; // No need to change state further once I am dead

    [self stopAllActions];
    id action = nil;
    characterState = newState;

    switch (newState) {
        case kStateSpawning:
            [self runAction:[CCFadeOut actionWithDuration:0.0f]];
```

```
    // Fades out the sprite if it was visible before
    [self setDisplayFrame:
     [[CCSpriteFrameCache sharedSpriteFrameCache]
        spriteFrameByName:@"teleport.png"]];

    action =  [CCSpawn actions:
                [CCRotateBy actionWithDuration:1.5f angle:360],
                [CCFadeIn actionWithDuration:1.5f],
                 nil];
break;

case kStateIdle:
    CCLOG(@"EnemyRobot->Changing State to Idle");
    [self setDisplayFrame:
     [[CCSpriteFrameCache sharedSpriteFrameCache]
       spriteFrameByName:@"an1_anim1.png"]];
break;

case kStateWalking:
    CCLOG(@"EnemyRobot->Changing State to Walking");
    if (isVikingWithinBoundingBox)
      break; // AI will change to Attacking on next frame

    float xPositionOffSet = 150.0f;
    if (isVikingWithinSight) {
        if ([vikingCharacter position].x < [self position].x)
            xPositionOffSet = xPositionOffSet * -1;
            // Invert to -150
    } else {
        if (CCRANDOM_0_1() > 0.5f)
            xPositionOffSet = xPositionOffSet * -1;

        if (xPositionOffSet > 0.0f) {
            [self setFlipX:YES];
        } else {
            [self setFlipX:NO];
        }
    }
    action = [CCSpawn actions:
                [CCAnimate actionWithAnimation:robotWalkingAnim
                 restoreOriginalFrame:NO],
                [CCMoveTo actionWithDuration:2.4f
                 position:ccp([self position].x +
                              xPositionOffSet,
                              [self position].y)],
                nil];
break;
```

```
    case kStateAttacking:
        CCLOG(@"EnemyRobot->Changing State to Attacking");
        action = [CCSequence actions:
                    [CCAnimate actionWithAnimation:raisePhaserAnim
                     restoreOriginalFrame:NO],
                    [CCDelayTime actionWithDuration:1.0f],
                    [CCAnimate actionWithAnimation:shootPhaserAnim
                     restoreOriginalFrame:NO],
                    [CCCallFunc actionWithTarget:self
                     selector:@selector(shootPhaser)],
                    [CCAnimate actionWithAnimation:lowerPhaserAnim
                     restoreOriginalFrame:NO],
                    [CCDelayTime actionWithDuration:2.0f],
                    nil];
        break;

    case kStateTakingDamage:
        CCLOG(@"EnemyRobot->Changing State to TakingDamage");
        if ([vikingCharacter getWeaponDamage] > kVikingFistDamage){
            // If the viking has the mallet, then
            action =
              [CCAnimate actionWithAnimation:headHitAnim
                        restoreOriginalFrame:YES];
        } else {
            // Viking does not have weapon, body blow
            action = [CCAnimate actionWithAnimation:torsoHitAnim
                        restoreOriginalFrame:YES];
        }
        break;

    case kStateDead:
        CCLOG(@"EnemyRobot -> Going to Dead State");
        action = [CCSequence actions:
                    [CCAnimate actionWithAnimation:robotDeathAnim
                     restoreOriginalFrame:NO],
                    [CCDelayTime actionWithDuration:2.0f],
                    [CCFadeOut actionWithDuration:2.0f],
                    nil];
        break;

    default:
        CCLOG(@"Enemy Robot -> Unknown CharState %d",
         characterState);
        break;
}
```

```
    if (action != nil)
        [self runAction:action];
}
```

The first part of the changeState method checks to make sure the EnemyRobot is not dead. If the robot is dead, the method does nothing. Otherwise, any currently running actions are also stopped, since the EnemyRobot is about to transition to a new state.

After these setup lines, the method drops into a switch statement that carries out the particular logic depending on which state the EnemyRobot is transitioning to. The first state listed is the kStateSpawning, which is how the EnemyRobot first appears onscreen. Here you can see an action consisting of a fade-in and a rotation, along with the EnemyRobot's display frame being set to the teleport graphic.

The teleport graphic is a round swirl graphic, and this action makes it rotate around the screen. You can see the teleport graphic in Figure 5.1; remember that this image is included in the texture atlas for this scene.

Figure 5.1   EnemyRobot teleport graphic

The next state is the idle state, which simply sets the display frame of the Enemy-Robot to a standing pose.

The walking state contains more logic: first it checks to see if the Viking is near the EnemyRobot. If so, it returns knowing that the updateStateWithDelta time method will automatically transition the state of the EnemyRobot to "attacking." If the Viking is not within the adjusted bounding box of the EnemyRobot, it then checks to see if the Viking is within the eyesight of the robot. If the robot can "see" the Viking, it moves toward it; otherwise, it just moves in a random direction. If the direction of travel is to the right, the EnemyRobot's flipX flag is turned to YES, flipping all of the pixels horizontally. As with the Viking, this makes the EnemyRobot appear to be moving to the left or right instead of left and backwards.

The attacking state is next on the changeState method, and it sets up the raise, fire, and then lower animations for the EnemyRobot. As with the SpaceCargoShip, there are a series of compound actions to perform the full attack. The EnemyRobot first raises the gun, then delays, and then runs a CCCallFunc action. The CCCallFunc action calls the shootPhaser method that you created in Listing 5.8. This method tells the gameplayLayer to create a phaser beam and send it off toward the Viking. After firing, the EnemyRobot lowers the gun and pauses for another 2 seconds.

> **Note**
>
> CCCallFunc is a special action that can call a method in any object. It is useful when you want to call some portion of your code before, during, or after an action sequence. Along with CCCallFunc are CCCallFuncN, which passes along the CCNode as a parameter, and CCCallFuncND, which passes along the CCNode and a pointer to some data element you define.

Following the attacking state, there is the taking damage state in the switch block. The taking damage state determines if the Viking is carrying a weapon or not and plays the corresponding animation. If the Viking is carrying a weapon, the Enemy-Robot takes on damage to the head; otherwise, it shows the torso taking a hit. The difference here is purely for effects, as the Mallet weapon attack animation has the Viking swinging the mallet over the top of the EnemyRobot, while a punch is straight on at about chest height.

Finally there is a dead state, which plays an animation of the EnemyRobot exploding followed by a fade-out. These are all of the various states that the EnemyRobot transitions between, depending on what is happening in the game play.

The changeState method is called from within the updateStateWithDelta-Time method, which is shown in Listing 5.10.

Listing 5.10   **EnemyRobot.m implementation file (part 3 of 4)**

```
-(void)updateStateWithDeltaTime:(ccTime)deltaTime
andListOfGameObjects:(CCArray*)listOfGameObjects {
    [self checkAndClampSpritePosition];

    if ((characterState != kStateDead) && (characterHealth <= 0)) {
        [self changeState:kStateDead];
        return;
    }

    vikingCharacter = (GameCharacter*)[[self parent]
     getChildByTag:kVikingSpriteTagValue];
    CGRect vikingBoundingBox = [vikingCharacter adjustedBoundingBox];
    CGRect robotBoundingBox = [self adjustedBoundingBox];
    CGRect robotSightBoundingBox = [self eyesightBoundingBox];

    isVikingWithinBoundingBox =
     CGRectIntersectsRect(vikingBoundingBox, robotBoundingBox) ?
     YES : NO;
    isVikingWithinSight =
     CGRectIntersectsRect(vikingBoundingBox, robotSightBoundingBox)?
     YES : NO;
```

```
if ((isVikingWithinBoundingBox) &&
    ([vikingCharacter characterState] == kStateAttacking)) {
    // Viking is attacking this robot
    if ((characterState != kStateTakingDamage) &&
        (characterState != kStateDead)) {
        [self setCharacterHealth:
         [self characterHealth] -
         [vikingCharacter getWeaponDamage]];
        if (characterHealth > 0) {
            [self changeState:kStateTakingDamage];
        } else {
            [self changeState:kStateDead];
        }
        return; // Nothing to update further, stop and show damage
    }
}

if ([self numberOfRunningActions] == 0) {

    if (characterState == kStateDead) {
        // Robot is dead, remove
        [self setVisible:NO];
        [self removeFromParentAndCleanup:YES];
    } else if ([vikingCharacter characterState] == kStateDead) {
        // Viking is dead, walk around the scene
        [self changeState:kStateWalking];
    } else if (isVikingWithinSight) {
        [self changeState:kStateAttacking];
    } else {
        // Viking alive and out of sight, resume walking
        [self changeState:kStateWalking];
    }
}
}
```

The updateStateWithDeltaTime method starts with a quick call to the check-AndClampPosition method inherited from GameCharacter. This method ensures the EnemyRobot remains within the boundaries of the screen. The following if statement then checks that the EnemyRobot is not already dead and that the health is greater than zero. If the EnemyRobot's health is zero or less, the robot is transitioned to a dead state.

The next set of lines gets the Viking from the CCSpriteSheet, which is the parent to all of the characters on this scene. The Viking is retrieved by using the getChildByTag and passing the unique tag used by the Viking character. Recall from earlier chapters that any CCNode can maintain a unique integer tag for each of its children. By having the `kVikingSpriteTagValue` as a constant, each of the children of the `CCSpriteSheet` can call it and retrieve a pointer to the Viking character. The next three lines create three `CGRects` that are used to determine where the Viking is in relation to the `EnemyRobot` and if the `EnemyRobot` can see the Viking.

If Statement Shortcuts

The two lines with the ternary "`?`" operator in *EnemyRobot.m* are a simple shortcut way to combine an `if` statement and an assignment operator. You should read the following line as:

```
isVikingWithinSight = CGRectIntersectsRect(vikingBoundingBox,
robotSightBoundingBox)? YES : NO;
```

If `CGRectIntersectsRect` returns true, set `isVikingWithinSight` to `YES`; otherwise, set it to `NO`. You could rewrite this one line of code as:

```
if (CGRectIntersectsRect(vikingBoundingBox, robotSightBoundingBox)) {
    isVikingWithinSight = YES;
} else {
    isVikingWithinSight = NO;
}
```

This simple shortcut can save you some tedious typing on simple compares and assignments. Keep in mind that `CGRectIntersectsRect` evaluates to either `TRUE` or `FALSE`, so you can leave out the `== TRUE` in the `if` statement.

There are two more critical sections in this method. The first is an `if` block that checks to see if the Viking is attacking the `EnemyRobot` and if the Viking is attacking with a weapon or just his bare fists. The health of the `EnemyRobot` is reduced and then checked to see if it is greater than zero. If the `EnemyRobot` still has a health level of greater than zero, he is transitioned to a taking damage state; otherwise, he is transitioned to the dead state. Both of those transitions were covered in the earlier listing of the `changeState` method.

The next critical section of this method is the `if` block once the `numberOfRunningActions` is zero for the `EnemyRobot`. As you learned with the `RadarDish`, if the `EnemyRobot` is currently executing an action such as an animation, the `numberOfRunningActions` will be greater than zero. This `if` block first checks to see if the `EnemyRobot` is dead and finished the dead animation. If so, the `EnemyRobot` is removed from the `CCLayer`. The next check is if the Viking is dead, and if so, then the robot is just transitioned to a walking state, where he will wander around the screen. The next check is to see if the Viking is within sight, and if so, then the robot moves to attack the Viking. Lastly, if the Viking is not within the sight box of the `EnemyRobot`, the robot will change to a walking state and patrol the scene. The next listing details the remaining three methods in `EnemyRobot` used to calculate the adjusted bounding box and initialize the animations. Copy the contents of Listing 5.11 and paste it below the updateStateWithDelta time in *EnemyRobot.m*.

Listing 5.11   **EnemyRobot.m implementation file (part 4 of 4)**

```
-(CGRect)AdjustedBoundingBox {
    // Shrink the bounding box by 18% on the X axis, and move it to the
    // right by 18% and crop it by 5% on the Y Axis.
    // On the iPad this is 30 pixels on the X axis and
    // 10 pixels from the top (Y Axis)
    CGRect enemyRobotBoundingBox = [self boundingBox];
    float xOffsetAmount = enemyRobotBoundingBox.size.width * 0.18f;
    float yCropAmount = enemyRobotBoundingBox.size.height * 0.05f;
    enemyRobotBoundingBox =
      CGRectMake(enemyRobotBoundingBox.origin.x + xOffsetAmount,
                 enemyRobotBoundingBox.origin.y,
                 enemyRobotBoundingBox.size.width - xOffsetAmount,
                 enemyRobotBoundingBox.size.height - yCropAmount);
    return enemyRobotBoundingBox;
}


#pragma mark -
#pragma mark initAnimations
-(void)initAnimations {

    [self setRobotWalkingAnim:
     [self loadPlistForAnimationWithName:@"robotWalkingAnim"
       andClassName:NSStringFromClass([self class])]];

    [self setRaisePhaserAnim:
     [self loadPlistForAnimationWithName:@"raisePhaserAnim"
      andClassName:NSStringFromClass([self class])]];

    [self setShootPhaserAnim:
     [self loadPlistForAnimationWithName:@"shootPhaserAnim"
      andClassName:NSStringFromClass([self class])]];

    [self setLowerPhaserAnim:
     [self loadPlistForAnimationWithName:@"lowerPhaserAnim"
      andClassName:NSStringFromClass([self class])]];

    [self setTorsoHitAnim:
     [self loadPlistForAnimationWithName:@"torsoHitAnim"
      andClassName:NSStringFromClass([self class])]];

    [self setHeadHitAnim:
     [self loadPlistForAnimationWithName:@"headHitAnim"
      andClassName:NSStringFromClass([self class])]];
```

```
        [self setRobotDeathAnim:
         [self loadPlistForAnimationWithName:@"robotDeathAnim"
          andClassName:NSStringFromClass([self class])]];
}
-(id) init
{
    if( (self=[super init]) )
    {
        isVikingWithinBoundingBox = NO;
        isVikingWithinSight = NO;
        gameObjectType = kEnemyTypeAlienRobot;
        [self initAnimations];
        srandom(time(NULL));
    }
    return self;
}
@end
```

The `AdjustedBoundingBox` method does exactly what the name implies: it takes the `EnemyRobot`'s bounding box and adjusts it to compensate for the transparent space. The `initAnimations` method just calls the `loadPlistForAnimationWith-Name` to load the many animations used by the robot. Lastly, the `init` method sets up the initial states of the instance variables and calls the `initAnimation` method.

Adding the PhaserBullet

The `EnemyRobot` will be using his gun to fire an electrifying phaser bullet at Ole. The `PhaserBullet` itself is an object that will travel left or right on the screen. Before creating the code behind the `PhaserBullet`, take a moment and create a new animation plist file called *PhaserBullet.plist* under the *Plists* group, as shown in Figure 5.2. You can also drag over this file from the resource folder for this chapter.

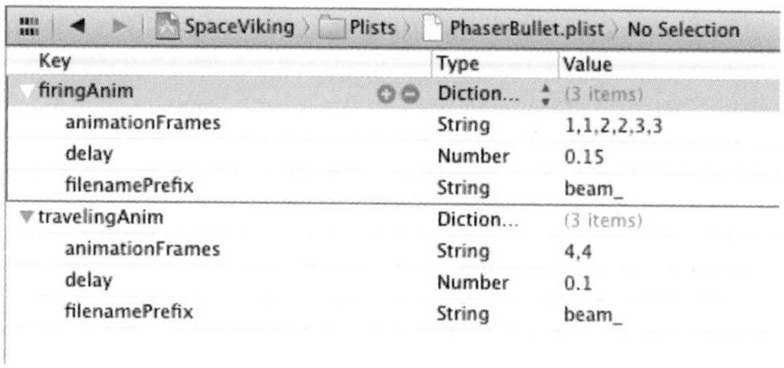

Figure 5.2   PhaserBullet.plist containing the animations for the PhaserBullet

The `PhaserBullet` is a simple class; to create it in your *SpaceViking* project:

1. Right-click on *EnemyObjects* group and click **New File**.
2. Select **Cocoa Touch category** under iOS and **Objective-C class** as the file type and click **Next**.
3. For the Subclass field, enter *GameCharacter*.
4. Enter *PhaserBullet.m* for the filename and click **Save**.

Open the *PhaserBullet.h* header file and replace it with the contents of Listing 5.12.

Listing 5.12   **PhaserBullet.h header file**

```
//   PhaserBullet.h
//   SpaceViking

#import <Foundation/Foundation.h>
#import "GameCharacter.h"

@interface PhaserBullet : GameCharacter {
    CCAnimation *firingAnim;
    CCAnimation *travelingAnim;

    PhaserDirection myDirection;

}
@property PhaserDirection myDirection;
@property (nonatomic,retain) CCAnimation *firingAnim;
@property (nonatomic,retain) CCAnimation *travelingAnim;
@end
```

Switch over to the *PhaserBullet.m* implementation file and replace the contents with Listing 5.13.

Listing 5.13   **PhaserBullet.m implementation file**

```
//   PhaserBullet.m
//   SpaceViking
#import "PhaserBullet.h"

@implementation PhaserBullet
@synthesize myDirection;
@synthesize travelingAnim;
@synthesize firingAnim;
- (void) dealloc {
    [travelingAnim release];
    [firingAnim release];
```

```
        [super dealloc];
    }


    -(void)changeState:(CharacterStates)newState {
        [self stopAllActions];
        id action = nil;
        characterState = newState;
        switch (newState) {
            case kStateSpawning:
                CCLOG(@"Phaser->Changed state to Spawning");
                action =
                [CCAnimate actionWithAnimation:firingAnim
                            restoreOriginalFrame:NO];
                break;
            case kStateTraveling:
                CCLOG(@"Phaser->Changed state to Traveling");
                CGPoint endLocation;
                if (myDirection == kDirectionLeft) {
                    CCLOG(@"Phaser direction LEFT");
                    endLocation = ccp(-10.0f,
                                        [self position].y);
                } else {
                    CCLOG(@"Phaser direction RIGHT");
                    endLocation = ccp(screenSize.width+24.0f,
                                        [self position].y);
                }
                [self runAction:
                 [CCMoveTo actionWithDuration:2.0f position:endLocation]];
                action = [CCRepeatForever actionWithAction:
                            [CCAnimate actionWithAnimation:travelingAnim
                                restoreOriginalFrame:NO]];

                break;
            case kStateDead:
                CCLOG(@"Phaser->Changed state to dead");
                // Remove from parent
                [self setVisible:NO];
                [self removeFromParentAndCleanup:YES];
            default:
                break;
        }
        if (action != nil)
            [self runAction:action];
    }


    -(BOOL)isOutsideOfScreen { // 5
        CGPoint currentSpritePosition = [self position];
```

```
    if ((currentSpritePosition.x < 0.0f) || (
        currentSpritePosition.x > screenSize.width)) {
        [self changeState:kStateDead];
        return YES;
    }
    return NO;
}

-(void)updateStateWithDeltaTime:(ccTime)deltaTime
andListOfGameObjects:(CCArray*)listOfGameObjects {
    if ([self isOutsideOfScreen])
        return;

    if ([self numberOfRunningActions] == 0) {
        if (characterState == kStateSpawning) {
            [self changeState:kStateTraveling];
            return;
        } else {
            [self changeState:kStateDead];
            return;
            // Should not do anything else from traveling
        }
    }
}

-(void)initAnimations {
    [self setFiringAnim:
     [self loadPlistForAnimationWithName:@"firingAnim"
      andClassName:NSStringFromClass([self class])]];

    [self setTravelingAnim:
     [self loadPlistForAnimationWithName:@"travelingAnim"
      andClassName:NSStringFromClass([self class])]];
}

-(id) init
{
    if( (self=[super init]) )
    {
        CCLOG(@"### PhaserBullet initialized");
        [self initAnimations];
        gameObjectType = kEnemyTypePhaser;
    }
    return self;
}
@end
```

The `PhaserBullet` is a simple character that moves from the firing location to either the left or right side of the screen. If it comes in contact with Ole, the Viking will change the `PhaserBullet`'s state to dead, as it absorbs the hit. If the `Phaser-Bullet` travels outside of the screen boundaries, it removes itself from the game. This wraps up what you need to do to create the `EnemyRobot`. The next step is to add a little bit of code in `GameplayLayer` to create the `EnemyRobot` and in the `Viking` class to enable the Viking to pick up the power-ups.

GameplayLayer and Viking Updates

The `gameplayLayer` class has to know about the power-ups, the space cargo ship, and the enemy robot in order to be able to add them on the screen.

The first step is to include the `imports` for the new classes you have added in this chapter. Open up the *GameplayLayer.m* implementation file and add the `import` statements in Listing 5.14 to the import for *RadarDish.h*.

Listing 5.14   **GameplayLayer.m imports**

```
#import "SpaceCargoShip.h"
#import "EnemyRobot.h"
#import "PhaserBullet.h"
#import "Mallet.h"
#import "Health.h"
```

The next step is to enhance the `createObjectOfType` method so that it can create the power-ups, the `SpaceCargoShip`, the `PhaserBullet`, and the `EnemyRobot`. Move to the `createObjectOfType` method and replace it with the contents of Listing 5.15.

Listing 5.15   **GameplayLayer.m createObjectOfType method**

```
-(void)createObjectOfType:(GameObjectType)objectType
          withHealth:(int)initialHealth
          atLocation:(CGPoint)spawnLocation
          withZValue:(int)ZValue {

    if (kEnemyTypeRadarDish == objectType) {
        CCLOG(@"Creating the Radar Enemy");
        RadarDish *radarDish =
          [[RadarDish alloc] initWithSpriteFrameName:@"radar_1.png"];
        [radarDish setCharacterHealth:initialHealth];
        [radarDish setPosition:spawnLocation];
        [sceneSpriteBatchNode addChild:radarDish z:ZValue
          tag:kRadarDishTagValue];
        [radarDish release];
```

```objc
    } else if (kEnemyTypeAlienRobot == objectType) {
        CCLOG(@"Creating the Alien Robot");
        EnemyRobot *enemyRobot =
         [[EnemyRobot alloc] initWithSpriteFrameName:@"an1_anim1.png"];
        [enemyRobot setCharacterHealth:initialHealth];
        [enemyRobot setPosition:spawnLocation];
        [enemyRobot changeState:kStateSpawning];
        [sceneSpriteBatchNode addChild:enemyRobot z:ZValue];
        [enemyRobot setDelegate:self];
        [enemyRobot release];
    } else if (kEnemyTypeSpaceCargoShip == objectType) {
        CCLOG(@"Creating the Cargo Ship Enemy");
        SpaceCargoShip *spaceCargoShip =
         [[SpaceCargoShip alloc]
            initWithSpriteFrameName:@"ship_2.png"];
        [spaceCargoShip setDelegate:self];
        [spaceCargoShip setPosition:spawnLocation];
        [sceneSpriteBatchNode addChild:spaceCargoShip z:ZValue];
        [spaceCargoShip release];
    } else if (kPowerUpTypeMallet == objectType) {
        CCLOG(@"GameplayLayer -> Creating mallet powerup");
        Mallet *mallet =
         [[Mallet alloc] initWithSpriteFrameName:@"mallet_1.png"];
        [mallet setPosition:spawnLocation];
        [sceneSpriteBatchNode addChild:mallet];
        [mallet release];
    } else if (kPowerUpTypeHealth == objectType) {
        CCLOG(@"GameplayLayer-> Creating Health Powerup");
        Health *health =
         [[Health alloc] initWithSpriteFrameName:@"sandwich_1.png"];
        [health setPosition:spawnLocation];
        [sceneSpriteBatchNode addChild:health];
        [health release];
    }
}
```

The beginning of this method has the same `if` statement you wrote in Chapter 4, creating the RadarDish enemy. The next `if else` blocks create the SpaceCargo-Ship, the power-ups, and the EnemyRobot. Note how the RadarDish is given a unique tag: this tag will be used later so that the GameplayLayer can get a reference back to the RadarDish object to determine its state.

The next method to replace is createPhaserWithDirection. In Chapter 4 this method was just a stub with a CCLOG statement inside. You now need to add the logic so that a PhaserBullet can be created by the GameplayLayer with a particular direction. Replace the contents of the createPhaserWithDirection method with the code in Listing 5.16.

Listing 5.16   GameplayLayer.m createPhaserWithDirection method

```
-(void)createPhaserWithDirection:(PhaserDirection)phaserDirection
andPosition:(CGPoint)spawnPosition {
    PhaserBullet *phaserBullet = [[PhaserBullet alloc] initWithSpriteFrame
Name:@"beam_1.png"];
    [phaserBullet setPosition:spawnPosition];
    [phaserBullet setMyDirection:phaserDirection];
    [phaserBullet setCharacterState:kStateSpawning];
    [sceneSpriteBatchNode addChild:phaserBullet];
    [phaserBullet release];
}
```

The createPhaserWithDirection method has the GameplayLayer create a new PhaserBullet object and set its direction. Once the PhaserBullet is added as a child to sceneSpriteBatchNode, it will be rendered onscreen and its update method will be called on every frame by the GameplayLayer.

There is a final method to add to the GameplayLayer class, which will continue adding EnemyRobots as long as the RadarDish is still not destroyed. Add the contents of Listing 5.17 below the createPhaserWithDirectionMethod in *GameplayLayer.m.*

Listing 5.17   GameplayLayer.m addEnemy method

```
-(void)addEnemy {
    CGSize screenSize = [CCDirector sharedDirector].winSize;
    RadarDish *radarDish = (RadarDish*)
     [sceneSpriteBatchNode getChildByTag:kRadarDishTagValue];
    if (radarDish != nil) {
        if ([radarDish characterState] != kStateDead) {
            [self createObjectOfType:kEnemyTypeAlienRobot
              withHealth:100
              atLocation:ccp(screenSize.width * 0.195f,
              screenSize.height * 0.1432f)
              withZValue:2];
        } else {
            [self unschedule:@selector(addEnemy)];
        }
    }
}
```

As you will see shortly, the addEnemy method will be called by the Cocos2D Scheduler. The first line retrieves the reference to the RadarDish object from the sceneSpriteBatchNode via the unique tag that was given to the RadarDish object when it was added as a child to the sceneSpriteBatchNode. If the RadarDish is not nil and not in a kStateDead, then the GameplayLayer will spawn off a new

EnemyRobot. If the RadarDish is dead, the GameplayLayer will unschedule the timer calling this method.

The final glue in GameplayLayer are a few lines to add in the init method. Add the lines shown in Listing 5.18 immediately after the [self scheduleUpdate] call.

Listing 5.18   GameplayLayer.m init method additions

```
[self schedule:@selector(addEnemy) interval:10.0f];
[self createObjectOfType:kEnemyTypeSpaceCargoShip
  withHealth:0
  atLocation:ccp(screenSize.width * -0.5f,
                screenSize.height * 0.74f)
  withZValue:50];
```

With the last two lines in place, the GameplayLayer will create the SpaceCargo-Ship and add another EnemyRobot every 10 seconds until the Viking destroys the RadarDish.

Running Space Viking

Now that you have all of the elements in place, you should be able to just click **Run** and play *Space Viking* on your iPad Simulator. Even better, you can connect your iPad and play *Space Viking* on the real thing. Figure 5.3 shows the *Space Viking* game with the RadarDish, EnemyRobot, and SpaceCargoShip.

Figure 5.3   Space Viking running on the iPad Simulator

If you have any trouble running *Space Viking*, go back and check your code against the listings in this chapter. Make sure you have included all of the classes and code in your copy of *Space Viking*. While playing the game, be sure to try out the crouching move to avoid those pesky phaser bullets.

A Word on Cocos2D's Scheduler

The Cocos2D Scheduler provides your game with timed events and calls. All `CCNode` objects know how to schedule and unschedule events, and using the Cocos2D Scheduler has several distinct advantages over just using `NSTimer`. The first advantage is that the scheduler calls get deactivated whenever the `CCNode` is no longer visible or is removed from the scene. The scheduler calls are also deactivated when Cocos2D is paused and are rescheduled when Cocos2D is resumed. If you were using `NSTimer` directly, you would have to keep track of when any object you had a timer set against was deallocated and deactivate that timer or risk a crash when the `NSTimer` fired.

Another advantage of the Cocos2D Scheduler is that it delivers a `deltaTime` of the milliseconds that have passed since the last call. This `deltaTime` is useful in moving objects and in modeling objects in physics engines, as you will see in Chapter 10, "Basic Game Physics: Adding Realism with Box2D."

Lastly, using the Cocos2D Scheduler with the `[self scheduleUpdate]` call ensures that your update function will be called before each frame needs to be rendered, not after or, even worse, midframe.

You can schedule the timers via the `[self schedule:]` call on any `CCNode` or by calling the `CCScheduler` singleton directly with `[[CCScheduler sharedScheduler] ... ]`. Having Cocos2D automatically manage your timers via the `CCScheduler` can save you a lot of time over `NSTimer` and let you focus on the mechanics of your game.

For the More Curious: Effects in Cocos2D

Cocos2D has a powerful, built-in effects system that you can use to create dramatic visual effects in your games. Effects in Cocos2D are packaged as actions, and you already know how to use those: they are the basis for all of the behaviors and animations in *Space Viking*.

The Cocos2D effects act on the OpenGL ES frame buffer object (FBO), and it is important to understand a little bit about the FBO to know how the actions work.

Each object that needs to be rendered onscreen is first rendered on the frame buffer object and then sent to the GPU for processing and to be displayed onscreen. The images are present in the FBO as an array of vertex data. The scope of the effect depends on what object you apply it to. If you apply an effect action to just a `CCSprite`, only that particular `CCSprite` is affected. If you apply it to a `CCSprite`-`BatchNode`, all `CCSprites` being rendered under that node will have the effect.

Finally, if you apply the effect to the CCLayer, everything in the layer will have the effect applied.

You don't have to know exactly how the vertex array is stored in the FBO, although you are free to see the implementation details in the Cocos2D source code. The important points to remember are that there is a grid of image data in the FBO, and the effect actions act on this grid.

Within the Cocos2D effects there are two subtypes: a tiled and a nontiled version. The tiled version breaks down the contents of the frame buffer object into individual tiles, which can be manipulated separately, whereas the nontiled version has the entire frame as a large tile.

Effects for Fun in Space Viking

To get a better feel for the Cocos2D effects, you will take one effects line and apply it first to a background tile and then to the CCSpriteBatchNode.

To start, open the *BackgroundLayer.m* implementation file and add these two lines at the bottom of the init method directly following the lines where you created the background CCSprite, as shown in Listing 5.19.

Listing 5.19   **BackgroundLayer.m waves action**

```
id wavesAction = [CCWaves actionWithWaves:5 amplitude:20
                         horizontal:NO vertical:YES
                         grid:ccg(15,10) duration:20];
[backgroundImage runAction:
   [CCRepeatForever actionWithAction:wavesAction]];
```

The first line sets up the wavesAction variable as an CCWave action, while the second line applies it to the background image. The CCWaves action has several parameters to control the amplitude of the waves, whether it is to "wave" in the horizontal or vertical axis, and the size of the grid along with the wave durations. The grid size determines how to break up the image in order to apply the effect. Larger grid sizes result in better effects at the cost of larger CPU time to generate each frame. Effects can take a lot of processing power, especially on older devices such as the iPhone 3G; do remember this when setting up effects in your system. If you click **Run**, you can see only the top left background image is experiencing the waves effect, as shown in Figure 5.4.

On the last step, you had an effect applied to only a background image; all of the other graphical elements in *Space Viking* are untouched. For the next example, comment out the two lines you just added so that the background is back to normal and open up the *GameplayLayer.m* implementation file. On the init method, add these two lines before the Cocos2D Scheduler calls, as shown in Listing 5.20.

Figure 5.4   Top left background; CCSprite with waves effect applied

Listing 5.20   **GameplayLayer.m waves action**

```
id wavesAction = [CCWaves actionWithWaves:5 amplitude:20 horizontal:NO
vertical:YES grid:ccg(15,10) duration:20];
       [sceneSpriteBatchNode runAction: [CCRepeatForever
actionWithAction:wavesAction]];
```

This is setting up a CCWaves action against the CCSpriteBatchNode that is used to render the Viking and all of the enemies onscreen. If you click **Run**, you should see an image similar to Figure 5.5. Pay close attention to the joystick and the attack and jump buttons. Note how the joystick and buttons are not impacted by the CCWaves action, since they are not part of the CCSpriteBatchNode.

> **Note**
>
> If you are using a CCSpriteBatchNode, then you need to apply the effects to the entire CCSpriteBatchNode instead of the individual sprites. Since the CCSprite-BatchNode is doing all of the rendering, it must have the effects applied to the CCSpriteBatchNode itself; otherwise, you will not see any of the effects onscreen.

Be sure to comment out the two lines you added to *GameplayLayer.m* and return *Space Viking* back to normal. If you want to check out all of the effect actions included with Cocos2D, you can run the EffectsTest and EffectsTestAdvanced samples included with Cocos2D.

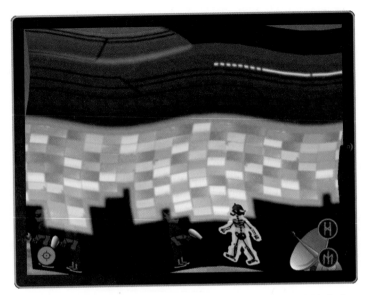

Figure 5.5   CCWaves action applied to the CCSpriteBatchNode in
Space Viking

Running the EffectsTest

Navigate to the directory where you downloaded Cocos2D back in Chapter 1, "Hello,
Cocos2D," and open the *cocos2d-iphone* project. With the *cocos2d-iphone* project opened,
set the Scheme dropdown to EffectsTest, as shown in Figure 5.6.

Figure 5.6   EffectsTest selected under the Scheme dropdown in Xcode

Select **Run** in Xcode, and you should see the EffectsTest running in the simulator. You can see the various effects that are possible with Cocos2D. You can also try
out the EffectsAdvancedTest target for more examples of Cocos2D effects.

Returning Sprites and Objects Back to Normal

Once you start playing with effects, you will notice that they stay applied to the CCSprites and other objects even after you stop the action. To return your CCSprite to its normal, nonaltered state, you need to call the special StopGrid action. For example, if you wanted to stop the CCWaves action applied to the CCSpriteBatch-Node in *Space Viking,* you would need:

```
[sceneSpriteBatchNode runAction:[CCStopGrid action]];
```

Summary

In this chapter you built on the Cocos2D actions and animations you created previously to add more characters to your *Space Viking* game. You added a SpaceCargoShip, power-ups, and an enemy robot that can pursue and attack Ole the Viking. In the later part of this chapter, you learned about the Cocos2D Scheduler and the built-in effects in Cocos2D. Hopefully, you are beginning to think about how you can reuse the techniques shown here in your own games. In the next chapter, you will learn about the Cocos2D text subsystem and will add health meters and an interactive debugger to *Space Viking.* Some quick challenges await before you can proceed in creating your Viking adventure.

Exercises and Challenges

1. What happens when you turn off the `[self flipX:true];` statement in the EnemyRobot? How does it affect the animation?

2. The EnemyRobot has a long delay after he raises his phaser and before he fires it at Ole. What would happen if you made that delay very small, such as 0.015 seconds?

3. The GameplayLayer spawns a new EnemyRobot every 10 seconds for as long as the RadarDish is still alive. What happens if you change this to 1 second?

4. How does changing the grid size change the quality of the waves effects?

Text, Fonts, and the Written Word

In the last two chapters, you learned how to add artificial intelligence, animations, and enemies to your game. In this chapter you get to have a reprieve from the complexities of game mechanics and focus on the text rendering available in Cocos2D. Cocos2D has extensive support for all of the built-in iOS fonts as well as embedded TrueType fonts. The text system allows you to add labels and text to your game with ease.

The font-rendering system in Cocos2D is split into two portions or classes: the `CCLabelTTF` *and the* `CCLabelBMFont` *classes. This chapter covers both classes and how to use them in* Space Viking.

CCLabelTTF

The `CCLabelTTF` class is meant as a quick and easy way to get text into your game with a minimal amount of setup or code. You already used the `CCLabelTTF` class way back in Chapter 1 as part of the *HelloWorld* sample. In the *HelloWorld* code you had the following lines:

```
CCLabelTTF  *label = [CCLabelTTF labelWithString:@"Hello World"
fontName:@"Marker Felt" fontSize:64];
```

To create a `CCLabelTTF`, all that is required is that you specify the text, the font, and the font size. The `CCLabelTTF` object will use the `CCTexture2D` class to create an image texture from your text and display that texture onscreen. After the initialization code above, you can use the `CCLabelTTF` like any other `CCNode`, add it to your layer, position it, and so forth. The `CCLabelTTF` class is great for text that is static or that you do not want to change often. Each time you call the `setText` method, a new texture is created, and this can have a significant performance impact if you are creating or changing the text on every frame.

Adding a Start Banner to Space Viking

To better understand how to use a `CCLabelTTF`, you will create a quick "Game Start" banner when the *Space Viking* game play first starts. This banner will be centered on the screen and will zoom and fade out over the course of 2 seconds. To get started, open the *SpaceViking* project and the *GameplayLayer.m* implementation file.

In the `init` method add the lines shown in Listing 6.1 before the `[self scheduleUpdate]` call.

Listing 6.1   **Game start label in GameplayLayer.m init method**

```
CCLabelTTF *gameBeginLabel =
    [CCLabelTTF labelWithString:@"Game Start" fontName:@"Helvetica"
        fontSize:64];                                                 // 1
[gameBeginLabel setPosition:ccp(screenSize.width/2,screenSize.height/2)];
// 2
[self addChild:gameBeginLabel];                                       // 3
id labelAction = [CCSpawn actions:
                    [CCScaleBy actionWithDuration:2.0f scale:4],
                    [CCFadeOut actionWithDuration:2.0f],
                    nil];                                             // 4
[gameBeginLabel runAction:labelAction];                               // 5
```

The code segment in Listing 6.1 accomplishes the following:

1. A new `CCLabelTTF` is created with the text "Game Start" using the Helvetica font with a size of 64. From this line forward, the `CCLabelTTF` acts just like any other `CCNode`, such as a `CCSprite`: you can position it and apply actions to it.

2. Sets the position of the label to the center of the screen by halving the screen width and height.

3. Adds the label to the `GameplayLayer` so that it will be rendered onscreen.

4. Creates an action called `labelAction`, which consists of two actions running simultaneously. The first action is a `CCScaleBy`, which zooms in the text to four times the original size. The second action is a `CCFadeOut` that fades out the text over the course of 2 seconds.

5. The `CCLabelTTF` runs the actions that you created in the previous line.

If you click **Run** on *Space Viking* on your iPad Simulator, you should see the "Game Start" text banner, as shown in Figure 6.1.

Figure 6.1   Space Viking with Game Start banner

Understanding Anchor Points and Alignment

All `CCNodes` from `CCSprites` to `CCLabelTTF` have anchor points to allow them to be positioned onscreen. Anchor points are useful in positioning and aligning your objects onscreen, especially labels. The anchor point is an offset into an object texture—in other words, what point in the texture to use to place it onscreen. Cocos2D defaults to an anchor point in the middle of your texture, so by default your objects are always placed according to their center points. For example, if you set the position of the sprite to (100,100), the center of the sprite would be at (100,100) by default.

If you set the anchor point to the bottom left corner of a sprite, and set the position of the sprite to (100,100), then the bottom left corner of the sprite would be at (100,100) instead of the center of the sprite being at that location.

Take a close look at Figure 6.2, showing the anchor point values for a "Game Start" `CCLabelTTF`.

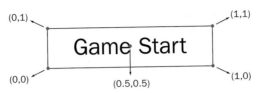

Figure 6.2   Game Start CCLabelTTF anchor points

Looking at Figure 6.2, you can see the default anchor point at the middle of the texture would have a value of (0.5,0.5). Look at anchor point values as percentages, with 1 being 100%, or all the way to the end of the texture. Take a close look at the bottom right of Figure 6.2, at the value (1,0). This anchor point (1,0) is all the way over on the x-axis of the texture, but at the start of the y-axis, so bottom right.

On the top right you can see the anchor point value of (1,1), meaning it is all the way on the x- and y-axes of the texture, therefore upper right.

Remember, anchor points range between zero and one, with (0,0) on the bottom left and (1,1) on the top right.

Normally, you will not need to change the anchor point in your objects; an exception is when you are trying to align labels.

If you wanted the CCLabelTTF to be aligned to the left, you would set the anchor point to (0,0.5). This translates to zero on the x-axis (left) and halfway up on the y-axis, which means a left alignment but centered vertically. If you had it at (0,0) instead, it would be aligned to the left but also to the bottom. Here are some examples of common CCLabelTTF alignments:

```
//Left Alignment
[gameBeginLabel setAnchorPoint: ccp(0, 0.5f)];

// Right Alignment
[gameBeginLabel setAnchorPoint: ccp(1, 0.5f)];

// Top Alignment
[gameBeginLabel setAnchorPoint: ccp(0.5f, 0)];

// Bottom Alignment
[gameBeginLabel setAnchorPoint: ccp(0.5f, 1.0f)];

// Center - Default
[gameBeginLabel setAnchorPoint: ccp(0.5f, 0.5f)];
```

Anchor Points and Rotation

Anchor points are used in rotation and with other effects in addition to being used to position a CCSprite. Keep in mind that if you change the CCSprite default anchor point (center of image), any rotations you apply to the CCSprite will happen at the new anchor point location.

Listing the Fonts Available in iOS

The `CCLabelTTF` class relies on the fonts available in the iOS, and Apple is always adding to the available fonts with each iOS release. The best way to know what fonts you can use is to query the iOS for available fonts under the `UIFont` class. Jonathan Saggau wrote an excellent bit of compact code to list out the fonts. A modified version of it is given here and can be dropped in the `init` method of *GameScene.m* to print out the available fonts to your console.

```
NSMutableArray *fontNames = [[NSMutableArray alloc] init];
    NSArray *fontFamilyNames = [UIFont familyNames];
    for (NSString *familyName in fontFamilyNames) {
        NSLog(@"Font Family Name = %@", familyName);
        NSArray *names = [UIFont fontNamesForFamilyName:familyName];
        NSLog(@"Font Names = %@", fontNames);
        [fontNames addObjectsFromArray:names];
    }
[fontNames release];
```

Fonts are part of a font family, and the `UIFont` class returns a list of all of the font families available in iOS as well as the fonts under each font family. The code above first gets a list of all the font families, and then a list of all the fonts under each family, printing those font names out to the console.

CCLabelBMFont

`CCLabelTTF`s are great for when you just need the standard iOS fonts and do not have to change the text of the labels very often. In the situations where you need to use a custom font or change the text on each frame, the `CCLabelBMFont` class is what you will want to use.

A bitmapped font atlas is an image containing all of the characters you want to display along with coordinates data that allows the characters to be cut out of the master image. The bitmap font atlas works in exactly the same way as the texture atlas you created in Chapter 2, "Hello, Space Viking," but in this case each of the images in the atlas represents a character. Since the characters are already stored as images, you cannot alter their size without using a different font atlas. If your game will have the same characters in two or more sizes, you need to create several font atlases for each of the sizes you need.

Cocos2D has support for any bitmapped fonts that use the *fnt* file format. While Cocos2D itself does not have a bundled tool to create the font atlases, there are plenty of great tools that can help you create them. This chapter covers Hiero (free) and the excellent Glyph Designer (available in the Mac App Store).

Using Glyph Designer

Glyph Designer is a Mac OS X–based application for design font atlases developed by 71Squared. Unlike Hiero, it is a native Mac OS X application, offering better performance and compatibility with Mac OS X. In order to use Glyph Designer, you need to purchase it in the Mac App Store or at *http://glyphdesigner.71squared.com/*.

To create the font texture atlas:

1. Start up Glyph Designer, or select **File > New** if it is already running.

2. In the top left search box, enter *Helvetica* and select it as the font.

3. Move the size slider so that the font size is set to 32.

4. By default, Glyph Designer automatically resizes the texture atlas to the smallest possible size that would fit all of the glyphs.

5. On the right, click on the **Gradient Bar** and select a **yellow** tone from the color wheel that pops up.

   The color you choose is not important; yellow was chosen because it is more visible against the *Space Viking* background.

6. On the bottom right, in the Included Glyphs section, click on the **NEHE** button.

   This area is where you enter the characters you need in your font atlas. The NEHE is a small subset of the full ASCII character set. Be sure to always include any characters you will need in your game inside of the font texture atlas. If in your game you try to render a character in a label without that glyph being present in the font texture atlas, Cocos2D will leave a blank space for it.

7. Under the file menu, select **Export** and enter *SpaceVikingFont* for the **Save As** field.

   This step creates two files: a PNG of all the glyphs in one font texture atlas and a plist file that will allow Cocos2D to extract each glyph from the font texture atlas. Figure 6.3 shows Glyph Designer with Helvetica selected.

Lastly, you need to import the newly created font texture atlas and plist files into Xcode. Drag both the *SpaceVikingFont.png* and *SpaceVikingFont.fnt* files into your *SpaceViking* project under the *Images* folder.

Using the Hiero Font Builder Tool

If you are looking for a free alternative to Glyph Designer, the Hiero Font Builder Tool is a Java application that you can run in your browser. It is a free tool that you can use to create a font texture atlas for Cocos2D. First point your browser to *www.n4te.com/hiero/hiero.jnlp*.

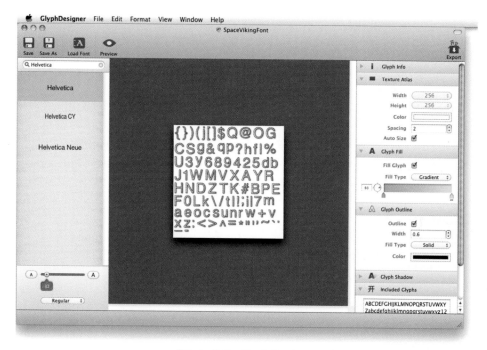

Figure 6.3   Glyph Designer

Warning

Safari's default behavior is to just download the *Hiero.jnpl* file. You will need to double-click it in the Downloads window to launch Hiero.

If prompted, accept the warning shown in Figure 6.4.

Figure 6.4   Warning upon running Hiero

Once Hiero is up and running, you will see a list of the fonts available in your system in the top left text box. To create the font atlas needed for *Space Viking*, follow these steps:

1. In the top left font selection box, scroll down and pick **Helvetica**.

2. In the Sample Text area, click on **NEHE** to have some sample characters entered in for you. If the text you need consists only of a few characters, you can type them here.

3. Under the Color, click on the **white** box and select a **yellow** color.

4. In the Rendering section, switch to **glyph cache** and set the page width and height to **256**. As with image texture atlases, you want the smallest power-of-two sized image that will contain all of the characters you need. This setting indicates that Hiero will create a 256 × 256 texture with all of the characters in the sample text. At this point, Hiero should look like Figure 6.5.

5. From the File menu, select **Save BMFont Files** and name the saved file *SpaceVikingFont.fnt*. Hiero will create both a *.fnt* and a *.png* file.

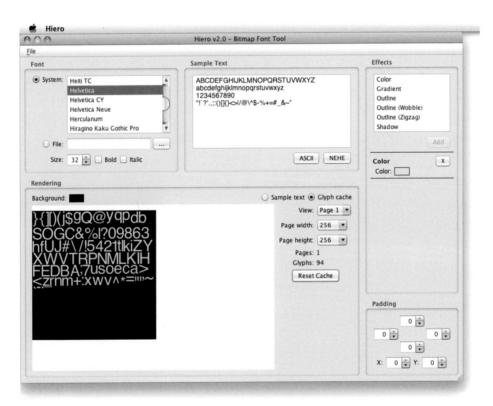

Figure 6.5   Hiero running/screen

If you created your font texture atlas with Hiero, you will need to import the PNG and plist files into Xcode. Drag both the *SpaceVikingFont.png* and *SpaceVikingFont.fnt* files into your *SpaceViking* project under the *Images* folder.

Note

All the characters you want to display have to be present in this font atlas. If you are using lowercase and uppercase versions of the characters, both need to be included. If you try to set the text to a character that is not in your font atlas, it will show up as blank onscreen. You can use Hiero or any other bitmap font utility that can generate both the PNG and FNT files for Cocos2D to use. If you wish to skip the font atlas creation, you can use the FNT and PNG files included with the source code for the book.

Using CCLabelBMFont Class

After you have created and imported the *SpaceVikingFont.fnt* and *SpaceVikingFont.png* files into *Space Viking*, you need to add the code to use the `CCLabelBMFont` class. To start, you will replace the Game Start `CCLabelTTF` with a `CCLabelBMFont`.

Open the *GameplayLayer.m* to the `init` method and replace the line creating the `CCLabelTTF` with the contents of Listing 6.2.

Listing 6.2   GameplayLayer.m init method, CCLabelBMFont instead of CCLabelTTF

```
// With CCLabelBMFont
        CCLabelBMFont *gameBeginLabel =
        [CCLabelBMFont labelWithString:@"Game Start"
         fntFile:@"SpaceVikingFont.fnt"];
```

The remaining lines that you created in the previous section setting the position and the two actions to the `gameBeginLabel` can remain in place. If you click **Run**, you should see the "Game Start" banner, although this time it should be yellow instead of white and in size 32 instead of 64.

Using `CCLabelBMFont` restricts you to having the fonts only in the original size saved to the font texture atlas via the external tool. Because the `CCLabelBMFont` is really just a texture, you can scale it and apply any other actions and effects to it as you would to any other `CCNode`. In the Game Start banner, the font size is 32 but the banner is scaled to four times its size as part of the `CCScaleBy` action.

Note

You should be careful not to scale your fonts too large, as they will lose clarity. In general, if you know you will need your fonts in several sizes, you can create font texture atlases for each of the needed sizes.

A good way to put the `CCLabelBMFont` to use is in setting up a live debugging system in *Space Viking*. The next section walks you through creating a live debugging text for the `EnemyRobot`.

For the More Curious: Live Debugging

At this point you know how to add text labels into your games, so if you just are interested in the basics, feel free to skip to the next chapter. But if you want to learn a cool way to use text labels to make debugging and developing your game easier, check out this section!

In your games it is often useful to know what state each of the characters is in during game play. One way you can do this is to overlay above the objects small text labels showing their state and other relevant data. In this section you set up a system to show the position and the current state of the enemy robots. To accomplish this, you need to set up an instance variable in EnemyRobot to point to the debug label and a method to update the label with the latest position and status. To start, open up the *EnemyRobot.h* header file.

Updating EnemyRobot

In the *EnemyRobot.h* header file, in the @interface section, add an instance variable to hold a pointer to the label object called myDebugLabel. The myDebugLabel variable can be added directly below the id <GameplayLayerDelegate> delegate declaration.

```
CCLabelBMFont *myDebugLabel;
```

Below the @interface section, add the property definition so that this pointer variable can be set by the GameplayLayer as follows:

```
@property (nonatomic,assign) CCLabelBMFont *myDebugLabel;
```

Listing 6.3 shows the full contents of the *EnemyRobot.h* header file with the two lines added for the myDebugLabel variable in **bold**.

Listing 6.3 **EnemyRobot.h header file**

```
//   EnemyRobot.h
//   SpaceViking

#import <Foundation/Foundation.h>
#import "GameCharacter.h"
@interface EnemyRobot : GameCharacter {
    CCAnimation *robotWalkingAnim;

    CCAnimation *raisePhaserAnim;
    CCAnimation *shootPhaserAnim;
    CCAnimation *lowerPhaserAnim;

    CCAnimation *torsoHitAnim;
    CCAnimation *headHitAnim;
    CCAnimation *robotDeathAnim;
```

```
    BOOL isVikingWithinBoundingBox;
    BOOL isVikingWithinSight;

    GameCharacter *vikingCharacter;
    id <GameplayLayerDelegate> delegate;
    CCLabelBMFont *myDebugLabel;


}
@property (nonatomic,assign) id <GameplayLayerDelegate> delegate;
@property (nonatomic, retain) CCAnimation *robotWalkingAnim;
@property (nonatomic, retain) CCAnimation *raisePhaserAnim;
@property (nonatomic, retain) CCAnimation *shootPhaserAnim;
@property (nonatomic, retain) CCAnimation *lowerPhaserAnim;
@property (nonatomic, retain) CCAnimation *torsoHitAnim;
@property (nonatomic, retain) CCAnimation *headHitAnim;
@property (nonatomic, retain) CCAnimation *robotDeathAnim;
@property (nonatomic,assign) CCLabelBMFont *myDebugLabel;
-(void)initAnimations;
@end
```

Switch over to the *EnemyRobot.m* implementation file. Immediately below the
@synthesize delegate statement, add the following line:

```
@synthesize myDebugLabel;
```

These three lines take care of making the myDebugLabel variable accessible from
outside EnemyRobot so that it can be set by the GameplayLayer.

Next, you need a small method so that each EnemyRobot can update its debug
label to show the current position and state. Move to above the updateStateWith-
DeltaTime method in EnemyRobot and add the setDebugLabelAndTextAnd-
Position method, as shown in Listing 6.4.

Listing 6.4   setDebugLabelTextAndPosition method

```
-(void)setDebugLabelTextAndPosition {
    CGPoint newPosition = [self position];
    NSString *labelString =
     [NSString stringWithFormat:@"X: %.2f \n Y:%.2f \n",
      newPosition.x, newPosition.y];

    switch (characterState) {
        case kStateSpawning:
            [myDebugLabel setString:
             [labelString stringByAppendingString:@" Spawning"]];
            break;
```

```
        case kStateIdle:
            [myDebugLabel setString:
             [labelString stringByAppendingString:@" Idle"]];
            break;

        case kStateWalking:
            [myDebugLabel setString:
             [labelString stringByAppendingString:@" Walking"]];
            break;

        case kStateAttacking:
            [myDebugLabel setString:
             [labelString stringByAppendingString:@" Attacking"]];
            break;

        case kStateTakingDamage:
            [myDebugLabel setString:
             [labelString stringByAppendingString:@" Taking Damage"]];
            break;

        case kStateDead:
            [myDebugLabel setString:
             [labelString stringByAppendingString:@" Dead"]];
            break;

        default:
            [myDebugLabel setString:
             [labelString stringByAppendingString:@" Unknown State"]];
            break;
    }

    float yOffset = screenSize.height * 0.195f;
    newPosition = ccp(newPosition.x,newPosition.y+yOffset);
[myDebugLabel setPosition:newPosition];
}
```

The setDebugLabelTextAndPosition method creates a string with the Enemy-Robot's current position and state. The .2f you see is just a formatting parameter to limit the decimal positions to two places. The \n adds a carriage return to keep the debug label tidy. Lastly, the debug label's position is set to directly above the Enemy-Robot's center point by 150 pixels.

Move to the updateStateWithDeltaTime method and add this line directly below the checkAndClampSpritePosition call:

```
[self setDebugLabelTextAndPosition];
```

This one line will call the `setDebugLabelTextAndPosition` method and update the debug label on every frame. If you recall from Chapter 5, "More Actions, Effects, and Cocos2D Scheduler," the `EnemyRobot` removes itself from the `CCSpriteBatchNode` once it is done playing the death animation. When the `EnemyRobot` is removed from the `CCSpriteBatchNode`, it needs to inform the debug label to remove itself from the `GameplayLayer`. Open the `dealloc` method in the `EnemyRobot` and add the following two lines above the `[super dealloc]` call:

```
myDebugLabel = nil;
```

The first line asks for the debug label to remove itself from the parent `Gameplay-Layer`. The second line sets the debug label pointer to nil, since the object reference is no longer valid.

Updating GameplayLayer

Now that the `EnemyRobot` is set up to update the debug label, the label itself needs to be created and associated with the `EnemyRobot`. Open the *GameplayLayer.m* implementation file and move to the `createObjectOfTypeMethod`.

In the `if` block that defines the steps needed to spawn an `EnemyRobot`, add the following three lines before the line `[enemyRobot release]`.

```
CCLabelBMFont *debugLabel =
        [CCLabelBMFont
         labelWithString:@"NoneNone"
         fntFile:@"SpaceVikingFont.fnt"];
        [self addChild:debugLabel];
        [enemyRobot setMyDebugLabel:debugLabel];
```

The first line creates the `CCLabelBMFont` `debugLabel` with a temporary "NoneNone" string and the font file you created earlier in this chapter. The `debugLabel` is then added to the `GameplayLayer`, allowing it to be rendered onscreen. Lastly, a pointer to it is passed to the newly created `EnemyRobot`, allowing the `EnemyRobot` to update the label. Your `if` block for creating `EnemyRobot` should be identical to Listing 6.5.

Listing 6.5 GameplayLayer.m createObjectOfTypeMethod for EnemyRobot objects

```
} else if (kEnemyTypeAlienRobot == objectType) {
        CCLOG(@"Creating the Alien Robot");
        EnemyRobot *enemyRobot = [[EnemyRobot alloc]
         initWithSpriteFrameName:@"an1_anim1.png"]; //teleport_2
        [enemyRobot setCharacterHealth:initialHealth];
        [enemyRobot setPosition:spawnLocation];
        [enemyRobot changeState:kStateSpawning];
        [sceneSpriteBatchNode addChild:enemyRobot z:ZValue];
        [enemyRobot setDelegate:self];
```

```
CCLabelBMFont *debugLabel =
[CCLabelBMFont
 labelWithString:@"NoneNone"
 fntFile:@"SpaceVikingFont.fnt"];
[self addChild:debugLabel];
[enemyRobot setMyDebugLabel:debugLabel];
[enemyRobot release];
}
```

If you click **Run** now, you will see that the EnemyRobot characters have three lines of debug text above their heads indicating state and their current position. Figure 6.6 shows *Space Viking* on the iPad Simulator with the debug labels. Notice how the position coordinates update on every frame while the EnemyRobot is walking without impacting the game's performance.

Figure 6.6   Space Viking with debug labels showing on top of the EnemyRobot characters

Other Uses for Text Debugging

You can use the text debugging in your games to get a real-time view of the states of various entities or game objects while playing. This technique can be really useful to find hard-to-diagnose bugs in your logic or when you are left scratching your head as to why that enemy does not attack even though the player is nearby. Some developers have even gone even further to show how much memory is free on the device as the game is being played to tip them off when they are about to encounter a low-memory condition or if they have memory leaks.

Summary

You have learned about the font-rendering system in Cocos2D and the differences between using `CCLabelTTF` and `CCLabelBMFont`. You also learned about using text labels as a live debugging system for your games and implemented a debugging system for the `EnemyRobot`. In the next chapter you will work to create the main menu and the foundation needed to allow Ole to explore more than just one level in the *Space Viking* universe.

Challenges

1. Try making the debug labels appear only in debug builds of *Space Viking* or enabling it to be toggled on and off by a `#define` statement.

   Hint

   You could define a `#define` around the `COCOS2D_DEBUG` flag.

2. Replace the y-axis indicator from the `EnemyRobot` with the robot's current health level.
3. Try adding a debug label to the Viking so you can see what state and position Ole is in.

Part III

From Level to Game

Learn how to expand the *Space Viking* level you have built into a full
game by adding menus, using sound, and scrolling.

Main Menu, Level Completed, and Credits Scenes

So far in this book you have built a full working scene for Ole the Viking to explore. He has to battle evil robots and figure out a way to stop them from spawning. In this chapter you learn about Cocos2D menus and how to create and link multiple scenes. By the end of this chapter you will have Space Viking *set up to start on a main menu, show three different levels for Ole to explore, and show a level complete screen once Ole has killed all the enemies or died trying. If you are ready, read on.*

Scenes in Cocos2D

In Chapter 1, "Hello, Cocos2D," you learned that each distinct level or view is stored inside of a `CCScene` and that the Cocos2D Director is in charge of running one scene at a time. Up to this point, you had one `CCScene`, the `GameScene` where all the action takes place. While one scene has been great to get *Space Viking* started, Ole needs more levels to explore. There are menus, scrolling, and physics to discover and implement before you reach the end of this book. This chapter covers how to create and link menus and levels in your games.

In *Space Viking* each level is represented by a `CCScene`. In your own games, you can split levels in whichever way suits you: you could have a `CCScene` that handles all levels or a set of levels that share the same graphics. Remember that a `CCScene` is just a subclass of `CCNode` with the `anchorPoint` set to the middle of the screen. It is has no further logic and is just a container for all the objects you will have in a particular part of your game. In *Space Viking* you will have the following scenes:

- **Main Menu**

  First screen displayed when *Space Viking* launches. It shows Ole spinning around and gives the player the option to play, set options, or see the website for this book.

- **Options Menu**

  A menu screen that allows the user to turn music on/off and sound effects on/off, as well as an option to view the *Space Viking* credits.

- **Credits**

  A list of the people involved in bringing *Space Viking* to life.

- **Level Completed**

  Shown when the player completes a level or dies, indicating the player's progress.

- **GameplayScenes**

  A scene for each of the levels in *Space Viking*. You have already created the first gameplay scene, when Ole awakens in the alien world.

In order to bring these scenes to life, you need to create a `MainMenuScene`, `LevelCompleteScene`, `OptionsScene`, and `CreditsScene`. The next section walks you through the process of creating the code needed to power these scenes. Figure 7.1 shows the navigation hierarchy of these scenes from the Main Menu.

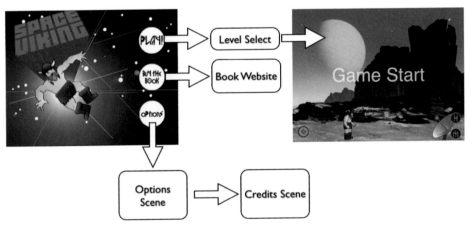

Figure 7.1   Menu screen flow in Space Viking

Before you can start creating these scenes, you need to set up the `GameManager` singleton, which informs the director which scene to display.

Introducing the GameManager

In the previous chapters you had the game starting out with the first scene, where Ole fights off the `RadarDish` and `EnemyRobot`. In order to make it easy to switch between scenes, you create a GameManager class to handle the task of asking the Cocos2D Director to switch CCScenes. The GameManager class will be a singleton class, so there will be only one instance of it during the lifetime of the *Space Viking* game, and it will be accessible from all the scenes. All of the scenes will know about the GameManager, and the GameManager will know about them, but the individual scenes will not know about each other. This way, each scene is self-contained and you can add more scenes or change them at will without worrying about interdependencies between scenes. The Singleton pattern is a powerful design pattern used throughout Cocos2D for the CCDirector, CCTextureCache, and other classes.

Note

For more information on the Singleton design pattern as well as other useful patterns in Cocoa programming, take a look at *Cocoa Design Patterns*, by Erik M. Buck and Donald A. Yacktman (Addison-Wesley, 2009).

The game manager needs to know what scenes to switch between, so before coding up the GameManager, open the *Constants.h* file and add the lines shown in Listing 7.1 to the bottom of it.

Listing 7.1   **Constants.h SceneType enumeration type**

```
#define kMainMenuTagValue 10
#define kSceneMenuTagValue 20

typedef enum {
    kNoSceneUninitialized=0,
    kMainMenuScene=1,
    kOptionsScene=2,
    kCreditsScene=3,
    kIntroScene=4,
    kLevelCompleteScene=5,
    kGameLevel1=101,
    kGameLevel2=102,
    kGameLevel3=103,
    kGameLevel4=104,
    kGameLevel5=105,
    kCutSceneForLevel2=201
} SceneTypes;

typedef enum {
    kLinkTypeBookSite,
    kLinkTypeDeveloperSiteRod,
    kLinkTypeDeveloperSiteRay,
    kLinkTypeArtistSite,
    kLinkTypeMusicianSite
} LinkTypes;
```

```
// Debug Enemy States with Labels
// 0 for OFF, 1 for ON
#define ENEMY_STATE_DEBUG 0
```

The `SceneTypes` is just an enumeration type that defines the scenes the `Game-Manager` will support switching between. You can see there are placeholders for game levels 2 through 5 that you have yet to create.

The `LinkTypes` is a set of types that are used to determine what URL to open. In the Main Menu the user will have the choice to open this book's site, and in the Credits scene the player can visit Ray's and my development site as well as the artist and musician sites.

Lastly, the `ENEMY_STATE_DEBUG` flag is used to answer the first challenge question from Chapter 6, "Text, Fonts, and the Written Word." You will use this flag to turn the Enemy Debug labels on and off. You will notice that this flag answers the challenge question from Chapter 6.

Creating the GameManager

To start creating the `GameManager`, select the *Singletons* folder you created in Chapter 3, "Introduction to Cocos2D Animations and Actions":

1. Right-click and, from the contextual menu, select **New File**. Choose the **Cocoa Touch category** under iOS and **Objective-C class** as the file type, and click **Next**.

2. For the Subclass field, enter *NSObject* and click **Next**.

3. Enter *GameManager.m* for the filename and click **Save**.

Open the *GameManager.h* header file and replace the code with the contents of Listing 7.2.

Listing 7.2 GameManager.h header file

```
//  GameManager.h
//  SpaceViking
//
#import <Foundation/Foundation.h>
#import "Constants.h"

@interface GameManager : NSObject {
    BOOL isMusicON;
    BOOL isSoundEffectsON;
    BOOL hasPlayerDied;
    SceneTypes currentScene;
}
```

```
@property (readwrite) BOOL isMusicON;
@property (readwrite) BOOL isSoundEffectsON;
@property (readwrite) BOOL hasPlayerDied;

+(GameManager*)sharedGameManager;                              // 1
-(void)runSceneWithID:(SceneTypes)sceneID;                     // 2
-(void)openSiteWithLinkType:(LinkTypes)linkTypeToOpen ;        // 3
@end
```

In Listing 7.2 pay close attention to the +(GameManager*)sharedManager method. The plus sign is key here—it indicates that the sharedManager method is a class method and not an instance method. This method is available at the class level, without your code having to have an allocated and initialized GameManager instance before calling it. In fact, this class method will allocate and initialize an instance of the GameManager class if there is not one already created for your game.

1. Sets up a class method called sharedGameManager. This class method returns the one and only instance of the GameManager. The full details are in the implementation file for GameManager in Listing 7.3.

2. Declares a runSceneWithID method that takes a sceneID of type SceneTypes. This method is called by various scenes when they need to have the director (via the GameManager) switch the scene that is currently running. An example is when the player finishes a level and the Gameplay scene has to be replaced by the LevelComplete scene.

3. Opens a URL based on the linkType sent. This method closes *Space Viking* and opens Mobile Safari to one of the predefined links in the game. You can use this same code if you want to send players to your site in your own games.

Note

As you will see in the *GameManager.m* implementation, the openSiteWithLinkType closes the *Space Viking* game and launches MobileSafari. If you wanted to keep your game running and open a web page with MobileSafari from within your game, you could create a UIWebView and add it to the view hierarchy, as doing so would let you display a website while keeping your game running.

The implementation of the GameManager can be thought of in two logical parts. In the first part are the methods needed to make the GameManager a singleton. The second part covers the runSceneWithID and openSiteWithLinkType methods and contains the GameManager-specific functionality. When you are creating your own singletons, copy the first part, and replace the second with your own game code.

Switch to the *GameManager.m* implementation file and replace the code with the contents of Listing 7.3.

Listing 7.3   **GameManager.m implementation—singleton portion**

```objc
//   GameManager.m
//   SpaceViking
//
#import "GameManager.h"
#import "GameScene.h"
#import "MainMenuScene.h"
#import "OptionsScene.h"
#import "CreditsScene.h"
#import "IntroScene.h"
#import "LevelCompleteScene.h"

@implementation GameManager
static GameManager* _sharedGameManager = nil;              // 1
@synthesize isMusicON;
@synthesize isSoundEffectsON;
@synthesize hasPlayerDied;

+(GameManager*)sharedGameManager {
    @synchronized([GameManager class])                     // 2
    {
        if(!_sharedGameManager)                            // 3
            [[self alloc] init];
        return _sharedGameManager;                         // 4
    }
    return nil;
}


+(id)alloc
{
    @synchronized ([GameManager class])                    // 5
    {
        NSAssert(_sharedGameManager == nil,
                @"Attempted to allocate a second instance of the Game
Manager singleton");                                       // 6
        _sharedGameManager = [super alloc];
        return _sharedGameManager;                         // 7
    }
    return nil;
}
                                                           // 8
-(id)init {
    self = [super init];
    if (self != nil) {
        // Game Manager initialized
```

```
            CCLOG(@"Game Manager Singleton, init");
            isMusicON = YES;
            isSoundEffectsON = YES;
            hasPlayerDied = NO;
            currentScene = kNoSceneUninitialized;
        }
        return self;
}
```

The singleton code has one purpose, to ensure that there is only one instance of GameManager allocated and running in your game at any time; hence the "single" part of the name. The code lines in Listing 7.3 carry out the following:

1. Declares a static object of type GameManager and initializes it to nil. This is the object that gets sent back to calling classes once GameManager is initialized.

2. Defines a synchronized block. This ensures that even if two class instances call this method at the same time, only one will go through at a time. This code becomes really important when you have a multithreaded app or game and you have the risk of executing the same code block by two different class instances (such as a scene and another object).

3. If the sharedManager is nil, this line allocates and initializes it. The sharedManager is the GameManager instance that gets returned by the Game-Manager class. If this sounds confusing, just remember that this code simply ensures that the GameManager class creates and returns only one instance of the GameManager, much the same way iOS creates only one instance of your Application Delegate.

4. Returns the newly allocated and initialized GameManager instance.

5. Allocates the memory needed for an instance of GameManager. This method is called by the sharedManager method in step 3. This method is surrounded by the @synchronized directive so that it can be executed by only one thread at a time.

6. An NSAssert to ensure that the GameManager instance is nil or nonexistent before an attempt is made to allocate it. As the message indicates, the NSAssert will stop execution if a second instance of GameManager is being allocated, as it would no longer be a singleton.

7. Returns the newly allocated instance of GameManager.

8. Initializes the instance variables of GameManager, including the default for the Music and Sound Effects options. The init method is the same as the other classes you have written for *Space Viking*; hopefully, by this point you can spot and repeat the init method pattern from memory.

When looking over Listing 7.3, keep in mind that a singleton is just like other classes, except that within your game there can be only one instance of the class. With the singleton portion out of the way, copy the contents of Listing 7.4 into GameManager's init method.

Listing 7.4   GameManager.m implementation—runSceneWithID

```
-(void)runSceneWithID:(SceneTypes)sceneID {
    SceneTypes oldScene = currentScene;
    currentScene = sceneID;
    id sceneToRun = nil;
    switch (sceneID) {
        case kMainMenuScene:
            sceneToRun = [MainMenuScene node];
            break;
        case kOptionsScene:
            sceneToRun = [OptionsScene node];
            break;
        case kCreditsScene:
            sceneToRun = [CreditsScene node];
            break;
        case kIntroScene:
            sceneToRun = [IntroScene node];
            break;
        case kLevelCompleteScene:
            sceneToRun = [LevelCompleteScene node];
            break;
        case kGameLevel1:
            sceneToRun = [GameScene node];
            break;

        case kGameLevel2:
            // Placeholder for Level 2
            break;
        case kGameLevel3:
            // Placeholder for Level 3
            break;
        case kGameLevel4:
            // Placeholder for Level 4
            break;
        case kGameLevel5:
            // Placeholder for Level 5
            break;
        case kCutSceneForLevel2:
            // Placeholder for Platform Level
            break;
```

```
            default:
                CCLOG(@"Unknown ID, cannot switch scenes");
                return;
                break;
        }

    if (sceneToRun == nil) {
            // Revert back, since no new scene was found
            currentScene = oldScene;
            return;
        }

    // Menu Scenes have a value of < 100
        if (sceneID < 100) {
            if (UI_USER_INTERFACE_IDIOM() != UIUserInterfaceIdiomPad) {
                CGSize screenSize =
                [CCDirector sharedDirector].winSizeInPixels;
                if (screenSize.width == 960.0f) {
                    // iPhone 4 Retina
                    [sceneToRun setScaleX:0.9375f];
                    [sceneToRun setScaleY:0.8333f];
                    CCLOG(@"GM:Scaling for iPhone 4 (retina)");

                } else {
                    [sceneToRun setScaleX:0.4688f];
                    [sceneToRun setScaleY:0.4166f];
                    CCLOG(@"GM:Scaling for iPhone 3G(non-retina)");
                }
            }
        }

        if ([[CCDirector sharedDirector] runningScene] == nil) {
            [[CCDirector sharedDirector] runWithScene:sceneToRun];

        } else {
            [[CCDirector sharedDirector] replaceScene:sceneToRun];
        }
}
```

The GameManager singleton asks the Cocos2D Director to switch between
different scenes, from the MainMenu, to LevelComplete, to Gameplay. The
runSceneWithID method is what controls the scene to switch to, and it can be
called from any scene. The switch statement initializes the new scene to be displayed.
The if block at the end of the function checks to see if the director is already running a scene, and if so, it calls replaceScene with the new scene. The check for

UI_USER_INTERFACE_IDIOM() determines if *Space Viking* is not running on the iPad and then applies a scaling down to the entire scene. Since the scene contains the layer and the sprites, everything gets scaled down in one call. The menu scenes contain very few images, so scaling down iPad-sized images provides a savings on the size of *Space Viking*. Unlike the other checks for UI_USER_INTERFACE_IDIOM(), here you are scaling if the game detects it is *not* running on the iPad. If you have a lot of images for your menus, you may decide to use iPhone and iPhone4 (-hd)-sized images, just as is done in the gameplay scenes.

> **Warning**
>
> The issue of when to use runScene and replaceScene is a common source of frustration to developers starting out with Cocos2D. runScene can be called only if the director is not currently running a scene, while replaceScene is called when there is already a scene being displayed. The if statement at the end of runSceneWithID takes care of calling the proper director method by checking to see if the director is currently running a scene.

The last part of the GameManager implementation deals with opening Mobile-Safari to one of the links from the MainMenu or other menus. Paste the contents of Listing 7.5 into the runSceneWithID method in *GameManager.m*.

Listing 7.5   **GameManager.m openSiteWithLinkType method**

```
-(void)openSiteWithLinkType:(LinkTypes)linkTypeToOpen {
    NSURL *urlToOpen = nil;
    if (linkTypeToOpen == kLinkTypeBookSite) {
        CCLOG(@"Opening Book Site");
        urlToOpen =
         [NSURL URLWithString:
          @"http://www.informit.com/title/9780321735621"];
    } else if (linkTypeToOpen == kLinkTypeDeveloperSiteRod) {
        CCLOG(@"Opening Developer Site for Rod");
        urlToOpen = [NSURL URLWithString:@"http://www.prop.gr"];
    } else if (linkTypeToOpen == kLinkTypeDeveloperSiteRay) {
        CCLOG(@"Opening Developer Site for Ray");
        urlToOpen =
         [NSURL URLWithString:@"http://www.raywenderlich.com/"];
    } else if (linkTypeToOpen == kLinkTypeArtistSite) {
        CCLOG(@"Opening Artist Site");
        urlToOpen = [NSURL URLWithString:@"http://EricStevensArt.com"];
    } else if (linkTypeToOpen == kLinkTypeMusicianSite) {
        CCLOG(@"Opening Musician Site");
        urlToOpen =
         [NSURL URLWithString:@"http://www.mikeweisermusic.com/"];
```

```
    } else {
        CCLOG(@"Defaulting to Cocos2DBook.com Blog Site");
        urlToOpen =
        [NSURL URLWithString:@"http://www.cocos2dbook.com"];
    }

    if (![[UIApplication sharedApplication] openURL:urlToOpen]) {
        CCLOG(@"%@%@",@"Failed to open url:",[urlToOpen description]);
        [self runSceneWithID:kMainMenuScene];
    }
}

@end
```

The `openSiteWithLinkType` method determines which URL to open via the `linkTypeToOpen` variable and makes a call to `UIApplication` to open the URL. The call to `UIApplication` closes *Space Viking* and opens `MobileSafari`, navigating to the URL sent via the `openURL` call. If this call fails, the game is returned to the `MainMenu`.

> **Warning**
>
> The code you have entered so far will not compile because you have yet to create the classes for the `MainMenu`, `Options`, `Credits`, and `LevelComplete` scenes. The error dialogs in Xcode should disappear as soon as you create these classes.

The next section covers the basics for the different `CCMenu` classes that make up the menu system in Cocos2D. You will use the `CCMenu` classes to create the `MainMenu`, `Options`, `Credits`, and `LevelComplete` scenes.

Menus in Cocos2D

Cocos2D has a built-in menu system that you can use to create the menus for your game, and that is what you will use to create the Main Menu and Credits screens for *Space Viking*. A similar hierarchy to how `CCLayers` are children of `CCScenes` exists in `CCMenu`. The classes are as follows:

- **CCMenu**

  The main class driving a menu, it contains the menu list items that represent your text, buttons, and toggles. The `CCMenu` is what you create last and add to your `CCLayer`.

- **CCMenuAtlasFont**

  A bitmapped font atlas class, used to create a text string to act as a text button onscreen.

- **CCMenuItemFont**

  A menu item class that can display a text string you want to display onscreen to act as a text button.

- **CCMenuItemImage**

  An image button composed of a normal and active/pressed-down image.

- **CCMenuItemLabel**

  A button that uses a `CCLabelTTF` to display the text.

- **CCMenuItemSprite**

  Similar to the `CCMenuItemImage` class except it uses already created `CCSprites` for the normal and active/pressed-down images.

- **CCMenuItemToggle**

  A toggle switch made of text or a label. When pressed, it switches between the two text options or toggles. The Music and Sound Effects On/Off menu items in the Options scene are examples of `CCMenuItemToggle`.

`CCMenuItems` act as buttons by calling a selector for methods in your code. If this sounds confusing, do not worry: you will see it in action in the next section. In a nutshell, it means that for each `CCMenuItem` press, one of your methods will get called. In that method you will then carry out the necessary action, such as switching the scene.

Scene Organization and Images

In the next section you create several scenes and layers to support all of the menus in *Space Viking*. In order to avoid a jumbled mess of scenes and layers, you should set up groups in Xcode to keep the new scenes and layers organized.

In your *SpaceViking* project

1. Select the *Scenes* group and right-click, selecting **Add > New Group**.

2. Label the new group *Intro* inside of the *Scenes* group.

3. Repeat the steps to create the groups *MainMenu*, *Options*, *Credits*, *LevelComplete*, and *Scene1*.

4. Move the *GameScene.h* and *GameScene.m* files into the *Scene1* group.

5. Move the *Layers* group you created previously inside of the *Scene1* group.

Your newly created groups should look like Figure 7.2.

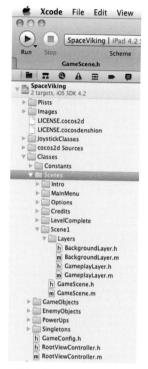

Figure 7.2   Scenes groups in Xcode

Adding Images and Fonts for the Menus

The various menus in *Space Viking* require a new set of images in addition to what you have used up to now. In the resources file you downloaded for this chapter, you will find two new folders: *Menus* and *Fonts*. Use the following steps to add the new images and new font atlas needed into your *SpaceViking* project.

1. In Xcode, select the *Images* group, right-click, and select **Add Files**.
2. Navigate to the directory where you downloaded the resources for this chapter and select the *Menus* folder and click **Add**.
3. Repeat Step 2 for the *Fonts* folder.
4. Move the *SpaceVikingFont.fnt* and *SpaceVikingFont.png* files you created in Chapter 6 inside of the *Fonts* group in Xcode.

Figure 7.3 shows the *Images* group in Xcode with the *Menus* and *Fonts* subfolders added.

With your *SpaceViking* project organized, you are ready to move on to creating the Main Menu classes.

Figure 7.3   Menu and fonts images in Xcode Images group

Creating the Main Menu

The Main Menu serves as the model for the menus in *Space Viking*. Once you understand how it works, you can have confidence in adding menus to your own games. You will first create the CCMenuItems, and then a CCMenu object that represents the entire menu that will be created and added to your scenes.

Creating the MainMenuScene

To start, select the *MainMenu* group in the Groups and Files tab.

1. Right-click and select **New File.**
2. Right-click and, from the contextual menu, select **New File**. Choose the **Cocoa Touch category** under iOS and **Objective-C class** as the file type, and click **Next**.
3. For the Subclass field, enter *CCScene* and click **Next**.
4. Enter *MainMenuScene.m* for the filename and click **Save**.
5. Create the *MainMenuLayer.m* class by following steps 1 to 3 but entering *CCLayer* for the Subclass field and *MainMenuLayer.m* for the filename.

Open the *MainMenuScene.h* header file and replace the template code with the contents of Listing 7.6.

Listing 7.6   MainMenuScene.h header file

```
//    MainMenuScene.h
//    SpaceViking
//
#import <Foundation/Foundation.h>
#import "cocos2d.h"
#import "MainMenuLayer.h"
```

```
@interface MainMenuScene : CCScene {
    MainMenuLayer *mainMenuLayer;
}
@end
```

The `MainMenu` scene is just a container object to hold the `MainMenuLayer` class. In the header file you can see the declaration for the `MainMenuLayer` instance variable.

Switch to the *MainMenu.m* implementation file and copy the code in Listing 7.7 in place of the template-generated code.

Listing 7.7   **MainMenuScene.m implementation file**

```
//    MainMenuScene.m
//    SpaceViking
//
#import "MainMenuScene.h"

@implementation MainMenuScene
-(id)init {
    self = [super init];
    if (self != nil) {
        mainMenuLayer = [MainMenuLayer node];
        [self addChild:mainMenuLayer];
    }
    return self;
}
@end
```

The `MainMenuScene` implementation file is just an `init` method that sets up the `MainMenuLayer` and adds it to the `MainMenuScene` as a child. All of the actual menu buttons and background images and animations are in the `MainMenuLayer`.

MainMenuLayer class

The `MainMenuLayer` is the class that contains the logic to power the Main Menu buttons, scene selections, and a background animation of Ole floating in space. To start, open the *MainMenuLayer.h* header file and replace the code with the contents of Listing 7.8.

Listing 7.8   **MainMenuLayer.h header file**

```
//    MainMenuLayer.h
//    SpaceViking
//
#import <Foundation/Foundation.h>
#import "cocos2d.h"
```

```
#import "Constants.h"
#import "GameManager.h"

@interface MainMenuLayer : CCLayer {
    CCMenu *mainMenu;
    CCMenu *sceneSelectMenu;
}
@end
```

In the header file of `MainMenuLayer` are two instance variables to cover the Main Menu and the scene selection menu. There is also an include of the *GameManager.h* header file so that the `MainMenuLayer` can call `GameManager` directly. In the implementation file is where everything comes together. Listing 7.9 shows the beginning portion of the *MainMenuLayer.m* class file. Make sure you copy the contents of Listings 7.9 through 7.13 into the *MainMenuLayer.m* class file.

Listing 7.9　MainMenuLayer.m (part 1: private methods)

```
//  MainMenuLayer.m
//  SpaceViking
//
#import "MainMenuLayer.h"
@interface MainMenuLayer()
-(void)displayMainMenu;
-(void)displaySceneSelection;
@end

@implementation MainMenuLayer
```

The first thing you may notice in Listing 7.9 is the `@interface` declaration inside of the implementation file. If you are thinking that `@interface` declarations normally belong in the header files, you are correct. Objective-C does not have explicit support for private class methods: any methods you declare in your header file are considered public methods. In order to have private methods, you need to include their declarations in the .m implementation file in an `@interface` section before the `@implementation` section.

In some of the previous code in *Space Viking* you have not had to add explicit private declarations for your methods; they have always preceded the calls to them in the class source code files. The private method–style declaration is really useful if you have method calls that may precede the implementation of those methods. An example would be if you had a call to `[self displayMainMenu]` before you defined the implementation of the `displayMainMenu` method in your code.

The next section of `MainMenuLayer` covers the calls to show the Options Menu, open the book site, and play the first scene in the game. Add the contents of Listing 7.10 to your *MainMenuLayer.m* class.

Listing 7.10   MainMenuLayer.m (part 2: buyBook, showOptions, playScene)

```
-(void)buyBook {
    [[GameManager sharedGameManager]
                    openSiteWithLinkType:kLinkTypeBookSite];
}

-(void)showOptions {
    CCLOG(@"Show the Options screen");
    [[GameManager sharedGameManager] runSceneWithID:kOptionsScene];
}

-(void)playScene:(CCMenuItemFont*)itemPassedIn {
    if ([itemPassedIn tag] == 1) {
        CCLOG(@"Tag 1 found, Scene 1");
        [[GameManager sharedGameManager] runSceneWithID:kIntroScene];
    } else {
        CCLOG(@"Tag was: %d", [itemPassedIn tag]);
        CCLOG(@"Placeholder for next chapters");
    }
}
```

The buyBook method is just a call to the openSiteWithLink method you declared in GameManager, which exits *Space Viking* and launches MobileSafari. The showOptions method places a call to GameManager to swap the MainMenu scene with the Options scene. The GameManager will initialize the Options scene and load it in place of the currently running MainMenu scene.

The playScene method launches the GameplayScene depending on which of the three levels the player has selected. In Listing 7.10 you can see the code for the first level you already created and placeholders for the next two scenes you will be creating later in this book. To understand exactly how playScene is called from the MainMenu scene, you need to refer to the code in Listings 7.11, 7.12, and 7.13.

Listing 7.11   MainMenuLayer.m (part 3: displayMainMenu)

```
-(void)displayMainMenu {
    CGSize screenSize = [CCDirector sharedDirector].winSize;
    if (sceneSelectMenu != nil) {
        [sceneSelectMenu removeFromParentAndCleanup:YES];
    }
    // Main Menu
    CCMenuItemImage *playGameButton = [CCMenuItemImage
        itemFromNormalImage:@"PlayGameButtonNormal.png"
        selectedImage:@"PlayGameButtonSelected.png"
        disabledImage:nil
        target:self
        selector:@selector(displaySceneSelection)];
```

```
CCMenuItemImage *buyBookButton = [CCMenuItemImage
  itemFromNormalImage:@"BuyBookButtonNormal.png"
  selectedImage:@"BuyBookButtonSelected.png"
  disabledImage:nil
  target:self
  selector:@selector(buyBook)];

CCMenuItemImage *optionsButton = [CCMenuItemImage
  itemFromNormalImage:@"OptionsButtonNormal.png"
  selectedImage:@"OptionsButtonSelected.png"
  disabledImage:nil
  target:self
  selector:@selector(showOptions)];

mainMenu = [CCMenu
  menuWithItems:playGameButton,buyBookButton,optionsButton,nil];
[mainMenu alignItemsVerticallyWithPadding:
         screenSize.height * 0.059f];
[mainMenu setPosition:
         ccp(screenSize.width * 2,
             screenSize.height / 2)];
id moveAction =
    [CCMoveTo actionWithDuration:1.2f
             position:ccp(screenSize.width * 0.85f,
                          screenSize.height/2)];
id moveEffect = [CCEaseIn actionWithAction:moveAction rate:1.0f];
[mainMenu runAction:moveEffect];
[self addChild:mainMenu z:0 tag:kMainMenuTagValue];
}
```

The `displayMainMenu` method creates the `CCMenuItems` and the `CCMenu` needed for the Main Menu and adds the menu to the `MainMenuLayer` itself. It also adds an animation at the end to slide the menu buttons from right to left.

The key to remember is that a `CCMenu` is just a collection of `CCMenuItems`, and those menu items are what define the various buttons or text labels you will have as part of your menu. Since the `CCMenu` contains all of the menu items, it controls the alignment and position of those items. By default, all of the menu items are placed at the center of the `CCMenu`. The line `[mainMenu alignItemsVerticallyWithPadding:60.0f];` aligns all of the `CCMenuItems` vertically with a padding of 60 pixels between each of them. There is an equivalent method for aligning the menu items horizontally if your menu is left to right instead of top to bottom.

There are two more methods you need to include in *MainMenuLayer.m*: the `displaySceneSelection` and `init` methods. Be sure to copy the entire contents of those two methods into your *MainMenuLayer.m* file from Listings 7.12 and 7.13.

Listing 7.12   **MainMenuLayer (part 4: displaySceneSelection)**

```
-(void)displaySceneSelection {
    CGSize screenSize = [CCDirector sharedDirector].winSize;
    if (mainMenu != nil) {
        [mainMenu removeFromParentAndCleanup:YES];
    }

    CCLabelBMFont *playScene1Label =
    [CCLabelBMFont labelWithString:@"Ole Awakes!"
     fntFile:@"VikingSpeechFont64.fnt"];
    CCMenuItemLabel *playScene1 =
    [CCMenuItemLabel itemWithLabel:playScene1Label target:self
                        selector:@selector(playScene:)];
    [playScene1 setTag:1];

    CCLabelBMFont *playScene2Label =
    [CCLabelBMFont labelWithString:@"Dogs of Loki!"
     fntFile:@"VikingSpeechFont64.fnt"];
    CCMenuItemLabel *playScene2 =
    [CCMenuItemLabel itemWithLabel:playScene2Label target:self
                        selector:@selector(playScene:)];
    [playScene2 setTag:2];

    CCLabelBMFont *playScene3Label =
    [CCLabelBMFont labelWithString:@"Descent Into Hades!"
     fntFile:@"VikingSpeechFont64.fnt"];
    CCMenuItemLabel *playScene3 = [CCMenuItemLabel
itemWithLabel:playScene3Label target:self
                        selector:@selector(playScene:)];
    [playScene3 setTag:3];

    CCLabelBMFont *playScene4Label =
     [CCLabelBMFont labelWithString:@"Descent Into Hades!"
      fntFile:@"VikingSpeechFont64.fnt"];
    CCMenuItemLabel *playScene4 = [CCMenuItemLabel
     itemWithLabel:playScene4Label target:self
     selector:@selector(playScene:)];
    [playScene4 setTag:4];

    CCLabelBMFont *playScene5Label =
    [CCLabelBMFont labelWithString:@"Escape!"
     fntFile:@"VikingSpeechFont64.fnt"];
    CCMenuItemLabel *playScene5 = [CCMenuItemLabel
     itemWithLabel:playScene5Label target:self
     selector:@selector(playScene:)];
    [playScene5 setTag:5];
```

```
CCLabelBMFont *backButtonLabel =
[CCLabelBMFont labelWithString:@"Back"
                        fntFile:@"VikingSpeechFont64.fnt"];
CCMenuItemLabel *backButton =
[CCMenuItemLabel itemWithLabel:backButtonLabel target:self
                        selector:@selector(displayMainMenu)];


CCLabelBMFont *backButtonLabel =
 [CCLabelBMFont labelWithString:@"Back"
   fntFile:@"VikingSpeechFont64.fnt"];
CCMenuItemLabel *backButton =
[CCMenuItemLabel itemWithLabel:backButtonLabel target:self
                        selector:@selector(displayMainMenu)];


sceneSelectMenu = [CCMenu menuWithItems:playScene1,
                    playScene2,playScene3,playScene4,
                    playScene5,backButton,nil];
[sceneSelectMenu alignItemsVerticallyWithPadding:
   screenSize.height * 0.059f];
[sceneSelectMenu setPosition:ccp(screenSize.width * 2,
                                  screenSize.height / 2)];

id moveAction = [CCMoveTo actionWithDuration:0.5f
                  position:ccp(screenSize.width * 0.75f,
                                screenSize.height/2)];
id moveEffect = [CCEaseIn actionWithAction:moveAction rate:1.0f];
[sceneSelectMenu runAction:moveEffect];
[self addChild:sceneSelectMenu z:1 tag:kSceneMenuTagValue];
}
```

In the beginning of the displaySceneSelection, the code checks to see if mainMenu is initialized (it should be), and if so, removes it from the layer.

The next few lines deal with creating the text labels for each of the level selection tags. In *Space Viking* you will be using the free Vinland font for the text labels. In the book's resource files for this chapter, you will find the font map and bitmap texture files for the Vinland font at size 64 and with a red color. The playScene1Label uses these font files to create a bitmapped font label of the "Ole Awakes!" text in Vinland size 64. These lines are identical to the debug fonts you created in the previous chapter for the EnemyRobot. Once the bitmap font label (playScene1Label) is created, it is added to a CCMenuItemLabel, which has a selector set to the playScene method.

The next line is important: it sets the tag value for the CCMenuItemLabel, 1 for this scene, 2 for the second scene, and so on. Toward the end of the display-SceneSelection method, the CCMenu is instantiated with the three scene selection CCMenuItemLabels. Listing 7.13 shows the init method.

Listing 7.13   **MainMenuLayer (part 5: init method)**

```
-(id)init {
    self = [super init];
    if (self != nil) {
        CGSize screenSize = [CCDirector sharedDirector].winSize;

        CCSprite *background =
          [CCSprite spriteWithFile:@"MainMenuBackground.png"];
        [background setPosition:ccp(screenSize.width/2,
                                    screenSize.height/2)];
        [self addChild:background];
        [self displayMainMenu];

        CCSprite *viking =
          [CCSprite spriteWithFile:@"VikingFloating.png"];
        [viking setPosition:ccp(screenSize.width * 0.35f,
                                screenSize.height * 0.45f)];
        [self addChild:viking];

        id rotateAction = [CCEaseElasticInOut actionWithAction:
                              [CCRotateBy actionWithDuration:5.5f
                                          angle:360]];

        id scaleUp = [CCScaleTo actionWithDuration:2.0f scale:1.5f];
        id scaleDown = [CCScaleTo actionWithDuration:2.0f scale:0.5f];

        [viking runAction:[CCRepeatForever actionWithAction:
                              [CCSequence
                               actions:scaleUp,scaleDown,nil]]];

        [viking runAction:
          [CCRepeatForever actionWithAction:rotateAction]];
    }
    return self;
}
@end
```

The first key part of the init method is the call to [self displayMainMenu], which creates the Main Menu buttons and places them onscreen. The rest of Listing 7.13 creates a sprite of the Viking floating in space and adds some repeating actions to him. The Viking will rotate and at the same time scale up and then down. In previous chapters you saw actions created in compound or nested sets, such as the actions for the space cargo ship. One thing to observe here is that CCNodes, including CCSprites, can run more than one action at a time. In the floating Viking, he is running a CCSequenceAction, scaling up and then down, and at the same time running a CCRotateBy action to cause him to spin around.

Additional Menus and GameplayLayer

The Intro, Credits, LevelComplete, and Options menus are set up in the same way as the MainMenu, each with its own CCScene and CCLayer classes. The Credits menu consists of just three links to the people who had a part in creating the *Space Viking* game. The LevelComplete and Intro have two key points worth noting in detail. In addition to these three menu scenes, there is a minor change to your existing GameplayLayer.m class for it to call GameManager and transition to the LevelComplete scene.

Importing the Intro, LevelComplete, Credits, and Options Scenes and Layers

The remaining menu scenes and layers are very similar to the MainMenu that you created earlier in this chapter. To save you some time typing in similar code, these classes are included as part of the resources for this chapter.

Locate the folder to which you downloaded the resources for this chapter and:

1. Drag the *IntroScene.h*, *IntroScene.m*, *IntroLayer.h*, and *IntroLayer.m* files into Xcode under the *Intro* subfolder inside of the *Scenes* group.

2. Drag the *LevelCompleteScene.h*, *LevelCompleteScene.m*, *LevelCompleteLayer.h*, and *LevelCompleteLayer.m* files into Xcode under the *LevelComplete* subfolder inside of the *Scenes* group.

3. Drag the *CreditsScene.h*, *CreditsScene.m*, *CreditsLayer.h*, and *CreditsLater.m* files into Xcode under the *Credits* subfolder inside of the *Scenes* group.

4. Drag the *OptionsScene.h*, *OptionsScene.m*, *OptionsLayer.h*, and *OptionsLayer.m* files into Xcode under the *Options* subfolder inside of the *Scenes* group.

Your *SpaceViking* project should look like Figure 7.4. Feel free to look through these classes. At this point you should have a good understanding of how they work based on what you've learned in previous chapters.

If you press ⌘-B, your *SpaceViking* project should now compile with no errors. If you encounter any errors or warnings, check that you have imported all of the files. The next step is to make changes to the Gameplay layer and to the SpaceViking-AppDelegate so they can support the new scenes.

GameplayLayer

There is a small addition to the GameplayLayer class in order to support the new GameManager and to transition to the LevelComplete scene once the Viking or RadarDish object is dead. In the Gameplayer you wrote in the previous chapters,

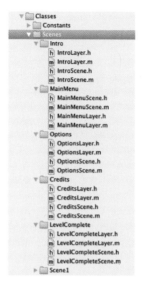

Figure 7.4   Space Viking after all of the menu classes have been added

there was no code to transition out of game play if the `Viking` died or the `RadarDish` was destroyed. To add these changes, start by opening the *GameplayLayer.h* header file.

In the import section, add an import for the *GameManager.h* header file, so that you have this line among the other import statements:

```
#import "GameManager.h"
```

The `import` statement allows the `GameplayLayer` to call upon the `GameManager` singleton and transition *Space Viking* from Gameplay to Level Complete.

Open the *GameplayLayer.m* implementation file and add the code shown in Listing 7.14 to the `update:(ccTime)deltaTime` method so that it can call the `GameManager` singleton when the `Viking` dies or the `RadarDish` is destroyed.

Listing 7.14   GameplayLayer.m update:(ccTime)deltaTime method

```
-(void) update:(ccTime)deltaTime
{
    // ...(See source for previous lines)
    // Chapter 7 Additions
    // Check to see if the Viking is dead
    GameCharacter *tempChar = (GameCharacter*)
                    [sceneSpriteBatchNode
                        getChildByTag:kVikingSpriteTagValue];
    if ((([tempChar characterState] == kStateDead) &&
        ([tempChar numberOfRunningActions] == 0)) {
```

```
            [[GameManager sharedGameManager] setHasPlayerDied:YES];
            [[GameManager sharedGameManager]
                    runSceneWithID:kLevelCompleteScene];
        }


        // Check to see if the RadarDish is dead
        tempChar = (GameCharacter*)[sceneSpriteBatchNode
                        getChildByTag:kRadarDishTagValue];
        if (([tempChar characterState] == kStateDead) &&
            ([tempChar numberOfRunningActions] == 0)) {
            [[GameManager sharedGameManager]
                runSceneWithID:kLevelCompleteScene];
        }
    }
}
```

If the code in Listing 7.14 looks long and convoluted, it is only because the
GamePlayLayer does not have a direct link to the Viking or RadarDish, since they
are both children of the CCSpriteBachNode called sceneSpriteBatchNode. The
GamePlayLayer pulls the two objects from the sceneSpriteBatchNode using the
unique integer tags you assigned to the Viking and RadarDish when they were
created.

First the Viking is checked to see if he is in a dead state and is not currently running any actions. If you are wondering what dead actions a Viking would be doing, it
is the death animation of the Viking turning to smoke and just a helmet falling to the
ground. You don't want the GamePlayLayer to transition to LevelComplete until
the Viking death animation is complete.

The next check is to see if the RadarDish is dead and not currently playing the
blowing up animation.

If either the Viking or RadarDish are dead, the GameManager is called and
asked to replace the GameScene with the LevelCompleteScene.

In your games you may have a similar setup, with your gameplay transitioning to a
game over or level complete when the player dies.

Changes to SpaceVikingAppDelegate

Finally, there is one more change to the SpaceVikingAppDelegate to support having the GameManager, not the Application Delegate, control the Cocos2D Director.

Open the *SpaceVikingAppDelegate.m* implementation file and add the import statement for the GameManager class:

```
#import "GameManager.h"
```

In the applicationDidFinishLaunching method, replace the runWithScene
call with the following line:

```
[[GameManager sharedGameManager] runSceneWithID:kMainMenuScene];
```

While you are in the `SpaceVikingAppDelegate`, you can remove the imports for `HelloWorldScene` and `GameScene`, as they are no longer called from the Application Delegate directly.

With all of the changes in this chapter in place, click **Run** and test your *SpaceViking* project. It should start with the Main Menu with the Viking rotating around the logo. If you play the first level and destroy the `RadarDish` or Ole dies, you will see the `LevelComplete` scene, and touching anywhere on `LevelComplete` will take you back to the `MainMenu`.

For the More Curious: The IntroLayer and LevelComplete Classes

The `IntroLayer` class has some specific functionality that differs from just driving a menu. The `IntroLayer` pages through several images before starting the gameplay, while the `LevelComplete` class displays different images depending on whether Ole beat a level or died trying.

Looking in the `init` method of the *IntroLayer.m* class, you will see the following line:

```
self.isTouchEnabled = YES;
```

This line alerts Cocos2D that you want to receive touch events on the `IntroLayer`. In `IntroLayer` you are only concerned with a touch began notification, as it means the player wants to skip ahead of the introduction animation. Since Cocos2D already knows that the `IntroLayer` is to receive touch events, all you need to implement is the following method:

```
-(void)ccTouchesBegan:(NSSet *)touches withEvent:(UIEvent *)event {
    CCLOG(@"Touches received, skipping intro");
    [self startGamePlay];
}
```

All that `startGamePlay` does is call `[[GameManager sharedGameManager] runSceneWithID:kGameLevel1];`. There is an animation that plays in the intro scene, and when it finishes, there is a `CCCallFunc` action that calls the `startGamePlay` method. If you followed the logic so far, the `IntroLayer` just plays an intro animation, and if the animation finishes or the player touches the screen, the `startGamePlay` method is called, calling the `GameManager` to swap the intro scene out and start the `GamePlayScene`.

If you wanted to know when a player moves a touch or lifts a finger off the screen, you can add the `ccTouchesMoved`, `ccTouchesEnded`, and `ccTouchesCancelled` methods to your layers. Be sure to copy the full *IntroScene.h*, *IntroScene.m*, *IntroLayer.h*, and *IntroLayer.m* files into the *Intro* groups in your *SpaceViking* project.

LevelCompleteLayer Class

The `LevelCompleteLayer` is set up similarly to the `IntroLayer`. It also responds to touches by asking the `GameManager` to swap the `MainMenu` in place of `Level-Complete`. There is one benefit to having the `GameManager` singleton that has not yet been discussed, and that is to have it act as a single place to store what's happening in the game. Read that last line again: the `GameManager` singleton is the one place where you will store the Viking's score, what happened on the last level, and any other data you may want to access in various scenes. If you recall Listing 7.2 when you set up *GameManager.m*, it had the `hasPlayerDied`. In a moment, you will see how the `GameplayLayer` sets that variable. Listing 7.15 shows how it is used in the `LevelCompleteLayer`.

Listing 7.15   **LevelCompleteLayer.m—how hasPlayerDied is used**

```
BOOL didPlayerDie = [[GameManager sharedGameManager] hasPlayerDied];
      CCSprite *background = nil;
      if (didPlayerDie) {
          background =
          [CCSprite spriteWithFile:@"LevelCompleteDead.png"];
      } else {
          background =
          [CCSprite spriteWithFile:@"LevelCompleteAlive.png"];
      }
```

If the `GameManager` `hasPlayerDied` indicates that the Viking has died on the game right before `LevelComplete` was shown, then the `LevelCompleteDead` image is used as the background; otherwise, the `LevelCompleteAlive` image is shown. Figure 7.5 shows these two images.

Figure 7.5   LevelComplete background image when the Viking lives and dies

The use of the Singleton pattern for a game manager can be greatly beneficial in keeping your game data in one place and at the same time accessible by any class in your game. If you want to save the player's progress or create a new level based on how the player did on the previous level, you can do that with a singleton game manager.

> **Note**
>
> While the `CreditsScene` and `Layer` classes are not covered in this chapter, they contain the same basic Cocos2D objects and calls you have already seen in `MainMenu`.

Summary

In this chapter you learned about the `CCMenu` and `CCMenuItem` classes and how to wire menus together in *Space Viking*. More important, you learned about creating a `GameManager` singleton and how to talk to it from any scene in your game. While writing your own games, feel free to refer back to this chapter for code and techniques you can reuse in your game singleton and how to connect scenes together. In the next chapter you learn how to add music and sound to *Space Viking*. To turn up the volume, turn the page.

Challenges

1. Add a counter to the `LevelComplete` scene to show how many `EnemyRobots` Ole has disposed off.

> **Hint**
>
> Add a variable to track it in `GameManager`, and call it from `GameplayLayer` and `LevelCompleteLayer`.

2. Add a label showing a "Level Cleared" message when Ole destroys the `RadarDish`.

> **Hint**
>
> Look at the game start `CCLabelTTF` that comes onscreen when gameplay begins. Could it be changed and reused?

Pump Up the Volume!

In the last chapter you learned how to create menus and link scenes together in your games. Now it is time to head back into the gameplay and add music and sound effects to Space Viking. In this chapter you will learn how to use the audio engine included with Cocos2D and how you can add audio to your own games. Read on to hear what Ole the Viking sounds like, and find out what sounds break the silence of the alien planet.

Introducing CocosDenshion

Apple provides two great frameworks to play audio on iOS devices, `AVAudioPlayer` and OpenAL. `AVAudioPlayer` is a quick and simple way to play audio but gives you only limited control, while OpenAL is a lower-level API with more features.

Cocos2D comes bundled with the CocosDenshion sound engine, which is an easy-to-use wrapper for both frameworks. CocosDenshion was created by Steve Oldmeadow and has been included with Cocos2D since the early days. Recently CocosDenshion has incorporated a new, simpler API called `SimpleAudioEngine`, which you use in this chapter. CocosDenshion leverages the power of `AVAudioPlayer` and OpenAL for you, so you don't have to dive down into the lower-level sound APIs unless you want to.

Just like the rest of the Cocos2D source code, the source for CocosDenshion is included with Cocos2D and you are encouraged to look through it. While Cocos2D uses the `CC` namespace for all of its classes, CocosDenshion uses the `CD` namespace except for `SimpleAudioEngine`, which is not preceded by the letters `CD`.

What Is in a Name

`SimpleAudioEngine` was originally designed by Joao Caxaria as an interface into CocosDenshion, and the name has remained the same to indicate the origins of the API. Since you will just be using `SimpleAudioEngine`, all you need to know is that this is the easiest way to leverage CocosDenshion.

There are some great examples included with CocosDenshion that you might want to check out, including a game called "Tom the Turret" created by Ray Wenderlich and Steve Oldmeadow. The code for *Space Viking* borrows heavily from the Tom the Turret sample.

Importing and Setting Up the Audio Filenames

Before you can dive into coding the audio playback in *Space Viking*, you need to add the audio files to your project. In this section you also set up a series of `#define` constants for the audio filenames, as you have done with other constants in *Space Viking*.

Adding the Audio Files to Space Viking

To add background music and sound effects to *Space Viking*, you start by adding the *Sounds* folder to your *SpaceViking* Xcode project. Grab the *Sounds* folder from the resources file for this chapter and drag it into your *SpaceViking* project, selecting to copy the items into your destination folder (into your project). Your Xcode navigator should resemble Figure 8.1.

Figure 8.1   Sounds folder added to SpaceViking project

> **Warning**
>
> If you do not add the *Sounds* folder to your project and select copy items to destination folder, the audio files will not be copied into your project. Not having the audio files in your project will result in a silent *Space Viking* and a sad Ole.

Audio Constants

`SimpleAudioEngine` uses filenames as the identifier for the audio. In order not to have to list the filenames for the audio assets in multiple places, you use a *SoundEffects. plist* file to contain all of the filenames. Keeping the sound effects in a plist file makes it easy to swap out audio files later on, while only having to make the change in one place. In addition, there are just four background music tracks in *Space Viking*, and those filenames are in a set of `#defines` in *Constants.h*.

Open *Constants.h* and add the lines in Listing 8.1. The audio filenames are set up as #define statements to make it easy to switch filenames without having to find every reference to them in the code. Do not worry about hand-typing all of these #defines; in the resources folder for this chapter is a file called *AddtionsToConstants-HeaderFile.rtf* that includes all of them.

Listing 8.1   **#defines for audio filenames in Constants.h**

```
// Audio Items
#define AUDIO_MAX_WAITTIME 150

typedef enum {
    kAudioManagerUninitialized=0,
    kAudioManagerFailed=1,
    kAudioManagerInitializing=2,
    kAudioManagerInitialized=100,
    kAudioManagerLoading=200,
    kAudioManagerReady=300

} GameManagerSoundState;

// Audio Constants
#define SFX_NOTLOADED NO
#define SFX_LOADED YES

#define PLAYSOUNDEFFECT(...) \
[[GameManager sharedGameManager] playSoundEffect:@#__VA_ARGS__]

#define STOPSOUNDEFFECT(...) \
[[GameManager sharedGameManager] stopSoundEffect:__VA_ARGS__]

// Background Music
// Menu Scenes
#define BACKGROUND_TRACK_MAIN_MENU @"VikingPreludeV1.mp3"

// GameLevel1 (Ole Awakens)
#define BACKGROUND_TRACK_OLE_AWAKES @"SpaceDesertV2.mp3"

// Physics Puzzle Level
#define BACKGROUND_TRACK_PUZZLE @"VikingPreludeV1.mp3"

// Physics MineCart Level
#define BACKGROUND_TRACK_MINECART @"DrillBitV2.mp3"

// Physics Escape Level
#define BACKGROUND_TRACK_ESCAPE @"EscapeTheFutureV3.mp3"
```

At this point, the #defines and typedef enum declarations should be pretty familiar to you. The GameManagerSoundState type definition makes it easier to track what state the audio engine is in. In this enumeration you also declare the value of each choice. Notice how the states before "initialized" are less than 100 in value. That makes it easier later on to check whether the engine is still initializing or loading audio. The #defines serves as reference for background music filenames.

The #define PLAYSOUNDEFFECT (...) line is a macro definition that expands into a call for the playSoundEffect method in GameManager. In *Space Viking* you use the GameManager to handle the initialization of the CocosDenshion engine and to start and stop the playback of sound effects. The macro is nothing more than a shortcut to keep you from having to type out the [[[GameManager sharedGame-Manager] playSoundEffect:SFX_NAME] over and over.

The STOPSOUNDEFFECT(...) macro is a shortcut to the stopSoundEffect method in GameManager that takes the ALuint identifier of the audio effect you want to stop. You will learn more about the audio effects identifier when adding the walking sounds to the EnemyRobot and Viking later in this chapter.

If your games have a long list of filenames, you may also choose to keep them in a plist file similar to the animation frames you did in earlier chapters instead of a long list of #defines. In *Space Viking* you do just that, adding a set of methods to Game-Manager to load and unload sound effect files as you move between scenes.

Before going any further, copy the *SoundEffects.plist* file from the resources folder for this chapter into your *SpaceViking* Xcode project. Figure 8.2 shows the contents of the *SoundEffects.plist* file.

Key	Type	Value
▶ kCreditsScene	Diction...	(1 item)
▶ kCutSceneForLevel2	Diction...	(0 items)
▼ kGameLevel1	Diction...	(50 items)
ENEMYROBOT_DAMAGE	String	22k_enemy_robot_taking_damageV1.wav
ENEMYROBOT_DYING	String	22k_enemy_robot_dyingV1.wav
ENEMYROBOT_MUMBLE_1	String	22k_enemy_mumbleV1.wav
ENEMYROBOT_MUMBLE_2	String	22k_enemy_mumbleV2.wav
ENEMYROBOT_PHASERFIRE_1	String	22k_enemy_phaser_fireV1.wav
ENEMYROBOT_PHASERFIRE_2	String	22k_enemy_phaser_fireV2.wav
ENEMYROBOT_TELEPORT	String	22k_enemy_teleportV1.wav
ENEMYROBOT_WALKING_1	String	22k_enemy_walkingV1.wav
ENEMYROBOT_WALKING_2	String	22k_enemy_walkingV2.wav
SPACECARGOSHIP_CLOSE_1	String	22k_cargo_space_freighter_closeV1.wav
SPACECARGOSHIP_CLOSE_2	String	22k_cargo_space_freighter_closeV2.wav
SPACECARGOSHIP_CLOSE_3	String	22k_cargo_space_freighter_closeV3.wav
SPACECARGOSHIP_FAR	String	22k_cargo_space_freighter_farV1.wav
VIKING_CROUCHING_1	String	22k_viking_crouchingV1.wav
VIKING_CROUCHING_2	String	22k_viking_crouchingV2.wav
VIKING_CROUCHING_3	String	22k_viking_crouchingV3.wav
VIKING_CROUCHING_4	String	22k_viking_crouchingV4.wav
VIKING_CURSING_1	String	22k_viking_cursingV1.wav
VIKING_CURSING_2	String	22k_viking_cursingV2.wav
VIKING_DYING_1	String	22k_viking_dyingV1.wav
VIKING_DYING_2	String	22k_viking_dyingV2.wav

Figure 8.2   SoundEffects.plist added to the SpaceViking project

> **Warning**
>
> Be sure to copy the *SoundEffects.plist* file into your Xcode project; otherwise, *Space Viking* will not work when you reach the end of this chapter.

The code that utilizes the *SoundEffects.plist* is inside `GameManager`. Before learning about those methods, it is important to understand the two ways that audio files can be loaded into CocosDenshion.

Synchronous versus Asynchronous Loading of Audio

Music and sound files are usually the second biggest items in your games after the images. Loading them into memory for your game can take time, and the last thing you want to do is have the player encounter an unresponsive game while the sound files are being loaded. Luckily, it is easy to load sounds asynchronously in a background thread with the help of `NSOperationQueues`. This chapter covers both methods of loading audio in your games. First you learn the simpler synchronous method, and then you learn how to create an asynchronous loader method that runs in a separate thread.

Loading Audio Synchronously

Open the *GameplayLayer.h* file and add this single import for the `SimpleAudioEngine`:

```
#import "SimpleAudioEngine.h"
```

In the `@interface` definition, add this variable declaration:

```
SimpleAudioEngine *soundEngine;
```

CocosDenshion is already included with Cocos2D, and importing `SimpleAudio-Engine` is all you need to do in order to start using it in your projects.

The next step is to create a method to handle the sound initialization in `Gameplay-Layer`. Above the `init` method in *GameplayLayer.m*, create a method called `loadAudio`, as shown in Listing 8.2.

Listing 8.2   The loadAudio method in the GameplayLayer.m implementation file

```
-(void)loadAudio {
    // Loading Sounds Synchronously
    [CDSoundEngine setMixerSampleRate:CD_SAMPLE_RATE_MID];     // 1

    [[CDAudioManager sharedManager] setResignBehavior:kAMRBStopPlay
  autoHandle:YES];          // 2
```

```
    soundEngine = [SimpleAudioEngine sharedEngine];              // 3

    // 4
    [soundEngine preloadBackgroundMusic:BACKGROUND_TRACK_OLE_AWAKES];

    // 5
    [soundEngine playBackgroundMusic:BACKGROUND_TRACK_OLE_AWAKES];
}
```

The `loadAudio` method here is very simple, since it loads the music synchronously and plays it immediately after loading. The method works as follows:

1. The audio mixing rate is set up for the CocosDenshion `SoundEngine`.

   The iPhone and iPad audio hardware has the best performance when all of the audio has the same sample rate. In *Space Viking* all of the audio is set to the middle bit rate of 22,050Hz, but in your games you may want a lower bit rate to save on memory. The bit rate depends on the type of sound you need in your games.

   Xcode comes with `afconvert`, a handy utility to convert and modify the bit rate for your audio files called. You can learn more about it by typing *afconvert -h* in a terminal window. You can read more about audio converting and playback on iOS here: *http://developer.apple.com/library/ios/#codinghowtos/AudioAndVideo/*.

2. The CocosDenshion `AudioManager` is set up and instructed to automatically handle events such as the player locking the screen. If the application receives a Resign Active event from iOS, it stops playing the audio. If you do not include this line, it is up to your code to stop and restart playback when your game is interrupted or sent to the background and resumed.

3. Grab a reference to the Simple Audio Engine so that you can ask it to load and play audio.

4. Preload the background music track. This method call loads the mp3 file into the buffer and gets it ready to start playing. No sound is played yet, but it is loaded in memory and ready to go.

5. Starts playing the background music. This method call also has the option to loop the background music. By default, CocosDenshion continuously loops your background track.

Inside the `init` method of *GameplayLayer.m*, add a call to the `loadAudio` method:

```
[self loadAudio];
```

If you click **Run** now and select the Ole Awakens level, you will start to hear the background track coming in. If you run *Space Viking* on your iPad, you will notice a delay of a second or two before the level starts. That delay is caused by loading the music synchronously instead of in a background thread.

Before we get to asynchronous loading, let's quickly cover how to play sound effects. In the start of the level, let's have Ole speak a quick curse to show his frustration with his situation. You can imagine how irritated you would be, waking up in an alien world surrounded by robots. Don't worry—the curse is PG-rated and spoken in words only a Viking would know.

Add the lines shown in Listing 8.3 to your `loadAudio` method in order to play the Viking cursing sound effect.

Listing 8.3   Additions to loadAudio method showing how to play a sound effect

```
[soundEngine preloadEffect: @"22k_viking_cursingV1.wav"];
[soundEngine playEffect: @"22k_viking_cursingV1.wav"];
```

Just like the background music track, the effect sound is first preloaded into memory and set up for playing. The second line actually plays the sound effect. If you click **Run** and select the Ole Awakens level, you will hear the Viking mumble a curse at the same time the background music is playing.

At this point, you have seen how easy it is to add music and sound effects to your game with just a few simple lines. The next section deals with loading audio asynchronously. Then you will add sound effects for the `Viking`, `RadarDish`, and `EnemyRobot`.

Before moving any further, comment out the call to `[self loadAudio]` in the *GameplayLayer.m* init method. You will be handling the CocosDenshion initialization and effect playback from the `GameManager` singleton.

Loading Audio Asynchronously

In your games, you do not want the whole game to pause because you are loading audio assets from flash and into memory. Even though flash memory is fast, it is much slower than the CPU can execute code. You do not want the CPU to sit idle while it is waiting for the flash memory to return the next few bytes from your audio files. The best way to get around the freeze during loading times is to load the audio assets asynchronously in another thread.

In *Space Viking* you use an asynchronous approach to initializing CocosDenshion and loading the sound effect audio files. The CocosDenshion audio engine is initialized asynchronously, and the sound effects are loaded asynchronously as a scene starts to run. The `GameManager` controls the loading and unloading of sound effects to keep the memory footprint as small as possible. Any calls to try to play effects before they are loaded are just ignored by the `GameManager`.

You can reuse the code from this chapter if in your game you know you will be using only certain sound effects in specific parts of your game. You can set up the preloading to happen right before you need the audio, in a loading scene, or as you see here during gameplay. If you know you are not going to need a sound asset anymore, you can also unload it from memory.

Remember to remove or comment out the code you just added to *GameplayLayer.m*. You are going to have the audio set up and preloaded in the GameManager, and the individual GameObjects, such as the Viking and EnemyRobot, will take care of calling GameManager to play their audio.

Adding Audio to GameManager

For the next step you need to move the audio initialization and preloading code to GameManager. You will use NSOperationQueue to manage the background threads for you, setting up and preloading the audio in the background in just a few easy steps.

To get started, open the *GameManager.h* header file and add the **bold** lines shown in Listing 8.4.

Listing 8.4   Additions to GameManager.h

```
// GameManager.h

#import <Foundation/Foundation.h>
#import "Constants.h"
#import "SimpleAudioEngine.h"

@interface GameManager : NSObject {
    BOOL isMusicON;
    BOOL isSoundEffectsON;
    BOOL hasPlayerDied;

    // Added for audio
    BOOL hasAudioBeenInitialized;
    GameManagerSoundState managerSoundState;
    SimpleAudioEngine *soundEngine;
    NSMutableDictionary *listOfSoundEffectFiles;
    NSMutableDictionary *soundEffectsState;
}
@property (readwrite) BOOL isMusicON;
@property (readwrite) BOOL isSoundEffectsON;
@property (readwrite) BOOL hasPlayerDied;
@property (readwrite) GameManagerSoundState managerSoundState;
@property (nonatomic, retain) NSMutableDictionary
                              *listOfSoundEffectFiles;
@property (nonatomic, retain) NSMutableDictionary *soundEffectsState;
+(GameManager*)sharedGameManager; // 1
-(void)runSceneWithID:(SceneTypes)sceneID; // 2
-(void)openSiteWithLinkType:(LinkTypes)linkTypeToOpen ;// 3
-(void)setupAudioEngine;
-(ALuint)playSoundEffect:(NSString*)soundEffectKey;
-(void)stopSoundEffect:(ALuint)soundEffectID;
-(void)playBackgroundTrack:(NSString*)trackFileName;

@end
```

The first line is the import of the `SimpleAudioEngine`, which brings the Cocos-Denshion classes into `GameManager`. In the `@interface` block add two instance variables, one to keep track of the `GameManagerSoundState` and another to be a pointer to the `soundEngine`. Lastly, add two `@property` statements for the `managerSoundState` and the `soundEngine`. Note also the `NSMutableDictionary` variables that keep track of the sound effect filenames and whether or not they are loaded in memory.

Switching over to the *GameManager.m* implementation file, first add the three lines shown in Listing 8.5 next to the other `@synthesize` statements at the top of the class.

Listing 8.5   **Addition to the top of GameManager.m class file**

```
@synthesize managerSoundState;
@synthesize listOfSoundEffectFiles;
@synthesize soundEffectsState;
```

Next, add the two lines shown in Listing 8.6 to the `init` method.

Listing 8.6   **Additions to the init method of GameManager**

```
hasAudioBeenInitialized = NO;
soundEngine = nil;
managerSoundState = kAudioManagerUninitialized;
```

The first line sets the `boolean` variable indicating whether the audio engine is initialized to `NO`, since no initialization has been done yet. The second line sets the `soundEngine` to `nil`, since it too has not been initialized yet.

Next you need to set up the audio engine. This method is called from the `SpaceVikingAppDelegate`. The `setupAudioEngine` method kicks off the background thread to set up the audio engine and preload the audio. Add the contents of Listing 8.7 to *GameManager.m* above the `init` method.

Listing 8.7   **setupAudioEngine method in GameManager.m**

```
-(void)setupAudioEngine {
    if (hasAudioBeenInitialized == YES) {
        return;
    } else {
        hasAudioBeenInitialized = YES;
        NSOperationQueue *queue = [[NSOperationQueue new] autorelease];
        NSInvocationOperation *asyncSetupOperation =
          [[NSInvocationOperation alloc] initWithTarget:self
                                       selector:@selector(initAudioAsync)
                                       object:nil];
```

```
            [queue addOperation:asyncSetupOperation];
            [asyncSetupOperation autorelease];
    }
}
```

The first part of setupAudioEngine checks to make sure the audio engine has not yet been initialized. If the engine is already initialized, there is no need to do anything else, so the method just returns. If the engine is not initialized, the process to get it set up is started.

The next few lines set up NSOperationQueue and NSInvocationOperation to run the contents of the initAudioAsync method in another thread. This means that as soon as asynchSetupOperation is added to the queue, it starts running in the background and this method returns. This allows the game logic to continue while the audio engine is being initialized and the audio preloaded in the background.

The next step is, of course, the actual initAudioAsync method that is added to the NSOperationQueue. Add the contents of Listing 8.8 above the setupAudio-Engine method in GameManager.

Listing 8.8   initAudioAsync method in GameManager

```
-(void)initAudioAsync {
    // Initializes the audio engine asynchronously
    managerSoundState = kAudioManagerInitializing;
    // Indicate that we are trying to start up the Audio Manager
    [CDSoundEngine setMixerSampleRate:CD_SAMPLE_RATE_MID];

    //Init audio manager asynchronously as it can take a few seconds
    //The FXPlusMusicIfNoOtherAudio mode will check if the user is
    // playing music and disable background music playback if
    // that is the case.
    [CDAudioManager initAsynchronously:kAMM_FxPlusMusicIfNoOtherAudio];

    //Wait for the audio manager to initialize
    while ([CDAudioManager sharedManagerState] != kAMStateInitialised)
    {
        [NSThread sleepForTimeInterval:0.1];
    }

    //At this point the CocosDenshion should be initialized
    // Grab the CDAudioManager and check the state
    CDAudioManager *audioManager = [CDAudioManager sharedManager];
    if (audioManager.soundEngine == nil ||
        audioManager.soundEngine.functioning == NO) {
        CCLOG(@"CocosDenshion failed to init, no audio will play.");
        managerSoundState = kAudioManagerFailed;
```

```
    } else {
        [audioManager setResignBehavior:kAMRBStopPlay autoHandle:YES];
        soundEngine = [SimpleAudioEngine sharedEngine];
        managerSoundState = kAudioManagerReady;
        CCLOG(@"CocosDenshion is Ready");
    }
}
```

The first part of the `initAudioSync` method sets the `managerSoundState` to initializing and sets the CocosDenshion sample rate. The sample rate should match the sample rate in your audio files. Usually you want this to be set to `CD_SAMPLE_RATE_MID`. In *Space Viking* the audio files were exported at 22050Hz, so the `CD_SAMPLE_RATE_MID` is used here. It is really important to have your audio files at the same sample rate for best performance. When playing audio with different sample rates, the iPhone and iPad audio hardware automatically pads and extrapolates your lower sample audio clips to the highest sample rate you are currently playing.

The next set of lines kick off the initialization of the CocosDenshion Audio Manager. The audio manager can be started in a variety of states.

The `CDAudioManager` can be initialized to the following states:

1. `kAMM_FxOnly`

   Plays sound effects only; other applications can continue playing audio.

2. `kAMM_FxPlusMusic`

   Only this game will play audio.

3. `kAMM_FxPlusMusicIfNoOtherAudio`

   If another application is already playing audio when the game starts, play effects only; otherwise, play music and effects. This is the option you will most likely want to use for your games. This way, for instance, your players can listen to their own music while playing your game.

4. `kAMM_MediaPlayback`

   This setting forces the game to completely take over the audio hardware and act just like a music player application.

5. `kAMM_PlayAndRecord`

   Same as `kAMM_MediaPlayback` except that it adds access to the microphone.

After kicking off CocosDenshion initialization, the next lines wait for the Cocos-Denshion Audio Manager to start and then set the state of the `managerSoundState` in GameManager. This state is used to determine if it is safe to load audio. In other words, it determines if the CocosDenshion is initialized and the audio files can be loaded into memory.

Caveat about Multiple Threads

Although asynchronous loading of audio is recommended and encouraged, CocosDenshion is not designed to be thread safe, meaning that you should not attempt to load and play audio at the same time or load audio from a number of separate threads. When loading audio asynchronously, you should always have one worker thread, as shown here. The background music and sound effects engines are separate, though, so it is perfectly safe to play background music while loading sound effects, and vice versa.

After the initAudioAsync method returns, the managerSoundState is set to kAudioManagerReady. There are two steps to load the sound effects. First, you need to get a list of the sound effects for the current scene from the *SoundEffects.plist* file. After you have the list (as a NSDictionary) of what files to load, you have to call CocosDenshion to load them in memory and prepare them to be played. As before, copy the contents of Listing 8.9 to *GameManager.m* right above the initAudioAsync method.

Listing 8.9 formatSceneTypeToString and getSoundEffectsListForSceneWithID methods in GameManager.m

```
- (NSString*)formatSceneTypeToString:(SceneTypes)sceneID {
    NSString *result = nil;
    switch(sceneID) {
        case kNoSceneUninitialized:
            result = @"kNoSceneUninitialized";
            break;
        case kMainMenuScene:
            result = @"kMainMenuScene";
            break;
        case kOptionsScene:
            result = @"kOptionsScene";
            break;
        case kCreditsScene:
            result = @"kCreditsScene";
            break;
        case kIntroScene:
            result = @"kIntroScene";
            break;
        case kLevelCompleteScene:
            result = @"kLevelCompleteScene";
            break;
        case kGameLevel1:
            result = @"kGameLevel1";
            break;
        case kGameLevel2:
            result = @"kGameLevel2";
            break;
```

```objc
        case kGameLevel3:
            result = @"kGameLevel3";
            break;
        case kGameLevel4:
            result = @"kGameLevel4";
            break;
        case kGameLevel5:
            result = @"kGameLevel5";
            break;
        case kCutSceneForLevel2:
            result = @"kCutSceneForLevel2";
            break;
        default:
            [NSException raise:NSGenericException format:@"Unexpected
SceneType."];
    }
    return result;
}


-(NSDictionary *)getSoundEffectsListForSceneWithID:(SceneTypes)sceneID {
    NSString *fullFileName = @"SoundEffects.plist";
    NSString *plistPath;

    // 1: Get the Path to the plist file
    NSString *rootPath =
    [NSSearchPathForDirectoriesInDomains(NSDocumentDirectory,
                                    NSUserDomainMask, YES)
     objectAtIndex:0];
    plistPath = [rootPath stringByAppendingPathComponent:fullFileName];
    if (![[NSFileManager defaultManager] fileExistsAtPath:plistPath]) {
        plistPath = [[NSBundle mainBundle]
                    pathForResource:@"SoundEffects" ofType:@"plist"];
    }

    // 2: Read in the plist file
    NSDictionary *plistDictionary =
    [NSDictionary dictionaryWithContentsOfFile:plistPath];

    // 3: If the plistDictionary was null, the file was not found.
    if (plistDictionary == nil) {
        CCLOG(@"Error reading SoundEffects.plist");
        return nil; // No Plist Dictionary or file found
    }

    // 4. If the list of soundEffectFiles is empty, load it
    if ((listOfSoundEffectFiles == nil) ||
        ([listOfSoundEffectFiles count] < 1)) {
```

```
    NSLog(@"Before");
    [self setListOfSoundEffectFiles:
     [[NSMutableDictionary alloc] init]];
    NSLog(@"after");
    for (NSString *sceneSoundDictionary in plistDictionary) {
        [listOfSoundEffectFiles
          addEntriesFromDictionary:
          [plistDictionary objectForKey:sceneSoundDictionary]];
    }
    CCLOG(@"Number of SFX filenames:%d",
          [listOfSoundEffectFiles count]);
}

// 5. Load the list of sound effects state, mark them as unloaded
if ((soundEffectsState == nil) ||
    ([soundEffectsState count] < 1)) {
    [self setSoundEffectsState:[[NSMutableDictionary alloc] init]];
    for (NSString *SoundEffectKey in listOfSoundEffectFiles) {
        [soundEffectsState setObject:[NSNumber
            numberWithBool:SFX_NOTLOADED] forKey:SoundEffectKey];
    }
}

// 6. Return just the mini SFX list for this scene
NSString *sceneIDName = [self formatSceneTypeToString:sceneID];
NSDictionary *soundEffectsList =
[plistDictionary objectForKey:sceneIDName];

return soundEffectsList;
}
```

The beginning of Listing 8.9 has the formatSceneTypeToString method, which may look a bit odd to you at first. Earlier in the book, you set up a typedef enumeration for various scenes in *Space Viking*. Internally, typedefs are stored as integers, unbeknownst to you. Here is the problem you have:

1. The list of sound effects to load are in the *SoundEffects.plist*, each as an entry in an NSDictionary. There are NSDictionary entries for each scene in *Space Viking*.

2. You want to reference each scene by the typedef enum name, not the integer value. For example, you want to reference the Main Menu scene by getting the NSDictionary named kMainMenuScene and not have to remember it has an actual value of 1.

3. How do you get an NSString out of an integer constant (typedef enum)? That is where formatSceneTypeToString comes in. It has just a switch

branch to create and return an NSString based on the SceneTypes typedef enum you send it.

The getSoundEffectsListForSceneWithID method loads the *SoundEffects.plist* file and returns just the NSDictionary for the scene that was requested. This should be familiar to you by now, as this method contains the same logic you used to load the animation plist files.

Pay close attention to step 4 in the getSoundEffectsListForSceneWithID method. The listOfSoundEffectFiles is an instance variable in GameManager that keeps the list of all sound files you load. Not the files themselves, just the filenames, which are used as the unique key in CocosDenshion to load and unload audio. As each scene is loaded, the list of audio filenames is added to listOfSoundEffectFiles.

Step 5 in getSoundEffectsListForSceneWithID loads the state of each of the audio files, marking them as unloaded. This NSDictionary is used by the GameManager to determine if a sound effects file has been loaded into memory and is safe to play. As you move from scene to scene, the status of each sound effect is updated to reflect whether or not it is currently loading in memory.

Now that you have the methods in place to retrieve the filenames of the audio files to use for each scene, you need two methods to call CocosDenshion and carry out the loading and unloading. Copy the contents of Listing 8.10 at the end of the getSoundEffectsListForSceneWithID method.

Listing 8.10   loadAudioForSceneWithID and unloadAudioForSceneWithID methods in GameManager.m

```
-(void)loadAudioForSceneWithID:(NSNumber*)sceneIDNumber {
    NSAutoreleasePool* pool = [[NSAutoreleasePool alloc] init];

    SceneTypes sceneID = (SceneTypes)[sceneIDNumber intValue];
    // 1
    if (managerSoundState == kAudioManagerInitializing) {
            int waitCycles = 0;
            while (waitCycles < AUDIO_MAX_WAITTIME) {
                [NSThread sleepForTimeInterval:0.1f];
                if ((managerSoundState == kAudioManagerReady) ||
                    (managerSoundState == kAudioManagerFailed)) {
                    break;
                }
                waitCycles = waitCycles + 1;
            }
    }

    if (managerSoundState == kAudioManagerFailed) {
        return; // Nothing to load, CocosDenshion not ready
    }
```

```
    NSDictionary *soundEffectsToLoad =
    [self getSoundEffectsListForSceneWithID:sceneID];
    if (soundEffectsToLoad == nil) { // 2
        CCLOG(@"Error reading SoundEffects.plist");
        return;
    }
    // Get all of the entries and PreLoad // 3
    for( NSString *keyString in soundEffectsToLoad )
    {
        CCLOG(@"\nLoading Audio Key:%@ File:%@",
            keyString,[soundEffectsToLoad objectForKey:keyString]);
        [soundEngine preloadEffect:
         [soundEffectsToLoad objectForKey:keyString]]; // 3
        // 4
        [soundEffectsState setObject:
         [NSNumber numberWithBool:SFX_LOADED] forKey:keyString];

    }
    [pool release];
}

-(void)unloadAudioForSceneWithID:(NSNumber*)sceneIDNumber {
    NSAutoreleasePool* pool = [[NSAutoreleasePool alloc] init];
    SceneTypes sceneID = (SceneTypes)[sceneIDNumber intValue];
    if (sceneID == kNoSceneUninitialized) {
        return; // Nothing to unload
    }


    NSDictionary *soundEffectsToUnload =
    [self getSoundEffectsListForSceneWithID:sceneID];
    if (soundEffectsToUnload == nil) {
        CCLOG(@"Error reading SoundEffects.plist");
        return;
    }
    if (managerSoundState == kAudioManagerReady) {
        // Get all of the entries and unload
        for( NSString *keyString in soundEffectsToUnload )
        {
            [soundEffectsState setObject:
             [NSNumber numberWithBool:SFX_NOTLOADED] forKey:keyString];
            [soundEngine unloadEffect:keyString];
            CCLOG(@"\nUnloading Audio Key:%@ File:%@",
                keyString,
                [soundEffectsToUnload objectForKey:keyString]);

        }
    }
```

```
        [pool release];
}
```

The loadAudioForSceneWithID and unloadAudioForSceneWithID methods work in the same way: they both grab an NSDictionary from the *SoundEffects.plist* file and call on CocosDenshion to either load or unload the audio files from memory.

You are almost there. Next you need to add three more small methods to Game-Manager to finish the setup. The playBackgroundTrack method preloads and starts playing a background music track. The playSoundEffect method checks to see if a sound effect has been loaded in memory and plays it. Finally, the stopSoundEffect method calls on CocosDenshion to halt the playback of a sound effect using that sound's ALuint identifier. Copy the code in Listing 8.11 to GameManager directly above the formatSceneTypeToString method.

Listing 8.11 playBackgroundTrack, stopSoundEffect, and playSoundEffect methods in GameManager.m

```
-(void)playBackgroundTrack:(NSString*)trackFileName {
    // Wait to make sure soundEngine is initialized
    if ((managerSoundState != kAudioManagerReady) &&
        (managerSoundState != kAudioManagerFailed)) {

        int waitCycles = 0;
        while (waitCycles < AUDIO_MAX_WAITTIME) {
            [NSThread sleepForTimeInterval:0.1f];
            if ((managerSoundState == kAudioManagerReady) ||
                (managerSoundState == kAudioManagerFailed)) {
                break;
            }
            waitCycles = waitCycles + 1;
        }
    }
    if (managerSoundState == kAudioManagerReady) {
        if ([soundEngine isBackgroundMusicPlaying]) {
            [soundEngine stopBackgroundMusic];
        }
        [soundEngine preloadBackgroundMusic:trackFileName];
        [soundEngine playBackgroundMusic:trackFileName loop:YES];
    }
}

-(void)stopSoundEffect:(ALuint)soundEffectID {
    if (managerSoundState == kAudioManagerReady) {
        [soundEngine stopEffect:soundEffectID];
    }
}
```

```
-(ALuint)playSoundEffect:(NSString*)soundEffectKey {
    ALuint soundID = 0;
    if (managerSoundState == kAudioManagerReady) {
        NSNumber *isSFXLoaded =
          [soundEffectsState objectForKey:soundEffectKey];
        if ([isSFXLoaded boolValue] == SFX_LOADED) {
            soundID =
              [soundEngine playEffect:
                [listOfSoundEffectFiles objectForKey:soundEffectKey]];
        } else {
            CCLOG(@"GameMgr: SoundEffect %@ is not loaded.",
              soundEffectKey);
        }
    } else {
        CCLOG(@"GameMgr: Sound Manager is not ready, cannot play %@",
          soundEffectKey);
    }
    return soundID;
}
```

The methods in Listing 8.11 wait for the CocosDenshion audio manager to be initialized and for the sound audio files to have been preloaded into memory before attempting to play any of them. If for any reason the CocosDenshion audio manager fails to initialize or the audio effect is not loaded, these methods simply return without playing.

You are done with adding methods, but there are two steps left before you can have GameManager fully functional. The first step is to add calls to the load and unload audio methods.

In *GameManager.m* locate the runSceneWithID method and add the lines shown in bold in Listing 8.12.

Listing 8.12   Additional lines in runSceneWithID method in GameManager.m

```
// ... runSceneWithID method ...
    default:
        CCLOG(@"Unknown ID, cannot switch scenes");
        return;
        break;
    }

    if (sceneToRun == nil) {
        // Revert back, since no new scene was found
        currentScene = oldScene;
        return;
    }
```

```
// Load audio for new scene based on sceneID
[self performSelectorInBackground:
     @selector(loadAudioForSceneWithID:)
     withObject:[NSNumber
     numberWithInt: currentScene]];

if ([[CCDirector sharedDirector] runningScene] == nil) {
    [[CCDirector sharedDirector] runWithScene:sceneToRun];

} else {
    [[CCDirector sharedDirector]
     replaceScene:
     [CCTransitionFlipAngular transitionWithDuration:0.5f
                                          scene:sceneToRun]];
}

[self performSelectorInBackground:
     @selector(unloadAudioForSceneWithID:)
     withObject:[NSNumber
     numberWithInt: oldScene]];

currentScene = sceneID;
}
```

As you can see in Listing 8.12, both the loading and unloading of audio files is done in a background thread via the `performSelectorInBackground` call. There is one final step to having the GameManager handle the audio setup and preloading. The `setupAudioEngine` method must be called when *Space Viking* starts. For that, open the *SpaceVikingAppDelegate.m* file and add the line shown in Listing 8.13 right above the `runSceneWithID` call in the `applicationDidFinishLaunching` method.

Listing 8.13   setupAudioEngine call in SpaceVikingAppDelegate

```
[[GameManager sharedGameManager] setupAudioEngine];
```

You should do a quick build of your *SpaceViking* project to make sure you have not made any typos. The next section covers adding audio to the GameObjects so that Ole the Viking and the enemies will have voices.

Adding the soundEngine to GameObjects

Now that you have the GameManager initializing the sound engine and preloading the audio, it is time to give Ole and the other characters their voices. Since all of the objects in *Space Viking* inherit from GameObject, we can add properties and methods in GameObject that are used by all.

First, open *GameObject.h* and add an import for the *GameManager.h* class.

```
#import "GameManager.h"
```

This is all that is needed to make the GameManager available in the GameObject and therefore in the Viking, EnemyRobot, and other objects in *Space Viking*. The GameManager will handle the playing of sound effects and the background music. The next section covers how to play the sound effects in time with the actions and animations.

Adding Sounds to RadarDish and SpaceCargoShip

The RadarDish and SpaceCargoShip are ideal objects to start with when adding sound effects. The RadarDish has only one sound effect when it is hit by Ole, while the SpaceCargoShip has four, representing the different sounds of the engines as it gets closer to Ole the Viking.

Adding Audio to RadarDish

Open the *RadarDish.m* file and go to the changeState method. In the kState-TakingDamage branch, add a call to the soundEngineLink, as shown in **bold** in Listing 8.14.

Listing 8.14   RadarDish changeState method showing call to soundEngineLink

```
-(void)changeState:(CharacterStates)newState {
    [self stopAllActions];
    id action = nil;
    [self setCharacterState:newState];

    switch (newState) {
        case kStateSpawning:
            CCLOG(@"RadarDish->Starting the Spawning Animation");
            action = [CCAnimate actionWithAnimation:tiltingAnim
                            restoreOriginalFrame:NO];
            break;

        case kStateIdle:
            CCLOG(@"RadarDish->Changing State to Idle");
            action = [CCAnimate actionWithAnimation:transmittingAnim
                            restoreOriginalFrame:NO];
            break;

        case kStateTakingDamage:
            CCLOG(@"RadarDish->Changing State to TakingDamage");
            characterHealth =
            characterHealth - [vikingCharacter getWeaponDamage];
            if (characterHealth <= 0.0f) {
```

```
                [self changeState:kStateDead];
            } else {
                PLAYSOUNDEFFECT(VIKING_HAMMERHIT1);
                action = [CCAnimate actionWithAnimation:takingAHitAnim
                                    restoreOriginalFrame:NO];
        }
            break;

        case kStateDead:
            CCLOG(@"RadarDish->Changing State to Dead");
            PLAYSOUNDEFFECT(VIKING_HAMMERHIT2);
            PLAYSOUNDEFFECT(ENEMYROBOT_DYING);
            action = [CCAnimate actionWithAnimation:blowingUpAnim
                                restoreOriginalFrame:NO];
            break;

        default:
            CCLOG(@"Unhandled state %d in RadarDish", newState);
            break;
    }
    if (action != nil) {
        [self runAction:action];
    }
}
```

In the previous section you added the GameManager import to GameObject. Since RadarDish inherits from GameCharacter, which in turn inherits from GameObject, RadarDish has access to GameManager and can call it via the PLAYSOUNDEFFECT macro. The PLAYSOUNDEFFECT macro expands into a call to the playSoundEffect in GameManager, playing the sound effect for the RadarDish. The GameManager already took care of loading the sound effects when the Gameplay scene was loaded, so it is just a quick call to CocosDenshion and you can hear the sound effects.

After adding this line, click **Run**. You should be able to have Ole strike the RadarDish and hear a crashing/clunking sound. Can you hear the explosion sound when Ole destroys the RadarDish?

Adding Audio to SpaceCargoShip

The SpaceCargoShip inherits directly from GameObject, so it too has access to the GameManager. The SpaceCargoShip plays four sounds. During the first two and most distant passes, the faraway engine sound is played. On the next three passes, a louder and closer sound is played to give the player the illusion that the ship is getting closer.

In SpaceCargoShip you need a method to play the four sounds in sequence with the animations and actions you previously created in the init method. Before creating this method, open the *SpaceCargoShip.h* header file and add the following instance variable inside the @interface declaration block.

```
int soundNumberToPlay;
```

This is a number you will increment to indicate which engine sound the Space-CargoShip should play. Open the *SpaceCargoShip.m* file and add the contents of Listing 8.15 into the init method.

Listing 8.15   SpaceCargoShip.m playSpaceCargoShipSound

```
#pragma mark -
#pragma mark SoundMethods
-(void)playSpaceCargoShipSound {
    if (soundNumberToPlay  < 2) {
        PLAYSOUNDEFFECT(SPACECARGOSHIP_FAR);
    } else if (soundNumberToPlay == 2) {
        PLAYSOUNDEFFECT(SPACECARGOSHIP_CLOSE_1);
    } else if (soundNumberToPlay == 3) {
        PLAYSOUNDEFFECT(SPACECARGOSHIP_CLOSE_2);
    } else if (soundNumberToPlay == 4) {
        PLAYSOUNDEFFECT(SPACECARGOSHIP_CLOSE_3);
    }
    soundNumberToPlay = soundNumberToPlay + 1;
    if (soundNumberToPlay > 4) {
        soundNumberToPlay = 0;
    }
}
```

Listing 8.15 shows the soundNumberToPlay variable being incremented each time the playSpaceCargoShip method is called. When the soundNumberToPlay is greater than four, it is reset to zero.

The init method for SpaceCargoShip ties it all together. Go to the init method in SpaceCargoShip and locate the id action declaration. In this nested set of actions, add the CCCallFunc action shown in Listing 8.16 before each CCMoveTo action, starting with the second one.

Listing 8.16   SpaceCargoShip init method—adding CCCallFunc

```
[CCCallFunc actionWithTarget:self
            selector:@selector(playSpaceCargoShipSound)],
// Example:
id action = [CCRepeatForever actionWithAction:
                [CCSequence actions:
                    [CCDelayTime actionWithDuration:2.0f],
                    [CCMoveTo actionWithDuration:0.01f
                            position:ccp(-500.0f,550.0f)],
```

```
[CCScaleTo actionWithDuration:0.01f scale:0.5f],
[CCFlipX actionWithFlipX:YES],
[CCCallFunc actionWithTarget:self
            selector:@selector(playSpaceCargoShipSound)],
[CCMoveTo actionWithDuration:8.5f
          position:ccp(screenSize.width+1000.0f,550.0f)],
```

In the resources folder for this chapter, the changes to the init method in the SpaceCargoShip class are included in the *UpdatedSpaceCargoShipInit.rtf* file. All of the changes are included as well with the source code for this chapter.

There is one line of code left to complete the SpaceCargoShip. In the beginning of the init method, be sure to initialize the soundNumberToPlay variable by adding the following line in the init method.

```
soundNumberToPlay = 0;
```

That wraps it up for SpaceCargoShip. If you click **Run**, you will hear the SpaceCargoShip as it makes its way across the screen. In the next section, you work on adding sounds to the EnemyRobot and finally to Ole the Viking.

Adding Sounds to EnemyRobot

The EnemyRobot is a bit more complex than the RadarDish or SpaceCargoShip. The robot patrols the level, looking for Ole, and attacks Ole when he is spotted. So this time, there are several more sounds to add!

To start, you need to add an instance variable to EnemyRobot. Open the *EnemyRobot.h* file and in the @interface declaration section add the following line:

```
ALuint walkingSound;
```

Unlike the rest of the sounds in EnemyRobot, the walking sound effect may need to be cut short if the EnemyRobot suddenly spots Ole. To stop an effect that is currently playing, you need to know the audio layer identifier for that sound. The audio layer identifier is a type of unsigned integer called ALuint. You can get the ALuint by setting it when you call playEffect, as you will see later in the playWalking-Sound method.

Before creating the walking sounds, you will want to add and understand the simpler playPhaserFireSound method shown in Listing 8.17. Open *EnemyRobot.m* and add the contents of Listing 8.17 right above the changeState method.

Listing 8.17   **EnemyRobot.m playPhaserFireSound method**

```
#pragma mark -
#pragma mark SoundMethods
-(void)playPhaserFireSound {
    int soundToPlay = random() % 2;
```

```
    if (soundToPlay == 0) {
        PLAYSOUNDEFFECT(ENEMYROBOT_PHASERFIRE_1);
    } else {
        PLAYSOUNDEFFECT(ENEMYROBOT_PHASERFIRE_2);
    }
}
```

In the `playPhaserFireSound` method the modulus (%) operator is used to get the remainder of a random number divided by two. The two possible outcomes are 0 and 1, and they are used to select one of the two enemy phaser sounds to play.

Next you need to create a similar method to alternate between the two walking sounds for the `EnemyRobot`. Once more, copy the contents of Listing 8.18 below the newly created `playPhaserFireSound` method.

Listing 8.18   EnemyRobot.m playWalkingSound method

```
-(void)playWalkingSound {
    int soundToPlay = random() % 2;
    if (soundToPlay == 0) {
        walkingSound = PLAYSOUNDEFFECT(ENEMYROBOT_WALKING_1);
    } else {
        walkingSound = PLAYSOUNDEFFECT(ENEMYROBOT_WALKING_2);
    }
}
```

The main difference between `playWalkingSound` and `playPhaserFireSound` is that you are keeping a reference to the audio layer identifier of the walking sound effect being played, via the `walkingSound` variable. This identifier is used to stop the walking sound anytime the `EnemyRobot` transitions state, so if he stops walking suddenly, the sound will not keep playing.

On Stopping Sounds before They Finish

Stopping a sound effect during playback is a common occurrence in games. Often your animations or actions may be stopped due to an event in the game, and you will want to stop your sound effects, too. The easiest way to do this with CocosDenshion is to keep a reference to the audio layer identifier when you call `playEffect` and then use it in a `stopEffect` method call.

The bulk of the changes to `EnemyRobot` are in the `changeState` method, where a call is added to play a sound effect on several of the state changes. Listing 8.19 shows an excerpt of the `changeState` method with the added lines shown. The rest of the code in the `changeState` method remains unchanged and is not shown here.

Listing 8.19 EnemyRobot.m changeState method (partial)

```
[self stopAllActions];
STOPSOUNDEFFECT(walkingSound);
id action = nil;
characterState = newState;

switch (newState) {
    case kStateSpawning:
    [soundEngineLink
    PLAYSOUNDEFFECT(ENEMYROBOT_TELEPORT);
    [self runAction:[CCFadeOut actionWithDuration:0.0f]]; ...
    break;
...


    case kStateWalking:
        CCLOG(@"EnemyRobot->Changing State to Walking");
        if (isVikingWithinBoundingBox)
         break;
        [self playWalkingSound];
...
        case kStateAttacking:
        CCLOG(@"EnemyRobot->Changing State to Attacking");
        action = [CCSequence actions:
                    [CCAnimate actionWithAnimation:raisePhaserAnim
                            restoreOriginalFrame:NO],
                    [CCDelayTime actionWithDuration:1.0f],
                    [CCAnimate actionWithAnimation:shootPhaserAnim
                            restoreOriginalFrame:NO],
                    [CCCallFunc actionWithTarget:self
                             selector:@selector(shootPhaser)],
                    [CCCallFunc actionWithTarget:self
                     selector:@selector(playPhaserFireSound)],
                    [CCAnimate actionWithAnimation:lowerPhaserAnim
                            restoreOriginalFrame:NO],
                    [CCDelayTime actionWithDuration:2.0f],
                    nil];
        break;

case kStateTakingDamage:
        CCLOG(@"EnemyRobot->Changing State to TakingDamage");
        PLAYSOUNDEFFECT(ENEMYROBOT_DAMAGE);
        if ([vikingCharacter getWeaponDamage] > 10){
            // If the viking has the mallet, then
            action =
             [CCAnimate actionWithAnimation:headHitAnim
                        restoreOriginalFrame:YES];
```

```
        } else {
            // Viking does not have weapon, body blow
            action =
            [CCAnimate actionWithAnimation:torsoHitAnim
             restoreOriginalFrame:YES];
        }
        break;
...
case kStateDead:
        CCLOG(@"EnemyRobot -> Going to Dead State");
        PLAYSOUNDEFFECT(ENEMYROBOT_DYING);
...
```

The first addition to the changeState method is the line [soundEngineLink stopEffect:walkingSound], which stops the walking sound if it is playing. This line ensures that if the EnemyRobot transitions out of the walking state, the walking sound will not continue playing. The next sets of changes are in the kStateSpawning, kStateWalking, kStateAttacking, kStateTakingDamage, and kStateDead branches.

In the kStateSpawning, kStateTakingDamage, and kStateDead transitions, a single call to PLAYSOUNDEFFECT is all that is needed to play the teleport sound and the hit sound effect.

In the kStateWalking transition, the playWalkingSound method is called to play one of the two walking sounds.

Lastly, in the kStateAttacking transition, the call to playPhaserFireSound is included in the CCSequence action as a CCCallFunc action so that it starts to play exactly when the phaser bolt shoots out of the gun.

That wraps up the EnemyRobot sound effects. If you click **Run**, you should hear the EnemyRobot teleporting in and the sound effects when he fires at Ole or gets whacked in the head by the Viking mallet.

In the next section you the give Ole full audio treatment by adding sound effects to his actions.

Adding Sound Effects to Ole the Viking

The Viking character is the main protagonist in *Space Viking*, and as such he has the largest set of sound effects. Earlier in the EnemyRobot class, any sounds involving two or more effects that could be played were wrapped in a method to make the code clear and easier to understand. Feel free to reference back and use this code when adding sound effects to your own game.

First open the *Viking.h* file and add the following line in the @interface declaration section.

```
ALuint walkingSound;
```

Just as with `EnemyRobot`, the `walkingSound` instance variable allows the Viking to stop the walking sound anytime he transitions out of that state.

Now move to the *Viking.m* implementation file to create a set of methods to play the sounds. Be sure to copy the code in Listings 8.20 to 8.22 into *Viking.m* into the `changeState` method.

Listing 8.20   Viking.m playJumpingSound

```
#pragma mark -
#pragma mark SoundEffectsMethods
-(void)playJumpingSound {
    int soundToPlay = random() % 4;
    if (soundToPlay == 0) {
        PLAYSOUNDEFFECT(VIKING_JUMPING_1);
    } else if (soundToPlay == 1) {
        PLAYSOUNDEFFECT(VIKING_JUMPING_2);
    } else if (soundToPlay == 2) {
        PLAYSOUNDEFFECT(VIKING_JUMPING_3);
    } else {
        PLAYSOUNDEFFECT(VIKING_JUMPING_4);
    }
}
```

The `soundToPlay` variable is set to one of four possible values randomly, and then based on that value (0-3), one of the four jumping sounds is played.

Copy the contents of Listing 8.21 into the `playJumpingSound` method in order to add the methods to play the swinging mallet sound and the breathing sounds.

Listing 8.21   Viking.m playSwingingSound and playBreathingSound methods

```
-(void)playSwingingSound {
    int soundToPlay = random() % 8;
    switch (soundToPlay) {
        case 0:
            PLAYSOUNDEFFECT(VIKING_SWINGING_1);
            break;
        case 1:
            PLAYSOUNDEFFECT(VIKING_SWINGING_2);
            break;
        case 2:
            PLAYSOUNDEFFECT(VIKING_SWINGING_3);
            break;
        case 3:
            PLAYSOUNDEFFECT(VIKING_SWINGING_4);
            break;
```

```
        case 4:
            PLAYSOUNDEFFECT(VIKING_SWINGING_5);
            break;
        case 5:
            PLAYSOUNDEFFECT(VIKING_SWINGING_6);
            break;
        case 6:
            PLAYSOUNDEFFECT(VIKING_SWINGING_7);
            break;
        case 7:
            PLAYSOUNDEFFECT(VIKING_SWINGING_8);
            break;
        default:
            PLAYSOUNDEFFECT(VIKING_SWINGING_9);
            break;
    }
}
-(void)playBreathingSound {
    int soundToPlay = random() % 4;
    if (soundToPlay == 0) {
        PLAYSOUNDEFFECT(VIKING_GRUMBLING_1);
    } else if (soundToPlay == 1) {
        PLAYSOUNDEFFECT(VIKING_GRUMBLING_2);
    } else if (soundToPlay == 2) {
        PLAYSOUNDEFFECT(VIKING_CURSING_1);
    } else {
        PLAYSOUNDEFFECT(VIKING_CURSING_2);
    }
}
```

As with the `playJumpingSound` method, the `playSwingingSound` and `play-BreathingSound` methods randomly select between the sound effect options for swinging and breathing. The breathing sound (grumbling) is played when the player has not touched any of the controls for a period of time in an attempt to direct the player's attention back to the game. After all, there are aliens to bash!

Two more methods remain to round out the sound effects for Ole the Viking. Copy the contents of Listing 8.22 into the `playBreathingSound` method in the *Viking.m* implementation file.

Listing 8.22   playTakingDamagSound, playDyingSound, and playCrouchingSound methods in Viking.m

```
-(void)playTakingDamageSound {
    int soundToPlay = random() % 5;
    if (soundToPlay == 0) {
        PLAYSOUNDEFFECT(VIKING_HIT_1);
```

```
    } else if (soundToPlay == 1) {
        PLAYSOUNDEFFECT(VIKING_HIT_2);
    } else if (soundToPlay == 2) {
        PLAYSOUNDEFFECT(VIKING_HIT_3);
    } else if (soundToPlay == 3) {
        PLAYSOUNDEFFECT(VIKING_HIT_4);
    } else {
        PLAYSOUNDEFFECT(VIKING_HIT_5);
    }
}

-(void)playDyingSound {
    int soundToPlay = random() % 5;
    if (soundToPlay == 0) {
        PLAYSOUNDEFFECT(VIKING_DYING_1);
    } else if (soundToPlay == 1) {
        PLAYSOUNDEFFECT(VIKING_DYING_2);
    } else if (soundToPlay == 2) {
        PLAYSOUNDEFFECT(VIKING_DYING_3);
    } else if (soundToPlay == 3) {
        PLAYSOUNDEFFECT(VIKING_DYING_4);
    } else {
        PLAYSOUNDEFFECT(VIKING_DYING_5);
    }
}

-(void)playCrouchingSound {
    int soundToPlay = random() % 4;
    if (soundToPlay == 0) {
        PLAYSOUNDEFFECT(VIKING_CROUCHING_1);
    } else if (soundToPlay == 1) {
        PLAYSOUNDEFFECT(VIKING_CROUCHING_2);
    } else if (soundToPlay == 2) {
        PLAYSOUNDEFFECT(VIKING_CROUCHING_3);
    } else {
        PLAYSOUNDEFFECT(VIKING_CROUCHING_4);
    }
}
```

The playTakingDamage and playDyingSound methods choose randomly between the five available sound effects for Ole taking a hit and Ole dying. The playCrouchingSound method plays four different crouching movement sounds. The multiple sound effects for each event prevent the game from being too repetitive and the player from having to hear the sounds played over and over.

Adding the Sound Method Calls in changeState for Ole

The last step in making Ole speak is to add the calls to the methods you just created. The calls are inside of the changeState method. Listing 8.23 shows the lines added to the changeState method. Look closely at Listing 8.23 and add these lines in your *Viking.m* implementation file.

Listing 8.23   **Viking.m changeState method (partial)**

```
STOPSOUNDEFFECT(walkingSound);

[self setCharacterState:newState];

switch (newState) {
...

    case kStateWalking:
        PLAYSOUNDEFFECT(VIKING_WALKING_1);
...

        break;

    case kStateCrouching:
        [self playCrouchingSound];
...

        break;

    case kStateBreathing:
        [self playBreathingSound];
...

        break;

    case kStateJumping:
        [self playJumpingSound];
...

        break;

    case kStateAttacking:
        if (isCarryingMallet == YES) {
            action = [CCAnimate
                    actionWithAnimation:malletPunchAnim
                    restoreOriginalFrame:YES];
            [self playSwingingSound];
        } else {
            PLAYSOUNDEFFECT(VIKING_PUNCHING);
...

        break;
```

```
        case kStateTakingDamage:
            [self playTakingDamageSound];
...
            break;

        case kStateDead:
            [self playDyingSound];
...
            break;

        default:
            break;
    }
```

In the changeState method, the first line added is a call to stop playing the walking sound effect. This call does nothing if the walking sound is not currently playing. In the switch block for the states, the following occurs.

If the state is switching to:

1. kStateWalking

    The walking sound effect is played and the audio layer identifier for this sound effect is stored in the instance variable. This audio layer identifier is used to stop playing the walking sound when Ole changes state.

2. kStateCrouching

    There are four crouching sounds, and the playCrouchingSound method chooses among them at random.

3. kStateBreathing

    Calls the playBreathingSound method, which randomly chooses one of the four mumbling sound effects to try to entice the player to return to the game.

4. kStateJumping

    Calls the playJumpingSound method to randomly play one of Ole's jumping sound effects.

5. kStateAttacking

    If Ole is carrying the mallet, the playSwingingSound is called to randomly play one of Ole's mallet-swinging sound effects. If Ole's just got his bare fists to rely on, it calls soundEngineLink directly and plays the Viking punch sound effect.

6. kStateTakingDamage

    Calls the playTakingDamageSound to randomly play one of the five sound effects of Ole being hit by one of the enemies.

7. `kStateDead`

Calls the `playDyingSound` to randomly play one of the five sound effects of Ole dying and turning to dust. Let's hope you don't hear this sound effect very often.

This concludes all the setup you need to give Ole the Viking a voice and a full complement of sound effects. If you click **Run**, you should be able to hear Ole making the various sound effects as you play *Space Viking*.

Adding Music to the Menu Screen

All of the scenes in *Space Viking* have background music to go along with them. You have already carried out most of the work needed to play background music in the `GameManager` class. All you need to do is call it from the various scenes. While you could add the next call at the scene level, you will be adding it to the layer, as that is where you have most of the code.

Adding Music to Gameplay

Open the *GameplayLayer.h* file and add an import for the `GameManager` class:

```
#import "GameManager.h"
```

Switch over to the *GameplayLayer.m* file and in the `init` method, add the following line:

```
[[GameManager sharedGameManager] playBackgroundTrack:BACKGROUND_TRACK_
OLE_AWAKES];
```

If you click **Run** and play the Ole Awakes level, you should hear the background music starting.

Adding Music to the MainMenu

To add music to the `MainMenu`, follow the same steps as for adding it to the `Gameplay`. Start by opening the *MainMenuLayer.h* file and add an import for the `GameManager` class:

```
#import "GameManager.h"
```

Switch over to the *MainMenuLayer.m* file and in the `init` method, add the following line:

```
[[GameManager sharedGameManager] playBackgroundTrack:BACKGROUND_TRACK_
MAIN_MENU];
```

In addition to playing the new background music, the `GameManager` will stop any currently playing background music when the player returns to it from one of the levels.

Once more, click **Run**, and you should now hear music in the `Main Menu` along with the `Gameplay` layer. Since the other menus in *Space Viking* do not have their own music, the main menu background track will continue playing when you transition to them.

For the More Curious: If You Need More Audio Control

`SimpleAudioEngine` is an excellent interface for getting sounds into your games with a minimal amount of code and setup. Even though you used the short `playEffect` call, there is a fuller version available with `SimpleAudioEngine`.

```
[soundEngine playEffect:
            pitch:
            pan:
            gain: ]
```

`Pitch` is a multiplier that can change the octave of the sound being played: 1.0 is unchanged, 0.5 is an octave lower.

`Pan` controls the left and right stereo position of the sound: -1 is all the way on the left, while 1 is all the way on the right. Zero is in the center, with the sound coming out of both the left and right speakers equally.

`Gain` controls the audio gain: 1.0 is unchanged, 0.5 is half the audio gain.

Although `SimpleAudioEngine` provides quite a bit of power, sometimes you need more control over how the audio is played. For greater control over audio playback, there are two additional APIs for CocosDenshion, `CDAudioManager` and `CDSoundEngine`.

In *Space Viking* you used the `ALUint` identifier to stop audio playback. The `CDSoundSource` objects in CocosDenshion provide better control when you need to stop sounds, even allowing you to fade your sounds. It is recommended that you use `CDSoundSource` when you need to stop sound effects or loop them, as it provides finer-grained control over your audio effects.

Additionally, there is a limit of 32 sounds that can be played simultaneously on the iOS devices. `SimpleAudioEngine` always attempts to honor a play request, and if you attempt to play more than 32 sounds at once, your earlier sounds may be prematurely cut off.

`CDAudioManager` provides a mechanism to identify sounds by their unique numerical IDs instead of filenames and is the underlying CocosDenshion module `SimpleAudioEngine` uses.

`CDSoundEngine` provides full access to the OpenAL layer, allowing you to group your sounds into interruptible and noninterruptible channels, and provides you with precise control over the audio buffers and playback. `CDSoundEngine` also provides an easy way to loop any audio, not just the background track.

Covering these two portions of CocosDenshion is beyond the scope of this book, but there are several example projects included with Cocos2D to help you get started with these two APIs.

The DrumPad, Fade to Grey, and FancyRat Metering targets included in the Cocos2D Xcode project are a great starting point for delving deeper into the Cocos-Denshion framework.

There are also additional examples included with the source files of this book, found at the InformIT website *(www.informit.com/title/9780321735621)* and at the Cocos2DBook website *(www.cocos2dbook.com)*.

Summary

In this chapter you learned about CocosDenshion, the sound engine included with Cocos2D. You learned how to preload audio and initialize the sound engine. You also learned how to play a music track and sound effects for the characters in *Space Viking* and how to load the music via a background thread. When you create your own games, you can reuse the code from this book to help you on your way. In the next chapter you take Ole even further on the alien planet by adding scrolling to *Space Viking*.

Challenges

1. Add code in `GameManager` to avoid playing music or special effect sounds if the player has selected to turn the music or the sound effects off in the Options Menu screen.

   Hint

   Take a look at `GameManager`'s `isMusicON` and `isSoundEffectsON` variables.

2. Add the ability to pan the sounds so that the engine noise from the `Space-CargoShip` pans from the left when the ship comes from the left side and from the right when the ship comes from the right side of the screen.

9

When the World Gets Bigger: Adding Scrolling

In the last chapter you learned how to add sound effects and music to Space Viking, *giving Ole a heavy metal soundtrack as inspiration to beat the aliens. In this chapter you learn how to make Ole's world even larger by adding scrolling and creating a second game level and a cut-scene. Scrolling is an easy and powerful technique that can be used to make your levels larger and to add depth to your games.*

Let's take a moment to cover the basics. Up to now the levels have been set to the dimensions of the iOS device screen. On the iPad the alien world is only 1024 × 768 pixels in size. Ole and his enemies cannot move beyond the screen to the left or right. For the background, you are using one large image (1024 × 768 pixels on the iPad) on top of which the GameplayLayer *and all the characters are composited. If you made the level twice as wide, you would need a larger background image to cover the new space, and larger levels would quickly cause you to run out of memory. There is a better way, using TileMaps, as you will learn in the third section of this chapter.*

Terminology Review

Before jumping into the scrolling functionality, it is useful to cover some of the terminology used in this chapter.

- **Parallax Scrolling**
  A technique used in 2D games to create depth by scrolling separate layers of the background at different rates. Having the layers closest to the player move faster than layers further away gives the player the illusion of depth. To visualize this, think about the scenery as you ride in a car or train. The road or track moves really fast, the items farther away move slower. By replicating the same movement on a 2D scene, the game can fool the player's brain into seeing depth were there is none.

- **Tiles**
  Image or texture used in a TileMap. These are usually PNG images combined in a texture atlas. Tile images are usually squared, and the common sizes are 32 × 32 and 64 × 64 pixels.

- **TileMap**
  A large image made up of tiles of a standard size. The tile images/textures can repeat so that a large TileMap needs only a small amount of unique tiles. TileMaps can contain multiple TileSets and can contain image and other custom data for each tile.

- **TileSet**
  A set of tiles stored as one image. Consider how texture atlases are used to combine multiple sprites images into a single larger image: the TileSet is the texture atlas of tiles.

Don't worry if you do not understand the TileMap terminology just yet. It will become clear by the time you reach the last section of this chapter. With the definitions out of the way, it is time to get into the code.

First you learn how to scroll with one large image. Then you can learn how to add multiple layers and scroll them at different speeds with parallax. Finally you learn about using TileMaps and develop a scrolling background using TileMap layers.

Adding the Logic for a Larger World

Until now you have been working with a single game level. You will leave this first level unchanged and instead create a new level for use in this chapter and beyond.

In Chapter 3, "Introduction to Cocos2D Animations and Actions," you created code in GameCharacter to automatically clamp the character's position to iOS device dimensions. If you recall, before the GameCharacter class can clamp the position, it needs to know the size of the level. Since the first level was the size of the screen, you simply used the screen dimensions for the level size. However, this will not work if the level size varies from level to level. Since you already have the GameManager controlling the transition from one level to another, it makes sense to create a method there to provide the size of the level.

Open the *GameManager.h* header file and add the line shown in Listing 9.1 immediately below the @property declarations.

Listing 9.1   GameManager.h declaration for getDimensionsOfCurrentScene method

```
-(CGSize)getDimensionsOfCurrentScene;
```

Just as the name implies, this method returns the dimensions of the current scene. Since this method bases the dimension on the CCDirector's winSize, it automatically has the proper dimensions for iPhone, iPhone 4, and iPad screen sizes. Remember that winSize returns the size in points, while the winSizeInPixels call returns the actual pixel size of the display.

Move to the *GameManager.m* implementation file and add the getDimensionsOfCurrentScene right above the @end declaration, as shown in Listing 9.2.

Listing 9.2   GameManager.m getDimensionsOfCurrentScene method

```
-(CGSize)getDimensionsOfCurrentScene {
    CGSize screenSize = [[CCDirector sharedDirector] winSize];
    CGSize levelSize;
    switch (currentScene) {
        case kMainMenuScene:
        case kOptionsScene:
        case kCreditsScene:
        case kIntroScene:
        case kLevelCompleteScene:
        case kGameLevel1:
            levelSize = screenSize;
            break;
        case kGameLevel2:
            levelSize = CGSizeMake(screenSize.width * 2.0f,
                                   screenSize.height);
            break;

        default:
            CCLOG(@"Unknown Scene ID, returning default size");
            levelSize = screenSize;
            break;
    }
    return levelSize;
}
```

The getDimensionsOfCurrentScene method takes a look at what the currentSceneID is set to and returns the appropriate level dimensions as a CGSize. The screen dimensions on the devices are always constant, such as 1024 × 768 on the iPad, but the sizes of the levels will vary. As you can see in Listing 9.2, the menus and the first game level are the same size as the screen, while on the second level, identified by the kGameLevel2 ID that you will be building, they are actually twice as wide.

With the level size out of the way, the next step is to modify the checkAndClampSpritePosition method in GameCharacter to take into account the levelDimensions.

Open the *GameCharacter.m* implementation file and replace the checkAndClampSpritePosition method with the contents of Listing 9.3.

Listing 9.3   GameCharacter.m checkAndClampSpritePosition method

```
-(void)checkAndClampSpritePosition {
    CGPoint currentSpritePosition = [self position];

    CGSize levelSize = [[GameManager sharedGameManager]
                         getDimensionsOfCurrentScene];
```

```
float xOffset;
if (UI_USER_INTERFACE_IDIOM() == UIUserInterfaceIdiomPad) {
    // Clamp for the iPad
   xOffset = 30.0f;
} else {
    // Clamp for iPhone, iPhone 4, or iPod touch
   xOffset = 24.0f;
}

if (currentSpritePosition.x < xOffset) {
   [self setPosition:ccp(xOffset, currentSpritePosition.y)];
} else if (currentSpritePosition.x > (levelSize.width - xOffset)) {
   [self setPosition:ccp((levelSize.width - xOffset),
                          currentSpritePosition.y)];
}
}
```

The `checkAndClampSpritePosition` method now takes into account the level width and keeps game characters such as Ole and the `EnemyRobot` 30 pixels away from the left and right sides. The level dimensions are retrieved from the `GameManager`.

To ensure you have typed everything correctly up to this point, click **Run** and try out the first level. Ole and the alien robots should remain within the screen.

Common Scrolling Problems

Before you begin learning about scrolling, it is worthwhile taking a quick detour to see what happens if you widen the level without taking care to reposition Ole and the joystick controls.

Open `GameManager` and modify the lines for the `levelSize` so that they match Listing 9.4. Note how the level width is larger than what it should be for `kGameLevel1`.

Listing 9.4   Level width change for kGameLevel1 in GameManager.m

```
case kGameLevel1:
    levelSize = CGSizeMake(screenSize.width * 2.0f,
                           screenSize.height);
    break;
```

All you have changed here is the width of the first game level to twice the screen size; on the iPad this means the width went from 1024 to 2048 pixels. The first level is not designed for scrolling. Take a minute to run the game, and play the first level. Figure 9.1 shows what happens when you move Ole to the right.

Figure 9.1   Ole scrolls past the screen and is nowhere to be seen.

The first game level scene was not set for scrolling, so when Ole moves to the right, the scene does not follow him, and he quickly disappears offscreen. This was an exercise to illustrate how you need to track Ole's position in order to scroll the entire layer properly to match his position. Keep this in mind as you work through the next section.

Make sure to return the kGameLevel1 to just be the width of the screenSize before moving on.

```
case kGameLevel1:
        levelSize = screenSize;
```

Creating a Larger World

Instead of just creating a scrolling layer, you will create a whole new level for Ole to play in. In the process you will learn several techniques to achieve scrolling in your games.

The first step is to import the *ParallaxBackgrounds* folder located with the resources for this chapter into your *SpaceViking* project. You can drag the *ParallaxBackgrounds* folder as a subfolder to the *Images* folder in Xcode.

> **Warning**
>
> Be sure to import all of the images in the *ParallaxBackgrounds* folder or your *SpaceViking* project will not run when you reach the end of this chapter.

Next create a new group under Scenes called *Scene2,* as shown in Figure 9.2. All of the classes for this scene and level will be created under this group to keep your *SpaceViking* project organized.

Figure 9.2   Scene2 group in Xcode

Creating the Second Game Scene

In order to keep things simple and compartmentalized, you will create a new scene class instead of adding code to the existing `GameScene`.

Right-click on the *Scene2* group in Xcode and create a new Objective-C class called *GameScene2.m* as subclass of `CCScene`. If you are unsure about the steps in creating a new class, refer back to the previous chapters in this book, in particular Chapter 2, "Hello, Space Viking."

Open the *GameScene2.h* header file and replace it with the contents of Listing 9.5.

Listing 9.5   **GameScene2.h header file**

```
//   GameScene2.h
//   SpaceViking
//
#import <Foundation/Foundation.h>
```

```
#import "cocos2d.h"
#import "Constants.h"
#import "GameControlLayer.h"
#import "GameplayScrollingLayer.h"
#import "StaticBackgroundLayer.h"

@interface GameScene2 : CCScene {
    GameControlLayer *controlLayer;
}
@end
```

In the import statements, the GameControlLayer GameplayScrollingLayer, and StaticBackgroundLayer are three classes you have not created yet. Do not worry if Xcode starts displaying warnings for the missing classes; you will add them in the next few listings.

The StaticBackgroundLayer is a simple class, which contains the farthest background image that will not be scrolled.

In the previous scene, the GameplayLayer contained both the controls and the gameplay action. Since you are going to have the gameplay scroll, it is useful to move the joystick controls to their own layer. Having the joystick and buttons in their own layer means you do not have to move or adjust them when the gameplay layer scrolls. The joystick will always be on top of the gameplay regardless of what scroll position the other layers are in.

You are going to split the background into two layers: a static backmost layer that does not scroll, and a GameplayScrollingLayer where the action and scrolling takes place.

Move on to the implementation of *GameScene2.m* and replace the code with the content of Listing 9.6.

Listing 9.6   GameScene2.m implementation file

```
//   GameScene2.m
//   SpaceViking
//
#import "GameScene2.h"

@implementation GameScene2
-(id)init {
    self = [super init];
    if (self != nil) {
        // Background Layer
        StaticBackgroundLayer *backgroundLayer =
                            [StaticBackgroundLayer node];
        [self addChild:backgroundLayer z:0];
```

```
        // Initialize the Control Layer
        controlLayer = [GameControlLayer node];
        [self addChild:controlLayer z:2 tag:2];

        // Gameplay Layer
        GameplayScrollingLayer *scrollingLayer =
                            [GameplayScrollingLayer node];
[scrollingLayer connectControlsWithJoystick:[controlLayer leftJoystick]
                    andJumpButton:[controlLayer jumpButton]
                    andAttackButton:[controlLayer attackButton]];
        [self addChild:scrollingLayer z:1 tag:1];

    }
    return self;

}
@end
```

The GameScene2 init method starts by initializing the static background layer and adding it to the scene. Next it initializes the control layer, which contains the joystick and buttons. Lastly, it creates the GameplayScrollingLayer where all the action is going to take place. The connectControlsWithJoystick method links the joystick and buttons from the ControlLayer to the Viking inside of GameplayScrollingLayer. Take care to notice the z values of the three layers; even though the ControlLayer is initialized first, it is actually composited on top of the GameplayScrollingLayer.

Note on z Values

You learned how z values affect the compositing of objects in Cocos2D. The Game-Scene2 init method provides a clear example of times when this can be really useful. In *Space Viking*, you need to initialize the controls before you initialize the Gameplay-ScrollingLayer. Even though the ControlLayer is initialized first, it is composited on top of the scrolling GameplayScrollingLayer due to its z value. Keep this in mind when writing your own games and when you find that you need to initialize objects and add objects to a scene in a different way than their compositing order.

Next create the StaticBackgroundLayer class inside the *Scene2* folder as a subclass of CCLayer. Open the header file and replace the template-created code with the contents of Listing 9.7.

Listing 9.7   StaticBackgroundLayer.h header file

```
//   StaticBackgroundLayer.h
//   SpaceViking
//
#import <Foundation/Foundation.h>
#import "cocos2d.h"
```

```
@interface StaticBackgroundLayer : CCLayer {
}
@end
```

The header file is as simple as possible, containing just an import for Cocos2D and declaring StaticBackgroundLayer as a subclass to CCLayer. Move to the implementation file and replace the code with the contents of Listing 9.8.

Listing 9.8   **StaticBackgroundLayer.m implementation file**

```
//   StaticBackgroundLayer.m
//   SpaceViking
#import "StaticBackgroundLayer.h"

@implementation StaticBackgroundLayer
-(id)init {
    self = [super init];
    if (self != nil) {
        CGSize screenSize = [CCDirector sharedDirector].winSize;
        CCSprite *backgroundImage;
        if (UI_USER_INTERFACE_IDIOM() == UIUserInterfaceIdiomPad) {
            // Indicates game is running on iPad
            backgroundImage =
              [CCSprite spriteWithFile:@"chap9_scrolling1.png"];
        } else {
            backgroundImage =
              [CCSprite spriteWithFile:@"chap9_scrolling1iPhone.png"];
        }

        [backgroundImage setPosition:ccp(screenSize.width/2.0f,
                                         screenSize.height/2.0f)];
        [self addChild:backgroundImage];
    }
    return self;
}
@end
```

The StaticBackgroundLayer implementation file contains only the init method, creating the background CCSprite and adding it to the layer. This is the same logic that you implemented for the BackgroundLayer in the first level of *Space Viking* back in Chapter 2.

The next step is to create the GameControlLayer class as a subclass of CCLayer. Create it in the *Scene2* group, and open the header file. Copy the contents of Listing 9.9 into the *GameControlLayer.h* file.

Listing 9.9   **GameControlLayer.h header file**

```
//  GameControlLayer.h
//  SpaceViking
//
#import <Foundation/Foundation.h>
#import "cocos2d.h"
#import "SneakyJoystick.h"
#import "SneakyJoystickSkinnedBase.h"
#import "SneakyButton.h"
#import "SneakyButtonSkinnedBase.h"

@interface GameControlLayer : CCLayer {
    SneakyJoystick *leftJoystick;
    SneakyButton *jumpButton;
    SneakyButton *attackButton;

}
@property (nonatomic, readonly) SneakyJoystick *leftJoystick;
@property (nonatomic, readonly) SneakyButton *jumpButton;
@property (nonatomic, readonly) SneakyButton *attackButton;
@end
```

The GameControlLayer imports the SneakyJoystick and SneakyButton classes. It also contains the instance variables for the leftJoystick, the jump, and the attack buttons. Note the property declarations for the instance variables to allow access to them from outside the GameControlLayer class. They are set to readonly because the SneakyJoystick and buttons should only be read from and not changed.

Next move to the GameControlLayer implementation file and replace the template-generated code with the contents of Listing 9.10.

Listing 9.10   **GameControlLayer.m**

```
//  GameControlLayer.m
//  SpaceViking
//
#import "GameControlLayer.h"

@implementation GameControlLayer
@synthesize leftJoystick;
@synthesize jumpButton;
@synthesize attackButton;

-(void)initJoystickAndButtons {
    CGSize screenSize = [CCDirector sharedDirector].winSize;
    CGRect joystickBaseDimensions = CGRectMake(0, 0, 128.0f, 128.0f);
    CGRect jumpButtonDimensions = CGRectMake(0, 0, 64.0f, 64.0f);
```

```
CGRect attackButtonDimensions = CGRectMake(0, 0, 64.0f, 64.0f);
CGPoint joystickBasePosition;
CGPoint jumpButtonPosition;
CGPoint attackButtonPosition;
if (UI_USER_INTERFACE_IDIOM() == UIUserInterfaceIdiomPad) {
    // The device is an iPad running iPhone 3.2 or later.
    CCLOG(@"Positioning Joystick and Buttons for iPad");
    joystickBasePosition = ccp(screenSize.width*0.0625f,
                               screenSize.height*0.052f);

    jumpButtonPosition = ccp(screenSize.width*0.946f,
                             screenSize.height*0.052f);

    attackButtonPosition = ccp(screenSize.width*0.947f,
                               screenSize.height*0.169f);
} else {
    // The device is an iPhone or iPod touch.
    CCLOG(@"Positioning Joystick and Buttons for iPhone");

    joystickBasePosition = ccp(screenSize.width*0.07f,
                               screenSize.height*0.11f);

    jumpButtonPosition = ccp(screenSize.width*0.93f,
                             screenSize.height*0.11f);

    attackButtonPosition = ccp(screenSize.width*0.93f,
                               screenSize.height*0.35f);
}

SneakyJoystickSkinnedBase *joystickBase =
[[[SneakyJoystickSkinnedBase alloc] init] autorelease];
joystickBase.position = joystickBasePosition;
joystickBase.backgroundSprite =
[CCSprite spriteWithFile:@"dpadDown.png"];
joystickBase.thumbSprite =
[CCSprite spriteWithFile:@"joystickDown.png"];
joystickBase.joystick = [[SneakyJoystick alloc]
                        initWithRect:joystickBaseDimensions];
leftJoystick = [joystickBase.joystick retain];
[self addChild:joystickBase];

SneakyButtonSkinnedBase *jumpButtonBase =
[[[SneakyButtonSkinnedBase alloc] init] autorelease];
jumpButtonBase.position = jumpButtonPosition;
jumpButtonBase.defaultSprite =
[CCSprite spriteWithFile:@"jumpUp.png"];
jumpButtonBase.activatedSprite =
[CCSprite spriteWithFile:@"jumpDown.png"];
```

```
    jumpButtonBase.pressSprite =
    [CCSprite spriteWithFile:@"jumpDown.png"];
    jumpButtonBase.button = [[SneakyButton alloc]
                              initWithRect:jumpButtonDimensions];
    jumpButton = [jumpButtonBase.button retain];
    jumpButton.isToggleable = NO;
    [self addChild:jumpButtonBase];

    SneakyButtonSkinnedBase *attackButtonBase = [[[SneakyButtonSkinnedBase
alloc] init] autorelease];
    attackButtonBase.position = attackButtonPosition;
    attackButtonBase.defaultSprite = [CCSprite spriteWithFile:@"handUp.png
"];
    attackButtonBase.activatedSprite = [CCSprite
spriteWithFile:@"handDown.png"];
    attackButtonBase.pressSprite = [CCSprite spriteWithFile:@"handDown.png
"];
    attackButtonBase.button = [[SneakyButton alloc] initWithRect:attackBut
tonDimensions];
    attackButton = [attackButtonBase.button retain];
    attackButton.isToggleable = NO;
    [self addChild:attackButtonBase];
}

-(id)init {
    self = [super init];
    if (self != nil) {
        // enable touches
        self.isTouchEnabled = YES;
        [self initJoystickAndButtons]; // 4
        CCLOG(@"GameControlLayer initialized");
    }
    return self;
}
@end
```

The `initJoystick` method is the same as you wrote back in Chapter 2. It creates the `SneakyJoystick`, jump, and attack buttons. The `init` method marks this layer as receiving touch events and adds the joystick and buttons to itself. This is all that is needed for the player to control the game and move Ole the Viking around.

Creating the Scrolling Layer

You are going to create three kinds of scrolling layers in this chapter. First you start with a simple scrolling layer with a large background image twice as wide as the screen. Next you add a parallax node and scroll the background in layers, where each layer has a different scroll speed. Lastly, you scroll with a `TileMap` layer, learning how to save on memory while creating much larger levels. Along the way you also learn how to create infinite scrolling for a cut-scene.

To start, create the GameplayScrollingLayer class as a subclass of CCLayer inside of the *Scene2* group. Open the header file and replace the code with the contents of Listing 9.11.

Listing 9.11   **GameplayScrollingLayer.h**

```
//   GameplayScrollingLayer.h
//   SpaceViking
//
#import <Foundation/Foundation.h>
#import "cocos2d.h"
#import "Viking.h"
#import "GameControlLayer.h"

@interface GameplayScrollingLayer : CCLayer {
    CCSpriteBatchNode *sceneSpriteBatchNode;

    CCTMXTiledMap *tileMapNode;
    CCParallaxNode *parallaxNode;
}
-(void)connectControlsWithJoystick:(SneakyJoystick*)leftJoystick
                    andJumpButton:(SneakyButton*)jumpButton
                  andAttackButton:(SneakyButton*)attackButton;
@end
```

The GameplayScrollingLayer contains the imports for Cocos2D, the Viking, and the GameControlLayer class, which contains the joystick and buttons. In the interface declaration, you can see instance variables for the CCTMXTiledMap and CCParallaxNode, which you will use later in this chapter. Lastly, there is a method called connectControlsWithJoystick, which wires up the joystick and buttons to the Viking character.

Move to the GameplayScrollingLayer implementation file and replace the template code with the contents of Listings 9.12, 9.13, and 9.14.

Listing 9.12   **GameplayScrollingLayer.m (part 1 of 3)**

```
//   GameplayScrollingLayer.m
//   SpaceViking
//
#import "GameplayScrollingLayer.h"

@implementation GameplayScrollingLayer
-(void)connectControlsWithJoystick:(SneakyJoystick*)leftJoystick
                    andJumpButton:(SneakyButton*)jumpButton
                  andAttackButton:(SneakyButton*)attackButton {
```

```
    Viking *viking = (Viking*)[sceneSpriteBatchNode
                        getChildByTag:kVikingSpriteTagValue];
    [viking setJoystick:leftJoystick];
    [viking setJumpButton:jumpButton];
    [viking setAttackButton:attackButton];


}

// Scrolling with just a large width *2 background
-(void)addScrollingBackground {
    CGSize screenSize = [[CCDirector sharedDirector] winSize];
    CGSize levelSize = [[GameManager sharedGameManager]
                        getDimensionsOfCurrentScene];


    CCSprite *scrollingBackground;
    if (UI_USER_INTERFACE_IDIOM() == UIUserInterfaceIdiomPad) {
        // Indicates game is running on iPad
        scrollingBackground =
          [CCSprite spriteWithFile:@"FlatScrollingLayer.png"];
    } else {
        scrollingBackground =
          [CCSprite spriteWithFile:@"FlatScrollingLayeriPhone.png"];
    }
    [scrollingBackground setPosition:ccp(levelSize.width/2.0f,
                                    screenSize.height/2.0f)];
    [self addChild:scrollingBackground];
}

-(id)init {
    self = [super init];
    if (self != nil) {
        CGSize screenSize = [[CCDirector sharedDirector] winSize];

        if (UI_USER_INTERFACE_IDIOM() == UIUserInterfaceIdiomPad) {
            [[CCSpriteFrameCache sharedSpriteFrameCache]
             addSpriteFramesWithFile:@"scene1atlas.plist"];
            sceneSpriteBatchNode =
            [CCSpriteBatchNode
              batchNodeWithFile:@"scene1atlas.png"];
        } else {
            [[CCSpriteFrameCache sharedSpriteFrameCache]
             addSpriteFramesWithFile:@"scene1atlasiPhone.plist"];
            sceneSpriteBatchNode =
            [CCSpriteBatchNode
              batchNodeWithFile:@"scene1atlasiPhone.png"];
        }
```

```
        [self addChild:sceneSpriteBatchNode z:20];

        Viking *viking = [[Viking alloc]
          initWithSpriteFrame:
           [[CCSpriteFrameCache sharedSpriteFrameCache]
             spriteFrameByName:@"sv_anim_1.png"]];
        [viking setJoystick:nil];
        [viking setJumpButton:nil];
        [viking setAttackButton:nil];
        [viking setPosition:ccp(screenSize.width * 0.35f,
                                screenSize.height * 0.14f)];
        [viking setCharacterHealth:100];
        [sceneSpriteBatchNode addChild:viking
          z:1000 tag:kVikingSpriteTagValue];

        [self addScrollingBackground];

        [self scheduleUpdate];
    }
    return self;
}
```

The connectControlsWithJoystick method wires up the Viking with references to the joystick and button controls residing in the ControlLayer. The Game-Scene2 class has access to both layers and uses this method to connect the joystick from the ControlLayer to the Viking in the GameplayScrollingLayer.

The addScrollingBackground method is where you set up the scrolling background for use in this level. In Listing 9.12 this method starts out with just a large 2048-pixel-wide background image. In the next section of this chapter, you will change out the contents of this method to use a parallax layer.

The init method starts in much the same way as the GameplayLayer init in the first SpaceViking scene. The screenSize is determined from the Cocos2D Director, and the SpriteBatchNode is set up.

Next the Viking object is created and added to the layer. Note how the joystick and buttons are set to nil at this point. They will be connected when the connect-ControlsWithJoystick method is called. Finally, the scrolling background is added.

Before you can test out this game, you have to add the update method and a little bit of the scrolling logic to the GameplayScrollingLayer class. Add the contents of Listing 9.13 directly below the init method.

Listing 9.13   GameplayScrollingLayer.m adjustLayer method (part 2 of 3)

```
#pragma mark SCROLLING_CALCULATION
-(void)adjustLayer {
    Viking *viking = (Viking*)[sceneSpriteBatchNode
                      getChildByTag:kVikingSpriteTagValue];          // 1
```

```
    float vikingXPosition = viking.position.x;                    // 2
    CGSize screenSize = [[CCDirector sharedDirector] winSize];    // 3
    float halfOfTheScreen = screenSize.width/2.0f;                // 4
    CGSize levelSize = [[GameManager sharedGameManager]
                        getDimensionsOfCurrentScene];             // 5
    // 6
    if ((vikingXPosition > halfOfTheScreen) &&
        (vikingXPosition < (levelSize.width - halfOfTheScreen))) {
        // Background should scroll
        float newXPosition = halfOfTheScreen - vikingXPosition;   // 7
        [self setPosition:ccp(newXPosition,self.position.y)];     // 8
    }
}
```

The adjustLayer method is responsible for moving the gameplayScrolling-Layer so that it scrolls left and right as Ole moves around the level. The first few lines in this method get the size of the screen and then the size of the level. If Ole is more than halfway across the screen and less than half a screen from the end of the level, the layer is scrolled. Otherwise the layer is not moved, and Ole remains and moves around the screen. Line by line, here is what happens:

1. Retrieves the Viking object from the SpriteBatchNode using the unique Viking Tag Constant

2. Retrieves the x coordinate of the Viking and saves it as a float. The level is designed to scroll only horizontally, so the y coordinate is ignored. The x coordinate is stored as a float just to make the code clearer; in your own games feel free to combine lines and shorten this method.

3. Retrieves the screen size from the Cocos2D Director. This is the screen size (1024 × 768 on the iPad) and not the level size. It is used to figure out if Ole is more than halfway across the screen.

4. Gets half of the screen size and stores it as a float. Once more, each computation is given on an individual line for clarity. Feel free to combine these in your own code.

5. Gets the size of the level in pixels. Only the width is used in deciding when to scroll the level.

6. Determines if the layer needs to be scrolled or not. The first part of this if statement checks to see if Ole's position is more than halfway across the screen. If Ole is not, then there is no need to scroll: Ole can move around the scene with the background remaining static. The second part of the if statement checks to see if Ole's position is less than the level width minus half of the screen. In other words, if Ole is all the way to the right, there is no need to scroll the layer.

   To put it another way, if the screen size is a normal iPad, the width will be 1024 pixels. The level here is double that size at 2048 pixels. If Ole is in the first 512 pixels or in the last (1536–2048 pixels), there is no need to scroll the level. If he is anywhere in between, the layer needs to scroll.

7. Calculates how much to move the layer. The layer needs to move in relation to the Viking minus the half of the screen in which it will not scroll. If this seems confusing, don't worry: you will get to see how it works shortly. Since the Viking is already moved to the new position, the layer needs to be moved so that it stays onscreen and has the appearance of scrolling.

8. Changes the position of the layer in the x coordinate. The y coordinate remains the same.

There is one more method to add, and then you can test out scrolling. Copy the contents of Listing 9.14 directly below adjustLayer in *GameplayScrollingLayer.m*.

Listing 9.14   **GameplayScrollingLayer.m update method (part 3 of 3)**

```
#pragma mark -
-(void) update:(ccTime)deltaTime
{
    CCArray *listOfGameObjects =
    [sceneSpriteBatchNode children];
    for (GameCharacter *tempChar in listOfGameObjects) {
        [tempChar updateStateWithDeltaTime:deltaTime
                        andListOfGameObjects:listOfGameObjects];
    }

    [self adjustLayer];

    // Check to see if the Viking is dead
    GameCharacter *tempChar =
    (GameCharacter*)[sceneSpriteBatchNode
                    getChildByTag:kVikingSpriteTagValue];
    if (([tempChar characterState] == kStateDead) &&
        ([tempChar numberOfRunningActions] == 0)) {
        [[GameManager sharedGameManager] setHasPlayerDied:YES];
        [[GameManager sharedGameManager]
          runSceneWithID:kLevelCompleteScene];
    }

    // Check to see if the RadarDish is dead
    tempChar = (GameCharacter*)[sceneSpriteBatchNode
                                getChildByTag:kRadarDishTagValue];
    if (([tempChar characterState] == kStateDead) &&
        ([tempChar numberOfRunningActions] == 0)) {
        [[GameManager sharedGameManager]
          runSceneWithID:kLevelCompleteScene];
    }

}
@end
```

The update method is the same as you have written before except for the call to
adjustLayer. The for loop updates all of the GameObjects in the layer, and then
the layer is adjusted, followed by a check to see if the Viking or RadarDish are dead.
Since the layer is adjusted according to the Viking's position, it is important to do it
after the Viking has had a chance to update inside of the for loop.

Two quick steps remain before you can try out this level. You have to set up the
GameManager to be able to load and run the GameScene2 and the MainMenuLayer
to call the GameManager when you press on the "Dogs of Loki!" button.

Open the *GameManager.m* class and add an import for the GameScene2 class:

```
#import "GameScene2.h"
```

Next scroll down to the runSceneWithID method and update the switch block
so that for kGameLevel2, the GameScene2 is instantiated and set as the sceneToRun
variable.

```
case kGameLevel2:
            sceneToRun = [GameScene2 node];
            break;
```

> ### Warning
>
> Be sure to remove the return statement that was previously inside of the kGame-
> Level2 switch branch. You want the GameScene2 scene to be initialized and for the
> method to continue so that the audio is loaded and the director can transition to the new
> scene.

Open the *MainMenuLayer.m* class and add the if else branches shown in
Listing 9.15.

Listing 9.15   **Updated playScene method in MainMenuLayer.m**

```
-(void)playScene:(CCMenuItemFont*)itemPassedIn {
    if ([itemPassedIn tag] == 1) {
        [[GameManager sharedGameManager] runSceneWithID:kIntroScene];
    } else if ([itemPassedIn tag] == 2) {
        [[GameManager sharedGameManager] runSceneWithID:kGameLevel2];
    } else if ([itemPassedIn tag] == 3) {
        [[GameManager sharedGameManager] runSceneWithID:kGameLevel3];
    } else if ([itemPassedIn tag] == 4) {
        [[GameManager sharedGameManager] runSceneWithID:kGameLevel4];
    } else if ([itemPassedIn tag] == 5) {
        [[GameManager sharedGameManager] runSceneWithID:kGameLevel5];
    } else {
        CCLOG(@"Unexpected item.  Tag was: %d", [itemPassedIn tag]);
    }
}
```

The kGameLevel2 branch is called for the Dogs of Loki; the others are for later chapters. If you click **Run** and select the Dogs of Loki level, you should be able to move Ole to the right. Once he crosses over half of the screen, you should start to see the background scrolling. Figure 9.3 shows the level as Ole scrolls from left to right.

Figure 9.3 Space Viking level 2 showing scrolling

A Note on CCFollow

There is a built-in action in Cocos2D to move a layer or the camera around any CCNode called CCFollow. The CCFollow action makes the object running it follow one of your characters (or any CCNode) and scroll in the opposite direction. To use it in your games, you just need the lines:

```
id followAction = [CCFollow actionWithTarget:playerCharacter];
[layer runAction:followAction];
```

This action runs continuously and adjusts the layer to the position of the player character. You can even provide the CCFollow action with boundaries so that the scrolling or movement of the layer is limited. Unfortunately, it moves the layer in both the x- and y-axes, so when the playerCharacter jumps, the ground layer falls away. In *Space Viking* the scrolling needs to happen only in the x-axis; therefore, the CCFollow action is not used. It is mentioned here in case you find it helpful in your own games.

While this scrolling is a good start, it lacks depth, and you don't really get the illusion that Ole is in a big alien landscape. The next section covers adding a parallax node to this layer in order to have multiple levels of scrolling backgrounds for a faux-3D scrolling effect.

Scrolling with Parallax Layers

In the previous section you created a scrolling scene consisting of a background with two layers. One was the static backdrop of the alien desert, the other the ground along with the boulders and mountains in the background that moved with Ole. In order to give your games more depth, it is useful to have multiple background layers all scrolling at different rates. To visualize this effect, think of a time you were looking out the side window of a car or train. The grass or the side of the road scrolled by quickly, the trees beyond that slower, and the mountains or faraway items in the background scrolled the slowest of all. In your Cocos2D games there is no real depth to these layers, but by scrolling various layers at different speeds from the player, you can have the same effect. A little bit of work is needed on your part, and the player's brain will automatically do the rest.

You do not have to scroll the items manually; there is a handy class in Cocos2D called CCParallaxNode that takes care of the scrolling for you. A parallax node is a special Cocos2D parent node that has the logic to scroll its children at different ratios than the ratios at which the parent itself is scrolled. The best way to understand this is with a simple code change.

Start by opening the GameplayScrollingLayer.m class and creating a new method called addScrollingBackgroundWithParallax directly above the init method. Copy the lines in Listing 9.16 into the new addScrollingBackgroundWithParallax method.

Listing 9.16   GameplayScrollingLayer.m addScrollingBackgroundWithParallax

```
// Scrolling with 3 Parallax backgrounds
-(void) addScrollingBackgroundWithParallax {
    CGSize screenSize = [[CCDirector sharedDirector] winSize];
    CGSize levelSize = [[GameManager sharedGameManager]
                        getDimensionsOfCurrentScene];

    CCSprite *BGLayer1;
    CCSprite *BGLayer2;
    CCSprite *BGLayer3;

    if (UI_USER_INTERFACE_IDIOM() == UIUserInterfaceIdiomPad) {
        // Indicates game is running on iPad
        BGLayer1 = [CCSprite spriteWithFile:@"chap9_scrolling4.png"];
        BGLayer2 = [CCSprite spriteWithFile:@"chap9_scrolling2.png"];
        BGLayer3 = [CCSprite spriteWithFile:@"chap9_scrolling3.png"];
    } else {
        BGLayer1 = [CCSprite
                    spriteWithFile:@"chap9_scrolling4iPhone.png"];
        BGLayer2 = [CCSprite
                    spriteWithFile:@"chap9_scrolling2iPhone.png"];
```

```
        BGLayer3 = [CCSprite
                      spriteWithFile:@"chap9_scrolling3iPhone.png"];
   }
   // chap9_scrolling4 is the ground
   // chap9_scrolling2 are the large mountains
   // chap9_scrolling3 are the small rocks


   parallaxNode = [CCParallaxNode node];
   [parallaxNode
    setPosition:ccp(levelSize.width/2.0f,screenSize.height/2.0f)];
   float xOffset = 0;

   // Ground moves at ratio 1,1
   [parallaxNode addChild:BGLayer1 z:40 parallaxRatio:ccp(1.0f,1.0f)
          positionOffset:ccp(0.0f,0.0f)];

   xOffset = (levelSize.width/2) * 0.3f;
   [parallaxNode addChild:BGLayer2 z:20 parallaxRatio:ccp(0.2f,1.0f)
          positionOffset:ccp(xOffset, 0)];

   xOffset = (levelSize.width/2) * 0.8f;
   [parallaxNode addChild:BGLayer3 z:30 parallaxRatio:ccp(0.7f,1.0f)
          positionOffset:ccp(xOffset, 0)];
   [self addChild:parallaxNode z:10];
}
```

The first part of the addScrollingBackgroundWithParallax method creates three CCSprites to be used as the layers in the parallax background. Next the CCParallax node is instantiated. The three background elements are added along with a parallaxRatio and positionOffset. Note how even though you add the ground first, then the mountains, and then the small rocks layer, they are kept in the correct order due to the z values. The ground has a z value of 40, the rocks 30, and the mountains 20.

The positions of the three CCSprites are based on the position of the CCParallax-Node. To understand how the position of a CCParallaxNode child is calculated, look at the code inside of ParallaxNode addChild, shown in Listing 9.17.

Listing 9.17   CCParallaxNode addChild method

```
CGPoint pos = self.position;
    float x = pos.x * ratio.x + offset.x;
    float y = pos.y * ratio.y + offset.y;
    child.position = ccp(x,y);
```

The child layer position is based on the `CCParallaxNode` position times the ratio plus the offset.

In the second layer of this scrolling background, the ratio on the x-axis is 0.7. Since you already set the position of the `CCParallaxNode` to be 1024 on the x-axis, this means the second layer would be placed at 716.8 pixels (1024 times 0.7). That would skew the position of the layer to the left, so the offset is needed to put in the correct initial position.

The offset helps put the layer in the correct position to compensate for the ratio if needed. In the case of *Space Viking* you can see the offset being the remainder needed to add the initial x coordinate to the middle of the scene. In your games, you may want the offset to be different, for instance, if a particular background starts later in a level.

As you can see in Listing 9.15, the topmost background layer (`BGLayer3`) is moved 0.7 pixels for every pixel the `CCParallaxNode` is moved in the x-axis, while the backmost layer (`BGLayer2`) is moved only 0.3 pixels for every pixel the `CCParralaxNode` is moved.

To see how the parallax scrolling works, comment out the call to `addScrolling-Background` and add in a call to the `addScrollingBackgroundWithParallax` in the `init` method, as shown in Listing 9.18.

Listing 9.18 GameplayScrollingLayer init method changes

```
//[self addScrollingBackground];
[self addScrollingBackgroundWithParallax];
```

If you click **Run**, you will see the new level with four layers in the background, three scrolling as part of the `CCParallaxNode` and one static background element. Move Ole to the right of the screen and pay close attention to the scrolling layers. Figure 9.4 shows Ole with the four layers of background: the ground, the rock piles, the mountains, and the alien sky.

You have taken the first steps in creating a scrolling level. Hopefully, your mind is already full of ideas on how to bring scrolling into your own games. In the next section you learn how to create an infinitely scrolling level as a cut-scene for this second level. After that, you will learn about TileMaps and how to create even larger levels while using less memory at the same time.

Scrolling to Infinity

Scrolling left and right a few screen widths is very useful, and there are many games that go only that far. But perhaps your game requires an endlessly scrolling background, and if so, this section teaches you how to do that.

To learn how to implement infinite scrolling, you create a cut-scene to play before the second level you created earlier in this chapter. This scene features Ole in

Figure 9.4   Ole with the four background layers

a floating platform flying through the alien landscape with clouds zooming by in the background. The clouds keep zooming by until the player touches the screen. In this example the clouds scroll from right to left, but there is nothing mandating that it has to be that way. You can scroll left to right, top to bottom, or bottom to top in your own games.

To start, create a new group in Xcode called `CutSceneForLevel2` under the *Scenes* group. You will have the infinite scrolling cut-scene separate from the second alien desert level, so that it is easier to understand the scrolling logic and reuse it in your games.

To accomplish infinite scrolling, you are going to have a set of 25 clouds that move from right to left at random speeds. Once the clouds go offscreen on the left, they are moved to a new position on the right side, offscreen. They are once more moved from right to left. The whole time, Ole remains in the middle of the screen but seems as if he is flying by. That's because our brains are wired to interpret background movement as if we were moving, so you "feel" like Ole is moving, even though he is always in the exact same position. If you are making a 2D flying game or the next shooter, you can use this technique to make it look as though your character is flying through the air or over the terrain.

Enough with the theory: time to get into the code and see how it is actually done. You start with the scrolling background to understand the logic in there. Following that, you build the scene in order to be able to have Cocos2D play the cut-scene.

Creating the Scrolling Layer

The scrolling layer in the cut-scene is a set of clouds that scrolls from right to left at varying speeds. Figure 9.5 shows how the clouds look along with Ole and the platform.

Figure 9.5   Cut-scene for level 2 showing Ole on a platform in front of scrolling clouds

To make this scene as efficient as possible, you use a texture atlas to hold both the cloud images and the Viking and Platform graphics. In the beginning of this chapter, you imported the *ParallaxBackgrounds* folder into your *SpaceViking* project. Inside that folder are subfolders called *ScrollingCloudsBackgrounds* and *ScrollingCloudsTextureAtlases* for the static background and the texture atlases, respectively. There are iPhone-, iPhone 4-, and iPad-sized backgrounds and texture atlases, just as you created and used previously in *Space Viking*.

Create a new Objective-C class inside of the *CutSceneForLevel2* group and name it *PlatformScrollingLayer.m*, setting it as a subclass of CCLayer. Open the *PlatformScrolling-Layer.h* header file and replace the contents with the code from Listing 9.19.

Listing 9.19   **PlatformScrollingLayer.h header file**

```
//  PlatformScrollingLayer.h
//  SpaceViking
//
```

```
#import <Foundation/Foundation.h>
#import "cocos2d.h"
#import "Constants.h"

@interface PlatformScrollingLayer : CCLayer {
    CCSpriteBatchNode *scrollingBatchNode;
}
@end
```

The *PlatformScrollingLayer* header file has only imports for Cocos2D and the *Constants.h* file, along with an instance variable to hold the CCSpriteBatchNode used in this scene.

> **Note on** CCSpriteBatchNode
>
> Since the scrolling layer is made up of many clouds using the same six textures, it is much more efficient to have those textures inside of a texture atlas and rendered onscreen in a CCSpriteBatchNode. As you will see in this chapter, there are 25 clouds, Ole, and the platform (27 sprites). Using the CCSpriteBatchNode reduces the OpenGL ES bind calls from 27 to 1 and batches the draw calls for better performance.

Switch over to the *PlatformScrollingLayer.m* implementation file and add the contents of Listing 9.20.

Listing 9.20   PlatformScrollingLayer.m (declarations and init method) (part 1 of 6)

```
//  PlatformScrollingLayer.m
//  SpaceViking
//
#import "PlatformScrollingLayer.h"
#import "GameManager.h"

@interface PlatformScrollingLayer (PrivateMethods)
-(void)resetCloudWithNode:(id)node;
-(void)createCloud;
-(void)createVikingAndPlatform;
-(void)createStaticBackground;
@end

@implementation PlatformScrollingLayer

-(id)init {
    self = [super init];
    if (self != nil) {
        srandom(time(NULL));
        self.isTouchEnabled = YES;
        [self createStaticBackground];
```

```
    if (UI_USER_INTERFACE_IDIOM() == UIUserInterfaceIdiomPad) {
        // Indicates game is running on iPad
        [[CCSpriteFrameCache sharedSpriteFrameCache]
        addSpriteFramesWithFile:
        @"ScrollingCloudsTextureAtlas.plist"];
        scrollingBatchNode = [CCSpriteBatchNode
                batchNodeWithFile:@"ScrollingCloudsTextureAtlas.png"];
    } else {
        [[CCSpriteFrameCache sharedSpriteFrameCache]
        addSpriteFramesWithFile:
        @"ScrollingCloudsTextureAtlasiPhone.plist"];
        scrollingBatchNode = [CCSpriteBatchNode
          batchNodeWithFile:@"ScrollingCloudsTextureAtlasiPhone.png"];
    }

    [self addChild:scrollingBatchNode];

    for (int x=0; x < 25; x++) {
        [self createCloud];
    }

    [self createVikingAndPlatform];
    }
    return self;
}
```

The second @interface declaration becomes a Category to the Platform-
ScrollingLayer, enabling these methods to be called anywhere within the class. In
the previous classes you wrote for *Space Viking*, the init method is at the bottom of
the file because the methods it called had to be defined above.

@interface Declaration inside Implementation Files

Remember, if you want to easily move the order of your methods inside of your implementation file, you can declare your methods in the header file or in a separate @interface
declaration inside of your implementation (.m or .mm) file.

The second @interface declaration defines the four methods used internally by
PlatformScrollingLayer to create and reset the clouds and create the Viking, the
platform, and the static background image. In the init method the CCSpriteFrame-
Cache is asked to load the sprite frames from the *ScrollingCloudsTextureAtlas.plist*. These
are the coordinates of the clouds, Ole, and the platform inside of the texture atlas.
The scrollingBatchNode is initialized with the texture atlas PNG and added to the
layer.

If you follow the code in the init method, you will see a call to create the static
background followed by a for loop initializing 25 clouds via the createCloud

method. After the `for` loop, the `createVikingAndPlatform` method is called to add Ole and the platform, as you probably already guessed, by the method name.

Add the code in Listing 9.21 to *PlatformScrollingLayer.m* in order to create the static background in the scrolling scene.

Listing 9.21 createStaticBackground in PlatformScrollingLayer.m (part 2 of 6)

```
-(void)createStaticBackground {
    CGSize screenSize = [CCDirector sharedDirector].winSize;
    CCSprite *background;
    if (UI_USER_INTERFACE_IDIOM() == UIUserInterfaceIdiomPad) {
        // Indicates game is running on iPad
        background =
         [CCSprite spriteWithFile:@"tiles_grad_bkgrnd.png"];
    } else {
        background =
         [CCSprite spriteWithFile:@"tiles_grad_bkgrndiPhone.png"];
    }

    [background setPosition:
     ccp(screenSize.width/2.0f, screenSize.height/2.0f)];
    [self addChild:background];
}
```

The `createStaticBackground` method sets up a new `CCSprite` to act as the moon and sky background for this level and adds it to the layer. Since the background is the full size of the iPad screen, it is centered in the middle of the screen. Because it is being added first to the layer, it will have a lower z value than the `CCSprite-BatchNode`, causing the background image to be composited behind the clouds.

Next add the code in Listing 9.22 to your *PlatformScrollingLayer.m* implementation file below the `createStaticBackground` method, to add the `createCloud` method.

Listing 9.22 createCloud method in PlatformScrollingLayer.m (part 3 of 6)

```
-(void)createCloud {
    int cloudToDraw = random() % 6; // 0 to 5
    NSString *cloudFileName = [NSString
     stringWithFormat:@"tiles_cloud%d.png",cloudToDraw];
    CCSprite *cloudSprite = [CCSprite
     spriteWithSpriteFrameName:cloudFileName];
    [scrollingBatchNode addChild:cloudSprite];
    [self resetCloudWithNode:cloudSprite];
}
```

The cloud filenames are *tiles_cloud0.png* through *tiles_cloud5.png*. A random number between zero and five is used to create a cloud using one of the six images. The cloud PNG files are inside of the texture atlas PNG, and they can be retrieved via the sprite frame with the same name as the original filename. Remember when the texture atlas was created with TexturePacker, how the filenames of the original images were set as the image frame names? A `cloudSprite` is created, set to one of the six cloud images, and added to the `CCSpriteBatchNode` called `scrollingBatchNode`. The cloud-Sprite is then passed to the `resetCloudWithNode` method, which sets it into place and starts moving it from right to left. Add the `resetCloudWithNode` method shown in Listing 9.23 to your *PlatformScrollingLayer.m* class file.

Listing 9.23   resetCloudWithNode method in PlatformScrollingLayer.m (part 4 of 6)

```
-(void)resetCloudWithNode:(id)node {
    CGSize screenSize = [CCDirector sharedDirector].winSize; // 1
    CCNode *cloud = (CCNode*)node; // 2
    float xOffSet = [cloud boundingBox].size.width /2; // 3

    int xPosition = screenSize.width + 1 + xOffSet; // 4
    int yPosition = random() % (int)screenSize.height; // 5

    [cloud setPosition:ccp(xPosition,yPosition)]; // 6

    int moveDuration = random() % kMaxCloudMoveDuration; // 7
    if (moveDuration < kMinCloudMoveDuration) {
        moveDuration = kMinCloudMoveDuration; // 8
    }

    float offScreenXPosition = (xOffSet * -1) - 1; // 9

    // 10
    id moveAction = [CCMoveTo actionWithDuration:moveDuration
                        position:
                            ccp(offScreenXPosition,[cloud position].y)];
    id resetAction = [CCCallFuncN
                        actionWithTarget:self
                        selector:@selector(resetCloudWithNode:)];
    id sequenceAction = [CCSequence
                            actions:moveAction,resetAction,nil];

    [cloud runAction:sequenceAction]; // 11

    int newZOrder = kMaxCloudMoveDuration - moveDuration; // 12

    [scrollingBatchNode reorderChild:cloud z:newZOrder]; // 13
}
```

At a high level, the resetCloud method positions the cloud offscreen on the right side and setups a CCMove action to move the cloud at a random speed across the screen from right to left. The z composition ordering of the cloud is based on its speed with the faster clouds closer to the foreground and the slower clouds toward the background. At the end of the move, the resetCloud method is called on the cloud's behalf to reset it back offscreen to the right at a random position to start the right-to-left move again. The code in resetCloud works as follows:

1. Gets the screen size from the CCDirector. The screen size is used to figure out how far to the right and left would be offscreen and not visible to the player.

2. Casts the id type to a CCNode. The resetCloud method is called from both the createCloud method and a CCCallFuncN action. The CCCallFuncN action passes back a more generic id type even though you know it is a CCSprite, a subclass of CCNode. The cast to CCNode pointer is purely for code clarity; you can omit it in your code if you are comfortable with the generic id type.

3. Sets the x-axis offset to half the width of the cloud image. Recall from earlier chapters that the anchor point for Cocos2D objects is in the center of the image by default. When you move an image around, it is always moved and positioned relative to its center point. Since the anchor point is in the middle, you need to know half of the image's width so that you know how far it needs to be to the right or left to be offscreen.

   This point bears repeating because it is important to understand it. The cloud image is moved around its center point. If its position is half of the width of the image and the screen width, it is offscreen to the right. Likewise, if it is at zero minus half of the cloud width on the x-axis, it is just about offscreen on the left side. Remember zero on the x-axis is the left-most side of the screen. Figure 9.6 illustrates the cloud, its anchor point, and position.

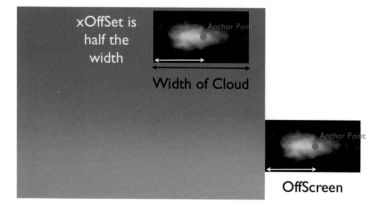

Figure 9.6   Cloud anchor point, width, and position

4. Sets the x position variable to offscreen on the right. By adding the screen width to half of the cloud width (xOffSet) and one more pixel, the cloud is placed directly to the right of the visible area of the screen.

5. Sets the y position variable to a random value along the screen height.

6. Sets the cloud position to the new x and y values calculated in steps 4 and 5.

7. Sets the move duration to a random value between zero and the maximum move duration. The maxMoveDuration and minMoveDuration #defines are added in Listing 9.26.

8. Checks to ensure that the move duration is at least as long as the minimum value. If not, it is set to the minimum value. The move duration is in seconds.

9. Calculates the x position that the cloud will be at when it is offscreen on the left. The clouds start on the right and move left; this value is when they go offscreen on the left side. Figure 9.6 illustrates when the cloud is offscreen on the left side.

10. Creates the actions to move and then reset the cloud. The move action moves the cloud from its current position offscreen on the right, across the screen, ending offscreen on the left side. The CCCallFuncN resets the cloud by calling the resetCloud method once the cloud has finished moving. The CCSequence action creates a simple move and reset sequence.

11. Runs the CCSequence action, starting the move from right to left.

12. Calculates the new z compositing value. If you recall back to Chapter 2, the z values in Cocos2D determine how to composite the CCSprites, with the higher values being in the foreground and lower values being closer to the background. In other words, a CCSprite with a higher z value will be composited in front of one with a lower z value within the same layer or CCSpriteBatchNode.

    In this line the current move duration is subtracted from the maximum duration. Suppose the maximum duration is 10 seconds and the move duration is 2 seconds. This means that the new z value would be 8 (10 − 2). If a cloud had a longer duration, such as 6 seconds, this means the new z value would be 4 (10 − 6). The cloud with a z value of 8 would be in front of the cloud with a z value of 4. Calculating and changing the z values allows for the clouds with the fastest speeds (shortest move durations) to be in front of the slower clouds. This is the key line that gives the impression of depth by having the faster items in the front and the slower ones in the back.

13. Asks the CCSpriteBatchNode to reorder the composite position of the cloud to the new z value, moving it to the front of slower clouds and behind faster clouds.

Tips and Tricks

I have often heard more experienced game developers say that most of game development was done with tricks, and the key was learning what tricks to use to get the effect you need. You don't have to replicate real life in your game in order for scrolling to feel real. One clear example is keeping Ole centered on this screen and how he was moved in the second level you built previously. Playing the game, you feel like Ole is moving through the level when in reality he is centered in the middle of the screen.

There are two more methods to add to `PlatformScrollingLayer` before it can be complete. The first is the `createVikingPlatform` method, shown in Listing 9.24. Copy the contents into your *PlatformScrollingLayer.m* class file.

Listing 9.24   createVikingAndPlatform in PlatformScrollingLayer.m (part 5 of 6)

```
-(void)createVikingAndPlatform {
    CGSize screenSize = [CCDirector sharedDirector].winSize; // 1
    int nextZValue = [scrollingBatchNode children].count + 1; // 2

    // 3
    CCSprite *platform = [CCSprite
                            spriteWithSpriteFrameName:@"platform.png"];
    [platform setPosition:
            ccp(screenSize.width/2,
                screenSize.height * 0.09f)];
    [scrollingBatchNode addChild:platform z:nextZValue];

    nextZValue = nextZValue + 1; // 4

    //5
    CCSprite *viking = [CCSprite
                            spriteWithSpriteFrameName:@"sv_anim_1.png"];
    [viking setPosition:
            ccp(screenSize.width/2,
                screenSize.height * 0.23f)];
    [scrollingBatchNode addChild:viking z:nextZValue];
}
```

The `createVikingAndPlatform` method works as follows:

1. Gets the size of the screen, which is used as a reference point to position Ole and the platform.

2. Calculates the next z value available in order to place the platform and Ole in front of all of the clouds. The `scrollingBatchNode` is asked for the `CCArray` of all its children, and the count of the number of elements in the `CCArray` is returned. The logic here is that no matter how many clouds have been added, if you set the platform and Viking to a z value greater than the clouds, they will

be composited in front of them. If you knew you were only going to have 50 or 100 clouds, you could always set the z value to a larger amount, such as 101, or even 2000, just as long as it is larger than any of the clouds' z values.

3. Creates a new CCSprite for the platform and sets it on the bottom center of the screen. The screen size is used to determine the bottom center position. The new CCSprite is added to the CCSpriteBatchNode scrollingBatchNode.

4. Increments the z value by one so that Ole will be composited in front of the platform.

5. Creates a new CCSprite for Ole and sets it on top of the platform on the bottom center of the screen. The new CCSprite of Ole is added to the CCSprite-BatchNode scrollingBatchNode.

The previous code listings set up the cloud, the platform, and Ole and got them rendered onscreen. This would be all that is needed except that you need a way to transition out of the cut-scene and into the second level of the game. Since the PlatformScrollingLayer already listens for touch events, all you need to do is add a ccTouchesBegan method, as shown in Listing 9.25. Add the contents of Listing 9.25 to your *PlatformScrollingLayer.m* class.

Listing 9.25   ccTouchesBegan method in PlatformScrollingLayer (part 6 of 6)

```
-(void)ccTouchesBegan:(NSSet *)touches withEvent:(UIEvent *)event {
    [[GameManager sharedGameManager] runSceneWithID:kGameLevel2];
}
@end
```

The ccTouchesBegan method just places a call to the GameManager to switch from the cut-scene to the game level 2 scene.

There is one more quick addition you need to make to *Constants.h* file to support the new cut-scene. Open the *Constants.h* file and add the #defines, as shown in Listing 9.26.

Listing 9.26   Constants.h #define used in PlatformScrollingLayer.m

```
// Defines for Cloud Scrolling Scene
#define kMaxCloudMoveDuration 10
#define kMinCloudMoveDuration 1
```

At this point you should build your project to make sure you did not make any typos or other mistakes. If the project compiles fine, you can move on to creating the scene and adding the logic to the GameManager class to be able to play the cut-scene in *Space Viking*.

Creating the Platform Scene

The cut-scene will be a new Cocos2D scene with just a single scrolling layer. Create a new Objective-C class inside of the *CutSceneForLevel2* group called *PlatformScene.m* as a subclass of CCScene. Open the *PlatformScene.h* header file and replace the template contents with Listing 9.27.

Listing 9.27   **PlatformScene.h header file**

```
//   PlatformScene.h
//   SpaceViking
//
#import <Foundation/Foundation.h>
#import "cocos2d.h"
#import "PlatformScrollingLayer.h"

@interface PlatformScene : CCScene {
}
@end
```

The header file format should be very familiar to you by now; the PlatformScene inherits from CCScene, and it imports the scrolling background class.

Switch over to the *PlatformScene.m* implementation file and replace it with the contents of Listing 9.28.

Listing 9.28   **PlatformScene.m implementation file**

```
//   PlatformScene.m
//   SpaceViking
//
#import "PlatformScene.h"

@implementation PlatformScene
-(id)init {
    self = [super init];
    if (self != nil) {
        // Platform Cloud Scrolling
        PlatformScrollingLayer *scrollingLayer =
         [PlatformScrollingLayer node];
        [self addChild:scrollingLayer];
    }
    return self;
}
@end
```

The `PlatformScene` implementation is straightforward, just a simple boilerplate
`init` method that creates the scrolling layer and adds it to the scene.

There are two more steps, and then you can run the cut-scene in *Space Viking*. First,
let's add the necessary code to the *MainMenuLayer.m* so that it plays the cut-scene when
the second level is selected.

Open the *MainMenuLayer.m* and find the `playScene` method. Modify the `if else`
branch for the 2 tag so that the `playScene` method looks like the **bold** code in Listing 9.29.

Listing 9.29   **playScene method in MainMenuLayer.m**

```
-(void)playScene:(CCMenuItemFont*)itemPassedIn {
    if ([itemPassedIn tag] == 1) {
        [[GameManager sharedGameManager] runSceneWithID:kIntroScene];
    } else if ([itemPassedIn tag] == 2) {
        [[GameManager sharedGameManager]
            runSceneWithID:kCutSceneForLevel2];
    } else if ([itemPassedIn tag] == 3) {
        [[GameManager sharedGameManager] runSceneWithID:kGameLevel3];
    } else if ([itemPassedIn tag] == 4) {
        [[GameManager sharedGameManager] runSceneWithID:kGameLevel4];
    } else if ([itemPassedIn tag] == 5) {
        [[GameManager sharedGameManager] runSceneWithID:kGameLevel5];
    } else {
        CCLOG(@"Unexpected item.  Tag was: %d", [itemPassedIn tag]);
    }
}
```

When the second level menu item is selected on the Main Menu screen, the Game-
Manager will be called and asked to run the `kCutSceneForLevel2`, which is the
cut-scene you just wrote.

Open the *GameManager.m* class and the import for the `PlatformScene` next to the
other `#import` statements as follows:

```
#import "PlatformScene.h"
```

Next move to the `runSceneWithID` method. In the `switch` block add the code
shown in Listing 9.30.

Listing 9.30   **Switch branch for cut-scene and level 2 in GameManager.m runSceneWithID
method**

```
case kCutSceneForLevel2:
            sceneToRun = [PlatformScene node];
            break;
Lastly,
```

You should now be able to click **Run** and select the second level from the Main Menu. The scrolling clouds scene should show up, playing in an endless loop. If you touch anywhere, the game should transition to the second level you built earlier in this chapter.

Now that you have learned how to add parallax scrolling and infinite scrolling, the next step is to learn about TileMaps. You can use TileMaps to create large scrolling worlds of almost infinite size while keeping your game's memory footprint small.

Tile Maps

In building the parallax levels, you used a series of double screen-width images to create the scrolling background strips. While this was easy to code, it was not efficient as far as memory is concerned. You can imagine that making a large level of, say, 10,000 or 20,000 pixels in width would use up all the available memory on an iPad or iPhone 4, saying nothing of the older iPhone and iPhone 3G.

There is a simpler way to create large worlds and levels without the use of large amounts of memory for your textures. The key is in using tiles, or unique textures that you can repeat over and over to create your landscape. Take a close look at Figure 9.7. It shows how the new ground layer will be made up of just four unique tiles. Likewise, the rock formation that you will add as a repeating background will be made of only two unique tiles each. If you are careful with how your tiles are designed, you can use them over and over while still making the player believe he or she is seeing a unique landscape.

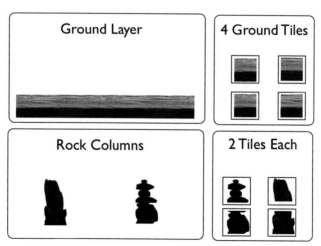

Figure 9.7   Ground and rock formation and the tiles that make them up

In *Space Viking* you are going to use tiles that are 64 × 64 pixels in size. It is important that your tiles all be the same size, and preferably a size that is a power of two. Most games can get away with 32 × 32 pixel tiles. Looking at Figure 9.7, imagine that you use the four ground tiles to re-create the entire ground layer on the second level you created in this chapter. In other words, by using various combinations of these tiles, you can create a background to stretch out as long as you need. No matter how large the background you design, it never takes any more graphic memory than the unique tiles you have here.

Tiles take very little memory, as they themselves are very small images. Even if a tile is drawn on 20 places onscreen, it is stored only once in texture memory. If you can get creative and build your backgrounds from tiles, you can have really wide or tall backgrounds while using very little memory.

Tiles in *Space Viking*

The artwork for *Space Viking* was not designed with tiles in mind, so it does not break apart into tiles as easily as if it were designed to fit in those tiles. If you design your game and artwork to fit into tiles from the start, you can achieve even greater memory savings.

In the next section you create the TileMap and learn how to incorporate it inside of the second-level code you have already built.

Installing the Tiled Tool

To create the tile map that Cocos2D will use, you need to use the free Tiled tool. The Tiled tool allows you to create tile maps and set up multiple layers in your tile maps. In *Space Viking* you use Tiled only to set up the layout of the tiles. In your games you can use it for setting up the locations of the walls, enemies, and a host of other elements. In fact, some people design complete games using Tiled where quite a bit of the game logic is centered around the features offered by tiled maps. Given that you can visually lay out a level to see how it looks before you code the functionality, this offers an easy way for developers to set up games like puzzles and platforms where you need to create a variety of large and intricate levels.

Download the Tiles Texture Atlas before Proceeding

The tiles have already been added to a texture atlas that you can download along with the source code for this chapter. The instructions in this section assume that you already have the *TilesTextureAtlas.png* that is located with the resources for this chapter saved on your Mac.

To Install Tiled on Your Mac

1. Open a browser to *http://mapeditor.org*.
2. Click the **Tiled Qt for Mac OS** X link on the right. This will download a DMG file to your Mac.

3. Double-click on the DMG to open it if it is not opened automatically by your browser.

4. Drag the Tiled application into your *Applications* folder.

That's it. Tiled is installed on your system. Figure 9.8 shows the mapeditor.org website and the contents of the Tiled DMG.

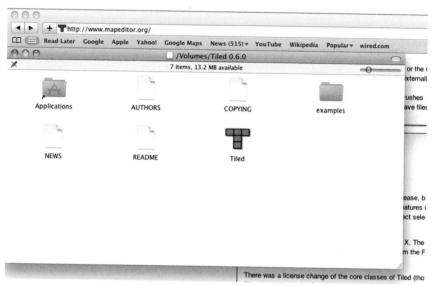

Figure 9.8   Mapeditor.org website and contents of Tiled DMG

Now that you have Tiled installed, the next step is to create the TileMap that you are going to use in *Space Viking*.

Creating the Tile Map

You are going to create a TileMap for the iPad that is 4096 pixels wide by 768 pixels tall. This map will be twice as wide as the scrolling map you created earlier in the chapter.

Start up the Tiled tool, and

1. Select **File > New**.

2. In the dialog box, under Map Size:

   Enter *64* for the width.

   Enter *12* for the height.

3. Under Tile Size:

   Enter *64* for the width and height.

   Your dialog box should look like Figure 9.9.

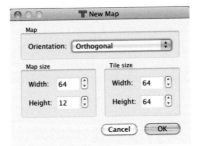

Figure 9.9   Tiled showing the new TileMap window

4. Click **OK** to create the empty TileMap.

5. From the Map menu, select **New Tileset**.

6. Click **Browse** and select the *TilesTextureAtlas.png* file you downloaded previously from the book's site. Set the tile width and height to 64 and the margins to 1. The Tiled New Tileset window should look like Figure 9.10.

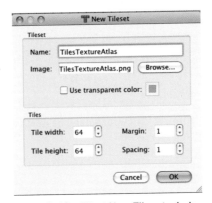

Figure 9.10   Tiled New Tileset window

7. Click **OK** to add the new TileSet to your TileMap.

Now you have a blank TileMap along with a set of tiles in a TileSet that you can use to paint the TileMap. By clicking on the tiles and then on the TileMap, you can set a particular tile in the TileMap to be a specific tile texture.

The next step is to create the Tile layers you will need to store the ground, the rock column, and the rock boulder.

Creating the Three TileMap Layers

1. Click on the **Layers** tab in the right panel of Tiled.

2. Select **Layer > Add Tiled Layer** from the menu to add each layer.

3. Add two tile layers, one called `RockColumnsLayer` and one called `RockBoulderLayer`.

4. Rename the first layer to `GroundLayer`.

5. Uncheck both the `RockColumnsLayer` and the `RockBoulderLayer` so that only `GroundLayer` is checked and selected.

If you switch over to the Tilesets tab, you can select a tile and place it on the TileMap. Create a ground layer on the bottom row of tiles, similar to the one shown in Figure 9.11.

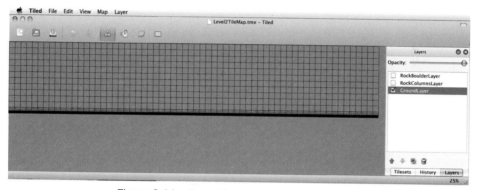

Figure 9.11   GroundLayer populated on TileMap

Next, deselect the `GroundLayer` and select the `RockColumnLayer`. Add the rock columns above the ground at random intervals. Your TileMap should now look like Figure 9.12.

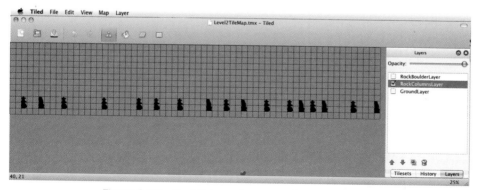

Figure 9.12   RockColumnsLayer populated on TileMap

There is one more layer to create, the rock boulders, which will scroll the slowest:

1. Ensure that both the `GroundLayer` and the `RockColumnsLayers` are unchecked.

2. Select and check the `RockBoulderLayer`.

3. Create rock boulders randomly across the TileMap, starting with the second tile from the bottom. Your TileMap should look similar to Figure 9.13.

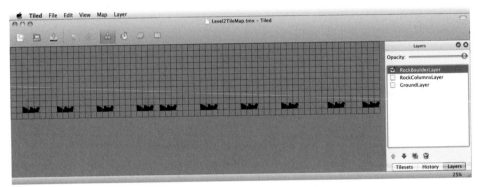

Figure 9.13   RockBoulderLayer populated on TileMap

The `RockBoulderLayer` and the `RockColumnsLayer` overlap, but in the code you will see how to pull the layers apart and assign them to a `CCParallaxNode`. This is all the work you need to do in Tiled. Make sure all three layers are selected (check-box to the left side of the layer name), then save the TileMap as *Level2TimeMap.tmx* and:

1. Add the *Level2TileMap.tmx* to your *SpaceViking* Xcode project.

2. Add the *TilesTextureAtlas.png* to your *SpaceViking* Xcode project.

You need both the TMX and the PNG files for the TileMap to work. If you had any trouble creating these files, they are available in the resources folder for this chapter.

What's in a TMX File?

If you open the *Level2TileMap.tmx* file in Xcode, you will see it is just an XML file with a reference back to the *TilesTextureAtlas.png* and a compressed section for the tiles in each of the layers. The compressed data is just a listing of what texture occupies each tile in the TileMap. If you were to make the TileMap larger, say 8192 pixels, only this compressed TileMap data would increase, and then only by a few kilobytes. Since you are using the same tiles, the texture memory stays the same. In other words, you can make a huge level without using up all of the available memory on your iPhone or iPad.

Cocos2D Compressed TileMap Class

Cocos2D has a built-in class to read TileMap files from Tiled both in a compressed and noncompressed format. Since Tiled exports the TileMaps in a compressed (TMX) format by default, this book covers only this one. If you are using uncompressed tiled maps, the Cocos2D class is different, but the process and code are the same. The class you are going to use is CCTMXTiledMap, and it makes loading and using TileMaps a breeze.

You are first going to add a TileMap to the *Scene2* GameplayScrollingLayer and then learn how to add the individual layers to a CCParallaxNode in order to have them scroll at different speeds.

Adding CCTMXTiledMap to the Second Level

Open the *GameplayScrollingLayer.m* implementation file and above the init method add the contents of Listing 9.31.

Listing 9.31   addScrollingBackgroundWithTileMap in GameplayScrollingLayer.m

```
// Scrolling with all TileMap Layers together
-(void)addScrollingBackgroundWithTileMap {
    if (UI_USER_INTERFACE_IDIOM() == UIUserInterfaceIdiomPad) {
        tileMapNode = [CCTMXTiledMap
                    tiledMapWithTMXFile:@"Level2TileMap.tmx"];
    } else {
        tileMapNode = [CCTMXTiledMap
                    tiledMapWithTMXFile:@"Level2TileMapiPhone.tmx"];
    }
    [self addChild:tileMapNode];
}
```

Adding a TileMap to your Cocos2D game takes nothing more than a single call to initialize a CCTMXTiledMap object and then adding that object to your layer. The *TileSet* file is specified inside of the TMX file, and Cocos2D automatically loads when you are creating your TileMap.

There is one more change to the init method to replace the parallax background with the new TileMap. Open the init method, comment out the call to addScrollingBackgroundWithParallax, and add the call to addScrolling-BackgroundWithTileMap as shown in Listing 9.32.

Listing 9.32   new call to addScrollingBackgroundWithTileMap in init method

```
//[self addScrollingBackgroundWithParallax];
[self addScrollingBackgroundWithTileMap];
```

While you created the *Level2TileMap.tmx* file in the previous section, you need the *Level2TileMapiPhone.tmx* and *Level2TileMapiPhone-hd.tmx* files if you are testing on the iPhone. Take a moment and copy them into Xcode from the resources folder for this chapter.

If you click **Run** and select the second level in *Space Viking*, you should see the new TileMap background that you created. You should see it scrolling when you move Ole to the right and left of the level. Figure 9.14 shows what *Space Viking* looks like with the TileMap level when all the layers are in the same position.

Figure 9.14   Space Viking showing TileMap level, with all layers in the same position

Did you notice anything strange about the TileMap background? You can see that the `RockColumnsLayer` and the `RockBoulderLayer` overlap each other. You also should have noticed that the entire TileMap moves as one element, so the illusion of depth is lost.

Adding a TileMap to a ParallaxNode

The solution to adding the illusion of depth when using a TileMap as a scrolling background is to take the individual layers and move them from the TileMap to a `CCParallaxNode`.

Open the `GameplayScrollingLayer` and add the method `addScrolling-BackgroundWithTileMapInsideParallax` above the `init` method, as shown in Listing 9.33.

Listing 9.33 **addScrollingBackgroundWithTileMapInsideParallax**

```
// Scrolling with TileMap Layers inside of a Parallax Node
-(void)addScrollingBackgroundWithTileMapInsideParallax {
    CGSize screenSize = [[CCDirector sharedDirector] winSize];
    CGSize levelSize = [[GameManager sharedGameManager]
                        getDimensionsOfCurrentScene];
    // 1
    if (UI_USER_INTERFACE_IDIOM() == UIUserInterfaceIdiomPad) {
        tileMapNode = [CCTMXTiledMap
                        tiledMapWithTMXFile:@"Level2TileMap.tmx"];
    } else {
        tileMapNode = [CCTMXTiledMap
                        tiledMapWithTMXFile:@"Level2TileMapiPhone.tmx"];
    }

    CCTMXLayer *groundLayer = [tileMapNode layerNamed:@"GroundLayer"];
    CCTMXLayer *rockColumnsLayer = [tileMapNode
                                        layerNamed:@"RockColumnsLayer"];
    CCTMXLayer *rockBoulderLayer = [tileMapNode
                                        layerNamed:@"RockBoulderLayer"];

    // 2
    parallaxNode = [CCParallaxNode node];
    [parallaxNode setPosition:
                    ccp(levelSize.width/2,screenSize.height/2)];
    float xOffset = 0.0f;

    // 3
    xOffset = (levelSize.width/2);
    [groundLayer retain];
    [groundLayer removeFromParentAndCleanup:NO];
    [groundLayer setAnchorPoint:CGPointMake(0.5f, 0.5f)];
    [parallaxNode addChild:groundLayer z:30 parallaxRatio:ccp(1,1)
                positionOffset:ccp(0,0)];
    [groundLayer release];

    // 4
    xOffset = (levelSize.width/2) * 0.8f;
    [rockColumnsLayer retain];
    [rockColumnsLayer removeFromParentAndCleanup:NO];
    [rockColumnsLayer setAnchorPoint:CGPointMake(0.5f, 0.5f)];
    [parallaxNode addChild:rockColumnsLayer z:20
                parallaxRatio:ccp(0.2,1)
                positionOffset:ccp(xOffset, 0.0f)];
    [rockColumnsLayer release];
```

```
// 5
xOffset = (levelSize.width/2) * 0.3f;
[rockBoulderLayer retain];
[rockBoulderLayer removeFromParentAndCleanup:NO];
[rockBoulderLayer setAnchorPoint:CGPointMake(0.5f, 0.5f)];
[parallaxNode addChild:rockBoulderLayer z:30
              parallaxRatio:ccp(0.7,1)
              positionOffset:ccp(xOffset, 0.0f)];
[rockBoulderLayer release];

// 6
[self addChild:parallaxNode z:1];
}
```

While the method in Listing 9.33 has a long and descriptive name, the logic inside is similar to what you have created previously. The CCTMXTiledMap is initialized first, and then the layers are pulled from the CCTMXTiledMap and added to a new ParallaxNode. Finally, the ParallaxNode is added to the GameplayScrolling-Layer. The CCTMXTiledMap is not added to the layer because it is without children at this point and is no longer needed. The code sections are as follows:

1. Initializes the TileMapNode with the contents of the *Level2TileMap.tmx* file. This section also retrieves the three tile layers from the TileMap by name. These are the names you set your layers to in the Tiled application.

2. Initializes the ParallaxNode, which will be the scrolling background, and then adds the ParallaxNode to the center of the level and sets up the x-axis offset to be used when adding in the layers.

3. Adds the ground layer to the ParallaxNode. The groundLayer is first retained so that it is not deallocated. It is then removed from the TileMap and added to the ParallaxNode. A CCNode cannot have two parents at once, and this is why you have to retain, reassign, and then release each of the three layers. The anchor point of the tile layers are set to the leftmost side by default; this is changed to the center to make positioning easier.

4. Adds the rock columns layer to the ParallaxNode using a ratio of 0.2 on the x-axis. This means the rock columns will move 2 pixels for every 10 pixels the ParallaxNode is moved on the x-axis.

5. Adds the rock boulder layer to the ParallaxNode using a ratio of 0.7 on the x-axis. The rock boulder layer will move 7 pixels for every 10 pixels the ParallaxNode is moved on the x-axis.

6. Adds the ParallaxNode to the layer, causing the scrolling background to appear.

Add the call to `addScrollingBackgroundWithTileMapInsideParallax` and comment out the line calling `addScrollingBackgroundWithTileMap`, as shown in Listing 9.34.

Listing 9.34   **Changes to init method in GameplayScrollingLayer**

```
//[self addScrollingBackgroundWithTileMap];
[self addScrollingBackgroundWithTileMapInsideParallax];
```

The last change you need to make is to increase the level size in the `GameManager`, since the TileMap background is now 4096 pixels wide instead of 2048. Open the *GameManager.m* implementation file and locate the `getDimensionsOfCurrentScene` method. Change the width of the `kGameLevel2` branch to 4096, as shown in Listing 9.35.

Listing 9.35   **getDimensionsOfCurrentScene changes in GameManager.m**

```
case kGameLevel2:
    levelSize = CGSizeMake(4096.0f, screenSize.height);
break;
```

If you click **Run** and select the second level from the Main Menu, you can move Ole left and right on the screen. You will see how much farther you can get Ole to scroll if you move him to the right.

Note

Remember that you need to import the *Level2TileMapiPhone.tmx* and *Level2TileMapiPhone-hd.tmx* files into your Xcode project in order to test out the TileMap scrolling on the iPhone or iPhone 4. The two tiles are set up with a width of four times the screen size of each iOS device: 3840 pixels wide for the iPhone 4 and 1920 pixels wide for the iPhone.

There is a lot more you can do with TileMaps than what you have learned here. You can use layers in Tiled to specify walls, enemies, and even game characters in your games. TileMaps are often used for top-down games, but as you learned in *Space Viking*, they can be used in games with other viewpoints as well.

Note

If you want to learn more about TileMaps, including building a whole game based on them, check out Mike Daley's book, *Learning iOS Game Programming*, at *http://www.informit.com/store/product.aspx?isbn=0321699424*.

Summary

In this chapter you learned three different techniques to add scrolling to your games. You learned how to use the `CCParallaxNode` in Cocos2D, how to move sprites endlessly, and how to use TileMaps to create large levels. Whether you are making a role-playing game (RPG) or the next flying shooter, you now have the concepts and techniques needed to make it happen.

In the next few chapters, you will learn about physics and how to implement both the Box2D and Chipmunk physics engines. There is a whole new level of fun and realism you can add to your games with physics engines, and Cocos2D comes bundled with two of the best 2D physics engines out there, Box2D and Chipmunk, for free.

Challenges

1. Change Ole and the platform's z values so that Ole is in the middle of the clouds instead of in front of them during the cut-scene.

2. Change the cut-scene so that the clouds scroll from the top of the screen to the bottom instead of right to left.

3. Add the `RadarDish` to the `GameplayScrollingLayer`. Position it so that it is at the far right side of the level.

4. Create a new TileMap and use it instead of the *Level2TileMap.tmx* file. Can you set it up to have more than three parallax layers?

Part IV

Physics Engines

With the Box2D and Chipmunk physics engines that come with Cocos2D, you can add some amazing effects to your games, such as gravity, realistic collisions, and even ragdoll effects. In these chapters you get a chance to add some physics-based levels to *Space Viking*, from simple to advanced.

- Chapter 10: "Basic Game Physics: Adding Realism with Box2D"
- Chapter 11: "Intermediate Game Physics: Modeling, Racing, and Leaping"
- Chapter 12: "Advanced Game Physics: Even Better than the Real Thing"
- Chapter 13: "The Chipmunk Physics Engine (No Alvin Required)"

Basic Game Physics: Adding Realism with Box2D

So far Space Viking *has been an action-packed game complete with aliens blasting, cargo ships flying, and fists bashing. Up until this point, any time you wanted to move an object in* Space Viking, *it was up to you. You would use Cocos2D actions or update the positions of objects manually.*

But what if you wanted to add more realistic physics behavior in your game? Maybe you want more realistic collisions between objects, objects flying through the air under the influence of gravity, vehicles bouncing off terrain, or enemies collapsing like ragdolls when they are defeated.

Well, you could always crack open a physics textbook, start plugging away at some complex equations, and start developing your own game physics library.

But if you're not a math guru, don't worry: there's a much easier way. You can save yourself a lot of time, energy, and hair pulling by using the power of Box2D!

Getting Started

Box2D is a popular and easy-to-use, full-featured game physics library integrated with Cocos2D that can help you make your game objects move in realistic ways.

When you create objects you want Box2D to simulate, you tell Box2D where to initially place them and then let Box2D handle the rest of the simulation and calculate the new positions of the objects over time. The high-level workflow can be seen in Figure 10.1.

As Figure 10.1 illustrates, there are four main steps to using Box2D:

1. The first time you add an object to your scene (but only the first time!), you tell Box2D where it is and what shape it has.

2. In your game `update` loop, you tell Box2D if you want to apply any forces to the game objects, such as gravity or movement.

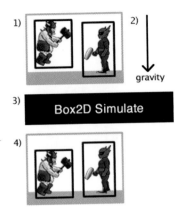

Figure 10.1   High-level workflow for Box2D

3. In your game update loop, you tell Box2D to simulate the world for a certain amount of time. Box2D then calculates the new positions for each object based on forces and collisions.

4. Also in your game update loop, you get the new positions of the objects from Box2D and update your sprites to match those positions.

In summary, Box2D controls the positions of your objects and where they move, and you just update your sprites to where Box2D says your objects are. Instead of moving your objects by setting their position or using CCMoveTo, you should influence your objects' positions by applying forces and impulses to Box2D objects. You'll see how this works in detail as you work through these next few chapters!

Box2D and C++

Box2D is written in C++ rather than in Objective-C like Cocos2D. This is because Box2D has a long history. Box2D was developed by Erin Catto as a simple game physics library in 2006, before Cocos2D even existed! Box2D has since been ported for several platforms, including Flash, Java, and Python, and has been made to work seamlessly with Cocos2D.

With Xcode you can use both Objective-C and C++ code within the same file, so you can use C++ libraries with no problems. However, if you're new to C++, some of the syntax will look unfamiliar to you.

You can work through the code samples in this and the next two chapters without having any C++ knowledge, but it's still a good idea to learn C++ if you plan to use Box2D in your own projects. Here's a quick cheat sheet for some of the most common new syntax elements that you'll see in this chapter:

- **Creating New Objects**
  Rather than using the [[object alloc] init] methods you are familiar with in Objective-C to allocate objects, in C++ you use the new keyword like this:

  ```
  MyClass *myClassPointer = new MyClass();
  ```

- **Pointers**

    In the previous example, you see that the variable is prefixed with a star (*). This indicates that the variable is a pointer to an object somewhere in memory. Later, when you want to call a method on a pointer to an object, you use the arrow (->). For example:

    ```
    myClassPointer->doSomething();
    ```

- **For More Information**

    For more information on C++, a great reference is *The C++ Programming Language* by Bjarne Stroustrup (Addison-Wesley Professional, 2000).

Mad Dreams of the Dead

The easiest way to understand Box2D is to see it in action for yourself, so it's time to continue the story of Ole the Viking!

In this chapter, you create a scene that represents a strange dream Ole had while frozen in his block of ice after he landed on the planet. It takes the form of a mini-puzzle game in which you try to figure out how to move frozen Ole to a spot that can thaw him back to action—with the aid of Box2D physics. You can see what the finished level looks like in Figure 10.2.

Making this level teaches you how to create objects with Box2D, how to move them with touches or the accelerometer, how to skin them with your own sprites, how to do simple collision detection with sensors, and much more!

Figure 10.2   The Box2D-enabled puzzle game you make in this chapter

Creating a New Scene

The first thing to do is create a new scene for the puzzle level. Open your *SpaceViking* project if you don't have it open already, expand *Classes\Scenes*, click **New Group**, then rename the new folder that was created to *Scene3*. Then with the *Scene3* group selected, go to **File > New > New File...**, choose **iOS > Cocoa Touch > Objective-C class**, and click **Next**. Enter *CCLayer* as the Subclass of, click **Next**, name the file *PuzzleLayer.m*, and click **Save**.

Then replace the contents of *PuzzleLayer.h* with the contents of Listing 10.1.

Listing 10.1   **PuzzleLayer.h**

```
#import <Foundation/Foundation.h>
#import "cocos2d.h"

@interface PuzzleLayer : CCLayer {
}

+ (id)scene;

@end
```

This should look familiar; you're creating a Cocos2D layer to be added to the scene called PuzzleLayer. However, you may be wondering where the scene class went. Until this point, you have been creating subclasses of CCScene in addition to subclassing CCLayer.

Well, for times when you know your scene is going to have only one layer, a shortcut is to create a static method that creates a plain CCScene and add the given layer as the only child of that scene. It's a bit simpler, and since that's all you'll need in this scene, let's give it a try.

Next, replace the contents of *PuzzleLayer.m* with the contents of Listing 10.2.

Listing 10.2   **PuzzleLayer.m**

```
#import "PuzzleLayer.h"

@implementation PuzzleLayer

+ (id)scene {
    CCScene *scene = [CCScene node];
    PuzzleLayer *layer = [self node];
    [scene addChild:layer];
    return scene;
}

- (id)init {
    if ((self = [super init])) {
```

```
    CGSize winSize = [CCDirector sharedDirector].winSize;
    CCLabelTTF *label = [CCLabelTTF
        labelWithString:@"Hello, Mad Dreams of the Dead!"
        fontName:@"Helvetica" fontSize:24.0];
    label.position = ccp(winSize.width/2, winSize.height/2);
    [self addChild:label];
    }
    return self;
}

@end
```

There should be no surprises here. The `init` method simply puts a label in the middle of the screen so you can verify it's working.

Finally, you need to modify *GameManager.m* to load your scene when it gets called with kGameLevel3. First, add a line to import *PuzzleLayer.h* at the top of the file, as shown in Listing 10.3.

Listing 10.3   GameManager.m (at top of file)

```
#import "PuzzleLayer.h"
```

Then inside `runSceneWithID`, modify the entry in the case statement for level 3 to create the new scene, as shown in Listing 10.4.

Listing 10.4   GameManager.m (inside runSceneWithID's case statement)

```
case kGameLevel3:
    sceneToRun = [PuzzleLayer scene];
    break;
```

That's it! Compile and run your project, select **Mad Dreams of the Dead** from the Main Menu, and you should see your new scene with the placeholder text, as shown in Figure 10.3.

> **Tip**
>
> You are going to be modifying this scene quite a bit in this chapter. To avoid having to select the Main Menu option every time you want to test this level, there's a shortcut to run your new scene right away. Simply open *Classes\Singletons\SpaceVikingAppDelegate.m*, navigate to the bottom of `applicationDidFinishLaunching`, and replace the `CCDirector:runSceneWithID` call at the bottom to:
>
> ```
> [[GameManager sharedGameManager]
>     runSceneWithID:kGameLevel3];
> ```
>
> Compile and run your project, and now it should start running your new scene right away!

Figure 10.3   Placeholder scene for Mad Dreams of the Dead

Adding Box2D Files to Your Project

Now you have a scene ready to try out Box2D—except you don't have the required Box2D files in your project! This is because you created the project with the plain *Cocos2D Application* template (i.e., you didn't pick the *Cocos2D Box2D Application* template). The plain *Cocos2D Application* template doesn't come with the Box2D files included by default.

Luckily, this is quite easy to fix. Just perform the following steps:

1. Open a Finder window and navigate to where you downloaded the Cocos2D source.

2. Open the folder and navigate to *external\Box2d\Box2D*.

3. Open a second Finder window, navigate to your *SpaceViking* project, and navigate to *libs*.

4. Copy the *Box2D* folder to the *libs* folder.

Once you're done, your directory structure should look as shown in Figure 10.4.

The next step is adding these files to your Xcode project. Expand the *cocos2d Sources* group, then drag the *Box2D* folder from your *SpaceViking\libs* directory to the group. When the dialog appears, make sure **Copy items into destination group's folder (if needed)** is *not* checked, **Create groups for any added folders** is selected, and then click **Finish**, as shown in Figure 10.5.

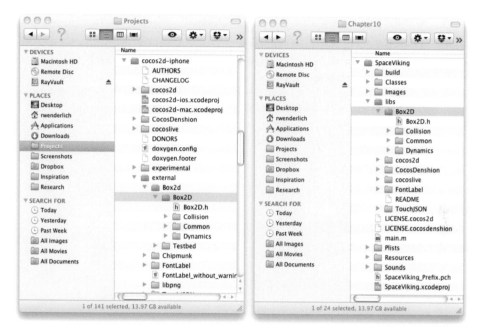

Figure 10.4   Where to place the Box2D files in the SpaceViking project

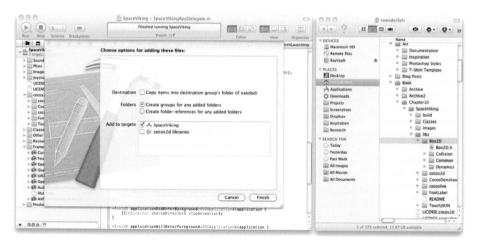

Figure 10.5   Adding the Box2D directory to your Xcode project

Next you need to set up the project so it knows where the Box2D header files are. Click on your *SpaceViking* project in the Project Navigator to bring up your project settings, select the **Build Settings** tab, make sure the **All** and **Combined** buttons are selected, and look for the entry for **Search Paths > Header Search Paths**. Double-click the entry to bring up an editor, click the plus button to add a new entry, double-click the entry for path, set it to *libs* if you are using Xcode 3 or *SpaceViking/ libs* if you are using Xcode 4, and click **OK**. When you are done, the settings should look like Figure 10.6.

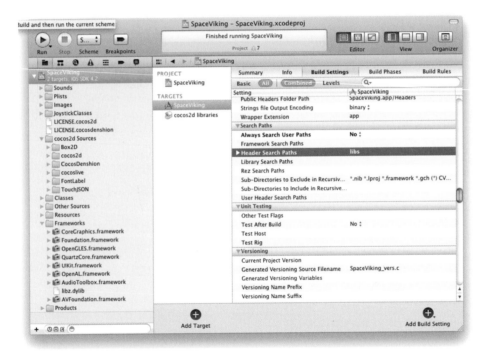

Figure 10.6   Adding libs folder to header search paths

Now you've copied over the main Box2D files, but there are two more important files that you should copy over as well: the ones responsible for drawing Box2D objects to the screen for debug purposes.

In Xcode, make a new group to put these files inside the *Classes* group, and name it *Box2D*. Then open up a Finder window, navigate to your Cocos2D directory, and navigate to *templates\cocos2d_box2d_app\Classes*. Inside you'll find the files *GLES-Render.h* and *GLES-Render.mm*. Select those two files and drag them to your new *Box2D* group in Xcode. Make sure **Copy items into destination group's folder (if needed)** is checked, and click **Finish**.

Now, let's test if it's working. In Xcode, expand the *Classes\Scenes\Scene3* group, and open *PuzzleLayer.h*. Import the Box2D header at the top of the file, as shown in Listing 10.5.

Listing 10.5   **PuzzleLayer.h (at top of file)**

```
#import "Box2D.h"
```

Now try to compile your project. Yowza! You will notice a huge list of errors, as shown in Figure 10.7.

Figure 10.7   Errors you'll see if you don't use the .mm extension when using C++ code

This is happening because you are importing the Box2D header file (which uses C++) in files that are set up to use only Objective-C. How do you instruct the compiler to allow both C++ and Objective-C? Simply rename the files with a *.mm* extension!

Give this a shot: rename *PuzzleLayer.m* to *PuzzleLayer.mm*. Then repeat this for *Classes\Singletons\GameManager.m*—rename it *GameManager.mm*. The reason you have to do this for *GameManager.m* is because *GameManager.m* imports *PuzzleLayer.h*, which imports *Box2D.h*.

Ok! Compile and run again, and this time it should compile with no errors.

> **Tip**
>
> As you've seen, if you're working with Box2D and you see hundreds of strange errors like we demonstrated here, chances are that you're trying to use C++ code in a file that doesn't end with .mm. Just remember, when you see a huge list of errors like that, double check to make sure that all files using Box2D have the **.mm** extension!

Congratulations! You have successfully imported the Box2D code into your project. But before you proceed, you should learn about one of the most important concepts when working with Box2D in Cocos2D projects: units.

Box2D Units

When making a game with Cocos2D, you usually think in terms of points. Ole, for example, is about a 100 × 180-point sprite on the iPad (and a good looking one at that)!

However, Box2D does not deal with points. Box2D is optimized to work with meters (m), kilograms (kg), and seconds(s). So, Box2D considers an object "*x* meters" wide instead of "*x* points" wide.

You may think to yourself, *Why not just define 1 point = 1 meter, and make it easy?* Unfortunately, this does not work too well. Box2D works best with objects between 0.1 and 10 meters, so you want to make most of your objects fit within that length—and ideally have your most common object types be about 1 meter in length.

Luckily, this is quite easy to do by applying a conversion factor. For example, if you wanted Ole to be 1 meter wide, you could just set the conversion factor to be 1 width of Ole per 1 meter, or 100 points/meter if Ole is 100 points wide. Figure 10.8 illustrates how you can use this conversion factor to convert any number of points to meters.

100px   ÷ 100 points/meter = 1 meter

Figure 10.8   Converting points to meters

In code, the conversion looks something like this:

```
#define PTM_RATIO     100.0
// When converting from Cocos2D coord to Box2D coord:
float x_box2D = x_cocos2D / PTM_RATIO;
float y_box2D = y_cocos2D / PTM_RATIO;
// When converting from Box2D coord to Cocos2D coord:
float x_cocos2D = x_box2D * PTM_RATIO;
float y_cocos2D = y_box2D * PTM_RATIO;
```

> **Tip**
>
> If you look at Box2D samples, you'll see that a common value for the PTM_RATIO is 32. Why is this number commonly chosen? Well, the size of the iPhone screen is 480 points wide, so a normal sprite would commonly be about 1/15 of that size (32 points). So if the PTM_RATIO is set to 32, that common sprite would be equal to 1 meter, which is great because Box2D is optimized for objects between 0.1 and 10 meters.
>
> But since your game's sprites may be larger or smaller, don't use this value blindly—choose it according to the actual sizes of your sprites!
>
> If you forget to set your PTM_RATIO properly, the sizes of your objects might be very small or very large in Box2D terms. This could cause some strange behavior in your game, such as objects bouncing and colliding in unexpected ways. So if you see odd behavior and are wondering why, double check that your objects aren't too big or too small when converted to meters under Box2D!

In the puzzle level you're about to create, on the iPad the most common objects will be 100 points in width and the largest 800 points, so you'll set the PTM_RATIO to be 100 (so most common objects are 1 meter and the largest still less than 10 meters). On the iPhone, the objects will be half the size in points.

So define the PTM_RATIO to be 100 points per meter at the bottom of *Constants.h* (and half that on the iPhone), as shown in Listing 10.6.

Listing 10.6   **Constants.h (at the bottom of the file)**

```
#define PTM_RATIO ((UI_USER_INTERFACE_IDIOM() == \
    UIUserInterfaceIdiomPad) ? 100.0 : 50.0)
```

With that done, you've got your project completely ready to use Box2D, so you can proceed with creating and populating your Box2D world!

Hello, Box2D!

The first step to using Box2D is to create a Box2D world. Think of a Box2D world as Box2D's view of the objects it simulates (in units of meters). If you recall Figure 10.1, you'll populate this world with objects, let Box2D handle the simulation for you, then update your sprites according to the positions of the Box2D objects.

Let's see how to create a Box2D world. First open up *PuzzleLayer.h* and import the Box2D debug drawing header that you added earlier and the constants file containing the `PTM_RATIO`, as shown in Listing 10.7.

Listing 10.7   **PuzzleLayer.h (at the top of the file)**

```
#import "GLES-Render.h"
#import "Constants.h"
```

Next add a few member variables inside the `@interface` declaration, as shown in Listing 10.8.

Listing 10.8   **PuzzleLayer.h (inside @interface declaration)**

```
b2World * world;
GLESDebugDraw * debugDraw;
```

These are two instance variables stored in the Box2D world and debug draw classes. You'll learn exactly what these mean shortly in this chapter. Now, open up *Puzzle-Layer.mm*, and add a method to create your Box2D world above the `init` method, as shown in Listing 10.9.

Listing 10.9   **PuzzleLayer.mm (above init method)**

```
- (void)setupWorld {
    b2Vec2 gravity = b2Vec2(0.0f, -10.0f);
    bool doSleep = true;
    world = new b2World(gravity, doSleep);
}
```

This function initializes the Box2D world. The first thing it does is set up the gravity force that will affect all objects in the world—a b2Vec2 initialized with an x value of 0 and a y value of −10. A b2Vec2 is a Box2D class used to represent vectors, so this vector is facing down along the y-axis with a magnitude of 10.

You may be wondering why you should use this as your value. Well, gravity is in m/s², and 10 m/s² down the y-axis is pretty close to the actual gravity of earth (9.8 m/s²)!

> **Note**
>
> As you work with Box2D, you'll be using a lot of vectors, so if you're not familiar with how they work, here's a quick explanation.
>
> Vectors are simply a pair of x and y values that can be used to represent either a position or a direction and magnitude.
>
> For example, Figure 10.9 shows what the vector (3, 4) looks like. This same vector could be used to indicate the position (3, 4) or to indicate the direction of 53° with a magnitude of 5.

Whether the vector is used as a position or direction/magnitude depends on the context. In the case of gravity, you know that the vector is being used to indicate a direction and magnitude.

Don't worry if you're still confused by this. You'll be using vectors a lot as you go through this chapter, and it will start to make more sense as you proceed!

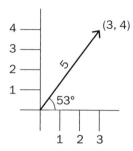

Figure 10.9   Diagram of a vector, which can represent either a point or a magnitude/angle

In summary, the first line sets up a gravity vector pointing down, much like Earth's gravity. The second and third lines create a new b2World object, passing in the gravity vector and `true` for `doSleep`.

Note that the `doSleep` parameter is set to `true`. This tells the b2World that when objects have settled in to their positions and aren't moving anymore, it can stop performing calculations on those objects until something causes them to move again. Usually you want this to be on by default, but if you don't, you can disable this for all objects here.

One more thing . . . since you created a new world, you need to create a `dealloc` method to delete it once your layer is deallocated, as shown in Listing 10.10.

Listing 10.10   PuzzleLayer.mm (at the bottom of the file)

```
- (void)dealloc {
    if (world) {
        delete world;
        world = NULL;
    }
    [super dealloc];
}
```

Deleting a world also deletes anything you have added into that world (such as bodies, joints, or fixtures, all of which we cover later on).

That's it—you have created a Box2D world! However, there's currently nothing in it. So let's fix this by adding a simple box into the world.

Creating a Box2D Object

Before you create a Box2D object, it's important to understand the terminology that Box2D uses when setting up objects.

Each individual object in a Box2D world is called a *body*. Box2D is a rigid body physics simulation, which just means that when two bodies collide, they don't squish—instead they bounce off each other rigidly.

Each body can be made up of several different pieces, or *fixtures*. In Figure 10.10, you can see that if you wanted to create a baseball cap, you might make a single body with two fixtures: one for the cap and one for the brim. The reason you might want to create a body from two fixtures rather than one is because it may be simpler, and for reasons you'll learn about in the next chapter, you need to do this in order to create certain shapes with Box2D.

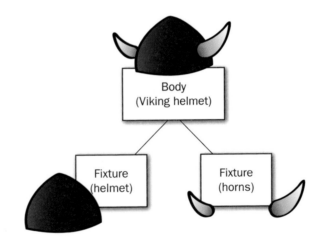

Figure 10.10   A Box2D body is composed of one or more fixtures.

> **Note**
>
> Since Box2D is a rigid physics simulation, any fixtures that are in the same body will not move relative to each other, which works great for fixtures that are permanently connected like the Viking helmet in Figure 10.10. But if you wanted to model an arm (made up of a lower arm and an upper arm), you wouldn't want to model it as two fixtures on the same body, because then the arm wouldn't be able to rotate at the elbow.
>
> For cases like an arm where you want two pieces to be able to move relative to each other, you create two bodies (one for the lower arm and one for the upper arm) and connect them with a joint. You will learn how to use joints in detail in the next chapter. In this chapter, you work with just simple bodies, usually with just one fixture, and not connected to any other bodies with joints.

Figure 10.11 illustrates the steps you take to create a body with Box2D. As you can see in the figure, first you create a *body definition*. A body definition specifies some properties of the body, such as its position and movement type. There are three different movement types: a *dynamic body* (Box2D handles the movement), a *kinematic body* (the game code handles the movement), or a *static body* (the body doesn't move at all).

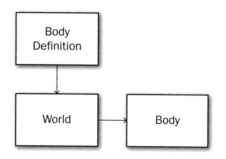

Figure 10.11   Creating a body with Box2D

When you're done, you pass the body definition to the world, which creates a body object for you.

Let's see what this looks like in code. Inside *PuzzleLayer.mm* above the init method, add the beginning of a method that will create a box in the Box2D world at a particular location, as shown in Listing 10.11.

Listing 10.11   **PuzzleLayer.mm (above init method)**

```
- (void)createBoxAtLocation:(CGPoint)location withSize:(CGSize)size {
    b2BodyDef bodyDef;
    bodyDef.type = b2_dynamicBody;
    bodyDef.position =
        b2Vec2(location.x/PTM_RATIO, location.y/PTM_RATIO);
    b2Body *body = world->CreateBody(&bodyDef);
}
```

This function creates a box at a specified location with a specified size. It sets the body as a dynamic body (which means its movement should be handled by Box2D), sets its initial position, and then calls the CreateBody method on the world to create a body object.

Note that since this function takes a location in points, it needs to convert the location from points to meters by using the PTM_RATIO, as discussed earlier.

Once you create the body, you can create one or more fixtures to attach to the body. To create a fixture, you follow a process much like you did while creating a body, as Figure 10.12 illustrates. Basically, first you create a *shape*, which can be a circle, a square, or an arbitrary shape made up of connected vertices. You pass that shape to a *fixture definition*, where you can set other properties such as bounciness or density. You then pass the fixture definition to the body, which returns to you a *fixture object*.

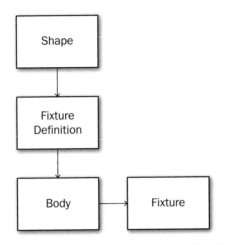

Figure 10.12   Creating a fixture with Box2D

To try this out, continue the `createBoxAtLocation` method by adding the code shown in Listing 10.12 to add a fixture to the body.

Listing 10.12   **PuzzleLayer.mm (at bottom of createBoxAtLocation method)**

```
b2PolygonShape shape;
shape.SetAsBox(size.width/2/PTM_RATIO, size.height/2/PTM_RATIO);

b2FixtureDef fixtureDef;
fixtureDef.shape = &shape;
fixtureDef.density = 1.0;

body->CreateFixture(&fixtureDef);
```

This function defines a shape object and uses a helper method to set the vertices up so that it is a box of the specified size. Note that it has to divide the width and height by 2, since this helper method takes a half width and half height of the box as parameters. Again note that this uses the `PTM_RATIO` to convert the size from points to meters.

> **Warning**
>
> Note that when using the `SetAsBox` method, it's easy to forget that you have to provide a half width and half height and to instead pass in the full height and width. If your objects seem to be double the size you expect, double check that you've passed in the half width and half height correctly in this method.

Note that this function sets the density of the box to 1.0. The higher the fixture's density, the "heavier" it is, but for now don't worry too much about it. We discuss density in detail later in this chapter.

At this point you have written methods to create the world and add an object to the world. However, if you called these methods in your `init` method right now, you wouldn't see anything, because there is no code that draws representations of the Box2D bodies in your scene.

This is where Box2D debug drawing comes to the rescue!

Box2D Debug Drawing

Box2D debug drawing is already implemented for you by the *GLES-Render* files you copied into your project earlier. You just need to add a bit of code to create an instance of the debug drawing class, connect it to your world, and call it in your draw method.

So add a method to set up a debug drawing above your `init` method, as shown in Listing 10.13.

Listing 10.13   PuzzleLayer.mm (above init method)

```
- (void)setupDebugDraw {
    debugDraw = new GLESDebugDraw(PTM_RATIO *[[CCDirector sharedDirector]
contentScaleFactor]);
    world->SetDebugDraw(debugDraw);
    debugDraw->SetFlags(b2DebugDraw::e_shapeBit);
}
```

Here you create a new instance of the `GLESDebugDraw` class and pass it to the world with the `SetDebugDraw` method. You then set some flags on the debug draw telling it what specifically to draw. For this level, you're just interested in shapes.

> **Note**
>
> You have to multiply the `PTM_RATIO` by the `contentScaleFactor` because GLES-DebutDraw deals with pixels, not points. Without this, debug drawing will not be sized correctly on the retina display.
>
> Also, you can use the Box2D debug draw class to render other interesting things, such as joints, axis-aligned bounding boxes, or center of mass. Check out *b2WorldCallbacks.h* in the Box2D source for the full list!

Next you need to make sure that the debug draw class gets a chance to draw. Add a draw method to your layer, as shown in Listing 10.14.

Listing 10.14   **PuzzleLayer.mm (below init method)**

```
-(void) draw {
    glDisable(GL_TEXTURE_2D);
    glDisableClientState(GL_COLOR_ARRAY);
    glDisableClientState(GL_TEXTURE_COORD_ARRAY);

    world->DrawDebugData();

    glEnable(GL_TEXTURE_2D);
    glEnableClientState(GL_COLOR_ARRAY);
    glEnableClientState(GL_TEXTURE_COORD_ARRAY);
}
```

Here you're overriding the layer's draw method so you can perform the debug drawing in every frame. Inside, it sets the OpenGL states to handle debug drawing and tells the world to go ahead and draw each object with the specified debug draw class. Don't worry if you don't understand this—this is boilerplate code that you can use as is.

One last step . . . since you created a debug draw object, you need to delete it in your dealloc routine. Add the code to delete your debug draw object inside your dealloc routine, as shown in Listing 10.15.

Listing 10.15   **PuzzleLayer.mm (inside dealloc routine)**

```
if (debugDraw) {
    delete debugDraw;
    debugDraw = nil;
}
```

Okay, you now have almost all of the pieces in place, so it's almost time to see something on the screen!

Putting It All Together

First delete your current init method, and replace it with the contents of Listing 10.16.

Listing 10.16   **PuzzleLayer.mm (init method)**

```
- (id)init {
    if ((self = [super init])) {
        [self setupWorld];
        [self setupDebugDraw];
```

```
        [self scheduleUpdate];
        self.isTouchEnabled = YES;
    }
    return self;
}


- (void)registerWithTouchDispatcher {
    [[CCTouchDispatcher sharedDispatcher] addTargetedDelegate:self
        priority:0 swallowsTouches:YES];
}
```

The first two lines call the methods you added earlier to set up the world and debug drawing. It then schedules an update method to be called every tick, which you'll write in a second. It also sets up the layer to accept touches by setting isTouchEnabled to YES and implementing registerWithTouchDispatcher—further down, you'll add a touch handler to create a box wherever the user taps.

Next add the implementation of the update method that will be called every tick, as shown in Listing 10.17.

Listing 10.17   **PuzzleLayer.mm (below init method)**

```
-(void)update:(ccTime)dt {

    int32 velocityIterations = 3;
    int32 positionIterations = 2;
    world->Step(dt, velocityIterations, positionIterations);

}
```

By calling scheduleUpdate in the init method earlier, Cocos2D will automatically look for a routine named update in your layer and call it every frame. Inside this method, you need to give Box2D time to perform its simulation, and you do that by calling the Step method on the world.

When calling the Step method, you pass it a parameter for the number of velocity iterations to perform and the number of position iterations to perform. The higher these values, the better the simulation will be—but the tradeoff is performance. Hence, you generally want to set these numbers as low as you can while still getting acceptable behavior for your game. In other words, you need to tweak these and see what works best for your situation!

Note

The game loop shown in Listing 10.17 uses a variable-based timestep, meaning it is called with a variable amount of delta time (dt) each tick. However, Box2D works best with a fixed timestep—that is, when it is called with the same amount of time every step.

> If you don't use a fixed timestep, as your simulations get more complicated, you may see some strange behavior, such as joints disconnecting or bodies bouncing strangely. We'll come back to the game loop in Chapter 11, "Intermediate Game Physics," with an improved version, but for this level you can get away fine with this simple implementation without any noticeable problems.

One last step: you need to add the code to create the box! To make things interesting, you'll add a routine to create a box wherever the user taps. Implement the ccTouchBegan method to do this, as shown in Listing 10.18.

Listing 10.18 **PuzzleLayer.mm (below init method)**

```
-(BOOL) ccTouchBegan:(UITouch *)touch withEvent:(UIEvent *)event {

    CGPoint touchLocation = [touch locationInView:[touch view]];
    touchLocation = [[CCDirector sharedDirector]
        convertToGL:touchLocation];
    touchLocation = [self convertToNodeSpace:touchLocation];
    b2Vec2 locationWorld =
        b2Vec2(touchLocation.x/PTM_RATIO, touchLocation.y/PTM_RATIO);

    [self createBoxAtLocation:touchLocation
        withSize:CGSizeMake(50, 50)];
    return TRUE;

}
```

This gets called whenever there is a touch in your layer. It first converts the touch from UIView coordinates to OpenGL coordinates with convertToGL. Then it converts the coordinates to the node space for the current layer. Finally, it converts the coordinates to Box2D coordinates by applying the PTM_RATIO. Note that it is dividing by the PTM_RATIO this time, since it is moving from meters to points.

Finally, with the resulting touch location, it calls the method you wrote earlier to create a box at the location.

That's it—you're finally ready to check it out! Compile and run your project, and you'll be able to tap the screen to have objects created into the Box2D world. The boxes will fall down as though affected by gravity, as shown in Figure 10.13.

However, you'll notice an immediate problem: there's nothing stopping these objects from falling off the screen! So let's fix that by adding some ground.

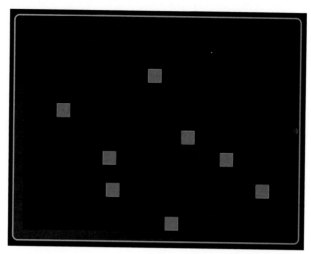

Figure 10.13   Box2D objects falling with gravity

Creating Ground

The goal here is to create a boundary that lines up with the edges of the screen so that the falling objects don't fall out of view.

> **Note**
>
> You don't have to set up the boundaries of the Box2D world to line up exactly to the screen. It's typical to want to have worlds that extend many screen widths so players can scroll from side to side. If you want to do that, you simply make the ground boundaries wider and move the position of the layer as the user scrolls from side to side. You learn exactly how to do that in the next chapter, in fact!
>
> But for this mini-game, you don't need scrolling, so you want the boundaries to line up with the width and height of one screen.

First open *PuzzleLayer.h* and add a new instance variable that will keep a handy reference to the ground body you're about to create, as shown in Listing 10.19.

Listing 10.19   **PuzzleLayer.h (inside @interface declaration)**

```
b2Body *groundBody;
```

Next open *PuzzleLayer.mm* and add the method to create the ground body above your init method, as shown in Listing 10.20.

Listing 10.20   **PuzzleLayer.mm (above init method)**

```
- (void)createGround {
    CGSize winSize = [[CCDirector sharedDirector] winSize];
    float32 margin = 10.0f;
    b2Vec2 lowerLeft = b2Vec2(margin/PTM_RATIO, margin/PTM_RATIO);
    b2Vec2 lowerRight = b2Vec2((winSize.width-margin)/PTM_RATIO,
                              margin/PTM_RATIO);
    b2Vec2 upperRight = b2Vec2((winSize.width-margin)/PTM_RATIO,
                              (winSize.height-margin)/PTM_RATIO);
    b2Vec2 upperLeft = b2Vec2(margin/PTM_RATIO,
                              (winSize.height-margin)/PTM_RATIO);

    b2BodyDef groundBodyDef;
    groundBodyDef.type = b2_staticBody;
    groundBodyDef.position.Set(0, 0);
    groundBody = world->CreateBody(&groundBodyDef);

    b2PolygonShape groundShape;
    b2FixtureDef groundFixtureDef;
    groundFixtureDef.shape = &groundShape;
    groundFixtureDef.density = 0.0;

    groundShape.SetAsEdge(lowerLeft, lowerRight);
    groundBody->CreateFixture(&groundFixtureDef);
    groundShape.SetAsEdge(lowerRight, upperRight);
    groundBody->CreateFixture(&groundFixtureDef);
    groundShape.SetAsEdge(upperRight, upperLeft);
    groundBody->CreateFixture(&groundFixtureDef);
    groundShape.SetAsEdge(upperLeft, lowerLeft);
    groundBody->CreateFixture(&groundFixtureDef);
}
```

The beginning of this method sets up the Box2D coordinates that correspond to the four corners of the ground boundary you're about to make. Note that it uses a margin to pad the edges a bit and that it uses PTM_RATIO to convert from points to meters as usual.

Next the method creates a body following the usual process. The only differences are that the body is set up as a static body (i.e., it does not move) and the position of the body is set to (0, 0).

Note

After setting the position of a body, the coordinates you use to create fixtures are local coordinates (i.e., relative to the body). In this case, the position of the body is (0,0), so if you specified a vertex for a fixture of (10,10), the world coordinates for the fixture would also be (10,10).

However, if the position of the body was at (5, 5) and you specified a vertex for a fixture at (10,10), the world coordinates for the fixture would be at (15,15).

This is a handy property of Box2D, since it allows you to create fixtures relative to a body, then easily change where you place a body without having to redo the fixture coordinates. It doesn't matter very much in this particular example, but it becomes useful when making complicated objects (such as vehicles) that you want to place in a scene multiple times.

After creating the body, the method sets up a fixture definition. It sets the shape to the groundShape (which isn't filled in yet) and the density to 0. When the density for an object is 0, this is a special case that means that the object is static (not moving).

Warning

Be careful of this! If you ever create a Box2D fixture and forget to set its density, it will default to 0 and the body will become static and not move. So if you ever notice that a fixture isn't moving at all, double check that you set the density to a nonzero value!

Finally, the method adds four fixtures to the body, one for each side of the box. To do this, it uses the SetAsEdge helper method to create a fixture with just two vertices and then adds it to the body. Remember from the earlier discussion that you can have multiple fixtures attached to the same body (like modeling a ball cap); this is the first example of doing this.

Next, you just need to call your new method at the bottom of init, as shown in Listing 10.21.

Listing 10.21   PuzzleLayer.mm (at bottom of init method)

```
[self createGround];
```

And that's it! Compile and run to try it out, and you should now see a green boundary along the edges of the screen—that's the ground you just created. Now when you create the objects, they will fall until they hit the ground, then they will stop, as shown in Figure 10.14. You can also see some cool physics effects by making objects fall on top of other objects!

Note

If you're wondering why some bodies are pink and some are gray, it's because Box2D colors bodies gray when they aren't currently moving and are asleep. As mentioned earlier, when bodies are asleep, Box2D can stop performing calculations on the bodies until something causes them to move again, which is a performance optimization.

At this point, you've gotten a basic "Hello, World" Box2D scene functioning from scratch—you've added Box2D bodies, set up gravity, and set up a ground box to contain the objects! Let's take this to the next level by adding more interactivity and decoration.

Figure 10.14   Box2D bodies landing on the ground

Basic Box2D Interaction and Decoration

This scene is starting to be a little bit fun, watching boxes fall off each other and the like, but you know what would make it even more fun? The ability to move your device around and modify your Box2D world's gravity based on how you hold it!

This is ridiculously easy to do, so let's give it a shot. First enable accelerometer support in your scene by adding a line to your `init` method as shown in Listing 10.22.

Listing 10.22   **PuzzleLayer.mm (at the bottom of the init method)**

```
self.isAccelerometerEnabled = TRUE;
```

This tells Cocos2D that you want to receive a callback for accelerometer events in your layer. When the accelerometer gets data, it calls a method in your layer called `accelerometer:didAccelerate`. Go ahead and write that now, as shown in Listing 10.23.

Listing 10.23   **PuzzleLayer.mm (after init method)**

```
- (void)accelerometer:(UIAccelerometer *)accelerometer
didAccelerate:(UIAcceleration *)acceleration {
    b2Vec2 gravity(-acceleration.y * 15, acceleration.x *15);
    world->SetGravity(gravity);
}
```

This simply converts the accelerometer input to a gravity vector. It multiplies the accelerometer result (which typically ranges between −1 and 1) by 15, in order to get a nice feel for gravity in the level. Since *Space Viking* is set up to run in landscape mode (and accelerometer data is given in portrait orientation), it reverses the x and y coordinates and flips the sign of the y coordinate to get the proper vector.

Then it simply calls `SetGravity` on the world to update the gravity vector!

Compile and run your project (on your device, since accelerometer input is not supported on the simulator), add a bunch of boxes, and rotate your device to see them all fly around, as shown in Figure 10.15; it's actually pretty fun!

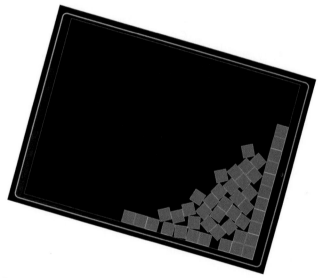

Figure 10.15   Making Box2D bodies move with gravity and the accelerometer

As you play with it, you may notice that if the bodies settle down, they turn gray (which means the objects are asleep). If you try to rotate the device again, they won't move.

There are a couple of ways to fix this (such as running a high-pass filter over the accelerometer input to detect if the orientation has changed enough to warrant wakening the sleeping bodies), but there's an even simpler way that works for the purposes of this app: set the bodies as unable to sleep.

To do this, all you need to do is add one line inside your `createBoxAtLocation` routine before you call `CreateBody`, as shown in Listing 10.24.

```
bodyDef.allowSleep = false;
```

Now compile and run your project again, and note that the bodies no longer go to sleep, so they will no longer get stuck.

> **Note**
>
> If you're interested in the high-pass filter option, check out Apple's *Event Handling Guide for iOS* (inside the Motion Events section), which does a great job explaining the topic in further detail. Implementing this would be more efficient than simply waking all bodies, since allowing bodies to sleep saves processing time.

Dragging Objects

Now that the scene has accelerometer input, it's getting kind of fun, since you can see the impact of physics on the various bodies. But it would be even cooler if you could move objects just by dragging them!

The good news is that you can do so easily in Box2D using a special kind of joint called a *mouse joint*.

Joints are a way to tell Box2D that two bodies are connected in some way and to enforce some kind of rule about their relative motion. For example, you can tell Box2D that two objects are connected by a *distance joint*, which sets them up so that they are always the same distance apart. Or you could tell Box2D that two objects are connected by a *revolute joint*, which sets them up so that they can rotate only along the same shared axis.

You'll learn more about joints in the next chapter, but for now you're going to use a specific kind of joint designed for user input: the mouse joint. The mouse joint is meant to connect the location the user touches with an object the user wants to move and have the object move toward the desired location as quickly as possible.

There are several steps required to use a mouse joint, so let's go through them step by step. First open up *PuzzleLayer.h* and add a new instance variable for the mouse joint, as shown in Listing 10.25.

Listing 10.25   **PuzzleLayer.h (inside @interface declaration)**

```
b2MouseJoint *mouseJoint;
```

Then switch back to *PuzzleLayer.mm* and find the ccTouchBegan method. Delete the createBoxAtLocation line and add the contents of Listing 10.26 in its place.

Listing 10.26   **PuzzleLayer.mm (inside ccTouchBegan, replaces call to createBoxAtLocation)**

```
b2AABB aabb;
b2Vec2 delta = b2Vec2(1.0/PTM_RATIO, 1.0/PTM_RATIO);
```

```
aabb.lowerBound = locationWorld - delta;
aabb.upperBound = locationWorld + delta;
SimpleQueryCallback callback(locationWorld);
world->QueryAABB(&callback, aabb);
```

To set up a mouse joint, the first thing you need to do is figure out what object the user wants to move. You can do this by asking Box2D what object is at a certain location.

To search for an object in the Box2D world, you need to use a method called AABB Testing, which stands for axis-aligned bounding box testing. This is a highly optimized method that can quickly return to you all of the objects whose bounding boxes intersect a given rectangle. Then it's up to you to figure out if any of the returned objects actually intersect.

To see how it works, consider Figure 10.16. Here you want to test if the touch point (represented by the small rectangle in the lower right) intersects the polygon shape. To be able to quickly return a list of possible objects that the point could hit, Box2D first performs an AABB test to see if the point is within the bounding box of any of the shapes (which it is, for this polygon). You then need to perform a second test to see if the point is actually within the bounds of the polygon itself by calling TestPoint (which it isn't, for this polygon).

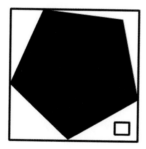

Figure 10.16   AABB testing vs. actual shape intersection

The code you wrote in Listing 10.26 sets up a lower bound and an upper bound for the AABB test, which is the equivalent of a 1-point box around the touch location, converted to meters. It then calls the QueryAABB function to perform the test. As a parameter, the QueryAABB function takes a pointer to a class as an argument. The QueryAABB method calls a method on this class for all of the possible intersections, and it's the job of the class to perform a secondary test to see whether or not there was actually an intersection.

This SimpleQueryCallback class doesn't come with Box2D—you have to write it yourself. So select your *Classes\Box2D* folder, go to **File > New > New File...**,

choose **iOS > C** and **C++ > Header File**, and click **Next**. Name the file
SimpleQueryCallback.h, and click **Save**.

Then replace *SimpleQueryCallback.h* with the contents of Listing 10.27.

Listing 10.27 SimpleQueryCallback.h

```
#import "Box2D.h"

class SimpleQueryCallback : public b2QueryCallback
{
public:
    b2Vec2 pointToTest;
    b2Fixture * fixtureFound;

    SimpleQueryCallback(const b2Vec2& point) {
        pointToTest = point;
        fixtureFound = NULL;
    }

    bool ReportFixture(b2Fixture* fixture) {
        b2Body* body = fixture->GetBody();
        if (body->GetType() == b2_dynamicBody) {
            if (fixture->TestPoint(pointToTest)) {
                fixtureFound = fixture;
                return false;
            }
        }
        return true;
    }
};
```

This is a very simple C++ class that derives from b2QueryCallback. It has
a constructor that takes the original point to test as a parameter and saves it in an
instance variable. It then overrides the virtual method ReportFixture, which is
called on every possible intersection. Inside this method, it checks to see if the body is
a dynamic body (those are the only types of objects you'll want to move with mouse
joints) and uses TestPoint to see if the point actually intersects. If it does, it saves a
pointer to the fixture in an instance variable and returns false (which tells Box2D it
can stop looking for matches); otherwise, it returns true (which tells Box2D to keep
searching).

Note that this returns only the first object found at the given point. If multiple
objects are at the current point, it just returns the first one found, but that is sufficient
for this level.

Switch back to *PuzzleLayer.mm*. Go ahead and add the import for this new class at
the top of your file, as shown in Listing 10.28.

Listing 10.28 **PuzzleLayer.mm (at the top of the file)**

```
#import "SimpleQueryCallback.h"
```

Looking back to your ccTouchBegan method, you see that your last line calls QueryAABB. After this method returns, the world will have called the SimpleQueryCallback object for each potential intersection, and the class will have figured out if the point actually intersects anything or not. Now it's time to make use of that information! Continue your ccTouchBegan method by adding the lines shown in Listing 10.29 at the end of the method (but before the return statement).

Listing 10.29 **PuzzleLayer.mm (at end of ccTouchBegan but before return):**

```
if (callback.fixtureFound) {

    b2Body *body = callback.fixtureFound->GetBody();

    b2MouseJointDef mouseJointDef;
    mouseJointDef.bodyA = groundBody;
    mouseJointDef.bodyB = body;
    mouseJointDef.target = locationWorld;
    mouseJointDef.maxForce = 100 * body->GetMass();
    mouseJointDef.collideConnected = true;

    mouseJoint = (b2MouseJoint *) world->CreateJoint(&mouseJointDef);
    body->SetAwake(true);
    return YES;

} else {
    [self createBoxAtLocation:touchLocation
        withSize:CGSizeMake(50, 50)];
}
```

This code first checks to see if a fixture was found by the SimpleQueryCallback class, and if so it gets a pointer to the body from the fixture. It then creates a mouse joint definition, setting the parameters on the mouse joint definition as follows:

bodyA: When you specify a joint, you usually specify two bodies. For mouse joints, you usually want the first body to be a nonmoving body, so you can specify a fixed target location and have the target move to that location. So for bodyA, you set it to the groundBody you saved away earlier.

bodyB: The body you want to move. In this case, it's the body that was detected by the AABB test and SimpleQueryCallback.

target: Where you want the object to move to. In this case, it's the location tapped by the user.

maxForce: The maximum amount of force to apply to move the body. In this case, you want to be able to move an object of any mass, so you give it a multiple of the body's mass. The larger the multiple, the faster objects will move to their target locations.

collideConnected: Whether or not `bodyA` and `bodyB` should collide. In this case, you still want the chosen body to collide with the ground, so you set it to `true`.

Warning

It's a common mistake to forget to set `collideConnected` to `true` when setting up joints connected with ground bodies. If you forget to set this, it defaults to false, which means that your body will no longer collide with the ground. So if you see your objects going through your world boundaries, double check that you don't have any joints set up that would prevent the objects from colliding with the ground!

After creating the mouse joint definition, it passes it to the world with the `CreateJoint` method, which actually creates the joint. It also sets the body to awake in case it was sleeping.

Note that if a fixture was not found, it runs the old method to create a new box at that touch point.

You're almost done! Just add the methods to handle touch movement and ending, as shown in Listing 10.30.

Listing 10.30 PuzzleLayer.mm (after ccTouchBegan)

```
-(void) ccTouchMoved:(UITouch *)touch withEvent:(UIEvent *)event {
    CGPoint touchLocation = [touch locationInView:[touch view]];
    touchLocation =
        [[CCDirector sharedDirector] convertToGL:touchLocation];
    touchLocation = [self convertToNodeSpace:touchLocation];
    b2Vec2 locationWorld = b2Vec2(touchLocation.x/PTM_RATIO,
                                  touchLocation.y/PTM_RATIO);
    if (mouseJoint) {
        mouseJoint->SetTarget(locationWorld);
    }
}

-(void) ccTouchEnded:(UITouch *)touch withEvent:(UIEvent *)event {
    if (mouseJoint) {
        world->DestroyJoint(mouseJoint);
        mouseJoint = NULL;
    }
}
```

The ccTouchMoved method simply updates the target of the existing mouse joint based on the new touch location, and the ccTouchEnded method destroys the joint, since the movement is complete.

That's it! Compile and run your app, and you should now be able to drag the objects all around the screen and flick them around in fun and amusing ways!

Mass, Density, Friction, and Restitution

So far, the bodies you've added to your Box2D world have used mostly default values. But sometimes you want some bodies to be heavier than others, or to slide along objects more (or less), or to be more (or less) bouncy.

You can set this behavior on each fixture you create in Box2D by setting three properties: density, friction, and restitution. How to use these properties can be confusing to beginners of Box2D, so we'll run a few experiments so that you can fully understand how they work.

Begin by opening *PuzzleLayer.mm* and modifying your createBoxAtLocation method so it looks like Listing 10.31.

Listing 10.31   **PuzzleLayer.mm (modify createBoxAtLocation to this)**

```
- (void)createBoxAtLocation:(CGPoint)location
    withSize:(CGSize)size friction:(float32)friction
    restitution:(float32)restitution density:(float32)density {

    b2BodyDef bodyDef;
    bodyDef.type = b2_dynamicBody;
    bodyDef.position = b2Vec2(location.x/PTM_RATIO,
                             location.y/PTM_RATIO);
    bodyDef.allowSleep = false;
    b2Body *body = world->CreateBody(&bodyDef);

    b2PolygonShape shape;
    shape.SetAsBox(size.width/2/PTM_RATIO, size.height/2/PTM_RATIO);

    b2FixtureDef fixtureDef;
    fixtureDef.shape = &shape;
    fixtureDef.density = density;
    fixtureDef.friction = friction;
    fixtureDef.restitution = restitution;

    body->CreateFixture(&fixtureDef);
}
```

This is almost exactly like the previous routine, except that it adds in a few extra parameters, allowing us to specify three properties on the fixture: the density, the friction, and the restitution. If you don't know what these mean, don't worry—you're about to learn what they mean through hands-on experimentation!

Next add some calls to the bottom of your init method to add three boxes to your scene when it first loads, as shown in Listing 10.32.

Listing 10.32 PuzzleLayer.mm (at the bottom of the init method)

```
CGPoint location1, location2, location3;
CGSize smallSize, medSize, largeSize;
if (UI_USER_INTERFACE_IDIOM() == UIUserInterfaceIdiomPad) {
    location1 = ccp(200, 400);
    location2 = ccp(500, 400);
    location3 = ccp(800, 400);
    smallSize = CGSizeMake(50, 50);
    medSize = CGSizeMake(100, 100);
    largeSize = CGSizeMake(200, 200);
} else {
    location1 = ccp(100, 200);
    location2 = ccp(250, 200);
    location3 = ccp(400, 200);
    smallSize = CGSizeMake(25, 25);
    medSize = CGSizeMake(50, 50);
    largeSize = CGSizeMake(100, 100);
}
[self createBoxAtLocation:location1 withSize:medSize
                friction:0.2 restitution:0.0 density:1.0];
[self createBoxAtLocation:location2 withSize:medSize
                friction:0.2 restitution:0.0 density:1.0];
[self createBoxAtLocation:location3 withSize:medSize
                friction:0.2 restitution:0.0 density:1.0];
```

This creates three boxes in the middle of your scene to play around with; each has the same values for friction, restitution, and density as the default values would be. Note that it sets up some locations and sizes for the boxes, which need to be different depending on whether you're running on the iPhone or iPad.

Now that you're creating objects when the scene starts up, you no longer want to create boxes on touches. So comment out the line in ccTouchBegan that creates boxes where you touch, as shown in Listing 10.33.

Listing 10.33 PuzzleLayer.mm (comment out the following line in ccTouchBegan)

```
//[self createBoxAtLocation:touchLocation withSize:CGSizeMake(50, 50)];
```

Compile and run, and throw the boxes around a little bit so you get an idea how they work. Pay particular attention to how they slide along the ground, what happens when you throw one object into another, and how bouncy it is when it collides on the ground.

Next replace the three `createBoxAtLocation` lines with the contents of Listing 10.34.

Listing 10.34   PuzzleLayer.mm (replace createBoxAtLocation lines in init method)

```
[self createBoxAtLocation:location1 withSize:smallSize
    friction:0.2 restitution:0.0 density:1.0];
[self createBoxAtLocation:location2 withSize:medSize
    friction:0.2 restitution:0.0 density:1.0];
[self createBoxAtLocation:location3 withSize:largeSize
    friction:0.2 restitution:0.0 density:1.0];
```

This time you're creating boxes of three different sizes: a small, medium, and large box. They still all have the default parameters though. Compile and run, and try throwing the small box at the large box. Notice how it barely moves? Now throw the large box at the small box. Yowza!

So this tells you something cool and interesting: Box2D computes the mass of an object for you automatically based (in part) on the size of an object. The larger the object, the higher the mass will be and the harder it will be to move around.

Let's try another experiment: seeing what density does. Replace the three create-BoxAtLocation lines with the contents of Listing 10.35.

Listing 10.35   PuzzleLayer.mm (replace createBoxAtLocation lines in init method)

```
[self createBoxAtLocation:location1 withSize:smallSize
    friction:0.2 restitution:0.0 density:10.0];
[self createBoxAtLocation:location2 withSize:medSize
    friction:0.2 restitution:0.0 density:1.0];
[self createBoxAtLocation:location3 withSize:largeSize
    friction:0.2 restitution:0.0 density:1.0];
```

Note that there are still three different sizes of boxes, but the small box now has a much higher density than the other boxes. This time when you try throwing the small box at the large box, you'll see it moves quite a bit, while the small box is not impacted as much by the other boxes.

This reveals the other component that affects the mass: density. The higher the density, the higher the mass will be, and the harder it will be to move around. Which makes perfect sense, because as you may have learned in physics, mass = volume × density!

Okay, next let's play around with friction. Replace the three `createBoxAtLocation` lines with the contents of Listing 10.36.

Listing 10.36 PuzzleLayer.mm (replace createBoxAtLocation lines in init method)

```
[self createBoxAtLocation:location1 withSize:medSize
    friction:0.0 restitution:0.0 density:1.0];
[self createBoxAtLocation:location2 withSize:medSize
    friction:1.0 restitution:0.0 density:1.0];
[self createBoxAtLocation:location3 withSize:medSize
    friction:10.0 restitution:0.0 density:1.0];
```

The boxes are back to being all the same size now, but the first one is set to be extremely slippery, the second to be somewhat slippery, and the third to be not slippery at all. Play around with them and see how they act.

> **Note**
>
> When two fixtures slide along each other, each with different friction values, Box2D computes the friction to apply based on the geometric mean of the two fixture's friction values.

One final test: restitution! Replace the three createBoxAtLocation lines with the contents of Listing 10.37.

Listing 10.37 PuzzleLayer.mm (replace createBoxAtLocation lines in init method)

```
[self createBoxAtLocation:location1 withSize:medSize
    friction:1.0 restitution:0.0 density:1.0];
[self createBoxAtLocation:location2 withSize:medSize
    friction:1.0 restitution:0.5 density:1.0];
[self createBoxAtLocation:location3 withSize:medSize
    friction:1.0 restitution:1.0 density:1.0];
```

Compile and run, and you'll see the third box is extremely bouncy, while the second bounces just a little, and the first not at all.

> **Note**
>
> When two bodies collide with each other with different restitution values, Box2D applies the restitution value to use by choosing the maximum of the two fixtures' restitution values.

That about covers the tests of mass, density, friction, and restitution. In summary, you've seen that

- *Mass* is automatically calculated by the *volume* of the shape (automatically computed by Box2D based on the size of the shape) times the *density*.
- The more *mass* an object has, the more *force* it will take to move the object.
- The less *friction* an object has, the more it will slide along other objects.
- The more *restitution* an object has, the bouncier it will be.

By thinking about the bodies in your game and how heavy/slippery/bouncy they should be, you can tweak these properties and get much nicer (and more realistic, if that's what you're aiming for) behavior!

Decorating Your Box2D Bodies with Sprites

You're getting close to being able to have all the tools necessary to make a simple game using Box2D, except you're missing one major piece: the ability to associate sprites with Box2D bodies! Obviously, shipping a game with Box2D debug drawing as your art layer wouldn't win you any Apple Design Awards.

Now you'll learn how to decorate Box2D bodies by decorating your objects with some artwork for this level: a frozen Ole, blocks of ice, rocks, meteors, and even a few deranged skulls!

The downloadable files associated with this chapter include the sprite sheets and background files you'll need for this scene (*scene3atlas.plist,scene3atlas.png, scene3atlas-hd.plist, scene3atlas-hd.png, puzzle_level_bkgrnd.png, puzzle_level_bkgrnd-hd.png,* and *puzzle_level_bkgrnd-ipad.png*). Find these files in Finder, and drag them into your *Images* group. Make sure **Copy items into destination group's folder (if needed)** is checked, and click **Finish**.

> **Note**
>
> For this level, we use the hd sprite sheet for the iPad and retina display, and the non-hd sprite sheet for the iPhone. Although the aspect ratio is different on the iPhone and iPad, they'll still look good as long as we place the objects in the correct spot for each device.
>
> The background is a special case, however. It's critical it matches up to the exact size of each screen so we have a separate image for each case.
>
> Note that the sprite sheets are premade for you in the resources for this chapter. However, if you'd like, you can make them yourself with TexturePacker or Zwoptex, using the instructions from Chapter 2. You can find the sprites used in the sprite sheets in the *Raw Art* folder.

The next step is to create a new subclass of GameCharacter that sprites associated with Box2D bodies will derive from so that they have a place to keep track of the associated Box2D body. Choose the *Classes\Game Objects* group, and make a new subgroup named *Box2D*. With the new *Box2D* subgroup selected, go to **File > New > New File...**, choose **iOS > Cocoa Touch > Objective-C class**, and click **Next**. Enter *GameCharacter* as the Subclass of, click **Next**, name the file *Box2DSprite.mm*, and click **Save**.

With that done, replace the contents of *Box2DSprite.h*, as shown in Listing 10.38.

Listing 10.38   **Box2DSprite.h**

```
#import "GameCharacter.h"
#import "Box2D.h"
```

```
@interface Box2DSprite : GameCharacter {
    b2Body *body;
}

@property (assign) b2Body *body;

// Return TRUE to accept the mouse joint
// Return FALSE to reject the mouse joint
- (BOOL)mouseJointBegan;

@end
```

This class derives from `GameCharacter`, since subclasses will need the ability to store their current character state. It contains a single instance variable and property for the associated Box2D body. It also defines a method that you will use to check if the Box2D body accepts mouse joint input or not.

Next replace the contents of *Box2DSprite.m*, as shown in Listing 10.39.

Listing 10.39   Box2DSprite.mm

```
#import "Box2DSprite.h"

@implementation Box2DSprite
@synthesize body;

// Override if necessary
- (BOOL)mouseJointBegan {
    return TRUE;
}

@end
```

This simply synthesizes the variable, and returns TRUE as the default behavior for `mouseJointBegan` (which means objects should be able to be moved by mouse joints).

Now switch back to *PuzzleLayer.h* and add a few instance variables inside the interface, as shown in Listing 10.40.

Listing 10.40   PuzzleLayer.h (inside @interface declaration)

```
CCSpriteBatchNode *sceneSpriteBatchNode;
b2Body *frozenVikingBody;
```

This keeps track of your sprite batch node and is a handy reference to your frozen Viking.

Next, switch to *PuzzleLayer.mm* and import the header for *Box2DSprite* at the top of the file, as shown in Listing 10.41.

Listing 10.41   PuzzleLayer.mm (at top of file)

```
#import "Box2DSprite.h"
```

Then modify your `createBoxAtLocation` one more time, as shown in Listing 10.42. The **bold** lines indicate the changes since last time.

Listing 10.42   PuzzleLayer.mm (modify createBoxAtLocation to this)

```
- (void)createBodyAtLocation:(CGPoint)location
    forSprite:(Box2DSprite *)sprite friction:(float32)friction
    restitution:(float32)restitution density:(float32)density
    isBox:(BOOL)isBox {

    b2BodyDef bodyDef;
    bodyDef.type = b2_dynamicBody;
    bodyDef.position = b2Vec2(location.x/PTM_RATIO,
                             location.y/PTM_RATIO);
    bodyDef.allowSleep = false;
    b2Body *body = world->CreateBody(&bodyDef);
    body->SetUserData(sprite);
    sprite.body = body;

    b2FixtureDef fixtureDef;

    if (isBox) {
        b2PolygonShape shape;
        shape.SetAsBox(sprite.contentSize.width/2/PTM_RATIO,
                       sprite.contentSize.height/2/PTM_RATIO);
        fixtureDef.shape = &shape;
    } else {
        b2CircleShape shape;
        shape.m_radius = sprite.contentSize.width/2/PTM_RATIO;
        fixtureDef.shape = &shape;
    }

    fixtureDef.density = density;
    fixtureDef.friction = friction;
    fixtureDef.restitution = restitution;

    body->CreateFixture(&fixtureDef);

}
```

There are a few interesting differences this time. First, the routine takes a parameter of a Box2DSprite (our new subclass of GameCharacter), and sets this as the user data of the Box2D body. It also uses the content size of the sprite to figure out the size of the box to create.

> **Note**
>
> The content size of a sprite includes any transparent space that may be in the sprite image. This isn't a problem for the puzzle level, as the sprites don't have any extra transparent space, but if you're making a game where your images do, you will have to modify the Box2D body to map to the actual image more closely. You'll learn how to do this with Vertex Helper in the next chapter!

The routine also has a new parameter specifying whether to create a box (as before) or, if not, a circle. Why would we want to make a circle? Well, for some of the shapes in this level, a circle is a better match than a box for the sprite. Creating a circle is simply a matter of creating a b2CircleShape instead of a b2PolygonShape and setting the radius of the circle.

Note that the method also has a name change (createBodyAtLocation rather than createBoxAtLocation), since it now can make circles as well as boxes.

Next create several routines, which will use this method to create Box2D objects associated with sprites, as shown in Listing 10.43.

Listing 10.43   PuzzleLayer.mm (above init method)

```
- (void)createMeteorAtLocation:(CGPoint)location {
    Box2DSprite *sprite = [Box2DSprite spriteWithSpriteFrameName:@"meteor.
png"];
    sprite.gameObjectType = kMeteorType;
    [self createBodyAtLocation:location forSprite:sprite friction:0.1
restitution:0.3 density:1.0 isBox:FALSE];
    [sceneSpriteBatchNode addChild:sprite];
}

- (void)createSkullAtLocation:(CGPoint)location {
    Box2DSprite *sprite = [Box2DSprite spriteWithSpriteFrameName:@"skull.
png"];
    sprite.gameObjectType = kSkullType;
    [self createBodyAtLocation:location forSprite:sprite friction:0.5
restitution:0.5 density:0.25 isBox:FALSE];
    [sceneSpriteBatchNode addChild:sprite];
}

- (void)createLongBlockAtLocation:(CGPoint)location {
    Box2DSprite *sprite = [Box2DSprite spriteWithSpriteFrameName:@"long_
block.png"];
    sprite.gameObjectType = kLongBlockType;
```

```
    [self createBodyAtLocation:location forSprite:sprite friction:0.2
restitution:0.0 density:1.0 isBox:TRUE];
    [sceneSpriteBatchNode addChild:sprite];
}


- (void)createIceBlockAtLocation:(CGPoint)location {
    Box2DSprite *sprite = [Box2DSprite spriteWithSpriteFrameName:@"ice_
block.png"];
    sprite.gameObjectType = kIceType;
    [self createBodyAtLocation:location forSprite:sprite friction:0.2
restitution:0.2 density:1.0 isBox:TRUE];
    [sceneSpriteBatchNode addChild:sprite];
}


- (void)createFrozenOleAtLocation:(CGPoint)location {
    Box2DSprite *sprite = [Box2DSprite spriteWithSpriteFrameName:@"frozen_
ole.png"];
    sprite.gameObjectType = kFrozenVikingType;
    [self createBodyAtLocation:location forSprite:sprite friction:0.1
restitution:0.2 density:1.0 isBox:TRUE];
    [sceneSpriteBatchNode addChild:sprite];
    frozenVikingBody = sprite.body;
}


- (void)createRockAtLocation:(CGPoint)location {
    Box2DSprite *sprite = [Box2DSprite spriteWithSpriteFrameName:@"rock.
png"];
    sprite.gameObjectType = kRockType;
    [self createBodyAtLocation:location forSprite:sprite friction:3.0
restitution:0.0 density:1.0 isBox:TRUE];
    [sceneSpriteBatchNode addChild:sprite];
}
```

This is pretty straightforward: each routine simply creates a `Box2DSprite`, passing in the appropriate sprite frame name from the sprite sheet, sets the game object type and `friction`/`restitution`/`density`/`isBox` parameters appropriately, and adds the new sprite to the sprite batch node.

Now delete the calls to `createBoxAtLocation` in your `init` method and replace them with the contents of Listing 10.44.

Listing 10.44   PuzzleLayer.mm (replace createBoxAtLocation lines in init method)

```
if (UI_USER_INTERFACE_IDIOM() == UIUserInterfaceIdiomPad) {
    [[CCSpriteFrameCache sharedSpriteFrameCache]
     addSpriteFramesWithFile:@"scene3atlas-hd.plist"];
    sceneSpriteBatchNode = [CCSpriteBatchNode
                            batchNodeWithFile:@"scene3atlas-hd.png"];
```

```
    [self addChild:sceneSpriteBatchNode z:0];
    [self createMeteorAtLocation:ccp(200, 600)];
    [self createSkullAtLocation:ccp(200, 500)];
    [self createRockAtLocation:ccp(400, 100)];
    [self createIceBlockAtLocation:ccp(400, 400)];
    [self createLongBlockAtLocation:ccp(400, 300)];
    [self createFrozenOleAtLocation:ccp(100, 400)];
    [self createRockAtLocation:ccp(300, 400)];
    [CCTexture2D
        setDefaultAlphaPixelFormat:kCCTexture2DPixelFormat_RGB565];
    CCSprite *background = [CCSprite
        spriteWithFile:@"puzzle_level_bkgrnd-ipad.png"];
    background.anchorPoint = ccp(0,0);
    [CCTexture2D
        setDefaultAlphaPixelFormat:kCCTexture2DPixelFormat_Default];
    [self addChild:background z:-1];
} else {
    [[CCSpriteFrameCache sharedSpriteFrameCache]
        addSpriteFramesWithFile:@"scene3atlas.plist"];
    sceneSpriteBatchNode = [CCSpriteBatchNode
                            batchNodeWithFile:@"scene3atlas.png"];
    [self addChild:sceneSpriteBatchNode z:0];
    [self createMeteorAtLocation:ccp(100, 300)];
    [self createSkullAtLocation:ccp(100, 250)];
    [self createRockAtLocation:ccp(200, 50)];
    [self createIceBlockAtLocation:ccp(200, 200)];
    [self createLongBlockAtLocation:ccp(200, 150)];
    [self createFrozenOleAtLocation:ccp(40, 200)];
    [self createRockAtLocation:ccp(150, 200)];
    [CCTexture2D
        setDefaultAlphaPixelFormat:kCCTexture2DPixelFormat_RGB565];
    CCSprite *background = [CCSprite
        spriteWithFile:@"puzzle_level_bkgrnd.png"];
    background.anchorPoint = ccp(0,0);
    [CCTexture2D
        setDefaultAlphaPixelFormat:kCCTexture2DPixelFormat_Default];
    [self addChild:background z:-1];
}
```

Listing 10.44 adds some bodies to the scene at particular locations. Note there is one case for the iPad and one case for the iPhone, so the appropriate sprite sheets are loaded and the sprites are put at the correct positions for each device.

It also sets up a background image of the level. Note that it sets the pixel format to RGB565 before loading the background image—it's good practice to use a lower quality pixel format when loading large images (such as background images) to conserve memory usage, which is quite limited on iOS devices.

> **Warning**
>
> If you don't make wise use of setting pixel formats and load a lot of massive images, eventually you will run out of memory and the OS will shut down your app. To learn more about pixel formats, check out this great post written by Ricardo Quesada on the Cocos2D site:
>
> *http://www.cocos2d-iphone.org/archives/61*

To review, at this point you've created a sprite sheet and then created several Box2D bodies with the same dimensions as each sprite. But you're missing a key piece: somehow, you need to connect the locations of the sprites to the locations of the Box2D bodies.

For each animation frame of your game, you should update your sprites based on the locations of the Box2D bodies—hence you need to add some code to your update method. Find your update method and add the contents of Listing 10.45 to the bottom of the method.

Listing 10.45   PuzzleLayer.mm (add at end of update method)

```
for(b2Body *b = world->GetBodyList(); b != NULL; b = b->GetNext()) {
    if (b->GetUserData() != NULL) {
        Box2DSprite *sprite = (Box2DSprite *) b->GetUserData();
        sprite.position = ccp(b->GetPosition().x * PTM_RATIO,
                              b->GetPosition().y * PTM_RATIO);
        sprite.rotation = CC_RADIANS_TO_DEGREES(b->GetAngle() * -1);
    }
}
```

This simply loops through all of the bodies in the world and checks to see if their user data isn't null. Remember how in `createBodyAtLocation` it now sets the user data for the Box2D body to be the sprite? This is where it's used.

It then sets the position and rotation of the sprite based on the Box2D body's position. Note that it has to apply the `PTM_RATIO` and also convert from the Box2D angle (radians) to the Cocos2D angle (degrees). There's also a difference between clockwise and counterclockwise angles that is corrected by the −1.

One last thing: you've been experimenting with the accelerometer, but for the final puzzle level, you don't want the accelerometer enabled for the style of puzzle you're going to build. So comment out the `isAccelerometerEnabled` line in your `init` routine, as shown in Listing 10.46.

Listing 10.46   PuzzleLayer.mm (in init method, comment out the following line)

```
//self.isAccelerometerEnabled = TRUE;
```

Compile and run your code, and you should now see a bunch of Box2D objects decorated with sprites, as shown in Figure 10.17. You can try moving the various objects around and check out their various density/restitution/friction properties!

Figure 10.17   Box2D objects decorated with sprites

At this point you've learned a ton about Box2D—how to create bodies of square and circle shapes, how to move them around the screen with mouse joints, and even how to decorate them with sprites. You now have enough knowledge about Box2D to make a simple puzzle game out of this, so let's add in some game logic and polish next!

Making a Box2D Puzzle Game

The goal of this puzzle game is to get Ole into the spot where the sun is shining so his ice block can melt. But of course, in order for this to work, you need some code to detect when Ole reaches that spot.

One way to accomplish this is to simply check the position of Ole each update and check if he is within a set position. This would work, but there's another way that leverages the power of Box2D.

Since Box2D is a physics engine that models what happens when objects collide into each other, it already has code to detect when objects collide so that it can respond appropriately. You can make use of this by registering for notifications from Box2D when collisions occur or by asking Box2D for a list of the currently active collisions for an object.

For this mini-game, you want to know when Ole collides with the bottom right corner of the scene. One way of doing this is to make a very thin object at that position and check to see when Ole collides with that dummy object.

But this isn't ideal, because you might want to detect if Ole hits near, but not exactly on, the bottom right corner. Luckily, Box2D provides a very nice solution to this: sensors!

Sensors are just Box2D objects that don't cause any collision responses. So you can have an "imaginary box" in the lower right corner that Ole and other objects can just pass through as if it weren't there. However, Box2D will still report when objects collide with the imaginary box object, so you can look for that and mark the level as won when Ole reaches that spot!

Let's see this in action. First add two instance variables in *PuzzleLayer.h*, as shown in Listing 10.47.

Listing 10.47   **PuzzleLayer.h (inside @interface declaration)**

```
b2Body *sensorBody;
BOOL hasWon;
```

These instance variables keep track of the sensor body and whether or not the user has won the level.

Then switch over to *PuzzleLayer.mm* and import GameManager.h at the top of the file, as shown in Listing 10.48.

Listing 10.48   **PuzzleLayer.mm (at top of file)**

```
#import "GameManager.h"
```

You had to import GameManager.h because you'll need to use GameManager later on to go to the level completed scene. Next add a new method to create the sensor that represents the spot where the sun is shining, as shown in Listing 10.49.

Listing 10.49   **PuzzleLayer.mm (before init method)**

```
- (void)createSensor {
    CGSize winSize = [[CCDirector sharedDirector] winSize];
    CGSize sensorSize = CGSizeMake(100, 50);
    if (UI_USER_INTERFACE_IDIOM() == UIUserInterfaceIdiomPhone) {
        sensorSize = CGSizeMake(50, 25);
    }

    b2BodyDef bodyDef;
    bodyDef.type = b2_staticBody;
    bodyDef.position =
        b2Vec2((winSize.width-sensorSize.width/2)/PTM_RATIO,
                (sensorSize.height/2)/PTM_RATIO);
    sensorBody = world->CreateBody(&bodyDef);
```

```
    b2PolygonShape shape;
    shape.SetAsBox(sensorSize.width/PTM_RATIO,
                    sensorSize.height/PTM_RATIO);

    b2FixtureDef fixtureDef;
    fixtureDef.shape = &shape;
    fixtureDef.isSensor = true;
    sensorBody->CreateFixture(&fixtureDef);
}
```

This sets up a body and attaches a box-shaped fixture to it in the usual manner. However, there is one difference—it sets `isSensor` to `true` on the fixture. This makes the object detect collisions but still allows anything to pass through.

Next add the code to call your new `createSensor` method and a method to display the instructions for the level (which you will write soon), as shown in Listing 10.50.

Listing 10.50   PuzzleLayer.mm (inside init method)

```
[self createSensor];
[self instructions];
```

If you implemented a stub for the instructions method you're about to write, you could compile and run your project now and you'd see a strange green box in the lower right corner representing the sensor. However, it wouldn't do anything, since you haven't added any code to look for the collision yet. So let's add that now by adding the contents of Listing 10.51 to the bottom of your update method.

Listing 10.51   PuzzleLayer.mm (at the bottom of the update method)

```
if (!hasWon) {
    b2ContactEdge* edge = frozenVikingBody->GetContactList();
    while (edge)
    {
        b2Contact* contact = edge->contact;
        b2Fixture* fixtureA = contact->GetFixtureA();
        b2Fixture* fixtureB = contact->GetFixtureB();
        b2Body *bodyA = fixtureA->GetBody();
        b2Body *bodyB = fixtureB->GetBody();
        if (bodyA == sensorBody || bodyB == sensorBody) {
            hasWon = true;
            [self win];
            break;
        }
        edge = edge->next;
    }
}
```

This code checks if the user has won, and if not, it checks if Ole is colliding with the sensor.

How does this work? Well, Box2D maintains a list of all of the contacts that one body makes to other bodies. Each contact contains information on exactly what points are touching as well as references to the fixtures that are touching (from which you can get the bodies). So this simply looks through Ole's current contacts and checks if any of them are the sensor body. If so, it sets the level as won and calls a method you'll write in a second to perform the winning animations.

Note

This way of doing things has a small problem. It uses only the *current* state of Ole's contacts. If Ole was moving very quickly and moved through the sensor area within a single Box2D step, this would not pick up the collision. Next chapter, we show a more robust way of detecting collisions with Box2D (at the cost of extra complexity), but for this level, this manner of checking collisions works quite fine!

The last step is to add the code to display the instructions at the beginning of the level and display an effect when the player wins (see Figure 10.18). Add the code in Listing 10.52 above your `init` method.

Listing 10.52 PuzzleLayer.mm (above init method)

```
- (void)instructions {
    CGSize winSize = [[CCDirector sharedDirector] winSize];
    CCLabelTTF *label = [CCLabelTTF labelWithString:@"Melt the Viking!"
fontName:@"Helvetica" fontSize:48.0];
    label.position = ccp(winSize.width/2, winSize.height/2);
    label.scale = 0.25;
    [self addChild:label];

    CCScaleTo *scaleUp = [CCScaleTo actionWithDuration:1.0 scale:1.2];
    CCScaleTo *scaleBack = [CCScaleTo actionWithDuration:1.0 scale:1.0];
    CCDelayTime *delay = [CCDelayTime actionWithDuration:5.0];
    CCFadeOut *fade = [CCFadeOut actionWithDuration:2.0];
    CCSequence *sequence = [CCSequence actions:scaleUp, scaleBack, delay,
fade, nil];
    [label runAction:sequence];
}

- (void)winComplete:(id)sender {
    [[GameManager sharedGameManager] setHasPlayerDied:NO];
    [[GameManager sharedGameManager]
        runSceneWithID:kLevelCompleteScene];
}

- (void)win {
    CGSize winSize = [[CCDirector sharedDirector] winSize];
```

```
    CCLabelTTF *label = [CCLabelTTF labelWithString:@"You Win!"
fontName:@"Helvetica" fontSize:48.0];
    label.position = ccp(winSize.width/2, winSize.height/2);
    label.scale = 0.25;
    [self addChild:label];

    CCScaleTo *scaleUp = [CCScaleTo actionWithDuration:1.0 scale:1.2];
    CCScaleTo *scaleBack = [CCScaleTo actionWithDuration:1.0 scale:1.0];
    CCDelayTime *delay = [CCDelayTime actionWithDuration:2.0];
    CCCallFuncN *winComplete = [CCCallFuncN actionWithTarget:self
selector:@selector(winComplete:)];
    CCSequence *sequence = [CCSequence actions:scaleUp, scaleBack, delay,
winComplete, nil];
    [label runAction:sequence];
}
```

This uses a set of CCActions (which you learned about in Chapter 5) to animate a label (which you learned about in Chapter 6) to zoom in and out, wait a bit, then transition to the level complete scene.

Compile and run the code, and if everything works well, you should be able to drag Ole to the bottom right corner of the scene and win the level!

Figure 10.18   Sensor detecting Ole reaching target location

Ramping It Up

You may notice one major problem with the level at this point: it's just way too easy! As it stands, you can simply pick up frozen Ole and drag him over to the finish zone.

To make things more challenging, you'll set things up so that you can't move certain objects directly, such as Ole or the long stone block, and you'll also add a bunch of extra objects to clutter up the space. While you're at it, you'll add a little extra interactivity by adding sound effects and making skulls "pop" and disappear when you tap them.

Up to this point, you've been using the same subclass of CCSprite for all of the sprites (Box2DSprite) because they all had the same behavior and it was easy to do. But now you want different behavior for each object, so to keep your code nice and organized, you'll subclass Box2DSprite for each one.

Note that you're about to embark upon writing a bunch of code for this! But don't worry—most of the code that follows is pretty straightforward, and if you don't want to type it all, you can copy/paste it from the sample project (or copy/paste the relevant bits from file to file).

So take a big stretch, maybe grab some munchies and a soda, and get ready for some coding!

Start by adding a new file for the first subclass of Box2DSprite. Select the *Classes\ GameObjects\Box2D* group, go to **File > New > New File...**, choose **iOS > Cocoa Touch > Objective-C class**, and click **Next**. Enter *Box2DSprite* as the Subclass of, click **Next**, name the file *Meteor.mm* (note the *.mm* extension, since it imports Box2D), and click **Save**.

Now repeat this for the other objects in this scene: *Skull.mm, Rock.mm, IceBlock.mm, LongBlock.mm,* and *FrozenOle.mm*.

Next, replace the contents of *Meteor.h* with the contents of Listing 10.53.

Listing 10.53   **Meteor.h**

```objc
#import "Box2DSprite.h"

@interface Meteor : Box2DSprite {

}

@end
```

There's nothing fancy here—it's just a subclassing of Box2DSprite. Repeat the above for the rest of the headers: *Skull.h, Rock.h, IceBlock.h, LongBlock.h,* and *FrozenOle.h*, replacing *Meteor* with the appropriate class name for each file.

Next onto the implementations for each of these classes. Start by replacing the contents of *FrozenOle.mm* with the contents of Listing 10.54.

Listing 10.54   **FrozenOle.mm**

```objc
#import "FrozenOle.h"

@implementation FrozenOle
```

```
-(id) init {
    if((self = [super init])) {
        [self setDisplayFrame:[
            [CCSpriteFrameCache sharedSpriteFrameCache]
                spriteFrameByName:@"frozen_ole.png"]];
        gameObjectType = kFrozenVikingType;
    }
    return self;
}

- (BOOL)mouseJointBegan {
    return FALSE;
}

@end
```

This simply sets the display frame to be the frozen Ole image and sets up the game object type appropriately. It's nice to encapsulate this logic inside the `FrozenOle` class itself so the main game level doesn't have to contain knowledge about what sprite frame to use or the object type for this sprite.

Note

You could keep the organization even cleaner by refactoring the logic to construct the Box2D body for this object into the `init` method for this class as well. However, in the interest of clarity and time in this chapter, you will keep things as they are.

Note that the `mouseJointBegan` method returns false when the user tries to start a mouse joint on the body (meaning you cannot move Ole by dragging directly).

Next replace *LongBlock.mm* with a similar implementation, as shown in Listing 10.55.

Listing 10.55   **LongBlock.mm**

```
#import "LongBlock.h"

@implementation LongBlock

-(id) init {
    if((self = [super init])) {
        [self setDisplayFrame:[
            [CCSpriteFrameCache sharedSpriteFrameCache]
                spriteFrameByName:@"long_block.png"]];
        gameObjectType = kLongBlockType;
    }
    return self;
}
```

```
- (BOOL)mouseJointBegan {
    return FALSE;
}
```

@end

This is very similar in behavior to the `FrozenOle` class, so there's not much to discuss here. Next replace *IceBlock.mm*, as shown in Listing 10.56.

Listing 10.56   **IceBlock.mm**

```
#import "IceBlock.h"

@implementation IceBlock

-(id) init {
    if((self = [super init])) {
        [self setDisplayFrame:[
            [CCSpriteFrameCache sharedSpriteFrameCache]
                spriteFrameByName:@"ice_block.png"]];
        gameObjectType = kIceType;
    }
    return self;
}
```

@end

Again, similar implementation, except this time it doesn't override `mouseJointBegan`, so it accepts the default behavior (to allow the mouse joint).

Next up, replace *Rock.mm* with the contents of Listing 10.57.

Listing 10.57   **Rock.mm**

```
#import "Rock.h"
#import "SimpleAudioEngine.h"

@implementation Rock

-(id) init {
    if( (self=[super init]) ) {
        gameObjectType = kRockType;
        [self setDisplayFrame:[
            [CCSpriteFrameCache sharedSpriteFrameCache]
                spriteFrameByName:@"rock.png"]];
    }
    return self;
}
```

```
- (BOOL)mouseJointBegan {
    PLAYSOUNDEFFECT(PUZZLE_ROCK1);
    return TRUE;
}

@end
```

Similar implementation, except here we spice things up a bit by playing a sound effect when the user begins to move the rock.

Next replace *Meteor.mm* with the contents of Listing 10.58, which is similar but plays a different sound effect.

Listing 10.58   **Meteor.mm**

```
#import "Meteor.h"
#import "SimpleAudioEngine.h"

@implementation Meteor

-(id) init {
    if( (self=[super init]) ) {
        gameObjectType = kMeteorType;
        [self setDisplayFrame:[
            [CCSpriteFrameCache sharedSpriteFrameCache]
                spriteFrameByName:@"meteor.png"]];
    }
    return self;
}

- (BOOL)mouseJointBegan {
    PLAYSOUNDEFFECT(PUZZLE_METEOR);
    return TRUE;
}

@end
```

Finally, replace *Skull.mm* with the contents of Listing 10.59.

Listing 10.59   **Skull.mm**

```
#import "Skull.h"
#import "SimpleAudioEngine.h"

@implementation Skull

-(id) init {
    if( (self=[super init]) ) {
```

```
            gameObjectType = kSkullType;
            [self setDisplayFrame:[
                [CCSpriteFrameCache sharedSpriteFrameCache]
                    spriteFrameByName:@"skull.png"]];
        }
        return self;
}


- (void)shrinkDone:(id)sender {
    [self removeFromParentAndCleanup:YES];
}


-(void)changeState:(CharacterStates)newState {
    [self setCharacterState:newState];

    switch (newState) {
    case kStateDead:
    {
        CCLOG(@"Skull->Changing State to Dead");

        PLAYSOUNDEFFECT(PUZZLE_SKULL);
        body->GetWorld()->DestroyBody(body);
        body = NULL;
        CCScaleTo *growAction = [
            CCScaleTo actionWithDuration:0.1 scale:1.2];
        CCScaleTo *shrinkAction =
            [CCScaleTo actionWithDuration:0.1 scale:0.1];
        CCCallFuncN *doneAction = [CCCallFuncN actionWithTarget:self
                selector:@selector(shrinkDone:)];
        CCSequence *sequence = [CCSequence actions:
            growAction, shrinkAction, doneAction, nil];
        [self runAction:sequence];
        break;
    }
    default:
        CCLOG(@"Unhandled state %d in Skull", newState);
        break;
    }
}


- (BOOL)mouseJointBegan {
    if (self.characterState == kStateDead) return FALSE;
    [self changeState:kStateDead];
    return FALSE;
}

@end
```

In the case of the skull, when the user begins to tap the skull, it sets the state of the skull to dead and returns false (mouse joint not allowed). When the state is changed to dead, it performs the following steps:

1. Destroys the Box2D body by calling `DestroyBody()`, passing in the saved away Box2D body as a parameter.

2. Sets the body pointer to `NULL`.

3. Runs a little animation showing the skull popping away with Cocos2D actions, with a scheduled callback upon complete.

4. The callback uses `removeFromParentAndCleanup` to remove the sprite from the scene.

Okay, time to integrate these new classes. Switch to *PuzzleLayer.mm* and add some imports to the top of the file, as shown in Listing 10.60.

Listing 10.60   PuzzleLayer.mm (at the top of the file)

```
#import "Meteor.h"
#import "Skull.h"
#import "Rock.h"
#import "IceBlock.h"
#import "LongBlock.h"
#import "FrozenOle.h"
#import "SimpleAudioEngine.h"
```

Then go to `createMeteorAtLocation`, delete the first two lines, and replace them with a new line to create a meteor with the new `Meteor` class, as shown in Listing 10.61.

Listing 10.61   PuzzleLayer.mm (modify createMeteorAtLocation)

```
- (void)createMeteorAtLocation:(CGPoint)location {

    Meteor *sprite = [Meteor node];
    [self createBodyAtLocation:location forSprite:sprite
        friction:0.1 restitution:0.3 density:1.0 isBox:FALSE];
    [sceneSpriteBatchNode addChild:sprite];


}
```

Now repeat this for the other methods (`createSkullAtLocation`, `createLong-BlockAtLocation`, etc.), using the appropriate class for each method.

Next go to the `init` method and add some code at the bottom to start up the background music and add some extra objects to make the level more interesting, as shown in Listing 10.62.

Listing 10.62   PuzzleLayer.mm (at the bottom of the init method)

```
for(int i = 0; i < 10; ++i) {
    if (UI_USER_INTERFACE_IDIOM() == UIUserInterfaceIdiomPad) {
        [self createSkullAtLocation:ccp(200, 700)];
    } else {
        [self createSkullAtLocation:ccp(100, 250)];
    }
}
for(int i = 0; i < 2; ++i) {
    if (UI_USER_INTERFACE_IDIOM() == UIUserInterfaceIdiomPad) {
        [self createMeteorAtLocation:ccp(300, 600)];
        [self createRockAtLocation:ccp(300, 600)];
        [self createIceBlockAtLocation:ccp(300, 600)];
    } else {
        [self createMeteorAtLocation:ccp(100, 250)];
        [self createRockAtLocation:ccp(100, 250)];
        [self createIceBlockAtLocation:ccp(100, 250)];
    }
}
```

Note that you're adding all of the bodies at the same locations. That is okay because Box2D automatically spreads out the bodies when the level starts so they aren't colliding. You could also modify this to put the bodies at specific locations if you like.

While you're in the init method, also comment out the line to set up debug drawing, since you don't need it anymore, as shown in Listing 10.63.

Listing 10.63   PuzzleLayer.mm (comment out this line in the init method)

```
//[self setupDebugDraw];
```

One final step! Go to the ccTouchBegan method, right after you call callback. fixtureFound->GetBody(), and add the three lines of code shown in Listing 10.64.

Listing 10.64   PuzzleLayer.mm (inside ccTouchBegan, after callback.fixtureFound->GetBody())

```
Box2DSprite *sprite = (Box2DSprite *) body->GetUserData();
if (sprite == NULL) return FALSE;
if(![sprite mouseJointBegan]) return FALSE;
```

This calls the mouseJointBegan method on the objects so they have a chance to respond to (or cancel) the mouse joint.

Phew—you're done! Compile and run the code, and now you should be able to hear sound effects when you move a rock or a meteor and see the skulls disappear when you tap them. And best of all, you've ramped up the difficulty, since you can no longer move Ole or the long ice block directly, and there are more objects blocking the way, so you'll have to use a little physics to win! See Figure 10.19.

Figure 10.19   The final puzzle level!

Summary

You have developed a cool mini-puzzle game, using Box2D to handle the game physics automatically. You should now be familiar with the most important concepts in Box2D, such as bodies, fixtures, density, restitution, and friction. You also have hands-on experience adding bodies to the world, skinning them with sprites, and adding simple collision checking and game logic.

In the next level, you take this a step further and see how you can use Box2D to create a side-scrolling action game, complete with vehicles, bridges, motors, and more!

Challenges

1. Try to modify the level to be a different puzzle by moving the positions of the Box2D bodies to different locations or adding more bodies or deleting some. Can you come up with an interesting challenge to stump your friends?

2. Try creating your own sprite (perhaps a snowball?) and add it to the scene, as you did with the other types of sprites/bodies.

3. To add to the challenge, create a new body type (perhaps an electrified power generator?) that the Frozen Ole can't touch without losing the level.

Intermediate Game Physics:
Modeling, Racing, and Leaping

In Chapter 10, "Basic Game Physics: Adding Realism with Box2D," you learned the basics of using the Box2D physics engine. Specifically, you learned how to create basic shapes, decorate them with sprites, and use gravity. In the process, you made your own simple puzzle game with Box2D physics!

Although the level you made is quite cool, it barely scratches the surface of what you can do with Box2D. You're not limited to simple shapes such as squares or circles with Box2D—you can make more complicated shapes and connect multiple bodies together to create objects such as vehicles. You're also not limited to using gravity to move your objects—you can also apply forces, impulses, and motor effects to move your objects through your level in realistic ways.

In this chapter, you create an action-packed level where you move a mine cart with wheels based on accelerometer input. You race the cart in a side-scrolling level (Figure 11.1) over rocky terrain, tap to jump through the air, and learn a lot more about using Box2D along the way!

Figure 11.1   The Box2D-enabled side-scrolling action level you make in
this chapter

Getting Started

To get started with this level, you first need to get a basic Box2D scene set up—then you can build from there, adding features bit by bit. In this section you add the required resource files for this chapter to your project and create a basic Box2D scene as a starting point.

You should be familiar with how to do the code in this section based on what you learned in Chapter 10, but this will be a great refresher to make sure you mastered everything. And don't worry—before you know it, you'll be done with the initial setup and on to the fun stuff!

Adding the Resource Files

Go ahead and download the resource files for this chapter (if you haven't already) so you can add the required images, sounds, and property lists to your project.

Once you download the resource files, you will see several directories of files (*Images\Backgrounds*, *Images\TextureAtlases*, *Sounds*, and *Plists*), as shown in Figure 11.2.

Figure 11.2   Resources for Chapter 11

Drag the contents of the *Images* directory into the similarly named *Images* group in Xcode, and drag the contents of the *Plists* directory into the similarly named *Plists* group in Xcode.

> **Note**
>
> You do not need to add the contents of the *Raw Art—Do Not Add!* folder to your project—that folder contains the images inside the sprite sheet in case you want to try making the sprite sheet yourself with TexturePacker or Zwoptex.

Now that you have the files you need for Chapter 11 added, it's time to create a basic Box2D scene for the level.

Creating a Basic Box2D Scene

You start simple for the scene for this level and just create a Box2D world and one sprite-decorated Box2D body for Ole's cart.

The scene for this level contains two layers: one for the main action of the scene (the cart racing and jumping) and one to contain the user interface (win/lose text).

> **Note**
>
> The reason you use separate layers for the user interface (UI) elements and the action elements in this scene is related to how scrolling is implemented for this scene. As you'll see later, you implement scrolling by moving the action layer itself left or right to keep the player centered as he or she moves through the scene.
>
> By keeping the action layer and the UI layer separate, moving the action layer won't affect the UI elements, and they will always stay at the right spots on your screen.

First, make a class for the user interface layer. Control-click on the *Classes\Scenes* group in Xcode, select **New Group**, then rename the new folder that was created to *Scene4*. Then with the *Scene4* group selected, go to **File > New > New File...**, choose **iOS > Cocoa Touch > Objective-C class**, and click **Next**. Enter *CCLayer* as the Subclass of, click **Next**, name the file *Scene4UILayer.m*, and click **Save**.

Open *Scene4UILayer.h* and replace it with the contents of Listing 11.1.

Listing 11.1 Scene4UILayer.h

```
#import "cocos2d.h"

@interface Scene4UILayer : CCLayer {
    CCLabelTTF *label;
}

- (BOOL)displayText:(NSString *)text
    andOnCompleteCallTarget:(id)target selector:(SEL)selector;

@end
```

This is just a standard subclass of CCLayer. It contains a reference to a label that is used to display text to the user and a function that displays a line of text to the screen and runs a callback upon completion. You use this to display text on the screen, such as when the level begins or when the player wins or loses.

Next switch to *Scene4UILayer.m* and replace it with the contents of Listing 11.2.

Listing 11.2   **Scene4UILayer.m**

```objc
#import "Scene4UILayer.h"

@implementation Scene4UILayer

- (id)init {
    if ((self = [super init])) {
        CGSize winSize = [CCDirector sharedDirector].winSize;
        label = [CCLabelTTF labelWithString:@"" fontName:@"Helvetica"
            fontSize:48.0];
        label.position = ccp(winSize.width/2, winSize.height/2);
        label.visible = NO;
        [self addChild:label];
    }
    return self;
}

- (BOOL)displayText:(NSString *)text
   andOnCompleteCallTarget:(id)target selector:(SEL)selector {
    [label stopAllActions];
    [label setString:text];
    label.visible = YES;
    label.scale = 0.0;
    label.opacity = 255;

    CCScaleTo *scaleUp = [CCScaleTo actionWithDuration:0.5 scale:1.2];
    CCScaleTo *scaleBack =
        [CCScaleTo actionWithDuration:0.1 scale:1.0];
    CCDelayTime *delay = [CCDelayTime actionWithDuration:2.0];
    CCFadeOut *fade = [CCFadeOut actionWithDuration:0.5];
    CCHide *hide = [CCHide action];
    CCCallFuncN *onComplete =
        [CCCallFuncN actionWithTarget:target selector:selector];
    CCSequence *sequence = [CCSequence actions:scaleUp, scaleBack,
        delay, fade, hide, onComplete, nil];
    [label runAction:sequence];
    return TRUE;
}

@end
```

The `init` method adds a blank label to the middle of the screen and sets it to invisible. The `displayText` method stops any running actions (in case the label is currently animating), sets the string to the value passed in, and resets the label to visible, fully opaque, and very tiny (with a scale of 0.0). Then it scales the label up and slightly back to make it appear to "pop" into view, waits a few seconds, then fades out and rehides the label. It then calls whatever callback was passed in (and it's okay to pass nil for the parameters there if you don't have a callback). These are just the standard Cocos2D actions that you learned about earlier in the book, chained together in a cool and easy way. Aren't Cocos2D actions great?

Next, add a class for the game object representing Ole's cart. Select the *Classes\ Game Objects\Box2D* group, go to **File > New > New File...**, choose **iOS > Cocoa Touch > Objective-C class**, and click **Next**. Enter *Box2DSprite* as the Subclass of, click **Next**, name the file *Cart.mm* (note the *.mm* extension, since this imports Box2D), and click **Save**.

Replace *Cart.h* with the contents of Listing 11.3.

Listing 11.3   Cart.h

```
#import "Box2DSprite.h"

@interface Cart : Box2DSprite {
    b2World *world;
}

- (id)initWithWorld:(b2World *)world atLocation:(CGPoint)location;

@end
```

You've made subclasses of `Box2DSprite` before, but there's something new here—this time it takes the Box2D world as a parameter to the `init` method. This is because the class will now contain the logic to create its Box2D body in addition to setting up the sprite.

Let's see how this works with the implementation. Switch over to *Cart.mm* and replace it with the contents of Listing 11.4.

Listing 11.4   Cart.mm

```
#import "Cart.h"

@implementation Cart

- (void)createBodyAtLocation:(CGPoint)location {
    b2BodyDef bodyDef;
    bodyDef.type = b2_dynamicBody;
    bodyDef.position =
```

```
            b2Vec2(location.x/PTM_RATIO, location.y/PTM_RATIO);
    body = world->CreateBody(&bodyDef);
    body->SetUserData(self);

    b2FixtureDef fixtureDef;
    b2PolygonShape shape;
    shape.SetAsBox(self.contentSize.width/2/PTM_RATIO,
                   self.contentSize.height/2/PTM_RATIO);
    fixtureDef.shape = &shape;

    fixtureDef.density = 1.0;
    fixtureDef.friction = 0.5;
    fixtureDef.restitution = 0.5;

    body->CreateFixture(&fixtureDef);
}

- (id)initWithWorld:(b2World *)theWorld atLocation:(CGPoint)location {
    if ((self = [super init])) {
        world = theWorld;
        [self setDisplayFrame:[[CCSpriteFrameCache
            sharedSpriteFrameCache] spriteFrameByName:@"Cart.png"]];
        gameObjectType = kCartType;
        characterHealth = 100.0f;
        [self createBodyAtLocation:location];
    }
    return self;
}

}

@end
```

The code in `createBodyAtLocation` should be familiar to you—it creates a Box2D body and fixture in the same way you did in Chapter 10. The `init` method should look familiar as well, based on the other game objects you have made.

Now you implement the action layer, which uses this `Cart` object in a basic Box2D setup that you learned how to create in the previous chapter. It creates a Box2D world, enables debug drawing, preloads the sound effects you need, and adds a cart. It also sets up a mouse joint like you learned in Chapter 10, since it will be useful for debugging purposes as you develop this level (so you can move objects around to test their behavior).

With the *Scene4* group selected, go to **File > New > New File...**, choose **iOS > Cocoa Touch > Objective-C class**, and click **Next**. Enter *CCLayer* as the Subclass of, click **Next**, name the file *Scene4ActionLayer.mm* (note the *.mm* extension, since this imports Box2D), and click **Save**.

Then replace *Scene4ActionLayer.h* with the contents of Listing 11.5.

Listing 11.5 **Scene4ActionLayer.h**

```
#import "cocos2d.h"
#import "Box2D.h"
#import "GLES-Render.h"
#import "Constants.h"

@class Scene4UILayer;
@class Cart;

@interface Scene4ActionLayer : CCLayer {
    b2World * world;
    GLESDebugDraw * debugDraw;
    CCSpriteBatchNode * sceneSpriteBatchNode;
    b2Body * groundBody;
    b2MouseJoint * mouseJoint;
    Cart * cart;
    Scene4UILayer * uiLayer;
}

- (id)initWithScene4UILayer:(Scene4UILayer *)scene4UILayer;

@end
```

This includes the Cocos2D and Box2D headers, the Box2D debug draw class header, and *Constants.h* (mainly for the PTM_RATIO). As instance variables, it has pointers to the Box2D world, debug draw class, sprite batch node, ground body, mouse joint, and cart object. It also has an instance variable for the Scene4UILayer (and an initializer that takes this as a parameter)—this is because this class needs to call the Scene4UILayer to do things like display text or update Ole's health status.

Next you're on to the most important part—creating the basic implementation of the Box2D scene by implementing *Scene4ActionLayer.mm*. There's a good bit of code to write in this section, but don't worry—most of this should be quite familiar to you by now, and this is almost the last step before you'll be ready to compile and run!

Take a deep breath and a swig of caffeine. When you're ready, replace *Scene4Action-Layer.mm* with the contents of Listing 11.6.

Listing 11.6 **Scene4ActionLayer.mm**

```
#import "Scene4ActionLayer.h"
#import "Box2DSprite.h"
#import "Scene4UILayer.h"
#import "Cart.h"
#import "SimpleQueryCallback.h"

@implementation Scene4ActionLayer
```

```objectivec
- (void)setupWorld {
    b2Vec2 gravity = b2Vec2(0.0f, -10.0f);
    bool doSleep = true;
    world = new b2World(gravity, doSleep);
}

- (void)setupDebugDraw {
    debugDraw = new GLESDebugDraw(PTM_RATIO*
        [[CCDirector sharedDirector] contentScaleFactor]);
    world->SetDebugDraw(debugDraw);
    debugDraw->SetFlags(b2DebugDraw::e_shapeBit);
}

- (void)createGround {
    CGSize winSize = [[CCDirector sharedDirector] winSize];
    float32 margin = 10.0f;
    b2Vec2 lowerLeft = b2Vec2(margin/PTM_RATIO, margin/PTM_RATIO);
    b2Vec2 lowerRight = b2Vec2((winSize.width-margin)/PTM_RATIO,
        margin/PTM_RATIO);
    b2Vec2 upperRight = b2Vec2((winSize.width-margin)/PTM_RATIO,
        (winSize.height-margin)/PTM_RATIO);
    b2Vec2 upperLeft = b2Vec2(margin/PTM_RATIO,
        (winSize.height-margin)/PTM_RATIO);

    b2BodyDef groundBodyDef;
    groundBodyDef.type = b2_staticBody;
    groundBodyDef.position.Set(0, 0);
    groundBody = world->CreateBody(&groundBodyDef);

    b2PolygonShape groundShape;
    b2FixtureDef groundFixtureDef;
    groundFixtureDef.shape = &groundShape;
    groundFixtureDef.density = 0.0;

    groundShape.SetAsEdge(lowerLeft, lowerRight);
    groundBody->CreateFixture(&groundFixtureDef);
    groundShape.SetAsEdge(lowerRight, upperRight);
    groundBody->CreateFixture(&groundFixtureDef);
    groundShape.SetAsEdge(upperRight, upperLeft);
    groundBody->CreateFixture(&groundFixtureDef);
    groundShape.SetAsEdge(upperLeft, lowerLeft);
    groundBody->CreateFixture(&groundFixtureDef);
}

- (void)createCartAtLocation:(CGPoint)location {
    cart = [[[Cart alloc]
        initWithWorld:world atLocation:location] autorelease];
```

```
        [sceneSpriteBatchNode addChild:cart z:1 tag:kVikingSpriteTagValue];
    }


-   (void)registerWithTouchDispatcher {
        [[CCTouchDispatcher sharedDispatcher]
         addTargetedDelegate:self priority:0 swallowsTouches:YES];
    }


-   (id)initWithScene4UILayer:(Scene4UILayer *)scene4UILayer {
        if ((self = [super init])) {
            CGSize winSize = [CCDirector sharedDirector].winSize;
            uiLayer = scene4UILayer;

            [self setupWorld];
            [self setupDebugDraw];
            [[GameManager sharedGameManager]
                playBackgroundTrack:BACKGROUND_TRACK_MINECART];
            [self scheduleUpdate];
            [self createGround];
            self.isTouchEnabled = YES;


            if (UI_USER_INTERFACE_IDIOM() == UIUserInterfaceIdiomPad) {
                [[CCSpriteFrameCache sharedSpriteFrameCache]
                    addSpriteFramesWithFile:@"scene4atlas-hd.plist"];
                sceneSpriteBatchNode = [CCSpriteBatchNode
                    batchNodeWithFile:@"scene4atlas-hd.png"];
                [self addChild:sceneSpriteBatchNode z:-1];
            } else {
                [[CCSpriteFrameCache sharedSpriteFrameCache]
                    addSpriteFramesWithFile:@"scene4atlas.plist"];
                sceneSpriteBatchNode = [CCSpriteBatchNode
                    batchNodeWithFile:@"scene4atlas.png"];
                [self addChild:sceneSpriteBatchNode z:-1];
            }

            [self createCartAtLocation:
                ccp(winSize.width/4, winSize.width*0.3)];
            [uiLayer displayText:@"Go!" andOnCompleteCallTarget:nil
                selector:nil];
        }
        return self;
}

-(void)update:(ccTime)dt {
    int32 velocityIterations = 3;
    int32 positionIterations = 2;
```

```
    world->Step(dt, velocityIterations, positionIterations);

    for(b2Body *b=world->GetBodyList(); b!=NULL; b=b->GetNext()) {
        if (b->GetUserData() != NULL) {
            Box2DSprite *sprite = (Box2DSprite *) b->GetUserData();
            sprite.position = ccp(b->GetPosition().x * PTM_RATIO,
                b->GetPosition().y * PTM_RATIO);
            sprite.rotation =
                CC_RADIANS_TO_DEGREES(b->GetAngle() * -1);
        }
    }

    CCArray *listOfGameObjects = [sceneSpriteBatchNode children];
    for (GameCharacter *tempChar in listOfGameObjects) {
        [tempChar updateStateWithDeltaTime:dt
                    andListOfGameObjects:listOfGameObjects];
    }
}

-(void) draw {
    glDisable(GL_TEXTURE_2D);
    glDisableClientState(GL_COLOR_ARRAY);
    glDisableClientState(GL_TEXTURE_COORD_ARRAY);

    if (world) {
        world->DrawDebugData();
    }

    glEnable(GL_TEXTURE_2D);
    glEnableClientState(GL_COLOR_ARRAY);
    glEnableClientState(GL_TEXTURE_COORD_ARRAY);
}

-(BOOL) ccTouchBegan:(UITouch *)touch withEvent:(UIEvent *)event {
    CGPoint touchLocation = [touch locationInView:[touch view]];
    touchLocation = [[CCDirector sharedDirector]
        convertToGL:touchLocation];
    touchLocation = [self convertToNodeSpace:touchLocation];
    b2Vec2 locationWorld =
        b2Vec2(touchLocation.x/PTM_RATIO, touchLocation.y/PTM_RATIO);

    b2AABB aabb;
    b2Vec2 delta = b2Vec2(1.0/PTM_RATIO, 1.0/PTM_RATIO);
    aabb.lowerBound = locationWorld - delta;
    aabb.upperBound = locationWorld + delta;
    SimpleQueryCallback callback(locationWorld);
    world->QueryAABB(&callback, aabb);
```

```objc
    if (callback.fixtureFound) {
        b2Body *body = callback.fixtureFound->GetBody();
        b2MouseJointDef mouseJointDef;
        mouseJointDef.bodyA = groundBody;
        mouseJointDef.bodyB = body;
        mouseJointDef.target = locationWorld;
        mouseJointDef.maxForce = 50 * body->GetMass();
        mouseJointDef.collideConnected = true;

        mouseJoint = (b2MouseJoint *)
            world->CreateJoint(&mouseJointDef);
        body->SetAwake(true);
        return YES;
    }
    return TRUE;
}


-(void) ccTouchMoved:(UITouch *)touch withEvent:(UIEvent *)event {
    CGPoint touchLocation = [touch locationInView:[touch view]];
    touchLocation = [[CCDirector sharedDirector]
        convertToGL:touchLocation];
    touchLocation = [self convertToNodeSpace:touchLocation];
    b2Vec2 locationWorld = b2Vec2(touchLocation.x/PTM_RATIO,
        touchLocation.y/PTM_RATIO);

    if (mouseJoint) {
        mouseJoint->SetTarget(locationWorld);
    }
}

-(void) ccTouchEnded:(UITouch *)touch withEvent:(UIEvent *)event {
    if (mouseJoint) {
        world->DestroyJoint(mouseJoint);
        mouseJoint = NULL;
    }
}

@end
```

Phew! Now that you've got that coded, take a breather and look things over to make sure you understand how everything works.

You should already be familiar with most of this based on what you learned in Chapter 10. Here's a quick reminder of what each method does, but if you're unsure about anything, refer back to Chapter 10 for full details. This is the foundation for everything else you're about to do, so make sure you take the time to understand it fully!

setupWorld creates a Box2D world with gravity similar to Earth's gravity. It stores a pointer to the `world` object in an instance variable for future reference.

setupDebugDraw creates a Box2D debug `draw` object and tells the `world` object to use it. The `draw` method sets up the OpenGL states properly for debug drawing and tells the `world` to do the debug drawing.

createGround creates a static Box2D body (out of four edge fixtures) around the boundaries of the screen to act as the "ground" so that any Box2D objects we add to the scene don't fall off the edge of the screen.

createCartAtLocation simply creates an instance of the `Cart` object you made earlier and adds it as a child of the sprite sheet object.

update gives Box2D time to run the simulation every frame. It then loops through all of the Box2D bodies, looking for those that have a Box2DSprite in their user data. For each sprite it finds, it updates the position of the sprite based on where Box2D says it should be.

ccTouchBegan, **ccTouchMoved**, and **ccTouchEnded** contain the mouse joint code used for testing and debugging, the same as you learned in Chapter 10.

initWithScene4UILayer simply calls the above methods to create the world, ground, and Box2D body for Ole's cart. It also preloads the sound effects and calls `displayText` on the UI layer to display some text in the middle of the screen.

You're almost ready to try this out! But first, you need to create a Cocos2D scene that contains these two layers. With the *Scene4* group selected, go to **File > New > New File...**, choose **iOS > Cocoa Touch > Objective-C class**, and click **Next**. Enter *CCScene* as the Subclass of, click **Next**, name the file *Scene4.mm* (note the *.mm* extension, since this imports Box2D), and click **Save**.

Replace *Scene4.h* with the contents of Listing 11.7.

Listing 11.7   **Scene4.h**

```
#import "cocos2d.h"

@interface Scene4 : CCScene {
}

@end
```

Nothing fancy here—it's simply a subclass of `CCScene`. Move on to *Scene4.mm* and replace it with the contents of Listing 11.8.

Listing 11.8   **Scene4.mm**

```
#import "Scene4.h"
#import "Scene4UILayer.h"
#import "Scene4ActionLayer.h"
```

```
@implementation Scene4

-(id)init {
    if ((self = [super init])) {
        Scene4UILayer * uiLayer = [Scene4UILayer node];
        [self addChild:uiLayer z:1];
        Scene4ActionLayer * actionLayer =
        [[[Scene4ActionLayer alloc]
            initWithScene4UILayer:uiLayer] autorelease];
        [self addChild:actionLayer z:0];
    }
    return self;
}

@end
```

This simply creates both of the layers (passing the UI layer as a parameter to the action layer) and adds both to the scene. Note that the UI layer is set with a higher z value than the action layer, so it shows up in front.

The final step is to modify *GameManager.mm* to run your new scene when the user chooses Level 4. First import *Scene4.h* at the top of *GameManager.mm*, as shown in Listing 11.9.

Listing 11.9   GameManager.mm (at top of file)

```
#import "Scene4.h"
```

Then find runSceneWithId and modify the case for kGameLevel4 to run Scene4, as shown in Listing 11.10.

Listing 11.10   GameManager.mm (in the case statement in runSceneWithId)

```
case kGameLevel4:
    sceneToRun = [Scene4 node];
    break;
```

Tip

As mentioned in the previous chapter, you may wish to set up your app to run this new scene right away, since you'll be working with it a lot in this chapter. Again, to do this, simply open *Classes\Singletons\SpaceVikingAppDelegate.m*, navigate to the bottom of applicationDidFinishLaunching, and replace the CCDirector:runScene-WithID call at the bottom to:

```
[[GameManager sharedGameManager]
    runSceneWithID:kGameLevel4];
```

That's it! If you compile and run the app and choose **Descent Into Hades!** from the Main Menu (or have it set up to launch right away), you should see your new scene appear with a ground body around the edges, and Ole's cart (well at least part of it) will drop into your scene, as shown in Figure 11.3.

Figure 11.3   A Basic Box2D scene with a world, ground box, and single body/sprite

Creating a Cart with Box2D

If Ole saw his cart right now, he wouldn't be very impressed. First, the Box2D body doesn't actually match up with the cart's shape—the Box2D body is a rectangle, while the cart's shape is actually thinner at the bottom than at the top. Second, it doesn't have wheels! Even the Flintstones had those.

In this section, you learn how to make the shape of the Box2D body match up to the shape of the cart, how to create Box2D bodies for the wheels, and how to connect them with Box2D joints. You'll have Ole cruising along in no time!

Creating Custom Shapes with Box2D

Until this point, the shapes you've made with Box2D have been boxes, circles, or edges. When making a circle, you set the radius, and when making a rectangle or edge, you used helper methods such as `SetAsBox` and `SetAsEdge` to set up the vertices for you.

But with Box2D you're not stuck with simple box or circle shapes alone—you can set the location of each vertex yourself to make more complicated shapes as well. You use a `b2PolygonShape` as usual, but instead of using `SetAsBox` or `SetAsEdge`, you create a vertex array and then call the `Set` method, as shown in Figure 11.4.

```
b2PolygonShape shape;
int num = 4;
b2Vec2 verts[] = {
    b2Vec2(78.3f / PTM_RATIO, 38.5f / PTM_RATIO),   // A
    b2Vec2(-79.4f / PTM_RATIO, 38.2f / PTM_RATIO),  // B
    b2Vec2(-59.9f / PTM_RATIO, -38.5f / PTM_RATIO), // C
    b2Vec2(57.8f / PTM_RATIO, -38.5f / PTM_RATIO)   // D
};
shape.Set(verts, num);
```

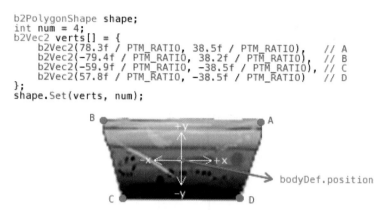

Figure 11.4   Defining vertices based on a center point in Box2D

Let's explain how Figure 11.4 works. When defining vertices for Box2D shapes, there are four important things to know: vertices are relative to the body's center, vertices need to be defined in counterclockwise order, there is a maximum count of vertices per shape, and vertices cannot define a concave shape. Let's go through these one by one.

Vertices are relative to the body's center: As you can see in the code shown in Figure 11.4, when you set vertices, you don't give world coordinates; instead you give local coordinates relative to the body's center point. So for the case of the cart, the upper right corner of the cart is about 78.3 pixels to the right of the center and 38.5 pixels above the center. This is a convenient trait, because it allows you to set up a shape without having to worry about where the body is in the world.

Vertices need to be defined in counterclockwise order: As you can see in Figure 11.4, the vertices are defined in counterclockwise order: upper right → upper left → lower left → lower right. If you forget to do this and define vertices in a different order, Box2D will likely crash (usually specifying an assertion error when computing the area).

There is a maximum count of vertices per shape: By default, each shape can have, at most, only eight vertices. This setting is configurable—it is set in *b2Settings.h* with the b2_maxPolygonVertices setting. Obviously, you want to keep this as small as possible, since the more vertices your shapes have, the larger the memory usage and slower the performance. If you try to add more vertices than the maximum, Box2D will likely crash (usually specifying an assertion error when checking the vertex count).

Vertices cannot define a concave shape: When you set up your shapes, you need to make sure that the shapes you define are convex, not concave. A concave shape is a shape in which one of the interior angles inside the shape is greater than

180 degrees. A good way to think of it is as a shape that has an indentation in it. Figure 11.5 illustrates the difference between convex and concave polygons.

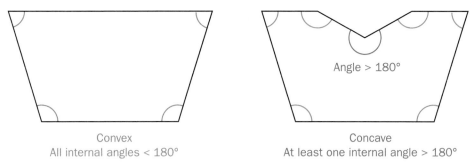

Figure 11.5   Convex vs. concave polygons

When defining vertices in Box2D, you have several options. First, you could guesstimate the pixel offsets for the vertices, compile, test, and iterate until you get them right. This works but is slow and painful. Second, you could load your image into an image editor and use a tool such as a ruler to measure the pixel offsets. This works too and is quicker than the first option, but it is still time consuming. Finally, there's a third method that can save you a lot of time—use a neat tool written by Johannes Fahrenkrug called Vertex Helper.

Using Vertex Helper

Vertex Helper is an open source tool that lets you import an image and click points on the image to represent the vertices you wish to define. When you're done, Vertex Helper generates Box2D code for you to define the vertices; you can simply cut and paste this code into your project. Let's see how this is done.

First, download and compile Vertex Helper (or if you'd rather, you can download the full version—Vertex Helper Pro—from the Mac App Store).

To grab the code, visit *https://github.com/jfahrenkrug/VertexHelper*, click **Downloads**, and click **Download zip**, as shown in Figure 11.6.

Once you've downloaded the zip file, extract the file to a folder and open the *VertexHelper.xcodeproj* file within. Compile and run the project, and you should see the main Vertex Helper UI appear, as shown in Figure 11.7.

Next find the image for Ole's cart from the resources folder that comes with this chapter (*Raw Art…\Scene\cart.png*) and drag it to the Vertex Helper window (where it says *Drop Sprite Image*).

You should now see the cart image in the center of the window. Now go to the control panel at the bottom and type 1 for **Rows**, 1 for **Cols**, set the **Type** to **Box2D**, and set the **Style** to **Initialization**. At this point Vertex Helper should have drawn a black boundary around your image, and you are ready to start defining vertices.

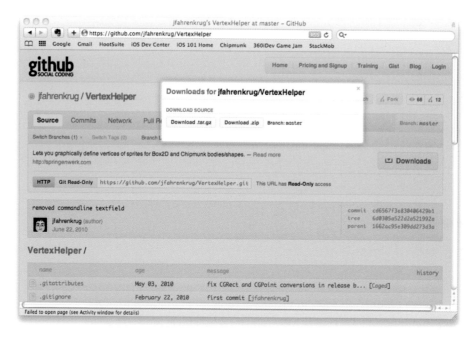

Figure 11.6   Downloading Vertex Helper

Figure 11.7   Main Vertex Helper screen

Now click on **Edit Mode** in the upper right corner, and then click on the upper right corner of the cart, which sets the first vertex at that point. Click on the upper left corner next, then the lower left corner, and lower right corner (counterclockwise order). Do not finish the shape off with a line back to the upper right—Box2D closes the shape automatically.

As you click your vertices, Vertex Helper draws a green line between the points you click, showing you the shape you are defining. When you're done, your screen should look similar to the screenshot shown in Figure 11.8.

If you look at the edit pane to the lower right, you'll see that Vertex Helper has set up a Box2D vertex array for you based on the vertices that you defined. It's a snap to use, so let's give it a shot!

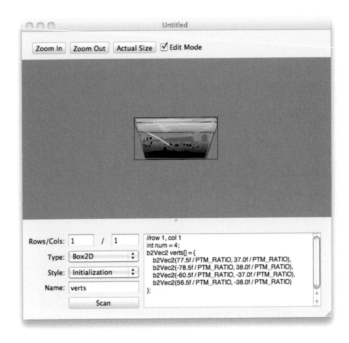

Figure 11.8   Cart vertices defined with Vertex Helper

Open up *Cart.mm* and comment out the line that calls `SetAsBox` in the create-`BodyAtLocation` method. Right below that commented line, paste the code that Vertex Helper generated for you in the edit pane (but replace all instances of `PTM_RATIO` with 100.0—more on why later). After you paste that, use the `Set` method on the shape and pass in the vertices and number of vertices, as shown in Listing 11.11.

Listing 11.11   **Cart.mm (in createBodyAtLocation method)**

```
// Comment out this line
//shape.SetAsBox(self.contentSize.width/2/PTM_RATIO,
//     self.contentSize.height/2/PTM_RATIO);
// Add your code from Vertex Helper here, but replace all
// instances of PTM_RATIO with 100.0
int num = 4;
b2Vec2 verts[] = {
    b2Vec2(77.5f / 100.0, 37.0f / 100.0),
    b2Vec2(-78.5f / 100.0, 38.0f / 100.0),
    b2Vec2(-60.5f / 100.0, -37.0f / 100.0),
    b2Vec2(56.5f / 100.0, -38.0f / 100.0)
};
// Then call this
shape.Set(verts, num);
```

> **Note**
>
> You may be wondering why you had to replace all instances of `PTM_RATIO` with 100.0.
> This is because you traced the large (HD) artwork in Vertex Helper. So to convert the pix-
> els to Box2D coordinates, you divide by the HD `PTM_RATIO`, which is 100.0. For *Space
> Viking*, you can't just use `PTM_RATIO` constant, since it's defined to be different on the
> iPad than on the iPhone.

Now compile and run your code. Instead of a rectangular shape around the cart, the Box2D body's shape should match up much better with your sprite, as shown in Figure 11.9.

Figure 11.9   A Box2D shape with custom-defined vertices

Now you know how to make an arbitrary shape using Box2D and how to use Vertex Helper to make your life a lot easier. But right now our cart has a big problem—it doesn't have wheels. So let's roll on out of the Stone Age and learn about Box2D revolute joints!

Adding Wheels with Box2D Revolute Joints

To add wheels to the cart, you need to make two more bodies—one for each wheel. Remember from Chapter 10 that they need to be separate bodies (rather than fixtures) because you want the cart and the wheels to be able to move independently from each other. For example, the wheels should be able to rotate without having to rotate the cart body.

However, you do need to set some kind of restriction on the movement of the bodies. You want the wheels and the cart to be fixed together at a particular point—but still able to rotate about that point independently. And that's exactly what joints are for—what we need is a type of joint called a revolute joint in this particular case.

Although there are many kinds of joints in Box2D, all of them work in a similar way. You set up a joint definition and specify which bodies are involved. Each joint is a relationship between two bodies—like marriage! You then set up some parameters on the joint definition, which vary depending on the joint type you're using. For revolute joints, the only parameter required is the common anchor point (i.e., the center of the wheel).

Let's give it a shot! First open *Cart.h* and add a few instance variables you'll need for the wheel sprites, bodies, and joints, as shown in Listing 11.12.

Listing 11.12   **Cart.h (inside @interface)**

```
Box2DSprite *wheelL;
Box2DSprite *wheelR;
b2Body *wheelLBody;
b2Body *wheelRBody;
b2RevoluteJoint *wheelLJoint;
b2RevoluteJoint *wheelRJoint;
```

While you're there, add properties for the wheel sprites and bodies so they can be accessed from the action layer, as shown in Listing 11.13.

Listing 11.13   **Cart.h (after @interface)**

```
@property (readonly) b2Body * wheelLBody;
@property (readonly) b2Body * wheelRBody;
@property (readonly) Box2DSprite * wheelL;
@property (readonly) Box2DSprite * wheelR;
```

Then switch to *Cart.mm* and synthesize the properties right after the `@implemen-tation` line, as shown in Listing 11.14.

Listing 11.14   Cart.mm (after @implementation)

```
@synthesize wheelL;
@synthesize wheelR;
@synthesize wheelLBody;
@synthesize wheelRBody;
```

Next add a new method to create a wheel before the `initWithWorld` method, as shown in Listing 11.15.

Listing 11.15   Cart.mm (before initWithWorld method)

```
- (b2Body *)createWheelWithSprite:(Box2DSprite*)sprite
    offset:(b2Vec2)offset {

    b2BodyDef bodyDef;
    bodyDef.type = b2_dynamicBody;
    bodyDef.position = body->GetWorldPoint(offset);
    b2Body * wheelBody = world->CreateBody(&bodyDef);
    wheelBody->SetUserData(sprite);
    sprite.body = wheelBody;

    b2CircleShape circleShape;
    circleShape.m_radius = sprite.contentSize.width/2/PTM_RATIO;

    b2FixtureDef fixtureDef;
    fixtureDef.shape = &circleShape;
    fixtureDef.friction = 1.0;
    fixtureDef.restitution = 0.2;
    fixtureDef.density = 10.0;
    wheelBody->CreateFixture(&fixtureDef);

    return wheelBody;
}
```

Most of this should look quite familiar to you—this method creates a Box2D body and circle shape/fixture in the usual manner. However, there are three things to point out.

First, the goal for this method is to create a wheel based on an offset from the main cart body. This is important so that you can place the body in any initial angle or rotation and still have the wheel be in the right place. To accomplish this, it calls a method on the main cart body called `GetWorldPoint`, to convert a local offset from the cart body to a world coordinate (which is required when creating a body).

Second, the friction for the wheels is quite high (1.0). This is because you will be using the wheels to drive the cart along the ground, so you want a high friction so that moving the wheels causes the cart to move responsively (rather than slipping along the ground too much).

Third, the density of the wheel (10.0) is much larger than the density of the cart (1.0). This is because the wheels behave best in Box2D when they have equal or more mass than the body they are supporting. Since the wheels are small and the cart body is large, we need to make it a much bigger number. If you forget to set this higher, you may see strange behavior like the wheels falling off the cart or bouncing strangely.

Next add a method to make use of this below createWheelWithSprite, as shown in Listing 11.16.

Listing 11.16 Cart.mm (below createWheelWithSprite)

```
- (void)createWheels {
    wheelL = [Box2DSprite spriteWithSpriteFrameName:@"Wheel.png"];
    wheelL.gameObjectType = kCartType;
    wheelLBody = [self createWheelWithSprite:wheelL
        offset:b2Vec2(-63.0/100.0, -48.0/100.0)];

    wheelR = [Box2DSprite spriteWithSpriteFrameName:@"Wheel.png"];
    wheelR.gameObjectType = kCartType;
    wheelRBody = [self createWheelWithSprite:wheelR
        offset:b2Vec2(63.0/100.0, -48.0/100.0)];

    b2RevoluteJointDef revJointDef;
    revJointDef.Initialize(body, wheelLBody,
        wheelLBody->GetWorldCenter());
    wheelLJoint = (b2RevoluteJoint *) world->CreateJoint(&revJointDef);

    revJointDef.Initialize(body, wheelRBody,
        wheelRBody->GetWorldCenter());
    wheelRJoint = (b2RevoluteJoint *) world->CreateJoint(&revJointDef);
}
```

This method first creates a sprite for each wheel and then calls the method you just wrote to create a Box2D object for that sprite.

Afterwards, it sets up a revolute joint for each wheel. As you can see, this is quite simple. It creates a b2RevoluteJointDef structure and calls the Initial-ize method, passing in the two bodies that are involved (the wheel and the body) and the point at which they should be fixed (the center of the wheel). It then passes the b2RevoluteJointDef to the world to actually create the joint. This returns a b2Joint object, which it saves away in an instance variable.

Note

The offsets for the wheels were figured out by using the ruler tool in an image editor to estimate the number of pixels that each wheel should be offset from the center of the cart. Since the HD artwork was used for this, it needs to be converted to HD coordinates by dividing by the HD PTM_RATIO, which is 100.0.

Next call this new method in initWithWorld:atLocation, as shown in Listing 11.17.

Listing 11.17   Cart.mm (at the bottom of initWithWorld:atLocation)

```
[self createWheels];
```

One last step: you need to add the new sprites for the wheels to the sprite batch node. Back in *Scene4ActionLayer.mm*, add the lines to do so the bottom of createCart-AtLocation, as shown in Listing 11.18.

Listing 11.18   Scene4ActionLayer.mm (at the bottom of createCartAtLocation)

```
[sceneSpriteBatchNode addChild:cart.wheelL];
[sceneSpriteBatchNode addChild:cart.wheelR];
```

That's it! Compile and run the app, and now your cart should have wheels, as shown in Figure 11.10. You can use the mouse joint to roll it around the screen and see how it works. Note how the wheels and cart are fixed at the center of the wheels, but the wheels can still spin. That's revolute joints in action!

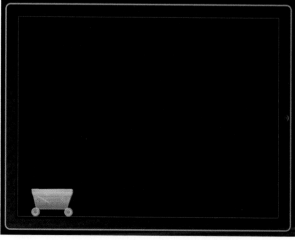

Figure 11.10   Cart with wheels connected with Box2D revolute joints

Making the Cart Move and Jump

Ole's cart is pretty cool so far, and it rolls around adhering to real game physics. However, there's still a long way to go—the goal is to make this level an action-packed side-scroller, complete with accelerometer-based movement, interesting obstacles and ground terrain to ride over, and the ability to tap to launch the cart into the air so Ole can get some major hangtime!

In this section, you learn how to make the cart move based on accelerometer input, how to make a side-scrolling level by tracing ground pieces, how to make the cart jump, and how to fix a few problems that arise along the way.

Making the Cart Move with the Accelerometer

The first step is to add the capability to move the cart based on accelerometer input. After reading Chapter 10, your first thought might be to just set the gravity based on the accelerometer input, making the cart move back and forth due to the pull of gravity. This would work great at first—until the player flips his or her device upside down, at which time the cart would fly up into the air!

If you take a step back and think about it, what you really want to happen is for the cart to move in relation to how much the device is currently tilted. If it's tilted a little bit, you want the cart to move slowly, and if it's tilted a lot, you want the cart to move quickly.

There are several ways you can move the cart in Box2D. You could apply a force or impulse (which you'll learn about later) on the cart to push it forward each frame based on the current accelerometer input. You could set the linear velocity for the body directly (although this can cause problems with the physics simulation sometimes, so avoid it when possible). But for this level you're going to take an approach that models the behavior of a real-world cart—you're going to move the cart by making the wheels spin!

Since you set up revolute joints for the cart wheels, rotating the wheels is easy. Revolute joints have a built-in "motor" that defines how quickly the wheels rotate in radians per second. You can make use of this to simply set the motor speed of the wheels based on the accelerometer input!

Let's see how this looks. First open *Cart.mm* and add the bolded lines in Listing 11.19 to `createWheels`, right after the first call to `Initialize` for the `b2RevoluteJointDef`.

Listing 11.19   Cart.mm (add bolded lines inside createWheels, right after first call to Initialize)

```
// Right after creating wheelRBody...
b2RevoluteJointDef revJointDef;
revJointDef.Initialize(body, wheelLBody,
                   wheelLBody->GetWorldCenter());
```

```
revJointDef.enableMotor = true;
revJointDef.maxMotorTorque = 1000;
revJointDef.motorSpeed = 0;
wheelLJoint = (b2RevoluteJoint *) world->CreateJoint(&revJointDef);

revJointDef.Initialize(body, wheelRBody,
                        wheelRBody->GetWorldCenter());
wheelRJoint = (b2RevoluteJoint *) world->CreateJoint(&revJointDef);
```

These calls enable the motor for the revolute joint and set the initial speed to 0. Think of a motor as an automatic mechanism that turns the wheels based on the motorSpeed. motorSpeed is in radians per second, and M_PI radians is equivalent to half a circle (180 degrees). So a motor speed of M_PI would rotate the wheel half a circle (M_PI) every second.

maxMotorTorque is the maximum amount of torque that the motor should apply to the wheel in order to reach the desired wheel speed. If this number is low and the wheel hits resistance (such as something stopping its rotation), it will likely "give up" and stop rotating. If this number is high, the wheel can keep increasing the torque until it overcomes the resistance. In this case, you set it to a fairly high number so the wheels can continue spinning despite resistance.

Next add a new method to *Cart.mm* to set the motor speed on both of the wheel joints when called, as shown in Listing 11.20.

Listing 11.20 **Cart.mm (anywhere inside class)**

```
- (void)setMotorSpeed:(float32)motorSpeed {
    if (characterState != kStateTakingDamage) {
        wheelLJoint->SetMotorSpeed(motorSpeed);
        wheelRJoint->SetMotorSpeed(motorSpeed);
    } else {
        wheelLJoint->SetMotorSpeed(0.2 * motorSpeed);
        wheelRJoint->SetMotorSpeed(0.2 * motorSpeed);
    }
}
```

Note that this usually just passes the motor speed onto the wheel joints, but if the cart is taking damage (which you'll implement later), it temporarily slows down the cart.

Then switch to *Cart.h* and add the declaration for this method in the header, as shown in Listing 11.21.

Listing 11.21 **Cart.h (after @interface)**

```
- (void)setMotorSpeed:(float32)motorSpeed;
```

Now that this is set up, open *Scene4ActionLayer.mm* and add a line in the `init` method to enable accelerometer support, as shown in Listing 11.22.

Listing 11.22   **Scene4ActionLayer.mm (at the bottom of the initWithScene4UILayer method)**

```
self.isAccelerometerEnabled = YES;
```

Next write the actual implementation of the accelerometer callback to set the speed of the wheels based on how much the device is tilted, as shown in Listing 11.23.

Listing 11.23   **Scene4ActionLayer.mm (anywhere inside class)**

```
- (void)accelerometer:(UIAccelerometer *)accelerometer
  didAccelerate:(UIAcceleration *)acceleration {
    float32 maxRevsPerSecond = 7.0;
    float32 accelerationFraction = acceleration.y*6;
    if (accelerationFraction < -1) {
        accelerationFraction = -1;
    } else if (accelerationFraction > 1) {
        accelerationFraction = 1;
    }
    float32 motorSpeed =
        (M_PI*2) * maxRevsPerSecond * accelerationFraction;
    [cart setMotorSpeed:motorSpeed];
}
```

This method first sets up the max speed of the wheels to be 7 revolutions per second. This number was determined by simply play testing and seeing what "felt right."

It then computes the fraction of the max speed to actually set the wheels according to how much the device is tilted. Acceleration usually ranges from 0 (completely level) to ± 1 (completely vertical one way or the other). However, you don't want the user to have to tilt the device completely vertical to achieve max speed, so you multiply the current acceleration value by 6 and limit the result to be within the range of −1 to 1, so that one-sixth of a tilt either way is the "max speed range."

Remember that motor speed is in radians per second, so if you set it to `M_PI*2`, that would be one full rotation a second. It multiplies one full rotation a second times the max speed and then the current fraction of speed based on how much the device is tilted.

Compile and run the code (on your device, since accelerometer input does not work in the simulator), and you should now be able to move your cart back and forth by tilting the device. Nice, you're making some great progress toward an action level!

Making It Scrollable

While you could probably make an entire game about moving back and forth within this box, in this chapter you're going to do even better. You're now going to learn how to make a scrollable level with Box2D—and have the view stay focused on the cart as it moves!

Figure 11.11 shows part of *Images\groundAtlas-hd.png*, which contains the pieces of ground that you're about to add to the level. You'll be adding each of these strips to the level horizontally like Lego blocks, laying down each piece side by side to construct the entire level.

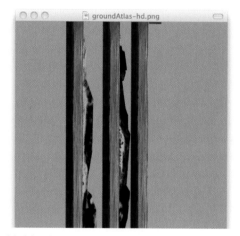

Figure 11.11   Strips of ground you'll be adding to this level

> **Note**
>
> The ground images in the sprite sheet appear to be vertical even though the source images are horizontal. This is because the sprite sheets were created with TexturePacker, which sometimes rotates your images so they fit in the sprite sheets better. Don't worry—this is completely transparent to you as a user—when you retrieve the images in the code, they will be rotated back to their initial orientation.

Currently you have a Box2D ground body that maps to the size of the screen, but now you want to create a ground body that extends far offscreen to the right and juts up and down according to the slopes of the ground artwork.

Your first thought might be to simply load the ground images into Vertex Helper, click on the points along each of the bodies to figure out their vertices, and then add them to the scene as different shapes. Well, you're partly right (you will be using Vertex Helper), but it wouldn't work well in practice because you'll find two problems:

- The shapes have too many vertices.
- The shapes are concave.

Remember back to earlier in this chapter—when defining shapes in Box2D, you can only have up to eight vertices (by default), and they can't be concave (i.e., have an interior angle of greater than 180 degrees). You could split the ground body up into smaller pieces so that both of these rules would be followed, but that would be a big pain.

Luckily, there is an easy solution—and you can still use Vertex Helper. The idea is, instead of creating polygons for each ground piece, you just make edges along the top of each piece. You can use Vertex Helper to define the list of vertices, and then write a helper method to create an edge for each vertex pair in the array.

Let's see what this looks like. First, open *Scene4ActionLayer.h* and add a few more instance variables, as shown in Listing 11.24.

Listing 11.24 Scene4ActionLayer.h (inside @interface)

```
CCSpriteBatchNode * groundSpriteBatchNode;
float32 groundMaxX;
```

groundSpriteBatchNode stores a reference to the sprite sheet that contains the strips of ground, and groundMaxX keeps track of the maximum x value for the ground pieces added to the scene.

Then replace your createGround method in *Scene4ActionLayer.mm*, as shown in Listing 11.25.

Listing 11.25 Scene4ActionLayer.mm (replace createGround method)

```
- (void)createGround {
    b2BodyDef groundBodyDef;
    groundBodyDef.type = b2_staticBody;
    groundBodyDef.position.Set(0, 0);
    groundBody = world->CreateBody(&groundBodyDef);
}
```

Note that you've removed all of the code relating to adding the edges mapping to the boundaries of the screen but are still creating a body (with no fixtures). So next write a function to create some ground edges based on a passed-in set of vertices, as shown in Listing 11.26.

Listing 11.26 Scene4ActionLayer.mm (right below the createGround method)

```
- (void)createGroundEdgesWithVerts:(b2Vec2 *)verts numVerts:(int)num
    spriteFrameName:(NSString *)spriteFrameName {
    CCSprite *ground =
        [CCSprite spriteWithSpriteFrameName:spriteFrameName];
    ground.position = ccp(groundMaxX+ground.contentSize.width/2,
                        ground.contentSize.height/2);
    [groundSpriteBatchNode addChild:ground];
```

```
b2PolygonShape groundShape;
b2FixtureDef groundFixtureDef;
groundFixtureDef.shape = &groundShape;
groundFixtureDef.density = 0.0;

for(int i = 0; i < num - 1; ++i) {
    b2Vec2 offset = b2Vec2(groundMaxX/PTM_RATIO +
                        ground.contentSize.width/2/PTM_RATIO,
                      ground.contentSize.height/2/PTM_RATIO);
    b2Vec2 left = verts[i] + offset;
    b2Vec2 right = verts[i+1] + offset;
    groundShape.SetAsEdge(left, right);
    groundBody->CreateFixture(&groundFixtureDef);
}

groundMaxX += ground.contentSize.width;
}
```

Let's go through this step by step. This method takes an array of vertices, the number of vertices (that you generate using Vertex Helper), and the name of the sprite that goes along with this. It then creates a normal CCSprite with the given sprite frame name and adds it to the ground sprite batch node.

> **Note**
>
> Notice that the ground sprites are not associated with a Box2D body in any way—the sprites just happen to be placed at the same position. Since the ground sprites never move, there's no need to associate them with a Box2D body to synchronize the position in the update loop. This also makes things simpler, since you can make the ground edges on the same Box2D body (groundBody) rather than having to create a separate Box2D body for each sprite.
>
> Remember that you don't need to make a Box2D body for every sprite you add into your game unless you want Box2D to handle the movement/physics simulation. You may find this useful in your games—sometimes, you might just want sprites without Box2D bodies for decoration or so you can move the sprites yourself with actions such as CCMoveTo.

Next the method loops through the list of vertices and creates an edge for each. Each vertex is offset by the maximum x value the ground has reached so far and by half the width and height (since the vertices are centered around the center of the sprite). At the end of the routine, it simply adds the width of the sprite to the ground maximum x value. Note that this code makes the assumption that vertices are listed from left to right and that ground chunks are also placed down left to right.

Now it's time to get a list of vertices for each piece of ground so that you can call this routine with the appropriate list of vertices. To do this, open Vertex Helper, find the resource folder for this chapter, and drag *Raw Art...\ground\ground1.png* to the Vertex Helper window. As usual, type 1 for **Rows**, 1 for **Cols**, set the **Type** to **Box2D**, set the **Style** to **Initialization**, and click **Edit Mode** to begin clicking vertices.

Add the vertices by clicking from left to right across the ground. Since the ground is quite wide, it will most likely extend beyond the width of your window. To scroll, you need to toggle the **Edit Mode** checkbox so you can pan the image, toggle it again to define a few more vertices, and repeat. When you are done, your window should look similar to Figure 11.12.

Figure 11.12   Defining vertices for ground edges with Vertex Helper

When you are done, write a method to call `createGroundEdgesWithVerts` passing in the vertex array generated by Vertex Helper, as shown in Listing 11.27. Just like last time, you'll also need to replace all instances of `PTM_RATIO` with 100.0, since you traced the HD artwork. Note that the vertex coordinates might be slightly different for you depending on how you clicked using Vertex Helper.

Listing 11.27   **Scene4ActionLayer.mm (right below createGroundEdgesWithVerts)**

```
- (void)createGround1 {
    // Replace with your values from Vertex Helper, but replace all
    // instances of PTM_RATIO with 100.0
    int num = 23;
    b2Vec2 verts[] = {
        b2Vec2(-1022.5f / 100.0, -20.2f / 100.0),
        b2Vec2(-966.6f / 100.0, -18.0f / 100.0),
        b2Vec2(-893.8f / 100.0, -10.3f / 100.0),
```

```
        b2Vec2(-888.8f / 100.0, 1.1f / 100.0),
        b2Vec2(-804.0f / 100.0, 10.3f / 100.0),
        b2Vec2(-799.7f / 100.0, 5.3f / 100.0),
        b2Vec2(-795.5f / 100.0, 8.1f / 100.0),
        b2Vec2(-755.2f / 100.0, -1.8f / 100.0),
        b2Vec2(-755.2f / 100.0, -9.5f / 100.0),
        b2Vec2(-632.2f / 100.0, 5.3f / 100.0),
        b2Vec2(-603.9f / 100.0, 17.3f / 100.0),
        b2Vec2(-536.0f / 100.0, 18.0f / 100.0),
        b2Vec2(-518.3f / 100.0, 28.6f / 100.0),
        b2Vec2(-282.1f / 100.0, 13.1f / 100.0),
        b2Vec2(-258.1f / 100.0, 27.2f / 100.0),
        b2Vec2(-135.1f / 100.0, 18.7f / 100.0),
        b2Vec2(9.2f / 100.0, -19.4f / 100.0),
        b2Vec2(483.0f / 100.0, -18.7f / 100.0),
        b2Vec2(578.4f / 100.0, 11.0f / 100.0),
        b2Vec2(733.3f / 100.0, -7.4f / 100.0),
        b2Vec2(827.3f / 100.0, -1.1f / 100.0),
        b2Vec2(1006.9f / 100.0, -20.2f / 100.0),
        b2Vec2(1023.2f / 100.0, -20.2f / 100.0)
    };
    [self createGroundEdgesWithVerts:verts
        numVerts:num spriteFrameName:@"ground1.png"];
}
```

Once you are done, repeat with *ground2.png* and *ground3.png* to create two more methods, createGround2 and createGround3, as shown in Listing 11.28.

Listing 11.28   **Scene4ActionLayer.mm (right below createGround1)**

```
- (void)createGround2 {
    // Replace with your values from Vertex Helper, but replace all
    // instances of PTM_RATIO with 100.0
    int num = 24;
    b2Vec2 verts[] = {
        b2Vec2(-1022.0f / 100.0, -20.0f / 100.0),
        b2Vec2(-963.0f / 100.0, -23.0f / 100.0),
        b2Vec2(-902.0f / 100.0, -4.0f / 100.0),
        b2Vec2(-762.0f / 100.0, -7.0f / 100.0),
        b2Vec2(-674.0f / 100.0, 26.0f / 100.0),
        b2Vec2(-435.0f / 100.0, 22.0f / 100.0),
        b2Vec2(-258.0f / 100.0, -1.0f / 100.0),
        b2Vec2(-242.0f / 100.0, 19.0f / 100.0),
        b2Vec2(-170.0f / 100.0, 43.0f / 100.0),
        b2Vec2(-58.0f / 100.0, 45.0f / 100.0),
        b2Vec2(98.0f / 100.0, -20.0f / 100.0),
        b2Vec2(472.0f / 100.0, -20.0f / 100.0),
```

```
        b2Vec2(471.0f / 100.0, -7.0f / 100.0),
        b2Vec2(503.0f / 100.0, 4.0f / 100.0),
        b2Vec2(614.0f / 100.0, 66.0f / 100.0),
        b2Vec2(679.0f / 100.0, 59.0f / 100.0),
        b2Vec2(681.0f / 100.0, 46.0f / 100.0),
        b2Vec2(735.0f / 100.0, 31.0f / 100.0),
        b2Vec2(822.0f / 100.0, 24.0f / 100.0),
        b2Vec2(827.0f / 100.0, 12.0f / 100.0),
        b2Vec2(934.0f / 100.0, 14.0f / 100.0),
        b2Vec2(975.0f / 100.0, 1.0f / 100.0),
        b2Vec2(982.0f / 100.0, -19.0f / 100.0),
        b2Vec2(1023.0f / 100.0, -20.0f / 100.0)
    };
    [self createGroundEdgesWithVerts:verts numVerts:num
        spriteFrameName:@"ground2.png"];
}


- (void)createGround3 {
    // Replace with your values from Vertex Helper, but replace all
    // instances of PTM_RATIO with 100.0
    int num = 2;
    b2Vec2 verts[] = {
        b2Vec2(-1021.0f / 100.0, -22.0f / 100.0),
        b2Vec2(1021.0f / 100.0, -20.0f / 100.0)
    };
    [self createGroundEdgesWithVerts:verts numVerts:num
        spriteFrameName:@"ground3.png"];
}
```

Now that you are making this level scrollable, it would be cool to have a parallax scrolling background. To implement this, add a new method, as shown in Listing 11.29.

Listing 11.29 Scene4ActionLayer.mm (right after createGround3)

```
- (void)createBackground {
    CCParallaxNode * parallax = [CCParallaxNode node];
    [CCTexture2D setDefaultAlphaPixelFormat:
        kCCTexture2DPixelFormat_RGB565];
    CCSprite *background;
    if (UI_USER_INTERFACE_IDIOM() == UIUserInterfaceIdiomPad) {
        background =
            [CCSprite spriteWithFile:@"scene_4_background-ipad.png"];
    } else {
        background =
            [CCSprite spriteWithFile:@"scene_4_background.png"];
    }
```

```
background.anchorPoint = ccp(0,0);
[CCTexture2D setDefaultAlphaPixelFormat:
    kCCTexture2DPixelFormat_Default];
[parallax addChild:background z:-10 parallaxRatio:ccp(0.05f, 0.05f)
    positionOffset:ccp(0,0)];
[self addChild:parallax z:-10];
}
```

This creates a parallax node to store the background image so that it slowly scrolls as the player moves through the level. Note that it sets the texture pixel format to RGB565, which is a 16-bit pixel format (saves memory in comparison to the default 32-bit format with a tradeoff in quality). This format in particular gives the best possible quality for red, green, and blue channels for 16-bit images, with the tradeoff of not having any alpha channel (transparency) support at all, but that is okay because this image doesn't have any transparent parts.

Next, create a method to create the level by laying these pieces side by side, as shown in Listing 11.30.

Listing 11.30   Scene4ActionLayer.mm (right after createBackground)

```
- (void)createLevel {
    [self createBackground];
    [self createGround3];
    [self createGround1];
    [self createGround3];
    [self createGround2];
    [self createGround3];
}
```

This simply calls the above methods to create a starting level layout by laying down the pieces of ground one after the other. You'll be returning to this method to add more content to the level as this chapter progresses.

Next you need to add some code to follow the cart as it moves through the level. You can do this by setting the layer's position based on the position of the cart, as shown in Listing 11.31.

Listing 11.31   Scene4ActionLayer.mm (right after createLevel)

```
- (void)followCart {
    CGSize winSize = [CCDirector sharedDirector].winSize;
    float fixedPosition = winSize.width/4;
    float newX = fixedPosition - cart.position.x;
    newX = MIN(newX, fixedPosition);
    newX = MAX(newX, -groundMaxX-fixedPosition);
    CGPoint newPos = ccp(newX, self.position.y);
```

```
    [self setPosition:newPos];
}
```

This method moves the layer to keep the cart in a fixed position as the cart moves through the level. Figure 11.13 illustrates how this works.

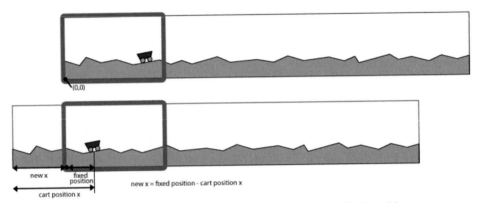

Figure 11.13   Moving the layer to keep the cart at a fixed position onscreen

As Figure 11.13 shows, if the layer did not move, the cart would simply move offscreen. However, you can keep the cart centered by figuring out the difference between where you want the cart to be centered (in this case, at one-fourth the screen width) and the cart's current position and setting the layer to that position.

This method also bounds the scroll value so that the scrolling stops when you near the edges of the level, as you can see in the calls to MAX and MIN.

Note

There is also a built-in Cocos2D action called CCFollow that behaves similarly to the code you just wrote here. The reason you wrote separate code to do this rather than using CCFollow is twofold. First, CCFollow centers the object in the screen, and you want the cart to be to the left-hand side of the screen so that Ole can see more of what's ahead. Second, you need precise control over when the layer's position is updated so that it runs at the same rate that your update method is called in order to ensure smooth scrolling.

Next add a call to followCart at the end of your update method, as shown in Listing 11.32.

Listing 11.32   **Scene4ActionLayer.mm (at the end of update)**

```
[self followCart];
```

One last step: add the code to set up the ground batch sprite node and call `createLevel` at the end of `initWithScene4UILayer`, as shown in Listing 11.33.

Listing 11.33 **Scene4ActionLayer.mm (at the end of initWithScene4UILayer)**

```
[CCTexture2D setDefaultAlphaPixelFormat:
    kCCTexture2DPixelFormat_RGB5A1];
if (UI_USER_INTERFACE_IDIOM() == UIUserInterfaceIdiomPad) {
    [[CCSpriteFrameCache sharedSpriteFrameCache]
        addSpriteFramesWithFile:@"groundAtlas-hd.plist"];
    groundSpriteBatchNode = [CCSpriteBatchNode
                        batchNodeWithFile:@"groundAtlas-hd.png"];
} else {
    [[CCSpriteFrameCache sharedSpriteFrameCache]
        addSpriteFramesWithFile:@"groundAtlas.plist"];
    groundSpriteBatchNode = [CCSpriteBatchNode
                        batchNodeWithFile:@"groundAtlas.png"];
}
[CCTexture2D setDefaultAlphaPixelFormat:
    kCCTexture2DPixelFormat_Default];
[self addChild:groundSpriteBatchNode z:-2];

[self createLevel];
```

The first section of code loads the ground texture atlas. Note that it sets the texture pixel format to `RGB5A1`, which is a 16-bit pixel format (saves memory in comparison to the default 32-bit format with a tradeoff in quality). This format in particular gives good quality for red, green, and blue channels but poor quality for alpha channel, which is okay because for these images, the alpha channel is only used as an on/off indicator for transparency.

Compile and run the code, and you should now be able to use your accelerometer to move and bounce the cart back and forth along a side-scrolling level!

However, as you go through the level, you may find times when you hit an outcropping or a strange edge and your cart flips over! Obviously, Ole would not be very happy about that if he was stuck inside.

There are several ways you can fix this with Box2D, such as making the terrain smoother to make this less likely to occur, having bigger wheels, modifying the weight distribution of the cart to discourage this behavior, and so on. But for this level, you want to keep the current wheel sizes, terrain, and weight distribution, so you'll fix this by adding some code to prevent the cart from rotating more than a specified angle range—and pushing it back within the range if by chance it does exceed it.

But how can you "push" the cart in a certain direction? To understand that, let's discuss forces and impulses.

Figure 11.14   A side-scrolling Box2D level with a moving cart

Forces and Impulses

An *impulse* is an instantaneous change in momentum (momentum is mass × velocity). Think of it as an instant boost that you can apply to an object to make it jump or fly through the air.

A *force* is a change in momentum over a period of time. Think of it as a gradual energy that you can use to make objects float into the air or be pushed toward a wall.

Both impulses and forces affect an object's velocity (how fast it's moving), but the difference is that an impulse affects the velocity immediately while a force is meant to be applied over a longer period of time. Usually, you would call an impulse at a single point in time in code (like when the user taps to jump), but you would apply forces in your update method every frame while the force is still active.

There are two kinds of impulses: *linear impulses* (a push in a certain direction) and *angular impulses* (a rotation in a certain direction). To push the cart back to a certain angle, you want to apply an angular impulse. So let's give that a shot.

Fixing the Tipping

Open *Cart.mm* and add the method shown in Listing 11.34.

Listing 11.34   **Cart.mm (anywhere in class)**

```
- (void) updateStateWithDeltaTime:(ccTime)deltaTime
    andListOfGameObjects:(CCArray *)listOfGameObjects {
    float32 minAngle = CC_DEGREES_TO_RADIANS(-20);
```

```
float32 maxAngle = CC_DEGREES_TO_RADIANS(20);
double desiredAngle = self.body->GetAngle();
if (self.body->GetAngle() > maxAngle) {
    desiredAngle = maxAngle;
} else if (self.body->GetAngle() < minAngle) {
    desiredAngle = minAngle;
}

float32 diff = desiredAngle - self.body->GetAngle();
if (diff != 0) {
    body->SetAngularVelocity(0);
    float32 diff = desiredAngle - self.body->GetAngle();
    float angimp = self.body->GetInertia() * diff;
    self.body->ApplyAngularImpulse(angimp * 2);
}
}
}
```

This method checks the angle of the cart and compares it to a desired range (−20 to 20 degrees). If the cart is out of range, it first stops the cart from rotating further (by setting the angular velocity to 0) and then applies a slight angular impulse to push the cart back toward the center. The more the cart is off center, the stronger the angular impulse will be.

Now compile and run: your cart should be able to get through the entire level without flipping!

Making the Cart Jump

To make the cart jump, you apply the other type of impulse—a linear impulse. You apply a boost to the bottom of the cart to launch it up into the air to give a neat jump effect.

The first thing you need to do is write a helper function to detect if a Box2D body is intersecting another body of a given type. This function detects if the cart is touching the ground, and more later on.

Select the *Classes\Box2D* group, go to **File > New > New File...**, choose **iOS > Cocoa Touch > Objective-C class**, and click **Next**. Enter *NSObject* as the Subclass of, click **Next**, name the file *Box2DHelpers.mm* (note the *.mm* extension, since this imports Box2D), and click **Save**.

Replace *Box2DHelpers.h* with the contents of Listing 11.35.

Listing 11.35 **Box2DHelpers.h**

```
#import "Box2D.h"
#import "CommonProtocols.h"

bool isBodyCollidingWithObjectType(b2Body *body,
    GameObjectType objectType);
```

This simply predeclares the helper function you're about to write. Next write the implementation by replacing *Box2DHelpers.mm* with the contents of Listing 11.36.

Listing 11.36 **Box2DHelpers.mm**

```
#import "Box2DHelpers.h"
#import "Box2DSprite.h"

bool isBodyCollidingWithObjectType(b2Body *body, GameObjectType
objectType) {
    b2ContactEdge* edge = body->GetContactList();
    while (edge)
    {
        b2Contact* contact = edge->contact;
        if (contact->IsTouching()) {
            b2Fixture* fixtureA = contact->GetFixtureA();
            b2Fixture* fixtureB = contact->GetFixtureB();
            b2Body *bodyA = fixtureA->GetBody();
            b2Body *bodyB = fixtureB->GetBody();
            Box2DSprite *spriteA =
                (Box2DSprite *) bodyA->GetUserData();
            Box2DSprite *spriteB =
                (Box2DSprite *) bodyB->GetUserData();
            if ((spriteA != NULL &&
                spriteA.gameObjectType == objectType) ||
                (spriteB != NULL &&
                spriteB.gameObjectType == objectType)) {
                return true;
            }
        }
        edge = edge->next;
    }
    return false;
}
```

This code should look pretty familiar: it's the same method of looping through the contacts list to look for collisions that you learned in Chapter 10.

> **Note**
>
> As mentioned in Chapter 10, this method of checking for collisions won't detect the case where an object was colliding at one point since the last call but bounced off and is no longer colliding. However, for the purposes of this level, this doesn't matter to us, so we'll continue to use this simple method.
>
> If this is something you care about, you need to implement a Box2D contact listener. For more information on how to do this, check out the Box2D manual at *www.box2d.org*.

Now go to *Scene4ActionLayer.mm* and import *Box2DHelpers.h* at the top of the file, as shown in Listing 11.37.

Listing 11.37   **Scene4ActionLayer.mm (at the top of the file)**

```
#import "Box2DHelpers.h"
```

Next delete the `ccTouchBegan`, `ccTouchMoved`, and `ccTouchEnded` methods, since you won't need the mouse joint for debugging anymore. Then add the contents of Listing 11.38 as your new `ccTouchBegan` method.

Listing 11.38   **Scene4ActionLayer.mm (delete ccTouchXX methods and replace with this)**

```
-(BOOL) ccTouchBegan:(UITouch *)touch withEvent:(UIEvent *)event {
    if (isBodyCollidingWithObjectType(cart.body, kGroundType) ||
        isBodyCollidingWithObjectType(groundBody, kCartType)) {
        [cart jump];
    }
    return TRUE;
}
```

This simply checks to see if the ground body is colliding with any object marked as a cart type, and if so, it instructs the cart to jump.

Now switch to *Cart.h* and predeclare the jump function you just called as well as another helper method, as shown in Listing 11.39.

Listing 11.39   **Cart.h (after @interface)**

```
- (void)jump;
- (float32)fullMass;
```

Then switch to *Cart.mm* and add the support methods to implement jumping, as shown in Listing 11.40.

Listing 11.40   **Cart.mm (anywhere inside class)**

```
- (void)playJumpEffect {
    int soundToPlay = random() % 4;
    if (soundToPlay == 0) {
        PLAYSOUNDEFFECT(VIKING_JUMPING_1);
    } else if (soundToPlay == 1) {
        PLAYSOUNDEFFECT(VIKING_JUMPING_2);
    } else if (soundToPlay == 2) {
        PLAYSOUNDEFFECT(VIKING_JUMPING_3);
    } else {
        PLAYSOUNDEFFECT(VIKING_JUMPING_4);
```

```
    }
}

- (float32)fullMass {
    return body->GetMass() + wheelLBody->GetMass() +
        wheelRBody->GetMass();
}

- (void)jump {
    [self playJumpEffect];
    b2Vec2 impulse = b2Vec2([self fullMass]*1.0, [self fullMass]*5.0);
    b2Vec2 impulsePoint =
        body->GetWorldPoint(b2Vec2(5.0/100.0, -15.0/100.0));
    body->ApplyLinearImpulse(impulse, impulsePoint);
}
```

The code first plays a sound effect, then applies a linear impulse to the cart body to make it jump. When you apply an impulse, you specify the impulse to apply and the point at which to apply it. The impulse should usually be a multiple of the mass of the object; the exact numbers depend on how high you want your cart to jump. Here it is making it jump upward by a good amount and a slight amount to the right. The impulse point is set slightly to the right and bottom of the cart in order to make the cart tend to slightly tip backward on a jump to get a nicer effect.

There's one last thing. When implementing jumping in Box2D, sometimes you want to let the user jump even if the object isn't actually hitting the ground, but is "close enough." For example, when the user rides over rough terrain, the wheels might be bouncing off the ground quite often, but the user would perceive that the cart should be able to jump anyway. To address this, you add a sensor to the bottom of the cart so that if the cart is "close enough" to the ground, a jump will be allowed.

Add the code to create a sensor on the bottom of the cart at the bottom of createBodyAtLocation, as shown in Listing 11.41.

Listing 11.41   Cart.mm (at the bottom of createBodyAtLocation)

```
b2PolygonShape sensorShape;
sensorShape.SetAsBox(self.contentSize.width/2/PTM_RATIO, self.contentSize.
height/2/PTM_RATIO,
                    b2Vec2(0, -self.contentSize.height/PTM_RATIO), 0);
fixtureDef.shape = &sensorShape;
fixtureDef.density = 0.0;
fixtureDef.isSensor = true;
body->CreateFixture(&fixtureDef);
```

Compile and run the code, and your cart should now jump when you tap the screen, as you can see in Figure 11.15.

Figure 11.15   Cart jumping using Box2D impulses

More Responsive Direction Switching

If you experiment with the level, you'll see that once the cart gets moving, it takes a bit of time to switch directions. This models what would happen in real life, but in games, players are used to instant gratification!

So let's use impulses again to make the direction switching a bit faster for players. Inside *Scene4ActionLayer.mm*, add the contents of Listing 11.42 to the bottom of accelerometer:didAccelerate.

Listing 11.42   **Scene4ActionLayer.mm (at the bottom of accelerometer:didAccelerate)**

```
if (abs(cart.body->GetLinearVelocity().x) < 5.0) {
    b2Vec2 impulse =
        b2Vec2(-1 * acceleration.y * cart.fullMass * 2, 0);
    cart.body->ApplyLinearImpulse(impulse,
        cart.body->GetWorldCenter());
}
```

This simply checks to see if the cart is moving very slowly (less than 5 meters per second in either direction). If that is the case, it applies a slight impulse to get the body moving a bit faster in the intended direction. This helps reduce the time switching directions or starting up.

Compile and run the code, and now the cart should switch directions more quickly. Finally, you have a cart worthy of Ole to ride in!

Summary

At this point you have created a side-scrolling action level with Box2D, complete with vehicles, motors, joints, impulses, and more! You should now be familiar with how to use Box2D to model arbitrary shapes with Vertex Helper, connect multiple bodies with joints, and use impulses to move your game objects.

In the next chapter, you pick up where you left off and add Ole into the game, riding the cart—using Box2D to model his body for a cool effect. You also add bridges to cross, spikes to avoid, and a dangerous boss for Ole to battle at the end with an epic cinematic fight intro!

Challenges

1. Make the level longer by adding more ground pieces to the level. Draw your own piece of ground in an image editor, use Vertex Helper to determine the vertices for the edges, and then add it to the level. See how cool and fun you can make the level!

1. Replace the cart with your own vehicle. Maybe instead of racing a mining cart, you'd like Ole to drive a truck or a sports car? The vehicle you choose may be slower or faster than a cart, so modify the acceleration and impulse values accordingly.

2. Add a long platform to the level that has a revolute joint in the middle so that when Ole is at either end, the platform starts to fall down on that side. This makes for a fun challenge for Ole to navigate and give you a chance to practice making your own bodies and joints!

Advanced Game Physics: Even Better than the Real Thing

In Chapter 11, "Intermediate Game Physics," you made an action-packed level where you can race a mining cart across interesting terrain and tap to leap through the air. However, there are two major problems. First, the level is far too easy! There are no dangers to avoid, no enemies to fight. Second, our hero Ole is nowhere to be seen! It's time to wake him up from his mad dreams and bring him back into action.

In this level, you pick up where you left off in Chapter 11 and add Ole into the mine cart (Figure 12.1) using Box2D so his body reacts to the bumps and jumps using a cool ragdoll effect. You also add bridges to cross, spikes to avoid, and even a boss fight at the end with a cinematic intro sequence!

By the time you finish reading this chapter, you'll have covered the most important aspects of using Box2D and will be ready to make your own physics-based game including vehicles, enemies, ragdoll bodies, and more!

Figure 12.1   Adding Ole, spikes, and more to the Box2D side-scrolling action level!

Joints and Ragdolls: Bringing Ole Back into Action

Now that you have the cart ready for Ole to ride in, let's add him into the scene!

One way you could approach this is to draw Ole in as part of the cart sprite—but where would be the fun in that? In this chapter, you take things to the next level by adding Ole to the cart using ragdoll physics, so he bounces and moves in realistic and amusing ways as the cart travels through the level.

You accomplish this by breaking Ole's body into pieces (poor Ole!), making separate bodies for each, and connecting them with joints, as shown in Figure 12.2.

Figure 12.2　Breaking Ole into various Box2D bodies and connecting them with joints

As you can see in Figure 12.2, you want to create bodies for each piece (the outlined boxes) and set things up so that some of the bodies rotate around each other (the dots) and some of the bodies move up and down in relation to each other (the arrows).

In order to accomplish this, you need to know three things: (1) how to restrict the rotation of revolute joints, (2) how to use a new type of joint called a prismatic joint, and (3) how to create multiple bodies and joints at the right spots. Before you begin coding this up, let's go over these items one by one.

Restricting Revolute Joints

For most of the body parts, you'll use revolute joints, which you learned about in Chapter 11 when you added the wheels to the cart. Remember, revolute joints fix two bodies together at a certain point but allow each body to rotate around that point.

This is exactly what you want for connecting an arm to the body, except you also want to restrict the rotations to a certain angle range. For example, if your arm started spinning around and around 360 degrees without any limits, people would think it was time to call an exorcist!

Luckily, it is quite easy to restrict revolute joints to a certain angle range with Box2D. When you set up a b2RevoluteJointDef, you just set a few extra properties: **enableLimit**, **lowerAngle**, and **upperAngle**. Listing 12.1 shows an example of connecting an arm to the main body.

Listing 12.1   **Example of limiting revolute joint angles**

```
revJointDef.Initialize(trunkBody, armBody,
    armBody->GetWorldPoint(b2Vec2(-9.0/PTM_RATIO, 29.0/PTM_RATIO)));
revJointDef.lowerAngle = CC_DEGREES_TO_RADIANS(-30);
revJointDef.upperAngle = CC_DEGREES_TO_RADIANS(60);
revJointDef.enableLimit = true;
world->CreateJoint(&revJointDef);
```

The angles you set for lowerAngle and upperAngle are in respect to the initial placement of the two bodies. Whatever angle the bodies are placed at when you first add them to the scene is considered "angle 0."

When you rotate body #2 counterclockwise (the arm in this case), the angle is positive. So in this example, the arm can rotate at most 60 degrees clockwise from the initial orientation.

Similarly, when you rotate body #2 clockwise, the angle is negative. So in this example, the arm can rotate at most −30 degrees clockwise from the initial orientation.

Figure 12.3 shows the angles each revolute joint in Ole should be restricted to for planning purposes.

Figure 12.3   Angles to restrict each revolute joint for Ole

Using Prismatic Joints

A prismatic joint is a type of joint that restricts two bodies so they can move relative to each other only along a specified axis. For example, you could connect a garage door body with a ground body and set the axis to be the y-axis, so the garage door can only slide up and down. Or you could connect a raft body with a ground body and set the axis to be the x-axis, so the raft can only slide right and left.

Prismatic joints are useful for connecting Ole's legs with the cart. You can set up the axis to be the y-axis, so that when the cart goes over a bump, Ole will "pop" out of the cart a little bit. Just like you can set up revolute joints to revolve only a certain amount, you can set up prismatic joints to allow only a limited amount of movement.

You set up prismatic joints in a similar manner to how you set up revolute joints. Listing 12.2 shows an example of creating a prismatic joint to connect Ole's legs to the cart.

Listing 12.2   **Example of creating a prismatic joint**

```
b2PrismaticJointDef prisJointDef;
prisJointDef.Initialize(body, legsBody,
    legsBody->GetWorldCenter(), axis);
prisJointDef.enableLimit = true;
prisJointDef.lowerTranslation = 0.0;
prisJointDef.upperTranslation = 43.0/100.0;
world->CreateJoint(&prisJointDef);
```

The `Initialize` method takes the two bodies in the joint relationship (in this case, the cart and the legs), the anchor point, and the axis where the objects can move relative to each other (the y-axis in this case).

Note that you can restrict how much the objects can move along the axis relative to each other by setting `enableLimit`, `lowerTranslation`, and `upperTranslation`, similar to how you could limit revolute joints. In this case, the legs can't go down the y-axis any further than they currently are, but they can move up the y-axis up to 43.0 points (relative to the HD artwork), so Ole can pop out of the cart over a bump.

Figure 12.4 shows the offsets each prismatic joint in Ole should be restricted to for planning purposes.

How to Create Multiple Bodies and Joints at the Right Spots

To add Ole to the scene, you need to add multiple pieces—legs, trunk, arm, head, and helmet. When you add these bodies to the scene, you need to give the world coordinates for where to place each. One method to do this is to place all of the bodies in the configuration you want in an image editor, use ruler tools to measure the world point for where you want to place each object, and use that for each location.

This approach works if you know the exact points for where you want to place each body, but it's rather fragile. What happens if you want to start your body at a different

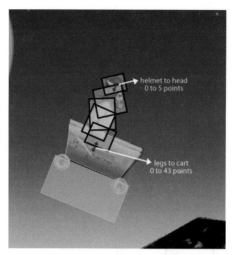

Figure 12.4   Offsets to restrict each prismatic joint for Ole

location? A second method is to measure the distance of each object relative to a main body (such as the cart) and then add the main body's current position to that point. This is better, but if you try to change the cart's initial angle, the related bodies will no longer be in the correct location.

An approach that works well even if you want to place an object in a different spot or at a different initial angle is to (1) measure the distance between each object and the object it's connected to, and (2) use a helper function called GetWorldPoint on the body it's connected to to convert a local offset from that body to a world coordinate.

For example, Listing 12.3 shows the code you should (and shouldn't) use to place Ole's legs in the right position. The first line shows the not-so-good way (adding an offset to the body's current position). The second line shows the better way (using the GetWorldPoint to convert a local offset to a world coordinate, which correctly factors in the body's rotation).

Listing 12.3   **Good and bad ways to place bodies relative to each other**

```
// Bad way (adding body's position manually)
legsBody = [self createPartAtLocation:
            b2Vec2(body->GetPosition().x-10.0/100.0,
                   body->GetPosition().y+6.0/100.0)
                      withSprite:legs];
// Good way (using GetWorldPoint, which factors in rotation)
legsBody = [self createPartAtLocation:
            body->GetWorldPoint(b2Vec2(-10.0/100.0,
                                6.0/100.0))
                      withSprite:legs];
```

In summary, to place multiple bodies and joints at the right spot, it's a matter of using `GetWorldPoint` to convert local offsets from bodies to world coordinates and using an image editing tool to measure the offsets to place each body.

In this chapter, you can use the sample code, which has the offsets premeasured, or you can replace the coordinates with your own measurements to make sure you fully understand how it works—it's your choice!

> **Note**
>
> If all of this measuring and tweaking is too much for you, there are some tools you can purchase to make your life a bit easier.
>
> The first is a tool called Mekanimo *(www.mekanimo.net)* that helps you visually sketch out physics bodies, connect them with joints, and even test out how they work inside the tool. When you're done, you can export the shapes and joints you defined as Box2D code that you can cut and paste into your projects (with a few modifications). At the time of writing, Mekanimo has both Windows and Mac versions and costs $29.95 for noncommercial use and $199.95 for independent developer use.
>
> The second is a tool/sample project called LevelSVG *(www.sapusmedia.com/levelsvg)*, written by none other than Ricardo Quesada, the creator of Cocos2D. LevelSVG allows you to create levels for your games in Inkscape, a free vector editing tool, and read the saved files in Cocos2D code to create Box2D bodies and objects. LevelSVG works especially well for platformer games if you want to have an easier time developing your levels and is also a good example of Cocos2D game programming. At the time of writing, LevelSVG costs $249 if you buy it alone and $149 if you buy it along with other source code projects written by Ricardo.
>
> Last but not least, there's a great tool by the author of TexturePacker called Physics Editor *(www.physicseditor.de)*. This tool is similar to Vertex Helper but even easier, since it can automatically trace your shapes for you! You can even set your Box2D object properties from right within Physics Editor and easily load your objects in code, saving yourself a lot of time and work. TexturePacker has a free trial version, and the full version costs $17.95, or $29.99 if you buy it along with TexturePacker.
>
> We didn't cover using these tools in these chapters because we wanted you to learn how things work from the ground up, but in practice, they are definitely recommended because they can save you a lot of time!

Adding Ole: The Implementation

With that background knowledge in mind, let's give Ole the ride of his life!

First things first: adding some required instance variables and properties. Open up *Cart.h* and add the member variables for the body part sprites and Box2D bodies, as shown in Listing 12.4.

Listing 12.4 **Cart.h (inside @interface)**

```
Box2DSprite * legs;
Box2DSprite * trunk;
Box2DSprite * head;
```

```
Box2DSprite * helm;
Box2DSprite * arm;
b2Body * legsBody;
b2Body * trunkBody;
b2Body * headBody;
b2Body * helmBody;
b2Body * armBody;
```

Then underneath, add properties for the sprites, as shown in Listing 12.5.

Listing 12.5 **Cart.h (after @interface)**

```
@property (readonly) Box2DSprite * legs;
@property (readonly) Box2DSprite * trunk;
@property (readonly) Box2DSprite * head;
@property (readonly) Box2DSprite * helm;
@property (readonly) Box2DSprite * arm;
```

At the top of *Cart.mm*, synthesize your new properties, as shown in Listing 12.6.

Listing 12.6 **Cart.mm (right after @implementation)**

```
@synthesize legs;
@synthesize trunk;
@synthesize head;
@synthesize helm;
@synthesize arm;
```

Now on to the fun stuff. First modify both `createBodyAtLocation` and `createWheelWithSprite` and add the lines in Listing 12.7 as you create your fixture definition.

Listing 12.7 **Cart.mm (in both createBodyAtLocation and createWheelWithSprite, right after creating the fixtureDef)**

```
fixtureDef.filter.categoryBits = 0x2;
fixtureDef.filter.maskBits = 0xFFFF;
fixtureDef.filter.groupIndex = -1;
```

These three settings set up the collision filters for Box2D. You need to set these up so that the cart doesn't collide with any of the body parts you're about to add. Let's go through what each setting means.

Every Box2D body can belong to a set of object categories, and by setting **categoryBits**, you control which categories the body belongs to. The default category is 0x1, so here you set the cart to a different category (mainly to illustrate that you can do this).

You can set which categories of objects an object will collide with by setting the **maskBits** field. This is a 16-bit value, so setting it to 0xFFFF means that it collides with all categories (the same as the default behavior).

The final item, **groupIndex**, is a special field you can use to override the mask bits. When two bodies share the same group index, if the number is negative, they will not collide, and if the number is positive, they will collide. In this case, it's set to negative (and the bodies that make up Ole will have the same negative value), so they will not collide even though they would otherwise.

> ### Tip
>
> In your games, you may find it useful to use #defines for the various categories that your objects might belong to. For example, you could #define kGroundCategory 0x1, #define kCartCategory 0x2, and so on, and then set the categoryBits and maskBits for all of your fixtures using these constants. This makes your code a little bit easier to work with, especially when your scenes start getting more complex.

Next create a new function to create a part of Ole, as shown in Listing 12.8.

Listing 12.8   Cart.mm (before initWithWorld:atLocation)

```
-(b2Body *)createPartAtLocation:(b2Vec2)location
   withSprite:(Box2DSprite *)sprite {
   b2BodyDef bodyDef;
   bodyDef.type = b2_dynamicBody;
   bodyDef.position = location;
   bodyDef.angle = body->GetAngle();

   b2Body *retval = world->CreateBody(&bodyDef);
   retval->SetUserData(sprite);
   sprite.body = retval;

   b2PolygonShape shape;
   shape.SetAsBox(sprite.contentSize.width/2/PTM_RATIO,
       sprite.contentSize.height/2/PTM_RATIO);

   b2FixtureDef fixtureDef;
   fixtureDef.shape = &shape;
   fixtureDef.density = 0.05;
   fixtureDef.filter.categoryBits = 0x2;
   fixtureDef.filter.maskBits = 0xFFFF;
   fixtureDef.filter.groupIndex = -1;

   retval->CreateFixture(&fixtureDef);
   return retval;
}
```

Most of this is standard body creation code that you have seen many times. There are three things in particular to point out though.

First, the density is set to very low so Ole's bouncing around only affects the cart's movement a little bit. Without this, you might see an effect where the force of Ole bouncing around overwhelms the joint constraints, and Ole could end up under the cart!

Second, the category filtering is set up so that Ole doesn't collide with the cart, as described previously.

Third, each part of Ole is created as a box (rather than tracing it more exactly with Vertex Helper). Boxes are used because in this level, Ole won't really be colliding with much, so the exact shapes don't matter, and boxes are much simpler.

Next, add a new method to create Ole, as shown in Listing 12.9.

Listing 12.9 Cart.mm (right after createPartAtLocation)

```
-(void)createOle {
    legs = [Box2DSprite spriteWithSpriteFrameName:@"OleCartLegs.png"];
    legs.gameObjectType = kCartType;
    legsBody = [self createPartAtLocation:
        body->GetWorldPoint(b2Vec2(-10.0/100.0, 6.0/100.0))
        withSprite:legs];

    trunk = [Box2DSprite spriteWithSpriteFrameName:@"OleCartBody.png"];
    trunk.gameObjectType = kCartType;
    trunkBody = [self createPartAtLocation:
        legsBody->GetWorldPoint(b2Vec2(0, 45.0/100.0))
        withSprite:trunk];

    head = [Box2DSprite spriteWithSpriteFrameName:@"OleCartHead.png"];
    head.gameObjectType = kCartType;
    headBody = [self createPartAtLocation:
        trunkBody->GetWorldPoint(
            b2Vec2(18.0/100.0, 24.0/100.0)) withSprite:head];

    helm = [Box2DSprite
        spriteWithSpriteFrameName:@"OleCartHelmet.png"];
    helm.gameObjectType = kCartType;
    helmBody = [self createPartAtLocation:
        headBody->GetWorldPoint(b2Vec2(15.0/100.0, 25.0/100.0))
        withSprite:helm];

    arm = [Box2DSprite spriteWithSpriteFrameName:@"OleCartArm.png"];
    arm.gameObjectType = kCartType;
    armBody = [self createPartAtLocation:
        trunkBody->GetWorldPoint(
            b2Vec2(5.0/100.0, -15.0/100.0)) withSprite:arm];
}
```

This simply uses the above method to create a Box2D body for each piece of Ole. Note that it uses `GetWorldPoint` to make each piece relative to the piece it's connecting to for maximum code reuse. All of the points listed here were simply measured with a ruler tool in an image-editing program using the HD artwork, so they need to be divided by the HD `PTM_RATIO` (100.0) to be converted to the proper Box2D coordinates as usual.

Next, at the bottom of `createOle`, add the code to create the necessary joints, as shown in Listing 12.10.

Listing 12.10   **Cart.mm (at bottom of createOle)**

```
b2Transform axisTransform;
axisTransform.Set(b2Vec2(0, 0), body->GetAngle());
b2Vec2 axis = b2Mul(axisTransform.R, b2Vec2(0,1));

b2PrismaticJointDef prisJointDef;
prisJointDef.Initialize(body, legsBody,
    legsBody->GetWorldCenter(), axis);
prisJointDef.enableLimit = true;
prisJointDef.lowerTranslation = 0.0;
prisJointDef.upperTranslation = 43.0/100.0;
world->CreateJoint(&prisJointDef);

b2RevoluteJointDef revJointDef;
revJointDef.Initialize(legsBody, trunkBody,
    legsBody->GetWorldPoint(b2Vec2(0, 20.0/100.0)));
revJointDef.lowerAngle = CC_DEGREES_TO_RADIANS(-15);
revJointDef.upperAngle = CC_DEGREES_TO_RADIANS(15);
revJointDef.enableLimit = true;
revJointDef.enableMotor = true;
revJointDef.motorSpeed = 0.5;
revJointDef.maxMotorTorque = 50.0;
world->CreateJoint(&revJointDef);
revJointDef.enableMotor = false;

revJointDef.Initialize(trunkBody, armBody,
    armBody->GetWorldPoint(b2Vec2(-9.0/100.0, 29.0/100.0)));
revJointDef.lowerAngle = CC_DEGREES_TO_RADIANS(-30);
revJointDef.upperAngle = CC_DEGREES_TO_RADIANS(60);
revJointDef.enableLimit = true;
world->CreateJoint(&revJointDef);

revJointDef.Initialize(trunkBody, headBody,
    headBody->GetWorldPoint(b2Vec2(-12.0/100.0, -9.0/100.0)));
revJointDef.lowerAngle = CC_DEGREES_TO_RADIANS(-5);
revJointDef.upperAngle = CC_DEGREES_TO_RADIANS(5);
```

```
revJointDef.enableLimit = true;
world->CreateJoint(&revJointDef);

prisJointDef.Initialize(headBody, helmBody,
    helmBody->GetWorldCenter(), axis);
prisJointDef.enableLimit = true;
prisJointDef.lowerTranslation = 0.0/100.0;
prisJointDef.upperTranslation = 5.0/100.0;
world->CreateJoint(&prisJointDef);
```

Based on the discussion earlier in this chapter, most of this should be straightforward. It's simply creating revolute joints and prismatic joints to connect each body to another and setting up the limits so the bodies act appropriately.

There are two things of interest to note in this method, however. The first is that for the first revolute joint (connecting the legs to the trunk), the motor for the joint is enabled, with a speed of 0.5 and a small max torque. This is to make Ole tend to lean backward a bit, so he looks upright rather than falling over due to the weight of his head being in the front.

The second thing of interest is that the axis is rotated according to the body's angle rather than just pointing straight up. This is important so that if you rotate the body when you initially place it into the scene, it will still be connected properly.

Now call your new method at the bottom of `initWithWorld:atLocation`, as shown in Listing 12.11.

Listing 12.11   Cart.mm (at bottom of initWithWorld:atLocation)

```
[self createOle];
```

And finally, switch to *Scene4ActionLayer.mm* and modify `createCartAtLocation` to add the new sprites to the scene, as shown in Listing 12.12.

Listing 12.12   Scene4ActionLayer.mm (at bottom of createCartAtLocation)

```
[sceneSpriteBatchNode addChild:cart.legs];
[sceneSpriteBatchNode addChild:cart.trunk];
[sceneSpriteBatchNode addChild:cart.head];
[sceneSpriteBatchNode addChild:cart.helm];
[sceneSpriteBatchNode addChild:cart.arm z:2];
```

Note that Ole's arm is added with a higher z value, so it appears to be hanging outside the cart.

Compile and run your code (on the device, as the simulator is slower and can have some oddities), and as you can see in Figure 12.5, Ole should now be back in action, swaying and bouncing in a really cool manner as your cart jumps through the level!

Figure 12.5   Ole leaping through the level with a ragdoll effect

Adding Obstacles and Bridges

So far the level is kind of fun, with a cart that you can move around and jump—but there's absolutely no challenge! So let's spice things up a bit by adding some simple spikes along the ground that you have to jump and a neat swaying bridge you can cross.

Adding a Bridge

You start with adding the bridge, since it's simpler and will reinforce what you just learned about how to use joints.

As you can see in Figure 12.6, the basic idea is that you create a sequence of small rectangles for bridge planks end to end, connect each plank to the next with a revolute joint, and connect the first and last bridge planks to the ground. Then Box2D handles the simulation, and gravity causes the planks toward the middle to sag a bit, much like a bridge made out of connected planks would.

Since you know how to create revolute joints and create Box2D bodies, this should be a snap. First, add two new instance variables to *Scene4ActionLayer.h*, as shown in Listing 12.13.

Listing 12.13   **Scene4ActionLayer.h (inside @interface)**

```
b2Joint * lastBridgeStartJoint;
b2Joint * lastBridgeEndJoint;
```

Before Gravity

After Gravity

Figure 12.6   Adding a bridge using revolute joints

These just hold a reference to the first and last joints in the bridge added to the scene. They come in handy later in this chapter.

Next add a new method to *Scene4ActionLayer.mm* to create the bridge, as shown in Listing 12.14.

Listing 12.14   **Scene4ActionLayer.mm (before createLevel)**

```
- (void)createBridge {
    Box2DSprite *lastObject;
    b2Body *lastBody = groundBody;
    for(int i = 0; i < 15; i++) {
        Box2DSprite *plank =
            [Box2DSprite spriteWithSpriteFrameName:@"plank.png"];
        plank.gameObjectType = kGroundType;

        b2BodyDef bodyDef;
        bodyDef.type = b2_dynamicBody;
        bodyDef.position =
            b2Vec2(groundMaxX/PTM_RATIO +
                    plank.contentSize.width/2/PTM_RATIO,
                80.0/100.0 -
                    (plank.contentSize.height/2/PTM_RATIO));

        b2Body *plankBody = world->CreateBody(&bodyDef);
        plankBody->SetUserData(plank);
        plank.body = plankBody;
        [groundSpriteBatchNode addChild:plank];

        b2PolygonShape shape;
        float32 diff;
        if (UI_USER_INTERFACE_IDIOM() == UIUserInterfaceIdiomPad) {
            diff = 40.0-plank.contentSize.height;
        } else {
            diff = 20.0-plank.contentSize.height;
        }
```

```
        shape.SetAsBox(
            plank.contentSize.width/2/PTM_RATIO, 40.0/100.0,
            b2Vec2(0, -plank.contentSize.height/2/
                PTM_RATIO-diff/PTM_RATIO), 0);

        b2FixtureDef fixtureDef;
        fixtureDef.shape = &shape;
        fixtureDef.density = 2.0;
        plankBody->CreateFixture(&fixtureDef);

        b2RevoluteJointDef jd;
        jd.Initialize(lastBody, plankBody,
            plankBody->GetWorldPoint(
                b2Vec2(-plank.contentSize.width/2/PTM_RATIO, 0)));
        jd.lowerAngle = CC_DEGREES_TO_RADIANS(-0.25);
        jd.upperAngle = CC_DEGREES_TO_RADIANS(0.25);
        jd.enableLimit = true;
        b2Joint *joint = world->CreateJoint(&jd);
        if (i == 0) { lastBridgeStartJoint = joint; }

        groundMaxX += (plank.contentSize.width * 0.8);
        lastBody = plankBody;
        lastObject = plank;
    }

    b2RevoluteJointDef jd;
    jd.Initialize(lastBody, groundBody,
        lastBody->GetWorldPoint(
            b2Vec2(lastObject.contentSize.width/2/PTM_RATIO, 0)));
    lastBridgeEndJoint = world->CreateJoint(&jd);
}
```

This code creates 15 bridge planks and lays them end to end, but slightly overlapping, so there are no gaps in the bridge when it sags due to gravity. It connects each bridge plank to the next with a revolute joint, setting it up with a very tight restriction (−0.25 degrees per connection) to get a "tight" feel to the bridge. Also note that the first and last joints are connected to the ground.

One thing you may be wondering about is the section that begins with a test if the height of the plank is less than 40 points (relative to the HD artwork). This code makes sure that the actual Box2D body representing the plank is at least 40 points tall. This height is needed to prevent the wheels of the cart from falling through the planks, which could happen in practice if the plank was too thin. The code just lines up the taller Box2D bodies so that the tops of the bodies align with the tops of the planks.

Next, just modify your `createLevel` method to call the new `createBridge` method between the calls to create the ground, as shown in Listing 12.15.

Listing 12.15   **Scene4ActionLayer.mm (replace createLevel with this)**

```
- (void)createLevel {
    [self createBackground];
    [self createGround3];
    [self createBridge];
    [self createGround1];
    [self createBridge];
    [self createGround3];
    [self createBridge];
    [self createGround2];
    [self createGround3];
    [self createBridge];
    [self createGround3];
}
```

Compile and run your code, and as you can see in Figure 12.7, now you should be able to ride over cool dynamic bridges!

Figure 12.7   Creating bridges with Box2D revolute joints

Adding Spikes

Now that you have bridges, let's increase the challenge for the player by scattering some spikes across the level for the player to avoid.

To start, you create a new subclass of Box2DSprite for the spikes. Select the *Classes\Game Objects\Box2D* group, go to **File > New > New File...**, choose **iOS > Cocoa Touch > Objective-C class**, and click **Next**. Enter *Box2DSprite* as the Subclass of, click **Next**, name the file *Spikes.mm* (note the *.mm* extension, since this will be importing Box2D), and click **Save**.

Open *Spikes.h* and replace the file with the contents of Listing 12.16.

Listing 12.16   **Spikes.h**

```
#import "Box2DSprite.h"

@interface Spikes : Box2DSprite {
    b2World *world;
}

- (id)initWithWorld:(b2World *)world atLocation:(CGPoint)location;

@end
```

This creates a subclass of Box2DSprite and declares an init method. Next open *Spikes.mm* and replace the file with the contents of Listing 12.17.

Listing 12.17   **Spikes.mm**

```
#import "Spikes.h"

@implementation Spikes

- (void)createBodyAtLocation:(CGPoint)location {
    b2BodyDef bodyDef;
    bodyDef.type = b2_dynamicBody;
    bodyDef.position = b2Vec2(location.x/PTM_RATIO,
        location.y/PTM_RATIO);

    self.body = world->CreateBody(&bodyDef);
    body->SetUserData(self);

    b2PolygonShape shape;
    shape.SetAsBox(self.contentSize.width/2/PTM_RATIO,
        self.contentSize.height/2/PTM_RATIO,
        b2Vec2(0, +5.0/100.0), 0);
```

```
    b2FixtureDef fixtureDef;
    fixtureDef.shape = &shape;
    fixtureDef.density = 1000.0;

    body->CreateFixture(&fixtureDef);
}

- (id)initWithWorld:(b2World *)theWorld atLocation:(CGPoint)location {
    if ((self = [super init])) {
        world = theWorld;
        [self setDisplayFrame:[[CCSpriteFrameCache
            sharedSpriteFrameCache] spriteFrameByName:@"spikes.png"]];
        gameObjectType = kSpikesType;
        [self createBodyAtLocation:location];
    }
    return self;
}

@end
```

You should be familiar with this by now; it creates a rectangular Box2D body for the sprite. Note that you could try to mimic the shape of the spikes more accurately using Vertex Helper or other methods, but for this level it's just not worth the time and effort, as a box approximation is good enough. Note that the box is set up to be slightly smaller than the actual sprite (so it appears sunken into the ground) and that spikes are set up with a very high density so that they barely move when hit.

Now switch to *Cart.mm* and first add an import for *Box2DHelpers.h* to the top of the file, as shown in Listing 12.18.

Listing 12.18   Cart.mm (at top of file)

```
#import "Box2DHelpers.h"
```

Then add a few methods to allow the cart to transition to a damage-taking state, as shown in Listing 12.19.

Listing 12.19   Cart.mm (anywhere in class)

```
- (void)playHitEffect {
    int soundToPlay = random() % 5;
    if (soundToPlay == 0) {
        PLAYSOUNDEFFECT(VIKING_HIT_1);
    } else if (soundToPlay == 1) {
        PLAYSOUNDEFFECT(VIKING_HIT_2);
    } else if (soundToPlay == 2) {
        PLAYSOUNDEFFECT(VIKING_HIT_3);
```

```
    } else if (soundToPlay == 3) {
        PLAYSOUNDEFFECT(VIKING_HIT_4);
    } else {
        PLAYSOUNDEFFECT(VIKING_HIT_5);
    }
}

-(void)changeState:(CharacterStates)newState {
    if (characterState == newState) return;

    [self stopAllActions];
    [self setCharacterState:newState];

    switch (newState) {
      case kStateTakingDamage: {
          [self playHitEffect];
          characterHealth = characterHealth - 10;
          CCAction *blink = [CCBlink actionWithDuration:1.0
              blinks:3.0];
          [self runAction:blink];
          [wheelL runAction:[blink copy]];
          [wheelR runAction:[blink copy]];
          [legs runAction:[blink copy]];
          [trunk runAction:[blink copy]];
          [head runAction:[blink copy]];
          [helm runAction:[blink copy]];
          [arm runAction:[blink copy]];
          break;
      }
      default:
          break;
    }
}
```

The first method plays a random sound effect when Ole gets hit. The second method decreases the character's health upon a hit and starts a blink animation to indicate that the cart is taking damage. Note that it has to run the animation on all of the sprites that make up Ole's cart.

Next add the lines to handle state transitions at the bottom of updateStateWith-DeltaTime, as shown in Listing 12.20.

Listing 12.20   Cart.mm (at the bottom of updateStateWithDeltaTime)

```
if (characterState == kStateDead)
    return; // Nothing to do if the Viking is dead
```

```
if ((characterState == kStateTakingDamage) &&
    ([self numberOfRunningActions] > 0))
    return; // Currently playing the taking damage animation

if ([self numberOfRunningActions] == 0) {
    // Not playing an animation
    if (characterHealth <= 0) {
        [self changeState:kStateDead];
    } else {
        [self changeState:kStateIdle];
    }
}

if (isBodyCollidingWithObjectType(wheelLBody, kSpikesType)) {
    [self changeState:kStateTakingDamage];
} else if (isBodyCollidingWithObjectType(wheelRBody, kSpikesType)) {
    [self changeState:kStateTakingDamage];
}
```

This returns if any action is running on the object (such as the cart blinking as it's taking damage—it gets temporary invulnerability). If there are no actions running, it switches to either dead or idle depending on the cart's health. Finally, it uses the helper method you wrote earlier to check if the cart body is colliding with any spikes, and if so, changes the state to taking damage.

Now switch over to *Scene4ActionLayer.mm* and add the import for *Spikes.h* at the top of the file, as shown in Listing 12.21.

Listing 12.21   Scene4ActionLayer.mm (at the top of the file)

```
#import "Spikes.h"
```

Then add a method to create spikes at a particular offset, as shown in Listing 12.22.

Listing 12.22   Scene4ActionLayer.mm (before createLevel)

```
- (void)createSpikesWithOffset:(int)offset {
    Spikes * spikes;
    if (UI_USER_INTERFACE_IDIOM() == UIUserInterfaceIdiomPad) {
        spikes = [[[Spikes alloc] initWithWorld:world
            atLocation:ccp(groundMaxX + offset, 100)] autorelease];
    } else {
        spikes = [[[Spikes alloc] initWithWorld:world
            atLocation:ccp(groundMaxX + offset/2, 100/2)] autorelease];
    }
    [sceneSpriteBatchNode addChild:spikes];
}
```

Note that the coordinates are divided by two if it's not the iPad—this way we can specify the coordinates once (for the HD artwork) and convert to the other device.

One last step! Modify your `createLevel` method to call this new method a couple times, as shown in Listing 12.23.

Listing 12.23 **Scene4ActionLayer.mm (replace createLevel with this)**

```
- (void)createLevel {
    [self createBackground];
    [self createGround3];
    [self createSpikesWithOffset:-1200];
    [self createSpikesWithOffset:-400];
    [self createBridge];
    [self createGround1];
    [self createSpikesWithOffset:-1050];
    [self createSpikesWithOffset:-100];
    [self createBridge];
    [self createGround3];
    [self createSpikesWithOffset:-1700];
    [self createSpikesWithOffset:-900];
    [self createBridge];
    [self createGround2];
    [self createSpikesWithOffset:-1300];
    [self createSpikesWithOffset:-900];
    [self createGround3];
    [self createSpikesWithOffset:-1200];
    [self createSpikesWithOffset:-400];
    [self createBridge];
    [self createGround3];
}
```

Compile and run your code, and as you can see in Figure 12.8, now the level is a lot more fun and challenging, since Ole has some spikes to avoid!

An Improved Main Loop

As you've been experimenting with adding bridges and spikes, you may have noticed some odd behavior with Box2D along the way. You may have seen the wheels pop off at times or the bridges sway more than expected.

The root cause of all of this goes back to the way you give Box2D time to run in your update loop. Currently, you are just using an extremely simplified run loop that gives Box2D a different amount of time to process each frame (also known as a *variable rate timestep*), as shown in Listing 12.24.

Figure 12.8   Ole jumping spike obstacles in level

Listing 12.24   **Current main loop for Box2D—a variable rate timestep**

```
int32 velocityIterations = 3;
int32 positionIterations = 2;
world->Step(dt, velocityIterations, positionIterations);
```

As you can see in Listing 12.24, each time the update method is called, the Step method is called in the world with a different amount of time—whatever the variable dt happens to be.

As mentioned in Chapter 10, "Basic Game Physics," Box2D doesn't work well with a variable rate timestep; it works much better with a *fixed timestep*, which means giving it the same exact amount of time each time you call the Step method. Although you can get away with variable rate timesteps with smaller apps or games, the more Box2D has to do, the more likely this is to cause problems.

So let's replace this with a fixed timestep implementation. Go to your update method in *Scene4ActionLayer.mm*, comment out the lines from Listing 12.24, and add the new implementation shown in Listing 12.25.

Listing 12.25   **Scene4ActionLayer.mm (in update method, comment out the code from Listing 12.24 and replace with this)**

```
static double UPDATE_INTERVAL = 1.0f/60.0f;
static double MAX_CYCLES_PER_FRAME = 5;
static double timeAccumulator = 0;
```

```
timeAccumulator += dt;
if (timeAccumulator > (MAX_CYCLES_PER_FRAME * UPDATE_INTERVAL)) {
    timeAccumulator = UPDATE_INTERVAL;
}

int32 velocityIterations = 3;
int32 positionIterations = 2;
while (timeAccumulator >= UPDATE_INTERVAL) {
    timeAccumulator -= UPDATE_INTERVAL;
    world->Step(UPDATE_INTERVAL,
        velocityIterations, positionIterations);
}
```

Every time the Step method is called on the world, it's always called with the same amount of time (UPDATE_INTERVAL; i.e., 1/60 of a second). If the time passed in to the method is greater than this, it divides it by the UPDATE_INTERVAL and calls Step multiple times. It also keeps track of the leftover amount and uses it next time update is called.

> **Note**
>
> There is one further optimization you can do to your physics loop: interpolate the results to remove the effects of that tiny extra slice of time in each frame. For more information on how to do this, check out *http://gafferongames.com/game-physics/fix-your-timestep/* or search the Cocos2D forums for a good discussion.

The fixed timestep greatly improves the stability of the physics simulation. If you compile and run your code, you should see a lot less strange behavior.

The Boss Fight!

What better way to end an awesome level than with an amazing boss fight? In this section we do exactly that: pit Ole against the dangerous Digger Robot!

The idea here is that the Digger Robot paces back and forth on the final platform. If Ole collides with the Digger, Ole gets hurt. However, if Ole slams into the back of the Digger, he can push the Digger back a bit and eventually push him off the edge of the level to win!

Figure 12.9 gives you an idea of what this menacing foe looks like and how you'll model him in the Box2D world.

As you can see in Figure 12.9, you model the Digger as a box with two wheels, which makes it easy to move him left and right. Since the robot will be pacing back and forth, you also add two sensors for the Digger: one on the left of the robot and one on the right. You simply use the appropriate sensor depending on which direction the Digger is facing.

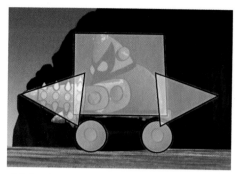

Figure 12.9   Mapping the Digger sprite to Box2D bodies

To make the Digger Robot, the first thing you need to do is create a new subclass of `Box2DSprite` for the Digger. Select the *Classes\Game Objects\Box2D* group, go to **File > New > New File...**, choose **iOS > Cocoa Touch > Objective-C class**, and click **Next**. Enter *Box2DSprite* as the Subclass of, click **Next**, name the file *Digger.mm* (note the *.mm* extension, since this will be importing Box2D), and click **Save**.

Replace the contents of *Digger.h*, as shown in Listing 12.26.

Listing 12.26   **Digger.h**

```
#import "Box2DSprite.h"

@interface Digger : Box2DSprite {
    b2Body *wheelLBody;
    b2Body *wheelRBody;
    b2RevoluteJoint *wheelLJoint;
    b2RevoluteJoint *wheelRJoint;
    b2Body *drillLBody;
    b2Body *drillRBody;
    b2Fixture *drillLFixture;
    b2Fixture *drillRFixture;
    Box2DSprite *wheelLSprite;
    Box2DSprite *wheelRSprite;
}

@property (assign) Box2DSprite *wheelLSprite;
@property (assign) Box2DSprite *wheelRSprite;

- (id)initWithWorld:(b2World *)world atLocation:(CGPoint)location;

@end
```

Here you make a subclass of `Box2DSprite` for the Digger Robot and declare references to a few variables you'll need to keep track of. Specifically, these variables keep track of the Box2D bodies and joints for the Digger's wheels and the body and fixture for the two drill sensor bodies.

Next, switch to *Digger.mm* and add the method to create a body for the Digger Robot, as shown in Listing 12.27.

Listing 12.27   **Digger.mm (inside @implementation)**

```
@synthesize wheelLSprite;
@synthesize wheelRSprite;

- (void)createBodyWithWorld:(b2World *)world
    atLocation:(CGPoint)location {
    b2BodyDef bodyDef;
    bodyDef.type = b2_dynamicBody;
    bodyDef.position =
        b2Vec2(location.x/PTM_RATIO, location.y/PTM_RATIO);

    b2Body *cartBody = world->CreateBody(&bodyDef);
    cartBody->SetUserData(self);
    self.body = cartBody;

    b2PolygonShape shape;
    int num = 4;
    b2Vec2 verts[] = {
        b2Vec2(87.0f / 100.0, -32.0f / 100.0),
        b2Vec2(81.0f / 100.0, 110.0f / 100.0),
        b2Vec2(-87.0f / 100.0, 112.0f / 100.0),
        b2Vec2(-84.0f / 100.0, -33.0f / 100.0)
    };
    shape.Set(verts, num);

    b2FixtureDef fixtureDef;
    fixtureDef.shape = &shape;
    fixtureDef.density = 0.5;
    fixtureDef.friction = 0.5;
    fixtureDef.restitution = 0.5;

    cartBody->CreateFixture(&fixtureDef);
    cartBody->SetAngularDamping(1000);
}
```

Most of this should look pretty familiar to you by now. It creates a body for the Digger with a polygon shape that traces a box around the top of the body. The vertices for the shape were created with Vertex Helper; you can trace the shape to define your own vertices if you wish.

As far as the settings go, the robot is set up to have a low density (so that when Ole collides with it, he gives it a good *thwack*). It's also set up to use angular damping. Angular damping is a value that affects the body's resistance to rotation, so you set this to a high value here to prevent the Digger from flipping when Ole collides with it.

Next add a method to create the wheels for the Digger, as shown in Listing 12.28.

Listing 12.28   Digger.mm (after createBodyWithWorld)

```
- (void)createWheelsWithWorld:(b2World *)world {
    b2BodyDef bodyDef;
    bodyDef.type = b2_dynamicBody;

    bodyDef.position =
        body->GetWorldPoint(b2Vec2(-50.0/100.0, -80.0/100.0));
    wheelLBody = world->CreateBody(&bodyDef);

    bodyDef.position =
        body->GetWorldPoint(b2Vec2(50.0/100.0, -80.0/100.0));
    wheelRBody = world->CreateBody(&bodyDef);

    b2CircleShape circleShape;
    b2FixtureDef fixtureDef;
    fixtureDef.shape = &circleShape;
    fixtureDef.friction = 0.2;
    fixtureDef.restitution = 0.5;
    fixtureDef.density = 5.0;

    circleShape.m_radius = 25.0/100.0;
    wheelLBody->CreateFixture(&fixtureDef);
    circleShape.m_radius = 25.0/100.0;
    wheelRBody->CreateFixture(&fixtureDef);

    b2RevoluteJointDef revJointDef;
    revJointDef.Initialize(body, wheelLBody,
        wheelLBody->GetWorldCenter());
    revJointDef.enableMotor = true;
    revJointDef.motorSpeed = 0;
    revJointDef.maxMotorTorque = 1000;
    wheelLJoint = (b2RevoluteJoint *) world->CreateJoint(&revJointDef);
    revJointDef.Initialize(body, wheelRBody,
        wheelRBody->GetWorldCenter());
    wheelRJoint = (b2RevoluteJoint *) world->CreateJoint(&revJointDef);

    wheelLSprite = [Box2DSprite
        spriteWithSpriteFrameName:@"digger_wheel.png"];
```

```
    wheelLSprite.body = wheelLBody;
    wheelLBody->SetUserData(wheelLSprite);

    wheelRSprite = [Box2DSprite
        spriteWithSpriteFrameName:@"digger_wheel.png"];
    wheelRSprite.body = wheelRBody;
    wheelRBody->SetUserData(wheelRSprite);
}
```

This method creates two wheels for the Digger. Even though the Digger doesn't appear to have wheels, you still want it to slide around the ground as if it has wheels. This is a good example of how sometimes it's convenient to have your Box2D bodies appear differently than what the user sees in order to get certain effects.

The code in the method should look quite familiar to you at this point; it creates a body and fixture for each wheel. The numbers for the radius and position of the wheels in the method were determined by measuring the desired size and distance of the virtual wheels in an image editor. Feel free to measure it yourself to make sure you fully understand it.

It also sets the density for the wheels to be higher (since wheels should be close in mass to the bodies they support in Box2D to act properly) and creates revolute joints to connect each wheel to the main body.

Finally, it creates a sprite for each wheel and ties the sprites and Box2D bodies together.

Next add a method to create the drill sensors, as shown in Listing 12.29.

Listing 12.29   **Digger.mm (after createWheelsWithWorld)**

```
- (void)createDrillWithWorld:(b2World *)world {
    b2BodyDef bodyDef;
    bodyDef.type = b2_dynamicBody;
    bodyDef.position = body->GetPosition();
    drillLBody = world->CreateBody(&bodyDef);
    drillRBody = world->CreateBody(&bodyDef);

    b2PolygonShape shape;
    int num = 3;
    b2Vec2 verts[] = {
        b2Vec2(-65.0f / 100.0, 31.0f / 100.0),
        b2Vec2(-189.0f / 100.0, -2.0f / 100.0),
        b2Vec2(-85.0f / 100.0, -72.0f / 100.0)
    };
    shape.Set(verts, num);

    b2FixtureDef fixtureDef;
    fixtureDef.density = 0.25;
```

```
fixtureDef.shape = &shape;
fixtureDef.isSensor = true;
drillLFixture = drillLBody->CreateFixture(&fixtureDef);

int num2 = 3;
b2Vec2 verts2[] = {
    b2Vec2(85.0f / 100.0, -72.0f / 100.0),
    b2Vec2(189.0f / 100.0, -2.0f / 100.0),
    b2Vec2(65.0f / 100.0, 31.0f / 100.0),
};
shape.Set(verts2, num2);
drillRFixture = drillRBody->CreateFixture(&fixtureDef);

b2WeldJointDef weldJointDef;
weldJointDef.Initialize(body, drillLBody, body->GetWorldCenter());
world->CreateJoint(&weldJointDef);
weldJointDef.Initialize(body, drillRBody, body->GetWorldCenter());
world->CreateJoint(&weldJointDef);
}
```

This method creates two bodies and fixtures for the drill sensors: one for when the driller is facing left and one for when the driller is facing right. The vertices for the left drill were determined by tracing the drill shape using Vertex Helper (feel free to trace them yourself if you'd like). Note that it sets the position of the drills to be the position of the body, so tracing the drill in Vertex Helper would result in the proper coordinates.

Once you have vertices for the left drill, you can easily determine the vertices for the right drill by switching the x offset from negative to positive (i.e., −65.0 would become 65.0), since the center of the body matches up to the center of the driller sprite. However, you need to swap the order of the vertices, because vertices must always be added in counterclockwise order, as you can see in Figure 12.10.

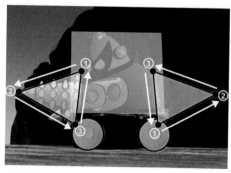

Figure 12.10   Making sure vertex order is counterclockwise for both left and right drill sensors

Next add the `init` method to create a new Digger, as shown in Listing 12.30.

Listing 12.30   Digger.mm (after createDrillWithWorld)

```
- (id)initWithWorld:(b2World *)world atLocation:(CGPoint)location {
    if ((self = [super init])) {
        [self setDisplayFrame:
            [[CCSpriteFrameCache sharedSpriteFrameCache]
                spriteFrameByName:@"digger_anim5.png"]];
        gameObjectType = kDiggerType;
        characterHealth = 100.0f;
        [self createBodyWithWorld:world atLocation:location];
        [self createWheelsWithWorld:world];
        [self createDrillWithWorld:world];
    }
    return self;
}
```

This simply sets an initial frame for the Digger and calls the methods you wrote previously to create the body, wheels, and drill sensors.

Now it's time to add the Digger to your level! Open *Scene4ActionLayer.h* and predeclare Digger at the top of the file, as shown in Listing 12.31.

Listing 12.31   Scene4ActionLayer.h (at the top of the file)

```
@class Digger;
```

While you're there, add a few new instance variables, as shown in Listing 12.32.

Listing 12.32   Scene4ActionLayer.h (inside @interface)

```
Digger * digger;
bool gameOver;
b2Body *offscreenSensorBody;
```

These keep track of the Digger, whether the game is over, and a pointer to a body that will help detect if the cart or the Digger falls off the screen.

Then switch to *Scene4ActionLayer.m* and add a few imports to the top of the file, as shown in Listing 12.33.

Listing 12.33   Scene4ActionLayer.mm (at the top of the file)

```
#import "Digger.h"
#import "GameManager.h"
```

Then add a method to create a new Digger, as shown in Listing 12.34.

Listing 12.34   **Scene4ActionLayer.mm (before createLevel)**

```objc
- (void)createDigger {
    CGSize winSize = [CCDirector sharedDirector].winSize;
    digger = [[[Digger alloc] initWithWorld:world
        atLocation:ccp(groundMaxX - winSize.width * 0.8,
                        winSize.height/2)] autorelease];
    [sceneSpriteBatchNode addChild:digger];
    [sceneSpriteBatchNode addChild:digger.wheelLSprite];
    [sceneSpriteBatchNode addChild:digger.wheelRSprite];
}
```

This method places the Digger 80 percent of a screen width left of the last ground/
bridge section added to the scene and in the air a bit (he'll drop down due to gravity).

Next you add a method to create the sensor that helps detect if the cart or the Digger falls offscreen, as shown in Listing 12.35.

Listing 12.35   **Scene4ActionLayer.mm (after createDigger)**

```objc
- (void)createOffscreenSensorBody {
    CGSize winSize = [CCDirector sharedDirector].winSize;
    float32 sensorWidth = groundMaxX + winSize.width*4;
    float32 sensorHeight = winSize.height * 0.25;
    float32 sensorOffsetX = -winSize.width*2;
    float32 sensorOffsetY = -winSize.height/2;

    b2BodyDef bodyDef;
    bodyDef.type = b2_staticBody;
    bodyDef.position.Set(
        sensorOffsetX/PTM_RATIO + sensorWidth/2/PTM_RATIO,
        sensorOffsetY/PTM_RATIO + sensorHeight/2/PTM_RATIO);
    offscreenSensorBody = world->CreateBody(&bodyDef);

    b2PolygonShape shape;
    shape.SetAsBox(sensorWidth/2/PTM_RATIO, sensorHeight/2/PTM_RATIO);

    b2FixtureDef fixtureDef;
    fixtureDef.shape = &shape;
    fixtureDef.isSensor = true;
    fixtureDef.density = 0.0;

    offscreenSensorBody->CreateFixture(&fixtureDef);
}
```

This creates a large rectangular area below the level that can be used to detect if the
cart or Digger falls into that area.

Next, add some code to the bottom of your `update` method to check for the win and lose conditions, as shown in Listing 12.36.

Listing 12.36   **Scene4ActionLayer.mm (at the bottom of the update method)**

```
if (!gameOver) {
    if (isBodyCollidingWithObjectType(offscreenSensorBody, kCartType)) {
        gameOver = true;
        [uiLayer displayText:@"You Lose"
           andOnCompleteCallTarget:self selector:@selector(gameOver:)];
    } else if (isBodyCollidingWithObjectType(offscreenSensorBody,
                                             kDiggerType)) {
        gameOver = true;
        [uiLayer displayText:@"You Win!"
           andOnCompleteCallTarget:self selector:@selector(gameOver:)];
    }
}
```

This checks to see if the cart has collided with the offscreen sensor (which causes the player to lose) or if the Digger has collided with the offscreen sensor (which causes the player to win).

Next add the `gameOver` method as shown in Listing 12.37.

Listing 12.37   **Scene4ActionLayer.mm (before the update method)**

```
-(void)gameOver:(id)sender {
    [[GameManager sharedGameManager] runSceneWithID:kMainMenuScene];
}
```

Almost done! As the final step, add the lines shown in Listing 12.38 at the end of your `createLevel` method.

Listing 12.38   **Scene4ActionLayer.mm (at the end of the createLevel method)**

```
[self createDigger];
[self createGround3];
[self createGround3];
[self createOffscreenSensorBody];
```

That's it! Compile and run your code, and as you can see in Figure 12.11, if you can make it to the end of the level, you'll see Ole's menacing foe ready for battle!

Or maybe not so ready. Right now the poor Digger just sits there doing absolutely nothing. Since Ole deserves a more menacing nemesis than that, let's start making this Digger a bit more dangerous.

Figure 12.11   Ole first encountering the Digger robot

A Dangerous Digger

The Digger will move back and forth along the platform, switching directions every so often, while Ole tries to slam into the Digger from behind. If Ole is successful, he'll bump the Digger a bit toward the edge, but if he fails and collides with the drill, Ole takes some damage.

To implement this action, you add a new `updateStateWithDeltaTime` method inside the `Digger` class to check for collisions and implement game logic and a `changeState` method to switch between states such as drilling, walking, rotating, and taking damage. You also add a few animations to the Digger, for when the Digger rotates from left to right or successfully drills into Ole.

Start by opening *Digger.h* and add three new instance variables to keep track of when the Digger started moving in the current direction and the two animations for rotating and drilling, as shown in Listing 12.39.

Listing 12.39   **Digger.h (inside @interface)**

```
double movingStartTime;
CCAnimation *rotateAnim;
CCAnimation *drillAnim;
```

Next, switch to *Digger.mm* and add the imports listed in Listing 12.40 to the top of the file.

Listing 12.40   **Digger.mm (at the top of the file)**

```
#import "Cart.h"
#import "Box2DHelpers.h"
```

Then add the first part of the updateStateWithDeltaTime method, which contains most of the game logic for the Digger, as shown in Listing 12.41.

Listing 12.41   **Digger.mm (anywhere in class)**

```
- (void) updateStateWithDeltaTime:(ccTime)deltaTime
   andListOfGameObjects:(CCArray *)listOfGameObjects {
   // 1
   if ((characterState == kStateTakingDamage) &&
       ([self numberOfRunningActions] > 0)) {
      return;
   }

   // 2
   if (characterState == kStateDrilling &&
       [self numberOfRunningActions] == 0) {
      [self changeState:kStateRotating];
   }

   // 3
   if (characterState == kStateTakingDamage &&
       [self numberOfRunningActions] == 0) {
      wheelLJoint->SetMotorSpeed(0);
      wheelRJoint->SetMotorSpeed(0);
      [self changeState:kStateRotating];
   }

   // 4
   if (characterState != kStateWalking &&
       [self numberOfRunningActions] == 0) {
      [self changeState:kStateWalking];
   }
}
```

Let's go through this method section by section.

1. Check to see if the Digger is in the taking-damage state and has an action running (which would mean the blinking action is running). If this is the case, the method immediately returns because it shouldn't do anything else until the blinking animation finishes.

2. Check to see if the Digger is in the drilling state and has no actions running (which would mean the drilling animation has finished). If this is the case, it immediately rotates the Digger (so Ole has a chance to retaliate).

3. Check to see if the Digger is in the taking-damage state and has no actions running (which would mean the blinking action has finished). If this is the case, it stops the wheel motors to pause the Digger and switches the state to rotating (to give the Digger a chance to retaliate this time).

4. Check to see if the Digger is in any state but walking and has no running actions (which would happen when the rotating animation finishes, etc.). If this is the case, it changes the Digger to walking.

Next, wrap up the method by adding the remaining logic, shown in Listing 12.42.

Listing 12.42 **Digger.mm (at the end of updateStateWithDeltaTime)**

```
// 5
if (characterState == kStateWalking) {

    Cart *cart = (Cart *)
        [[self parent] getChildByTag:kVikingSpriteTagValue];
    b2Body *cartBody = cart.body;

    // 6
    double curTime = CACurrentMediaTime();
    double timeMoving = curTime - movingStartTime;
    static double TIME_TO_MOVE = 2.0f;

    // 7
    b2Body * drill = drillLBody;
    float direction = -1.0;
    if ([self flipX]) {
        drill = drillRBody;
        direction = -1 * direction;
    }

    // 8
    if (isBodyCollidingWithObjectType(drill, kCartType)) {
        [[SimpleAudioEngine sharedEngine] playEffect:@"drill.caf"];
        [cart changeState:kStateTakingDamage];
        [self changeState:kStateDrilling];
        wheelLJoint->SetMotorSpeed(0);
        wheelRJoint->SetMotorSpeed(0);
        cartBody->ApplyLinearImpulse(
          b2Vec2(direction * cart.fullMass * 8, -1.0 * cart.fullMass),
                cartBody->GetWorldPoint(b2Vec2(0, -15.0/100.0)));
    }
```

```
// 9
else if (isBodyCollidingWithObjectType(cartBody, kDiggerType)) {
    [[SimpleAudioEngine sharedEngine] playEffect:@"collision.caf"];
    [self changeState:kStateTakingDamage];
    cartBody->ApplyLinearImpulse(
        b2Vec2(-direction * cart.fullMass * 8, -1.0 * cart.fullMass),
            cartBody->GetWorldPoint(b2Vec2(0, -15.0/100.0)));
    body->ApplyLinearImpulse(
        b2Vec2(direction * body->GetMass() * 10, 0),
            body->GetWorldPoint(b2Vec2(0, -5.0/100.0)));
}

// 10
else if (timeMoving > TIME_TO_MOVE) {
    wheelLJoint->SetMotorSpeed(0);
    wheelRJoint->SetMotorSpeed(0);
    [self changeState:kStateRotating];
}

// 11
else {
    wheelLJoint->SetMotorSpeed(-1 * direction * M_PI * 3);
    wheelRJoint->SetMotorSpeed(-1 * direction * M_PI * 3);
}
}
```

Again, let's explore the rest of this method section by section.

5. Check to see if the Digger is in the walking state; the rest of the logic applies only if that is the case. Also grab a reference to Ole's cart by looking it up using the kVikingSpriteTagValue tag from the Digger's parent (the sprite batch node). Remember, when you added the tag to the sprite batch node earlier in this chapter, you set the tag to kVikingSpriteTagValue. This is an easy way to get a reference to a particular sprite.

6. Calculate how long the Digger has been moving in the current direction by subtracting the initial time the Digger started moving from the current time.

7. Figure out the direction the drill is moving in. Normally it moves left, since that is the way the sprite faces, but if the sprite is flipped (i.e., flipX is set), it moves right. Based on the direction, we get a reference to the drill sensor that should be active.

8. Check to see if the active drill is colliding with the cart. If it is, change the cart to the taking-damage state, change the drill to the drilling state, and also use an impulse to slightly "knock back" the cart.

9. Check to see if the cart is colliding with the drill. If it is, change the drill to the taking-damage state and use impulses to apply a slight "knock back" effect to both the cart and the Digger.

10. Check to see if the cart has moved in the current direction for a preset period of time, and if so, switch directions by switching to the rotating state.

11. If none of the above conditions are met, set the wheels of the Digger to move in the current direction as the default action.

Phew! You've made a lot of progress so far and are well on your way to having a cool boss fight! Just a few more steps to go.

The next thing you need is a method to change states and supporting methods for that method, as shown in Listing 12.43.

Listing 12.43 **Digger.mm (anywhere in class)**

```
-(void)disableDrills {
    drillLFixture->SetSensor(true);
    drillRFixture->SetSensor(true);
}


-(void)enableDrills {
    if ([self flipX]) {
        drillRFixture->SetSensor(false);
    } else {
        drillLFixture->SetSensor(false);
    }
}


-(void)changeState:(CharacterStates)newState {
    if (characterState == newState) return;

    [self stopAllActions];
    id action = nil;
    [self setCharacterState:newState];

    switch (newState) {
        case kStateTakingDamage:
            action = [CCBlink actionWithDuration:1.0 blinks:3.0];
            break;
        case kStateDrilling:
            action = [CCRepeat actionWithAction:
                [CCAnimate actionWithAnimation:drillAnim
                    restoreOriginalFrame:YES] times:3];
            break;
        case kStateWalking:
            movingStartTime = CACurrentMediaTime();
            break;
        case kStateRotating:
        {
```

```
        CCCallFunc *disableDrills =
            [CCCallFunc actionWithTarget:self
                selector:@selector(disableDrills)];
        CCAnimate *rotToCenter =
            [CCAnimate actionWithAnimation:rotateAnim
                restoreOriginalFrame:NO];
        CCFlipX *flip = [CCFlipX actionWithFlipX:!self.flipX];
        CCAnimate *rotToSide = (CCAnimate *) [rotToCenter reverse];
        CCCallFunc *enableDrills =
            [CCCallFunc actionWithTarget:self
                selector:@selector(enableDrills)];
        action = [CCSequence actions:disableDrills, rotToCenter,
                flip, rotToSide, enableDrills, nil];

        break;
    }
    default:
        break;
    }

    if (action != nil) {
        [self runAction:action];
    }
}
```

This method runs the appropriate visual effects for each change of state. For taking damage, the cart runs a blinking action. For drilling, it runs the drill animation. Rotating launches a sequence of actions: it first disables both drill sensors as the cart starts rotating, then runs a rotation animation to rotate to the center position, flips the sprite, runs the rotation animation again to face the other way, and reenables the appropriate drill.

Next, add a method to load the animations needed in this class, as shown in Listing 12.44.

Listing 12.44   **Digger.mm (before initWithWorld:atLocation)**

```
-(void)initAnimations {
    rotateAnim = [self loadPlistForAnimationWithName:@"rotateAnim"
        andClassName:NSStringFromClass([self class])];
    [[CCAnimationCache sharedAnimationCache] addAnimation:rotateAnim
name:@"rotateAnim"];

    drillAnim = [self loadPlistForAnimationWithName:@"drillAnim"
        andClassName:NSStringFromClass([self class])];
    [[CCAnimationCache sharedAnimationCache] addAnimation:drillAnim
name:@"drillAnim"];

}
```

This uses the same helper methods you've used before to create animations based on a property list. If you would like, you can look at the property list and compare it to the images in the sprite sheet to see how each animation is put together.

> **Note**
>
> The animations are added to the CCAnimationCache so that they are retained somewhere for future use. Alternatively, you could just retain these variables and release them in dealloc.

One final step! Just add the following call to the end of initWithWorld: atLocation to load the animations, as shown in Listing 12.45.

Listing 12.45   Digger.mm (at the end of initWithWorld:atLocation)

```
[self initAnimations];
```

That's it! Compile and run your code, and as you can see in Figure 12.12, now Ole can fight a forbidding foe!

Figure 12.12   Ole getting drilled by the digger

Finishing Touches: Adding a Cinematic Fight Sequence

The level is looking really good now. It has action, danger, cool physics effects, and even a boss fight! But let's make this even more awesome by adding a cinematic introduction to the final fight to add some spice and excitement to the level.

The idea is that when Ole approaches the final boss, action pauses for a moment, and the camera pans to the left to show the bridge that Ole just crossed go up in flames and drop to the ground! The camera then pans to reveal the boss menacingly approach Ole with the drill, and then again to the far side of the screen to reveal the pit where you can push the Digger off.

Not only does this make the level cooler, but it also explains to the player:

- This is a boss fight,
- This is the boss's location, and
- The way to defeat him is to push him off the cliff—

all without saying a word.

The good news is, you can do most of this with material that you've already learned in this book, such as how to move the camera and how to run actions. So let's dig in.

First, open *Scene4ActionLayer.h* and add the new instance variables shown in Listing 12.46.

Listing 12.46   Scene4ActionLayer.h (inside @implementation)

```
CCParticleSystem *fireOnBridge;
b2Body *finalBattleSensorBody;
bool inFinalBattle;
bool actionStopped;
```

These variables are a particle system used for the fire particle effect (more on this later), a sensor to detect when it's time to play the final battle animation, a Boolean to keep track of whether the player is in the final battle, and a Boolean to keep track of whether the action is temporarily stopped.

Next, switch to *Scene4ActionLayer.mm* and add a routine to create a sensor to detect if the player has reached a certain location, which triggers the start of the final battle sequence, as shown in Listing 12.47.

Listing 12.47   Scene4ActionLayer.mm (before createLevel)

```
- (void)createFinalBattleSensor {
    CGSize winSize = [CCDirector sharedDirector].winSize;
    float32 sensorWidth = winSize.width * 0.03;
    float32 sensorHeight = winSize.height;
    float32 sensorOffset = winSize.width * 0.15;

    b2BodyDef bodyDef;
    bodyDef.type = b2_staticBody;
    bodyDef.position.Set(
        groundMaxX/PTM_RATIO + sensorOffset/PTM_RATIO
            + sensorWidth/2/PTM_RATIO,
```

```
        sensorHeight/2/PTM_RATIO);
    finalBattleSensorBody = world->CreateBody(&bodyDef);

    b2PolygonShape shape;
    shape.SetAsBox(sensorWidth/2/PTM_RATIO, sensorHeight/2/PTM_RATIO);

    b2FixtureDef fixtureDef;
    fixtureDef.shape = &shape;
    fixtureDef.isSensor = true;
    fixtureDef.density = 0.0;

    finalBattleSensorBody->CreateFixture(&fixtureDef);
}
```

This is just a tall thin box that is placed right after the final bridge leading to the boss. When the player collides with it, the cinematic fight sequence begins.

Next, add a method to create a particle system that creates a fire effect to show the bridge burning, as shown in Listing 12.48.

Listing 12.48 Scene4ActionLayer.mm (after createFinalBattleSensor)

```
- (void)createParticleSystem {
    fireOnBridge = [CCParticleSystemQuad
        particleWithFile:@"fire.plist"];
    if (UI_USER_INTERFACE_IDIOM() == UIUserInterfaceIdiomPad) {
        fireOnBridge.position = ccp(groundMaxX - 400.0, 80);
    } else {
        fireOnBridge.position = ccp(groundMaxX - 200, 40);
    }
    [fireOnBridge stopSystem];
    [self addChild:fireOnBridge z:10];
}
```

This method is called right after adding the final bridge, so the particle system is located in the middle of the bridge. The particle system immediately stops after initialization, but it is started up again later when needed.

The particle system itself was generated with Particle Designer, and its definition is saved to a property list. You can read more about Particle Designer and creating particle systems in Chapter 14, "Particle Systems, Game Center, and Performance."

Next add the "meat" of the cinematic fight sequence code at the bottom of your update method, as shown in Listing 12.49.

Listing 12.49   **Scene4ActionLayer.mm (at the end of the update method)**

```
CGSize winSize = [CCDirector sharedDirector].winSize;
if (!inFinalBattle &&
    isBodyCollidingWithObjectType(finalBattleSensorBody, kCartType)) {

    inFinalBattle = true;
    actionStopped = true;
    [cart setMotorSpeed:0];
    cart.body->SetLinearVelocity(b2Vec2(0, 0));

    [self runAction:
     [CCSequence actions:
      [CCDelayTime actionWithDuration:1.0],
      [CCMoveBy actionWithDuration:0.5
            position:ccp(winSize.width * 0.6, 0)],
      [CCCallFunc actionWithTarget:self
                           selector:@selector(startFire)],
      [CCDelayTime actionWithDuration:2.0],
      [CCCallFunc actionWithTarget:self
                           selector:@selector(destroyBridge)],
      [CCDelayTime actionWithDuration:1.0],
      [CCMoveBy actionWithDuration:2.0
            position:ccp(-1 * winSize.width * 1.3, 0)],
      [CCDelayTime actionWithDuration:1.0],
      [CCCallFunc actionWithTarget:self
                           selector:@selector(playRoar)],
      [CCDelayTime actionWithDuration:1.0],
      [CCMoveBy actionWithDuration:2.0
            position:ccp(-1 * (winSize.width*6-winSize.width*0.7), 0)],
      [CCDelayTime actionWithDuration:1.0],
      [CCMoveBy actionWithDuration:2.0
            position:ccp(winSize.width*6, 0)],
      [CCCallFunc actionWithTarget:self
                           selector:@selector(backToAction)],
      nil]];
}
```

This first checks to see if the player collided with the final battle sensor. If the
player has, it marks that the player is in the final battle and that the game action is
stopped. Next, it sets the motor speed on the cart's wheels to 0, stops the layer from
following the player, and also uses SetLinearVelocity on the cart body to immediately stop the cart.

> **Note**
>
> SetLinearVelocity is a function that immediately sets the velocity of a Box2D body to a specified value. Usually, it is better to use impulses or forces to indirectly influence the velocity of an object rather than using SetLinearVelocity, because SetLinearVelocity can cause strange behavior with the physics engine. However, it's okay in cases in which you just want to immediately stop a body.

Once everything is stopped, it runs a sequence of actions. Specifically, the scene pans to the left, starts a fire on the bridge, destroys the bridge, pans back over to the boss and plays an evil roar sound effect, pans to the far side of the screen to reveal the pit, then pans back and starts the action back up. These are all done with Cocos2D actions, as you learned in Chapter 4, "Simple Collision Detection and the First Enemy."

Next, add the helper functions referenced earlier to start the fire, destroy the bridge, play the laugh, and return to action, as shown in Listing 12.50.

Listing 12.50   Scene4ActionLayer.mm (above the update method)

```
- (void)startFire {
    PLAYSOUNDEFFECT(FLAME_SOUND);
    [fireOnBridge resetSystem];
}

- (void)destroyBridge {
    [fireOnBridge stopSystem];
    world->DestroyJoint(lastBridgeStartJoint);
    lastBridgeStartJoint = NULL;
    world->DestroyJoint(lastBridgeEndJoint);
    lastBridgeEndJoint = NULL;
}

- (void)playRoar {
    PLAYSOUNDEFFECT(ENEMYDRILL_ROAR1);
}

- (void)backToAction {
    actionStopped = false;
    [self followCart];
}
```

These are pretty simple. The startFire method plays a fire sound effect and restarts the fire particle system; the destroyBridge method calls DestroyJoint to remove the two joints connecting the bridge to the ground (so it falls); playLaugh plays a sound; and backToAction disables the actionStopped flag and refollows the cart.

Next, you need to add some code to check for the `actionStopped` variable. If the variable is set, the layer shouldn't follow the cart and the cart shouldn't be able to move. So add a check to the top of both the `accelerometer:didAccelerate` and `followCart` methods, as shown in Listing 12.51.

Listing 12.51   **Scene4ActionLayer.mm (at the top of both accelerometer:didAccelerate and followCart)**

```
if (actionStopped) return;
```

One last step. Inside your `createLevel` method, immediately after the last call to `createBridge`, add two lines to create the particle system and add the final battle sensor—*important*—*immediately after the last call to* `createBridge`, as shown in Listing 12.52.

Listing 12.52   **Scene4ActionLayer.mm (in the createLevel method, immediately after the last call to createBridge)**

```
[self createParticleSystem];
[self createFinalBattleSensor];
```

Comment out the `setupDebugDraw` method if you like, and compile and run the code. As you can see in Figure 12.13, you should now have an action-packed, physics-enabled, side-scrolling level, complete with a cinematic boss fight!

Figure 12.13   The burning bridge in the cinematic boss fight

Summary

At this point you have created a side-scrolling action level with Box2D, complete with vehicles, motors, joints, collisions, enemy logic, cinematic effects, and more! You should now be familiar with how to use Box2D in real games and how to use the most important capabilities of the engine.

To learn more about Box2D, check out the Box2D manual available on the official Box2D site *(http://www.box2d.org)*. It contains a full reference to some additional features of Box2D that may be useful in your games, such as additional joint types, raycasting, and more. The Box2D forums are also a great source of knowledge and a good place to ask Box2D-related questions.

Hopefully these three chapters have gotten you excited about the possibilities of using Box2D in your games, and we look forward to seeing your Box2D-enabled games available at the App Store!

Challenges

1. Add some additional artificial intelligence to the boss enemy. For example, have him charge at Ole when Ole is nearby or stop moving to the right once he nears the edge of the level.

2. Due to space and time constraints, this chapter didn't implement an indicator of Ole's health in the UI layer or create a lose condition if Ole's health hits zero. Go ahead and implement these features to reinforce the material you've learned in earlier chapters.

3. Make another type of enemy and add it to the level. For example, maybe add a long pole of spikes connected to a revolute joint on the ground that tries to slam into the ground when Ole draws near.

The Chipmunk Physics Engine (No Alvin Required)

Now that you have experienced using Box2D to make a cart-racing-and-jumping level, you can see how using a game physics library allows you to add some amazing effects to your game.

One of the nice things about Cocos2D is that it comes with not one but two different 2D game physics libraries. You've tried Box2D already in Chapters 10, 11, and 12, so now it's time to try the other library: Chipmunk.

In this chapter, you use Chipmunk to create a Metroid-style platform jumping level (Figure 13.1), where Ole has to leap from platform to platform to escape the planet before it explodes. In the process, you learn how to use Chipmunk, how it differs from Box2D, and you'll be ready to use whichever library you prefer in your games.

If you haven't read Chapters 10, 11, and 12 yet, you should go through those chapters first, as this chapter builds on some of the concepts covered there.

So let's get to it—the clock is ticking!

Figure 13.1   The Chipmunk Metroid-style platform jumping level you'll make in this chapter

What Is Chipmunk?

Chipmunk is an open source 2D game physics library originally written by Scott Lembcke. Like Box2D, Chipmunk comes integrated with Cocos2D by default, so it is quite easy to use in your Cocos2D games. Its feature set is very similar to Box2D, and even works in the same way but has slightly different terminology:

- You start by creating a physics world (but it's called a "space" in Chipmunk) to place your physics bodies. You give Chipmunk time to simulate the space in each frame. Chipmunk then moves the bodies in the space with physics, and you update the positions of your sprites afterward based on the body locations.
- You add bodies and fixtures into the space (but fixtures are called "shapes" in Chipmunk). Just like in Box2D, you can have multiple shapes on a body if you have a particularly complicated object to model, and bodies and shapes do not have to match exactly to sprites.
- You add joints to restrict the movement of bodies (but joints are called "constraints" in Chipmunk, as they are a bit more generic in Chipmunk). Chipmunk has similar types of constraints to those in Box2D, but there are some important differences, which you learn about in this chapter.

The good news is that since you're already familiar with using Box2D, Chipmunk will be much easier to pick up! The engines are so similar that it's mostly a matter of learning the slightly different APIs to call in Chipmunk to accomplish the same effects.

In this chapter, you dive right into using Chipmunk and get hands-on experience with the most important concepts: creating a space, adding bodies and shapes to the space, adding constraints, and more.

Chipmunk versus Box2D

Considering that you have a choice between using either Chipmunk or Box2D as the physics engine in your Cocos2D game, you might wonder which you should use. It really comes down to a personal preference, so it's best to play around with both engines and then see which you prefer, which you can do by completing these chapters! However, here are a few differences between Chipmunk and Box2D to keep in mind:

- Chipmunk is written in C, while Box2D is written in C++. Some programmers are more comfortable with C than with C++ (or vice versa), so they may prefer working with one engine over another. In addition, Chipmunk has some helper Objective-C wrapper classes you can use if you want to avoid C and C++ entirely.
- Chipmunk does not require you to convert points to meters. Therefore, you don't need to use the point-to-meter ratio (PTM_RATIO) to convert your

coordinates in Chipmunk, which can make your code less error prone and easier to read.

- Chipmunk code is often more terse. The code to create the same effect in Chipmunk is often fewer lines of boilerplate than it is in Box2D, which can be nice when you want to quickly prototype your game.

- Box2D joints and Chipmunk constraints have some differences. For example, when you create a revolute joint in Box2D, you can also set limits on how much the joint can move and set a motor on the joint. In Chipmunk, to accomplish the same effect, you have to use three different constraints. Some effects are more difficult to accomplish in Chipmunk than they are in Box2D because of the additional options that Box2D joints have. However, Chipmunk has a few joints (such as a damped rotary spring or ratchet joint effects) that have no direct equivalent in Box2D.

- Box2D has a continuous collision detection feature that prevents objects from penetrating static objects such as the ground. In certain cases, your objects in Chipmunk might get stuck in static objects or even go through.

- Box2D seems more stable/weather torn. Take this with a grain of salt, as this is just my personal opinion/experience, but after working with both engines, I've encountered fewer oddities that I've had to work around with Box2D than I have with Chipmunk.

But no matter which engine you choose, you can't go wrong! You can accomplish most of the things you might want to do with either engine, both offer an amazing feature set and are easy to use, and both have a wealth of knowledge available on their forums as you begin to use them.

In this chapter, you get a chance to try out Chipmunk, and when you're done, you'll have experience using both Box2D and Chipmunk in a nontrivial level. That way you can pick which you like best for your game, and have fun!

Getting Started with Chipmunk

Before you can get started writing Chipmunk code, you need to make a placeholder scene for the level and hook it up to the Main Menu.

Much as you did in Chapter 11, "Intermediate Game Physics," you create two layers in this scene: a user interface (UI) layer and an action layer. For this level, the UI level contains the countdown timer until the planet explodes, and the action layer contains just about everything else.

First, make a class for the user interface layer. Control-click on the *Scenes* group in Xcode, select **New Group**, then rename the new folder that was created to *Scene5*. Then with the new *Scene5* group selected, go to **File > New > New File...**, choose **iOS > Cocoa Touch > Objective-C class**, and click **Next**. Enter *CCLayer* as the Subclass of, click **Next**, name the file *Scene5UILayer.m*, and click **Save**.

Replace *Scene5UILayer.h* with contents of Listing 13.1.

Listing 13.1   **Scene5UILayer.h**

```
#import "cocos2d.h"

@interface Scene5UILayer : CCLayer {
    CCLabelTTF *label;
}

- (void)displaySecs:(double)secs;

@end
```

Note that the UI layer contains a single label used for the countdown timer, and a method that the action layer uses to display the number of seconds remaining.

Next switch to *Scene5UILayer.m* and replace it with the contents of Listing 13.2.

Listing 13.2   **Scene5UILayer.m**

```
#import "Scene5UILayer.h"

@implementation Scene5UILayer

- (void)displaySecs:(double)secs {
    // 1
    secs = MAX(0, secs);

    // 2
    double intPart = 0;
    double fractPart = modf(secs, &intPart);
    int isecs = (int)intPart;
    int min = isecs / 60;
    int sec = isecs % 60;
    int hund = (int) (fractPart * 100);
    [label setString:[NSString stringWithFormat:@"%02d:%02d:%02d",
        min, sec, hund]];
}

- (id)init {
    if ((self = [super init])) {
        // 3
        CGSize winSize = [CCDirector sharedDirector].winSize;
        float fontSize = 40.0;
        if (UI_USER_INTERFACE_IDIOM() == UIUserInterfaceIdiomPad) {
            fontSize *= 2;
        }
```

```
        label = [CCLabelTTF labelWithString:@""
            fontName:@"AmericanTypewriter-Bold" fontSize:fontSize];
        label.anchorPoint = ccp(1, 1);
        label.position = ccp(winSize.width - 20, winSize.height - 20);
        [self addChild:label];
    }
    return self;
}
@end
```

Let's go through this section by section.

1. This makes the minimum number of seconds zero, because it wouldn't make sense to display a negative number of seconds in this scene. After all, when the time hits zero, it's explosion time!

2. This converts the seconds into three parts: minutes, seconds, and hundredths of seconds, and shows the results in the label as a formatted string. If you haven't seen the `modf` function before, it is a handy C-library function that breaks a double value into an integral part and a fractional part.

3. This creates the label (which is blank to start) and positions it near the upper right. Note that it sets the anchor point to `ccp(1,1)`, which is the top right. That way when it sets the position of the label later, that sets where the top right corner of the label is.

That's it for the UI layer, so now make a class for the action layer. With the *Scene5* group selected, go to **File > New > New File...**, choose **iOS > Cocoa Touch > Objective-C class**, and click **Next**. Enter *CCLayer* as the Subclass of, click **Next**, name the file *Scene5ActionLayer.m*, and click **Save**.

Replace *Scene5ActionLayer.h* with the contents of Listing 13.3.

Listing 13.3 Scene5ActionLayer.h

```
#import "cocos2d.h"

@class Scene5UILayer;

@interface Scene5ActionLayer : CCLayer {
    Scene5UILayer * uiLayer;
    double startTime;
}


- (id)initWithScene5UILayer:(Scene5UILayer *)scene5UILayer;

@end
```

This layer contains a reference to the UI layer and the time the layer started. It also contains an initializer that takes the UI layer as a parameter.

Now switch to *Scene5ActionLayer.m* and replace it with the contents of Listing 13.4.

Listing 13.4   **Scene5ActionLayer.m**

```
#import "Scene5ActionLayer.h"
#import "Scene5UILayer.h"

@implementation Scene5ActionLayer

- (id)initWithScene5UILayer:(Scene5UILayer *)scene5UILayer {
    if ((self = [super init])) {
        uiLayer = scene5UILayer;
        startTime = CACurrentMediaTime();
        [self scheduleUpdate];
    }
    return self;
}

- (void)update:(ccTime)dt {
    static double MAX_TIME = 60;
    double timeSoFar = CACurrentMediaTime() - startTime;
    double remainingTime = MAX_TIME - timeSoFar;
    [uiLayer displaySecs:remainingTime];
}

@end
```

`initWithScene5UILayer` stores the reference to the UI layer and the current time and schedules the `update` method to be called in each frame.

`update` first defines that Ole has 1 minute (60 seconds) to escape the planet. It figures out how much time Ole has been in the scene so far (by subtracting the start time from the current time), then figures out how much time is remaining and displays that value.

Next make use of these two new layers by creating a class for the scene. With the *Scene5* group selected, go to **File > New > New File...**, choose **iOS > Cocoa Touch > Objective-C class**, and click **Next**. Enter *CCScene* as the Subclass of, click **Next**, name the file *Scene5.m*, and click **Save**.

Replace *Scene5.h* with the contents of Listing 13.5.

Listing 13.5   **Scene5.h**

```
#import "cocos2d.h"

@interface Scene5 : CCScene {
}

@end
```

So far this is nothing but a subclass of CCScene. Now switch to *Scene5.m* and replace it with the contents of Listing 13.6.

Listing 13.6 **Scene5.m**

```
#import "Scene5.h"
#import "Scene5UILayer.h"
#import "Scene5ActionLayer.h"

@implementation Scene5

-(id)init {
    if ((self = [super init])) {
        Scene5UILayer * uiLayer = [Scene5UILayer node];
        [self addChild:uiLayer z:1];

        Scene5ActionLayer * actionLayer =
            [[[Scene5ActionLayer alloc]
                initWithScene5UILayer:uiLayer] autorelease];
        [self addChild:actionLayer z:0];
    }
    return self;
}

@end
```

This creates the UI layer and the action layer and passes the UI layer as a parameter to the action layer.

You're almost done. The last step is to hook the new scene into the GameManager. Switch to *GameManager.mm* and import *Scene5.h* at the top of the file, as shown in Listing 13.7.

Listing 13.7 **GameManager.mm (at top of file)**

```
#import "Scene5.h"
```

Then go to the runSceneWithID method and modify the case for kGameLevel5 to run your new scene, as shown in Listing 13.8.

Listing 13.8 **GameManager.mm (inside runSceneWithID's switch statement)**

```
case kGameLevel5:
    sceneToRun = [Scene5 node];
    break;
```

> **Tip**
>
> As mentioned in the previous chapters, you may wish to set up your app to run this new scene right away, since you'll be working with it a lot in this chapter. Again, to do this simply open *Classes\Singletons\SpaceVikingAppDelegate.m*, navigate to the bottom of `applicationDidFinishLaunching`, and replace the `CCDirector:runScene-WithID` call at the bottom to:
>
> ```
> [[GameManager sharedGameManager]
>     runSceneWithID:kGameLevel5];
> ```

That's it. Compile and run your code, and select **Escape!** from the main menu (unless you've set it up to run right away). You should see a countdown timer appear in the upper right (Figure 13.2), proving that you're making progress and that it's only a matter of time before everything goes boom.

Figure 13.2   The placeholder scene with the countdown timer for the level

It's also just a matter of time before you start writing some Chipmunk code. But before you can do that, you need to add the Chipmunk files to your project.

Adding Chipmunk into Your Project

With Finder, navigate to the folder where you downloaded Cocos2D and navigate to the *external\Chipmunk* subdirectory. Control-click the *Chipmunk* directory and select **Copy Chipmunk**.

Then navigate to your *SpaceViking* project folder and navigate to the *libs* subdirectory. Control-click the *libs* directory and select **Paste Item**. At this point, you should have the *Chipmunk* directory as a subdirectory of *SpaceViking\libs*, as shown in Figure 13.3.

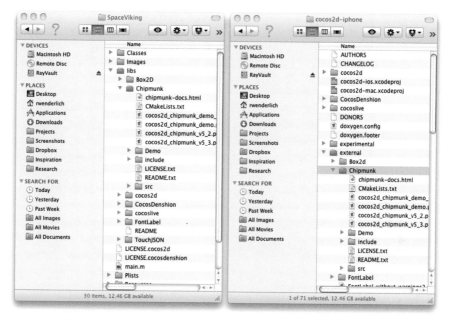

Figure 13.3   Copying the Chipmunk files to your project directory

The next step is adding these files to your Xcode project. Expand the *cocos2d Sources* group, then drag the *Chipmunk* folder from your *SpaceViking\libs* directory to the group. When the dialog appears, make sure **Copy items into destination group's folder (if needed)** is *not* checked, **Create groups for any added folders** is selected, and click **Finish**, as shown in Figure 13.4.

Figure 13.4   Adding the Chipmunk files to your Xcode project

Although you just added the entire Chipmunk directory, you actually only need the *include* and *src* subdirectories, so let's remove the references for the rest. To do this, expand your new *Chipmunk* group in Xcode and select all of the subfolders and files except for *include* and *src*. Control-click and choose delete, then choose **Remove References Only**, as shown in Figure 13.5.

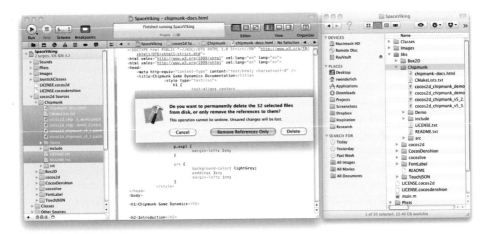

Figure 13.5   Removing all subfolders except for include and src

When you're done, your group tree in Xcode should look similar to Figure 13.6.

Figure 13.6   Your Chipmunk group in Xcode after adding the
Chipmunk files

One last step. Click on your *Space Viking* project in the Project Navigator to bring up your project settings, select the **Build Settings** tab, make sure the **All** and **Combined** buttons are selected, and look for the entry for **Search Paths > Header Search Paths**. Double-click the entry to bring up an editor, click the **Plus** button to add a new entry, double-click the entry for path, set it to *libs/Chipmunk/include/chipmunk* if you are using Xcode 3 or *SpaceViking/libs/Chipmunk/include/chipmunk* if you are using Xcode 4, and click **Done**. When you are done, the settings should look like Figure 13.7.

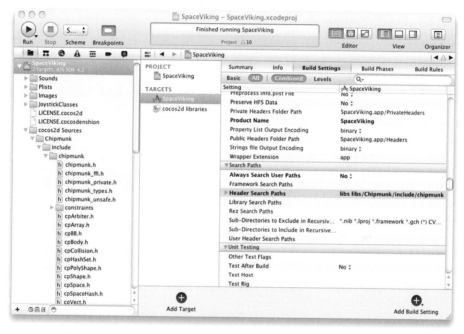

Figure 13.7   Adding the Chipmunk include directory to the cocos2d libraries target

Now compile your project; if it compiles, you've successfully integrated Chipmunk into your project. Now let's try it out and see how it works.

Creating a Basic Chipmunk Scene

Let's start simple by creating a basic Chipmunk scene. Here we create a Chipmunk space, add a simple box object to it, turn on debug drawing, and add a border at the bottom to prevent the box from falling off the screen.

Before you can use any Chipmunk functions, you need to call a method called *cpInitChipmunk* to initialize Chipmunk. This function needs to be called only once for the entire game, so a good place to put this is inside the `init` method for `GameManager`.

Switch to *GameManager.mm* and import *chipmunk.h* at the top of the file, as shown in Listing 13.9.

Listing 13.9   **GameManager.mm (at top of file)**

```
#import "chipmunk.h"
```

Then call `cpInitChipmunk` inside the `init` method, as shown in Listing 13.10.

Listing 13.10   **GameManager.mm (inside init method)**

```
cpInitChipmunk();
```

> **Note**
>
> `cpInitChipmunk` allocates some global data necessary for Chipmunk to run properly. If you forget to call `cpInitChipmunk`, your game will most likely crash with an `EXC_BAD_ACCESS` error the first time two objects collide.

Now that you've initialized Chipmunk, the next step is to create a Chipmunk space. A Chipmunk space is a "Chipmunk's view" of the physics objects it simulates, the equivalent of a Box2D world. You populate the space with Chipmunk bodies, let Chipmunk handle the simulation for you, then update your sprites according to the positions of the Chipmunk bodies.

As mentioned earlier, one difference between a Chipmunk space and a Box2D world is units. In Box2D, units are optimized for meters, so you have to convert points to meters with a point-to-meter ratio (`PTM_RATIO`). In Chipmunk, units can be whatever you want, so it's often simpler to use points directly as units rather than applying a conversion.

> **Note**
>
> Even though you can use points directly with Chipmunk, you still need to make sure the points you use are relative to the size of the current artwork. As in previous chapters, sometimes we'll be measuring offsets using the HD artwork, so we'll need to use different values for iPad and the iPhone.

Note that things won't compile yet because you still need to add some code; don't worry, you'll be able to compile again soon (when you get to Listing 13.16).

Next, switch to *Scene5ActionLayer.m* and add a method to create the space, as shown in Listing 13.11.

Listing 13.11   **Scene5ActionLayer.m (before initWithScene5UILayer)**

```
- (void)createSpace {
    space = cpSpaceNew();                                  // 1
```

```
    if (UI_USER_INTERFACE_IDIOM() == UIUserInterfaceIdiomPad) {
        space->gravity = ccp(0, -1500);                              // 2
    } else {
        space->gravity = ccp(0, -750);
    }
    cpSpaceResizeStaticHash(space, 400, 200);                        // 3
    cpSpaceResizeActiveHash(space, 200, 200);
}
```

It's important to understand everything that's going on here, so let's review it line by line:

1. This creates a new Chipmunk space by calling cpSpaceNew and stores the result in the space instance variable that you'll use later on.

2. Initializes the gravity for the Chipmunk space to a certain amount downward on the y-axis. The exact number here was chosen by play-testing and choosing what "felt right." Note that the gravity needs to be different on the iPad than on the iPhone due to the gravity being relative to the number of points on the screen.

3. To optimize collision detection, Chipmunk divides the space into a grid; that way if two objects are in different grid cells, Chipmunk can quickly determine that they don't collide. You can (and should) use cpSpaceResizeStaticHash and cpSpaceResizeActiveHash to tweak how large the grid sizes should be. It's best to have the size of the grid cells (the second parameter) be a little larger than the average size of an object you'll add to the scene and the number of grid cells (the third parameter) to be about 10 times the number of objects you'll add to the scene. Note that there is both a static hash (for static objects that do not move) and an active hash (for active objects that do move) that you can set separately.

Now that you have created a Chipmunk space, you write a method to add a simple box to the space at a particular location. To add an object to a Chipmunk space:

1. Create a Chipmunk body for the object and add it to the space.

2. Create one or more shapes for the Chipmunk body and add them to the space.

Let's see how this works. Write a new method to create a box, as shown in Listing 13.12.

Listing 13.12   Scene5ActionLayer.m (after createSpace)

```
- (void)createBoxAtLocation:(CGPoint)location {
    float boxSize = 60.0;
    float mass = 1.0;
    cpBody *body = cpBodyNew(mass,
        cpMomentForBox(mass, boxSize, boxSize));           // 1
    body->p = location;                                    // 2
```

```
    cpSpaceAddBody(space, body);                    // 3

    cpShape *shape =
    cpBoxShapeNew(body, boxSize, boxSize);          // 4
    shape->e = 0.0;                                 // 5
    shape->u = 0.5;                                 // 6
    cpSpaceAddShape(space, shape);                  // 7
}
```

Again, this is foundational knowledge that is important to understand, so let's step through this line by line:

1. Creates a new Chipmunk body for the box. It sets the mass of the box (how hard the box is to move) to 1.0 and uses a helper function to compute the moment of inertia for the box (how hard the box is to rotate). You should always use helper functions to compute the moment of inertia, as it's tricky to estimate by hand.

2. Sets the position of the body to be the passed-in location. Note that there is no need to convert units: you can just use points.

3. Adds the body to the Chipmunk space.

4. Creates a new shape for the box, associating it with the body. It uses a helper function to create the vertices for a rectangle shape. You can also use helper functions to create circle shapes (cpCircleShapeNew) or polygon shapes with arbitrary vertices (cpPolyShapeNew).

5. The e member variable on the body stands for elasticity (how bouncy the box is). Here it is set to 0.0 (no bounciness).

6. The f member variable on the body stands for friction (how much resistance the body gives when sliding across another). Here it is set to 0.5 for a medium amount of resistance.

7. Adds the shape to the Chipmunk space.

Now that you have a method to create a box, add a method to create the "level," which right now is just a single instance of that box, as shown in Listing 13.13.

Listing 13.13 Scene5ActionLayer.m (after createBoxAtLocation)

```
- (void)createLevel {
    CGSize winSize = [CCDirector sharedDirector].winSize;
    [self createBoxAtLocation:ccp(winSize.width * 0.5, winSize.height *
0.15)];
}
```

Next add a method to create a "ground" border along the bottom to prevent the box from falling off the screen due to gravity, as shown in Listing 13.14.

Listing 13.14   **Scene5ActionLayer.m (after createLevel)**

```
- (void)createGround {
    // 1
    CGSize winSize = [CCDirector sharedDirector].winSize;
    CGPoint lowerLeft = ccp(0, 0);
    CGPoint lowerRight = ccp(winSize.width, 0);

    groundBody = cpBodyNewStatic();                           // 2

    float radius = 10.0f;
    cpShape * shape = cpSegmentShapeNew(groundBody,
        lowerLeft, lowerRight, radius);                       // 3
    shape->e = 1.0f;                                          // 4
    shape->u = 1.0f;                                          // 5
    shape->layers ^= GRABABLE_MASK_BIT;                       // 6
    cpSpaceAddShape(space, shape);                            // 7
}
```

There's a lot of interesting new stuff here, so let's go through it section by section:

1. Computes the coordinates for the lower left and lower right of the screen based on the screen size.

2. This creates a Chipmunk body for the ground body by calling cpBodyNew-Static and stores the result in an instance variable you'll use later on. cpBodyNewStatic is used instead of cpBodyNew because this is a static object that should not move. Note that the body isn't actually added to the space, which is okay for static bodies like the ground that never need to move.

3. Creates a line segment shape from the lower left to the lower right by calling cpSegmentShapeNew, attaching it to the ground body created earlier. The last parameter is the radius of how wide to make the line segment; it's given a thickness of 10.0. This is a convenient feature in Chipmunk that is not present in Box2D (the ability to give an edge shape a thickness).

4. Sets the elasticity (how bouncy the ground is) to 1.0 (perfect bounciness).

5. Sets the friction of the ground to 1.0.

6. Removes the GRABABLE_MASK_BIT from the layers that this shape is in. This effectively prevents you from trying to move the ground with a mouse constraint, which you will learn more about later. If you forget to do this and are using mouse constraints, you may see Chipmunk crash with an unsolvable constraint error, since it is impossible to move a body with infinite mass.

7. Adds the shape to the Chipmunk space.

Next you need to give Chipmunk time to run each frame. To do so, add the contents of Listing 13.15 to the end of your update method.

Listing 13.15   **Scene5ActionLayer.m (at end of the update method)**

```
static double UPDATE_INTERVAL = 1.0f/60.0f;
static double MAX_CYCLES_PER_FRAME = 5;
static double timeAccumulator = 0;

timeAccumulator += dt;
if (timeAccumulator > (MAX_CYCLES_PER_FRAME * UPDATE_INTERVAL)) {
    timeAccumulator = UPDATE_INTERVAL;
}

while (timeAccumulator >= UPDATE_INTERVAL) {
    timeAccumulator -= UPDATE_INTERVAL;
    cpSpaceStep(space, UPDATE_INTERVAL);
}
```

This game loop is the fixed timestep game loop, similar to the game loop you added in Chapter 12, "Advanced Game Physics," but it calls `cpSpaceStep` in each frame rather than `world->Step`. Just as with Box2D, it is usually best to use a fixed timestep game loop like this in order to have a stable physics simulation.

Next you need to add debug draw support into the scene, so you can see the new shapes you're adding, and mouse support so you can move the objects by dragging. Most of the code you need for this is already contained in some handy support classes; you just need to add them to your project.

In Xcode, Control-click your *Classes* group, select **New Group**, and then rename the new folder to *Chipmunk*. Then open the folder for the resource files for this chapter and drag *cpMouse.c*, *cpMouse.h*, *drawSpace.c*, and *drawSpace.h* to the new *Chipmunk* group. Verify **Copy items into destination group's folder (if needed)** is checked, that only the **SpaceViking** target is checked, and click **Finish**, as shown in Figure 13.8.

Figure 13.8   Adding cpMouse.c/h and drawSpace.c/h from the resources files for this chapter

After you add the files, there's an important step to take to make sure they compile correctly. In Xcode, select *cpMouse.c*, and go to **View > Utilities > File Inspector**. Click on the **File Type** dropdown, and set it to **Objective-C source**, as you can see in Figure 13.9. Repeat the process with *drawSpace.c*.

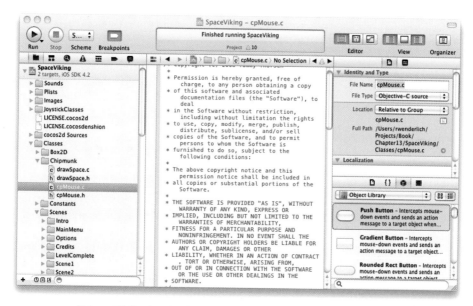

Figure 13.9   Setting file type of cpMouse.c and drawSpace.c to
Objective-C source

Switch to *Scene5ActionLayer.h* and import *chipmunk.h*, *cpMouse.h*, and *drawSpace.h* at the top of the file, as shown in Listing 13.16.

Listing 13.16   **Scene5ActionLayer.h (at top of file)**

```
#import "chipmunk.h"
#import "cpMouse.h"
#import "drawSpace.h"
```

Still inside *Scene5ActionLayer.h*, add the instance variables you need inside the interface declaration, as shown in Listing 13.17.

Listing 13.17   **Scene5ActionLayer.h (inside interface declaration)**

```
cpSpace *space;
cpBody *groundBody;
cpMouse *mouse;
```

Switch back to *Scene5ActionLayer.m* and implement your `draw` method to call Chipmunk's debug draw code in *drawSpace.c/h*, as shown in Listing 13.18.

Listing 13.18   Scene5ActionLayer.m (after update method)

```
- (void)draw {
    drawSpaceOptions options = {
        0,      // drawHash
        0,      // drawBBs
        1,      // drawShapes
        4.0f,   // collisionPointSize
        0.0f,   // bodyPointSize
        1.5f,   // lineThickness
    };
    drawSpace(space, &options);
}
```

This method calls the helper code contained in *debugDraw.c/h* to draw representations of the Chipmunk physics objects to the screen so you can visualize what's going on in the physics simulation. You can configure what to show in the `drawSpace-Options` structure. In this example, it turns on drawing of the shapes, sets the point that is drawn to indicate collisions to have a size of 4 points, and sets the general line thickness to be 1.5 points.

Next, add some touch-handling code that uses some helper functions in *cpMouse.c/h* to enable you to move objects by dragging, as shown in Listing 13.19.

Listing 13.19   Scene5ActionLayer.m (after draw method)

```
- (void)registerWithTouchDispatcher {
    [[CCTouchDispatcher sharedDispatcher] addTargetedDelegate:self
        priority:0 swallowsTouches:YES];
}

- (BOOL)ccTouchBegan:(UITouch *)touch withEvent:(UIEvent *)event {
    CGPoint touchLocation = [self convertTouchToNodeSpace:touch];
    cpMouseGrab(mouse, touchLocation, false);
    return YES;
}

- (void)ccTouchMoved:(UITouch *)touch withEvent:(UIEvent *)event {
    CGPoint touchLocation = [self convertTouchToNodeSpace:touch];
    cpMouseMove(mouse, touchLocation);
}

- (void)ccTouchEnded:(UITouch *)touch withEvent:(UIEvent *)event {
    cpMouseRelease(mouse);
}
```

This registers the node with the touch dispatcher to receive the callbacks, then for each callback, it calls the appropriate helper routine in *cpMouse.c/h* to enable mouse movement for this scene. Note how you have to convert the touches to node coordinates as usual before passing them on to the helper routines.

You're almost done! To wrap things up, add the code to call the new methods you wrote at the end of `initWithScene5UILayer`, as shown in Listing 13.20.

Listing 13.20   **Scene5ActionLayer.m (at end of initWithScene5UILayer)**

```
[self createSpace];
[self createGround];
mouse = cpMouseNew(space);
self.isTouchEnabled = YES;
[self createLevel];
```

This calls the functions you wrote to create the space and ground, initializes the mouse joint, sets the layer as accepting touches, and calls the method to create the level (which right now contains just a single box).

Compile and run your code, and you should be able to see a box fall down into your scene. You should also be able to move the box around by dragging it with your finger, as you can see in Figure 13.10.

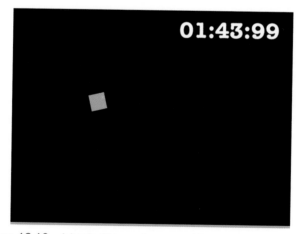

Figure 13.10   A basic Chipmunk scene with a space, body, shape, mouse joint movement, and debug drawing

Believe it or not, now you already know how to use some of the most important features of Chipmunk:

- How to create a space
- How to add a body and shape to the space

- How to enable debug drawing
- How to use mouse joint support

Based on this knowledge, you could use Chipmunk to make the puzzle level you created with Box2D in Chapter 10, "Basic Game Physics," except for one piece: how to map a sprite to the Chipmunk body. So let's learn this by bringing our hero back into action and enabling him to run and leap to safety.

Adding Sprites and Making Them Move

It's time to add a sprite for Ole into this level, but before you do, let's review the approach.

In Chapters 10, 11, and 12, you made the Box2D bodies line up very closely to the shapes of the sprites. You then looped through each Box2D body in the scene and updated the associated sprite to be in the same position as the body.

In this chapter, you take a different approach. You make the shape representing Ole just a small box toward his feet, since you don't really care about the collisions with the rest of his body, and that shape is simple to work with. Also, instead of looping through all of the physics bodies, you go the other way around: you loop through each of the sprites and their position based on the appropriate physics body. This is a preferred method of working, since it doesn't make the assumption that a sprite maps one-to-one to a physics body.

Much as you did in Chapter 11, you create a base class for all sprites that are related to Chipmunk bodies in order to contain some of the common code.

So let's get started by creating this class! Control-click on the *Classes\GameObjects* group in Xcode, select **New Group**, then rename the new folder *Chipmunk*. Then with the new *Chipmunk* group selected, go to **File > New > New File...**, choose **iOS > Cocoa Touch > Objective-C class**, and click **Next**. Enter *GameCharacter* as the Subclass of, click **Next**, name the file *CPSprite.m*, and click **Save**.

Replace *CPSprite.h* with the contents of Listing 13.21.

Listing 13.21 **CPSprite.h**

```
#import "cocos2d.h"
#import "chipmunk.h"
#import "GameCharacter.h"

@interface CPSprite : GameCharacter {
    cpBody * body;
    cpShape * shape;
    cpSpace * space;
}
```

```
- (void)addBoxBodyAndShapeWithLocation:(CGPoint)location
    size:(CGSize)size
    space:(cpSpace *)theSpace
    mass:(cpFloat)mass
    e:(cpFloat)e
    u:(cpFloat)u
    collisionType:(cpCollisionType)collisionType
    canRotate:(BOOL)canRotate;

@end
```

Note the base class defines a single body and shape for the sprite and keeps a reference to the Chipmunk space. It also has a superlong helper method to create a box body and shape based on several passed in values.

Next replace *CPSprite.m* with the contents of Listing 13.22.

Listing 13.22   **CPSprite.m**

```
#import "CPSprite.h"

@implementation CPSprite

-(void)updateStateWithDeltaTime:(ccTime)deltaTime
    andListOfGameObjects:(CCArray*)listOfGameObjects {
    self.position = ccp(body->p.x, body->p.y);
    self.rotation = CC_RADIANS_TO_DEGREES( -body->a );
}

- (void)addBoxBodyAndShapeWithLocation:(CGPoint)location
    size:(CGSize)size
    space:(cpSpace *)theSpace
    mass:(cpFloat)mass
    e:(cpFloat)e
    u:(cpFloat)u
    collisionType:(cpCollisionType)collisionType
    canRotate:(BOOL)canRotate {

    space = theSpace;

    float moment = INFINITY;
    if (canRotate) {
        moment = cpMomentForBox(mass, size.width, size.height);
    }

    body = cpBodyNew(mass, moment);
    body->p = location;
```

```
    cpSpaceAddBody(space, body);

    shape = cpBoxShapeNew(body, size.width, size.height);
    shape->e = e;
    shape->u = u;
    shape->collision_type = collisionType;
    shape->data = self;
    cpSpaceAddShape(space, shape);
}

@end
```

This first implements `updateStateWithDeltaTime` to update the position of the sprite based on the position of the Chipmunk body.

Then `addBoxBodyAndShapeWithLocation` creates a Chipmunk body and shape based on the passed in values, in the way you created the box shape earlier in this chapter. Note that if `canRotate` is false, the body is given an infinite moment of inertia, which makes the body unable to rotate.

Note that the `data` variable on the shape is set to `self`, so that a pointer to the class can be found if you just have the shape (which you'll need later on). Also note that the `collisionType` of the body is set to a passed in value. You'll be learning more about collision types and what they mean later in this chapter.

Now that you have your handy new `CPSprite` class, you create a subclass to represent Ole. With the *Classes\GameObjects\Chipmunk* group selected, go to **File > New > New File...**, choose **iOS > Cocoa Touch > Objective-C class**, and click **Next**. Enter *CPSprite* as the Subclass of, click **Next**, name the file *CPViking.m*, and click **Save**.

Replace *CPViking.h* with the contents of Listing 13.23.

Listing 13.23   **CPViking.h**

```
#import "CPSprite.h"

@interface CPViking : CPSprite {
}

- (id)initWithLocation:(CGPoint)location space:(cpSpace *)space
    groundBody:(cpBody *)groundBody;

@end
```

Not much to see here: this just subclasses `CPSprite` and defines an initializer for the class. Next switch to *CPViking.m* and replace it with the contents of Listing 13.24.

Listing 13.24   **CPViking.m**

```objc
#import "CPViking.h"

@implementation CPViking

- (id)initWithLocation:(CGPoint)location space:(cpSpace *)theSpace
    groundBody:(cpBody *)groundBody {
    if ((self = [super initWithSpriteFrameName:@"sv_anim_1.png"])) {
        CGSize size;
        if (UI_USER_INTERFACE_IDIOM() == UIUserInterfaceIdiomPad) {
            size = CGSizeMake(60, 60);
            self.anchorPoint = ccp(0.5, 30/self.contentSize.height);
        } else {
            size = CGSizeMake(30, 30);
            self.anchorPoint = ccp(0.5, 15/self.contentSize.height);
        }
        [self addBoxBodyAndShapeWithLocation:location
            size:size space:theSpace mass:1.0 e:0.0 u:0.5
            collisionType:0 canRotate:TRUE];
    }
    return self;
}

@end
```

This class represents Ole's sprite and will eventually contain the game logic for Ole's movement and behavior. In this level, the Chipmunk body does not match up exactly to Ole's size for this level. Instead, the Chipmunk body is just a smallish box toward the bottom of Ole's feet. This is because you don't really care about what the top of Ole's body collides with in this level, and it makes for nicer game behavior, as a short box is less likely to tip over than a long rectangular box.

> **Note**
>
> If you do care about the collisions with the top half of Ole, one good solution is to add a second shape to the same Chipmunk body for his upper half. This way, you can still use the box shape on the bottom for setting surface velocity for more stable player movement, as you'll see later on in this chapter.

The first thing the `initWithLocation` method does is set the sprite frame to Ole's "standing still" position. It then sets the anchor point to be in the middle of the sprite along the x-axis and 30 (or 15 for the iPhone) points from the bottom along the y-axis (since the goal is to match the anchor point with the center of the Chipmunk body). Finally, it calls the `addBoxBodyAndShapeWithLocation` method you wrote earlier in CPSprite to create a 60 × 60 (or 30 × 30 for the iPhone) box representing Ole.

> **Note**
>
> If you're still confused about why the anchor point was set, remember that the anchor point is the offset within the sprite that represents its position. For this sprite, you are creating a 60 × 60 box toward the bottom of the sprite, so you want the sprite's position to match up with the center of the box (i.e., the Chipmunk body's position). Since anchor point's values range from 0 to 1 (a percentage of the sprite's width/height), you divide 30 points by the height of the sprite to get the percentage.

Now, let's integrate this new class into the level. Switch to *Scene5ActionLayer.h* and add the declaration for `CPViking` above the interface declaration, as shown in Listing 13.25.

Listing 13.25   Scene5ActionLayer.h (above interface declaration)

```
@class CPViking;
```

Then add two new instance variables you'll need for the `viking` sprite and the scene's sprite batch node, as shown in Listing 13.26.

Listing 13.26   Scene5ActionLayer.h (inside interface declaration)

```
CPViking *viking;
CCSpriteBatchNode *sceneSpriteBatchNode;
```

Switch to *Scene5ActionLayer.m* and import *CPViking.h* at the top of the file, as shown in Listing 13.27.

Listing 13.27   Scene5ActionLayer.m (at top of file)

```
#import "CPViking.h"
```

Next go to the `initWithScene5UILayer` method and add the contents of Listing 13.28 right before the call to `createLevel`. Note that it is important to add it before `createLevel`, because later on `createLevel` will assume the sprite sheet was created beforehand.

Listing 13.28   Scene5ActionLayer.m (in initWithScene5UILayer, right before call to createLevel)

```
if (UI_USER_INTERFACE_IDIOM() == UIUserInterfaceIdiomPad) {
    [[CCSpriteFrameCache sharedSpriteFrameCache]
     addSpriteFramesWithFile:@"scene5atlas-hd.plist"];
    sceneSpriteBatchNode = [CCSpriteBatchNode
                            batchNodeWithFile:@"scene5atlas-hd.png"];
```

```
    viking = [[[CPViking alloc] initWithLocation:ccp(200,200)
        space:space groundBody:groundBody] autorelease];
} else {
    [[CCSpriteFrameCache sharedSpriteFrameCache]
     addSpriteFramesWithFile:@"scene5atlas.plist"];
    sceneSpriteBatchNode = [CCSpriteBatchNode
                        batchNodeWithFile:@"scene5atlas.png"];
    viking = [[[CPViking alloc] initWithLocation:ccp(100,100)
        space:space groundBody:groundBody] autorelease];
}
[self addChild:sceneSpriteBatchNode z:0];
[sceneSpriteBatchNode addChild:viking z:2];
```

This creates the sprite batch node for this level and stores it in an instance variable. It then creates a CPViking object, using the initializer you just wrote, and adds it to the sprite batch node.

Speaking of the sprite batch node, go ahead and drag *scene5atlas.png*, *scene5atlas.plist*, *scene5atlas-hd.png*, and *scene5atlas-hd.plist* from the resources files for this chapter into the *Images* group. Make sure **Copy items into destination group's folder (if needed)** is checked when you do so.

One last step. You need to call the update method on each of the GameObjects in your scene, so add the code to your update method, as shown in Listing 13.29.

Listing 13.29 Scene5ActionLayer.m (at bottom of update method)

```
CCArray *listOfGameObjects = [sceneSpriteBatchNode children];
for (GameCharacter *tempChar in listOfGameObjects) {
    [tempChar updateStateWithDeltaTime:dt
                andListOfGameObjects:listOfGameObjects];
}
```

Compile and run, and you should see Ole in your scene with a small box tied to the bottom of his feet, as shown in Figure 13.11.

He acts a little weird if right now you move him around with the mouse joint, but that's okay because you're about to enable Ole to run and jump his way off this planet. For this level, you move Ole by tilting the device left and right and make him jump by tapping the screen.

But before you dive into code, let's take a moment to discuss some Chipmunk concepts you need to know to implement his movement.

Figure 13.11   Ole sprite added to scene, mapped to a (smaller)
Chipmunk object

Jumping by Directly Setting Velocity

In the mine cart level you made in Chapters 11 and 12, you implemented jumping by applying an impulse to the Box2D body. You can apply forces and impulses in Chipmunk as well, but for this level you take a different approach: you implement jumping by setting the velocity of the sprite directly.

One of the nice things about Chipmunk is that it works well with directly setting the velocity of bodies, which can be really convenient for player controls like this. Setting the velocity of a body is easy: you just call a function like the one in Listing 13.30.

Listing 13.30   **Example of directly setting velocity**

```
cpBodySetVel(body, newVel);
```

For the y velocity of Ole, this function is set to a hardcoded value as long as Ole is jumping. For this level, the longer the player's finger is held down, the higher Ole will jump. So basically, the y velocity is set to the hardcoded value as long as the finger is held down, up until a maximum number of seconds. This makes it a little more fun for the player, as he or she can make both short jumps and longer jumps.

For the x velocity of Ole, this function is set based on the amount the device is currently tilted while Ole is in the air. This is a nice trait to have, so the player can reverse Ole's direction in midjump.

Ground Movement by Setting Surface Velocity

Chipmunk has a neat property you can set on objects called surface velocity that works nicely for conveyor belt effects or for character controls such as this.

Basically, the surface velocity for an object represents the speed at which the surface of the object itself is moving. You can set it to make an object slide along the ground or move across a conveyor belt.

For this level, when Ole is on the ground, you will set the surface velocity to move Ole based on accelerometer input. This is more convenient than modifying Ole's velocity directly, so that his velocity does not affect the speed of moving platforms and so on. Setting the surface velocity is quite easy, as you can see in Listing 13.31.

Listing 13.31 **Example of setting surface velocity**

```
shape->surface_v = newSurfaceVel;
```

Detecting Collisions with the Ground

Since you're going to move Ole in different ways based on whether he's in the air or on the ground, you need to know when Ole is colliding with the ground.

Detecting collisions is very easy with Chipmunk. You first set the `collisionType` of each shape to a number representing the type of shape it is, so you can refer to it later. For this level, you set the ground and platforms as one number (`kCollision-TypeGround`) and Ole as another number (`kCollisionTypeViking`).

The next step is to tell Chipmunk what collision-related events you are interested in by specifying one or more callback functions. The events you can register for are:

- **Begin:** Called when two objects start colliding. In your handler for this event, you can return false to make Chipmunk permanently ignore the collision. This can be handy to have fine-grained control of which objects collide with each other, as Chipmunk's built-in collision filtering is somewhat limited.

- **PreSolve:** Called each frame while two objects are touching, immediately before Chipmunk calculates the collision response for the two objects. In your handler for this event, you can return false to make Chipmunk ignore this collision for the current frame only. This can be useful to implement if you want the collisions ignored sometimes but not always (such as you'll be doing in this level for one-way platforms!). It is also a good spot where you can modify collision-related values such as elasticity or friction.

- **PostSolve:** Called each frame while two objects are touching, immediately after Chipmunk calculates the collision response for the two objects. This is a good place to put code that relies on how hard two objects collide against each other, such as playing a sound effect with its volume based on the collision force.

- **Separate:** Called when two objects separate and are no longer colliding.

In this level, you use collision detection callbacks for two reasons: (1) to detect if the player is currently on the ground, by implementing the `Begin` and `Separate` callbacks, and (2) to allow the player to jump through the bottom of a one-way platform, by implementing the `PreSolve` callback.

> **Note**
>
> The callback functions you write are C functions, so you can't access member variables from your class in these functions. A common workaround is to pass your game object as a parameter, and then access properties on your object or call a method on it.
>
> Also note that you cannot delete Chipmunk objects directly from these callback functions (or Chipmunk will likely crash). Instead, you should use the `cpSpaceAddPostStep-Callback` function to schedule a callback to be called when it's safe to delete Chipmunk objects, passing in parameters for the objects you wish to delete. This is useful when you want to delete objects in the case of a collision (such as bullets intersecting a monster).

Chipmunk Arbiter and Normals

When you receive callbacks from Chipmunk for collision events, you get passed a data structure called `cpArbiter` that contains useful information on the collision.

The `cpArbiter` structure contains a list of all of the points where the two objects are colliding, and each collision point has a useful value called a normal, which is a vector perpendicular to the contact point, in the direction of the collision.

This is quite useful to detect if Ole is colliding with the top of a platform or the bottom of the platform. As you will see in the following code, we use this structure to allow Ole to jump through the bottom of a platform but still collide with the top.

Implementation—Collision Detection

Now that you are armed with some background knowledge, let's try this out and get Ole moving.

The first step is to add the code to detect when Ole is hitting the ground and when he isn't and to allow Ole to jump through the bottom of platforms. Open *Classes\Constants\Constants.h* and add a new `enum` for the collision types you need for this level, as shown in Listing 13.32.

Listing 13.32   **Constants.h (add to bottom of file)**

```
typedef enum {
    kCollisionTypeGround = 0x1,
    kCollisionTypeViking
} CollisionType;
```

Then, switch to *CPViking.m* and modify your call to `addBoxBodyAndShapeWith-Location` to specify the new collision type for Ole instead of 0, as shown in Listing 13.33.

Listing 13.33 **CPViking.m (modify call to addBoxBodyAndShapeWithLocation in initWithLocation)**

```
[self addBoxBodyAndShapeWithLocation:location
    size:size space:theSpace mass:1.0 e:0.0 u:1.0
    collisionType:kCollisionTypeViking canRotate:TRUE];
```

Similarly, switch to *Scene5ActionLayer.m* and set the collision type for the ground shape created in `createGround`, as shown in Listing 13.34.

Listing 13.34 **Scene5ActionLayer.m (before calling cpSpaceAddShape in createGround)**

```
shape->collision_type = kCollisionTypeGround;
```

Next let's convert the dynamic shape you added to the level into a static platform so you can test that the one-way platform code you're about to add works. Replace `createBoxAtLocation` with the contents of Listing 13.35.

Listing 13.35 **Scene5ActionLayer.m (replace createBoxAtLocation)**

```
- (void)createBoxAtLocation:(CGPoint)location {
    cpFloat hw, hh;
    if (UI_USER_INTERFACE_IDIOM() == UIUserInterfaceIdiomPad) {
        hw = 100.0/2.0f;
        hh = 10.0/2.0f;
    } else {
        hw = 50.0/2.0f;
        hh = 5.0/2.0f;
    }

    cpVect verts[] = {
        cpv(-hw,-hh),
        cpv(-hw, hh),
        cpv( hw, hh),
        cpv( hw,-hh),
    };

    cpShape *shape = cpPolyShapeNew(groundBody, 4, verts, location);
    shape->e = 1.0;
    shape->u = 1.0;
    shape->collision_type = kCollisionTypeGround;
    cpSpaceAddShape(space, shape);
}
```

> **Note**
>
> This method is a good example of how to create shapes with arbitrary vertices by using `cpPolyShapeNew`, passing in an array of vertices. If you wanted to, you could use Vertex Helper to trace exact shapes and create bodies based on those shapes, just as you did in Chapter 11. However, note that for Chipmunk, vertices must be defined in clockwise order (rather than counterclockwise as with Box2D).

Now that each of the shapes in the scene has the correct collision type set, you can set up some callback functions to be called when Ole hits or separates from the ground shapes.

The callbacks keep track of which ground shapes Ole is currently colliding with at any given time. Open *CPViking.h* and add an instance variable to store the array of ground shapes, as shown in Listing 13.36.

Listing 13.36 **CPViking.h (inside interface declaration)**

```
cpArray *groundShapes;
```

While you're there, also add a property for the ground shapes array, since you need to access it from outside the class (in the C-function callbacks), as shown in Listing 13.37.

Listing 13.37 **CPViking.h (after interface declaration)**

```
@property (readonly) cpArray *groundShapes;
```

Switch to *CPViking.m* and synthesize your new property, as shown in Listing 13.38.

Listing 13.38 **CPViking.m (right after @implementation)**

```
@synthesize groundShapes;
```

Then add the code to initialize the `groundShapes` array and register for the collision callbacks inside your `initWithLocation` method, as shown in Listing 13.39.

Listing 13.39 **CPViking.m (at end of initWithLocation)**

```
groundShapes = cpArrayNew(0);
cpSpaceAddCollisionHandler(space, kCollisionTypeViking,
    kCollisionTypeGround, begin, preSolve, NULL, separate, NULL);
```

This registers for three of the four possible collision-related events for Ole colliding with the ground: the `begin`, `preSolve`, and `separate` events. Go ahead and write these methods next, as shown in Listing 13.40.

Listing 13.40 **CPViking.m (before initWithLocation)**

```
static cpBool begin(cpArbiter *arb, cpSpace *space, void *ignore) {
    CP_ARBITER_GET_SHAPES(arb, vikingShape, groundShape);    // 1
    CPViking *viking = (CPViking *)vikingShape->data;        // 2
    cpVect n = cpArbiterGetNormal(arb, 0);                   // 3
    if (n.y < 0.0f) {                                        // 4
        cpArray *groundShapes = viking.groundShapes;         // 5
        cpArrayPush(groundShapes, groundShape);
    }
    return cpTrue;
}

static cpBool preSolve(cpArbiter *arb, cpSpace *space, void *ignore) {
    if(cpvdot(cpArbiterGetNormal(arb, 0), ccp(0,-1)) < 0){    // 6
        return cpFalse;
    }
    return cpTrue;
}

static void separate(cpArbiter *arb, cpSpace *space, void *ignore) {
    CP_ARBITER_GET_SHAPES(arb, vikingShape, groundShape);    // 7
    CPViking *viking = (CPViking *)vikingShape->data;
    cpArrayDeleteObj(viking.groundShapes, groundShape);
}
```

Overall, the begin method detects when Ole is colliding with the top of a platform (and adds it to an array if so), and the separate method removes the platform from the array. The preSolve method is responsible for ignoring any collisions Ole has with the bottom of platforms.

There's a good bit of new material here, so let's go over it step by step:

1. This is a helper macro that declares variables for the two shapes involved in the collision, naming them vikingSprite and groundShape. Note that the order of the shapes is the same as the order of the collision types that you passed into cpSpaceAddCollisionHandler.

2. Retrieves the pointer to the CPViking object from the data pointer in the shape. Remember that you set the data pointer of the shape to self when you created the shape in CPSprite's addBoxBodyAndShapeWithLocation method. Also remember that this is a C function, so it doesn't have access to the instance variables of the CPViking class, which is why you need to do this.

3. Gets the normal vector for the first contact point. Remember that a normal is a vector perpendicular to the contact point, in the direction of the collision.

4. If the y component of the normal vector is less than 0, Ole is colliding with the top of the platform.

5. Any time Ole is colliding with the top of the platform, this adds it to the list of shapes Ole is currently colliding with.

6. This tests to see if Ole is jumping through the bottom of the platform and, if so, cancels the collision response by returning false. Otherwise it returns true to have Chipmunk continue to process the collision response.

7. The separate method removes the ground shape from the array of shapes currently in contact if it is present.

At this point, the `Viking` class has a list of all of the ground shapes that Ole is currently in contact with, and it allows Ole to jump through the bottom of platforms. Well, if he could jump, that is! So let's add this capability next.

> **Note**
>
> This is just one of several ways to detect if an object is colliding with the ground. I chose to cover this method in this chapter because I thought it was a good introduction to the various callback methods available in Chipmunk.
>
> Another method suggested by Scott Lembcke, the creator of Chipmunk, is to keep a Boolean flag on the object and set it to false before stepping the Chipmunk space (as long as the body isn't sleeping). Then, register a presolve callback on the object and the ground, and set it back to true if the collision normal is pointing upward. The advantage of this method is only one callback is necessary rather than three like in the example.

Implementation—Movement and Jumping

The first thing you need to do to implement movement and jumping is add a few new instance variables to *CPViking.h*, as shown in Listing 13.41.

Listing 13.41   **CPViking.h (inside interface declaration)**

```
double jumpStartTime;
float accelerationFraction;
```

These variables keep track of the most recent time Ole began jumping and the fraction Ole should accelerate based on accelerometer input (between −1 and 1).

While you're there, also predeclare a few methods, as shown in Listing 13.42.

Listing 13.42   **CPViking.h (after interface declaration)**

```
- (void)accelerometer:(UIAccelerometer*)accelerometer
    didAccelerate:(UIAcceleration*)acceleration;
- (BOOL)ccTouchBegan:(UITouch *)touch withEvent:(UIEvent *)event;
- (void)ccTouchEnded:(UITouch *)touch withEvent:(UIEvent *)event;
```

Note that these are the methods that accept accelerometer and touch input; you need to forward the accelerometer and touch input from the action layer straight to the CPViking class for processing. Now switch to *CPViking.m* and implement those methods, as shown in Listing 13.43.

Listing 13.43   **CPViking.m (after initWithLocation)**

```
- (BOOL)ccTouchBegan:(UITouch *)touch withEvent:(UIEvent *)event {
    if (groundShapes->num > 0) {
        jumpStartTime = CACurrentMediaTime();
    }
    return TRUE;
}


- (void)ccTouchEnded:(UITouch *)touch withEvent:(UIEvent *)event {
    jumpStartTime = 0;
}


- (void)accelerometer:(UIAccelerometer*)accelerometer
    didAccelerate:(UIAcceleration*)acceleration {
    accelerationFraction = acceleration.y*2;
    if (accelerationFraction < -1) {
        accelerationFraction = -1;
    } else if (accelerationFraction > 1) {
        accelerationFraction = 1;
    }
    if ([[CCDirector sharedDirector] deviceOrientation] ==
        UIDeviceOrientationLandscapeLeft) {
        accelerationFraction *= -1;
    }
}
```

ccTouchBegan checks to see if Ole is currently colliding with any ground shapes and, if so, sets the jump start time to the current time. This has the effect of beginning the jump, as you'll see later on. ccTouchEnded effectively ends the jump by setting the jump start time to 0.

accelerometer:didAccelerate computes the fraction to accelerate the player. It multiplies the y value of the acceleration by 2 so that you only have to tilt the device about halfway to get Ole to move at max speed, and it clamps the range to between −1 and 1. Also note that it flips the acceleration values if the screen is the opposite orientation than expected.

Next override the `updateStateWithDeltaTime` method to add the jumping code, as shown in Listing 13.44.

Listing 13.44   CPViking.m (before initWithLocation)

```
-(void)updateStateWithDeltaTime:(ccTime)dt
    andListOfGameObjects:(CCArray*)listOfGameObjects {

    [super updateStateWithDeltaTime:dt
        andListOfGameObjects:listOfGameObjects];                    // 1

    float jumpFactor;
    if (UI_USER_INTERFACE_IDIOM() == UIUserInterfaceIdiomPad) {
        jumpFactor = 300.0;
    } else {
        jumpFactor = 150.0;
    }

    CGPoint newVel = body->v;                                        // 2
    if (groundShapes->num == 0) {                                    // 3
        newVel = ccp(jumpFactor*accelerationFraction,body->v.y);     // 4
    }
    double timeJumping = CACurrentMediaTime()-jumpStartTime;         // 5
    if (jumpStartTime != 0 && timeJumping < 0.25) {                  // 6
        newVel.y = jumpFactor*2;
    }
    cpBodySetVel(body, newVel);                                      // 7

}
```

There's a good bit to cover here, so let's go over it line by line:

1. Starts by calling the superclass's implementation of `updateStateWithDelta-Time`, which is the code in `CPSprite` that updates the position and rotation of the sprite based on the position and rotation of the Chipmunk body.

2. Sets a jump factor based on whether the device is an iPad or iPhone. It's more on the iPad because there are about double the points on the screen. Also gets the current velocity of the body as a vector.

3. Tests to see if Ole is in the air (i.e., Ole is not currently colliding with any ground shapes).

4. If so, sets the new x velocity to be the current acceleration fraction multiplied by −300, effectively making the x velocity range from −300 to 300.

5. Tests to see how long Ole has been jumping by subtracting the jump start time from the current time.

6. If the jump start time isn't 0 (i.e., Ole is currently trying to jump) and Ole hasn't been jumping for more than a quarter second, it sets the y component of the velocity to a straight 600.0 to make Ole leap into the air. After a quarter second, gravity starts to gradually lower the y component so Ole returns to earth.

7. Sets the velocity of the Chipmunk body to the newly calculated velocity.

That covers the movement of Ole while he's in the air, but to move Ole while he's on the ground, you use surface velocity instead. So add the code to handle ground movement to the bottom of the updateStateWithDeltaTime method next, as shown in Listing 13.45.

Listing 13.45   **CPViking.m (at bottom of updateStateWithDeltaTime)**

```
if (groundShapes->num > 0) {                                    // 1
    if (ABS(accelerationFraction) < 0.05) {                     // 2
        accelerationFraction = 0;
        shape->surface_v = ccp(0, 0);
    } else {                                                    // 3
        float maxSpeed = 200.0f;
        shape->surface_v = ccp(-maxSpeed*accelerationFraction, 0);
        cpBodyActivate(body);
    }
} else {
    shape->surface_v = cpvzero;                                 // 4
}
```

Again, several things to point out, so let's go over it line by line.

1. Checks to see if Ole is on the ground (i.e., Ole is currently colliding with at least one ground shape).

2. Tests if the acceleration fraction is very small. In this case, it halts Ole to prevent him from constantly moving when the player is trying to make him be still. Note that you should use the capital case ABS method so that it works properly with float values.

3. Otherwise, sets the x component of the surface velocity based on the current acceleration fraction multiplied by −200, effectively making the x component of the surface velocity range from −200 to 200. It also activates the body, which wakes it up if it was sleeping.

4. If Ole is not colliding with the ground, resets the surface velocity to 0.

There's one more bit of code to add to the bottom of the update method. Add the contents of Listing 13.46 to the end of the method next.

Listing 13.46   CPViking.m (at bottom of updateStateWithDeltaTime)

```
float margin = 70;
CGSize winSize = [CCDirector sharedDirector].winSize;
if (body->p.x < margin) {
    cpBodySetPos(body, ccp(margin, body->p.y));
}
if (body->p.x > winSize.width - margin) {
    cpBodySetPos(body, ccp(winSize.width - margin, body->p.y));
}
```

This code prevents Ole from going off the sides of the screen by clamping the x coordinate to min/max values.

You're almost done: now you just need to call these methods. Switch to *Scene5ActionLayer.m*, comment out your current implementations of ccTouchBegan, ccTouchMoved, and ccTouchEnded, and replace them with the contents of Listing 13.47.

Listing 13.47   Scene5ActionLayer.m (replace ccTouchBegan, ccTouchMoved, and ccTouchEnded with these, effectively deleting ccTouchMoved)

```
- (BOOL)ccTouchBegan:(UITouch *)touch withEvent:(UIEvent *)event {
    [viking ccTouchBegan:touch withEvent:event];
    return YES;
}

- (void)ccTouchEnded:(UITouch *)touch withEvent:(UIEvent *)event {
    [viking ccTouchEnded:touch withEvent:event];
}

- (void)accelerometer:(UIAccelerometer *)accelerometer
didAccelerate:(UIAcceleration *)acceleration {
    [viking accelerometer:accelerometer didAccelerate:acceleration];
}
```

These simply forward the accelerometer and touch input on to the new code you added in the CPViking class.

One last step: add a line inside your initWithScene5UILayer method to enable accelerometer input, as shown in Listing 13.48.

Listing 13.48   Scene5ActionLayer.m (at bottom of initWithScene5UILayer)

```
self.isAccelerometerEnabled = YES;
```

That's it. Compile and run, and now you should be able to use the accelerometer to move Ole back and forth, tap to jump in the air, and land on top of the platform (but still be able to jump through the bottom of the platform). See Figure 13.12.

Figure 13.12   A moving and jumping Viking with a platform

It's starting to work nicely, except you may notice that Ole sometimes gets flipped over, landing unheroically on his behind. Momma always told me to avoid angry Vikings, so we're going to fix this next by using Chipmunk's constraints.

Chipmunk and Constraints

Constraints in Chipmunk are special objects you can create to restrict how objects can move—similar to joints in Box2D but more fine-grained and specialized.

You can use a variety of constraints in Chipmunk. Let's take a quick tour of some of the most useful constraints available.

Pivot joint: Restricts two bodies so that they can only rotate around a particular point, similar to revolute joints in Box2D (Figure 13.13).

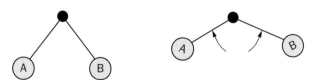

Figure 13.13   Pivot joint: Rotate around a point

Rotary limit joint: Unlike in Box2D, when you make pivot joints you cannot restrict the rotation to a certain degree range. Instead, you need to create a second constraint: a rotary limit joint. With this, you can specify the minimum and maximum rotation range for two objects (Figure 13.14).

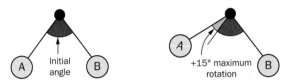

Figure 13.14   Rotary limit joint: Restrict rotation

Simple motor: Unlike Box2D, Chipmunk does not allow you to set motors directly on joints. An alternative method is an additional constraint called a simple motor. It lets you rotate an object at a desired speed (Figure 13.15).

Figure 13.15   Simple motor: Rotate at a set speed

Pin joint: You can think of this as pinning two points together with a large metal rod, so that as you move one body, the rod keeps the two points always the same distance apart. This is similar to a distance joint in Box2D (Figure 13.16).

Figure 13.16   Pin joint: Keep objects at set distance

Groove joint: Allows one body to slide (and rotate) up and down a "groove" on the first body. This is somewhat similar to prismatic joints in Box2D (Figure 13.17).

Figure 13.17   Groove joint: Object B moves and rotates along a groove on object A

Damped spring: Creates a "spring effect" between two objects that should be a specified distance apart. If you push the objects together, the constraint pushes them apart. If you pull them too far apart, the constraint pulls them together. This is similar to a soft distance joint in Box2D (with `frequencyHz` and `dampingRatio` set) (Figure 13.18).

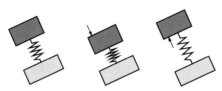

Figure 13.18   Damped spring: Creates a spring effect for the distance between objects

Damped rotary spring: This works similarly to a damped spring, but instead of attempting to keep bodies a particular distance from each other, it attempts to keep two bodies at the same relative angle (Figure 13.19).

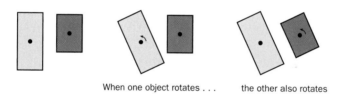

When one object rotates . . .   the other also rotates

Figure 13.19   Damped rotary spring: Creates a spring effect for the angle between objects

> **Note**
>
> This is just a sample of the most useful Chipmunk constraints. There are several more, including slide, ratchet, and gear joints. If you're interested in checking out the others, Scott Lembcke made a great demonstration video you can watch on YouTube at *http://www.youtube.com/watch?v=ZgJJZTS0aMM*.

Now that you have an idea of the types of constraints that are available, let's try them out by adding a constraint to prevent Ole from tipping over. Based on the list of useful constraints, you can see that an easy way to solve this problem is to use a rotary limit joint—you can use it to restrict Ole from rotating more than 30 degrees in either direction.

There are two steps to use a constraint in Chipmunk: create and initialize the constraint, then add it to the scene. Just as in Box2D, every constraint acts on two bodies. In this case, the bodies are the ground body and Ole.

So let's see this in code. Switch to *CPViking.m* and add two lines of code to the bottom of your `initWithLocation` method, as shown in Listing 13.49.

Listing 13.49   **CPViking.m (at bottom of initWithLocation)**

```
cpConstraint *constraint = cpRotaryLimitJointNew(groundBody, body,
    CC_DEGREES_TO_RADIANS(-30),   CC_DEGREES_TO_RADIANS(30));
cpSpaceAddConstraint(space, constraint);
```

That's how easy constraints are to use! Compile and run your code, and now Ole should be able to leap around without falling over anymore. It's good to have a happy Viking again.

Revolving Platforms

Now that you have Ole moving and jumping, you can create platforms for him to jump on to escape the level. For this level, you create a variety of different platform types, such as revolving platforms, spring platforms, and pivoting platforms. Creating them will help you learn more about Chipmunk constraints and see how useful they are.

You start by making a revolving platform, and for that you need to create a new subclass of CPSprite. Select the *Classes\GameObjects\Chipmunk* group, go to **File > New > New File...**, choose **iOS > Cocoa Touch > Objective-C class**, and click **Next**. Enter *CPSprite* as the Subclass of, click **Next**, name the file *CPRevolvePlatform.m*, and click **Save**.

Replace *CPRevolvePlatform.h* with the contents of Listing 13.50.

Listing 13.50   **CPRevolvePlatform.h**

```
#import "CPSprite.h"

@interface CPRevolvePlatform : CPSprite {
}

@end
```

As you can see, this is just a subclass of CPSprite with no extra instance variables. Next switch to *CPRevolvePlatform.m* and replace it with the contents of Listing 13.51.

Listing 13.51   **CPRevolvePlatform.m**

```
#import "CPRevolvePlatform.h"

@implementation CPRevolvePlatform
```

```
- (id)initWithLocation:(CGPoint)location space:(cpSpace *)theSpace
    groundBody:(cpBody *)groundBody {
    if ((self = [super
        initWithSpriteFrameName:@"platform_revolve.png"])) {
        [self addBoxBodyAndShapeWithLocation:location
            size:self.contentSize space:theSpace mass:1.0 e:0.2 u:1.0
            collisionType:kCollisionTypeGround canRotate:TRUE];

        // 1
        cpConstraint *c1 = cpPivotJointNew(groundBody, body, body->p);
        cpSpaceAddConstraint(space, c1);

        // 2
        cpConstraint *c2 = cpSimpleMotorNew(groundBody, body,
CC_DEGREES_TO_RADIANS(45));
        cpSpaceAddConstraint(space, c2);
    }
    return self;
}

@end
```

This creates a body using the helper method you wrote earlier in `CPSprite` and then sets up two constraints:

1. Creates a pivot joint connecting the body with the `groundBody` so that the body can rotate around its center point (its position).
2. Creates a simple motor so that the body rotates at a rate of 45 degrees a second with respect to the fixed `groundBody`.

To test this out, switch to *Scene5ActionLayer.m* and import the class at the top of the file, as shown in Listing 13.52.

Listing 13.52   **Scene5ActionLayer.m (at top of file)**

```
#import "CPRevolvePlatform.h"
```

Then add a helper method to create a revolving platform, as shown in Listing 13.53.

Listing 13.53   **Scene5ActionLayer.m (before createLevel)**

```
- (void)createRevolvePlatformAtLocation:(CGPoint)location {
    CPRevolvePlatform *revolvePlatform =
        [[[CPRevolvePlatform alloc] initWithLocation:location
            space:space groundBody:groundBody] autorelease];
    [sceneSpriteBatchNode addChild:revolvePlatform];
}
```

Finally, inside your `createLevel` method, comment out the call to `createBox-AtLocation` and call your new method, as shown in Listing 13.54.

Listing 13.54   **Scene5ActionLayer.m (replace createBoxAtLocation inside createLevel with this)**

```
[self createRevolvePlatformAtLocation:
    ccp(winSize.width * 0.5, winSize.height * 0.25)];
```

Compile and run your code, and you should now be able to jump on top of a revolving platform (Figure 13.20)!

Figure 13.20   A revolving platform made pivot and simple motor constraints

Pivot, Spring, and Normal Platforms

Let's create three more platform types to spice it up: a platform that pivots around a center point, a platform that gets pushed down when you jump on it, and a normal (static) platform.

Start by creating files for each of these. Select the *Classes\GameObjects\Chipmunk* group, go to **File > New > New File...**, choose **iOS > Cocoa Touch > Objective-C class**, and click **Next**. Enter *CPSprite* as the Subclass of, click **Next**, name the file *CPPivotPlatform.m*, and click **Save**. Repeat this process for *CPSpringPlatform.m* and *CPNormalPlatform.m*.

Replace *CPPivotPlatform.h* with the contents of Listing 13.55.

Listing 13.55 **CPPivotPlatform.h**

```
#import "CPSprite.h"

@interface CPPivotPlatform : CPSprite {
}

@end
```

This is just a subclass of CPSprite, with nothing extra added. Next replace *CPPivotPlatform.m* with the contents of Listing 13.56.

Listing 13.56 **CPPivotPlatform.m**

```
#import "CPPivotPlatform.h"

@implementation CPPivotPlatform

- (id)initWithLocation:(CGPoint)location space:(cpSpace *)theSpace
    groundBody:(cpBody *)groundBody {
    if ((self = [super
        initWithSpriteFrameName:@"platform_pivot.png"])) {
        [self addBoxBodyAndShapeWithLocation:location
            size:self.contentSize space:theSpace mass:10.0 e:0.2 u:1.0
            collisionType:kCollisionTypeGround canRotate:TRUE];

        // 1
        cpConstraint *c1 = cpPivotJointNew(groundBody, body, body->p);
        cpSpaceAddConstraint(space, c1);

        // 2
        cpConstraint *c2 = cpDampedRotarySpringNew(groundBody, body, 0,
            60000.0, 100.0);
        cpSpaceAddConstraint(space, c2);

        // 3
        cpConstraint *c3 = cpRotaryLimitJointNew(groundBody, body,
            CC_DEGREES_TO_RADIANS(-30), CC_DEGREES_TO_RADIANS(30));
        cpSpaceAddConstraint(space, c3);
    }
    return self;
}

@end
```

This creates a body for the pivot platform using the helper method you wrote earlier (but notice how it uses a large mass for this body to make it a bit harder to move). It then sets up three constraints:

1. Creates a pivot joint connecting the platform body with the ground body so that the platform body can rotate around its center point (its position).

2. Creates a damped rotary spring between the platform body and the ground body. The third parameter to cpDampedRotarySpringNew is the desired relative angle and is set to 0 to encourage the platform to return to its original horizontal position when the player is not on it. The fourth parameter is the stiffness. The larger the stiffness parameter, the more force is applied to rotate the platform, so a large value is added here to make the platform reset at a decent speed. The fifth parameter is the damping. The larger the damping parameter, the more the spring will resist motion in general, so a medium-sized value is added here to provide a degree of resistance when Ole jumps on the platform.

3. Creates a rotary limit joint between the ground body and the platform body, restricting the platform so it can't rotate more than 30 degrees in either direction.

That's it for the pivot platform; on to the spring platform. Replace *CPSpringPlatform.h* with the contents of Listing 13.57.

Listing 13.57 **CPSpringPlatform.h**

```
#import "CPSprite.h"

@interface CPSpringPlatform : CPSprite {
}

@end
```

Again, just a subclass of CPSprite. Next replace *CPSpringPlatform.m* with the contents of Listing 13.58.

Listing 13.58 **CPSpringPlatform.m**

```
#import "CPSpringPlatform.h"

@implementation CPSpringPlatform

- (id)initWithLocation:(CGPoint)location space:(cpSpace *)theSpace
    groundBody:(cpBody *)groundBody {
    if ((self = [super
        initWithSpriteFrameName:@"platform_spring.png"])) {
        [self addBoxBodyAndShapeWithLocation:location
```

```
                size:self.contentSize space:theSpace mass:1.0 e:0.2 u:1.0
                collisionType:kCollisionTypeGround canRotate:FALSE];

        // 1
        float springLength = 200;
        if (UI_USER_INTERFACE_IDIOM() == UIUserInterfaceIdiomPhone) {
            springLength /= 2;
        }
        cpConstraint * constraint = cpDampedSpringNew(groundBody, body,
                ccp(body->p.x, body->p.y-springLength), ccp(0,0),
                springLength, 25.0, 0.5);
        cpSpaceAddConstraint(space, constraint);

        // 2
        cpConstraint * c2 = cpGrooveJointNew(groundBody, body,
            ccp(body->p.x, body->p.y-springLength),
            ccp(body->p.x, body->p.y+springLength), ccp(0,0));
        cpSpaceAddConstraint(space, c2);
    }
    return self;
}

@end
```

This creates a body for the platform using the helper method you wrote earlier (but notice how it sets canRotate to FALSE, which makes the platform have an infinite moment of inertia and hence unable to rotate). It then sets up two constraints:

1. Creates a damped spring constraint between the platform body and the ground body. This makes it so the platform "wants to be" a certain distance from the ground and resists movement more and more the further away it gets from the desired point. The third parameter to cpDampedSpringNew is the anchor point on the first body (the ground body) in local coordinates, which is set as 200 points (or half that for iPhone) below the platform's current position. The fourth parameter is the anchor point on the second body (the platform body) in local coordinates, which is set to the exact center of the platform body. The fifth parameter is the desired length of the platform, and the fourth and fifth values are the stiffness and damping, which act the same way as discussed in the damped rotary spring example.

2. Without another joint, there would be nothing stopping the platform from moving left and right, but for this platform, you want it to only move up and down. So the call to cpGrooveJointNew creates a second constraint that restricts the platform body to only move up and down a "groove" on the ground body. The third and fourth parameters are the start and end points of the groove that the platform body can move in, in ground body coordinates. They are set here to a

little bit above and below the platform body's current position. The fifth parameter is the platform body-local coordinate that slides up and down the groove—
set here to be the center position of the platform body.

Just one more platform type to add, and then you'll get to test them out. This time
you add a normal platform. This platform is a special case because it doesn't move at
all, so you can add it as a static shape attached to the existing ground body. Start by
replacing *CPNormalPlatform.h* with the contents of Listing 13.59.

Listing 13.59   **CPNormalPlatform.h**

```
#import "CPSprite.h"

@interface CPNormalPlatform : CPSprite {
}


@end
```

Next replace *CPNormalPlatform.m* with the contents of Listing 13.60.

Listing 13.60   **CPNormalPlatform.m**

```
#import "CPNormalPlatform.h"

@implementation CPNormalPlatform

-(void)updateStateWithDeltaTime:(ccTime)dt andListOfGameObjects:(CCArray*)
listOfGameObjects {
    // Do nothing...
}

- (id)initWithLocation:(CGPoint)location space:(cpSpace *)theSpace
    groundBody:(cpBody *)groundBody {
    if ((self = [super
        initWithSpriteFrameName:@"platform_normal.png"])) {
        space = theSpace;

        self.position = location;
        cpFloat hw = self.contentSize.width/(cpFloat)2.0;
        cpFloat hh = self.contentSize.height/(cpFloat)2.0;

        cpVect verts[] = {
            cpv(-hw,-hh),
            cpv(-hw, hh),
            cpv( hw, hh),
            cpv( hw,-hh),
        };
```

```
        shape = cpPolyShapeNew(groundBody, 4, verts, location);
        shape->e = 1.0f;
        shape->u = 1.0f;
        shape->collision_type = kCollisionTypeGround;
        cpSpaceAddStaticShape(space, shape);
    }
    return self;
}

@end
```

This first overrides `updateStateWithDeltaTime` to do nothing, since there is no need to update the position of the sprite based on the body, since the body never moves!

It then creates a new static shape for the sprite based on the size of the sprite. Note that it uses `cpPolyShapeNew`, passing in the vertices for the shape rather than calling `cpBoxShapeNew`. This is because you need to place the shape at a specified offset relative to the ground body, and you can't specify an offset when you call `cpBoxShapeNew`.

Okay, now you can test the new platforms. First import the headers at the top of *Scene5ActionLayer.m*, as shown in Listing 13.61.

Listing 13.61   Scene5ActionLayer.m (at top of file)

```
#import "CPPivotPlatform.h"
#import "CPSpringPlatform.h"
#import "CPNormalPlatform.h"
```

Then add the helper methods to create the platforms, as shown in Listing 13.62.

Listing 13.62   Scene5ActionLayer.m (before createLevel)

```
- (void)createPivotPlatformAtLocation:(CGPoint)location {
    CPPivotPlatform *pivotPlatform = [[[CPPivotPlatform alloc]
        initWithLocation:location space:space groundBody:groundBody]
        autorelease];
    [sceneSpriteBatchNode addChild:pivotPlatform];
}

- (void)createSpringPlatformAtLocation:(CGPoint)location {
    CPSpringPlatform *springPlatform = [[[CPSpringPlatform alloc]
        initWithLocation:location space:space groundBody:groundBody]
        autorelease];
    [sceneSpriteBatchNode addChild:springPlatform];
}
```

```
- (void)createNormalPlatformAtLocation:(CGPoint)location {
    CPNormalPlatform *normPlatform = [[[CPNormalPlatform alloc]
        initWithLocation:location space:space groundBody:groundBody]
        autorelease];
    [sceneSpriteBatchNode addChild:normPlatform];
}
```

Finally, comment out the call to createRevolvePlatformAtLocation in your createLevel method and replace it with the contents of Listing 13.63.

Listing 13.63   **Scene5ActionLayer.m (replace contents of createLevel with the following)**

```
[self createPivotPlatformAtLocation:
    ccp(winSize.width * 0.7, winSize.height * 0.45)];
[self createSpringPlatformAtLocation:
    ccp(winSize.width * 0.4, winSize.height * 0.25)];
[self createNormalPlatformAtLocation:
    ccp(winSize.width * 0.2, winSize.height * 0.35)];
```

Compile and run your code, and you can jump Ole around to try out the new platform types (Figure 13.21)!

Figure 13.21   Pivot, spring, and normal platforms made with Chipmunk joints

The Great Escape!

At this point, you have enough building blocks to make this into a complete level, so let's put things together and add in a bit of polish and excitement along the way.

Following Ole

Since Ole will be moving vertically up this level, you need to set the layer to follow Ole as he moves up and down the scene. While you're at it, you'll apply a neat "screen shake" effect to the layer to make it seem like the planet is about to explode and add some tension to the scene.

Inside *Scene5ActionLayer.m*, add a new method to update the layer's position that will be called in each frame, as shown in Listing 13.64.

Listing 13.64   **Scene5ActionLayer.m (above update method)**

```
- (void)followPlayer:(ccTime)dt {
    // 1
    static double totalTime = 0;
    totalTime += dt;

    // 2
    double shakesPerSecond = 5;
    double shakeOffset = 3;
    double shakeX =
        sin(totalTime*M_PI*2*shakesPerSecond) * shakeOffset;

    // 3
    CGSize winSize = [CCDirector sharedDirector].winSize;
    float fixedPosition = winSize.height/4;
    float newY = fixedPosition - viking.position.y;
    float groundMaxY = 2048;
    newY = MIN(newY, 50);
    if (UI_USER_INTERFACE_IDIOM() == UIUserInterfaceIdiomPhone) {
        groundMaxY = 900;
        newY = MIN(newY, 25);
    }
    newY = MAX(newY, -groundMaxY-fixedPosition);
    CGPoint newPos = ccp(shakeX, newY);
    [self setPosition:newPos];
}
```

There are three things to point out about this method:

1. This first part keeps track of the total time elapsed in the scene, which is needed in order to calculate how much to shake the screen.

2. To shake the screen, you need to move the layer a little bit to the right for a short period of time, then a little bit to the left, then repeat. Whenever you find yourself needing to do something on a periodic basis like this, a good trick is to use the sin function. The sin function gives a periodic wave that cycles between −1 and 1 every 2*M_PI (6.28), so if you pass in seconds, it cycles between −1 and 1 every 6.28 seconds. However, if you multiply the seconds by 2*M_PI, it cycles between −1 and 1 every second. It multiplies that by the number of times you want to shake per second to get a nice jittery effect. Finally, it converts the result from the range of (−1,1) to (−3,3) by multiplying by 3.

3. The rest of this code is the same method of moving the layer with respect to the player's current position that you learned about in earlier chapters.

Now that you have this new method, add a line to call it at the bottom of your update method, as shown in Listing 13.65.

Listing 13.65   Scene5ActionLayer.m (at bottom of update method)

```
[self followPlayer:dt];
```

Compile and run your code to see the layer follow Ole with a neat shake effect.

Laying Out the Platforms

Now that the layer follows Ole around, replace the createLevel method to add some platforms in an interesting and challenging layout. Listing 13.66 shows one possible implementation; see if you can come up with your own.

Listing 13.66   Scene5ActionLayer.m (replace createLevel with this, or your own layout)

```
- (void)createLevel {
    CGSize winSize = [CCDirector sharedDirector].winSize;
    [self createNormalPlatformAtLocation:ccp(200, 100)];
    [self createNormalPlatformAtLocation:
        ccp(winSize.width * 0.2, winSize.height * 0.15)];
    [self createNormalPlatformAtLocation:
        ccp(winSize.width * 0.4, winSize.height * 0.30)];
    [self createNormalPlatformAtLocation:
        ccp(winSize.width * 0.6, winSize.height * 0.45)];
    [self createNormalPlatformAtLocation:
        ccp(winSize.width * 0.8, winSize.height * 0.75)];
    [self createNormalPlatformAtLocation:
        ccp(winSize.width * 0.6, winSize.height * 0.90)];
    [self createNormalPlatformAtLocation:
        ccp(winSize.width * 0.4, winSize.height * 1.15)];
    [self createNormalPlatformAtLocation:
        ccp(winSize.width * 0.2, winSize.height * 1.30)];
```

```
    [self createPivotPlatformAtLocation:
        ccp(winSize.width * 0.4, winSize.height * 1.60)];
    [self createNormalPlatformAtLocation:
        ccp(winSize.width * 0.7, winSize.height * 1.90)];
    [self createNormalPlatformAtLocation:
        ccp(winSize.width * 0.4, winSize.height * 2.15)];
    [self createSpringPlatformAtLocation:
        ccp(winSize.width * 0.45, winSize.height * 2.60)];
    [self createSpringPlatformAtLocation:
        ccp(winSize.width * 0.75, winSize.height * 2.80)];
    [self createSpringPlatformAtLocation:
        ccp(winSize.width * 0.55, winSize.height * 3.05)];
    [self createNormalPlatformAtLocation:
        ccp(winSize.width * 0.4, winSize.height * 3.15)];
    [self createNormalPlatformAtLocation:
        ccp(winSize.width * 0.2, winSize.height * 3.35)];
    [self createRevolvePlatformAtLocation:
        ccp(winSize.width * 0.5, winSize.height * 3.50)];
    [self createNormalPlatformAtLocation:
        ccp(winSize.width * 0.8, winSize.height * 3.65)];
}
```

Once you've implemented this platform, compile and run your project, and try out your new level.

Animating Ole

Right now Ole is just a nonanimated sprite, which isn't very entertaining for such an action-packed level. Let's fix that by integrating Ole's movement and jump animations into this level.

The first step is to add the property list file that defines the animations you'll need for Ole in this level. From the resources folder for this chapter, drag *CPViking.plist* to the *Plists* group in Xcode. Verify **Copy items into destination group's folder (if needed)** is checked, and click **Finish**.

Once you've added the file, open *CPViking.h* and add some new instance variables you'll need for the animations and to keep track of the last time Ole changed directions, as seen in Listing 13.67.

Listing 13.67   **CPViking.h (inside interface declaration)**

```
CCAnimation * walkingAnim;
CCAnimation * jumpingAnim;
CCAnimation * afterJumpingAnim;
float lastFlip;
```

Now switch to *CPViking.m* and add a method to load the animations from the property list, as shown in Listing 13.68.

Listing 13.68   **CPViking.m (before initWithLocation)**

```
-(void)initAnimations {
    walkingAnim = [self loadPlistForAnimationWithName:@"walkingAnim"
        andClassName:NSStringFromClass([self class])];
    [[CCAnimationCache sharedAnimationCache]
        addAnimation:walkingAnim name:@"walkingAnim"];

    jumpingAnim = [self loadPlistForAnimationWithName:@"jumpingAnim"
        andClassName:NSStringFromClass([self class])];
    [[CCAnimationCache sharedAnimationCache]
        addAnimation:jumpingAnim name:@"jumpingAnim"];

    afterJumpingAnim = [self
        loadPlistForAnimationWithName:@"afterJumpingAnim"
        andClassName:NSStringFromClass([self class])];
    [[CCAnimationCache sharedAnimationCache]
        addAnimation:afterJumpingAnim name:@"afterJumpingAnim"];
}
```

This method loads the three animations you need for this level from the *CPViking. plist* file that you just added to the project, using the helper method in GameObject.

Now it's time to add the code to manage Ole's states and play the correct animations for each state, as shown in Listing 13.69.

Listing 13.69   **CPViking.m (before initWithLocation)**

```
-(void)changeState:(CharacterStates)newState {
    [self stopAllActions];
    id action = nil;
    [self setCharacterState:newState];

    switch (newState) {
        case kStateIdle:
            [self setDisplayFrame:
                [[CCSpriteFrameCache sharedSpriteFrameCache]
                    spriteFrameByName:@"sv_anim_1.png"]];
            break;

        case kStateWalking:
            action = [CCAnimate actionWithAnimation:walkingAnim
                restoreOriginalFrame:NO];
            break;
```

```
    case kStateJumping:
        action = [CCAnimate actionWithAnimation:jumpingAnim
            restoreOriginalFrame:NO];
        break;

    case kStateAfterJumping:
        action = [CCAnimate actionWithAnimation:afterJumpingAnim
            restoreOriginalFrame:NO];
        break;

    default:
        break;
    }
    if (action != nil) {
        [self runAction:action];
    }
}
```

You should be familiar with how this works by now, based on what you learned starting back in Chapter 4, "Simple Collision Detection and the First Enemy."

You're almost done; you just need to add the code to handle state management. First add a line to the top of updateStateWithDeltaTime to record the position of the object before you call the superclass's updateStateWithDeltaTime, as shown in Listing 13.70.

Listing 13.70 CPViking.m (at very top of updateStateWithDeltaTime)

```
CGPoint oldPosition = self.position;
```

Then at the bottom of updateStateWithDeltaTime, add the code to handle transitioning Ole's states and flipping his sprite, as shown in Listing 13.71.

Listing 13.71 CPViking.m (at bottom of updateStateWithDeltaTime)

```
// 1
if(ABS(accelerationFraction) > 0.05) {
    double diff = CACurrentMediaTime() - lastFlip;
    if (diff > 0.1) {
        lastFlip = CACurrentMediaTime();
        if (oldPosition.x > self.position.x) {
            self.flipX = YES;
        } else {
            self.flipX = NO;
        }
    }
}
```

```
// 2
if (characterState != kStateJumping && jumpStartTime != 0) {
    [self changeState:kStateJumping];
}


// 3
if (characterState == kStateIdle && accelerationFraction != 0) {
    [self changeState:kStateWalking];
}


// 3
if ([self numberOfRunningActions] == 0) {
    if (characterState == kStateJumping) {
        if (groundShapes->num > 0) {
            [self changeState:kStateAfterJumping];
        }
    } else if (characterState != kStateIdle) {
        [self changeState:kStateIdle];
    }
}
```

There's a good bit of code here, so let's go through this section by section:

1. Checks to see if Ole is moving left or right compared to his last position, and flips the sprite accordingly. It also adds a check to prevent the sprite from flipping too often. Note that you should use the capital case ABS method so that it works properly with float values.

2. If the sprite isn't in the jumping state but yet it's jumping (the jumpStartTime isn't 0), it changes the sprite to the jumping state.

3. If the state is idle but yet the accelerationFraction isn't 0, it changes the state to walking.

4. If no actions (i.e., animations) are running, it looks to see if it should change the state. If it just finished jumping, it changes the state to after jumping. Otherwise, if the sprite isn't idle, it switches to the idle state.

As the last step, add the call to initialize the animations at the end of initWith-Location, as seen in Listing 13.72.

Listing 13.72   CPViking.m (at end of initWithLocation)

```
[self initAnimations];
```

Compile and run your code, and now Ole should be able to leap around in style (Figure 13.22)!

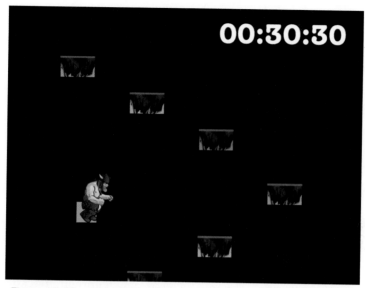

Figure 13.22   Adding jumping and moving animations to Ole's sprite

Music and Sound Effects

Now let's add some music and sound effects to make it even cooler. Add the line to start the background music playing in initWithScene5UILayer, as shown in Listing 13.73.

Listing 13.73   **Scene5ActionLayer.m (at bottom of initWithScene5UILayer)**

```
[[GameManager sharedGameManager]
    playBackgroundTrack:BACKGROUND_TRACK_ESCAPE];
```

Similarly, switch to *CPViking.m* and add a method to play a random jump sound effect, as shown in Listing 13.74.

Listing 13.74   **CPViking.m (before updateStateWithDeltaTime)**

```
- (void)playJumpEffect {
    int soundToPlay = random() % 4;
    if (soundToPlay == 0) {
        PLAYSOUNDEFFECT(VIKING_JUMPING_1);
    } else if (soundToPlay == 1) {
        PLAYSOUNDEFFECT(VIKING_JUMPING_2);
    } else if (soundToPlay == 2) {
        PLAYSOUNDEFFECT(VIKING_JUMPING_3);
```

```
    } else {
        PLAYSOUNDEFFECT(VIKING_JUMPING_4);
    }
}
```

Finally, inside the `changeState` method in the case for `kStateJumping`, call the `playJumpEffect` method, as shown in Listing 13.75.

Listing 13.75   CPViking.m (inside changeState method's kStateJumping case)

```
[self playJumpEffect];
```

Compile and run your code, and enjoy the grooves and grunts!

Adding the Background

The black background is getting kind of boring, so let's add a real background to the scene. In the resources files for this chapter, drag all of the files beginning with *chipmunk_background* and *chipmunk_ground* to the *Images* group in your project, make sure **Copy items into destination group's folder (if needed)** is checked, and click **Add**.

Next, write a method to add these two images to the scene, as shown in Listing 13.76.

Listing 13.76   Scene5ActionLayer.m (before initWithScene5UILayer method)

```
- (void)createBackground {
    // 1
    CCParallaxNode * parallax = [CCParallaxNode node];
    [CCTexture2D
      setDefaultAlphaPixelFormat:kCCTexture2DPixelFormat_RGB565];
    CCSprite *background;
    if (UI_USER_INTERFACE_IDIOM() == UIUserInterfaceIdiomPad) {
        background =
            [CCSprite spriteWithFile:@"chipmunk_background-ipad.png"];
    } else {
        background =
            [CCSprite spriteWithFile:@"chipmunk_background.png"];
    }
    background.anchorPoint = ccp(0,0);
    [CCTexture2D
        setDefaultAlphaPixelFormat:kCCTexture2DPixelFormat_Default];
    [parallax addChild:background z:-10 parallaxRatio:ccp(0.1f, 0.1f)
        positionOffset:ccp(0,0)];
    [self addChild:parallax z:-10];
```

```
// 2
CCSprite *groundSprite;
if (UI_USER_INTERFACE_IDIOM() == UIUserInterfaceIdiomPad) {
    groundSprite =
        [CCSprite spriteWithFile:@"chipmunk_ground-hd.png"];
} else {
    groundSprite =
        [CCSprite spriteWithFile:@"chipmunk_ground.png"];
}
groundSprite.anchorPoint = ccp(0,0);
groundSprite.position = ccp(0,0);
[self addChild:groundSprite z:-10];

// 3
[background runAction:
 [CCRepeatForever actionWithAction:
  [CCSequence actions:
   [CCTintTo actionWithDuration:0.5 red:200 green:0 blue:0],
   [CCTintTo actionWithDuration:0.5 red:255 green:255 blue:255],
   nil]]];
}
```

This method has three parts:

1. Adds the background to the scene, contained within a parallax node so that it scrolls at a slower rate than the foreground.

2. Adds a sprite to the bottom of the scene for the ground and positions the bottom left corner to start at the bottom left corner of the screen.

3. Runs an action on the background to make it pulse slightly for a subtle neat effect.

Now that you have this method, all you need to do is call it from initWith-Scene5UILayer, as you can see in Listing 13.77.

Listing 13.77   Scene5ActionLayer.m (at bottom of initWithScene5UILayer)

```
[self createBackground];
```

Compile and run the code (and comment out the debug draw code if you'd like), and you should now have a neat rocky background in your scene (Figure 13.23).

Figure 13.23   A background added to the almost complete level!

Adding Win/Lose Conditions

One last thing to add: a check to see if Ole has escaped the planet or if he's run out of time. You're going to do a real simple check for this here, and just check if the y position of Ole is greater than a certain amount.

You'll need to use `GameManager` to switch to the win/lose scene, so import that at the top of the file, as you can see in Listing 13.78.

Listing 13.78   **Scene5ActionLayer.m (at top of file)**

```
#import "GameManager.h"
```

Next, add the checking for the win/lose conditions at the bottom of your `update` method, as you can see in Listing 13.79.

Listing 13.79   **Scene5ActionLayer.m (at bottom of the update method)**

```
if (remainingTime <= 0) {
    [[GameManager sharedGameManager] setHasPlayerDied:YES];
    [[GameManager sharedGameManager]
        runSceneWithID:kLevelCompleteScene];
} else if (viking.position.y > 2900) {
    [[GameManager sharedGameManager] setHasPlayerDied:NO];
    [[GameManager sharedGameManager]
        runSceneWithID:kLevelCompleteScene];
}
```

Compile and run your level—see if you can help Ole escape from the planet before it's too late!

Summary

At this point, you have created a complete Metroid-style platformer escape level with Chipmunk. In the process, you gained hands-on experience using the most important aspects of Chipmunk: creating a space, adding bodies and shapes, moving the bodies, and restricting their movement with constraints.

Now that you know the basics of using Chipmunk, you should check out the official reference documentation for Chipmunk, available at *http://files.slembcke.net/ chipmunk/release/ChipmunkLatest-Docs/*. It contains a handy reference of the API calls you'll need and is good to keep on hand as you program your games.

In addition, you may wish to consider using one of the Objective-C wrappers for Chipmunk, which can make the APIs a bit easier to work with. Scott Lembcke has written an official Objective-C binding for Chipmunk called Objective-Chipmunk *(http://howlingmoonsoftware.com/objectiveChipmunk.php)*, and there is also an (older) Objective-C binding for Chipmunk called SpaceManager *(http://code.google.com/p/ chipmunk-spacemanager/)* available as well. Remember if you decide to use Chipmunk in your games, you might consider donating to Scott, as he makes his living off Chipmunk donations and consulting.

Congratulations! You've learned what many consider one of the trickiest (and also the most fun) parts of Cocos2D: how to use the physics libraries. Now that you have practical experience using both Chipmunk and Box2D, you can make an educated decision which you prefer most for your future games.

Challenges

1. Add a new platform type of your own design, using some of Chipmunk's constraints.

2. Create a platform that is a different shape than a rectangle, using Vertex Helper and Chipmunk's polygon shapes.

3. Add a jet pack item to the level. When Ole collides with it, apply a one-shot impulse to Ole to boost him quickly up into the air!

Part V

Particle Systems, Game Center, and Performance

Learn how to quickly create and add particle systems to your games, how to integrate with Apple's Game Center for online leaderboards and achievements, and some performance tips and tricks to keep your game running fast.

- Chapter 14: "Particle Systems: Creating Fire, Snow, Ice, and More"
- Chapter 15: "Achievements and Leaderboards with Game Center"
- Chapter 16: "Performance Optimizations"
- Chapter 17: "Conclusion"

Particle Systems: Creating Fire, Snow, Ice, and More

In the previous chapters you learned about the Box2D and Chipmunk physics engines and how to incorporate them into Space Viking and your games. In this chapter you will learn about particle systems and how easily you can add realistic fire, smoke, snow, rain, and other effects to your games. Particle system is just a name for a technique to generate certain graphical effects, such as explosions, flames, and of course fire, smoke, or even rain. Instead of trying to model those effects, a large set of tiny images, or particles, is used to fool the player into seeing the desired effect.

Terminology Review

Before moving on to creating and coding particle systems, it is important to understand a few key terms.

- **Particle System**
  A technique and object that you use to add and render a set of particles on the screen. The particle system contains an emitter as well as a configuration for how the particles should behave. In Cocos2D the particle systems classes (`CCParticleSystemPoint` and `CCParticleSystemQuad`) are responsible for rendering the particle systems, and both inherit from `CCNode`.

- **Particle**
  The image (as a texture) that is used to create your particle system. Varying the transparency and design of the particle image can create soft edge effects such as smoke.

- **Emitter**
  The brains behind the particle system. The emitter is what creates, moves, and eventually removes the particles in a particle system. The emitter controls the spawning and movement of particles based on the configuration you specify.

- **CCParticleSystemPoint**
  Cocos2D particle system that renders the particles using `GL_POINT_SPRITE`. It stores only one vertex coordinate for the each particle, the center point of the image. This particle system can have a maximum particle image size of only 64 × 64 pixels. The `CCParticleSystemPoint` cannot be rotated or scaled.

- **CCParticleSystemQuad**
  Cocos2D particle system that renders the particles using quads (two triangles).
  The `CCParticleSystemQuad` can have particle images of any size, and it
  allows for rotating and scaling of the entire particle system as a whole.

Do not worry if it is not clear to you how the emitter works or is configured. This chapter guides you through several examples of setting up and adding particle systems to *Space Viking*.

About ARCH_OPTIMAL_PARTICLE_SYSTEM

`CCParticleSystemPoint` is slightly faster than `CCParticleSystemQuad` on the older iPhone 3G and iPod touch (first and second generation). `CCParticle-SystemQuad` is faster on the newer iPhone 3GS, iPhone 4, and iPad. There is an easy way to choose between the two of them during compile time. Cocos2D has a handy macro to choose the fastest particle system for you to use during compile time based on the architecture you are compiling for (armv6 or armv7).

To use it, simply declare your particle system as inheriting from the `ARCH_OPTIMAL_PARTICLE_SYSTEM` macro instead of `CCParticleSystemPoint` or `CCParticle-SystemQuad` directly:

Instead of:

`@interface MyParticleSystem: CCParticleSystemPoint`

use:

`@interface MyParticleSystem: ARCH_OPTIMAL_PARTICLE_SYSTEM`

The best way to understand particle systems is to create one firsthand. First you learn about the built-in particle systems bundled with Cocos2D, and then you learn about Particle Designer, a tool you can use to create and customize your own particle systems.

Built-In Particle Systems

Cocos2D comes with 11 particle systems set up and ready for you to use inside of the Cocos2D source code, in the *CCParticleExamples.m* class. All it takes to use these particle systems is to initialize the emitter and add them to your `CCLayer`. The 11 built-in particle systems include fire, fireworks, smoke, rain, and even a flower emitter that generates a steady stream of sparkles.

Running the Built-In Particle Systems

To check out the built-in particle systems, open the *cocos2d-ios* Xcode project located in the folder you downloaded and extracted from the Cocos2D source in the beginning of this book.

Select **ParticleTest** under the **Scheme** dropdown menu in Xcode and click **Run**, as shown in Figure 14.1.

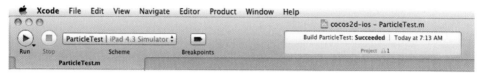

Figure 14.1   ParticleTest in the Scheme dropdown menu in Xcode

Pay close attention to the `ParticleSmoke` and `ParticleSnow` examples, as you will be incorporating those into *Space Viking*.

To see how the example particle systems are added to the scene, open the *ParticleTest.m* class in the *cocos2d-ios* Xcode project, located inside the *Tests* group. Move to the `DemoSnow` implementation and observe the lines shown on Listing 14.1.

Listing 14.1   **ParticleSnow being created in the ParticleTest demo**

```
self.emitter = [CCParticleSnow node];
[background addChild: emitter z:10];
```

The particle system settings are actually in the `CCParticleSnow` class; if you click on it and select **Jump to Definition**, you can see the details. In Cocos2D you can declare your particle systems programmatically, as shown with `CCParticleSnow`, or via a *plist* file produced by other tools, such as Particle Designer.

Making It Snow in the Desert

To get your feet wet on using particle systems, you are going to add the `CCParticle-Snow` to the *Space Viking* Ole Awakes level. It is an alien planet—who says it can't snow a little bit. To add the snow:

1. Open the *SpaceViking* Xcode project.

2. Drag the *Particles* folder available with the resources for this chapter into your *SpaceViking* project, under the *Images* group.

   This step is key, as the `CCParticleSnow` system relies on the *snow.png* texture to create the snowflakes. Figure 14.2 shows the *Particles* folder added to *SpaceViking*.

3. Open the *GameplayLayer.m* file and add the lines shown in Listing 14.2 to the end of the `init` method.

Listing 14.2   **GameplayLayer.m init method additions**

```
// Add Snow Particle System
CCParticleSystem *snowParticleSystem = [CCParticleSnow node];
[self addChild:snowParticleSystem];
```

Figure 14.2   Particles image folder added to SpaceViking Xcode project

If you are using the built-in particle systems, it just takes these two lines of code to get it into your game. If you click **Run** and select the Ole Awakes level, you will see Ole the Viking on the familiar alien desert, this time with snow. Figure 14.3 shows the *Space Viking* first level with the snow particle system.

Figure 14.3   Space Viking with the snow particle system

At some point in your game development, you may want to create your own particle systems in addition to using the built-in ones. While you can make your particles by hand, and Cocos2D already comes with some great definitions for particle systems, the best way to understand each of the variables you have to play with is by using a tool like Particle Designer. The Particle Designer Mac application created by

Mike Daley and Tom Bradley provides a great way to create and see your particle systems in real time. It also exports any particle systems you create in a *plist* format that Cocos2D can read and use natively.

The next section takes you through installing Particle Designer and creating the engine exhaust for the space cargo ship.

Getting Started with Particle Designer

Although Particle Designer is a tool you must pay for, you can try it out for free before buying it. To get Particle Designer on your Mac, download it from the 71Squared website at *http://particledesigner.71squared.com/*.

You can try out all of the particle systems settings in the free trial version, but you will not be able to save or export your particle systems until you purchase a license.

After you have downloaded Particle Designer:

1. Unzip the downloaded zip file and drag the Particle Designer app into your *Applications* folder.

2. If you want to save or export the particles you design, be sure to obtain a license from the Particle Designer website.

When you first start Particle Designer, it opens an iPhone simulator showing the particle system in action and a gallery of some of the user-submitted particle systems. Figure 14.4 shows Particle Designer's initial screen.

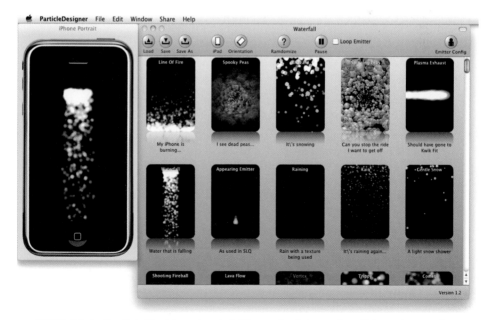

Figure 14.4   Particle Designer showing iPhone simulator and particle systems gallery

The iPhone and iPad simulators in Particle Designer are not the Xcode iPhone/iPad simulator but a window running the OpenGL code to render the particle system. The next version of Particle Designer includes a live export to iOS devices, so you can see your particle systems directly on your iPhone or iPad. Keep in mind that just because a particle system runs fast on your Mac does not mean it will run as fast on your iOS device. There is no substitute for testing it in your game on real hardware.

A Quick Tour of Particle Designer

Particle Designer contains the ability to pull particle system configurations from the 71Squared online gallery, and this list is always updated with new particle designs. Particle Designer's toolbar allows you to quickly view your particle system in iPhone and iPad mode as well as get into the configuration for each particle system. Figure 14.5 shows the available toolbar buttons.

Figure 14.5   Particle Designer toolbar

The toolbar shown in Figure 14.5 has the Load, Save, and Save As buttons as well as the following options:

1. Switches between iPhone- and iPad-sized preview display. Click on this button to see how your particle system would look on an iPhone or an iPad.

2. Toggles between portrait and landscape orientations for the preview display.

3. Randomly sets all of the particle emitter's values, so you can try a new combination at random.

4. Pauses or starts the particle emitter. If you want to pause or restart the preview display, use this button to do it.

5. Opens the emitter configuration panel. This is the heart of Particle Designer and contains all of the settings for the particle system.

The configuration panel is where you will spend most of your time in Particle Designer, as it contains the settings that Cocos2D will use to render your particle system. Figure 14.6 shows the configuration panel.

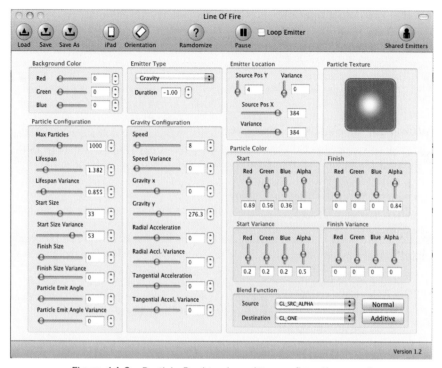

Figure 14.6   Particle Designer's emitter configuration panel

Particle Designer Controls

As you can see from Figure 14.6, there are quite a lot of options behind creating a particle system. Don't be overwhelmed if this looks like the control panel for a nuclear reactor: it is much simpler than it looks at first glance. Here is what each section sets up in the particle system:

- **Background Color Section**
  The background color is not exported to Cocos2D *plist* files. It is only used so that you can better see your particle system against a color similar to the background in your game. The default is a black background.

- **Particle Configuration Section**
  This section sets up how many particles are going to be used within the particle effect as well as how long they will live, known as the lifespan of a particle. This section also sets up the starting size of the particles and the variance and angle at which they are emitted. The size at which the particles will finish is also configured in this section.

- The variance determines how much each of the settings will vary from particle to particle. Having a good amount of variance in your particle system can make it seem more realistic. Having no variance will have each of the particles act exactly as the previous ones.
- **Emitter Type Section**
  The emitter type section lets you choose between a gravity or radial style particle system. Gravity has the particles flowing in one direction defined for both the x- and y-axes. This can create an effect similar to water flowing out of the tap. The radial type of emitter has particles emitting from a ring and usually collapsing inward. The best way to understand the difference between these two options is to try them out on Particle Designer by toggling the value in the Emitter Type dropdown.
- **Gravity/Radial Configuration Section**
  This section contains the configuration options for both the gravity and the radial emitters. If you have the gravity emitter selected, then you have the option to configure radial and tangential acceleration values. Radial acceleration occurs in all directions from the emitter, while tangential acceleration takes the particles on a curved path from the center point out. Text descriptions of these effects are hard to visualize, so be sure to play with these values to see for yourself what effect these settings have. If you select a radial emitter in the Emitter Type section, you can set the radius and rotation (in degrees) of the emitter.
- **Emitter Location Section**
  This section controls the location of the emitter itself. You can change the look of a particle system just by increasing the variance of the emitter location. Keep in mind you can also change the emitter location later in code via the `setPosition` call.
- **Particle Texture Section**
  This is the texture used to render each particle. Drag and drop your PNG texture into this section to have Particle Designer use it for your particle system. When you export the Cocos2D *plist* from Particle Designer, the texture is automatically embedded in the *plist* file.
- **Particle Color Section**
  This section controls the start and finish color values for the particles. These settings can turn a snowy particle system into a rain of fiery meteors.
- **Blend Function Section**
  This section sets the OpenGL ES parameters for the rendering of the particle system. While OpenGL is beyond the scope of this book, you can see how some of the settings work here by playing around in Particle Designer.

Remember, the best way to learn about particle systems is to play around with the settings and see what impact the changes have. When you are done creating your next particle system, a quick export will get it into the *plist* file that Coco2D can use to bring it into your iOS game. If you are using the trial version and cannot export, you will find the *EngineExhaust.plist* in the resources folder for this chapter. The next section covers how to create the engine exhaust for the space cargo ship and add it to *Space Viking*.

Creating and Adding a Particle System to Space Viking

To create the space cargo ship exhaust plume, you take one of the existing Particle Designer systems and modify it. To start:

1. Open Particle Designer and look at the Shared Emitters Gallery.
2. Select the **Plasma Exhaust Particle System**.

In the Particle Configuration section:

1. Change the Max Particles to **100** (from 1000).
2. Change the Particle Lifespan to **1.5** (from 10).
3. Change the Lifespan Variance to **0** (from 10), indicating that all particles will live for the same amount of time.

You can leave the Emitter Type and Gravity Configuration settings exactly as they are. In the Emitter Location section:

1. Change the Source Pos Y variance to **30** (from 0). This allows the plume to be wider in the vertical direction.
2. Change the Source Pos Y to **240**.
3. Change the Source Pos X position to **363**.
4. Change the Source Pos X variance to **68**.

Finally, you have to modify the Particle Color section so that the exhaust plume will have a yellow color instead of a blue plasma look.

1. Change the Start Particle Color Red amount to **0.86**.
2. Change the Start Particle Color Green amount to **0.14**.
3. Change the Start Particle Color Blue amount to **0**.

Your configuration panel should look as shown in Figure 14.7. You can test to see how the particle system looks by clicking the play button.

Before you can use the new particle system in *Space Viking*, you have to save it as a *plist* and import it into your *Space Viking* project.

1. Click **Save As**, and label the file *EngineExhaust.plist*.
2. Set the File Format to **cocos2d (plist)**.
3. After saving the *EngineExhaust.plist* file, import it into your *SpaceViking* project under the *Images* group.

The last step is to add the code to instantiate the particle system inside of *SpaceViking*.

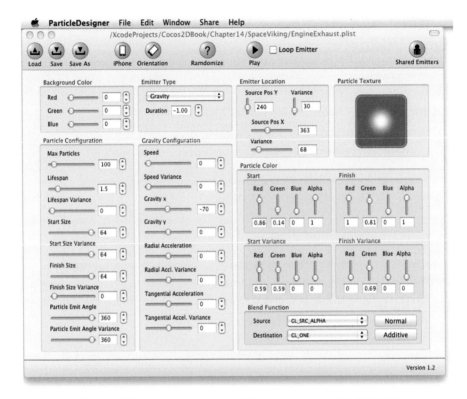

Figure 14.7   Engine exhaust particle system in Particle Designer

Adding the Engine Exhaust to Space Viking

What could be cooler than a fire and smoke exhaust trail on the space cargo ship? In this section you add the fire plume particle system *(EngineExhaust.plist)* you created as well as a smoke particle system.

To start, open the *GameplayLayer.h* header file and add the lines shown in Listing 14.3 inside the @interface declaration.

Listing 14.3   **Engine exhaust particle systems in GameplayLayer.h header file**

```
CCParticleSystem     *emitter;
CCParticleSystem     *smokeEmitter;
```

Move to the *GameplayLayer.m* implementation file and locate the createObject-OfType method. In the createObjectOfTypeMethod add the lines shown in **bold** in Listing 14.4 inside the if else branch for the SpaceCargoShip.

Listing 14.4   **createObjectofType method in GameplayLayer.m implementation file**

```
} else if (kEnemyTypeSpaceCargoShip == objectType) {
      CCLOG(@"Creating the Cargo Ship Enemy");
      SpaceCargoShip *spaceCargoShip =
       [[SpaceCargoShip alloc]
          initWithSpriteFrameName:@"ship_2.png"];
      [spaceCargoShip setDelegate:self];
      [spaceCargoShip setPosition:spawnLocation];
      [sceneSpriteBatchNode addChild:spaceCargoShip
                            z:ZValue
                            tag:kEnemyTypeSpaceCargoShip];
      [spaceCargoShip release];

      // Chapter 14
      // Add the flaming particle system
      emitter = [ARCH_OPTIMAL_PARTICLE_SYSTEM
                particleWithFile:@"EngineExhaust.plist"];     // 1
      smokeEmitter = [CCParticleSmoke node];                  // 2
      [self addChild:emitter];                                // 3
      [self addChild:smokeEmitter];                           // 4

   } else if (kPowerUpTypeMallet == objectType) {
```

The first step is to replace the addChild call so that the SpaceCargoShip can have its tag set to the kEnemyTypeSpaceCargoShip value. With the tag value in place, you can retrieve the SpaceCargoShip from the list of children objects rendered by the sceneSpriteBatchNode and update the position of the particle systems.

As with the built-in particle systems, creating a particle system takes just a few steps:

1. Initializes the emitter with the *EngineExhaust.plist* file you created in Particle Designer.

   The particle image/texture is actually embedded inside of the *plist* file, so it does not have to be included. The ARCH_OPTIMAL_PARTICLE_SYSTEM macro is used here so that the best-performing particle system is selected depending on the architecture being compiled (armv6 or armv7).

2. Initializes the smokeEmitter to the built-in smoke particle system.
   Along with the EngineExhaust fire plume, the smokeEmitter adds a second particle system to create the trailing smoke.

3. Adds the EngineExhaust particle system to the GameplayLayer.

4. Adds the smokeEmitter particle system to the GameplayLayer.

Now that the particle systems are added to the `Gameplay` layer, the last step is to position both particle systems behind the `SpaceCargoShip` so that they follow it left and right.

Move to the `update` method inside *GameplayLayer.m* and add the lines shown in **bold** in Listing 14.5.

Listing 14.5 update method in GameplayLayer.m implementation file

```
#pragma mark Update Method
-(void) update:(ccTime)deltaTime {
    CCArray *listOfGameObjects =
    [sceneSpriteBatchNode children];                                    // 1
    for (GameCharacter *tempChar in listOfGameObjects) {                // 2
        [tempChar updateStateWithDeltaTime:deltaTime
andListOfGameObjects:listOfGameObjects];                                // 3
    }


    // Chapter 7 Additions
    // Check to see if the Viking is dead
    GameCharacter *tempChar = (GameCharacter*)
    [sceneSpriteBatchNode
     getChildByTag:kVikingSpriteTagValue];
    if (([tempChar characterState] == kStateDead) &&
        ([tempChar numberOfRunningActions] == 0)) {
        [[GameManager sharedGameManager] setHasPlayerDied:YES];
        [[GameManager sharedGameManager]
          runSceneWithID:kLevelCompleteScene];
    }


    // Check to see if the RadarDish is dead
    tempChar = (GameCharacter*)[sceneSpriteBatchNode
                          getChildByTag:kRadarDishTagValue];
    if (([tempChar characterState] == kStateDead) &&
        ([tempChar numberOfRunningActions] == 0)) {
        [[GameManager sharedGameManager]
          runSceneWithID:kLevelCompleteScene];
    }


    // Chapter 14 Updates for Particle System
    GameCharacter *spaceCargoShip = (GameCharacter*)
     [sceneSpriteBatchNode getChildByTag:kEnemyTypeSpaceCargoShip];
    if (spaceCargoShip != nil) {
        CGRect cargoShipBoundingBox = [spaceCargoShip boundingBox];
        float xOffset = 0.0f;
```

```
    if ([spaceCargoShip flipX] == NO) {
        // Ship facing to the left
        xOffset = cargoShipBoundingBox.size.width;
    }
    CGPoint newPosition =
    ccp(cargoShipBoundingBox.origin.x + xOffset,
        cargoShipBoundingBox.origin.y +
        (cargoShipBoundingBox.size.height*0.6f));
    [emitter setPosition:newPosition];
    [smokeEmitter setPosition:newPosition];
    }
}
```

After the `for` loop has iterated through all of the `GameObjects` and updated their positions, the `SpaceCargoShip` is retrieved from the `SpriteBatchNode` via the `kEnemytypeCargoShip` tag value.

The logic to update the particle systems position works as follows:

1. Retrieve the bounding box so that the screen location and size of the `Space-CargoShip` are known (its size indicates how scaled up it currently is).

2. If the ship is currently facing to the left, the `xOffset` is set to the ship's width. Since the `SpaceCargoShip` is facing left, you want the particle systems to be behind it, which means they should be set to the position of the `SpaceCargo-Ship` plus the `width`.

3. The `newPosition` for the particle system is set to the `SpaceCargoShip` origin plus the `xOffset` in the x-axis and the `SpaceCargoShip` origin and to 60 percent of its height on the y-axis.

   Recall that sprites have their bounding box origin at the bottom left unless you change the anchor point.

   If the `SpaceCargoShip` is facing to the left side of the screen, the `newPosition` is set to be on the rightmost edge of the bounding box. If the `SpaceCargoShip` is facing to the left, it is moving in the left direction, and the exhaust is positioned on the right side.

4. Both the `EngineExhaust` and `Smoke` particle systems are set to the new position.

If you click **Run** you should see the Space Cargo Ship move with the engine exhaust and smoke trails following it. Figure 14.8 shows the `SpaceCargoShip` moving across the screen with the engine exhaust and smoke trails following it.

Figure 14.8   Space cargo ship showing the engine exhaust and smoke
particle systems

Summary

Particle systems can add a great deal of realism to your games and help pull the player into the game world. In this chapter you learned about particle systems and how to easily add them to your own Cocos2D games. You also learned about the Particle Designer tool and how to experiment with the various settings for particle systems quickly and easily from your Mac. In the next chapter you learn about Apple's Game Center API and how to add achievements and leaderboards to *Space Viking*.

Challenges

1. Change the `CCParticleSnow` class to increase the number of particles being used, simulating a large snowstorm on the alien planet.

   Hint: Look at the `[self initWithTotalParticles:700];` call for `CCParticleSnow`.

2. Change the `smokeEmitter` so that it is positioned behind the engine exhaust instead of on top of it.

Achievements and Leaderboards with Game Center

Space Viking is quickly becoming a pretty cool game. It uses a lot of different aspects of Cocos2D, including actions, animation, scrolling, sound, and game physics. It has multiple levels with different styles and has a kick-butt main character.

But when you make a game like this, you want to keep your players coming back for more. One good way to do that is by adding achievements and leaderboards into your game using Apple's new social gaming network: Game Center.

In this chapter, you add achievements into Space Viking *for completing each level to give players a sense of accomplishment and drive them to complete the game. You also add leaderboards for the Escape level, so players can compete for the fastest escapes.*

In the process, you learn a lot about Game Center, how to set up your leaderboards and achievements, and how to integrate them into your games. You learn about some pitfalls you might run into along the way and how to navigate through them successfully.

So let's take this game to the next level and integrate Game Center.

What Is Game Center?

When users think of Game Center, they often think of the app that comes preinstalled with iOS (4.1+). In the Game Center app, you can view your list of friends, see what kinds of games they've been playing, and see how far they've gotten in their games, as you can see in Figure 15.1.

You can also check out your own progress with Game Center. You can look through your list of Game Center games and compare your scores to those of your friends and the world, as you can see in Figure 15.2.

However, Game Center is more than just the app. It's also a set of APIs you can use in your apps that make it easy for you to add leaderboards, achievements, and multiplayer capabilities to your games. The APIs integrate with back-end services provided by Apple to store your leaderboards and achievements in a central spot online.

Figure 15.1   Friends list in Game Center and viewing friend's games

Figure 15.2   Viewing your progress in a game in Game Center

In this chapter, you get some hands-on experience using Game Center, by adding leaderboards and achievements into *Space Viking*. But before we get started, let's talk about why you'd want to use Game Center in the first place.

Why Use Game Center?

Using Game Center is a great idea for many reasons:

First, it's easy to do. Adding networked leaderboards or achievements to your game used to be a difficult task involving writing networking code and a server-side app—but now it's just a few simple API calls.

Second, it's fun for your players and keeps them coming back to your game. Many players feel an unstoppable urge to get all of their games 100 percent completed, so you can reward them for their dedication with achievements. Leaderboards are great as well, because they encourage users to keep replaying your game in order to get high scores or to beat their friends!

Third, Game Center can help you sell more apps. Game Center games are listed in a special section in the App Store, which you can get to straight from the Game Center app by tapping **Find Game Center Games** on the **Games** tab. You can also see what games your friends have, which might lead to more people downloading your game. Finally, the more features of Game Center you implement, the more players will enjoy your game and want to share it with others!

Now that you know that Game Center can give your app a lot of cool advantages with a minimal amount of effort, let's try it out in *Space Viking*.

Enabling Game Center for Your App

Unlike the other APIs that you've used in this book so far, your app requires a few configuration steps so it can use Game Center:

1. Obtain an iOS Developer Program account.
2. Create an App ID for your app.
3. Register your app in iTunes Connect.

The next three sections walk you through this process in detail so you can get back to code as quickly as possible.

If you've already created an entry for your app in iTunes Connect, you can skip straight to the last step in this section (Enable Game Center) and continue from there.

Obtain an iOS Developer Program Account

In order to use Game Center in your apps, you need to be able to register your app in iTunes Connect and the iPhone Developer Portal, both of which require you to be a registered member of the iOS Developer Program.

In order to complete this chapter and try out Game Center, you need to sign up for this program first and pay your $99 if you haven't already. At the time of writing this book, you can sign up at *http://developer.apple.com/programs/ios/*.

Note that it usually takes a couple weeks for the application to go through, so it's a good idea to register as soon as you can!

Create an App ID for Your App

Once you've created your iOS Developer Program account, the next step is to create an App ID for your app. An App ID is a unique identifier for an app that enables the OS to know if two apps are the same or different. App IDs are split into two parts, as you can see in Figure 15.3.

Bundle Seed ID		Bundle Identifer		App ID
FTXQ92UGJZ	+	.com.prop-group.spaceviking	=	FTXQ92UGJZ.com.prop-group.spaceviking

Figure 15.3   The two parts of an App ID

The first part (the Bundle Seed ID) is a random string of 10 characters generated by Apple. In the example in Figure 15.3, you can see that this was randomly set to FTXQ92UGJZ. If you have two different apps with the same App ID, they can share keychain access (a secure way to store information on iOS). If you aren't sure whether you'll ever need this or not, a safe bet is to use the same Bundle Seed ID for all of your apps, just in case you want keychain access in the future.

The second part (the Bundle Identifier) is a string you make up. It can be anything you want, but usually the best thing to do is start the name with a reverse DNS name to avoid any conflicts with something other developers might put. At the end, it's usually best to put something related to the name of your app to keep it straight. In the example in Figure 15.3, you can see that we set to *com.prop-group.spaceviking* (but you'll have to make up your own).

For the reverse DNS name, you can use a domain name you own as the start. If you don't have a domain name, don't worry: just use something fairly unique, such as your full name (e.g., com.joeschmoe.spaceviking).

Now that you know what App IDs are, let's create one for *Space Viking*. Here are the steps to do so at the time of writing, but note that this process changes from time to time. If it does, check the book forums or check the official documentation for more information.

1. Visit the iOS Dev Center *(http://developer.apple.com/devcenter/ios/)*, click the **Log in** button, as shown in Figure 15.4, and sign in with your account.

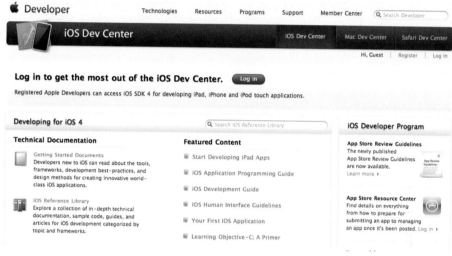

Figure 15.4   Click Log in

2. Click the link for **iOS Provisioning Portal** on the right-hand side, as shown in Figure 15.5. The iOS Provisioning Portal is a service that helps you set up your devices, App IDs, and provisioning/distribution/ad-hoc profiles.

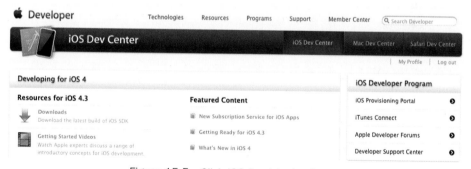

Figure 15.5   Click iOS Provisioning Portal

3. Right now, you just need an App ID, so click the link for **App IDs** on the left-hand side, then click the **New App ID** button in the upper right. Create a new App ID for your app according to the following instructions:

   ▪ For the **Description**, choose something to help you remember what this App ID is later, such as *Space Viking*.

- For the **Bundle Seed ID**, choose the same Bundle ID as your other apps if you want to share keychain access; otherwise choose **Generate New**.

- For the **Bundle Identifier**, enter in a unique name based on a DNS name you own, such as *com.prop-group.spaceviking*. If you do not own a domain name, you can make one up based on your full name or something else unique.

When you're done, click **Submit**, as shown in Figure 15.6.

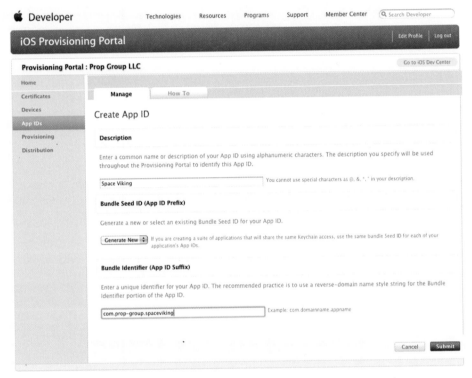

Figure 15.6 Create new App ID (but replace this with your own)

4. Now that you've created an App ID for your app, you need to go back to Xcode and set the Bundle Identifier in the *info.plist* file for *SpaceViking*. Go back to *SpaceViking* in Xcode, and select **Resources\Info.plist**. Edit the Bundle Identifier to be the second part of your App ID (the part after the 10 random characters). For our App ID, it is *com.prop-group.spaceviking*, as you can see in Figure 15.7.

Key	Value
▼ Information Property List	(12 items)
Localization native development re	English
Bundle display name	${PRODUCT_NAME}
Executable file	${EXECUTABLE_NAME}
Icon file	
Bundle identifier	com.prop-group.spaceviking
InfoDictionary version	6.0
Bundle OS Type code	APPL
Bundle version	0.0.2
LSRequiresIPhoneOS	☑
UIStatusBarHidden	☑
UIInterfaceOrientation	UIInterfaceOrientationLandscapeRight
▶ UIRequiredDeviceCapabilities	(2 items)

Figure 15.7   Set Bundle identifier in info.plist

Congratulations! You've successfully set up your app with a unique identifier, which is the first step toward enabling Game Center in your app. The next thing you need to do is register your app in iTunes Connect.

Register Your App in iTunes Connect

If you've developed other apps on the App Store before, you may be used to writing the app first, then registering the app in iTunes Connect and uploading it. If you want to use Game Center, however, you have to register your app early, even before you've written any Game Center code. But don't worry: you can just enter placeholder information to start and then fix it up later when you're ready to release.

Here are the steps to register your app on iTunes Connect. These steps also change from time to time, so if something is different, check the book forums or official documentation for more information.

1. Visit iTunes Connect *(https://itunesconnect.apple.com)* and log in with your account, as shown in Figure 15.8.

 iTunes Connect

Apple ID

Password

Forgot Password...   Sign In

Figure 15.8   Log in to iTunes Connect

2. Click **Manage Your Applications** in the main menu, as shown in Figure 15.9.

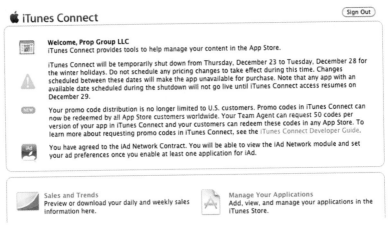

Figure 15.9   Click Manage Your Applications

3. From your list of apps, click **Add New App** to register a new app, and choose **iOS App** for the App type, as shown in Figure 15.10. Note that this screen may not appear if you are an iOS-only developer (if so, just continue to the next step). Also note that you may get a screen that asks you for your company name and language.

Figure 15.10   Click Add New App, then select iOS App as the App Type

4. Next you enter in the basic information for your app, according to the following instructions:

   - For the **App Name**, choose a unique app name. We chose *Space Viking* here, but you must choose a different name, as this name is already taken.

   - For **SKU Number**, you can put in some kind of abbreviation to keep track of your app; we just use SPACEVIKING001.

   - For **Bundle ID**, choose the Bundle Identifier you just made as part of your App ID; ours is *com.prop-group.spaceviking.*

   When you're done, click **Continue**, as shown in Figure 15.11.

Figure 15.11   Enter basic information for your app

5. You now advance to the **Rights and Pricing** screen, as shown in Figure 10.12. Here you can set your availability date, pricing, and educational discounts if you'd like. If you aren't sure, just select anything for now; you can go back and change this later.

6. The final screen is the **Version Information** screen, as shown in Figure 10.13. Just fill out this information the best you can. If you don't know what to put for a field yet, just put a few placeholder characters in there so you can get past this field. Don't worry; you can change all of this before you upload your final version. Note that Apple requires a large icon and a screenshot in order to accept your app; you can just upload temporary images of the right size there and replace them later as well. When you're done, click **Save**.

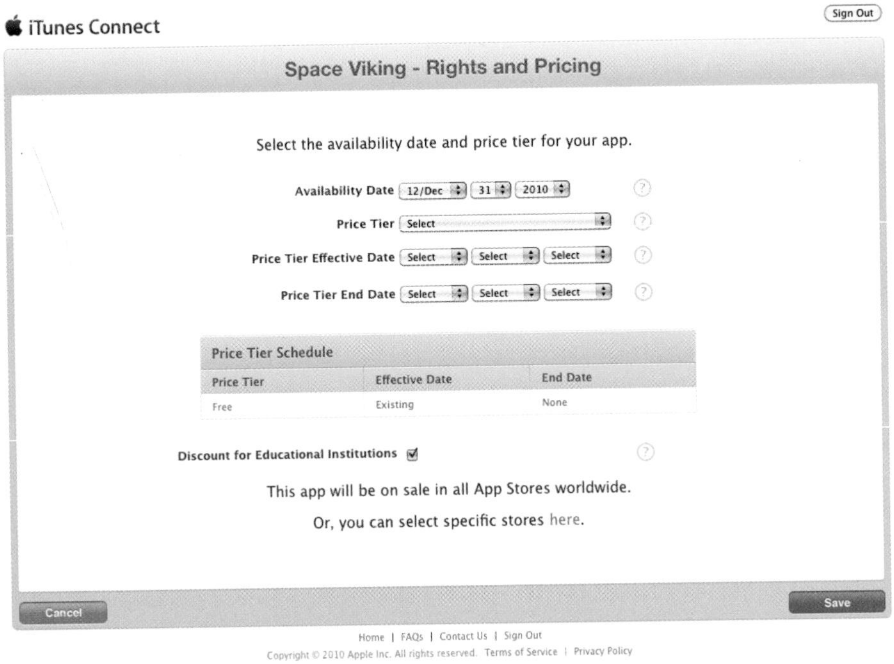

Figure 15.12   Entering rights and pricing

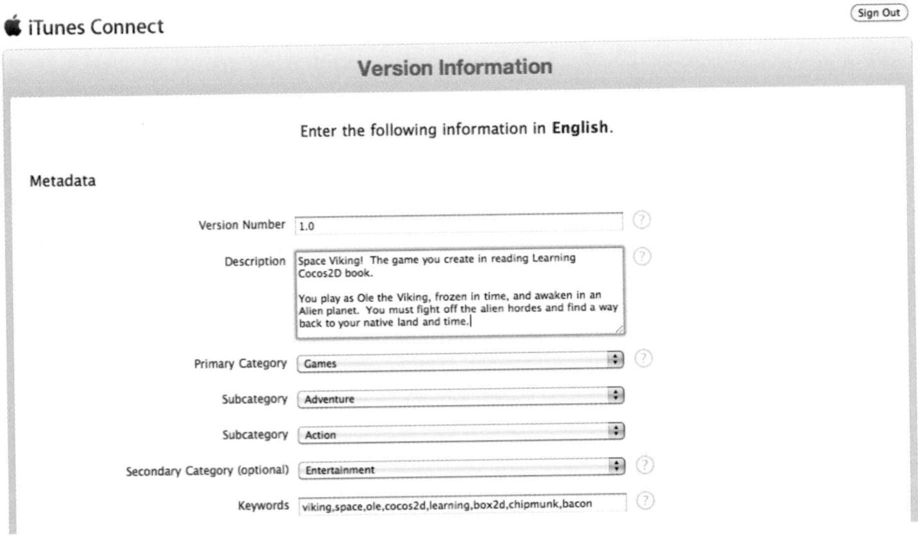

Figure 15.13   Enter placeholder information in Version Information
screen

At this point you should see a page for your app in the Prepare for Upload state, as shown in Figure 15.14. You won't be uploading the app yet (since you're still working on it), but at this point it's ready for you to enable Game Center support!

Figure 15.14   Your placeholder app entry in iTunes Connect

Enable Game Center Support

Now that you've gotten this far, enabling Game Center in your app is really easy. Just click on the **Manage Game Center** button, as shown in Figure 15.14, and then click the big blue **Enable** button as shown in Figure 15.15.

That's it; you're done. It gives you options to set up leaderboards and achievements, but you won't be setting those up until later in this chapter. For now, let's start some coding by integrating authentication into your app.

Figure 15.15   Click Enable to enable Game Center.

Game Center Authentication

Before you can do anything with Game Center, you must take three steps:

1. Make sure Game Center is available on the current device.

2. Try to authenticate the player with Game Center.

3. Keep informed if authentication status ever changes.

You'll start by learning what all of this means and how to implement it, then you'll try it out yourself by adding the code into *Space Viking*. So let's get authenticating!

Make Sure Game Center Is Available

Game Center is only available on iOS 4.1 and above, so if you want to use Game Center in your app, one option is to prevent your app from running on OS versions older than 4.1. You can do this by setting the Deployment Target of your app to iOS 4.1+ in the build settings. This is a simple fix, but the problem with this approach is that you might lose potential customers who are running on older versions of iOS.

In this chapter, you take a second approach: weak-link to Game Center and check if Game Center is available before you try to use it. This way, your code can still run on pre-iOS4 devices (but just not be able to use Game Center features).

To get this to work, you need to add some code to check if Game Center is available. Listing 15.1 shows Apple's recommended way to check.

Listing 15.1   **Recommended way to check if Game Center is available**

```
- (BOOL)isGameCenterAvailable
{
    // Check for presence of GKLocalPlayer API
    Class gcClass = (NSClassFromString(@"GKLocalPlayer"));
```

```
    // Check if the device is running iOS 4.1 or later
    NSString *reqSysVer = @"4.1";
    NSString *currSysVer = [[UIDevice currentDevice] systemVersion];
    BOOL osVersionSupported = ([currSysVer compare:reqSysVer
        options:NSNumericSearch] != NSOrderedAscending);

    return (gcClass && osVersionSupported);
}
```

The method in Listing 15.1 checks if the GKLocalPlayer class exists (one of the Game Center API classes), and then checks that the OS is 4.1 or later (since the class existed in an earlier OS but not in a fully complete state). If both of these are true, it's safe to use Game Center!

Try to Authenticate the Player

Once you've made sure that Game Center is available, the next thing you need to do is authenticate your user. The Game Center API makes this very easy: you just call a single line of code to authenticate players (which prompts them to enter their usernames/passwords if they're not logged in already), as shown in Listing 15.2.

Listing 15.2   **Example of authenticating the player**

```
[[GKLocalPlayer localPlayer]
    authenticateWithCompletionHandler:^(NSError *error) {
    // Do something if necessary...
}];
```

Note that this method takes a completion handler, which is a block of code that should be executed after the user successfully logs in or when there is an error.

> **Note**
>
> If you're unfamiliar with blocks, don't panic! The syntax looks weird, but once you get used to it, you'll start to like blocks because they keep related code close together. The best way to learn about blocks and how to use them is to read Apple's "A Short Practical Guide to Blocks," available at: *http://developer.apple.com/library/ios/#featuredarticles/ Short_Practical_Guide_Blocks/.*

Apple's guidance is to call authenticateWithCompletionHandler once when your app starts up, as early in the launch sequence as possible. This causes one of three things to happen:

- If the user is already logged in, it will display a Welcome Back dialog at the top of the app.
- If the user isn't logged in (and hasn't opted out), it will prompt the user to log in with an existing account or to create a new account.

- If the user isn't logged in (and has opted out by pressing cancel three times in a row), no dialog will be presented to the user—ever! The user will have to go to Game Center to log in again. This behavior is by design, as Game Center should be treated as systemwide login behavior.

> **Note**
>
> Note that you shouldn't try to add a Game Center button that calls `authenticate-WithCompletionHandler` again. If the user wants to log in to Game Center again, he or she should switch to the Game Center app to do so.
>
> For more information on the reasoning behind this, there is a good discussion on Apple's developer forums here: *https://devforums.apple.com/thread/71830.*

Keep Informed If Authentication Status Changes

There is one trick to authenticating users, and it has to do with multitasking on iOS 4+. With multitasking, the user can switch away from your app at any time, switch over to the Game Center app, and log out. Your app needs to know when this has happened so you can disable Game Center features until the user logs back in. Luckily, you can get notice of this by using the `NSNotificationCenter` to set a method to be called when the user's authentication status changes, as shown in Listing 15.3.

Listing 15.3   Example of registering for authentication status change callbacks

```
NSNotificationCenter *nc = [NSNotificationCenter defaultCenter];
[nc addObserver:self selector:@selector(authenticationChanged)
    name:GKPlayerAuthenticationDidChangeNotificationName object:nil];
```

This code registers for the `GKPlayerAuthenticationDidChangeNotificationName` notification, so every time the user logs in or logs out, the `authenticationChanged` method is called.

Note that this method is called even when the user initially logs in (after calling `authenticateWithCompletionHandler`), so it's a good central place to put code related to the authentication status changing.

The Implementation

Enough talk; time to try it out. The first step is to add the Game Kit framework to your project. Game Kit is the library that contains the Game Center API code.

To add Game Kit, select your *SpaceViking* project in the groups and files tree to bring up the project settings. Click on the **Build Phases** tab and expand the **Link Binary with Libraries** section. Click the **+** button at the bottom of the dialog, select **iOS SDK\GameKit.framework**, and click **Add**. Then in the **Link Binary with Libraries** section, find the entry for **GameKit.framework**, and set the Type to **Optional** (instead of Required), as shown in Figure 15.16.

Figure 15.16   Weak-linking to the GameKit framework

Now it's time to add some code. You'll be putting all of the Game Center–related code in a helper class to keep your code clean and reusable in future projects.

To add the helper class, select the *Singletons* group in Xcode, go to **File > New > New File...**, choose **iOS > Cocoa Touch > Objective-C class**, and click **Next**. Enter *NSObject* as the Subclass of, click **Next**, name the file *GCHelper.m*, and click **Save**.

Once you've created the class, replace *GCHelper.h* with the contents of Listing 15.4.

Listing 15.4 **GCHelper.h**

```
#import <Foundation/Foundation.h>
#import <GameKit/GameKit.h>

@interface GCHelper : NSObject {
    BOOL gameCenterAvailable;
    BOOL userAuthenticated;
}

+ (GCHelper *) sharedInstance;
- (void) authenticationChanged;
- (void) authenticateLocalUser;

@end
```

This method first imports the GameKit header, then creates a simple object with two member variables: one to keep track if the Game Center API is available on this device and one to keep track if the user is currently authenticated. It also defines a static method to get the single instance of the `GCHelper` for the application, predeclares the callback for authentication status changes, and defines a method that will authenticate the local user.

Next, switch to *GCHelper.m* and replace it with the contents of Listing 15.5.

Listing 15.5 **GCHelper.m**

```
#import "GCHelper.h"

@implementation GCHelper

#pragma mark Loading/Saving

static GCHelper *sharedHelper = nil;
+ (GCHelper *) sharedInstance {
    @synchronized([GCHelper class])
    {
        if (!sharedHelper) {
            [[self alloc] init];
        }
        return sharedHelper;
    }
    return nil;
}

+(id)alloc
{
    @synchronized ([GCHelper class])
    {
        NSAssert(sharedHelper == nil, @"Attempted to allocated a \
                second instance of the GCHelper singleton");
        sharedHelper = [super alloc];
        return sharedHelper;
    }
    return nil;
}

@end
```

This is just the beginning of *GCHelper.m*; you'll add the rest soon. This is the implementation of the Singleton design pattern to make sure there is only one instance of the `GCHelper` class in memory, just like you used to create the `GameManager` singleton in Chapter 7, "Main Menu, Level Completed, and Credits Scenes." If you're confused about how this code works, refer back to Chapter 7 for more details.

Now that you've added the code to create a singleton instance of GCHelper, add the code to initialize the object and keep track of authentication status changes, as shown in Listing 15.6.

Listing 15.6   GCHelper.m (after alloc method)

```
- (BOOL)isGameCenterAvailable {
    // check for presence of GKLocalPlayer API
    Class gcClass = (NSClassFromString(@"GKLocalPlayer"));

    // check if the device is running iOS 4.1 or later
    NSString *reqSysVer = @"4.1";
    NSString *currSysVer = [[UIDevice currentDevice] systemVersion];
    BOOL osVersionSupported = ([currSysVer compare:reqSysVer
        options:NSNumericSearch] != NSOrderedAscending);

    return (gcClass && osVersionSupported);
}

- (id)init {
    if ((self = [super init])) {
        gameCenterAvailable = [self isGameCenterAvailable];
        if (gameCenterAvailable) {
            NSNotificationCenter *nc =
                [NSNotificationCenter defaultCenter];
            [nc addObserver:self
                selector:@selector(authenticationChanged)
                name:GKPlayerAuthenticationDidChangeNotificationName
                object:nil];
        }
    }
    return self;
}

#pragma mark Internal functions

- (void)authenticationChanged {
    dispatch_async(dispatch_get_main_queue(), ^(void)
    {
        if ([GKLocalPlayer localPlayer].isAuthenticated &&
            !userAuthenticated) {
            NSLog(@"Authentication changed: player authenticated.");
            userAuthenticated = TRUE;
        } else if (![GKLocalPlayer localPlayer].isAuthenticated &&
                    userAuthenticated) {
            NSLog(@"Authentication changed: player not authenticated");
            userAuthenticated = FALSE;
        }
    });
}
```

isGameCenterAvailable is the same code shown earlier in this chapter that checks to see if this version of the OS has the Game Center code on it.

init first checks to see if Game Center is available. If it is, it registers authenticationChanged to be called whenever the authentication status changes.

authenticationChanged keeps a flag of whether or not the user is currently authenticated and logs when there is a change in status.

> **Note**
>
> You may be wondering why the call to dispatch_async is in this function. That line of code runs the contained block on the main thread. This is necessary because when you register for a callback for a notification, it's not guaranteed to run on the main thread.
>
> Since this method needs to modify variables on the object, it should run in the main thread to avoid multithreading access issues. dispatch_async is an easy way to do this. Note that it only works on iOS 3.2+, though. If you want your code to run on an earlier version of iOS, you should use an alternative method such as [self performSelectorOnMainThread:withObject:waitUntilDone].

The next step is to add the method to authenticate the local user, as shown in Listing 15.7.

Listing 15.7   GCHelper.m (after authenticationChanged)

```
#pragma mark User functions

- (void)authenticateLocalUser {

    if (!gameCenterAvailable) return;

    NSLog(@"Authenticating local user...");
    if ([GKLocalPlayer localPlayer].authenticated == NO) {
        [[GKLocalPlayer localPlayer]
            authenticateWithCompletionHandler:nil];
    } else {
        NSLog(@"Already authenticated!");
    }
}
```

You'll be adding some code to call authenticateLocalUser when *Space Viking* first starts up. Notice it immediately quits if Game Center isn't available or if the user is already authenticated. Otherwise, it calls authenticateWithCompletionHandler on the GKLocalPlayer singleton to start the authentication process, as described earlier in this chapter.

Note that there is no need to set a completion handler, since this class has already registered for the authentication changed notification.

Now that you're done with the implementation, it's time to try it out! Switch to *SpaceVikingAppDelegate.m* and import the `GCHelper` class at the top of your file, as shown in Listing 15.8.

Listing 15.8   SpaceVikingAppDelegate.m (at top of file)

```
#import "GCHelper.h"
```

Then at the beginning of `applicationDidFinishLaunching`, add a call to authenticate the user, as shown in Listing 15.9.

Listing 15.9   SpaceVikingAppDelegate.m (at beginning of applicationDidFinishLaunching)

```
[[GCHelper sharedInstance] authenticateLocalUser];
```

That's it! But before you run, open the Game Center app on your simulator or device, and sign out if you're logged in (by tapping on your **Account** banner and choosing **Sign Out**). That way, you are in a known state (logged out of Game Center) at this point.

Compile and run, and you should see a dialog prompting you to log in, as you can see in Figure 15.17.

Figure 15.17   Authenticating the player against the Sandbox Game Center environment

> **Note**
>
> Note that the dialog has the label "Sandbox" on it. This is because there are two differ-
> ent Game Center environments: a development "sandbox" environment for testing and a
> production environment that is used when your app has launched. You can tell which one
> you're on because the dialog boxes and Game Center app itself make it clear by contain-
> ing Sandbox labels if you're on the sandbox.
>
> Each environment has its own set of accounts, leaderboards, and achievements. So you
> can test happily away on the sandbox environment without worrying that it will affect the
> production leaderboards or achievements.
>
> When your app authenticates with Game Center, it automatically uses the Sandbox envi-
> ronment if you are building with a development provisioning profile.

If you don't already have a Sandbox account, go ahead and create one. Then log in,
shut down your app, and run it again. This time, you should see a "Welcome Back"
message, since you're already logged in, as shown in Figure 15.18.

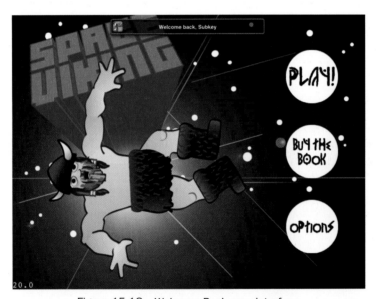

Figure 15.18   Welcome Back user interface

Congratulations: you now have an app that is Game Center enabled. You could
actually publish your app at this point and get many of the advantages of having a
Game Center app, such as making your app easier to find. However, adding achievements and leaderboards is pretty easy, too, so let's continue by adding those next.

Setting Up Achievements

Achievements are a way that you can set a challenge for users (such as "Get 1000 coins," "Kill 20 monsters," or "Beat this level") and then reward users for reaching that goal by keeping track of their achievements and giving them points. Users can see at a quick glance what achievements they've fulfilled and which are yet to be done.

In this section, you add achievements to *Space Viking*. To keep things simple, you just add an achievement for beating each level in the game. You also add a special "hidden" achievement for if the user dies three or more times in the mine cart level, just for fun.

First, you add achievements into iTunes Connect, then you learn a bit about how achievements work, and finally you add the implementation into the game.

Adding Achievements into iTunes Connect

Before you can implement achievements in your game, you need to set them up in iTunes Connect. Set these up for *Space Viking* now by taking the following steps:

1. Log on to iTunes Connect at *https://itunesconnect.apple.com*.

2. Click **Manage Your Applications**, select your application, click **Manage Game Center**, and then click **Set up** under **Achievements**. At this point, you should see a window similar to Figure 15.19.

Figure 15.19   Empty Achievements List

Note that the screen says "1000 Points Remaining." When you set up your achievements, you give each one a number of points. No matter how many achievements you add, your achievements can't sum to over 1000 points.

Note

Be careful with how you allocate points, because if you start out with achievements summing to 1000 points and you want to add another achievement later, there will be no more points left to give out. Therefore, it's a good idea to start with giving out a smaller number of points if you aren't sure how many you might add later.

3. Click **Add New Achievement** to bring up the **Add Achievement** screen, as shown in Figure 15.20.

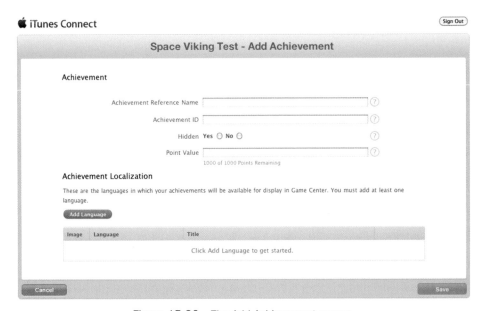

Figure 15.20　The Add Achievement screen

Let's go over each field on this screen in turn.

- The **Achievement Reference Name** is a string you use internally to keep track of the achievement—the player will never see this. Note that this name needs to be unique across all of your apps, however.
- **Achievement ID** is a unique ID to keep track of the achievement. You can use anything here, but again, it's a good idea to use reverse DNS notation so you're sure your names are unique.
- **Hidden** indicates whether users should see the achievement before they unlock it. This can be useful if you want to surprise users for accomplishing something rather than having them know it's there in advance.
- **Point value** is the number of points that this achievement is worth once it is completed, as discussed earlier.

There are several more values that are set on a per-language basis; you can see them by clicking **Add Language**. They are self-explanatory: the title of the achievement, the descriptions for before and after the user accomplishes the achievement, and a 512 × 512 image for the achievement.

> **Note**
>
> Note that achievement images in Game Center are circular to look a bit like coins. You can either make your icons circular as well or just upload a square image with transparency and Game Center will automatically add a circular border and background color (if your icon has transparency).

The resources folder for this chapter contains icons for each of the six achievements you'll be adding to *Space Viking*. Use them and the table in Figure 15.21 to set up six achievements for *Space Viking*. Remember to replace the Achievement ID with your own unique name!

Ref Name	Achievement ID	Hidden	Points	Title	Pre-Earned Descr	Post-Earned Descr	Image
SVLevel1	com.prop-group.spaceviking.achievement.level1	No	10	Simple Gamer	Complete Level 1: Ole Awakes!	You completed Level 1: Ole Awakes!	a_l1.png
SVLevel2	com.prop-group.spaceviking.achievement.level2	No	10	Side Scroller	Complete Level 2: Dogs of Loki!	You completed Level 2: Dogs of Loki!	a_l2.png.
SVLevel3	com.prop-group.spaceviking.achievement.level3	No	10	Physics Puzzler	Complete Level 3: Mad Dreams of the Dead!	You completed level 3: Mad Dreams of the Dead!	a_l3.png
SVLevel4	com.prop-group.spaceviking.achievement.level4	No	10	Box2D Master	Complete Level 4: Descent into Hades!	You completed Level 4: Descent into Hades!	a_l4.png
SVLevel5	com.prop-group.spaceviking.achievement.level5	No	10	Chipmunk Master	Complete Level 5: Escape!	Completed Level 5: Escape!	a_l5.png
SVBadDream	com.prop-group.spaceviking.achievement.baddream	Yes	10	Bad Dream	This is one bad dream...	You fell to your death 3 times - Ole must be having a bad dream!	a_bd.png

Figure 15.21   Space Viking achievement reference

How Achievements Work

When a user makes some progress on an achievement (i.e., kills 10 of the 20 monsters she needs to kill) or completes an achievement (i.e., completely finishes level 1), reporting that progress to Game Center is quite simple. You create a GKAchievement object with the Achievement ID you set up in iTunes Connect, set the percentComplete property, and call reportAchievementWithCompletionHandler, as shown in Listing 15.10.

Listing 15.10   **Example of reporting an achievement**

```
GKAchievement* achievement = [[[GKAchievement alloc]
    initWithIdentifier:identifier] autorelease];
achievement.percentComplete = percentComplete;
```

```
[achievement reportAchievementWithCompletionHandler:^(NSError *error) {
    // Do something...
}];
```

Pretty simple, eh? But there's one big problem: there is a chance that `report-AchievementWithCompletionHandler` could fail, such as if the Internet connection goes down or if Game Center itself is having troubles. If that happens, you don't want the player to lose the achievement, especially since some achievements entail a lot of work and are a big deal for your player!

Luckily, Apple makes this situation easy to deal with by making it easy to save `GKAchievement` objects to disk. This way, if any achievements can't be successfully sent to Game Center's servers, you can save them to disk and send them to Game Center again at a later time.

There are different approaches you can take to using Game Center. You can take the "Game Center knows best" approach, where you read the achievements the user has recorded in Game Center and use that as a baseline. Another option is the "game knows best" approach, where the game keeps its own storage of the user's achievements and just sends a copy to Game Center.

For *Space Viking*, you use the "game knows best" approach, which has the advantage that you can report achievements immediately as they happen without having to worry about Game Center's status, and just keep Game Center up to date when you can. You keep track of the user's progress internally and call a method on `GCHelper` to report achievements when the player makes progress. If `GCHelper` fails to send them, it saves them to disk until the next time the user authenticates, at which time the achievements are sent again.

So let's see what this looks like and move on to the implementation.

Implementing Achievements

Right now *Space Viking* doesn't save any game state, so before you can implement achievements, you need to add that capability. Then you can add the code to send the achievements to Game Center and save them to disk if they fail to send. Finally, you can update *Space Viking* to use the new Game State and achievement-sending classes.

There are four steps to implementing achievements in *Space Viking*:

1. Add a class to keep track of the game's state.

2. Add helper functions to make it easier to load/save data from disk.

3. Update `GCHelper` to support sending achievements (and saving unsent achievements to disk).

4. Update *Space Viking* to make use of these new classes.

This is all simple stuff, but there's a good chunk of code to write to get everything sorted, so grab a tasty snack and some caffeine, and let's get to work!

Creating a Game State Class

First, you create a new object called `GameState`, which the game will use to keep track of the user's progress. Select the *Singletons* group in Xcode, go to go to **File > New > New File...**, choose **iOS > Cocoa Touch > Objective-C class**, and click **Next**. Enter *NSObject* as the Subclass of, click **Next**, name the file *GameState.m*, and click **Save**.

Once you've created the class, replace *GameState.h* with the contents of Listing 15.11.

Listing 15.11   **GameState.h**

```
#import <Foundation/Foundation.h>

@interface GameState : NSObject <NSCoding> {
    BOOL completedLevel1;
    BOOL completedLevel2;
    BOOL completedLevel3;
    BOOL completedLevel4;
    BOOL completedLevel5;
    int timesFell;
}

+ (GameState *) sharedInstance;
- (void)save;

@property (assign) BOOL completedLevel1;
@property (assign) BOOL completedLevel2;
@property (assign) BOOL completedLevel3;
@property (assign) BOOL completedLevel4;
@property (assign) BOOL completedLevel5;
@property (assign) int timesFell;

@end
```

This is just a simple object that keeps track of the players' progress in the game: what levels they've completed and how many times they've fallen off the screen in Descent into Hades. You could extend this class to contain additional instance variables and properties for other data you'd like to save from game session to game session if you'd like.

Note that the class implements the `NSCoding` protocol, which is an easy way to encode/decode the data of a class to or from a data buffer. Also note that the class is a singleton (with a static method `sharedInstance` to get the single instance of the object) and has a method to save the data to disk.

Next add the implementation of *GameState.m*, as shown in Listing 15.12.

Listing 15.12   **GameState.m**

```objc
#import "GameState.h"
#import "GCDatabase.h"

@implementation GameState
@synthesize completedLevel1;
@synthesize completedLevel2;
@synthesize completedLevel3;
@synthesize completedLevel4;
@synthesize completedLevel5;
@synthesize timesFell;

static GameState *sharedInstance = nil;

+(GameState*)sharedInstance {
    @synchronized([GameState class])
    {
        if(!sharedInstance) {
            sharedInstance = [loadData(@"GameState") retain];
            if (!sharedInstance) {
                [[self alloc] init];
            }
        }
        return sharedInstance;
    }
    return nil;
}

+(id)alloc
{
    @synchronized ([GameState class])
    {
        NSAssert(sharedInstance == nil, @"Attempted to allocate a \
                second instance of the GameState singleton");
        sharedInstance = [super alloc];
        return sharedInstance;
    }
    return nil;
}

- (void)save {
    saveData(self, @"GameState");
}

- (void)encodeWithCoder:(NSCoder *)encoder {
    [encoder encodeBool:completedLevel1 forKey:@"CompletedLevel1"];
```

```
    [encoder encodeBool:completedLevel2 forKey:@"CompletedLevel2"];
    [encoder encodeBool:completedLevel3 forKey:@"CompletedLevel3"];
    [encoder encodeBool:completedLevel4 forKey:@"CompletedLevel4"];
    [encoder encodeBool:completedLevel5 forKey:@"CompletedLevel5"];
    [encoder encodeInt:timesFell forKey:@"TimesFell"];
}


- (id)initWithCoder:(NSCoder *)decoder {
    if ((self = [super init])) {
        completedLevel1 = [decoder
            decodeBoolForKey:@"CompletedLevel1"];
        completedLevel2 = [decoder
            decodeBoolForKey:@"CompletedLevel2"];
        completedLevel3 = [decoder
            decodeBoolForKey:@"CompletedLevel3"];
        completedLevel4 = [decoder
            decodeBoolForKey:@"CompletedLevel4"];
        completedLevel5 = [decoder
            decodeBoolForKey:@"CompletedLevel5"];
        timesFell = [decoder decodeIntForKey:@"TimesFell"];
    }
    return self;
}

@end
```

This first synthesizes the variable and has the static method to get the singleton instance of this class.

Note that when creating the singleton instance of this class, it first tries to load the data off the disk, with a function called loadData() that you'll write next. If the data doesn't exist, it creates an empty object. By default, when initializing an object, all instance variables are set to false or 0, so all the levels are marked as uncompleted and the timesFell is initialized to 0.

The save routine calls a function named saveData() that you'll also write next, passing the current instance of the object (self) as a parameter.

encodeWithCoder is the method that saves the object's data out to a data buffer. This is similar to the concept of serialization in other languages. Basically, it goes through each of the instance variables and calls a method to write it out, such as encodeBool for the booleans and encodeInt for the integers. There is also encode-Object for strings, arrays, and other types of objects, but that isn't needed here. Each time you call encodeWithCoder, you give it a key to save the data out to, and you use that key when reading the data back in.

initWithCoder is the opposite of encodeWithCoder: it reads an object back off disk. Here it simply calls the decode methods for each instance variable, passing in the appropriate key.

Creating Helper Functions to Load and Save Data

Now you implement the `loadData()` and `saveData()` methods referenced above
in a new file: *GCDatabase*. Select the *Singletons* group in Xcode, go to go to **File >
New > New File...**, choose **iOS > Cocoa Touch > Objective-C class**, and click
Next. Enter *NSObject* as the Subclass of, click **Next**, name the file *GCDatabase.m*, and
click **Save**.

Replace *GCDatabase.h* with the contents of Listing 15.13.

Listing 15.13   **GCDatabase.h**

```
#import <Foundation/Foundation.h>

id loadData(NSString * filename);
void saveData(id theData, NSString *filename);
```

These are two helper functions to save and load an object to a file, assuming the
object implements the `NSCoding` protocol. These two functions are regular C functions (i.e., not Objective-C), since they need no object state.

The nice thing about these functions is you'll be writing them in a way so that they
can be reused to load or save any object that implements `NSCoding` to a file, so you
can reuse these in future projects if you'd like.

Implement these functions in *GCDatabase.m*, as shown in Listing 15.14.

Listing 15.14   **GCDatabase.m**

```
#import "GCDatabase.h"

NSString * pathForFile(NSString *filename) {
    // 1
    NSArray *paths =
    NSSearchPathForDirectoriesInDomains(NSDocumentDirectory,
                                        NSUserDomainMask,
                                        YES);
    // 2
    NSString *documentsDirectory = [paths objectAtIndex:0];
    // 3
    return [documentsDirectory
        stringByAppendingPathComponent:filename];
}

id loadData(NSString * filename) {
    // 4
    NSString *filePath = pathForFile(filename);
    // 5
    if ([[NSFileManager defaultManager] fileExistsAtPath:filePath]) {
```

```
        // 6
        NSData *data = [[[NSData alloc]
            initWithContentsOfFile:filePath] autorelease];
        // 7
        NSKeyedUnarchiver *unarchiver = [[[NSKeyedUnarchiver alloc]
            initForReadingWithData:data] autorelease];
        // 8
        id retval = [unarchiver decodeObjectForKey:@"Data"];
        [unarchiver finishDecoding];
        return retval;
    }
    return nil;
}

void saveData(id theData, NSString *filename) {
    // 9
    NSMutableData *data = [[[NSMutableData alloc] init] autorelease];
    // 10
    NSKeyedArchiver *archiver = [[[NSKeyedArchiver alloc]
        initForWritingWithMutableData:data] autorelease];
    // 11
    [archiver encodeObject:theData forKey:@"Data"];
    [archiver finishEncoding];
    // 12
    [data writeToFile:pathForFile(filename) atomically:YES];
}
```

If you're not familiar with saving data or NSCoding, much of this may be new to you, so let's go over it line by line:

1. pathForFile takes a filename and returns a string for the full path of the file. In iOS, you can call the NSSearchPathForDirectoriesInDomains function to get standard system directories in which you can save files. One good place to save files for your apps is the NSDocumentDirectory, so it calls that function to get a path to that here.

2. NSSearchPathForDirectoriesInDomains actually returns a list of matching directories, but you're only interested in the first match, so you get the first entry in the array.

3. Now that you have the directory where the file should reside, you can get the full path by combining the two with a slash. NSString has a helper method that does this for you, called stringByAppendingPathComponent.

4. loadData tries to load the data from the disk (or return nil if there is no data saved to the disk yet). It starts by calling the pathForFile method to get a full path for where the file should be.

5. To check if a file exists on the disk, it uses the `NSFileManager` singleton's `fileExistsAtPath` method. `NSFileManager` is a useful class that can check if files exist, delete files, enumerate directories, and more.

6. To read an entire file off the disk and put it into a data buffer, there is a handy helper method on `NSData` called `initWithContentsOfFile`. This returns an `NSData`, which is a helper class that represents a buffer of bytes and a length.

7. Now that you have a buffer of data read from the disk, you need to unarchive any object encoded in the data with the `NSCoding` protocol. The first step for this is to create a `NSKeyedUnarchiver` and pass it the buffer of data, which is done here.

8. Finally it gets a reference to the object by calling `decodeObjectForKey` and then `finishDecoding` on the unarchiver, which decodes the object from the buffer using the `NSCoding` protocol, and returns the result. In effect, this calls `initWithCoder` on the object contained within.

9. To save an object, the first step is to create an empty data buffer. The data buffer is marked as mutable, since it will need to be modified after it is created.

10. The next step to encode the object is to create an `NSKeyedUnarchiver` and pass in an empty mutable data buffer to write to, which is done here.

11. The object is then written to the buffer by calling `encodeObject:forKey` and `finishEncoding`, which has the effect of calling `encodeWithCoder` on the object to write it to the buffer.

12. Now that the data buffer is full of archived data, it can be written to the disk with a helper method on `NSData` called `writeToFile:atomically`.

Modifying GCHelper to Send Achievements

At this point, you have written a class to store the game's state that implements `NSCoding` and a helper class that helps save objects that implement `NSCoding` out to a file. The next step is to make some modifications to your Game Center helper class to support saving achievements to Game Center, to keep track of achievements not yet confirmed as received by Game Center, and to save its data to disk.

You start by making some modifications to *GCHelper.h*, so open it up and modify the contents of the file so it looks like Listing 15.15.

Listing 15.15   **GCHelper.h**

```
#import <Foundation/Foundation.h>
#import <GameKit/GameKit.h>

// Make sure these #defines are on one line each to avoid errors
#define kAchievementLevel1
    @"com.prop-group.spaceviking.achievement.level1"
```

```
#define kAchievementLevel2
    @"com.prop-group.spaceviking.achievement.level2"
#define kAchievementLevel3
    @"com.prop-group.spaceviking.achievement.level3"
#define kAchievementLevel4
    @"com.prop-group.spaceviking.achievement.level4"
#define kAchievementLevel5
    @"com.prop-group.spaceviking.achievement.level5"
#define kAchievementBadDream
    @"com.prop-group.spaceviking.achievement.baddream"
#define kLeaderboardEscape
    @"com.prop-group.spaceviking.leaderboard.escape"

@interface GCHelper : NSObject <NSCoding> {
    BOOL gameCenterAvailable;
    BOOL userAuthenticated;
    NSMutableArray *scoresToReport;
    NSMutableArray *achievementsToReport;
}

@property (retain) NSMutableArray *scoresToReport;
@property (retain) NSMutableArray *achievementsToReport;

+ (GCHelper *) sharedInstance;
- (void)authenticationChanged;
- (void)authenticateLocalUser;

- (void)save;
- (id)initWithScoresToReport:(NSMutableArray *)scoresToReport
    achievementsToReport:(NSMutableArray *)achievementsToReport;
- (void)reportAchievement:(NSString *)identifier
    percentComplete:(double)percentComplete;
- (void)reportScore:(NSString *)identifier score:(int)score;

@end
```

The first change is the #defines up top for the Achievement IDs. You should replace these with whatever values you set up in Game Center when creating your achievements. Note that there's a leaderboard ID you haven't created yet; you'll use this later on.

The second change is to mark the GCHelper class as implementing NSCoding. The GCHelper class needs to know how to save itself out to disk, so any achievements (or scores, later on) that haven't been confirmed as received by Game Center can be sent out again later.

The third change is to add new arrays to store the scores and achievements that still need to be sent to Game Center. Note that you're adding the scores array now (even though you won't use it until later) just to avoid backtracking here later.

The final change is to add several new methods: one to save the GCHelper class to disk, an updated initializer, and methods to report achievements and scores (although right now, only the achievement method will be implemented).

Now, switch to *GCHelper.m* and import *GCDatabase.h* at the top of the file, which you'll need to use to help save this class to disk, as shown in Listing 15.16.

Listing 15.16   **GCHelper.m (at top of file)**

```
#import "GCDatabase.h"
```

Next synthesize your two arrays, as shown in Listing 15.17.

Listing 15.17   **GCHelper.m (right after @implementation)**

```
@synthesize scoresToReport;
@synthesize achievementsToReport;
```

Then modify the sharedInstance method, as shown in Listing 15.18.

Listing 15.18   **GCHelper.m (modify sharedInstance)**

```
+ (GCHelper *) sharedInstance {
    @synchronized([GCHelper class])
    {
        if (!sharedHelper) {
            sharedHelper = [loadData(@"GameCenterData") retain];
            if (!sharedHelper) {
                [[self alloc]
                    initWithScoresToReport:[NSMutableArray array]
                    achievementsToReport:[NSMutableArray array]];
            }
        }
        return sharedHelper;
    }
    return nil;
}
```

The difference is that instead of always creating a new instance, it first tries to load the class from disk, and if that fails, it creates a new instance (using the new initializer).

Next implement the method to save the class to disk using the GCDatabase helper code, as shown in Listing 15.19.

Listing 15.19   **GCHelper.m (below alloc method)**

```
- (void)save {
    saveData(self, @"GameCenterData");
}
```

Then modify the `init` method to take arrays as parameters, as shown in Listing 15.20.

Listing 15.20   **GCHelper.m (modify init method)**

```
- (id)initWithScoresToReport:(NSMutableArray *)theScoresToReport
  achievementsToReport:(NSMutableArray *)theAchievementsToReport {
    if ((self = [super init])) {
        self.scoresToReport = theScoresToReport;
        self.achievementsToReport = theAchievementsToReport;
        gameCenterAvailable = [self isGameCenterAvailable];
        if (gameCenterAvailable) {
            NSNotificationCenter *nc =
                [NSNotificationCenter defaultCenter];
            [nc addObserver:self
                selector:@selector(authenticationChanged)
                name:GKPlayerAuthenticationDidChangeNotificationName
                object:nil];
        }
    }
    return self;
}
```

The only difference here is that the `init` method now takes the arrays of scores and achievements to send as parameters and saves them to the instance variables. This way, the class can be initialized with any saved scores/achievements that failed to send and were saved to the disk in a previous session.

Next, go to the *Internal functions* section and add a method to send a single achievement, as shown in Listing 15.21.

Listing 15.21   **GCHelper.m (after authenticationChanged)**

```
- (void)sendAchievement:(GKAchievement *)achievement {
    [achievement reportAchievementWithCompletionHandler:
     ^(NSError *error) {
        dispatch_async(dispatch_get_main_queue(), ^(void)
        {
            if (error == NULL) {
                NSLog(@"Successfully sent achievement!");
                [achievementsToReport removeObject:achievement];
```

```
        } else {
            NSLog(@"Achievement failed to send... will try again \
                later. Reason: %@", error.localizedDescription);
        }
     });
  }];
}
```

This uses the `reportAchievementWithCompletionHandler` method to attempt to send an achievement to Game Center. Note that the handler isn't guaranteed to run on the main thread, so this uses `dispatch_async` to run the inner code on the main thread. If the achievement is successfully sent, it removes it from the array of achievements to report.

After the `sendAchievement` method, add a method to resend any unsent achievements, as shown in Listing 15.22.

Listing 15.22   GCHelper.m (after sendAchievement)

```
- (void)resendData {
    for (GKAchievement *achievement in achievementsToReport) {
        [self sendAchievement:achievement];
    }
}
```

This loops through each of the achievements that haven't been confirmed by Game Center and resends each one by calling `sendAchievement`.

Now call this method inside the "player now authenticated" case of `authenticationChanged`, as shown in Listing 15.23.

Listing 15.23   GCHelper.m (in authenticationChanged, right after userAuthenticated = TRUE)

```
[self resendData];
```

This way, if any data fails to send, the next time the app starts up, it will resend any leftover data. This is just one way of doing things; if you'd like, you could take a different strategy in your apps (such as try resending any leftover data on a periodic basis).

In the **User functions** section, add the implementation for `reportAchievement:percentComplete` and `reportScore:score`, as shown in Listing 15.24.

Listing 15.24   GCHelper.m (after authenticateLocalUser)

```
- (void)reportScore:(NSString *)identifier score:(int)rawScore {
    // TODO...
}
```

```
- (void)reportAchievement:(NSString *)identifier
    percentComplete:(double)percentComplete {

  GKAchievement* achievement = [[[GKAchievement alloc]
      initWithIdentifier:identifier] autorelease];
  achievement.percentComplete = percentComplete;
  [achievementsToReport addObject:achievement];
  [self save];

  if (!gameCenterAvailable || !userAuthenticated) return;
  [self sendAchievement:achievement];
}
```

The reportScore method is just a stub to be filled in later. The report-Achievement method creates a new achievement based on the passed-in identifier (such as *com.prop-group.spaceviking.achievement.level1*) and sets the percentComplete. It then adds it to the array of achievementsToReport.

At this point, it immediately saves itself to disk so that the achievements to send are saved away for safekeeping. If Game Center isn't available or the user isn't authenticated, it then quits. This has the advantage of being able to queue up the achievements for sending later, even if the user isn't logged in or is running on an older version of the OS.

Finally, if the user is online and Game Center is available, it calls the send-Achievement method to attempt to send the achievement to Game Center.

Next add the implementation of NSCoding for this object, as shown in Listing 15.25.

Listing 15.25   GCHelper.m (after reportAchievement)

```
#pragma mark NSCoding

- (void)encodeWithCoder:(NSCoder *)encoder {
  [encoder encodeObject:scoresToReport forKey:@"ScoresToReport"];
  [encoder encodeObject:achievementsToReport
      forKey:@"AchievementsToReport"];
}


- (id)initWithCoder:(NSCoder *)decoder {
  NSMutableArray * theScoresToReport =
      [decoder decodeObjectForKey:@"ScoresToReport"];
  NSMutableArray * theAchievementsToReport =
      [decoder decodeObjectForKey:@"AchievementsToReport"];
  return [self initWithScoresToReport:theScoresToReport
      achievementsToReport:theAchievementsToReport];
}
```

This encodes the two arrays of scores and achievements to report to disk in encodeWithDecoder, decodes them in initWithCoder, and calls the initializer.

Phew! That was a lot of code, but the good news is most of it is reusable for future projects and for the leaderboard implementation as well. There's only one part left: to make use of these new classes in *Space Viking*.

Using GameState and GCHelper in SpaceViking

Now you're ready to make use of your new objects to keep track of the user's progress locally and report the progress to Game Center when necessary.

In *Space Viking*, you'll be giving the users achievements after they win or lose a level, so most of the fun code will be in *Scenes\LevelComplete\LevelCompleteLayer.m*. First import *GameState.h* and *GCHelper.h* at the top of the file, as shown in Listing 15.26.

Listing 15.26　**LevelCompleteLayer.m (at top of file)**

```
#import "GameState.h"
#import "GCHelper.h"
```

Then add the code to keep track of achievements at the bottom of your init method, as shown in Listing 15.27.

Listing 15.27　**LevelCompleteLayer.m (at bottom of init method)**

```
CCLabelBMFont *achievementLabelText = [CCLabelBMFont
    bitmapFontAtlasWithString:@"" fntFile:@"VikingSpeechFont64.fnt"];
[achievementLabelText setPosition:
    ccp(screenSize.width/2, screenSize.height * 0.7f)];
[self addChild:achievementLabelText];

if ([GameManager sharedGameManager].lastLevel == kGameLevel1 &&
    ![GameManager sharedGameManager].hasPlayerDied) {
    CCLOG(@"Finished level 1");
    if (![GameState sharedInstance].completedLevel1) {
        [GameState sharedInstance].completedLevel1 = true;
        [[GameState sharedInstance] save];
        [[GCHelper sharedInstance] reportAchievement:kAchievementLevel1
            percentComplete:100.0];
        achievementLabelText.string =
            @"Achievement Unlocked: Simple Gamer!";
    }
} else if ([GameManager sharedGameManager].lastLevel == kGameLevel2 &&
    ![GameManager sharedGameManager].hasPlayerDied) {
    CCLOG(@"Finished level 2");
    if (![GameState sharedInstance].completedLevel2) {
        [GameState sharedInstance].completedLevel2 = true;
```

```
            [[GameState sharedInstance] save];
            [[GCHelper sharedInstance] reportAchievement:kAchievementLevel2
                percentComplete:100.0];
            achievementLabelText.string =
                @"Achievement Unlocked: Side Scroller!";
        }
    } else if ([GameManager sharedGameManager].lastLevel == kGameLevel3 &&
        ![GameManager sharedGameManager].hasPlayerDied) {
        CCLOG(@"Finished level 3");
        if (![GameState sharedInstance].completedLevel3) {
            [GameState sharedInstance].completedLevel3 = true;
            [[GameState sharedInstance] save];
            [[GCHelper sharedInstance] reportAchievement:kAchievementLevel3
                percentComplete:100.0];
            achievementLabelText.string =
                @"Achievement Unlocked: Physics Puzzler!";
        }
    } else if ([GameManager sharedGameManager].lastLevel == kGameLevel4 &&
        ![GameManager sharedGameManager].hasPlayerDied) {
        CCLOG(@"Finished level 4");
        if (![GameState sharedInstance].completedLevel4) {
            [GameState sharedInstance].completedLevel4 = true;
            [[GameState sharedInstance] save];
            [[GCHelper sharedInstance] reportAchievement:kAchievementLevel4
                percentComplete:100.0];
            achievementLabelText.string =
                @"Achievement Unlocked: Box2D Master!";
        }
    } else if ([GameManager sharedGameManager].lastLevel == kGameLevel5 &&
    ![GameManager sharedGameManager].hasPlayerDied) {
        CCLOG(@"Finished level 5");
        if (![GameState sharedInstance].completedLevel5) {
            [GameState sharedInstance].completedLevel5 = true;
            [[GameState sharedInstance] save];
            [[GCHelper sharedInstance] reportAchievement:kAchievementLevel5
                percentComplete:100.0];
            achievementLabelText.string =
                @"Achievement Unlocked: Chipmunk Master!";
        }
    } else if ([GameManager sharedGameManager].lastLevel == kGameLevel4 &&
    [GameManager sharedGameManager].hasPlayerDied) {
        CCLOG(@"Died on level 4. Fell %d times...", [GameState
sharedInstance].timesFell);
        int maxTimesToFall = 3;
        if ([GameState sharedInstance].timesFell < maxTimesToFall) {
            [GameState sharedInstance].timesFell++;
            [[GameState sharedInstance] save];
```

```
    double pctComplete = ((double)
        [GameState sharedInstance].timesFell /
            (int)maxTimesToFall) * 100.0;
    [[GCHelper sharedInstance]
        reportAchievement:kAchievementBadDream
        percentComplete:pctComplete];
    if ([GameState sharedInstance].timesFell >= maxTimesToFall) {
        achievementLabelText.string =
            @"Achievement Unlocked: Bad Dream!";
    }
  }
}
```

There's a lot of code here, but it's pretty straightforward. For each level, it checks to see if the player won, and if so, it checks to see whether or not the player already completed that level. If this is the first time the player completed the level, it marks the game's state as having completed the level and saves the updated state to disk. It then calls the reportAchievement:percentComplete method on the GCHelper to also try to send the achievement to Game Center and displays a label to the user.

The only different case is the "player died" achievement. In this case, the player has to die three times before the achievement will be unlocked. Each time the player dies, it updates the counter and updates the current progress on the achievement, but the achievement is only displayed to the user once it is 100 percent complete.

However, there's one problem with the above. Right now, there is no lastLevel property on GameManager! So let's add this next.

Start by adding a new instance variable for the current level and the last level inside Classes\Singletons\GameManager.h, as shown in Listing 15.28.

Listing 15.28 GameManager.h (inside @interface)

```
SceneTypes curLevel;
SceneTypes lastLevel;
```

Then add their properties right below the interface declaration, as shown in Listing 15.29.

Listing 15.29 GameManager.h (after @interface)

```
@property (assign) SceneTypes curLevel;
@property (assign) SceneTypes lastLevel;
```

In GameManager.m, synthesize these variables, as shown in Listing 15.30.

Listing 15.30   **GameManager.m (after @implementation)**

```
@synthesize curLevel;
@synthesize lastLevel;
```

Finally, add the contents of Listing 15.31 to the beginning of `runSceneWithID`.

Listing 15.31   **GameManager.m (at top of runSceneWithID)**

```
lastLevel = curLevel;
curLevel = sceneID;
```

Now GameManager keeps track of the last level played, so the LevelComplete-Layer code can work properly.

That's it! Compile and run your code, and beat a level in the game. Then exit out of the app, go to Game Center, and look to find the entry for your app. You should see the icon for the achievement you unlocked!

Figure 15.22   An unlocked achievement from your game!

You might also like to test what happens if the network connection is down and an achievement fails to send. To do this, you can start the game, then unplug the Ethernet cable from your computer (or disable your Ethernet adapter). Beat the level, and verify that the game records your achievement but fails to send it in the logs. Then plug your Ethernet cable back in and restart the game. When the user is authenticated, the game should resend your achievement data to Game Center, and you won't have lost your progress!

Displaying Achievements within the App

It's extremely easy to display achievements within your game by using a built-in view controller provided by Apple. Let's try it out!

In *Space Viking*, you display the achievements when the user selects the option in the Options menu. There's already an entry there: you just have to implement it! Switch to *Scenes\Options\OptionsLayer.m* and start by importing a few headers at the top of the file, as shown in Listing 15.32.

Listing 15.32   **OptionsLayer.m (at top of file)**

```
#import <GameKit/GameKit.h>
#import "SpaceVikingAppDelegate.h"
```

You need to import *GameKit.h* to use the achievement view controller, and you need to import *SpaceVikingAppDelegate.h* to access the root view controller of the app so that you can present the achievement view controller from it.

Next, add some new methods to show the achievements, as shown in Listing 15.33.

Listing 15.33   **OptionsLayer.m (above init)**

```
- (void)showAchievements {
    CCLOG(@"Show achievements!");

    SpaceVikingAppDelegate *delegate =
        [UIApplication sharedApplication].delegate;
    GKAchievementViewController *achievements =
        [[GKAchievementViewController alloc] init];
    if (achievements != NULL)
    {
        achievements.achievementDelegate = self;
        [delegate.viewController
            presentModalViewController: achievements animated: YES];
    }

}

- (void)achievementViewControllerDidFinish:
    (GKAchievementViewController *)viewController {
    SpaceVikingAppDelegate *delegate =
        [UIApplication sharedApplication].delegate;
    [delegate.viewController dismissModalViewControllerAnimated: YES];
    [viewController release];
}
```

You also need to modify `init` to add new menu options for achievements, as shown in Listing 15.34.

Listing 15.34 **OptionsLayer.m (in init, replace CCMenu * optionsMenu... and [optionsMenu alignItems... lines with the following)**

```
CCLabelBMFont *achievementsButtonLabel = [CCLabelBMFont
    labelWithString:@"Achievements" fntFile:@"VikingSpeechFont64.fnt"];
CCMenuItemLabel    *achievementsButton = [CCMenuItemLabel
    itemWithLabel:achievementsButtonLabel target:self
    selector:@selector(showAchievements)];

CCMenu *optionsMenu = [CCMenu menuWithItems:achievementsButton,
                                  musicToggle,
                                  SFXToggle,
                                  creditsButton,
                                  backButton,nil];
[optionsMenu alignItemsVerticallyWithPadding:40.0f];
```

Now we need to add a property for the `viewController` to the `SpaceVikingApp-Delegate`. First add a property declaration, as shown in Listing 15.35.

Listing 15.35 **SpaceVikingAppDelegate.h (after @interface)**

```
@property (nonatomic, assign) RootViewController *viewController;
```

Then switch to *SpaceVikingAppDelegate.m* and synthesize the variable, as shown in Listing 15.36.

Listing 15.36 **SpaceVikingAppDelegate.m (after @implementation)**

```
@synthesize viewController;
```

One final step: since this code uses UIKit to display a view controller, it's best to set Cocos2D to use `UIViewController` rotation (otherwise the view controller might display sideways!). So go to *GameConfig.h*, comment out the current define for `GAME_AUTOROTATION`, and set it up as shown in Listing 15.37.

Listing 15.37 **GameConfig.h (comment out current GAME_AUTOROTATION define and replace with this)**

```
#define GAME_AUTOROTATION kGameAutorotationUIViewController
```

That's it! Compile and run your app, and now you should be able to see the achievement in the app by selecting the line for achievements in the Options menu (Figure 15.23).

Figure 15.23   Viewing achievements in-game

> **Note**
>
> Displaying achievements with the built-in view controller like this is definitely the easiest way and will suffice for many apps, but you may want to make the achievement display look different (and more like the rest of your app). This is possible with Game Center: you just need to load the achievements and descriptions yourself and create a custom view. For more information, check the *Creating a Custom Achievement User Interface* section in the *Game Kit Programming Guide*.

Setting Up and Implementing Leaderboards

The good news is, after all of the work you did to track game state and implement achievements, adding leaderboards will be a breeze. For *Space Viking*, you'll just add a single leaderboard—the time to complete the Escape level.

To do this, you follow a process similar to (but shorter than) the process for adding achievements. You set up a leaderboard in iTunes Connect, learn how leaderboards work, and finally implement the code.

Setting up Leaderboards in iTunes Connect

Setting up leaderboards in iTunes Connect follows a similar process to setting up achievements. You'll just be adding a single leaderboard this time, so it will go quickly. Take the following steps:

1. Log on to iTunes Connect at *https://itunesconnect.apple.com*.

2. Click **Manage Your Applications**, select your application, click **Manage Game Center**, and then click **Set up** under **Leaderboards**. At this point, you should see a window similar to Figure 15.24.

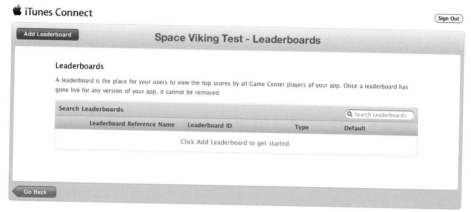

Figure 15.24   Empty leaderboards screen

3. Click **Add Leaderboard** to add a new leaderboard. It gives you a choice between a **Single Leaderboard** or **Combined Leaderboard**; choose **Single Leaderboard**. Then enter the settings as follows:

   - **Leaderboard Reference Name** is just an internal name used to keep track of the leaderboard, similar to the achievement reference name. Set this to **SVEscapeLeaderboard**.

   - **Leaderboard ID** is similar to an achievement ID, a unique name for your leaderboard. Set this to something similar to *com.prop-group.spaceviking.leaderboard.escape*, but change the DNS name to one of your own (or your name if you don't have a DNS name), and make sure it matches to the line for kLeaderboardEscape in *Classes\Singletons\GCHelper.h*.

   - Leaderboard values are always integers, but Score Format Type lets you format the integers in different ways. For the Escape level, we store the number of seconds it took to escape but display them like seconds by choosing **Elapsed Time – To the Second** as the Score Format Type.

   - For Sort Order, pick ascending so the fastest escapes (least time) are at the top.

   - Click **Add Language** to set the remaining options. For Name, choose **Escape from Robot Planet**. For Score Format Suffix, you could set a string to appear after the time, but that isn't necessary here, so leave it blank.

When you're done, click **Save** to save your leaderboard, as shown in Figure 15.25.

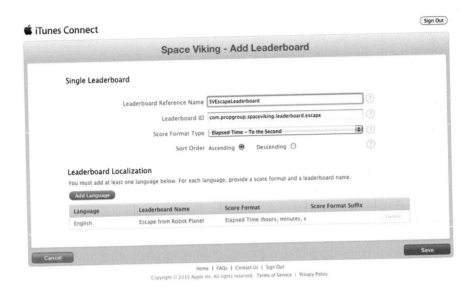

Figure 15.25   Adding a leaderboard

How Leaderboards Work

A leaderboard is simply an ordered collection of best scores. When the user has reached a score, you create a GKScore object and call a method to send the score to Game Center. Game Center keeps track of the max score for each user, and it is okay if you submit a lower score or send a score more than once; it silently discards it. The process looks similar to Listing 15.38.

Listing 15.38   **Example of sending a score to Game Center**

```
GKScore *score = [[[GKScore alloc]
    initWithCategory:identifier] autorelease];
score.value = rawScore;
[score reportScoreWithCompletionHandler:^(NSError *error) {
    // Do something...
}];
```

Of course, sending scores suffers from the same potential pitfall as sending achievements: the score might not make it to Game Center, so you need to add the code to save it to disk and resend later if necessary.

Also, note that although you create only a single leaderboard in this chapter, you can create multiple leaderboards if you want. Perhaps you'd like to make different leaderboards for different levels or difficulty levels in your game.

Implementing Leaderboards

Since you've already added the code to persist an array of scores to disk in GCHelper and added a placeholder method, implementing leaderboards will be easy.

Start by adding a new method called sendScore right above sendAchievement in *GCHelper.m*, as shown in Listing 15.39.

Listing 15.39   **GCHelper.m (above sendAchievement)**

```
- (void)sendScore:(GKScore *)score {
    [score reportScoreWithCompletionHandler:^(NSError *error) {
        dispatch_async(dispatch_get_main_queue(), ^(void)
        {
            if (error == NULL) {
                NSLog(@"Successfully sent score!");
                [scoresToReport removeObject:score];
            } else {
                NSLog(@"Score failed to send... will try again later.
Reason: %@", error.localizedDescription);
            }
        });
    }];
}
```

This is very similar to the sendAchievement method. It tries to send the score and runs a completion block on the main thread; if the score is successfully sent, it removes the score from the scoresToReport array.

Next add a few lines to resendData to have it resend any leftover scores as well, as shown in Listing 15.40.

Listing 15.40   **GCHelper.m (at end of resendData)**

```
for (GKScore *score in scoresToReport) {
    [self sendScore:score];
}
```

By adding this code to resendData, if any scores fail to send, they'll be resent the next time the user connects to Game Center.

Finally, implement the reportScore method, as shown in Listing 15.41.

Listing 15.41   **GCHelper.m (replace reportScore)**

```
- (void)reportScore:(NSString *)identifier score:(int)rawScore {

    GKScore *score = [[[GKScore alloc]
        initWithCategory:identifier] autorelease];
```

```
    score.value = rawScore;
    [scoresToReport addObject:score];
    [self save];

    if (!gameCenterAvailable || !userAuthenticated) return;
    [self sendScore:score];

}
```

This is similar to the `reportAchievement` method. It sets up the `GKScore` object, adds it to the array of scores to report, and saves the array. It bails if game center isn't available or the user isn't authenticated; otherwise, it calls the `sendScore` method to attempt to send the score.

Now all you have to do is report the score when the user completes the level. Switch to *Classes\Scenes\Scene5\Scene5ActionLayer.m*, and start by importing *GCHelper.h* at the top of the file, as shown in Listing 15.42.

Listing 15.42   Scene5ActionLayer.m (at top of file)

```
#import "GCHelper.h"
```

Then find the `update` method, and right before you call `setHasPlayerDied:NO`, add a line to report the user's score, as shown in Listing 15.43.

Listing 15.43   Scene5ActionLayer.m (in update method, right before call to setHasPlayerDied:NO)

```
[[GCHelper sharedInstance] reportScore:kLeaderboardEscape score:(int)
timeSoFar];
```

Compile and run your code, and beat the Escape level. When you're done, switch to the Game Center app, and you should see your best time in the leaderboard.

Displaying Leaderboards in-Game

Thanks to a built-in view controller provided by Apple, displaying leaderboards in-game is as simple as displaying achievements. Let's see how this works by displaying the leaderboards after the user taps the screen in the Level Complete scene for the Escape level.

Open *LevelCompleteLayer.m* and import *SpaceVikingAppDelegate.h* at the top of the file, as shown in Listing 15.44.

Listing 15.44   LevelCompleteLayer.m (at top of file)

```
#import "SpaceVikingAppDelegate.h"
```

Figure 15.26   Viewing leaderboards in Game Center

Then replace ccTouchesBegan with some new code to display a view controller, and add a method underneath, as shown in Listing 15.45.

Listing 15.45   **LevelCompleteLayer.m (replace ccTouchesBegan and add new method)**

```
-(void)ccTouchesBegan:(NSSet *)touches withEvent:(UIEvent *)event {
    if ([GameManager sharedGameManager].lastLevel == kGameLevel5) {
        GKLeaderboardViewController *leaderboardController =
            [[GKLeaderboardViewController alloc] init];
        if (leaderboardController != NULL)
        {
            leaderboardController.category = kLeaderboardEscape;
            leaderboardController.timeScope =
                GKLeaderboardTimeScopeAllTime;
            leaderboardController.leaderboardDelegate = self;
            SpaceVikingAppDelegate *delegate =
                [UIApplication sharedApplication].delegate;
            [delegate.viewController
                presentModalViewController:leaderboardController
                animated:YES];
        }
    } else {
        [[GameManager sharedGameManager] setHasPlayerDied:NO];
        [[GameManager sharedGameManager]
```

```
            runSceneWithID:kMainMenuScene];
    }
}


- (void)leaderboardViewControllerDidFinish:(GKLeaderboardViewController *)
viewController
{
    SpaceVikingAppDelegate *delegate =
        [UIApplication sharedApplication].delegate;
    [delegate.viewController dismissModalViewControllerAnimated: YES];
    [viewController release];
    [[GameManager sharedGameManager] setHasPlayerDied:NO];
    [[GameManager sharedGameManager] runSceneWithID:kMainMenuScene];
}
```

ccTouchesBegan checks to see if the last level was level 5 (the Escape level) and, if so, creates a GKLeaderboardViewController. When you create a GKLeaderboardViewController, you can select the leaderboard to display by setting the category, and the time scope to display by setting the timeScope property. Just as when displaying achievements, you need to set the delegate to your view controller and call presentModalViewController to display it.

When the user closes the leaderboard view controller, leaderboardViewControllerDidFinish is called. This routine simply goes back to the main menu.

Compile and run your code, beat the Escape level, and after the Level Complete scene appears, tap to see the leaderboards in-game!

Figure 15.27   Leaderboard display in-game

Summary

At this point you have had hands-on experience integrating Game Center player authentication, achievements, and leaderboards into a Cocos2D game. And you've learned how to send achievements and leaderboards in a safe way, so that the player's hard-earned achievements get sent even if the network connection is temporarily down.

Now that you know how to implement Game Center in your games, you can enjoy the many benefits, including making your game easier to find and download, keeping players coming back to enjoy your game, and making the game more fun and memorable for players!

Now that you've gotten this far, you might be interested in learning more about some of Game Center's additional features. Along with achievements and leaderboards, Game Center also makes it easy to add multiplayer matchmaking into your games and to add voice chat support. These features are beyond the scope of this book, but to learn more, a good place to start is the *Game Kit Programming Guide*.

Challenges

1. Add a new achievement to *Space Viking*—perhaps for dying three times in level 1.

2. Add a new leaderboard to *Space Viking*—perhaps for the fastest time to complete Descent into Hades.

3. So far, you only display when achievements are unlocked in the Level Complete scene. But what if you want to display achievement unlocks while inside in a level? Add the ability to display achievement unlocks in your level by scrolling a sprite down from the top of the window that says "Achievement Unlocked: Your Achievement Name." You may find it helpful to put this code in a helper class so it can be reused from level to level.

Performance Optimizations

Throughout this book, you learned how to create a game using Cocos2D, Box2D, and Chipmunk. You learned the basics of Cocos2D and advanced concepts from scrolling to physics engines to particle systems. This chapter takes you through some of the optimizations tips and tricks you may need in bringing that last bit of polish to your game now that you have a foundation of knowledge in Cocos2D game development.

In this chapter you learn how to tackle some of the common challenges and issues you will face in optimizing and getting the most of your Cocos2D game. This chapter uses a test bed sample game called PerformanceTestGame, which is included with the resources of this chapter.

CCSprite versus CCSpriteBatchNode

In Chapter 2, "Hello, Space Viking," you learned about CCSpriteBatchNode and how it is used in *Space Viking*. The CCSpriteBatchNode reduces the OpenGL texture binds to one call and batches all of the OpenGL draw calls together. If you do nothing else in your game, this one change has the largest benefit in terms of performance.

> **Note**
>
> The rest of this chapter requires the source code for the *PerformanceTestGame* project provided in the resource folder for this chapter. Please ensure you have downloaded the source code and built the project before proceeding.

The *PerformanceTestGame* project consists of the *Space Viking* alien desert background with Ole standing in the middle of it. From the sky are falling hundreds of little items, debris from the SpaceCargoShip. There are 500 items falling from the sky at random locations and at random speeds. This project is meant as an example of common performance issues you may encounter in your Cocos2D games.

To start, open the *PerformanceTestGame* project and click **Run**. Figure 16.1 illustrates what the game example looks like.

Figure 16.1   PerformanceTestGame project running on the iPad

Run this game on your actual iPad device. Right away you should notice that the performance is not very good: the frame rate is around 30 to 40 frames per second (fps), with occasional drops to 22 fps.

From the *PerformanceTestGame* project and the `GameplayLayer` class. Take a close look at the top of the implementation file and the `#define` shown in Listing 16.1.

Listing 16.1   **#define in GameplayLayer.m in the PerformanceTestGame**

```
#import "GameplayLayer.h"
#define USE_CCSPRITEBATCHNODE 0
#define REUSE_CCSPRITES 0
#define NUMBER_OF_ITEMS 500
```

The USE_CCSPRITEBATCHNODE #define determines if the CCSpriteBatchNode class is used or if just plain CCSprites are attached to the layer for all of the items falling from the sky. The REUSE_CCSPRITES directive allows this game to reuse the falling item CCSprites instead of creating new CCSprites every time a new item needs to be dropped. Setting USE_CCSPRITEBATCHNODE or REUSE_CCSPRITES to **1** turns them *on*.

Scroll to the bottom of the *GameplayLayer.m* implementation file and take a look at the `init` method shown in Listing 16.2.

Listing 16.2   Init method in GameplayLayer.m in the PerformanceTestGame

```
-(id)init {
    self = [super init];
    if (self != nil) {
        srandom(time(NULL));
        CGSize screenSize = [CCDirector sharedDirector].winSize;

        // 1
        CCSprite *background;
        if (UI_USER_INTERFACE_IDIOM() == UIUserInterfaceIdiomPad) {
            background = [CCSprite spriteWithFile:@"background.png"];

        } else {
            background =
             [CCSprite spriteWithFile:@"backgroundiPhone.png"];

        }

        [background setPosition:ccp(screenSize.width/2.0f,
                                    screenSize.height/2.0f)];
        [self addChild:background z:0 tag:0];

        // 2
        CCSprite *viking;
        if (UI_USER_INTERFACE_IDIOM() == UIUserInterfaceIdiomPad) {
            viking = [CCSprite spriteWithFile:@"sv_anim_1.png"];

        } else {
            viking = [CCSprite spriteWithFile:@"sv_anim_1iPhone.png"];

        }
        [viking setPosition:ccp(screenSize.width/2.0f,
                                screenSize.height * 0.15f)];
        [self addChild:viking z:1 tag:1];

        currentItemTag = 2;   // 3

        // 4
        #if (USE_CCSPRITEBATCHNODE == 1)
        [[CCSpriteFrameCache sharedSpriteFrameCache]
            addSpriteFramesWithFile:@"FallingItemsAtlas.plist"];
        sceneSpriteBatchNode = [CCSpriteBatchNode
            batchNodeWithFile:@"FallingItemsAtlas.png"];
        [self addChild:sceneSpriteBatchNode];
        #endif
```

```
          // 5
          dropElementsArray =
            [CCArray arrayWithCapacity:NUMBER_OF_ITEMS];
          [dropElementsArray retain];

          // 6
          for (int x =0; x < NUMBER_OF_ITEMS; x++) {
              CCSprite *dropSprite = [self createItem];
              [dropElementsArray insertObject:dropSprite atIndex:x];

              // 7
              #if (USE_CCSPRITEBATCHNODE == 1)
                  [sceneSpriteBatchNode addChild:dropSprite
                    z:currentItemTag tag:currentItemTag];
              #else
                  [self addChild:dropSprite
                          z:currentItemTag
                          tag:currentItemTag];
              #endif

              // 8
              currentItemTag = currentItemTag + 1;
          }
          [self scheduleUpdate];
      }
      return self;
  }
```

The init method sets up the important components of this test game as follows:

1. Creates the background image used for this game and adds it to the layer. Nothing special here: this is the same as you did in *Space Viking*. A differently sized background image is used depending on if you are running on the iPhone, iPhone 4, or iPad displays. The background has a Z-Order and Tag value of zero.

2. Creates the Viking CCSprite and adds it to the layer. The Viking has a Z-Order and Tag value of 1. All of the items that will drop have Z-Order and Tag values larger then 1.

3. Sets the currentItemTag to 2. The currentItemTag is an instance variable used to keep track of the next tag number to assign to the falling items. The background has a Tag value of zero, and the Viking a Tag value of 1, leaving a value of 2 and higher for the falling items.

4. Creates the CCSpriteBatchNode if the USE_CCSPRITEBATCHNODE #define is set to 1 (on). The USE_CCSPRITEBATCHNODE is used throughout this class to have the falling items as independent CCSprites or under a single CCSpriteBatchNode.

5. Initializes and retains a CCArray to hold all of the falling items. The CCArray is used for another optimization in this game, reusing the CCSprites (falling items) instead of creating new ones. CCArray is a Cocos2D fast array implementation.

   Memory allocation and deallocation is an expensive operation that you want to avoid and minimize if you can. By storing the CCSprites inside of a CCArray, they can be reused by simply moving them back to the top of the screen and restarting the CCMove action. The optimization section of this chapter covers how to reuse CCSprites.

6. Creates all of the falling objects, adding them to the CCArray. First the CCSprite is created in the createItem method and added to the CCArray. Note how the index on the CCArray is based on the loop counter (x) and not on the CCSprite's tag, since the tag value starts at 2 and not zero.

7. Adds the newly created CCSprite to either the Layer or the CCSpriteBatch-Node depending on the value of the USE_CCSPRITEBATCHNODE #define.

   The z-Order and Tag values are set to the currentItemTag variable, which is incremented on each pass of the for loop.

8. Increments the currentItemTag value so that each falling item has a higher z-Order and Tag value than the previous item.

The point to keep in mind from this method is that the falling items CCSprites are all stored in a CCArray as well as in either the Layer or CCSpriteBatchNode. Before turning on the optimizations in the *PerformanceTestGame*, take a close look at the update method shown in Listing 16.3.

Listing 16.3   **update method in GameplayLayer**

```
-(void) update:(ccTime)deltaTime {
    CCNode *node;
    CCARRAY_FOREACH(dropElementsArray, node)
    {
        if ([node tag] > 1) {
            if ([node position].y < 10.0f) {
                int arrayID = [node tag]-2;
                #if (REUSE_CCSPRITES == 1)
                    [self dropWithHighPerformanceItemWithID:arrayID];
                #else
                    [self dropWithLowPerformanceItemWithID:arrayID];
                #endif
            }
        }
    }
}
```

The `update` method cycles through each of the falling items stored in the `CCAr-ray`, checking to see if their position is less than 10 on the y-axis. If so, they are reset. The `dropWith` methods work as follows:

`dropWithLowPerformanceItemWithID`: Method removes the `CCSprite` item from the layer or `CCSpriteBatchNode`, creates a new `CCSprite`, and adds it back in the old one's place.

`dropWithHighPerformanceItemWithID`: Method simply moves the `CCSprite` back to the top, slightly offscreen, and restarts the `CCMove` animation to move the falling item down. The `CCSprite` is not removed from memory, just repositioned.

Testing the Performance Difference

Locate the `#define USE_CCSPRITEBATCHNODE` on the top of the *GameplayLayer.m* class and set it to **1**.

```
#define USE_CCSPRITEBATCHNODE 1
```

Click **Run** and try out the *PerformanceTestGame* on your iPad. You should see the performance jump back to 60 fps on an iPhone4 or an iPad. On the iPhone 3G, you will not see 60 fps but an improvement over running this project without using the `CCSpriteBatchNode`.

Reducing the OpenGL bind calls from many textures down to one texture and batching the OpenGL draw calls greatly improves performance. Even a small texture atlas can make a big difference in your performance. The texture atlas for the falling items was small, only 256 × 256 pixels. The reduction in texture binds from individual `CCSprites` to using the `CCSpriteBatchNode` are what provided the performance improvements. Figure 16.2 shows the texture atlas used for the falling items.

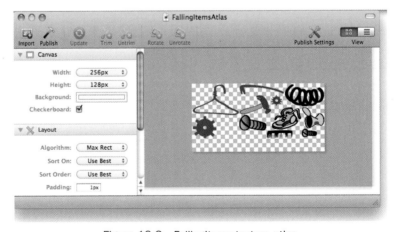

Figure 16.2   FallingItems texture atlas

Tips for Textures and Texture Atlases

In order to get the most performance out of using textures, texture atlases, and the `CCSpriteBatchNode` class, you should follow these simple rules.

Minimize the Empty Space in the Texture Atlas

Having a large, empty texture atlas is just as wasteful as having individual sprites. You want the smallest-sized texture atlas that you can use for your images with the least amount of empty space.

Use the Smallest Bit Depth Possible for Your Game

In *Space Viking* you had the bit depth of the PNGs at maximum RGBA8888. If you can use smaller bit depth in your images, do so, and make sure you save the texture atlas using the smaller bit depth (in Zwoptex or TexturePacker). In Cocos2D you can set the bit depth/texture format used by `CCTexture 2D` anytime by using the call:

```
// Default texture format for PNG/BMP/TIFF/JPEG/GIF images
// It can be RGBA8888, RGBA4444, RGB5_A1, RGB565
// You can change anytime.
[CCTexture2D
    setDefaultAlphaPixelFormat:kCCTexture2DPixelFormat_RGBA8888];
```

Use PVR Images if Possible

Use the Imagination Technologies PVRTC format if possible, as PVRTC textures can be stored in their compressed format directly in the iPhone and iPad GPU memory. PNG, JPG, and other image formats have to be uncompressed before they are stored in memory. PVRTC images using the PVRTC protocol work well for real-world images and photorealistic images, but not as well for pixel art and cartoon drawings. While PVRTC images generally take up more space on disk (flash memory), they can save you a significant amount of RAM in the form of texture memory, as they generally occupy less space than a PNG or JPG image. The PVRTC texture has either 4 bits or 2 bits of color data per pixel. Cocos2D also supports a special format of PVR images called PVR.CCZ, which is a PVR image that is has been gzip compressed so that it takes up less space on disk. It is decompressed by Cocos2D when it is loaded, before being passed to the GPU.

Use Smaller Images and Scale Up

Another trick is to use smaller images and scale them up. Depending on the images in your game, you can use half-sized images and scale them up.

```
CCSprite *sprite = [CCSprite spriteWithFile:@"image.png"];
// Setting the Scale as a property
[sprite setScale:2.0f];

// Setting the Scale via an Action
[sprite runAction:[CCScaleBy actionWithDuration:1.5f scale:2.0f]];
```

Use the FlipX and FlipY for Reverse Images

If you need the reverse of an image either horizontally or vertically, use the FlipX or FlipY parameter instead of storing two images of your character facing left and right. You used the FlipX setting in *Space Viking* to make Ole face left or right depending on his direction of movement.

```
[sprite setFlipX:YES]; // Flip the image Horizontally
[sprite setFlipY:YES]; // Flip the image Vertically
```

Allocate your CCSprites When a Layer Is Initialized

If you have a significant number of CCSprites being used in your game, it is beneficial to allocate them when the layer/scene or level is first initialized. This way, most of the memory allocation activity is done before gameplay begins and not during. In the *PerformanceTestGame*, all 500 falling items are initialized in the init method of the GameplayLayer. Preallocating your CCSprites or other game elements is always a balance between performance and trying to keep your memory footprint as small as possible. Do not read this tip as a free pass to allocate thousands of elements on the init method of your layers.

Flush Unused Textures

When writing your games, you may have different textures and texture atlases for the various scenes and levels. Cocos2D maintains a texture cache of every image/texture you load so that if you want to reuse it, it will not have to waste time loading it from flash storage. While this can save on loading time, it can consume a significant portion of the available memory.

The Cocos2D texture cache (CCTextureCache) is a singleton that can be called from anywhere in your game. After you have deallocated a scene and are no longer using those textures, a call to removeUnusedTextures will remove them from memory.

```
[[CCTextureCache sharedTextureCache] removeUnusedTextures];
```

Reusing CCSprites

Another optimization you can make in your game is to reuse CCSprites that you allocate for your enemies or bullets. Any image in your game that you are going to be using repeatedly is a good candidate for reuse.

In the *PerformanceTestGame* the CCSprites are all stored in a CCArray so that they can be easily reused. The REUSE_CCSPRITES #define determines if the low-performance or high-performance reuse method is called.

Open the *GameplayLayer.m* class and navigate to the dropWithLowPerformance-ItemWithID method shown in Listing 16.4.

Listing 16.4   **What not to do: dropWithLowPerformanceItemWithID method**

```
-(void)dropWithLowPerformanceItemWithID:(int)arrayID {
    CGSize screenSize = [CCDirector sharedDirector].winSize;
    CCSprite *item = [dropElementsArray objectAtIndex:arrayID];
    [dropElementsArray removeObjectAtIndex:arrayID];
    [item stopAllActions];
    [item removeFromParentAndCleanup:YES];
    item = nil;

    item = [CCSprite spriteWithFile:[self getNextItemFileName]];

    #if (USE_CCSPRITEBATCHNODE == 1)
        item = [CCSprite spriteWithSpriteFrameName:
                                [self getNextItemFileName]];
        [sceneSpriteBatchNode addChild:item
                            z:arrayID+2
                            tag:arrayID+2];
    #else
        item = [CCSprite spriteWithFile:[self getNextItemFileName]];
        [self addChild:item z:arrayID+2 tag:arrayID+2];
    #endif

    [dropElementsArray insertObject:item atIndex:arrayID];
    int randomX = random() % 1024;
    [item setPosition:ccp(randomX,screenSize.height)];
    float randomDuration = CCRANDOM_0_1() * 5.0f;
    id moveAction = [CCMoveTo actionWithDuration:randomDuration
                            position:ccp(randomX,0)];
    [item runAction:moveAction];
}
```

The dropWithLowPerformanceItemWithID method illustrates an incorrect way to use CCSprites in your games. In this method, as each falling item reaches the bottom of the screen, it is deallocated and a new CCSprite is created to take its place. There are a lot of memory copy operations in removing, deallocating, then allocating and readding a new CCSprite to the CCArray and the CCSpriteBatchNode or CCLayer.

The better way to reuse CCSprites is shown on the dropWithHighPerformance-ItemWithID method shown in Listing 16.5.

Listing 16.5   **Reusing CCSprites dropWithHighPerformanceItemWithID method**

```
-(void)dropWithHighPerformanceItemWithID:(int)arrayID {
    CGSize screenSize = [CCDirector sharedDirector].winSize;

    CCSprite *item = [dropElementsArray objectAtIndex:arrayID];
    [item stopAllActions];
```

```
    int randomX = random() % 1024;
    [item setPosition:ccp(randomX,screenSize.height)];
    float randomDuration = CCRANDOM_0_1() * 5.0f;
    id moveAction = [CCMoveTo actionWithDuration:randomDuration
                                position:ccp(randomX,0)];
    [item runAction:moveAction];
}
```

The `dropWithHighPerformance` method shows the correct way to reuse a `CCSprite`. In this case the `CCSprite` is just moved back to the top of the screen and the `CCMove` action is added to it once more. In your game you may have the `CCSprites` fading out or even carrying out an animation. You can easily reset them to the original frame, stop all of the actions, and reuse them.

The falling items are just meant as an example; in your game you may have a lot of bullets or laser beams or little enemies moving around the screen. Check to see if you can reuse those elements instead of creating new ones.

To turn on the `dropWithHighPerformanceItemWithID` method, set the `REUSE_CCSPRITES` to **1** (on).

```
#define REUSE_CCSPRITES 1
```

If you click **Run**, you can execute the *PerformanceTestGame* running with the `CCSprites` being reused. The next two sections contain some tips on using the Cocos2D Profiler and the Instruments tool to diagnose which parts of your code are causing performance issues.

Profiling within Cocos2D

Cocos2D comes with a built-in mini-profiling tool that can help you determine how much time is being spent in your methods. Perhaps you need an easy way to see if that enemy artificial intelligence method is taking too long or if the path-finding algorithm you used is causing the sluggishness. In this section you learn how to turn on time profiling in Cocos2D by adding it to the *PerformanceTestGame* project.

The Cocos2D Profiler is a set of classes that provide millisecond-level timers for you to wrap around methods or any parts of your code that you want to easily measure. Once a second, the results of all the profiler timers are displayed to the console.

To start, open the Cocos2D folder in the *PerformanceTestGame* and locate the *ccConfig.h* file. Inside the *ccConfig.h* file, change the `CC_ENABLE_PROFILERS` to 1 so that the required classes are compiled into Cocos2D. Save the change to the *ccConfig.h* file. Your `CC_ENABLE_PROFILERS` line in *ccConfig.h* should look as follows:

```
#define CC_ENABLE_PROFILERS 1
```

Next, open up the *GameplayLayer.h* header file and add the following two instance variables bracketed by a `#if` as shown in Listing 16.6.

Listing 16.6   Profiling variables in GameplayLayer.h header file

```
//   GameplayLayer.h
//   PerformanceTestGame
//
#import <Foundation/Foundation.h>
#import "cocos2d.h"
@interface GameplayLayer : CCLayer {
    CCSprite *Viking;
    int currentItemTag;
    CCArray *dropElementsArray;
    CCSpriteBatchNode *sceneSpriteBatchNode;

    #if CC_ENABLE_PROFILERS
      CCProfilingTimer *resetSpriteProfiler;
      CCProfilingTimer *updateLoopProfiler;
    #endif
}
@end
```

All of the profiling code you add should always be bracketed by the #if CC_ENABLE_PROFILERS block so that it is compiled in only when the profilers are included via the change to *ccConfig.h* and not compiled when the CC_ENABLE_PROFILERS is turned off. In the next four listings are the definitions for a profiler to track the time in the update loop and another to track the time in the CCSprite reset methods.

Switch over to the *GameplayLayer.m* file and scroll down to the init method. Add the lines shown in Listing 16.7 to the top of the init method directly below the screenSize declaration.

Listing 16.7   Profiling setup inside of init method in GameplayLayer.m

```
CGSize screenSize = [CCDirector sharedDirector].winSize;
        #if CC_ENABLE_PROFILERS
            resetSpriteProfiler = [[CCProfiler
                timerWithName:@"resetSprite"
                andInstance:self] retain];
            updateLoopProfiler = [[CCProfiler
                timerWithName:@"updateProfiler"
                andInstance:self] retain];
        #endif
```

The resetSpriteProfiler and updateLoopProfiler are initialized and given a unique name. The next step is to add the beginTiming and endTiming profiler calls in the dropWithLowPerformanceItemWithID and the dropWithHighPerfItemWithID methods.

In the *GameplayLayer.m* class, locate the `dropWithLowPerformanceItemWithID` and `dropWithHighPerformanceItemWithID` methods. In the beginning of these two methods, add the lines shown in Listing 16.8. Then, at the end of both methods, add the lines shown in Listing 16.9.

Listing 16.8   Profiler BeginTiming bracket in GameplayLayer.m

```
#if CC_ENABLE_PROFILERS
    CCProfilingBeginTimingBlock(resetSpriteProfiler);
#endif
```

Listing 16.9   Profiler EndTiming bracket in GameplayLayer.m

```
#if CC_ENABLE_PROFILERS
    CCProfilingEndTimingBlock(resetSpriteProfiler);
#endif
```

The final step to set up the profilers is to add the beginning and end blocks to the update method. Add the `beginTiming` and `endTiming` blocks to the `update` method inside of *GameplayLayer.m*, as shown in Listing 16.10.

Listing 16.10   BeginTiming and EndTiming blocks in update method inside of GameplayLayer.m

```
-(void) update:(ccTime)deltaTime {
    #if CC_ENABLE_PROFILERS
        CCProfilingBeginTimingBlock(updateLoopProfiler);
    #endif
    CCNode *node;
    CCARRAY_FOREACH(dropElementsArray, node)
    {
        if ([node tag] > 1) {
            if ([node position].y < 10.0f) {
                int arrayID = [node tag]-2;
                #if (REUSE_CCSPRITES == 1)
                    [self dropWithHighPerfItemWithID:arrayID];
                #else
                    [self dropWithLowPerformanceItemWithID:arrayID];
                #endif
            }
        }
    }
    #if CC_ENABLE_PROFILERS
        CCProfilingEndTimingBlock(updateLoopProfiler);
    #endif
}
```

If you click **Run**, you will see timing results on the Xcode console. Figure 16.3 shows the *PerformanceTestGame* console messages for the updateLoop and resetSprite profilers.

```
2011-01-27 13:43:14.029 PerformanceTestGame[5968:307] cocos2d: surface size: 1024x768
2011-01-27 13:43:15.895 PerformanceTestGame[5968:307] cocos2d: Frame interval: 1
resetSprite (0x0023cc10) : avg time, 0.302877ms
updateProfiler (0x0023cc10) : avg time, 1.235471ms
resetSprite (0x0023cc10) : avg time, 0.274077ms
updateProfiler (0x0023cc10) : avg time, 1.914239ms
resetSprite (0x0023cc10) : avg time, 0.264222ms
updateProfiler (0x0023cc10) : avg time, 1.389230ms
resetSprite (0x0023cc10) : avg time, 0.317768ms
updateProfiler (0x0023cc10) : avg time, 1.516871ms
resetSprite (0x0023cc10) : avg time, 0.331737ms
updateProfiler (0x0023cc10) : avg time, 1.164965ms
resetSprite (0x0023cc10) : avg time, 0.349077ms
updateProfiler (0x0023cc10) : avg time, 1.441612ms
resetSprite (0x0023cc10) : avg time, 0.267582ms
updateProfiler (0x0023cc10) : avg time, 2.089480ms
resetSprite (0x0023cc10) : avg time, 0.294057ms
updateProfiler (0x0023cc10) : avg time, 1.797684ms
resetSprite (0x0023cc10) : avg time, 0.306964ms
updateProfiler (0x0023cc10) : avg time, 1.189408ms
resetSprite (0x0023cc10) : avg time, 0.359378ms
```

Figure 16.3   Console showing output from updateLoop and resetSprite profilers

You can use the built-in Cocos2D profilers to quickly see how long sections of your game are taking to execute without having to write the timing code yourself. If you use the #if brackets shown in this section, you can easily turn all the profiling code on or off via the *ccConfig.h* file.

The next section takes your profiling skills further by covering a portion of Apple's Instruments tool.

Using Instruments to Find Performance Bottlenecks

Apple provides an excellent profiling tool along with Xcode called Instruments. Instruments is capable of a variety of performance and analysis methods, and it is a much larger topic than can be covered in one chapter. This section offers an overview and some pointers in using Instruments with your Cocos2D games.

> **Note**
>
> If you are not familiar with Instruments, Apple provides a detailed Instruments User's Guide at *https://developer.apple.com/library/prerelease/ios/#documentation/Developer-Tools/Conceptual/InstrumentsUserGuide/Introduction/Introduction.html#//apple_ref/doc/uid/TP40004652*.
>
> A great set of WWDC 2010 Videos on Instruments is available for free to any registered Apple iPhone Developer.

It is important that you run any performance metrics on the actual iPhone, iPad, or iPod touch you are targeting. Performance measurements on your Mac are meaningless, as the architecture and underlying hardware are vastly different from the iOS devices. Running the Leaks instrument to catch memory leaks is useful on the iPhone simulator; for everything else, run Instruments against a build on the device.

> **Warning**
>
> When profiling your code, make sure you are not running a `Debug` build. The `Debug` build adds a significant number of checks and is slower due to the `CCLOG` calls. In Xcode make sure you can always select **Build for Profiling** under the Product menu and use **Profile** instead of the **Run** command.

Xcode contains a couple of very handy templates for launching instruments preconfigured with what you would want to look at. The next sections cover some of these built-in templates.

Time Profiler

The Time Profiler template captures the CPU utilization of the device and how much time each portion of code spends on the CPU. It tracks both your code and any frameworks or system libraries called by your code. By default, the information is displayed in an inverted call tree, showing the called code on top and the caller below it. With Invert Call Tree selected, if method A calls method B, you will see B on top and A below it.

Make sure you have the `USE_CCSPRITEBATCHNODE` set to zero so that it is off. In Xcode select **Profile** and then pick the **Time Profiler**. After you have collected data for a few seconds, you should have in Instruments something similar to Figure 16.4.

If you look closely at Figure 16.4, you can see that the iPad is spending a lot of the CPU time running `gleUpdateDeferredState`. In fact, there are quite a few `gle` entries on the top of the Call Tree Samples list. This is an indication that the OpenGL ES driver is doing a lot of work, maybe more than it should. If you look further down, you can see that `nodeToParentTransform` is the method taking quite a bit of time, and you can see that it is called by the `CCDirectorIOS drawScene` method. All of those separate sprites have to be drawn one at time, causing a lot of work for the CPU and GPU. The CPU utilization is between 65 and 75 percent on the iPad.

Change the `USE_CCSPRITEBATCHNODE` `#define` to 1 (on) and select **Profile** under the Products menu. You will now have on the iPad a version of the *Performance-TestGame* that uses the `CCSpriteBatchNode`.

Once more in Xcode, select **Profile** and then pick the **Time Profiler**. You should have a trace that looks like Figure 16.5.

In Figure 16.5 the Time Profiler shows a completely different picture. Most of the time is spent in the `CCSpriteBatchNode`, and in particular in the `draw` method, which is drawing all of the `CCSprites`. The next item on the list is the `gleRun-VertexSubmitARM`, which is submitting the draw data to the GPU. Note how the CPU utilization is also much lower at around 24 percent.

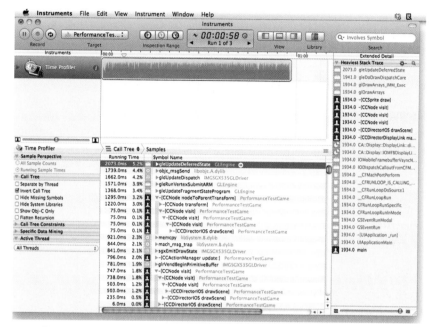

Figure 16.4   Time Profiler on PerformanceTestGame running at 40 fps

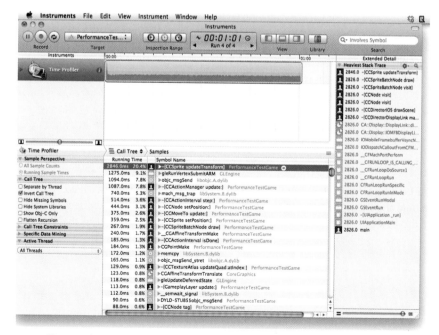

Figure 16.5   Time Profiler on PerformanceTestGame running at 60 fps

As you can see, by using the CCSpriteBatchNode, you are utilizing the GPU on the device much more efficiently, the CPU utilization is down, and the frames per seconds are up.

OpenGL Driver Instrument

To get a better feel for what the GPU is doing, there is an excellent OpenGL Instrument that can record what the utilization is on the renderer and tiler units in the GPU.

The OpenGL Driver Instrument is easily available from within Instruments. To use it:

1. First, change the *PerformanceTestGame* back to not using CCSpriteBatch nodes and close Instruments if it is running.

1. In Xcode, select **Profile** and then choose the **OpenGL ES Driver Instrument**.

2. Click on **info** on the OpenGL ES Driver and click **Configure**. Select the following attributes to track:

   Device Utilization %

   Renderer Utilization %

   Tiler Utilization %

   Keep ResourceBytes and CoreAnimationFramesPerSecond selected.

3. Click **done** and check that all of the selected parameters from step 3 are checked (turned on) in the OpenGL ES Driver.

   Figure 16.6 shows the parameters selected in the OpenGL ES Driver Instrument.

Figure 16.6   OpenGL ES Driver Instrument configuration

If *PerformanceTestGame* is not already running, click the **Record** button and capture about a minute or so of the *PerformanceTestGame* running without CCSprite-BatchNode on your iOS device. Figure 16.7 shows what the instruments trace for the OpenGL ES Driver looks like for the iPad.

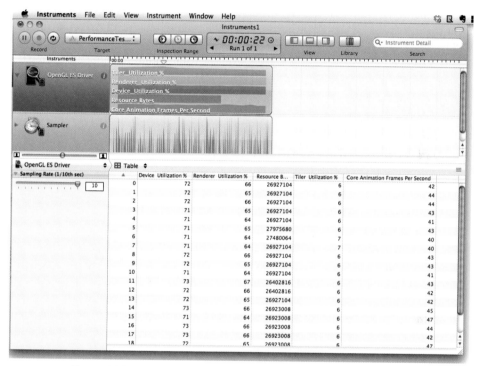

Figure 16.7   OpenGL ES Instrument on PerformanceTestGame with CCSpriteBatchNode turned off

You can see Device Utilization is around 72 percent, but Renderer Utilization is only at 66 percent. To risk oversimplifying, the Renderer Utilization represents the fragment shader portion of the GPU, and the Tiler Utilization represents the vertex processing section of the GPU. The Device Utilization represents how busy the GPU is doing the rendering and tiling work combined. The Renderer is affected by the amount of texture data the GPU is processing. The important thing to note here is that neither the Device Utilization nor the Renderer Utilization are close to 100 percent, and the frames per second are stalled at around 44 fps. It is an indication that perhaps *PerformanceTestGame* is not sending data between the CPU and GPU in an efficient manner, so the GPU could be waiting for memory access or instructions from the OpenGL Driver.

Change the *PerformanceTestGame* to use the CCSpriteBatchNode and select
Profile once more in Xcode under the Product menu. Xcode automatically builds the
PerformanceTestProject and starts another OpenGL ES Driver Instrument capture inside of the Instruments tool. Record for about a minute to see the changes. Figure 16.8 shows what the OpenGL ES Driver Instrument result looks like on the iPad.

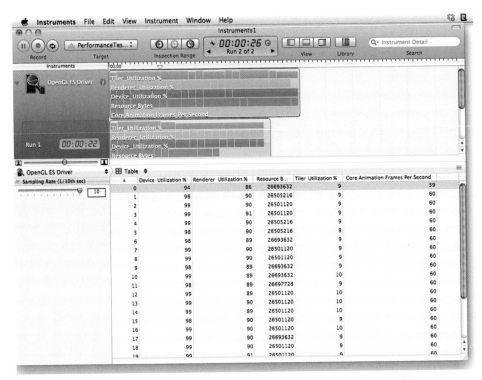

Figure 16.8   OpenGL ES Instrument on PerformanceTestGame with
CCSpriteBatchNode turned on

Figure 16.8 shows quite a different picture: the Device Utilization and Renderer
Utilization are much closer to 100 percent, and the frames per second have jumped
back up to 60. Since Cocos2D games are 2D, they contain a small amount of vertex
data, meaning that the Tiler (vertex processing) section of the GPU is not going to
get much work sent its way. Lowering the bit depth of the images used in the game
would improve your performance further, as less texture data would need to be moved
between the CPU and GPU. You can see that the GPU in the iPad is working at full
capacity.

If you need even more detailed data than Instruments can provide, there is another tool included with Xcode called Shark. Apple has a *User's Guide to Shark* at *https:// developer.apple.com/library/ios/#documentation/DeveloperTools/Conceptual/SharkUserGuide/ Introduction/Introduction.html*.

This section was a small sample of what kinds of profiling data you can access with the Instruments tool. There is a great set of information available to you in the Instruments tool, and even the ability to create your own instruments. Do not hesitate to read Apple's documentation so you can get the most out of this performance analysis tool.

Summary

In this chapter you learned a few of the performance tricks and tips you can use to keep your Cocos2D game running smoothly at 60 fps. You built a quick example of using the built-in Cocos2D Profiler and learned about Apple's Instruments tool. From the beginning of the book until now, you have learned the basics of Cocos2D and how to use every part of the framework in making *Space Viking*.

Your learning does not have to stop here: game development is a deep and rich field. You can learn more about artificial intelligence for your enemies, path finding, physics, and a whole lot more when it comes to rendering and effects. You can even start learning about OpenGL and mix in your own OpenGL rendering code inside of Cocos2D. Simply override the `draw` method in your `CCNode` or `CCSprites` to add your own OpenGL code alongside Cocos2D.

Challenges

1. Further optimize *PerformanceTestGame* so that the `CCMove` actions are reused and not allocated and deallocated each time that the `CCSprites` need to restart their motion.

2. The last challenge left for you is to create your own game using the knowledge and skills you learned and publish your game to the iOS or Mac AppStore. Ray and I look forward to seeing what games you create, and we wish you the best of luck. Your idea could be the next top AppStore game!

17

Conclusion

Throughout this book you have learned how to create a full game using Cocos2D, Box2D, and Chipmunk. You started out by learning the basics of the Cocos2D framework, and about scenes, layers, sprites, and sprite sheets. You then moved on to putting *Space Viking* together, getting Ole the Viking on the screen, and adding a set of joystick controls.

From this humble beginning, you learned how to add animations and enemies to *Space Viking*. You dived into a small sampling of how to configure an enemy's brain by designing a simple artificial intelligence (AI) system out of a state machine. You moved on from static enemies like the RadarDish to the EnemyRobot that patrols and seeks out Ole, and if it spots Ole, fires a shot off his phaser. You covered animations and actions in detail, even building a complex action sequence to drive the SpaceCargoShip around the level. Figure 17.1 shows the progression of *Space Viking*.

Figure 17.1   Progression of Space Viking

After learning about actions and animations, you worked on building some of the non-gameplay elements, by creating the menus used in *Space Viking* and a live text debug system. Along the way you discovered how Cocos2D renders fonts and how to use Font texture atlases for lightning-fast text labels.

Beyond the menus and labels, you moved on to `CocosDenshion`, the full-featured sound engine included with Cocos2D. You added a set of background music tracks to *Space Viking* and sound effects for every part of the game, from the menu click to the explosions when Ole smashes the `EnemyRobot`.

The next step for you was to make the alien world larger by learning how to implement scrolling in Cocos2D. You learned about parallax scrolling, infinite scrolling, and even using tile maps to have large scrolling backgrounds that take just a little bit of memory.

Scrolling added a whole new dimension to the *Space Viking* game, but to bring in the realism, the next chapters took you through an introduction and a complete guide in using the Box2D physics engine included with Cocos2D. You created a mine cart layer with an evil enemy drill robot Ole had to defeat. Not only did you learn and incorporate physics, but you even picked up tips on how to create a boss scene at the end of a level. After discovering the intricacies of Box2D, you worked on the Chipmunk physics engine and created a frantic escape level for Ole to try to make it out of the cave before it exploded. Figure 17.2 shows the two physics levels you created.

Figure 17.2   Physics levels in Space Viking

Having built several levels with and without physics, and even a puzzle level, you learned about Apple's GameCenter API and how to add achievements and leaderboards to your own games.

The last topic on Cocos2D was on particle systems. You learned how to use Particle Designer to design and create your own particle systems and how to incorporate them into your own games using Cocos2D. You added three different particle systems to *Space Viking* to give the `SpaceCargoShip` an exhaust plume and make it snow on the alien desert.

To round off your game development knowledge, you learned how to optimize your code and some of the common pitfalls that can hamper performance in your own games. You even saw how to use the Cocos2D profiler and Apple's Instruments tool.

Where to Go from Here

Cocos2D is a 2D game engine even though the OpenGL and OpenGL ES API it relies on to render the graphics supports 3D. If you want to take your games into the third dimension, you have at least three options: using the Cocos3D extension, learning OpenGL, or using a middleware tool such as Unity3D.

The Cocos3D extension allows you load and use 3D models in a special layer within Cocos2D. You can mix and match 2D and 3D objects and connect them together. Cocos3D is written in Objective-C and works alongside Cocos2D to create the OpenGL calls to render your game. It is brand new as of this writing and looks to be a really great addition to the Cocos2D family. You can find out more about it here: *http://brenwill.com/cocos3d*.

You can also learn how to program the OpenGL and OpenGL ES API directly. You could start by looking inside the CCNode class for what OpenGL calls relate to that node being rendered.

If you want to learn more about OpenGL ES, I strongly recommend Mike Daley's book *Learning iOS Game Programming*, as it covers making a full TileMap game using OpenGL ES. OpenGL and OpenGL ES are complex topics, and depending on what you are looking to do, there is a bit of math behind it. Don't be alarmed: you already picked up Cocos2D—this is simply the next step in becoming an even better game developer.

Unity3D provides a whole platform for you to develop on, from asset management to game logic. The rendering engine is 3D and creates the OpenGL calls for you behind the scenes. It is free to use if developing for the Mac, but there is a license required to deploy on the iOS devices. You can learn more about Unity3D here: *http://www.unity3d.com*.

Android and Beyond

There are now additional ports of Cocos2D to other platforms beyond Objective-C. While the language and syntax used in these ports is different from Objective-C, all of the Cocos2D fundamentals and techniques you learned would apply to these and other frameworks based on Cocos2D. Three ports getting a lot of attention are Cocos2D-Android-1, Cocos2D-X, and Cocos2D-JavaScript.

Cocos2D-Android-1

Port of Cocos2D to Java for the Android operating system. At the time of this writing, it is based on Cocos2D 0.99.4. More information can be found at *http://code. google.com/p/cocos2d-android-1/*.

Cocos2D-X

Cocos2D port written in C++. This port of Cocos2D runs on the iOS devices, just like Cocos2D, and also on Windows and Bada (Samsung), and there is work to bring it to Android. Many other portable game consoles, such as the Sony PlayStation Portable (PSP) and Nintendo DS, have compilers for C++, so it is not too far off to think that this port could be used there. In other areas of game development, C++ is a much more common language then Objective-C. More information can be found at *www.cocos2d-x.org/*.

Cocos2D-JavaScript

If you are interested in building web-based games, there is a port of Cocos2D to the JavaScript language. It is an excellent framework for bringing your Cocos2D games to any device with a modern browser. More information can be found at *www.cocos2d-javascript.org/*.

Cocos2D now offers native support for the Mac, so you can start making Mac OS X games as well as iOS ones. In fact, you can port your iOS games to Mac OS X with little effort if you have used Cocos2D.

Final Thoughts

We hope to have done a good job teaching you both the fundamentals and the in-depth usage of the Cocos2D framework to make games. We joke that the trials of Ole the Viking may have provided some comic relief as you made your way through the book and source code. With the knowledge and confidence you learned in this book, you are ready to create your own games with Cocos2D and get them in the AppStore. Remember that you can reuse any of the code in this book in your games for free. It is our hope you will find some of the classes, methods, or techniques useful.

You can keep up to date with this book and the *Space Viking* sample code at *http://cocos2dbook.com*. We wish you success in your games and look forward to playing them!

Appendix

Principal Classes of Cocos2D

In order to use Cocos2D, it is important to understand a few key classes in the Cocos2D framework. To avoid conflicts with your classes or other libraries and frameworks, all of the Cocos2D classes start with CC. When you see Director, Scene, Layer, Sprite, and other Cocos2D classes in this book, they are referred to by their class name, such as CCDirector, CCScene, CCLayer, and so forth. Knowing these classes wilsl make it easier for you to work through the tutorials in this book:

- CCDirector

  The director design in Cocos2D is similar to a director's role in movies. The director controls when a scene starts and ends and the transitions between each scene. Do not fret; you are still in full control over the director in your role as the game producer. In addition, the director is responsible for maintaining and running the game loop. The CCDirector class is responsible for setting up the OpenGL ES context into which the CCNodes (sprites and other classes) will draw. The director also sets up the orientation and projection settings in OpenGL ES. You will learn how to use the director throughout this book as well as when to use each of the four types of directors included in Cocos2D.

  The four types of directors in Cocos2D are:

  - CCDirectorTypeNSTimer

    This is the director to use if you plan on mixing UIKit views or objects with Cocos2D and you are targeting an iOS version prior to 3.1. It is the slowest director, and the update interval is customizable from 1 to 60 frames per second.

  - CCDirectorTypeMainLoop

    The main loop director is slightly faster than the NSTimer director and is fired off from a custom main loop on the main thread. It does not integrate well with UIKit objects, and the update interval cannot be customized.

  - CCDirectorTypeThreadMainLoop

    This director has the timer on a separate thread that triggers the main loop on the main thread. It is also faster than NSTimer director. It does not integrate well with UIKit objects, and the update interval cannot be customized.

- CCDirectorTypeDisplayLink

  This director utilizes CADisplayLink to synchronize the run loop timer and drawing with the refresh of the screen. It is available only on iOS 3.1 and higher. It integrates well with UIKit objects, and the update interval can be set to 60, 30, or 15 frames per second.

- CCNode

  The Cocos2D node is the main class used in Cocos2D. CCNode contains all of the necessary code to render itself using OpenGL ES. CCNode also contains the logic to enable it to schedule and unschedule events on itself as well as to perform Cocos2D actions. Everything that is rendered by the Cocos2D Director is a CCNode or a subclass of it.

- CCSprite

  A Cocos2D sprite is a subclass of CCNode and contains the necessary logic to hold and manipulate your image. The CCSprite works in parallel with other Cocos2D classes, such as the TextureCache, to display your images onscreen.

- CCSpriteBatchNode

  A sprite batch node is a combined collection of CCSprites. The sprite batch node also goes by the name of sprite sheet in older Cocos2D releases. Sprite batch nodes are used to reduce memory usage and increase OpenGL ES performance. You can combine many sprites into a single sprite batch node, greatly reducing the OpenGL ES CPU overhead required to render the sprites individually. The CCSpriteBatchNode requires a texture atlas, covered in Chapter 3.

- CCLayer

  A Cocos2D layer is a subclass of CCNode with the extra ability to receive touch and accelerometer events. All of the sprites and other elements in your game are contained within layers. In the beginning of the book, the game has only two layers: a background and a gameplay layer. The gameplay layer is where the sprites for your player and enemy characters reside.

- CCScene

  The scenes in Cocos2D hold all that is visible onscreen. The scene is a container of CCLayers and other graphical objects that you want to display or interact with on the screen. The director is responsible for loading, running, and then unloading the scenes. The game you develop in this book starts with a gameplay scene, followed by a menu, and then level-completed and credits scenes. CCScenes are simple container classes to hold your CCLayers and other elements of your game.

Index

inform IT.com THE TRUSTED TECHNOLOGY LEARNING SOURCE

PEARSON

InformIT is a brand of Pearson and the online presence for the world's leading technology publishers. It's your source for reliable and qualified content and knowledge, providing access to the top brands, authors, and contributors from the tech community.

✦Addison-Wesley   **Cisco Press**   EXAM/**CRAM**   **IBM** Press.   QUE   ░░ PRENTICE HALL   **SAMS**   Safari Books Online

LearnIT at InformIT

Looking for a book, eBook, or training video on a new technology? Seeking timely and relevant information and tutorials? Looking for expert opinions, advice, and tips? **InformIT has the solution.**

- Learn about new releases and special promotions by subscribing to a wide variety of newsletters. Visit **informit.com/newsletters**.

- Access FREE podcasts from experts at **informit.com/podcasts**.

- Read the latest author articles and sample chapters at **informit.com/articles**.

- Access thousands of books and videos in the Safari Books Online digital library at **safari.informit.com**.

- Get tips from expert blogs at **informit.com/blogs**.

Visit **informit.com/learn** to discover all the ways you can access the hottest technology content.

Are You Part of the **IT** Crowd?

Connect with Pearson authors and editors via RSS feeds, Facebook, Twitter, YouTube, and more! Visit **informit.com/socialconnect**.

inform IT.com THE TRUSTED TECHNOLOGY LEARNING SOURCE

PEARSON

✦Addison-Wesley   **Cisco Press**   EXAM/**CRAM**   **IBM** Press.   QUE   ░░ PRENTICE HALL   **SAMS**   Safari Books Online

FREE Online Edition

Your purchase of *Learning Cocos2D* includes access to a free online edition for 45 days through the Safari Books Online subscription service. Nearly every Addison-Wesley Professional book is available online through Safari Books Online, along with more than 5,000 other technical books and videos from publishers such as Cisco Press, Exam Cram, IBM Press, O'Reilly, Prentice Hall, Que, and Sams.

SAFARI BOOKS ONLINE allows you to search for a specific answer, cut and paste code, download chapters, and stay current with emerging technologies.

Activate your FREE Online Edition at
www.informit.com/safarifree

> **STEP 1:** Enter the coupon code: EPLUQGA.

> **STEP 2:** New Safari users, complete the brief registration form.
> Safari subscribers, just log in.

If you have difficulty registering on Safari or accessing the online edition,
please e-mail customer-service@safaribooksonline.com